QUANTUM INTELLIGENCE ON CLOUD PARADIGMS

OrangeBooks Publication

1st Floor, Rajhans Arcade, Mall Road, Kohka, Bhilai, Chhattisgarh 490020

Website: **www.orangebooks.in**

First Edition, 2026

ISBN: 978-93-7426-770-7

Price: Rs. 1999.00

Printed in India

QUANTUM INTELLIGENCE
ON
CLOUD PARADIGMS

AUTHOR

DR. MJ. BALACHANDRAN

OrangeBooks Publication
www.orangebooks.in

Preface

Artificial intelligence, robotics, machine learning, design principles, algorithms, architectures, cryptography, big data analytics, IoT, and quantum cloud platforms all converge into a rich and rapidly developing scientific frontier. This book is organized as structured reading material, yet it remains open and accessible to a wide audience.

I wrote this book out of deep excitement for the evolution of robotics, AI, and quantum computing as an integrated science. Like any emerging discipline, these fields contain both a formal theoretical foundation and an exploratory, often experimental dimension. My approach balances theory and practice, connecting them closely to provide a pathway from foundational principles to real-world applications.

In particular, I present the study of quantum cloud computing alongside its engineering applications. Today, research in quantum cloud, robotics, and AI is conducted by experts in diverse domains. No single individual can claim mastery of this vast and fragmented field, and some degree of specialization is inevitable.

This book is especially useful for engineers developing quantum-aware cloud systems. At the same time, it serves as foundational material for anyone entering advanced robotics, offering a conceptual bridge to interdisciplinary technologies. My goal is to present the fundamental building blocks—simple at their core—that, when combined, can give rise to the complex intelligent systems of the future.

Although the resulting systems will be intricate, their essence can be understood by grasping these fundamental connections between AI, quantum theory, robotics, and cloud infrastructures.

This book can be used as a foundational text on quantum computing, artificial intelligence, and robotics on the cloud for advanced undergraduate or graduate students in computer science and related disciplines such as computer engineering, philosophy of computing, cognitive science, or psychology. It is written with a strong technical orientation and will especially appeal to readers who are inclined toward designing, constructing, and implementing complex systems.

The chapters adopt a learning by doing approach, guiding readers through the process of building, experimenting, and innovating with intelligent and quantum-powered technologies. While technically challenging in places, the material is presented in a way that allows a scientifically curious reader to follow and benefit, even without deep prior technical expertise.

Although prior experience with computational systems is helpful, no formal background in areas such as logic, probability, mathematics, or control theory is strictly required. The necessary foundations are introduced and developed as needed throughout the book, ensuring that readers can progress and deepen their understanding step by step.

This balance makes the book both an advanced guide for technical learners and an accessible resource for scientifically oriented readers eager to explore the intersections of quantum systems, AI, robotics, and quantum cloud computing.

A student engaging with this book will develop high-value skills spanning from the analysis and architectural design of intelligent agents to hands-on abilities in implementing, testing, and improving robust software systems that address challenging application domains. The excitement of contributing to the emergence of a new field—where robotics, AI, and quantum technologies combine—adds unique appeal to this practical, systems-focused approach.

The book is arranged to allow readers to explore each technology—quantum cloud, AI, robotics—independently while highlighting their intersections through well-defined segments and real-world model illustrations. Core sections focus on topics such as quantum architecture, design patterns, artificial intelligence, robotics, and quantum cryptography, as well as applications in big data analytics. Lateral sections integrate quantum computing with big data, IoT, and machine learning, presenting concrete models and usage scenarios for deeper understanding.

This book aims to offer a comprehensive framework for understanding quantum cloud computing by presenting a multidimensional design space, rather than restricting itself to isolated logical or probabilistic perspectives. Within this design space, readers are encouraged to grasp the "big picture": how principles such as probabilistic reasoning and logical inference can coexist and interact in practical quantum cloud architectures.

This multidimensional perspective is critical for mastering the complexity and innovation found in quantum-enabled cloud systems, as it enables learners to see the underlying connections that make modern quantum computing possible.

The methodology used in this book, which emphasizes enhancing the power of the agent's capabilities and its representation language, offers a simpler yet more effective approach than traditional methods that catalogue diverse applications of quantum cloud computing. However, as a result, some specific application areas—such as computational vision or computational phonetics—are not covered within the book's scope.

This focused approach deliberately concentrates on core intelligent agent frameworks and their deployment in quantum cloud environments, prioritizing depth in foundational systems and architectures over a comprehensive enumeration of all potential application domains. This allows readers to develop robust skills and understanding in building and managing intelligent quantum cloud systems without being overwhelmed by every specialized application area.

The methodology decided upon in this book intentionally does not provide an exhaustive overview of quantum cloud computing. Instead, it selectively presents fundamental concepts that serve as the foundation for more advanced techniques, explaining these essential ideas in depth. The references included are curated to highlight works that have been practically applied or that offer strong, clear surveys of the field, emphasizing both classical foundational works and recent research reviews.

Readers are invited to embark on an intellectual journey focused on building a science of intelligent systems, concentrating on key principles rather than attempting to cover every aspect of quantum cloud computing comprehensively. This approach fosters a deep and nuanced understanding of the core design spaces and architectural considerations that underpin the field, rather than overwhelming learners with a broad but shallow survey.

Objective of the Book

The primary objective of this book is to provide a comprehensive, structured, and academically rigorous treatment of quantum cloud computing as an emerging paradigm that integrates the principles of quantum information science with the scalable infrastructure of cloud technologies.

It is designed for students, professionals, and corporate practitioners seeking to deepen their understanding of Quantum cloud technologies, Quantum Principles, algorithm, communication, architecture, design patterns, Quantum cryptography, Quantum in big data analytics, IoT and the associated challenges related to safety, security, and computational strategies. A key objective is to serve as a comprehensive and accurate resource that covers all major facets of Quantum cloud computing.

Specifically, the book aims to:

Introduce Foundations

Explain the fundamentals of quantum mechanics, quantum information, and quantum computing necessary to understand cloud-based quantum systems.

Bridge Classical and Quantum Cloud Models

Analyze how classical cloud architectures (IaaS, PaaS, SaaS) evolve into quantum-enabled frameworks (QaaS, hybrid quantum–classical clouds).

Develop Theoretical and Practical Perspectives

Explore the core theories, models, and algorithms of quantum cloud computing, alongside practical implementations and case studies on existing platforms (IBM Quantum, Amazon Braket, Microsoft Azure Quantum, etc.).

Address Research Challenges

Critically examine scalability, error correction, security, interoperability, and resource allocation in quantum cloud environments.

Highlight Applications

Demonstrate applications across AI, Robotics, cryptography, machine learning, optimization, materials science, and IoT enabled by quantum cloud infrastructures.

Stimulate Innovation and Research

Provide graduate students, researchers, and professionals with a roadmap of open problems, potential breakthroughs, challenges and interdisciplinary opportunities in quantum cloud computing.

Acknowledgement

Writing this book has been a rewarding yet challenging journey, and it would not have been possible without the support and encouragement of many individuals. I am deeply grateful to my parents and family for their unconditional love, patience, and inspiration, which gave me the strength to pursue this endeavour. Their constant encouragement has been the foundation of my success.

I wish to express my sincere appreciation to my mentors, colleagues, and friends for their insightful suggestions, constructive feedback, and motivation, which helped shape the direction and quality of this work. My heartfelt appreciation also goes to the publishing team for their professionalism, diligence, and expertise in transforming this manuscript into a completed book.

Finally, I extend my gratitude to you, the reader. Your interest gives true meaning to this effort, and I hope the knowledge shared here proves beneficial and inspiring.

Dr.MJ.Balachandran

Chapter Summary

This book provides a comprehensive exploration of quantum computing and quantum cloud computing, emphasizing their convergence with Artificial Intelligence (AI), Machine Learning (ML), Robotics, and the Internet of Things (IoT). It delves into the foundational quantum principles, algorithms, communication systems, cryptographic methods, architectural design patterns, and big data analytics that define this emerging technological frontier. The following technical chapters collectively present theoretical insights, practical frameworks, and real-world applications, enabling readers to understand how quantum-driven systems are reshaping computation, automation, and intelligent connectivity.

Chapter 1 establishes the foundation by presenting quantum computing as a truly interdisciplinary field, one that bridges theoretical physics, computer science, and engineering. It traces its roots in thermodynamics and electrodynamics, explores its pursuit of fault-tolerance through topological and error-correction approaches, and emphasizes the importance of collaborative and sustainable system design. This chapter also introduces the dual nature of quantum computing—as both a transformative technological paradigm and a domain marked by profound scientific, ethical, and practical challenges that continue to shape its evolution.

Chapter 2 provides a comprehensive examination of the fundamental principles of quantum computing, with an emphasis on the qubit as the basic unit of quantum information. It explores visualization methods such as the Bloch sphere, detailing how quantum states can be represented, manipulated, and measured. The chapter further delves into quantum operations implemented through gates and rotations, and introduces key quantum algorithms that form the foundation of quantum computation. In addition, it discusses quantum models and simulation techniques that play a vital role in bridging theoretical understanding with practical experimentation—laying the groundwork for advanced exploration in quantum systems and algorithmic design.

Chapter 3 explores quantum communication in depth, examining both traditional cryptographic methods and the emerging quantum protocols that are revolutionizing secure information exchange. The chapter highlights the transition from classical to quantum-based security paradigms—focusing on quantum key distribution (QKD), entanglement-based communication, and quantum teleportation. Beyond the technical scope, it critically engages with the ethical, digital sovereignty, and sustainability considerations that underpin the deployment of quantum communication infrastructures.

In doing so, it positions quantum communication as a transformative discipline with the capacity to redefine trust, transparency, and resilience in next-generation digital societies.

Chapter 4 delves into the quantum algorithms that constitute the computational core of quantum computing, revealing how quantum principles translate into practical algorithmic power. The chapter explores key concepts such as quantum stacks, characterization and factorization of quantum integers, and eigenvalue estimation, alongside the foundational algorithms that define the field—Grover's search, Shor's factorization, and quantum adiabatic methods. Both theoretical underpinnings and practical implementations are addressed, offering the mathematical formulations, circuit representations, and algorithmic strategies necessary to realize and harness quantum advantage. Through this, the chapter equips readers with a deep understanding of how quantum algorithms accelerate computation beyond classical limits and form the basis of emerging quantum applications.

Chapter 5 offers an extensive examination of quantum architecture and programming, presenting both the conceptual foundations and engineering strategies essential for building scalable, fault-tolerant quantum systems. It explores the design processes, compiler frameworks, error correction mechanisms, and resource distribution methodologies that collectively sustain reliable quantum computation. The chapter also delves into advanced architectural paradigms—including teleportation-based communication, quantum networked architectures, and hybrid quantum–classical models—illustrating how these innovations enable large-scale, interconnected quantum platforms. By bridging theoretical principles with practical design and implementation strategies, this chapter establishes the technical groundwork for realizing dependable and scalable quantum computers.

Chapter 6 covers the essentials of cloud computing, offering a comprehensive exploration of its core principles, service models (IaaS, PaaS, SaaS), and deployment approaches including public, private, hybrid, and multi-cloud architectures. The chapter examines the key requirements for cloud adoption, addressing regulatory frameworks, compliance standards, and security considerations that shape responsible and sustainable cloud integration. It further investigates the synergistic relationship between Artificial Intelligence (AI) and cloud infrastructure, illustrating how AI accelerates resource optimization, scalability, and intelligent automation within cloud ecosystems. Concluding with a balanced view of benefits, challenges, and operational trade-offs, this chapter provides readers with a solid foundation for designing and adopting AI-ready cloud strategies that align with technological, organizational, and governance priorities.

Chapter 7 explores advanced topics at the intersection of quantum computing and cloud technologies, presenting a detailed analysis of quantum cloud models, infrastructures, resource orchestration, and networking architectures. It emphasizes the Integration and Networking in Quantum Clouds, encompassing the fusion of quantum computing with classical cloud systems, the development of dynamic quantum networks, and the implementation of multitenancy-enabled quantum infrastructures that ensure secure, scalable, and adaptive service delivery. The chapter discusses secure and dynamic networking paradigms essential for reliable data exchange in distributed quantum environments. By mapping out the principles of infrastructure design, hybrid orchestration, and resource optimization, this chapter provides a comprehensive roadmap for adopting, integrating, and innovating within quantum cloud ecosystems, establishing the technological foundation for the next generation of multi-tenant, hybrid, and secure quantum computing environments.

Chapter 8 provides an in-depth exploration of quantum software engineering, emphasizing the novel design patterns, optimization techniques, and cryptographic frameworks uniquely enabled by quantum computation. It covers Encoding and Execution Patterns, Key Algorithms and Development Tools, and Integrated Security and Encryption Strategies that define the emerging discipline of quantum-aware software design. The chapter highlights how rigorous engineering principles, innovative coding methodologies, and domain-specific optimization approaches collectively contribute to building efficient, reliable, and secure applications for the quantum era. By bridging the gap between theory and implementation, this chapter establishes a comprehensive framework for developing, testing, and deploying software in quantum computing environments, ensuring adaptability, scalability, and cryptographic resilience in next-generation systems.

Chapter 9 discusses Quantum as a Service (QaaS), providing a comprehensive exploration of its deployment strategies, architectural design patterns, middleware integration, and broad spectrum of industrial and research applications. It examines how QaaS enables scalable and on-demand access to quantum computing resources through cloud-based frameworks, democratizing quantum capabilities across domains. The chapter guides readers through modern implementation models, orchestration techniques, and best practices essential for deploying, integrating, and optimizing quantum workloads in a service-oriented cloud ecosystem. By bridging theory with practical deployment insights, it highlights how QaaS fosters innovation, cost-efficiency, and accessibility, setting the foundation for the next generation of hybrid quantum–classical infrastructures.

Chapter 10 introduces the core architecture of quantum robotics, focusing on hybrid systems that integrate quantum processing modules with traditional robotic hardware and software. These architectures aim to enhance key robotic capabilities in perception, cognition, communication, and autonomous control. By leveraging quantum computing strengths—such as superposition, entanglement, and rapid optimization—quantum modules handle complex, probabilistic, and large-scale computations. Meanwhile, classical systems provide deterministic control and reliable interfacing with real-world environments. Such hybrid paradigms are increasingly applied across diverse domains, including swarm robotics, secure communication networks, and advanced AI-driven systems for cybersecurity. This convergence of quantum computing, robotics, AI, and secure communications paves the way for next-generation autonomous systems with unprecedented intelligence, adaptability, and trustworthiness.

Chapter 11 on Secure Cloud Computing Using Quantum Cryptography covers several key aspects including Current Cloud Cryptography Technology, Quantum Cryptography, Uncertainty Principle and Quantum Entanglement, Potential Points of Attack, Combining Quantum Cryptography with Cloud, Classical vs. Quantum Cryptography Distinctions. This chapter emphasizes quantum cryptography's role in safeguarding cloud environments through quantum key distribution (QKD), leveraging quantum mechanics principles, and deploying hybrid algorithms. These approaches protect sensitive data against emerging threats posed by quantum-enabled attacks, ensuring resilient and future-proof cloud security.

Chapter 12 explores the convergence of quantum computing with big data analytics, emphasizing its transformative potential. It covers key techniques, tools, and challenges involved in integrating quantum computation with large-scale data processing. By harnessing the unmatched computational power of quantum systems, this integration promises to reshape big data analytics, enabling novel data science methodologies, accelerating insights, and driving innovation in cloud-based data processing environments. The chapter highlights a future where quantum computing becomes a cornerstone of advanced, efficient, and scalable analytics.

Chapter 13 highlights the transformative applications of quantum computing across multiple domains, including healthcare, material science, finance, machine learning, natural language processing, task optimization, and security. Quantum computing offers the potential to solve previously intractable problems through enhanced computational power, advanced algorithms, and secure data handling. In healthcare, it enables precision medicine and optimized clinical workflows, while in other sectors it drives innovation by improving modelling, prediction, and optimization processes. Overall, the chapter underscores quantum computing's ability to revolutionize diverse industries by providing capabilities beyond classical computation.

Chapter 14 Quantum computing and AI/ML integration is opening new frontiers of computation, Framework for Integrating Quantum and AI, Automated Control and Quantum Technologies Calibration, Building Bridges Between Quantum and AI, Empathetic AI and Customized Algorithms, AI and Quantum Computing Synergies ushering in a paradigm where quantum-powered AI frameworks can address problems far beyond the reach of classical systems. This chapter explores current advancements, architectures, and challenges in realizing an effective synergy between quantum and AI. This confluence of quantum computing and AI is poised to transform industries, scientific research, and societal infrastructure, but must be matched by forward-looking frameworks for responsible and equitable adoption.

Chapter 15 explores that Quantum computing is revolutionizing the Internet of Things (IoT) by enabling network optimization, efficient computation at endpoints, robust security, and novel applications like quantum sensors and digital marketing. These advancements tackle IoT complexity in scale, security, and resource management, paving the way for more secure and powerful QIoT (Quantum IoT) systems. Quantum computing and QKD thus anchor a new era of IoT, bringing about ultra-efficient, secure, and versatile connected environments across industries.

Chapter 16 explores the application of quantum machine learning (QML) to advance classification tasks by leveraging quantum algorithms, including K-Nearest Neighbour (KNN), Support Vector Machines (SVM), Naive Bayes, and Logistic Regression, adapted for quantum architectures. These quantum-enhanced approaches open new possibilities for business analytics, enabling faster computation and handling of complex, high-dimensional datasets. However, they also introduce unique technical requirements, ethical challenges, and implementation obstacles. The chapter highlights that while quantum machine learning offers a promising paradigm for analytics-driven decision-making, its successful adoption requires careful consideration of both technical feasibility and responsible, ethical deployment.

Contents

Chapter - 1
Introduction

1.1 Quantum Computing

In the 20th century, data emerged as the new lottery prize, with data owners sitting on vast "gold mines." Traditional theories of physics have often been challenged throughout this century, and today, handling large volumes of data increasingly intersects with quantum computing. Classical physics studies binary states, but the proliferation of data—especially in business—has expanded the concept of "state." In quantum computing, superposition allows each state pair to generate numerous new state pairs, dramatically increasing the number of representable states. This concept is captured mathematically by vector states, which define the behavior of photons, the fundamental units of light.

Time-space graphs can be represented as vector spaces, and because photons can move in any direction, light polarization results in a variety of vector states. Calculus and trigonometric functions are often required to describe these states accurately. By applying algorithms and probability functions, one can determine the current compounded quantum state. The qubit serves as the fundamental data unit in quantum computing and can be represented mathematically. Its length is variable, particularly in contexts where memory constraints are minimal. Quantum computing provides highly precise results and operates on an ultra-fast, petaflop-scale timeframe, enabling computations that would be infeasible for classical systems.

A quantum computer is a device that exploits quantum mechanical phenomena to perform computations. At microscopic scales, physical matter exhibits characteristics of both particles and waves, and quantum computing leverages this duality through specialized hardware. These quantum devices operate in ways that defy classical physics, and a scalable quantum computer could potentially perform certain computations orders of magnitude faster than any classical computer available today.

One of the most influential ideas of the 20th century is quantum theory. It introduced a novel framework for scientific inquiry, anticipated previously unthinkable scenarios, and profoundly impacted modern technology. Just as physical laws can be expressed in multiple ways, knowledge itself can be represented in diverse forms. Information, in particular, can be manipulated automatically because it can be encoded, transmitted, and transformed while preserving its essential properties.

For example, spoken words are carried by variations in air pressure, and all forms of information rely on physical systems. As the physicist Rolf Landauer famously stated: "No information without physical representation." Since information can be translated freely from one form to another, it becomes a natural abstraction for fundamental physical concepts such as interaction, energy, and momentum, which are central to understanding the physical world.

Large-scale quantum computers hold the potential to break widely used encryption schemes and enable physicists to perform complex physical simulations. However, the current state of quantum computing remains largely experimental, with significant barriers to practical implementation.

The qubit (or quantum bit) is the fundamental unit of information in quantum computing, analogous to the classical bit. Unlike a classical bit, which exists in one of two states (0 or 1), a qubit can exist in a superposition of its two basis states, meaning it can effectively be in both states simultaneously. When measured, a qubit yields a probabilistic outcome, rather than a deterministic one.

Quantum computers exploit wave interference effects to amplify the probability of desired measurement outcomes. Designing quantum algorithms—processes that allow qubits to be manipulated efficiently and accurately—is central to harnessing the full computational power of quantum systems.

While a classical computer can theoretically solve the same problems as a quantum computer given unlimited time, the quantum advantage lies in temporal complexity. Quantum complexity theory demonstrates that certain quantum algorithms can be orders of magnitude more efficient than their classical counterparts. In theory, a large-scale quantum computer could tackle computational problems that classical systems could not solve within a practical timeframe. Although such claims of quantum supremacy have generated significant interest, near-term practical applications remain limited.

The evolution of computing reflects humanity's ongoing ability to harness different physical resources—materials, forces, and energy—to perform computations. The history of computers spans from Charles Babbage's early concepts to Konrad Zuse's 1941 construction of the first programmable computer. Over time, computing technologies progressed through a series of physical realizations: gears, relays, valves, transistors, integrated circuits, and microchips. Despite this evolution, modern high-speed computers perform the same fundamental task as their massive 30-ton predecessors with thousands of vacuum tubes: manipulating and interpreting encoded bits to produce useful computational results.

Since 1950, the number of atoms required to represent a single memory bit has steadily decreased. In 1965, Gordon Moore observed that computing power roughly doubles every 18 months, a principle now known as Moore's Law. Extending this trend suggests that atomic-scale computing may soon become feasible, with physical systems capable of encoding individual bits at the subatomic level within the next decade.

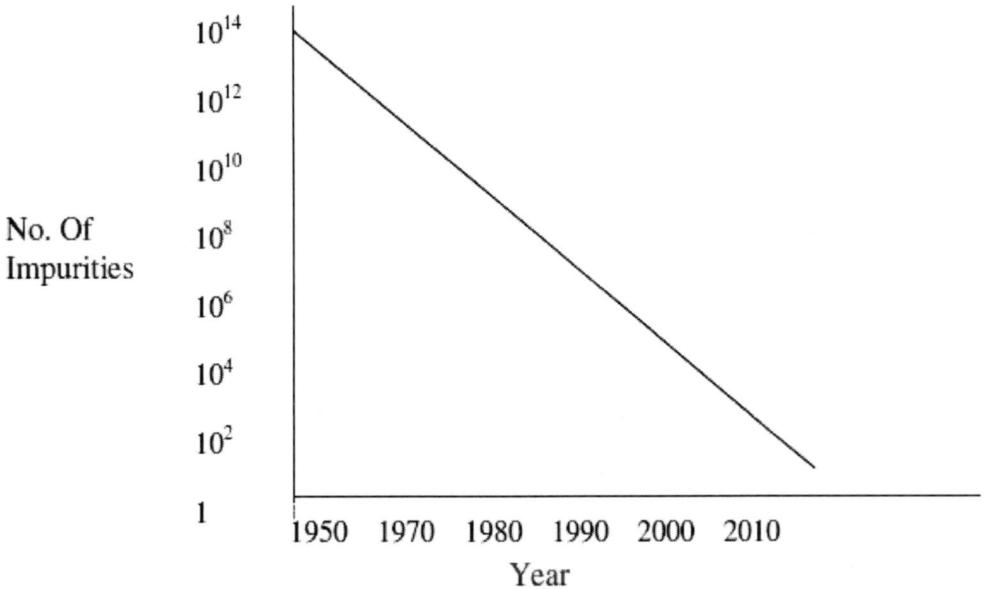

Fig.1.1 Displaying the number of dopant impurities in bipolar transistor logic along with the year.

The behavior of traditional logic gates is governed by classical rules, yet matter inherently follows the laws of quantum mechanics. As a result, future computing technologies will need to replace or augment classical components to continue scaling down device sizes. However, quantum technology offers far more than merely increasing bit density on silicon or raising microprocessor clock speeds. By leveraging quantum principles, it enables an entirely new class of computation with qualitatively and quantitatively novel algorithms.

As classical computer components shrink to the nanoscale, quantum effects increasingly dominate their behavior. This has motivated researchers to explore quantum behaviors as a foundation for computation. Remarkably, a fully quantum-level computer could be far more powerful than any classical system, capable of executing tasks that would be infeasible on conventional machines.

Quantum computers exhibit properties that are fundamentally different from classical computers: their memory can be exponentially larger than their physical size, they can manipulate an exponential set of inputs simultaneously—introducing a new paradigm of parallelism—and they can perform computations in Hilbert space or potentially higher-dimensional spaces such as Grassmann space.

Constructing a functional quantum computer requires only a few fundamental principles of quantum mechanics, but mastering their manipulation demands exceptional sophistication. Whether the realization of such a computer is inevitable or remains a formidable challenge is still an open question.

Quantum Computing Fundamentals

Classical computers use bits as the fundamental unit of information, which can exist in one of two states: 0 or 1. In contrast, quantum mechanics introduces concepts such as superposition and entanglement, which enable fundamentally new computational capabilities.

A qubit, the quantum equivalent of a classical bit, can exist not only in the states 0 or 1 but also in a superposition, a linear combination of these states. This is analogous to a television being in a superposition of channels when turned off, where multiple possibilities coexist simultaneously. Additionally, qubits can become entangled, meaning that the state of one qubit instantly determines the state of another, regardless of the distance separating them. Quantum memory and processing rely on these two key physical concepts.

Quantum gates manipulate qubits through unitary operations, creating rich entangled states and forming the building blocks of quantum circuits. A qubit can be converted to a classical state through measurement, but until then, it retains its quantum properties. Quantum algorithms are implemented in quantum programming environments by orchestrating quantum gates, quantum memory, and measurements, a framework that differs fundamentally from classical computing logic.

The structure of quantum systems allows for massive computational parallelism, especially in specialized operations like entanglement-based phase estimation. This capability enables quantum computers to tackle certain problems far more efficiently than classical computers, particularly tasks that are infeasible within reasonable execution times on classical systems.

Quantum computing also has significant implications for cryptography. Classical schemes like RSA and AES rely on mathematical problems that can be efficiently solved by quantum algorithms such as Shor's algorithm. Consequently, the development of post-quantum or quantum-resistant encryption algorithms is essential to maintain security in the quantum era.

1.2 History of Quantum Computing

The concept of quantum computing was first explored in the 1970s and early 1980s by physicists and computer scientists, including Paul A. Benioff of Argonne National Laboratory and Charles H. Bennett of the IBM Thomas J. Watson Research Center. Researchers such as Richard P. Feynman (Caltech) and David Deutsch (University of

Oxford) further advanced the idea while examining the fundamental limits of computation.

In 1982, Feynman proposed a theoretical model for a new type of computer based on quantum physics. He demonstrated that a quantum system could be used for computation and serve as a simulator for physical problems rooted in quantum mechanics. Feynman argued that quantum computers could solve many-body quantum mechanical problems that are intractable for classical computers, as quantum computations could be completed in polynomial time, whereas classical solutions would require exponentially increasing time.

Building on Feynman's ideas, Deutsch proposed in 1985 that such a device could be a general-purpose quantum computer capable of simulating any physical process in detail. This implied that quantum computers would be fundamentally more powerful than classical systems, spurring efforts to identify practical applications. Initial progress was limited to mathematical curiosities, but in 1994, Peter Shor introduced a quantum algorithm for integer factorization, demonstrating that quantum computers could factor large numbers far more efficiently than classical computers. This breakthrough transformed quantum computing from a theoretical curiosity into a field of active research.

The slow adoption of quantum computing is notable, given that subatomic particle physics had been understood since the 1920s. It was not until decades later that computer scientists seriously considered using quantum effects for computation, reflecting the complexity of the challenge. Publications by Benioff and Feynman inspired further work, including Deutsch's investigations into the many-worlds interpretation of quantum physics, which posits the simultaneous existence of multiple universes.

In 1985, Deutsch published the concept of a quantum Turing machine (QTM) in the Proceedings of the Royal Society, the first fully general and quantum computational model. By 1992, Deutsch, together with Australian mathematician Richard Jozsa, developed the Deutsch-Jozsa algorithm, demonstrating that a quantum computer could solve specific computational tasks exponentially faster than any classical machine. For these foundational contributions, Deutsch is often called the "father of quantum computing.

1.3 The Mathematical Foundation of Quantum Computing

A qubit is a fundamental data storage unit. In reality, it is a gadget that provides various data states in an orthogonal vector space. Two pronged variables determine the states. a0/0> + a1/1> are the ones. The numbers A0 and A1 are complicated. /a0/2 plus /a1/2. While a0 and a1 are lost, the two states are determined by the likelihood of /ao /and a1. A gate determines the state. The gate controls the flow of information. One qubit gate and two qubit gates are among the several types of gates. One qubit gate: The initial state determines the output vectors b0 and b1 in this ate. The final state needs to be consistent with the original state.

The values are listed below. The most basic type of gate that performs an action is the not gate.

INPUT OUTPUT

/0> /1>

/1> /0>

(a0b0a0b1

a1b0a1b1).

Two qubit gate is something different.

INPUT OUTPUT

/0>

$\frac{1}{\sqrt{2}}$/0> +

$\frac{1}{\sqrt{2}}$/1>

/1>

$\frac{1}{\sqrt{2}}$/0>-

$\frac{1}{\sqrt{2}}$/0>

/0>

/0> = (10

0 0),

/0>

/1> = (01

0 0),

/1>

/0> = (0 0

1 0),

/1>

/1> = (0 0 0 1)

1.4 Limits of Classical Computer and the Development of Quantum Computing

1.4.1 Public Key Cryptography and Traditional Big Integer Factorization

The "public key" systems, a brilliant mathematical finding, offered a solution to the key distribution problem in 1970. Users of these systems can send messages without first agreeing on a secret key. It operates on the idea of a safe with two keys—a public key for locking and a private key for opening. No one can take the message out of the safe; everyone has a key that locks it, but only one person has a key that opens it once more. The two keys are actually two huge integer numbers. A private key can be readily converted to a public key, but not the other way around. The technique takes advantage of the fact that some mathematical operations are simpler to execute in one way than the other. For example, multiplying numbers can be done considerably more quickly than factorizing a big number. The fundamental measure of a "fast" algorithm is not how long it takes to multiply a given pair of integers; rather, it's how long it takes the time to increase gradually as the numbers get bigger.

We know that factoring a three-digit number takes roughly 10^13 times less time or memory than multiplication when we go from two three-digit numbers to two thirty-digit numbers utilizing the more straightforward trial division method.

As we increase the number of digits in a factorization, a significant amount of computer resources is used. In actuality, public key cryptosystems might circumvent the issue of key distribution. Nevertheless, their safety relies on unverified mathematical suppositions, including the complexity of factoring big integers. However, one such protocol is RSA, which makes electronic banking feasible by presuming that banks and their clients would need millions of years to successfully execute a fraudulent transfer of funds or a successful forgery. Another is the Data Encryption Standard (DES), which is still widely used and secure for the majority of typical business transactions.

One way to quantify the process of factorizing a huge number is as follows. Let N be an integer having L decimal places (that is, N ~ 10 to the power of L). The trial division approach is used to factor the number. One well-known factoring method operates on conventional computers for a number of operations of the order of

$$s \sim O\left(\exp\left((64/9)^{1/3} (ln N)^{1/3} (ln\, ln N)^{2/3}\right)\right)$$

or explicitly,

$$s \sim A \exp\left(1.9\, L^{1/3} (ln L)^{2/3}\right)$$

As a result, the algorithm grows exponentially with the input size log N, where log N is the input's length. Our numbering scheme determines the logarithm's base. Therefore, base 2 provides the length in binary, base 2 provides the length in binary, and so on. A decimal base of 10 and so forth. For instance, this approach was successfully used in

1994 to factor a 129-digit number (known as RSA 129) on almost 1600 workstations located all over the world; the factorization process took eight months in total. This is used to calculate the per factor of the aforementioned exponential scaling, and the result shows that, with the same computer power, factoring a 250-digit number would take around 800,000 years, and that factoring a 1000-digit number would take 10 to the power 25 years—much longer than the universe's age.

The difficulty of factoring large numbers is crucial for public key cryptography such as used in banks around 250 digits. Using the trial division method for factorization $10^{L/2}$ ($=\sqrt{N}$) divisions are needed to solve the problem on exponential increase as function of L. Suppose a computer performs 10^{10} decisions per second. Thus the computer can factor any number N, in about e.g. a 100 digit number will be factored in 10^{40} seconds, much longer than 3.8 X 10^{17} second (12 billion years), the currently estimated age of the universe!

1.4.2 Factoring in Quantum

Based on the examination of traditional big integer factoring, it appears that factoring large numbers will always be beyond the reach of practical computing devices. Until mathematicians or computer scientists develop an effective factoring algorithm, public key crypto systems will continue to be secure. Nevertheless, it transpires that this is untrue. For the simple reason that it does not cover every calculation that is physically feasible, the Classical Theory of calculation is incomplete. Specifically, it doesn't cover calculations, as quantum devices are capable of handling them.

In reality, a quantum computer can factor far faster than any classical computer, according to recent studies in quantum computation. Factoring an integer with a quantum computer occurs in $O((ln N)\ 2+\varepsilon)$ steps, assuming ε is small, according to a method created by Peter Shor. Since the input size is almost quadratic, an algorithm of this kind may factor a 1000-digit integer in a few million steps. This suggests that factoring-based public key cryptosystems might be cracked.

1.4.3 Finding something with the desired attribute

Finding an item with a desired property among a group of N objects is another issue where a quantum logic-based method can achieve extremely high speed. Assume if we randomly select one item from a set of N items, the probability of selecting the correct item is half of the probability of selecting the incorrect item. Therefore, we need N/2 actions on average to retrieve the correct item. Nevertheless, Grover created an algorithm based on quantum logic that completes the identical task in an average of $\sqrt{N}$ operations.

1.4.4 Quantum system simulation with a classical computer

In 1982, Richard P. Feynman hypothesized that a standard computer could not simulate a quantum physical system of N particles with their quantum probabilities without experiencing an exponential slowdown in simulation performance. However, a polynomial slowdown can be used to mimic a system of N particles in classical physics. The primary cause of this is that, unlike classical physics, where a particle system's description size is linear in N, quantum computers—which use the rules of quantum mechanics as its foundation—have an exponential description size in N, which allows them to avoid the delay that occurs during the simulation of quantum systems. Feynman also discussed the challenge of using a probabilistic computer to simulate a quantum physical system, albeit it seems to be a challenging problem because of interference problems.

1.5 Foundations of Quantum Computing:

It is crucial to comprehend the basic ideas and principles underlying this ground-breaking technology before exploring how quantum computing is being used in the technological world.

Quantum bits, or qubits: Bits, which can have values of 0 or 1, are used in classical computing to represent and manipulate information. The quantum bit, or qubit, is the fundamental information unit in quantum computing. It may concurrently exist in a superposition of 0 and 1 states. Because of the superposition principle, quantum computers may represent and analyze several states at once, allowing for exponentially more concurrent computing.

Quantum Superposition and Entanglement: Quantum entanglement refers to the high correlation between the states of two or more quantum particles, whereas quantum superposition is the capacity of a quantum system to exist in several states simultaneously. Because they allow quantum algorithms to efficiently explore and manipulate increasingly huge state spaces, these phenomena are essential to the capability of quantum computing.

Quantum Gates and Circuits: Quantum computing uses quantum gates to control the states of qubits, just like conventional computing does using logic gates that operate on bits. These quantum gates, which are intended to take advantage of quantum phenomena like superposition and entanglement, are represented as unitary matrices. Complex quantum circuits that perform quantum algorithms can be created by merging many quantum gates.

Quantum Algorithms: Unlike its conventional counterparts, quantum algorithms are made to take use of the special characteristics of quantum computing in order to solve particular computational tasks more quickly. Grover's method for unstructured search issues, Shor's algorithm for prime factorization, and quantum machine learning algorithms for pattern recognition and data analysis are notable examples.

Quantum Error Correction and Fault Tolerance: Quantum computers are prone to mistakes and decoherence because of the brittleness of quantum systems and their susceptibility to external influences. Techniques for quantum error correction and fault-tolerance are crucial for preserving the accuracy and dependability of quantum computing, guaranteeing proper outcomes, and permitting scaling.

1.6 A completely new concept in parallelism: Quantum Computing

Even the fastest and most powerful computers have limitations when it comes to performing mathematical computations, searching the internet, modeling the country's economy, forecasting the weather, and other tasks. The problem lies not so much in the speed of microprocessors, but rather in the intrinsic inefficiency of computers. Programs that break down a task into simple actions that are subsequently performed serially, one at a time, are how modern (classical) computers work. Although attempts have been made to get two or more computers—or at the very least, two or more microprocessors—to work on various elements of an issue simultaneously, the field of parallel computing has only made sluggish, patchy progress in this regard. The main cause of this is that microprocessors' logic is fundamentally serial. Although standard computers can appear to be multitasking by running spreadsheet and word processor programs simultaneously, in actuality, the central processor is only quickly switching between tasks.

A parallel computer would be inherently simultaneous in every meaning of the word. It would be able to perform multiple tasks simultaneously, quickly sort through a lengthy number of options, and identify the solution. There are computers like this. We refer to them as quantum computers. Actually, quantum parallelism is the more fascinating aspect of quantum computing. Generally speaking, a quantum system is not in a single "classical state," but rather a "quantum state" that is made up of a superposition of numerous classical or classically inspired states. This is known as the linear superposition principle, and it is how quantum states are built. A quantum computer can produce outputs based on the specifics of all of its classically-like states if the superposition can be shielded from undesired entanglement with its surroundings (sometimes referred to as decoherence). This is parallelism on a serial machine, or quantum parallelism.

1.7 Conceptual representation of a quantum computer: Quantum superposition and quantum interference.

The basic unit of information in a quantum computer is referred to as a quantum bit, or "qubit," which is more quaternary in nature than binary, similar to the classical bit utilized in a conventional computer. This qubit's adherence to the principles of quantum movements directly results in this attribute. A qubit can exist in states that correspond to a blend of superposition of the classical states in addition to the logical states 0 or 1, as in a classical state bit. To put it another way, a qubit can exist as a zero, a one, or as both a zero and a one at the same time, with each state's probability represented by a numerical coefficient.

Given that everyday phenomena are regulated by conventional physics rather than quantum mechanics, which operates at the atomic level, this idea may seem counterintuitive. The spin s=1/2 of a single electron system can be used to physically represent a qubit, with the two states +1/2 and –1/2 representing the two eigenstates of Sz (the z component direction of an external magnetic field of spin ½). An alternative is to employ a single photon beam, with the overall state being the polarization state (vertical or horizontal) with respect to a selected axis. Consequently, a qubit can have two values, 0 or 1, which correspond to two eigenstates of, say, the spin of a single electron:

$$|1\rangle = |\uparrow\rangle$$
$$|0\rangle = |\downarrow\rangle$$
$$|0\rangle + |1\rangle = |\uparrow\rangle + |\downarrow\rangle$$

Additionally, a qubit can be a complex coefficient superposition of these two states, which sets it apart from classical bits seen in traditional computers. In mathematical words, we say that the state is described as a vector in the two-dimensional complex space c2, and the two pure states constitute the basis of the representation, as the general state of a qubit might be the superposition of two pure states with arbitrary complex coefficients. The following is an experimental demonstration of the quantum superposition phenomenon. Think about the below figure,

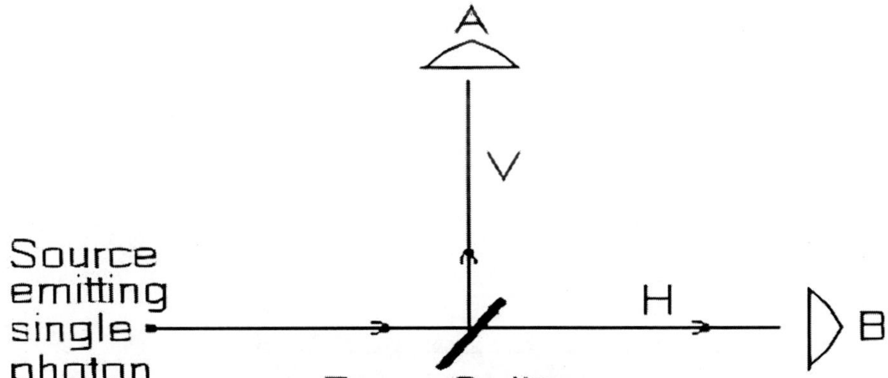

Fig.1.2 Beam division of light.

A photon is emitted by a light source and travels towards a mirror that is half-silvered. This mirror divides the light, sending half to detector B and reflecting the other half vertically toward detector A. A photon is equally likely to be detected at point A or point B since it represents a single quantized energy level (E=hv) and cannot be split. This is confirmed by observation: if signal is registered by detector A, then detector B does not, and vice versa. With this knowledge, one would prefer to believe that a photon randomly selects between traveling in a vertical or horizontal direction. However, according to quantum theory, the photon actually follows both directions concurrently, only collapsing into one path after measurement (collapse of the wave function). The single-particle interference that results from the linear superposition of the potential photon states of alternative routes is the name given to this effect. A little more complex experiment, shown in below fig., provides a better illustration of the single particle interference phenomena.

The photon in this experiment splits into a transmitted beam and a reflected beam after initially coming into contact with a half-polished mirror, or beam splitter. Before reaching a detector, the two beams are recombined with one half of the fully silvered mirrors, and then another half silvered mirror splits. A half-silvered mirror presents the possibility that a photon will follow one of two paths. When a photon travels vertically and strikes the mirror along one of the two paths following the first beam splitter, the arrangement is the same as in the above figure. According to the experiment in the above figure, there should be a 50% chance that the photon will strike either detector A or detector B. The same holds true for a photon moving in a horizontal direction. The real outcome, though, is very different.

It appears inevitable that the photon must have, in some sense, travelled both routes simultaneously if the two possible paths are exactly equal in length. This is because there is a 100% probability that the photon will reach detector A and a 0% probability that it will reach detector B. As a result, the photon is certain to strike detector A.

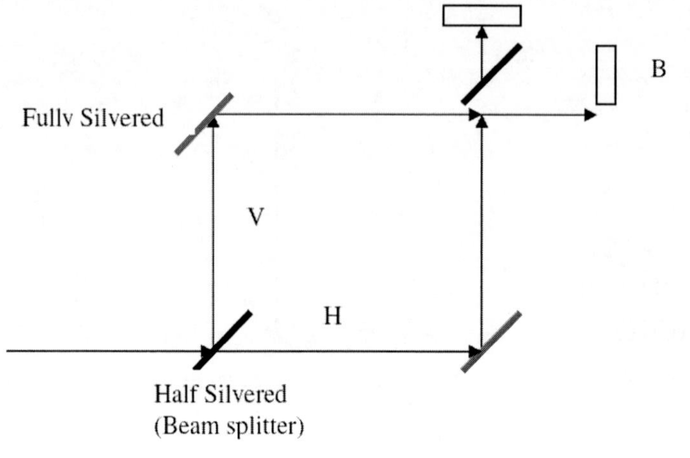

Fig.1.3 An illustration of the particle and wave natures of light.

This may be seen by blocking one of the paths with an absorbing screen, which makes it equally likely that detector A or B will be reached. When one of the channels is blocked, detector B can really be reached; since both paths are open, the photon must have realized that it cannot go to detector B and must have explored both of them. Therefore, it is entirely reasonable to state that the photon travelled both transmitted and reflected paths between the two half-silvered mirrors; alternatively, to use more scientific terminology, we might state that the photon is coherently superposed between being in the transmitted beam and the reflected beam.

The principle of linear superposition is responsible for this quantum interference. Because quantum computers harness those special characteristics that give them the potential to be extremely powerful computational devices, current research in quantum computing is not just a continuation of today's computer concept, but rather a completely new branch of thought and underlying idea. This is one of those unique characteristics that makes quantum computing research so exciting.

1.8 Entanglement in quantum

Daily occurrences include the observation of correlations between different events. The equations of classical physics help to describe these relationships in a clear manner. Let's think about the following illustration: Imagine that you are picturing a bank heist situation. The terrified teller is being threatened with a gun by the bank robber. One can determine if the gun has fired by glancing at the teller; if the teller is uninjured and still alive, then the pistol has not been fired. One can determine that the gun has fired if the teller is found dead on the ground from a gunshot wound. This is an easy case for a detective. The condition of the gun and the teller are therefore directly correlated: "gun fired" indicates "teller alive." It is assumed that the thief in this instance exclusively shoots to kill and never misses.

Think about a nucleus that could radioactively decay in a specific amount of time or not. As a result, there are only two conceivable states for the nucleus in terms of decay: "decayed" and "not decayed," just as there were two states for the gun: "fired" and "not fired," or "alive" and "dead" for the teller. But in the quantum mechanical world, an atom may also exist in a hybrid condition known as decayed-not-decayed, when it is in between the two states and neither is entirely in one or the other. The reason for this is the atomic principle of linear superposition of two quantum mechanical states.

Let's now take a closer look at a system with two nuclei. It's possible for two nuclei to be correlated such that if one decays, the other will follow suit. Moreover, if neither has degraded, then neither has the other. There is a perfect correlation here. Nevertheless, there is a chance that the nuclei are correlated, meaning that if one is in the superposition state of "decayed-not-decayed," the other will follow suit. Therefore, there is one more correlation between nuclei in quantum mechanics than in classical theory. We refer to this type of quantum "super correlation" as "entanglement."

In actuality, the German term for entanglement was initially "Verschrankung," coined by physicist Erwin Schrodinger, who won the Nobel Prize in physics for his fundamental work in quantum mechanics. It was Schrodinger who first recognized the peculiar nature of entanglement.

Imagine that the nucleus controls whether or not the gun fires, not the thief. The gun discharges when the nucleus decays because it activates a hair trigger. The pistol will not discharge if it does not decompose. However, it is possible to correlate the gun in a superposition state fired-not fired if the nucleus is in superposition.

But this correlation results in a dire circumstance. In this instance, the teller is simultaneously alive and dead! Schrodinger was concerned about the analogous scenario in which a cat in a box was the victim of quantum entanglement (Schrodinger cat: A paradox). The deterioration of the Schrodinger cat in a box could cause a deadly toxin to be released. The main issue is that we are not accustomed to seeing dead-alive cats or dead-alive tellers in the real world.

Such odd situations ought to be conceivable in theory if quantum mechanics is to be a comprehensive theory explaining every aspect of our experience. Where does the classical world start and the quantum universe end? Is there a true interface separating the classical and quantum realms? And so forth. Numerous interpretations of quantum theory have been proposed during the lengthy description of these and related issues.

Einstein, Podolsky, and Rosen's 1935 seminal study highlighted the issue by arguing that quantum physics is not incorrect, despite its odd entanglement behavior. This is referred to as the EPR paradox. The following example can help you understand the idea of the EPR paradox: Think about an atom of helium in its ground state. The quantum numbers of its two electrons are as follows: n=1, l=0, s=1/2, sz = +1/2 for one, and sz = -1/2 for the other.

Consequently, j = 0 & 1. Nonetheless, jz = (sz)1 + (sz)2 = 0. Thus, only the state j=0 is permitted. As a result, two electrons in an atom of helium are antiparallel to one another and form an entangled pair. Enough energy is given to the atom (equivalent to the atom's binding energy). in order for it to crumble while at rest. As a result, two electrons depart in opposing directions.

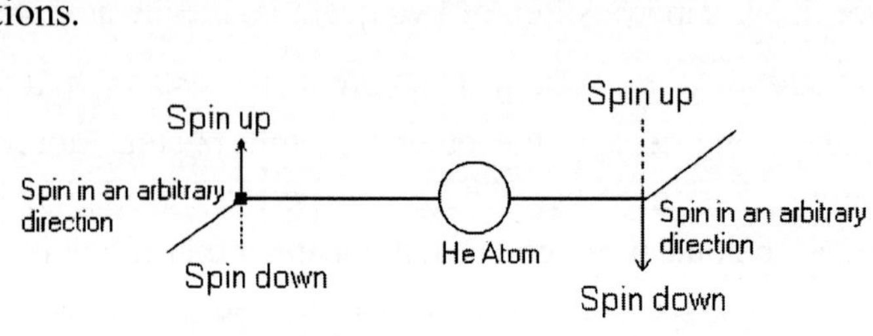

Fig.1.4 He atom explanation of the EPR paradox.

We separate two electrons. When a magnetic field is applied, one electron's spin flips instantly, flipping the spin of another electron as well (communication at a speed faster than light). This is a true occurrence that Einstein dubbed "spooky action at a distance." Einstein objected to the completeness of quantum theory since the mechanism behind it cannot yet be described by any theory and must be accepted as given. Nonetheless, we are aware that subsequent advances—such as Bell inequality and its experimental validation—have demonstrated the accuracy of quantum concepts, even when they imply communication between events that resemble space. The ability to determine another electron's spin state without measuring it is even more astounding.

Qubits can interact instantaneously (not just at the speed of light) while being separated by enormous distances thanks to quantum entanglement. As long as the associated particles are isolated, they will stay entangled regardless of how far apart they are. When combined, quantum superposition and entanglement produce a huge boost in processing capacity.

1.8.1 Bertleman's socks

At first glance, one might wonder: What makes quantum entanglement so unique? Similar circumstances—the occurrence of a correlation between two events—do occur outside of the quantum realm. Consider the instance of Mr.Bertleman, who has the odd habit of donning different coloured socks on his left and right foot. If he is wearing red socks on one foot, the other should be green, and if he is wearing yellow socks, the other should be blue. Mr. Bertleman presumably never disobeys the law. As a result, one can determine the colour of the second sock he is wearing just by observing the colour of one sock. On closer examination, though, the criticism mentioned above is not valid. In actuality, the choice of measurement is also quite important in quantum entanglement. It is possible to choose to measure the spin's x-, y-, or compound components along the s direction inclined at any inclination to the x-axis.

In accordance, the other particle organizes its spin. In Bertleman's example, there is a role for the spectator. When an observer chooses to view the yellow-blue color scheme of Bertleman socks, they consider their objective when choosing the color, and they find it as fascinating when this desire is communicated instantly.

1.8.2 Hidden Variables, EPR Situation, and Bell Theorem

John Bell's critical analysis of Einstein, Podolsky, and Rosen's (EPR) publication "Is Quantum Mechanics Complete?" produced the following contradicting results:

1. Because of the extreme strength of EPR correlations, also known as quantum entanglement, which quantum mechanics predicts, it is difficult to resist the conclusion that quantum mechanics needs some additional parameters, or so-called hidden variables.

2. The preceding result's clarification shows that the hidden variables description actually defies a few quantum mechanical expectations.

Given these two utterly compelling and incongruous findings, there's just one thing to do: inquire as to Nature's method of operation. There was no experimental result available to address this subject till the end of 1970. The contradiction that Bell found in the EPR report is so subtle that it only shows up in extremely unusual circumstances that haven't been looked at and demand that particular experiments be designed and built.

1.8.2.1 An instance of EPR

Think of a source that releases two photons, v1 and v2, that are traveling in opposing directions (Fig). Every photon strikes a polarizer, which measures the linear polarization in both of the two directions (a and b), as specified by the polarizer's orientation.

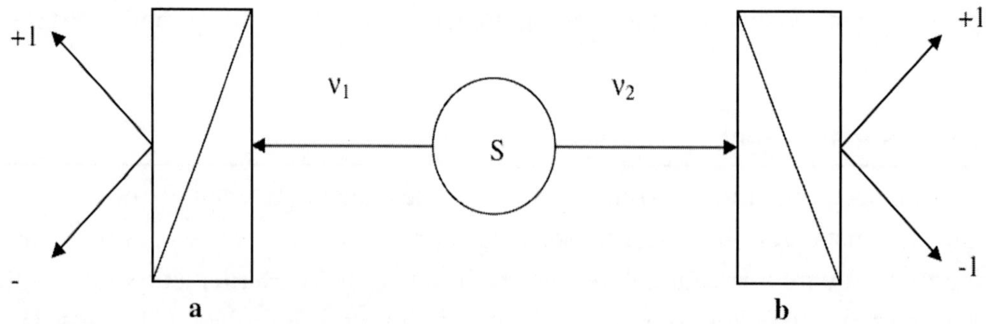

Fig.1.5 A visual depiction of the EPR scenario.

For every measurement, there are two possible results: +1 and –1. The presence of a two-photon state (EPR state), for which the polarization measurements done independently appear random but are tightly coupled, is permitted by quantum physics. For example, the probabilities P+(a) & P-(a) for photon v1 along an are projected to be equal to 0.5, regardless of orientation b. Similarly, the probabilities P+(b) & P-(b) for photon v2 are predicted to be equal to 0.5 and irrespective of orientation b.

Conversely, 0.5 Cos^2(a.b) is the joint probability P++(a) for witnessing + for both photons. Similarly, P--(0). For parallel polarisers [(a.b)=0], the joint probability is P++(0)=0.5. The joint probability for the cross polariser [(a.b)= □□2] is P-+(□/2)=P+-(□/2)=0. As a result, the outcomes for the two photons in the same pair are always the same, both + or – indicating perfect correlation. These kinds of associations between seemingly random events could also occur outside of the field of physics. Assume, for example, that biologists have noticed the emergence of a specific ailment (let's say G) in 50% of the population over the age of 20, and its absence in the other 50%. Upon examining a particular pair of identical brothers, it is discovered that there is a perfect correlation between the two outcomes: if one brother has the disease, the other brother also has it; conversely, if one brother has not got the ailment, the other brother is similarly untouched.

Given the exceptional association shown between twin brothers, researchers are likely to infer that the condition is rooted in genetics. A straightforward scenario may be proposed: during the initial stages of embryonic development, an arbitrary genetic process generated a pair of chromosomes, one of which is accountable for the presence or lack of the sickness that has been replicated and passed down to both brothers.

As a result, there is an exact analogy between the two scenarios: the correlation between the polarized states of two photons and the instance of twin brothers, both of which can be exemplified. Therefore, it would appear reasonable to attribute this correlation between the photon pairs to a shared characteristic, such as the two twin brothers' shared genome. This shared attribute varies from pair to pair, which explains why the single event is random. John Bell's primary conclusion on EPR states is as follows. The conclusion that quantum mechanics is not a full explanation of physical reality follows from a straightforward generalization of the EPR logic. In actuality, the idea that a pair's complete description must include "something" in addition to the state vector—which is the same for every pair—is implied by the insertion of "some common property," which varies between pairs. We can refer to this "something" as hidden variables or extra parameters. An account of the polarized states of two photons for any set (a, b) of orientations is sent when hidden variables are included.

1.8.2.2 Bell Disparities

Bell conducted a thorough analysis of the necessity of hidden variables in order to account for the anticipated correlation between the two polarized states of photons. It was demonstrated that the anticipated correlations, given the combined observations of photon polarized states as stated above, are subject to specific limitations but are not capable of taking any values. More specifically, Bell inequalities limit the corresponding correlation coefficients (which measure the amount of correlation) if we consider four possible sets of orientations [(a.b), (a.b'), (a'.b), (a'.b')]. These inequalities state that a given combination of these four coefficients, s, is between –2 and +2 for any reasonable hidden variable theory. Bell disparities therefore suggest a test to determine whether hidden variable theory is valid. Nonetheless, investigations verify that the value of s is 2.8, as predicted by quantum physics, which means that it defies Bell inequalities. Therefore, the above-mentioned hidden variable theories are unable to explain the EPR correlation (quantum entanglement) that quantum mechanics predicts. Compared to the mutual correlations between twin brothers, quantum mechanical correlations are much more difficult to comprehend.

Bell inequality is predicated on the idea of local models of hidden variables. According to the premise of locality, the orientation selected by one distant polariser cannot directly affect the outcome of a measurement made by another polariser. This is essentially just the result of Einstein's theory of causality, which states that no signal in a vacuum can travel faster than the speed of light. However, compared to local hidden variable theories, Bell inequalities apply to a wider range of theories.

Any theory, in which each photon has a “physical reality” localized in space-time, determining the outcome of the corresponding measurement, will lead to inequalities that (sometimes) conflict with quantum mechanics. Bell’s theorem can thus be phrased in the following way: some quantum mechanical predictions (EPR correlations-quantum entanglement) cannot be mimicked by any local realistic model in the spirit of Einstein ideas of theory of hidden variables.

1.9 Quantum Teleportation and Quantum Information Theory

Though this may seem harmless, information is physical, and any processing of it must always be done so physically. The implications of this are far from insignificant. A whole new subject known as the Quantum Theory of Information has emerged as a result of an explosion of theoretical and experimental advancements in recent years. Building qualitatively new kinds of logic gates, completely secure cryptosystems (comprising communications and cryptography), packing two bits of data into a single physical bit, and—as of late—the possibility of "teleportation" are all made possible by quantum mechanics.

Scientists did not take teleportation seriously until lately. Science fiction authors typically refer to the ability to cause an object or person to dissolve in one location while an exact duplicate arises someplace else as teleportation. This is typically accomplished by scanning the object in a way that extracts all of its information. This information is then transmitted to the receiving location and used to construct the replica, which is likely made of identically arranged atoms rather than the actual material of the original.

A teleportation device would function similarly to a fax machine, with the exception that it could scan documents and three-dimensional objects as well as generate an exact replica rather than an approximation, and that scanning the original would destroy it. According to classical physics, it is possible to teleport an object by measuring it in its entirety, sending the resulting information to a different location, and then reconstructing the thing. Additionally, classical information theory validates common sense: the greatest number of distinct messages that may be delivered is N if a message is to be conveyed using an item that can be placed in one of N distinctive states. A single photon, for instance, can only exist in the left- and right-handed polarization states. Consequently, no more than two distinct messages, or one bit of information, may be transmitted by a single photon.

Putting aside the fundamental query: is a comprehensive reconstruction of the original object possible? No, is the response. Furthermore, common sense is supported by classical information theory: if a message is to be sent using an item that may be placed in one of N distinct states, then the maximum number of distinct messages that may be delivered is N. For example, only the left- and right-handed polarization states are possible for a single photon. As a result, a single photon can only carry two different messages or one bit of information.

Putting aside the central question: is it feasible to rebuild the original object in its entirety? The answer is no.

Teleportation: It would be evident that a perfect copy could not be created if sufficient information could not be extracted from an object.

Stephen Wiesner and Charles H. Bennet's team have proposed an amazing method for teleporting quantum states using entangled states, or EPR states. An abstract description of quantum teleportation can be expressed in terms of two particles, A and B. A is in possession of an unidentified state |□>, which is represented as:

$$|\psi\rangle = \alpha|0\rangle + \beta|1\rangle$$

This is a two level quantum system, or a single quantum bit, or qubit. The state |□> is to be transported from A to B via teleportation. To do this, entangled states are used. One qubit of a two qubit entangled state is possessed by each of A and B.

$$|\psi\rangle(|0\rangle_A |0\rangle_B) + |1\rangle_A|1\rangle_B)$$

The aforementioned state can be rewritten for the first two qubits in the Bell basis (|00>±|11>)), (|01>±|10>), and for the final qubit in a conditional unitary transformation of the state $|\psi\rangle$.

$$(|00\rangle+|11\rangle)|\psi\rangle+(|00\rangle-|11\rangle)\sigma_Z|\psi\rangle + (|01\rangle+|10\rangle)\sigma_X |\psi\rangle + (|01\rangle-|10\rangle)(-i\sigma_Y|\psi\rangle)$$

in which the Pauli matrices $\sigma_X, \sigma_Y, \sigma_Z$ are in the |0>, |1> basis. On A's qubits, a measurement is made in the Bell basis. These measurements' results determine B's respective states, which are $|\psi\rangle$, $\sigma_Z |\psi\rangle$, $\sigma_X |\psi\rangle$, $-i\sigma_Z |\psi\rangle$. B receives the measurement result from A, and based on that result, applies the appropriate unitary transformation I, σ_Z, σ_Y or $i\sigma_Y$ to restore the original state $|\psi\rangle$. It should be highlighted that because B must wait for A's measurement result to arrive before he can recover the quantum state, quantum state transfer has not been completed quicker than light.

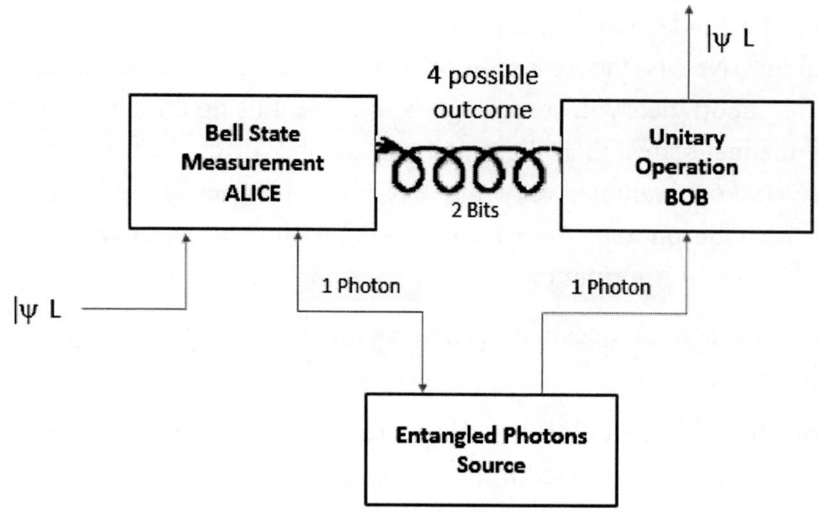

Fig.1.6 Quantum entanglement based transportation.

1.10 Thermodynamics of Quantum Computing

Since computers are machines, they are subject to the laws of thermodynamics, which impose limits on all machinery. Like any physical system, contemporary computers that run on digital electronics generate heat when they're operating. The fundamental query is: Is it possible to make improvements to digital computers to reduce heat production? It turns out that, in accordance with the rules of physics, it is feasible to imagine the perfect computer that is able to shape, preserve, and move digital signals without producing heat. However, there is one location where heat generation is required. The phase space connected to the information-storing system contracts whenever data is removed. When a single bit of data is erased, the system that stored it experiences at least □ S=klog2 decrease in entropy. Heat transfer to the surroundings is the result of this entropy reduction.

Therefore, if a computer could be built that never erases any data, it would be able to function without producing any heat at all. This is the exact scenario that exists in quantum computing. Although the readout of the computation's output is not reversible, quantum computation is. Thus, it is possible to perform quantum computation without producing heat, at least in theory. In actuality, the computer would still produce a significant amount of heat. Electric pulses would have to overcome resistance in order to travel via copper cables. Heat would still be produced by electrons diffusing from a source colliding with crystal flaws and with other electrons in the drain. However, under the best of circumstances, copper wires might be swapped out for imperfect crystals with perfect one or superconductors.

The creation of unique gates is the first step toward realizing the reversibility of quantum computers. Digital computers use gates such as NOR, AND, NAND, and XOR. Since each of these gates must produce heat, they are all irreversible.

$$(a,b) \longrightarrow (a \wedge b)$$

The amount of information on the right side of the chart is smaller than that on the left. Charles Bennett has shown that quantum computers can do any computation with just reversible steps by using Toffoli gates. These unique gates allow the computation to be performed both forward and backward by preserving all data that is given to them. As a result, the computation produces a huge quantity of data as each intermediate step is remembered, but it also eliminates heat generation, allowing the computation to continue. The computer can be restarted from the beginning to return to its starting state and prevent spontaneous combustion once the computation has finished.

1.11 Quantum Computer Realization in Experiment

The quantum computer's straightforward architecture makes it quicker, smaller, and less expensive, but its conceptual complexity is making it challenging to realize in practice. However, there have been other attempts in this direction with hopeful results. It is anticipated that the day when a quantum computer fully replaces a digital computer may not be too far off. The following is a summary of some of the attempts made to achieve a quantum computer through experimentation:

1.11.1 Heteropolymers

Teich invented and constructed the first heteropolymer-based quantum computer in 1988, and Lloyd upgraded it in 1993. Memory cells in a heteropolymer computer are made up of a linear array of atoms. An excited state of the appropriate atom is pumped into a cell to store information. Laser pulses at precisely tuned frequencies deliver instructions to the heteropolymer. The pulse's duration and shape dictate the type of calculation that is carried out on particular atoms.

1.11.2 Ion Traps

In 1995, Cirac and Zoller suggested the concept of an ion trap quantum computer. It was subsequently developed by Monroe and associates in 1995 and by Schwarzchild in 1996. Data is encoded in the energy levels of ions and in the vibrational modes that exist between them by the ion trap computer. From a conceptual standpoint, a different laser powers each ion. An initial examination revealed that the ion trap computer is capable of evaluating Fourier transforms. This ultimately leads to the Fourier transform-based Shor factoring algorithm.

1.11.3 Quantum Electrodynamics Cavity

In 1995, Turkette and associates presented a demonstration of a quantum electrodynamics (QED) cavity computer. The components of the computer are a QED cavity with a few cesium atoms inside of it, as well as a configuration of mirrors, polarizers, phase shift detectors, and lasers. Because the system is able to generate, modify, and maintain entanglements and superposition, it is a real quantum computer.

Nuclear Magnetic Resonance (NMR) computer: An NMR machine and a liquid-filled capsule make up an NMR computer. The liquid's molecules function as separate quantum memory registers. The sample is exposed to radio pulses, and the computation proceeds by reading the response. Qubits are implemented as the spin states of the atoms that make up molecules' nucleus. An NMR computer uses a statistical ensemble of, say, $2.7\text{x}10^{19}$ molecules as a basis for measurement in order to read out the memory register. This is not the case with the QED cavity computer ion-trap computer, where the memory register was a single isolated quantum system. Non-polynomial (NP) full problems can be solved by an NMR computer in polynomial time. Using NMR computers, the majority of quantum computing's practical achievements to date have been made.

1.11.4 Atomic Dots

Compared to the four quantum computer implementations that have been covered thus far, quantum computers based on quantum dot technology have a simpler architecture and require fewer advanced experimental, theoretical, and mathematical understanding. Split gate approach is used to create quantum gates from an array of quantum dots that are connected to their closest neighbors via gated tunneling barriers. One of the main benefits of this system is that the qubits are electrically controlled. The drawback of this architecture is that although quantum dots can communicate with their closest neighbors, it can be challenging to read out the data.

1.11.4.1 Josephson Intersections

In 1999, Nakamura and associates presented a demonstration of the Josephson junction quantum computer. A bulk superconductor is weakly linked to a Cooper pair box, a tiny superconducting island electrode, in this computer. A Josephson junction, which functions as a capacitor, is created between the superconductors by weak coupling.

The charging current splits into discrete transfers of individual Cooper pairs if the Cooper box is as small as a quantum dot. In the end, this allows one to transfer only one Cooper pair across the junction. Qubits are electrically regulated, just like in Josephson junction computers and quantum dot computers. Quantum computers based on Josephson junctions are a good option for upcoming advancements.

1.11.4.2 Kane Computer

This computer resembles a quantum dot computer in several aspects, but it resembles an NMR computer in other aspects as well. It is composed of one magnetically active p^{31} nucleus within an isotropically clean, magnetically inactive Si^{28} crystal. After that, the sample is subjected to an extremely powerful magnetic field, which causes the spin of p^{31} to align either parallel or antiparallel to the field's direction. Next, by delivering a radio frequency pulse to the A-gate, a control electrode located next to the nucleus, one can regulate the spin of the p^{31} nucleus. By providing voltage to J-gate electrodes positioned in between the p^{31} nuclei, one could control the electron-mediated interaction between spins.

1.11.5 Quantum Computer with Topological Properties

Qubits are encoded in an anyon system in this computer. "Anyons" are quasiparticles in two-dimensional media that follow Para statistics rather than Bose-Einstein or Fermi-Dirac. However, because of a repulsion that is similar to that of fermions, anyons are still somewhat closer to them. The braid group describes each anyon's specific movement. The concept of the topological quantum computer is to perform quantum computing by utilizing the features of the braid group, which characterize the motion of anyons. It is stated that a computer of this kind ought to be impervious to quantum mistakes pertaining to anyons' topological stability.

1.12 Prospects for Quantum Computing in the Future

The field of quantum computation already has a solid basis, but further research is being done to determine what else will be needed for it to continue growing. This includes atomic scale technology, quantum algorithms, dynamics comprehension and control, and valuable applications. Quantum computation's reversibility may be useful in resolving NP issues, which are simple in one direction but difficult in the other. Interference may help with global minimization problems (see Fermat's principle in wave mechanics). Quantum tunneling over obstacles could lead to improvements in simulated annealing techniques. New algorithms may be produced by the powerful characteristics of complex numbers, such as conformal mappings and analytic functions.

Quanta may be created and destroyed using quantum field theory, which expands the capabilities of quantum computation. Quantum optics provides an ideal environment for these kinds of activities. One way to think of the copy operation is the conventional double slit experiment, also known as the beam splitter. Because the intensity of the two copies is half that of the original value, it is allowed under quantum theory. There is a lack of developed theoretical methods to handle many-body quantum entanglement. Its enhanced characterization could lead to more effective quantum logic gate implementation and opportunities for correlated error correction.

Decoherence is an efficient process, although its dynamics are not well understood. The environment-favored eigenstates in a given setup should be able to be identified in order to control decoherence. Even after decades of quantum mechanics, the dynamics of the measurement process remain unclear. In a unitary quantum theory, measurement is simply defined as a non-unitary projection operator. Since the system and the observer are ultimately composed of quantum building pieces, it is necessary to establish a single quantum description that encompasses both measurement and decoherence.

In addition to providing theoretical gain, it would aid in enhancing detectors that function near the quantum limit of observation. It is of tremendous interest to physicists to research the crossover from the classical to the quantum state. We can get there by expanding the system from microscopic to mesoscopic levels and shrinking the environment from macroscopic to mesoscopic levels. The battle to create quantum devices would reveal everything hidden beneath the surface of quantum theory. In our quest to overcome decoherence, we might come upon further constraints on quantum theory.

If there is no corresponding technology, theoretical advancements on their own will be useless.

The current race to reduce the size of electronic circuits is closely related to the quantum reality of the natural world. We must shift from a scientific to a technological perspective when creating new kinds of equipment because quantum effects are not just for observation; we also need to learn how to manage them through real-world applications. Though it cannot yet be predicted, the future is bright and hopeful.

1.13 Quantum Com puting – Pros and Cons

Every work that a conventional computer can complete, a quantum computer can too. There is a catch, though. A quantum computer will just carry out the computation similarly to a conventional computer if we utilize classical algorithms on it. Quantum algorithms must be developed in order to fully exploit a quantum computer. The phenomena of quantum parallelism may be utilized by quantum algorithms. It takes a lot of research and development to construct these algorithms, thus it is not a simple task.

One of the techniques is the quantum factorization algorithm developed by AT&T Bell Laboratories' Peter Shor. The technique addresses the challenge of breaking down big integers into their prime elements. Assuming present technology, this issue is historically very tough to accomplish. Shor's algorithm solves the prime factorization issue in a matter of seconds by deftly utilizing the effects of quantum parallelism.

PROS

Speed: When it comes to certain types of computations, quantum computers outperform conventional computers significantly, especially when factoring large numbers and simulating quantum processes.

Parallelism: Some problems can be addressed considerably faster than others because quantum computers are able to conduct several calculations at once.

Large-scale optimization: Quantum algorithms solve complicated optimization problems more quickly and accurately than traditional methods.

Simulating quantum systems: Because a quantum computer is built on concepts from quantum physics, it can mimic quantum systems more accurately and successfully than a regular computer.

Cryptography: Although quantum computers may break some of the encryption employed by traditional computers, they also open up new avenues for confidential communication.

CONS

Hardware: Creating a large-scale, trustworthy quantum computer is a major engineering challenge since the size and stability of current quantum computers are limited.

Software: The field of building quantum algorithms and software is still in its infancy, and there is a dearth of skilled workers.

Cost: The present high cost of developing and maintaining quantum computers may hinder their widespread use.

Errors and noise: Unlike traditional computers, quantum computers are more vulnerable to errors and noise, and resolving these issues can be challenging.

Scalability: Large-scale, reliable quantum computers that can solve complicated problems are yet unknown, and quantum computers are currently only partially scalable.

Interoperability: Comparing and combining different quantum computers may be difficult due to the absence of standards in the field of quantum computing.

In certain situations, it would take a classical computer longer than the universe's lifetime to get a result. It is obvious that algorithmic advances are just as important as technological ones, and in order to speed the development of quantum computing, we do need additional supporting technologies like big data, cloud computing, machine learning (ML), and artificial intelligence (AI).

1.14 Quantum Cloud Integration for Collaboration and Connectivity

The emergence of cloud computing has brought about a fundamental transformation in the ways that data is shared, accessed, and stored, enabling remote teams to work together efficiently. When communication technology and the cloud are effectively connected, our digital interactions are maximized. This has several positive effects. Above all, scalability and flexibility allow individuals and organizations to swiftly adjust communication resources, such adding more data storage or bandwidth. In terms of economics, this integration saves money via lowering infrastructure costs, eliminating the need for a major hardware investment, and utilizing pay-as-you-go methods.

Cloud-based communication solutions facilitate real-time collaboration by enabling teams to work together on projects, exchange data, and connect easily from various locations and devices. Improved accessibility also ensures that users can access communication tools, software, and documents from any internet-connected device, which promotes productivity when on the go.

New opportunities arise when cloud computing and quantum computing are combined. Because they use quantum algorithms, cloud-based machine learning models with quantum-inspired capabilities are more powerful and effective. Cloud security methods that are "quantum-safe" have been developed in response to the advancements in quantum computing, strengthening data protection against potential attackers. Significant improvements in cloud computing techniques that are energy- and environmentally-efficient might result from using the unique properties of quantum computing, such as quantum entanglement and annealing.

1. The convergence of cloud integration and quantum computing will shape communication technology in the future by combining unmatched processing power and security with smooth collaboration and connection.
2. The distinctive feature of quantum computing is its ability to act as a catalyst, delivering quicker data processing and more robust security measures to enterprises.
3. Cloud integration plays a major role in the creation of a communication infrastructure that is scalable, reasonably priced, and readily available.
4. The combination of cloud computing with quantum computing creates ground-breaking possibilities including machine learning influenced by quantum mechanics, cloud computing that is safe for the environment, and cloud computing that is safe for quantum computing.

1.15 Progress of Cloud based and quantum communication

Encryption:

As quantum computing becomes more pervasive, it is becoming increasingly evident that encryption methods need to be robust to quantum assaults. Researchers are working on developing such algorithms to ensure that cloud-based communication remains secure over time, even in the face of potential quantum assaults.

Beyond the realm of cloud-based communication, quantum computing has the potential to spur breakthrough advances in many other fields. The outcomes of ongoing research initiatives ought to change the dynamics of interaction and communication and provide new application opportunities.

Accessibility:

It is projected that rising spending and upcoming advances in quantum technology will drive down prices in the next years, making quantum computers more affordable. This shift will allow businesses of all sizes to leverage quantum computing for cloud-based communication.

Quick and efficient communication is crucial in the dynamic digital world of today. Because cloud-based communication services enable seamless client interactions, real-time data transmission, and distant collaboration, they are indispensable in many businesses. Nevertheless, the processing capacity and temporal limitations of conventional computer systems limit the pace and effectiveness of these services. A solution to these problems is provided by quantum computing, which makes use of the concepts of quantum mechanics to perform complex computations on a scale never previously possible. Unlike conventional computing, which uses bits to store and process data, quantum computing uses quantum bits, or qubits.

1.16 How does cloud-based quantum computing operate?

Cloud-based quantum computing blends the scalability and accessibility of cloud computing with the capabilities of quantum computing. Without specific gear, users may execute quantum algorithms and access quantum resources via the cloud. During a computation, these processes allow quantum information to be altered and transformed.

1.17 Quantum Technology for Digital Delegation

Decentralized decision-making may appear to be a simple and primitive approach, but it can be effective. It can be challenging to picture ourselves in four dimensions. Consider bees, ants, and termites. Unlike popular belief, social insects do not rely on a single decision-maker, which is the queen. The queen likely makes the fewest decisions among colonists. Her primary duty is to lay eggs. Workers, foragers, and soldiers make their own decisions. They make both individual and group decisions, such as moving the nest or directing foragers to a specific location.

Large nests and hives, spanning dozens of cubic meters, are not produced by a single person or small team. Individuals build and maintain emergent structures using simple instructions. A bee or termite building an above-ground nest will add material until it reaches the edge or runs out. Complex decisions are reduced down into simpler equations. This is comparable to how modern artificial neural networks (ANNs) execute tasks like handwriting and image recognition. Termite nests, the insect equivalent of skyscrapers, are built through decentralized decision-making without a single individual or small group in charge. This concept is so foreign to humans that we invented the myth of the queen insect to explain it.

Imagine constructing a 40-story structure without a centralized plan, boss, or foreperson. How does this relate to the complex systemic difficulties discussed so far? Our civilization has made significant progress in addressing complex issues. While famine persists, the issue is a lack of food and calories. Food waste and obesity are ongoing and growing issues. Equitable distribution is a complex problem. This field encompasses politics, economics, social and gender systems, and geography, among others.

Solving complex issues with multiple variables is beyond the capabilities of individuals or small groups. Decentralized decision-making is necessary for addressing these issues. Complex challenges necessitate decision-making at the edge, as well as grasping the whole picture and potential consequences. This final aspect is where we view the future. Modern AI systems rely on artificial neural networks (ANNs) to tackle complicated systemic problems, rather than breaking them down and locating edges. Our goal is to enable AI to process data in a quantum, rather than linear, manner, akin to how humans do.

Although we do not advocate for quantum awareness, peer-reviewed research consistently demonstrates the reality of quantum biology. Quantum mechanics may have a role in bird navigation, plant energy conversion, enzyme function, and neurological functioning. Quantum computers can crack encryption faster than linear processors, thanks to the idea of superposition. Quantum-based artificial neural networks (ANNs) process data through superposition, resulting in faster and more comprehensive solutions. These systems will be able to consider several variables and combinations. Replicating these systems at industrial scale enables quantum-based, decentralized decision-making.

The Quantum Delegation Era

Quantum AI technologies for digital delegation will gradually become more widely adopted. Quantum computing is expected to become commoditized and a viable alternative to classical computing, resulting in the advent of quantum delegation. Quantum delegation's key enablers are already in place and are expected to grow further.

These enablers are both technical and economic. The Internet of Things, data storage, and data science are key technical enablers for scaling digital delegation within enterprises. The Internet of Things refers to inexpensive and widely available sensors that continuously collect data. The use of cloud technologies will lead to more affordable, high-volume data storage, enabling enterprises to manage large data lakes for analysis. Data scientists will benefit from specialized education and training programs to create advanced algorithms that utilize new data sources.

Economies of scale will be the primary economic driver, making it easier to purchase pre-trained systems with programmable algorithms rather than building quantum delegation tools individually. Commercial-off-the-shelf products will prevail, leading to startup enterprises focusing on particular business areas and developing enterprise quantum delegation tools. Differentiating between niche and enterprise quantum delegation tools is their ability to be in two states simultaneously, according to the principles of quantum mechanics. These two states are configurable and scalable. Quantum delegation technologies will provide personalized delegation at scale. Customized medical diagnosis offer personalized care and can be deployed globally. Quantum delegation techniques can benefit tiny financial advice firms and other small enterprises by using large volumes of data. Quantum delegation tools will transform the public sector.

Government bureaucracy exists for good cause. Large-scale problems have typically been broken down into smaller, more manageable components, yielding generic results. Public services, tax collection, and criminal justice all aim to provide solutions that benefit the majority of citizens. Citizens with unique problems or situations have significant challenges in navigating bureaucratic processes. Quantum delegation tools can improve decision-making between government and citizens. These tools will enhance, if not replace, decisions made by judges, case workers, police, and DMV officials.

As early adopters install quantum delegation technologies, certain businesses will monitor for potential concerns, including as data security and scale-related issues. The technologies will eventually be vital in both private and public life, whether for maintaining commercial competitiveness or staying ahead of a geopolitical foe. The technology industry typically offers goods tailored to the demands of medium and small organizations. Initially, only large corporations will have access to quantum AI solutions. However, these corporations will eventually commercialize them as a service that can be scaled up or down, or integrated into products and services, to capture small and midsize market share. As quantum delegation products become more popular, startups will emerge to provide niche goods, while large technology corporations will focus on creating enterprise solutions that can be scaled to meet the needs of various customer sizes.

Social Implications of Quantum Delegation

Adopting quantum digital delegation tools benefits both enterprises and society as a whole, particularly in the public sector. Quantum delegation enables faster deployment of personalized solutions for society. Quantum delegation promotes diversity while avoiding one-size-fits-all.- This movement improves society by providing personalized advice and addressing systemic issues including social welfare distribution, taxation, healthcare, poverty, homelessness, and racism. Quantum delegation techniques can improve transparency, risk management, adaptability, and reduce personal agendas in politics. Most policies are one-size-fits-most, or worse. Quantum delegation can improve risk analysis and decision-making in complex systems, but it also increases interconnection and introduces new dangers. Automating and delegating actions at system edges, rather than relying on centralized decision-making, might increase system risks. Our connection and sensitivity to external cues, whether real or fabricated, will increase. As quantum digital delegation products become more prevalent, enterprises must update to remain competitive. To gain a competitive advantage, it's crucial to be able to configure algorithms, connect various quantum digital delegation tools, secure them, and ensure the accuracy of the data fed into them.

Quantum computing's widespread availability will accelerate digital delegation in both commercial and public sectors. Quantum delegation products will be built to scale and offered to several tiers of purchasers, using existing trends in data-driven decision-making, data production through the Internet of Things, and commercial solutions. Large firms investing in these tools can use their data to train algorithms that can then benefit smaller organizations. As solutions improve and models get more complex, enterprises increasingly rely on automation technologies to enhance their data-driven insights. This enables businesses to make more decentralized, real-time choices and actions.

Quantum delegation will improve the public sector by optimizing complicated social issues like poverty and benefit distribution for individuals. This allows for more diverse solutions to systemic difficulties, reducing the need for "one-size-fits-all" approaches with unintended consequences.

1.18 Application Platform for Collaborative Quantum

In recent years, experts from a variety of industries have created novel quantum algorithms and applications, propelled by the ongoing advancements in quantum technology. Small and medium-sized businesses frequently lack the in-depth theoretical and practical understanding needed to apply these quantum applications. Facilitating the transfer of information between research and practice in order to recognize and fully utilize the promise of new developing technologies is one of the biggest challenges of our day. In order to reasonably develop a body of knowledge for quantum computing and make it usable for various stakeholders, it is imperative that all parties join together on a collaborative platform. For this reason, the quantum application platform needs to encompass every step of the process, from creating quantum algorithms to putting them into practice and carrying them out.

Such a quantum platform must meet a number of requirements due to the diversity of stakeholders and their disparate goals. Build on the stakeholders by first identifying important organizations that act as a knowledge anchor on a quantum platform, then identifying the necessary conditions for their quick implementation, and lastly demonstrating a general extensible architecture for a collaborative quantum software platform.

1.18.1 Key Entities

It is possible to use the following important entities to promote a clear organization of the knowledge generated on a quantum software platform. They facilitate the sharing and contribution of knowledge by allowing various professionals to connect to the platform.

Quantum Algorithm: As previously said, specialists with a thorough understanding of quantum physics usually design and specify quantum algorithms. Therefore, capturing quantum algorithms as artifacts is crucial for a quantum software platform.

In addition to sharing them broadly, quantum algorithms can also be associated with other useful information, such as expert debate about an algorithm's resource consumption, speedup over classical algorithms, or suitability for NISQ systems.

Application of Algorithms:

The diverse field of quantum hardware requires that vendor- and even hardware-specific implementations of quantum algorithms be captured, in addition to the depiction of quantum algorithms in their conceptual form, such as mathematical formulas or abstract circuits. This is because using a vendor-specific SDK is necessary for implementations for a certain vendor's quantum computer product. As a result, algorithms for quantum computers that are implemented by various suppliers often use different code or even entirely different quantum programming languages. Thus, allowing the sharing of various method implementations on a quantum software platform promotes knowledge transfer and lessens ramp-up, particularly for users who lack experience.

Data Transformator: Unlike classical software, which works directly with data, quantum algorithms work by manipulating quantum states. Rather, the information that needs to be processed needs to be encoded such that it may be prepared into a quantum register. Certain issue classes, like data clustering or classification, have particular processing needs. Finding general transformation and coding techniques for pertinent problem classes can be quite helpful. These tactics can then be explored and expressed as data transformators on the platform.

Hybrid Quantum Application: These must be provided alongside classical software components that operate on classical computers, as only the quantum components of an algorithm are carried out on a quantum computer. Quantum algorithms frequently require appropriate integration into an existing system environment, which includes appropriate data processing and preparation, in order to fully realize their potential.

For this reason, hybrid quantum applications are usually the solutions that are implemented in real-world scenarios. Consequently, knowledge sharing regarding suitable software solutions for specific use cases is restricted to hybrid quantum applications.

Quantum Pattern: In many computer science domains, software patterns are utilized to capture tried-and-true solutions to reoccurring issues. Therefore, quantum patterns appear to be a promising method for capturing tried-and-true solutions for the development of quantum algorithms, as well as for integrating them into current systems. The initial blueprints for creating quantum algorithms have already been released.

1.18.2 Prerequisites

Working together, multiple stakeholders can develop and contribute to a fair body of knowledge about quantum algorithms and applications. As opposed to conventional software engineering, computer scientists rather than quantum physicists usually do not specify quantum algorithms. Furthermore, since quantum states and their manipulation via unitary operators are now the fundamental building blocks of algorithms rather than loops, conditions, or procedure calls, a distinct mindset is needed to comprehend and apply those algorithms.

All platform users can contribute to the creation of additional value, including novice users and seasoned quantum experts. The prerequisites stated below must be fulfilled in order to do this.

Access to Knowledge: Frequently, only a few group of scientists and specialists possess the necessary knowledge to create and execute quantum algorithms. Companies must be given the authority to learn from and communicate with professionals (developers, service providers, consultants, and so forth) in order to recognize and take advantage of the practical applications of quantum computing. Furthermore, because there is a lot of research being done in this field, expert-to-expert communication is crucial for early dissemination and discussion of new discoveries.

Top Techniques for Developing Quantum Algorithms:

It takes extensive theoretical and practical knowledge and experience to build new algorithms. Reusable, documented best practices for reoccurring issues, or patterns, can aid and direct the creation of novel quantum algorithms.

1. **Assistance in Making Decisions for Quantum Applications and Suppliers:**

Finding suitable solutions for real-world use cases necessitates a two-stage decision-support process. The first step is to find quantum algorithms that work well for a particular issue. Second, for integration and execution, the right implementation and quantum hardware must be chosen. The second stage is primarily concerned with the resource usage of algorithms and implementations on various quantum devices.

2. **Vendor-Agnostic Use of Quantum Hardware:**

At the moment, proprietary SDKs created especially for each vendor's hardware provide access to a variety of algorithm implementations from several vendors. A standardized quantum programming language can help ensure that the quantum algorithm is portable between vendors, preventing vendor lockin.

3. **Data transformation for quantum algorithms:**

Sufficiently high-quality data is crucial, particularly for machine learning and artificial intelligence. This holds true for both quantum and conventional algorithms. For the quantum algorithm, such data must be made available and correspondingly encoded.

4. **Quantum Application as a Service (QaaS):**

The deployment of quantum applications is made more complex by their hybrid architecture, which combines classical and quantum components. Self-service portals that offer quantum apps "as a Service" make it easier to use the new technology.

1.18.3 Architecture

The collaborative quantum software platform's architecture is shown in the image below. The platform is essentially divided into two sections: the marketplace, which provides solutions in the form of quantum applications and consulting services, and the analysis and development platform, which is shown on the left of the figure for gathering, debating, analyzing, and sharing knowledge.

The platform for analysis and development caters to the requirements of researchers and experts in the fields of software engineering and quantum computing. Knowledge can be added to the platform in the first phase in the form of articles, software artifacts, datasets, or online content. This can be done automatically with a crawler or manually with a user interface.

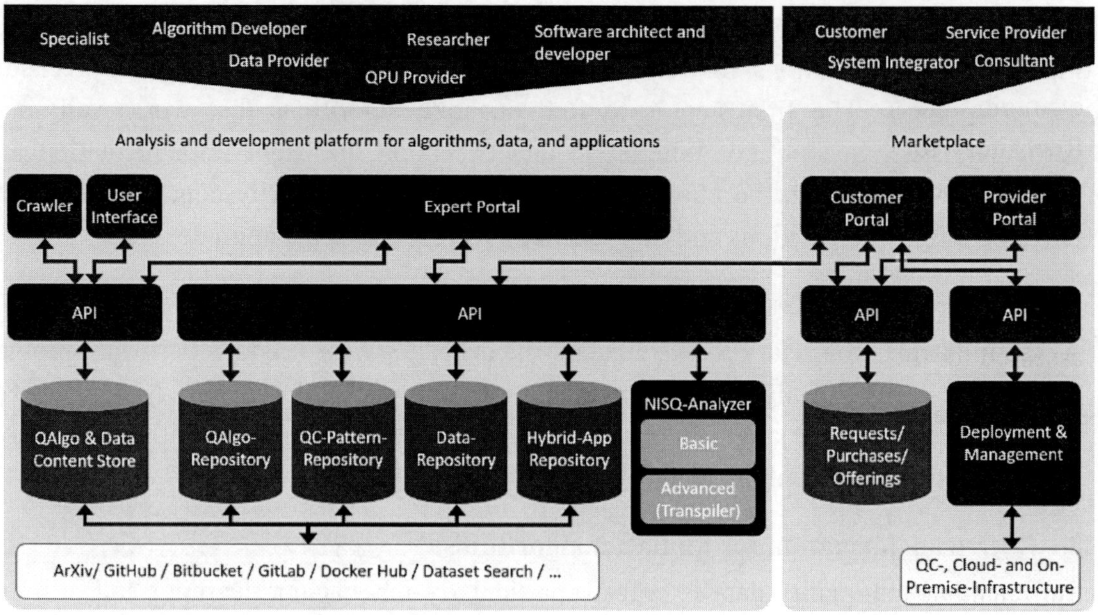

Fig.1.7 A collaborative quantum software platform's architecture.

It can be initially saved in the QAlgo & data content storage as raw data. It is necessary to extract relevant content from these raw data, like a quantum algorithm. Normalizing the representation of quantum circuits and mathematical expressions is necessary to promote cooperation between various fields and to establish a shared understanding. Finding and connecting pertinent knowledge also requires a qualified description of the knowledge asset with metadata. As a result, metadata formats need to be enhanced and standardized. After that, the knowledge artifacts are kept and made available to scientists and professionals through an expert portal, as well as to users and the community of interested parties seeking solutions for their use cases through a customer portal.

On the platform, scientists and specialists can debate, assess, and enhance the several important entities. The NISQ-Analyzer allows algorithms and their implementations to be connected and assessed using predetermined metrics. Best practices that have been identified, including those for entanglement creation, can subsequently be saved as quantum patterns in a Quantum Computing Pattern Repository. These patterns facilitate the creation of novel algorithms by offering tested fixes for common issues in quantum algorithm design. Patterns that address certain issues can then be combined and used to provide a wider use case. Best practices, however, are applicable not only to the construction of quantum algorithms but also to the integration of quantum algorithms with traditional applications and the preparation of data as input for quantum algorithms. In the NISQ age, data preparation is particularly important and needs to be taken into account.

The execution of quantum applications necessitates the dispersed deployment of hybrid quantum applications across classical and quantum hardware since the majority of quantum algorithms are hybrid algorithms. These apps can be kept in the Hybrid-App-Repository for later usage. Depending on the input data, algorithm implementation, and QPU characteristics, the vendor of the quantum computer—more especially, a single QPU—must be chosen for the quantum portion. The platform offers vendor-neutral access to quantum hardware and automates this selection process. In order to create an integrated deployment automation toolchain, traditional computing technologies are assessed for the deployment.

To facilitate portability, interoperability, and distribution across many settings, standards like the Topology and Orchestration Specification for Cloud Applications (TOSCA) have been specifically created for this reason. As a result, TOSCA, an international standard, provides a solid basis for combining classical and quantum deployment.

The marketplace on the right of the picture allows service providers and other stakeholders, such consultants, to offer solutions, while the expert site is designed to provide an adequate user interface and toolchain addressing the demands of specialists in quantum computing. Clients can submit requests for fixes for specific issues or use cases. It is also meant to enable the provision of consultancy services in addition to hybrid quantum applications and their implementations. This indicates that the interaction of the marketplace and the analysis and development platform enables business models in addition to their development and dissemination.

For instance, a TOSCA orchestrator like OpenTOSCA or Cloudify can facilitate the automatic deployment of hybrid quantum applications, enabling them to be offered as a service. Additionally, the NISQ-Analyzer and expert discussions can assist in choosing quantum algorithms that meet certain limitations of quantum hardware. Knowledge and software artifacts like hybrid quantum applications and implementations of quantum algorithms can be made profitable with the aid of the marketplace. There are incentives for participating professionals to contribute more knowledge to the platform with each turnover.

There will soon be new opportunities to use quantum computing to solve issues that have hitherto proven impossible. Due to the hybrid nature of quantum-based applications, cloud computing approaches will aid in the discipline of developing quantum computers, which are a component of the cloud infrastructure.

1.19 Understanding Quantum Noise: A Challenge

Quantum computing and artificial intelligence both have the power to produce outcomes that are difficult to independently verify, making them unique. Explanation and verification are not always difficult. Factoring numbers into their composite primes is a problem that can be solved using explainable algorithms. We can readily test candidate solutions to ensure they work. However, verifying and explaining complicated learning algorithms trained on big datasets to address high-dimensional problems is challenging. For many situations, it's crucial to not only swiftly achieve a result, but also comprehend why it was generated and evaluate its veracity.

Combining artificial intelligence and quantum computers can make explaining and verifying them more difficult for three reasons.

Quantum AI systems have exponentially huge Hilbert spaces with great dimensionality, making it impossible to sample more than a small portion of their state space. Quantum mechanics prohibits direct probing of intermediate states in quantum AI systems, which could interrupt calculations and lead to unexplainable outcomes. Quantum noise in AI systems is more difficult to mitigate than classical noise. The belief that quantum AI systems provide competitive benefits creates significant incentives to utilize them, especially in domains without reliable verification or understanding of their thinking. This article discusses the potential risks of quantum AI systems misinterpreting quantum noise as meaningful patterns and making actions that amplified highly correlated noise on a macroscopic scale.

Quantum computers use entanglement between qubits to achieve their power. Noise in a quantum computer can cause quantum-correlated mistakes to spread across the system unless fault-tolerant quantum error correction is implemented. Large-scale fault-tolerant, error-correcting quantum computers may take years, if not decades, to become a reality.

Fault-tolerant quantum computers require intricate engineering to maintain and control quantum entanglement for complex computations. A recent research suggests that a single effective fault-tolerant logical qubit may require 1,000 to 10,000 physical qubits, assuming a 1% error rate. The number of physical qubits needed per logical qubit varies based on error types and rates. However, even with advanced, scalable qubit architecture and control systems that are highly immune to errors, implementing a single fault-tolerant logical qubit will require a significant number of physical qubits. The current situation of the

Quantum computers contain fewer than 70 physical qubits and error rates of 1–2%. However, no fault-tolerant logical qubit has been shown. IBM aims to build a 1,000-qubit quantum computer by 2023, but achieving minimal error rates and precision control for real scalable logical qubits remains a challenge. Until scalable fault-tolerant quantum computers are available, we will continue to use noisy intermediate-scale quantum (NISQ) computers. These systems use noisy qubits and gate operations, with correlated errors spreading over time. Classical computer methods can evaluate NISQ data passively and control noisy quantum machines actively.

The first quantum AI systems will likely be NISQ-AI, which combines AI approaches with noisy qubits and gates. The initial steps of this development are already underway. Quantum learning algorithms will eventually embed qubits into their hardware, which I refer to as NISQ-AI.

An example of a NISQ-AI is a neural network with noisy qubit nodes.

The effectiveness of NISQ computers and AIs remains uncertain. Quantifying the capabilities of a NISQ computer, even when used to solve specific problems, is challenging due to controversies surrounding achieving quantum supremacy (the ability to perform calculations significantly faster than a realistic classical computer). As NISQ-AI systems get more complicated, this difficulty is likely to arise. Noise in NISQ-AIs leads to inaccuracies in state. Without fault-tolerant error correction, a single qubit can propagate throughout the system, resulting in entangled, nonlocally linked errors with increasing dimension. Analyzing high-dimensional data might make it difficult to distinguish between noise and real correlations.

Standard analysis methods presume statistical independence of noise sources. Averaging smoothes out random fluctuations, revealing genuine underlying signals. Classical machine learning algorithms employ nonlinearity to magnify signals and patterns, but rely on averaging to reduce noise. Nonlocal quantum noise can cause random fluctuations between widely separated qubits to be "spookily" coupled, challenging the concept of spatially independent fluctuations. AIs can mistake spatially correlated noise for significant correlations in data, leading to the emergence of ghost signals from quantum noise. Standard diagnostics may not discriminate between these patterns and others that are meaningful. Noise in classical data, such as financial markets, political polls, and health data, is frequently mistaken for meaningful information. Amplified quantum noise, with its unique and nonlocal features, is likely to be even more easily misinterpreted as signals.

As NISQ-AIs increase in number of qubits and coherence duration, it becomes difficult to accurately estimate the system's quantum state. This may make identifying whether nonlocal noise is amplified as false signal impossible. Using NISQ-AI systems for decision-making on critical topics may be problematic due to their intractability in verification and explainability. It's tough to distinguish between noise and signals. Quantum noise is more "dangerous" than classical noise due to its unique appearance. It is also resistant to traditional risk mitigation strategies that assume random noise is local and uncorrelated, with significant nonlocal correlation.

Why should we employ NISQ-AI systems outside of their intended domains, given these issues? Long-term investment, along with personal and institutional objectives, creates significant incentives to deploy technology for real-world applications. Evaluating the performance, reliability, and risks of NISQ-AI systems can be challenging, leading individuals, organizations, and nations to believe their system offers a competitive advantage while overlooking potential risks. False signals from quantum noise in NISQ-AI systems cannot be mistaken for conventional noise, as previously stated. Mistaking noise for signal and correlations for causality is a long-standing issue throughout human history.

Misuse of NISQ-AI systems might have varying effects depending on their use. If the systems are employed for exploratory inquiries, research, or well-constrained issues, such as quantum chemistry or material physics simulations, inconsistent performance may result in only lost time. Incorrect simulation results can lead to ineffective research directions. The risk is countered by the potential rewards of these machines producing significant results and advancing future technology. The risks of using NISQ-AI systems for crucial decision-making are speculative but should be considered. NISQ-AI systems could potentially be employed for fast-paced trading in financial markets.

Consider a system that consistently makes accurate forecasts, but occasionally trades due to quantum noise. If this happens on a large scale, it has the potential to create associated noise in markets, leading to unpredictable and destabilizing volatility. The 2008 market collapse was partly caused by risk models that mistakenly assumed uncorrelated factors, such as housing markets and financial instruments across multiple countries. The collapse highlights the risks of systems with hidden correlations, including the potential for huge, correlated consequences and the ineffectiveness of risk mitigation techniques based on uncorrelated factors. What is the potential risk of undetectable hidden correlations in markets?

Governments and armies are more risk-averse than firms, making them less likely to utilize NISQ-AI systems in vital procedures without proper testing and verification. If NISQ-AI systems demonstrate advantages under adequate testing conditions and quantum noise rates are low enough to avoid correlated errors, it may be tempting to use them without considering the risks. NISQ-AI systems that interpret correlated mistakes as signals can magnify nonlocal quantum noise to macroscopic levels. While noise and unpredictability are common in everyday life, nonlocal noise is not. NISQ-AI generates considerable nonlocal noise. Unconstrained systems necessitate a rethinking of risk mitigation strategies. Our actions may increase the frequency of black swan events in the future. Before NISQ-AI systems are used for critical decision-making applications, policy makers will need to carefully examine the risks and benefits from using unverifiable and unexplainable systems and reconsider how our familiar intuitions about risk can fail in a quantum world.

1.20 Identifying Quantum Advantage to Create a Sustainable MVP to Provide Quantum Computing Services

The future of computers is being heralded as Quantum Computing (QC). Following Google's 2019 assertion that it has achieved quantum supremacy, a number of organizations contested the assertion. By bringing down the current cryptographic cybersecurity architecture, some QC specialists identify catastrophic hazards that unchecked QC may generate in the future. These forecasts are only pertinent if QC develops into a sustainable and profitable industry in the future. No technology—or the standard by which that technology is judged to be superior—can be a one-way trip to disaster. Large-scale QC cannot become a minimal viable product (MVP) in the public domain if there are catastrophic hazards unless precautions are taken. Naturally, those protections ought to be a key component of the argument for why it is better than the outdated systems.

As that precaution, the National Institute of Standards & Technology, or NIST, is working to standardize post-quantum cryptography, or PQC. But since all 82 of the candidate PQCs are failing and businesses are already providing QC as a service, a different approach is desperately needed to lessen the threat of Q-Day and make QC sustainable.

How can we attain dominance or advantage if we don't know exactly what the requirements are to be eligible?

Can ethics and humanistic concerns be completely ignored at that threshold? If a nuclear chain reaction is uncontrollable, what good is it to humanity? Similarly, the concept of quantum advantage cannot be restricted to algorithmic superiority over legacy computing systems, especially since some experts believe that unchecked QC could pose a catastrophic threat by destroying the current cryptographic infrastructure, which would increase the existential risk to humanity. These forecasts are only pertinent if QC is made financially feasible and used for human benefit. Only when QC becomes commercially feasible and usable for the benefit of humanity will these forecasts be significant.

No technology—or the standard by which that technology is judged to be superior—can be a one-way trip to disaster. Without safeguards, QC can never become a minimal viable product (MVP) and enter the public domain if there are catastrophic hazards. Therefore, it goes without saying that those protections ought to be a fundamental component of the description of its advantage over traditional computers and a requirement to be fulfilled in order to reach the MVP barrier. As that precaution, the National Institute of Standards & Technology, or NIST, is working to standardize post-quantum cryptography, or PQC. An alternative approach is desperately needed, nevertheless, as 80 out of the 82 candidate PQCs failed in the first rounds and businesses are already providing QC as a service.

In recent years, quantum computing has advanced significantly in its promise to provide lightning-fast computation by leveraging quantum phenomena to transcend classical computation and achieve "Quantum supremacy," or, to use more politically correct terminology, "Quantum advantage." Quantum computing is not without its restrictions, despite these fascinating new developments. A current era of quantum computers that can handle intermediate executions of 50–100 qubits is defined by NISQ, or the Noisy Intermediate Scale Quantum. These computers can outperform classical computing capabilities, but they still suffer from quantum gate noise, which makes fault-tolerant quantum computing an unattainable goal at this time.

Regardless, quantum computers are not designed to completely replace conventional computers for general-purpose applications in the real world. If all goes well, they will be a crucial component of high-performance computing (HPC) for specific use cases involving numerous significant scientific work. The term "quantum supremacy" was first used in 2012 by John Preskill to characterize the point at which quantum computers are able to solve tasks and issues that traditional computers are now unable to. Achieving general-purpose quantum computer supremacy in 30 years is "not an unrealistic timescale," he later asserted. Google asserted in 2019 that their Sycamore quantum processor could solve a problem in three minutes, whereas a classical computer would need more than a thousand years to complete the same task.

In an attempt to refute Google's assertion that quantum computers are superior to classical computers, IBM hurried a preprint report asserting that they were able to solve the same problem in 2.5 days using a traditional technique. Quantum physicists protested the use of the term "supremacy" when Google's quantum supremacy breakthrough was published in Nature, arguing that it was careless to disregard the phrase's historical context and could perpetuate racial, gender, and class disparities. Instead, they urged the community to employ "quantum advantage." Preskill responded to the criticism by outlining the rationale for his use of the term "quantum supremacy."

Governments and big businesses have invested billions of dollars in undeveloped hardware, while private investors have reportedly financed at least 52 quantum-technology startups worldwide since 2012. Research on quantum technology is developing more quickly than anticipated, and Google's claim to dominance is being contested by rivals in a fierce and combative struggle for supremacy. It is important taking a step back and clearly defining what quantum supremacy or advantage should involve, or rather, what we want quantum supremacy to be, even though it is obvious that this goal is still far off.

In 2019, the European Quantum Communication Infrastructure, or EuroQCI, initiative was introduced. All of the EU's member states later joined the initiative after seven first signed the EuroQCI Declaration. The world must act swiftly to counter the looming threat of quantum computing because it takes years and a lot of work to upgrade the current commercial and governmental cryptography infrastructure. These laws represent a significant milestone in the global effort to develop and implement quantum-resilient cybersecurity. Furthermore, a lot of queries require immediate solutions because some businesses have already begun providing commercial QC services for specialized computing demands.

Without a gold standard, how would anyone know if a candidate QC has succeeded?

What does the term "gold standard" mean? Researchers believe that QC could devastate the world and lead to a catastrophe. In addition to being incredibly strong, QC is also extremely difficult to control if it cracks any of the encryption that keeps the modern Internet functioning. There is a genuine chance that QC will lead to the current cryptographic infrastructure collapsing, according to some experts, and mankind faces an increased existential threat. All of these forecasts will only matter if QC is made commercially feasible and used for the benefit of humanity. And can they become dominant if there is no effective control to stop evil actors from using them against humanity?

In other words, quantum computing cannot advance without reducing its potential to cause disasters, much as autonomous mobility cannot achieve supremacy without an effective stopping system. Humanity and humanitarian values can always prevail over technological superiority. No technology can be permitted to malfunction. Can "quantum supremacy or advantage" be attained by simply solving problems that are beyond the capabilities of traditional computers, without questioning the term's political correctness? Can a new technology become commercially deployable and provide any real value without protections in place, especially when experts link the technology to existential or catastrophic risk?

A nuclear chain reaction or an autonomous vehicle are useless without a brake system. Will it ever be anticipated that QC will surpass or outperform classical computing if the hazards prevent its broad commercial implementation? Since quantum supremacy and advantage are the most commonly used terms in quantum research and are the ultimate objective of all quantum researchers, it is imperative that the four corners of this concept be properly defined. The answers to all of the issues will become evident as QC develops.

Modern and Cutting Edge Technology

The field of QC research is developing at an exponential rate, and it appears that it will eventually provide "quantum advantage." However, NISQ (Noisy Intermediate Scale Quantum) characterizes the current era of quantum computers that can handle executions of 50-100 qubits before QC offers the quantum advantage. Fault-tolerant QC is now unattainable due to NISQ's quantum gate noise. When QC with enough qubits eventually becomes a reality, our issue statement highlights the shortcomings in handling potential Q-Day threats. Establishing a clear definition of the quantum supremacy/advantage is the first step in organizing a defense of the Internet against the looming Q-Day threat. This will help us comprehend what the advantage is and help us set precise objectives and KPIs to attain it.

This mostly depends on the following:

1. Comprehension of the development of the business model for providing end users with QC services;
2. Applicability of the measures taken to protect the Internet from quantum attacks. Here is the current state-of-the-art in each of these fields.

Quantum-as-a-Services: A Changing Business Model

The average cost of a single qubit is approximately $10,000. A QC that breaks encryption is thought to need about 317 million qubits. In addition to the qubits' real cost, a variety of expensive electronics, coaxial cabling, and other components that enable near-zero operating temperatures and are kept in a sizable, controlled space are also quite expensive. The cost of an encryption-breaking QC will still be around $3 billion, even if the price of each qubit drops by a thousand times. This is definitely out of the pricing range for average hackers and much beyond the means of average mortals. Cloud-based services are the only business model that can enable end users to access QC. The business concept known as Quantum-as-a-Service (QaaS) is developing quickly. Scientists, researchers, and producers of cloud services for creating, testing, and executing QC algorithms can already take advantage of the QaaS offers from at least six QCSPs (Quantum Computing Service Providers), such as Amazon and IBM. A number of these QCSPs even provide their QaaS at no cost.

Governments have the authority to control QCSPs in order to limit membership to verified users under terms and conditions that only permit the deployment of target quantum algorithms to pre-registered domains and require particular security measures and KYC (know your customers) processes in order to use the QC services. Regulating the QaaS business model is simpler than regulating the dispersed desk-top hackers. In order to withstand the decryption capabilities of strong QCs, the standardizing and policy-making organizations, such as NIST in the US and ENISA, its equivalent in Europe, are currently concentrating only on PQC (post-quantum cryptography). We must reconsider our QC protection approach in light of the developing QaaS business model and the recent failure of prospective PQC algorithms. In order to protect classical computers against future quantum hackers, it convinces us to explore beyond the state-of-the-art.

Safety Measures for QC

Not all of the security tools that are currently in use are susceptible to QC attacks. In general, there are two approaches to address the quantum danger to older computers:

- By using one of the most advanced PQC algorithms, each legacy computer linked to the Internet is uniquely protected from quantum attacks.

- Utilizing a new encryption-neutral ZVC (Zero Vulnerability Computing) technology, all QC operations will be isolated from the general Internet.

Cutting Edge Protections using PQC

Whether in a network or outside of one, cryptography is used in practically all inter-device communications to secure data and authenticate access to it. Cryptography continues to be the cornerstone of online safety. Therefore, state-of-the-art employs PQC algorithms as the initial protection strategy for individual computers. It also naturally builds upon the cybersecurity techniques that were prevalent in earlier art. Since the encryption algorithms of all the many IT systems that are currently connected to the Internet cannot be instantaneously updated and modernized, preparations must be made well in advance to deal with the new circumstance.

Without cryptography, it is impossible to secure a computer in a network using legacy technology. Quantum dangers emerge as a result, and standardization organizations are presently striving to standardize PQC procedures for the same reason. The European Telecommunications Standards Institute (ETSI), the Internet Engineering Task Force (IETF), the International Standards Organization (ISO), and the US-based NIST are spearheading these initiatives. Each of these projects covers a different PQC system and is in a different stage. It is crucial to look into options outside of PQC in light of NIST's recent setbacks and the lack of obvious results from the PQC standardization effort, which was started six years ago. Given that, it might be worthwhile to look at a novel theory regarding quantum robust computing.

Exceeding the State-of-the-Art

Cryptography has been the cornerstone of our computing infrastructure's security since the invention of the modern computer. Without cryptography, internet security would be unthinkable. Building computer hardware or software without obtaining authorization from third parties is also unthinkable in the prior art. These rights make a computer useful by enabling a variety of apps to run on it. A computer wouldn't function at all without these rights. On the other hand, these third-party permissions provide malicious actors access to the computer's processing power and enable them to develop attack vectors that use those permissions to introduce malware.

A computer will continue to be susceptible to an attack surface that a malicious actor could use malware to target as long as third-party rights are in place. Just as it is impossible to have a computer with no attack surface in prior art, it is also impossible to have 100% cybersecurity. A robust encryption system is necessary to authenticate such access because a computer is always vulnerable to being accessed by a non-native rogue application or code. However, the requirement for encryption to authenticate third-party access becomes negligible if all non-native programs or codes are intentionally denied access to a computer's resources. A new cybersecurity paradigm called Zero

Vulnerability Computing (ZVC) was created based on these security theories that are independent of encryption.

A technology will automatically make a connected device quantum safe if it can secure a computer without requiring user-facing access enabling encryption techniques. ZVC is an encryption-neutral method that was recently put forth as a substitute for the costly and resource-intensive PQC's widespread implementation on the Internet. ZVC, which received a Seal of Excellence from the European Commission, transforms multilayered legacy computing systems into solid state software on a chip and completely eliminates a computer's attack surface by prohibiting all third-party permissions.

Agnostic Cybersecurity for Encryption

As previously mentioned, all of the hardware and software in legacy computing systems are made to allow third parties to create different applications that make computers useful. Without using third-party authorization, a computer cannot be constructed. These built-in permissions are the source of the majority of computer vulnerabilities. Zero vulnerability is attained by ZVC by

1. Eliminating the attack surface by banning all third-party permits.

2. Constructing switchable offline storage on the computer within the linked device.

At every level, multilayered legacy computing systems are based on providing third-party permissions. Each layer is exposed to an attack surface as a result, creating variations akin to those found in the moving components configuration of older electrical devices. The old software's layered components are all combined by the ZVC permission less architecture to eliminate any attack surface and produce zero vulnerabilities.

Variabilities and complexity lead to a condition reminiscent of the pre-Solid-State age of electronics, when moving components in devices rendered them cumbersome, fragile, energy-inefficient, and susceptible to outside threats. Electronics was transformed by the development of solid-state technology, which also enabled the portable computers of today. Because solid-state electronics have no moving components, the intricate multi-layered architecture of legacy computer systems, which have third-party permissions at each layer, can be compared to the large, brittle, and energy-consuming electronics of the pre-solid-state era.

ZVC produces a situation similar to solid-state electronics with no moving parts since it removes every variable that the intricate, multi-layered traditional computing architecture introduced and completely destroys the attack surface by prohibiting third-party rights. The moving elements of outdated non-solid-state electronics are comparable to the variabilities in the layered architecture of archaic software systems. The direct implementation of ZVC on the nonvolatile memory chip of a computing device eliminates the need for piggybacking on the device's firmware or OS, enabling us to design a radically novel concept of Solid- State Software on a Chip (3SoC) with no conventional layers of firmware, drivers, OS, and application (all moving parts) between the hardware and the human-computer interface.

A small solid-state software environment that is resilient, energy-efficient, and devoid of attack surfaces—which malicious actors frequently use to compromise security—is produced by such a 3SoC method.

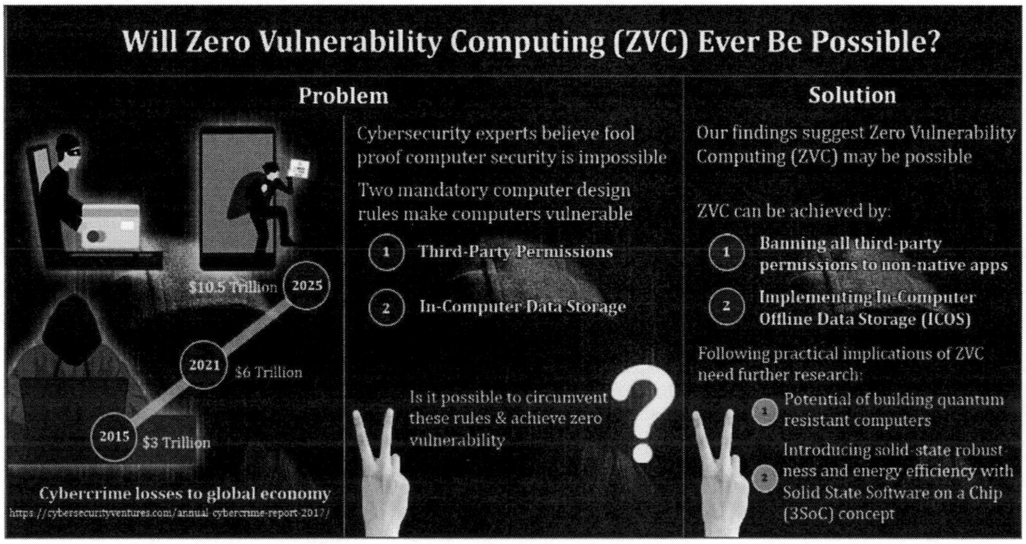

Fig.1.8 ZVC Graphical Abstract: The Internet of the Future.

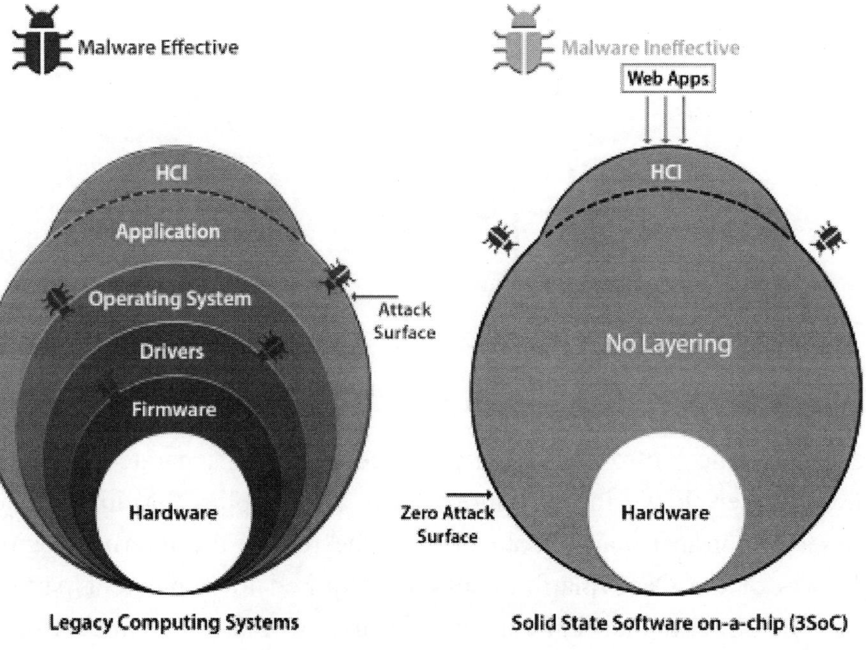

Fig.1.9 Layered Legacy System (A) against 3SoC (B).

(Image courtesy of Future Internet 14.8 (2022): 238)

3SoC Client-Server QaaS Network Driven by ZVC

This encryption-agnostic method effectively isolates QC from the Internet's core computing infrastructure, as seen in the figure below. A typical QCSP (Quantum Computing Service Provider) offers its cloud-based quantum computing services to its customers in this ZVC-powered new QaaS architecture using a business model that is quite similar to that of any other cloud computing service provider available today. As we saw in a previous section, QC's developing subscription-based QaaS business model, which meets the highly specialized, high-power computing needs of particular industry users, supports this kind of separation from the legacy Internet. A 3SoC client is given to subscribers as part of the proposed QaaS framework as a term of service so they can use the QCSP's quantum computing services.

Through a 3SoC server that only takes authentication requests from a 3SoC client device, the QCSP provides access to the quantum computer. We reject any additional requests from hackers or non-subscribers using outdated computing equipment.

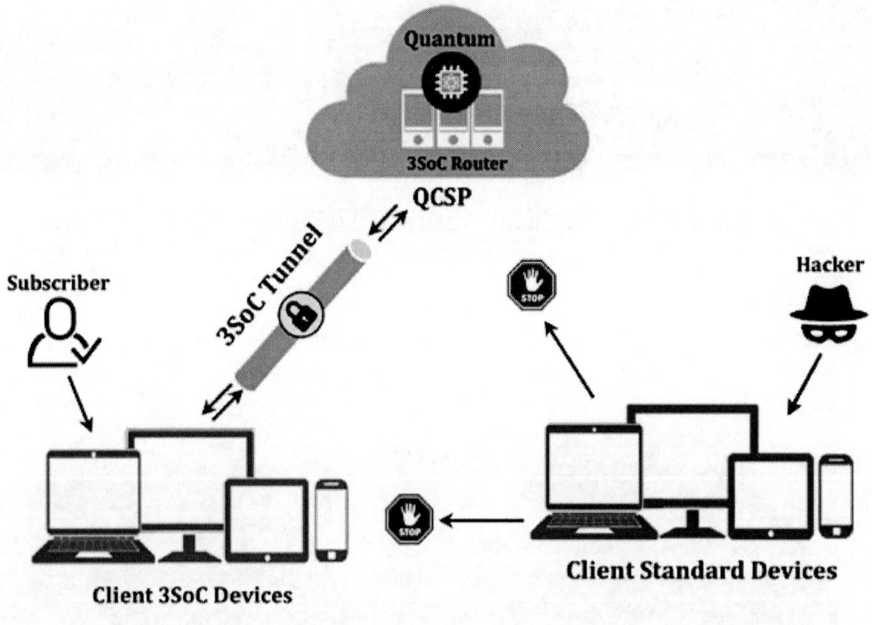

Fig.1.10 3SoC gateway to prevent hackers from accessing QC.

Provide unbreakable end-to-end security to access QC and separate it from the rest of the Internet, as further shown in the figure below. This implies that in order to access QC within a secure intranet that is isolated from the rest of the Internet, legitimate, KYC-verified users of the QaaS platform may be required to implement particular security measures. The 3SoC tunnel that connects the user to the QC is impervious to quantum methods that break encryption and is encryption agnostic.

A QaaS system like this prevents undesirable actors from accessing QC. Most significantly, this approach eliminates the requirement for a device-focused, Internet-wide rollout of resource-intensive PQCs that require a large amount of power and processing time. This would be a major burden on the majority of the 76 billion linked devices that are expected to make up the Internet by 2026. Therefore, a 3SoC intranet may be able to protect against malicious actors abusing quantum computing, even if the PQC algorithms that are now being pursued fall short of expectations.

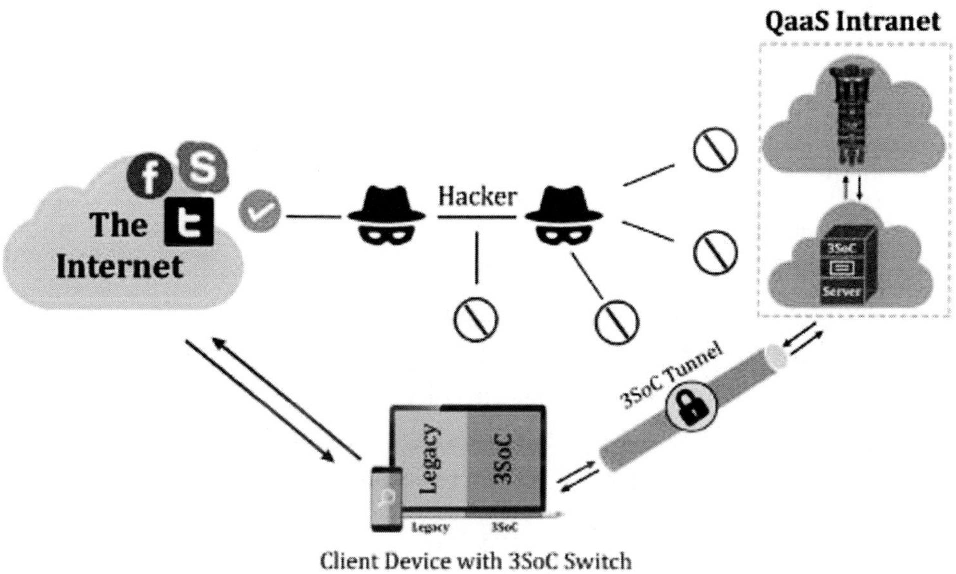

Fig.1.11 A switchable QaaS intranet that isolates QC from the general Internet.

The Tipping Point and Internet Security Using Quantum

By 2026, there will be 76 billion Internet-connected devices, and the vast majority of them will have limited energy and processing power, placing severe limitations on their hardware and software. The restricted computing capacity, limited energy source, and connectivity between these devices make it difficult to perform any cryptographic technique with longer keys.

Currently, 95% of Internet security is based on encryption, which has a substantial financial and resource impact on the devices that are linked to the Internet. Furthermore, quantum generative learning models (QGLMs) and quantum machine learning may outperform their classical counterparts in the future due to their quicker training speeds, giving them a distinct edge over the classical models in terms of becoming widely used. The most affected IoT devices will be those with little resources.

All of the data points to QC being at a turning point, which makes it imperative to get ready for a new computing paradigm. Furthermore, since businesses have already started providing QaaS cloud services, there is a greater need than ever to protect the Internet from upcoming quantum attacks. The initial NIST timeframe for PQC standardization, which was projected to be 15 years for a complete transition to quantum-safe Internet, may be in jeopardy due to recent failures. Implementing PQC globally is a huge project that affects every computer device in the Internet ecosystem. It is not only a costly and time-consuming endeavor, but it also requires a lot of resources.

1.21 Quantum Advantage

We are currently in the NISQ era, limited to small and noisy quantum processors. However, we are certain that fault-tolerance quantum computing is on the way. Quantum Artificial, Quantum artificial intelligence (QAI) and quantum machine learning (QML) are emerging topics that use quantum computing to solve issues beyond the scope of classical computing. While NISQ accelerators may not be a game changer in AI, fault-tolerant quantum computers will be a significant advancement.

Quantum computing has the potential to speed AI and machine learning, although it is unlikely to completely beat classical machine learning in the near future. Quantum machine learning may not always be superior to classical machine learning due to theoretical limitations, but it can beat classical models in some scenarios. Quantum AI and machine learning performance is primarily determined by applications, hence it's important to identify actual challenges where quantum AI might help. Quantum machine learning has the potential to alter fields such as weather prediction and finance.

The biopharmaceutical sector can take over ten years and billions of dollars to market a medicinal product based on an original scientific premise. Experimental design and characterization take up the majority of time, effort, and money. Traditional computer modeling of macromolecules including proteins, ligands, and peptides has made significant progress. However, many molecular biology and biophysics difficulties remain computationally infeasible.

Calculating the complete electrical wavelength of a medicine product is estimated to take longer than the universe itself, even with the most powerful supercomputers. Quantum computing has the potential to dramatically accelerate drug discovery, and machine learning can help attain this advantage. Similar approaches can be used in material science to anticipate the properties of unknown materials.

Quantum knowledge discovery will lead to new possibilities. The biopharmaceutical industry will no longer be deemed a high-risk sector, allowing for new discoveries to flourish. New drug discoveries and early diagnosis technologies have the potential to significantly improve life expectancy, in addition to economic benefits. Quantum physics and technology can help predict climate change and manage complicated global issues like pandemics.

Quantum physics and technology can help predict climate change and manage complicated global issues like pandemics. Quantum technology has the potential to widen the knowledge gap between developed and underdeveloped countries. Access to high-quality quantum resources, including hardware, algorithms, and scientists, is vital for scientific study. Equitable access to quantum technology is crucial to avoid perpetuating existing global inequities even after the race is won.

1.22 Reliability of Quantum Computing

Does the new quantum AI produce outcomes that are qualitatively different from those produced by traditional computer engines? The quantitative response is exponential, but is there a meaningful distinction between using a real quantum computer and, say, a conventional "supercomputer"? In order to build algorithms, program, prepare data, and understand findings, both kinds of systems are costly to own and run and necessitate complex, obscure expertise.

Ironically, quantum computing operations will always have the potential to malfunction or produce inaccurate results, but classical computers may be more "reliable" in that the same computational request on any given dataset should presumably yield the same response.

Although they are tremendously larger, the mathematical class of problems that quantum computing works on is similar to our traditional 0–1 logic-based computers in certain respects.

Quantum AI will be able to solve exponentially large problems thanks to quantum computing.

The dependability check could be the discrete response in a database search or decoding challenge. The search was incorrect if the messages don't decode. You can tell the system didn't work if you can't locate the correct bank account, property deed, or other distinguishing feature. These issues would be "closed" if they had a single solution or none at all.

But many of the issues we discussed previously are "open," meaning they deal more with likelihood than with deterministic, yes/no responses. How will we "know" if our response was the "correct" one? Importantly, it may be typical to supply responses with some kind of reliability estimate in place of a unique "answer" to a problem. A "code breaker" decryption system might only be helpful if the exact solution is given, but a climate forecaster will be helpful if it provides a range of responses, like the number of cloudy days or the amount of rain that will fall. Ranges will be appropriate for planning for more non-discrete tasks (e.g., what kinds of crops might we plant to have a decent harvest?).

Two key characteristics of the "collapse" of the set variables in a quantum computing problem are the capacity to handle enormous numbers of variables with extremely wide parameter ranges very quickly and the total inability to explain the cause and dependability of the collapse's outcomes. The statement "You never run a quantum computation on the same machine twice" encapsulates the extreme instability of the computational components of current quantum computing systems. Each computational component may or may not operate as intended. From the perspective of believing the answer, it is therefore truly quite challenging to perform a "calculation." In order to address this, designers employ the costly strategy of incorporating several levels of redundancy and quality assurance methods into their systems.

This reliability issue must be handled by "programmers" of quantum computing systems, which paradoxically implies that even a simple job like generating a really "random" number might not be random on a particular computer at a given time. One may set certain reliability constraints by rerunning varied settings to confirm the results of quantum computations, and one believes that quick, widely available quantum computing resources would make such repeats possible. Indeed, built-in "reruns" that show the dependability of outcomes will be a crucial component of quantum computing products from different vendors.

Chaos theory, however, contends that even minor adjustments to a system's variable inputs—or even how it manages its variables—may produce radically different overall outcomes. When quantum computing is combined with a lot of variables, such as rain or shine, stock levels rising or falling, or poisonous or harmless compounds, there is a very high chance that the findings will be unsuitable. Once more, human programmers, problem solvers, and result interpreters will be crucial. Is human intuition still useful?

Even though the quantum AI is capable of playing amazing chess or go, would it be able to "understand" the game or the reasons behind wins or loses?.

1.23 How Will Computing Develop in the Future?

Therefore, quantum computing is about facilitating the human race's future as much as it is about quantum necromancy. It is a specific computing future that coexists with other cutting-edge paradigms that are probably going to enhance conventional computing techniques (such as the incredibly low error rates of today's silicon chips). The increased ability of these future computing systems to accommodate computation failures is a crucial feature. For instance, systems that use neuromorphic, analog, and approximation computing can use a lot less energy per operation, but they may provide noisy or occasionally different outcomes when using the same inputs. Why would we put up with these results?

A portion of it refers back to Alexander Pope's statement, "To forgive is divine; to err is human." In particular, while working with different artificial intelligence subsystems, academics and businesses have discovered that, in the vast majority of situations, approximations are adequate. Examining how the results of the training process—a form of optimization—rely on hundreds or even millions of examples for the systems to learn from will help us comprehend this. Since the performance landscape cannot be significantly influenced by any one of those data points, we discover that making minor adjustments to some of the neural network circuit's parameters only slightly alters the result. Because it makes it challenging to train systems past a certain point, this lack of progress is frequently referred to as the "barren plateau problem." However, this drawback also has a benefit in that it indicates little mistakes don't significantly affect the system's overall performance. The approximate nature of the human reality that surrounds us is reflected in these inaccuracies.

However, these paradigms are already pushing traditional computing to new heights in conjunction with algorithmic advancements. As previously hinted, it is also impairing our comprehension of the intricacies of the systems we have developed—the data is extensive and, in many ways, the code.

Chapter - 2
Principles of Quantum Computing

Fundamentals of Quantum Mechanics

A key area of physics, quantum mechanics only gradually advanced until the early 19th century, thanks to several devoted publications by some of the most ardent physicists. It provides quantum computing's theoretical foundation. Superposition and quantum interference, two fundamental ideas of quantum mechanics that are not discernible from the theoretical and empirical perspectives of classical Bloch vectors and operations via gate-level symbols, lie at the heart of quantum computing. Only upper graduates and research scholars from the field of pure mathematics can predict the foundations of quantum computing by engaging with the pertinent physical theories, arguments, and rigor. Therefore, investigating the mathematical theory of quantum computing necessitates investigating foundational and interpretive quantum mechanics.

The fundamental idea of superposition in quantum physics basically says that a quantum particle, such an electron or a photon, can exist in several states at the same time until it is measured. In other words, their current state is a probabilistic linear mixture of several alternative states, which means that they can exist in the electron spin system both parallel to and perpendicular to the specified axis. The aforementioned cycle has demonstrated that quantum particles can also be highly entangled when represented by the set of coefficients associated with cat-head and cat-tail states only, with equal assumptions, in the normalization bracket notation. For this reason, logical qubits serve as sensors for use in quantum cryptography systems. Likewise, the chance of having super positioned states of excitations in even and odd numbers is twice that of the ground states. One of the electrical characteristics that facilitates the operation of quantum electrodynamics is this one.

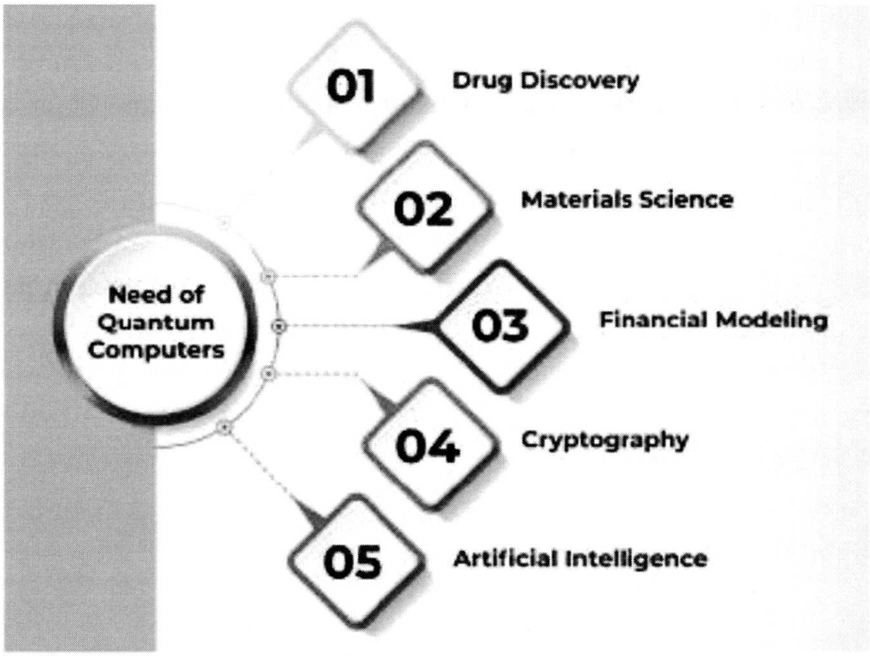

Fig.2.1 Mechanics of Quantum Principles.

2.1 Circuits and Gates in Quantum Physics

In order to carry out quantum computations, quantum gates are essential. The fundamental building pieces that perform operations on qubits are called quantum gates, or quantum operations. Although they are the equivalent of traditional logic gates, quantum circuit gates offer a number of special features.

Gates can be categorized into three sorts based on how they operate: measurement, parametric transformation, and linear transformation. Rotation gates and entanglement gates are the two main types of gates used in linear transformations. A qubit's state can be rotated about several axes in the Bloch sphere thanks to rotation gates. The Hadamard gate, which rotates a qubit from the base state $|0\rangle$ to $|0\rangle + |1\rangle / \sqrt{2}$, is an illustration of a rotation gate. The Pauli rotation gate, which rotates a qubit from one basic state to another, is a another illustration of a rotation gate.

The creation and manipulation of quantum entanglement between n qubits are accomplished by entanglement gates. When the first qubit is $|1\rangle$., the CNOT gate, an example of an entanglement gate, flips the second qubit. Another type of quantum gate that is dependent on operating parameters is the parametric gate, which is typically employed in varying circuit applications. Ry, Rz, and Rx are a few instances of parametric gates.

Multiple quantum gates are arranged to form quantum circuits. The ultimate output is recorded in the final state of the qubits involved, and they are composed of a set of input qubits and a series of subsequent operations represented by quantum gates. Quantum gates act on inputs of the quantum circuits, which are in the ground state $|0\rangle$ as $|0\rangle \otimes |0\rangle$. A certain family of quantum algorithms offers speedups over classical processing for a specific type of gate. The fundamental units of quantum algorithms within the quantum circuit are quantum gates, which are the actions performed by qubits.

In order to solve problems, the array of quantum gates must be connected in a unique way according to the quantum algorithm's design. Quantum gates are implemented in the bottom layer, while the creation of a quantum algorithm is represented in the top layer. All qubits must maintain coherent superposition, create entanglement, and carry out gate operations simultaneously in addition to building quantum gates and circuits. Additionally, we use a specific quantum error correcting technique in modern technology to stop faults from spreading.

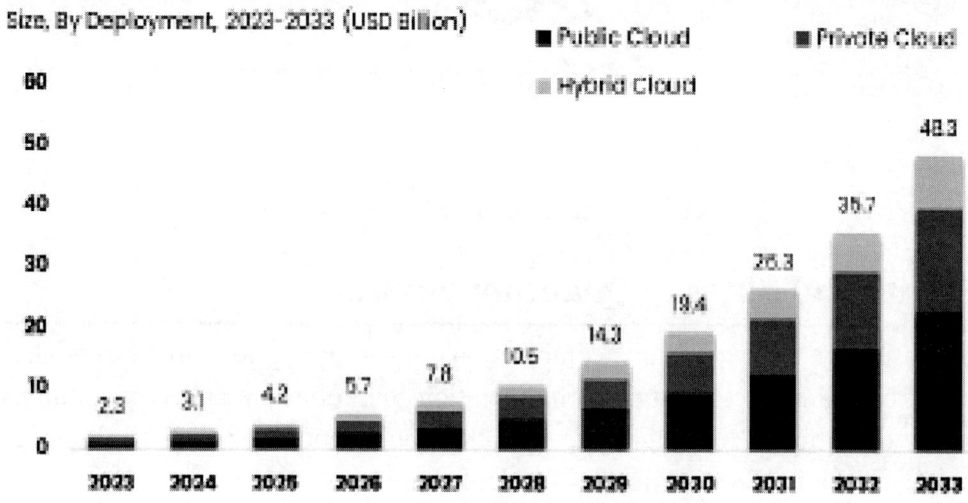

Fig.2.2 Quantum Computing.

2.2 Qubit

A classical bit, or single binary digit, is a system that can exist in two different states and is used to represent 0 and 1. In such a system, the only operations (gates) that can occur are the identity (0 -> 0, 1 —> 1) and NEVER (0 -> 1, 1 -> 0). On the other hand, a two-level quantum system that is characterized by a two-dimensional complex Hilbert space is called a quantum bit (qubit). One can select two normalized and mutually orthogonal quantum states in this space,

$$|0\rangle \equiv \begin{bmatrix} 1 \\ 0 \end{bmatrix}, \qquad |1\rangle \equiv \begin{bmatrix} 0 \\ 1 \end{bmatrix} \tag{1}$$

to symbolize a classical bit's values 0 and 1. A computational basis is formed by these two states. Any qubit state can be expressed using the superposition principle as

$$|\psi\rangle = \alpha|0\rangle + \beta|1\rangle \tag{2}$$

where the normalizing condition limits the complex values that make up the amplitudes α and β.

$$|\alpha|^2 + |\beta|^2 = 1 \tag{3}$$

With the exception of the base state $|1\rangle$, where $\alpha = 0$ and $\beta = 1$ real, one may select α a real and positive state vector since state vectors are only specified up to a global phase of no physical consequence. Consequently, a qubit's generic state can be expressed as

$$\begin{aligned} |\psi\rangle &= \cos\tfrac{\theta}{2}|0\rangle + e^{i\phi}\sin\tfrac{\theta}{2}|1\rangle \\ &= \begin{bmatrix} \cos\frac{\theta}{2} \\ e^{i\phi}\sin\frac{\theta}{2} \end{bmatrix} \qquad (0 \le \theta \le \pi,\ 0 \le \phi < 2\pi) \end{aligned} \tag{4}$$

Consequently, the qubit exists in a vector space that is parametrized by the continuous variables α and β (or θ and ϕ) in contrast to the traditional bit, which can only be set to equal 0 or 1. A continuum of states is therefore permitted. This goes against our "classical" style of thinking since we intuitively believe that a system with two states can only exist in one of them.

On the other hand, quantum mechanics is far more fascinating and opens up countless additional possibilities. At this point, one could be tempted to claim that a limitless amount of data might be stored in a single qubit. Actually, in order to express the complex integers α and β in Eq.(2), we typically need to supply an infinite amount of bits. There's a catch, though: in order to retrieve this information, we need to test the polarization state σ_n of a qubit along any axis n. According to quantum mechanics, this measurement yields just one bit of information ($\sigma_n = +1$ or $\sigma_n = -1$). To achieve α and β, an infinite number of measurements on similarly produced single-qubit states are needed.

If a two-level quantum system can be controlled in the manner described below, it can be used as a qubit in practice:

1. It can be prepared in a certain state, such as $|0\rangle$, which we refer to as the qubit's fiducial state;
2. Any state of the qubit can be changed into any other state. As we will see in the following section, these transformations are accomplished by unitary transformations;
3. The computational basis $\{|0\rangle, |1\rangle\}$ allows for the measurement of the qubit state. This implies that the qubit polarization can be measured along the z-axis. The Pauli

operator σ_z, whose eigenstates are $|0\rangle$ and $|1\rangle$, is the Hermitian operator linked to this measurement. Therefore, if Eq. (4) describes the qubit's state, the measurement yields 0 or 1

(i.e., $\sigma_z = +1$ or $\sigma_z = -1$) with probability.

$$p_0 = |\langle 0|\psi\rangle|^2 = \cos^2\frac{\theta}{2}, \qquad p_1 = |\langle 1|\psi\rangle|^2 = \sin^2\frac{\theta}{2} \tag{5}$$

The state of an atom in a cavity ($|0\rangle$ corresponds to the atomic ground state and $|1\rangle$) to the first excited state), or a Cooper pair tunneling between two superconducting islands ($|0\rangle$ if the pair is on one island and $|1\rangle$ if it is on the other island are examples of physical implementations of a qubit. Nuclear magnetic resonance quantum processors also use nuclear spin in molecules. Effective measurement devices have now been created, and magnetic or laser fields are used to implement the controlled unitary evolution of a qubit's state.

2.2.1 The Bloch Orbit

When considering qubits, the Bloch sphere representation is helpful since it offers a geometric representation of the qubit and the various transformations that can be applied to its state. The normalizing condition Eq (3) allows the qubit's state to be represented as a point on the Bloch sphere, a sphere with a unit radius. It is possible to embed this sphere in a three-dimensional space with Cartesian coordinates ($x = \cos\phi\sin\theta$, $y = \sin\phi\sin\theta$, $z = \cos\theta$). The state Eq(4) can therefore be expressed as

$$|\psi\rangle = \begin{bmatrix} \sqrt{\frac{1+z}{2}} \\ \frac{x+iy}{\sqrt{2(1+z)}} \end{bmatrix} \tag{6}$$

A vector that singles out a point on the Bloch sphere with its components (x, y, and z) is called a Bloch vector. As a result, every Bloch vector needs to meet the normalization requirement that x2 + y2 + z2 = 1. As illustrated in below Figure, we can alternatively state that a Bloch vector is defined by the angles θ and ϕ. The sinusoidal projection, which projects the Bloch sphere onto a plane, is also depicted in the same illustration.

4. The unitary transformations of a qubit's state can be seen with the aid of the sinusoidal projection. The projector $P = |\psi\rangle\langle\psi|$ yields another helpful representation of the state Eq (4). The operator P's matrix representation on the basis of $\{|0\rangle, |1\rangle\}$ is provided by

$$P = \begin{bmatrix} \cos^2 \frac{\theta}{2} & e^{-i\phi} \sin \frac{\theta}{2} \cos \frac{\theta}{2} \\ e^{i\phi} \sin \frac{\theta}{2} \cos \frac{\theta}{2} & \sin^2 \frac{\theta}{2} \end{bmatrix} = \frac{1}{2} \begin{bmatrix} 1+z & x-iy \\ x+iy & 1-z \end{bmatrix}, \tag{7}$$

Where $\langle i|P|j\rangle$ is the definition of the matrix element P_{ij} $(i, j = 0, 1)$.

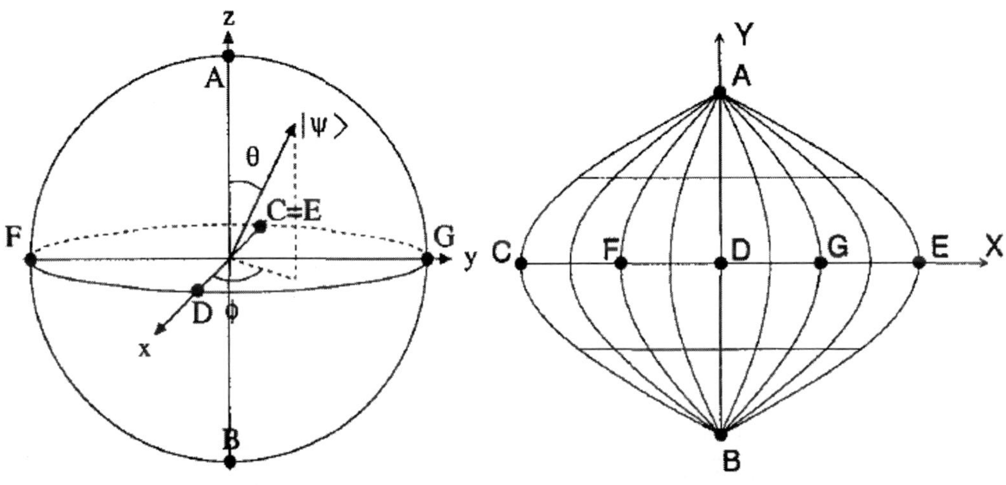

Fig.2.3 Sinusoidal projection of the Bloch sphere on the right and a Bloch-sphere representation of a qubit on the left. A = $(\alpha=1, \beta=0)$, B = (0, 1), C = E= $(\frac{1}{\sqrt{2}}, -\frac{1}{\sqrt{2}})$, D = $(\frac{1}{\sqrt{2}}, \frac{1}{\sqrt{2}})$, F = $(\frac{1}{\sqrt{2}}, -\frac{i}{\sqrt{2}})$, a n d G =$(\frac{1}{\sqrt{2}}, \frac{i}{\sqrt{2}})$ are the points that correspond to the states listed below. Keep in mind that the states $|0\rangle$ and $|1\rangle$ are represented by points A (the Bloch sphere's north pole) and B (its south pole), respectively.

2.2.2 Monitoring a qubit's state

If we have a large number of similarly prepared qubits at our disposal, we can theoretically measure the state $|\psi\rangle = \alpha|0\rangle + \beta|1\rangle$ of a qubit. The Bloch-sphere model provides a particularly useful foundation for comprehending this idea. The following will demonstrate that it is possible to measure the qubit's x, y, and z coordinates on the Bloch sphere (as we have shown, we can also derive α and β from these coordinates, up to an overall phase factor).

Pauli operators are used, and they are expressed in the computational basis as

$$\sigma_x = \begin{bmatrix} 0 & 1 \\ 1 & 0 \end{bmatrix}, \quad \sigma_y = \begin{bmatrix} 0 & -i \\ i & 0 \end{bmatrix}, \quad \sigma_z = \begin{bmatrix} 1 & 0 \\ 0 & -1 \end{bmatrix} \tag{8}$$

For the state $|\psi\rangle$ provided by Eq (4), one has

$$\begin{aligned} \sigma_x |\psi\rangle &= e^{i\phi} \sin\tfrac{\theta}{2} |0\rangle + \cos\tfrac{\theta}{2} |1\rangle , \\ \sigma_y |\psi\rangle &= -ie^{i\phi} \sin\tfrac{\theta}{2} |0\rangle + i \cos\tfrac{\theta}{2} |1\rangle , \\ \sigma_z |\psi\rangle &= \cos\tfrac{\theta}{2} |0\rangle - e^{i\phi} \sin\tfrac{\theta}{2} |1\rangle . \end{aligned} \tag{9}$$

The anticipated values for the state Eq (4) are so as follows:

$$\begin{aligned} \langle\psi|\sigma_x|\psi\rangle &= \langle\psi| \begin{bmatrix} 0 & 1 \\ 1 & 0 \end{bmatrix} |\psi\rangle = \sin\theta \cos\phi = x, \\ \langle\psi|\sigma_y|\psi\rangle &= \langle\psi| \begin{bmatrix} 0 & -i \\ i & 0 \end{bmatrix} |\psi\rangle = \sin\theta \sin\phi = y, \\ \langle\psi|\sigma_z|\psi\rangle &= \langle\psi| \begin{bmatrix} 1 & 0 \\ 0 & -1 \end{bmatrix} |\psi\rangle = \cos\theta = z. \end{aligned} \tag{10}$$

On the computational basis, the coordinates (x, y, z) can be retrieved with arbitrary accuracy by measuring σ_z, which is a conventional projective measurement. In fact, using Eq. (5), we get

$$p_0 - p_1 = \cos^2\tfrac{\theta}{2} - \sin^2\tfrac{\theta}{2} = \cos\theta = z \tag{11}$$

Therefore, the difference in the probability of obtaining outcomes 0 or 1 from a measurement of σ_z yields the coordinate z. We can estimate z as $N_0/N - N_1/N$ if we have a large number N of systems that are identically prepared in the state Eq (4) at our disposal. In this case, N_0 and N_1 count the number of outcomes 0 and 1. Therefore, as long as we measure a significant number of states, z can be measured to any desired accuracy.

The ability to do a unitary transformation on the qubit can be used to acquire the coordinates x and y. If the matrix describes the unitary transformation

$$U_1 = \frac{1}{\sqrt{2}}\begin{bmatrix} 1 & 1 \\ -1 & 1 \end{bmatrix} \tag{12}$$

is used to obtain the state $|\psi^{(1)}\rangle = U_1|\psi\rangle$ from the state (4). Following a projective measurement in the computational basis, the results are either 0 or 1, with probabilities of $p_0^{(1)} = |\langle 0|\psi^{(1)}\rangle|^2$ and $p_1^{(1)} = |\langle 1|\psi^{(1)}\rangle|^2$, respectively. Thus, we get

$$p_0^{(1)} - p_1^{(1)} = \cos\phi \sin\theta = x \tag{13}$$

Similar to this, if the matrix is used to change state Eq (4)

$$U_2 = \frac{1}{\sqrt{2}}\begin{bmatrix} 1 & -i \\ -i & 1 \end{bmatrix} \tag{14}$$

The state $|\psi^{(2)}\rangle = U_2|\psi\rangle$ is obtained. Consequently

$$p_0^{(2)} - p_1^{(2)} = \sin\phi \sin\theta = y \tag{15}$$

where the probability to acquire outcome 0 or 1 from the measurement of the qubit polarization along z are given by $p_0^{(2)} = |\langle 0|\psi^{(2)}\rangle|^2$ and $p_1^{(2)} = |\langle 1|\psi^{(2)}\rangle|^2$.

2.2.3 Qubit's State

Computation is the process of adjusting a physical system's states in order to address a challenge. A minuscule entity, such as an electron, photon, or ion, is used in quantum computing as a medium for the storage and transport of digital information. Two orthogonal states of a microorganism can be used to encode one-bit information, or zero or one. A quantum bit, often known as a qubit, is a quantum two-state system. In order to solve a problem, a quantum computer first places qubits in initial states and then manipulates those states to cause the qubits to exhibit the desired outcome.

Since those minuscule particles defy the laws of classical physics, quantum mechanics is employed to characterize the states in order to create such a quantum circuit. A qubit's state can be expressed as a vector $|\psi\rangle$.

$$|\psi\rangle=\alpha|0\rangle+\beta|1\rangle,\{\alpha,\beta\in\mathbb{C}\} \tag{1}$$

where the complex numbers α and β, also known as probability amplitude, fulfill the equation $|\alpha|2+|\beta|2=1$. Here, $|\alpha|2$ represents the likelihood of receiving the state $|0\rangle$ as a result of the qubit measurement $|\psi\rangle$, and $|\beta\rangle 2$ represents the likelihood of receiving $|1\rangle$. In quantum mechanics, the standard notation "| ⟩" is used to specify states. In the Dirac notation, it is also referred to as the column vector or ket vector. One can write the orthonormal basis $|0\rangle$ and $|1\rangle$ as |

$$|0\rangle=[1,0]^T,|1\rangle=[0,1]^T \quad (2)$$

Combinations of quantum states occur via the tensor product. Two qubit states, for example, can be expressed as $|\psi 1\rangle \otimes |\psi 2\rangle$, where the symbol "⊗" denotes a tensor product, or more compactly as $|\psi 1\rangle|\psi 2\rangle$ or $|\psi 1\psi 2\rangle$. As an illustration,

$$\begin{aligned} |\psi_1\rangle \otimes |\psi_2\rangle &= [\psi_{1,0}, \psi_{1,1}]^T \otimes [\psi_{2,0}, \psi_{2,1}]^T \\ &= [\psi_{1,0}\psi_{2,0}, \psi_{1,0}\psi_{2,1}, \psi_{1,1}\psi_{2,0}, \psi_{1,1}\psi_{2,1}]^T \end{aligned} \quad (3)$$

where $|\psi_i\rangle = \alpha|0\rangle + \beta|1\rangle = \alpha[1,0]^T + \beta[0,1]^T = [\alpha, \beta]^T = [\psi_{i,0}, \psi_{i,1}]^T$.

Thus, a column vector with 2^n elements can be used to represent an n-qubit state.

2.3 The State of Superposition

One component that is necessary for quantum computing is the superposition state. For simplicity's sake, a photon is presented as an example of a qubit in this section. One-bit information is represented by the polarization, or the geometric direction of the photon. Classical bit 0 is represented by a horizontally polarized photon, and bit 1 by a vertically polarized photon. Photons are fired at the emitter in the below picture and pass through Filter-V, which only permits photons that are vertically polarized to pass through. To simplify the scenario, we suppose that only one photon enters the Polarization Beam Splitter (PBS) at a time. While horizontally polarized photons are deflected by PBS, vertically polarized photons are transmitted (measured at the detector DV) (measured at the detector DH). As a result, below figure will measure all photons at DV.

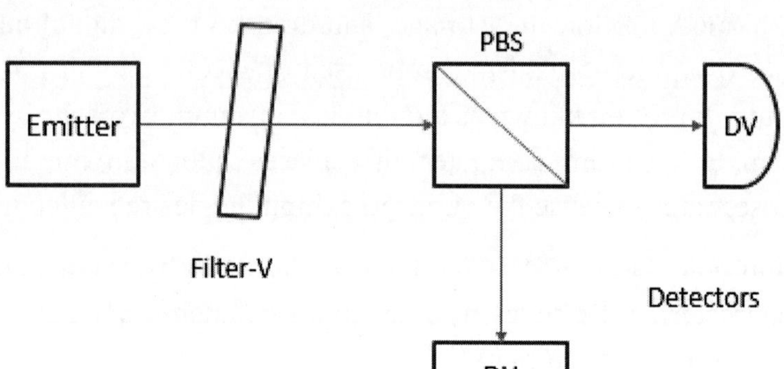

Fig.2.4 Photons detection at DV.

A vertically or horizontally polarized photon is detected at each detector with a probability of ½ if a filter known as "Filter-45°," which only transmits diagonally polarized photons, is positioned between Filter-V and PBS (Below Figure).

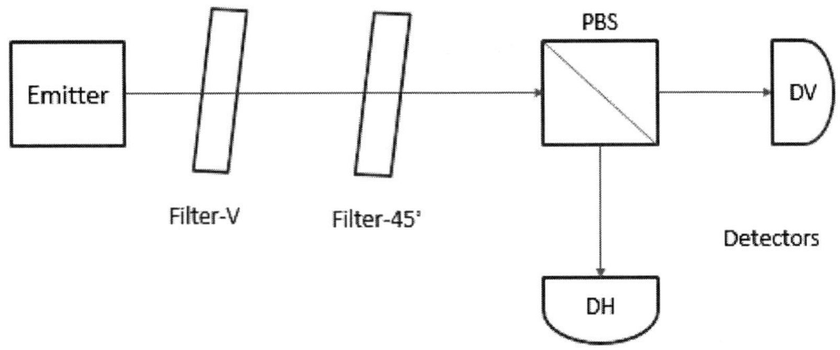

Fig.2.5 All photons are detected at DV; half are found at DV and the remaining half at DH.

The probability amplitudes of α and β should be $1/\sqrt{2}$ since the chance of detecting the vertically polarized photon $|\psi\rangle = |V\rangle$ or the horizontally polarized photon $|\psi\rangle = |H\rangle$ at the PBS is ½. Therefore, the photon's condition immediately prior to PBS can be expressed as

$$|\psi\rangle = \frac{1}{\sqrt{2}}|H\rangle + \frac{1}{\sqrt{2}}|V\rangle \quad (4)$$

The expression (4) is written as follows since |H⟩ is used to represent a classical bit "0" and |V⟩ is used to represent "1".

$$|\psi\rangle = \frac{1}{\sqrt{2}}|0\rangle + \frac{1}{\sqrt{2}}|1\rangle \quad (5)$$

In this state of preparation, a photon's digital information is encoded as either "0" or "1". According to our interpretation of equation (5), the states "0" and "1" exist simultaneously. We refer to this particular state as a superposition state. The state that exists when two qubits are in the superposition state (5) is expressed as the expression (4) is written as follows since |H⟩ is used to represent a classical bit "0" and |V⟩ is used to represent "1".

$$
\begin{aligned}
|\psi_1\rangle|\psi_2\rangle &= \left\{\frac{1}{\sqrt{2}}|0\rangle + \frac{1}{\sqrt{2}}|1\rangle\right\}\left\{\frac{1}{\sqrt{2}}|0\rangle + \frac{1}{\sqrt{2}}|1\rangle\right\} \\
&= \frac{1}{2}\{[1,1]^T \otimes [1,1]^T\} = \frac{1}{2}[1,1,1,1]^T \\
&= \frac{1}{2}\{[1,0,0,0]^T + [0,1,0,0]^T + [0,0,1,0]^T + [0,0,0,1]^T\} \\
&= \frac{1}{2}|0\rangle|0\rangle + \frac{1}{2}|0\rangle|1\rangle + \frac{1}{2}|1\rangle|0\rangle + \frac{1}{2}|1\rangle|1\rangle
\end{aligned} \tag{6}
$$

Four classical binary states (00, 01, 10, 11) are simultaneously represented by this two-qubit state. Two n potential inputs can be handled concurrently by a quantum computer when it prepares n qubits in a superposition state as its input for a quantum circuit (below figure). One of the main benefits of quantum computing is this quantum parallelism.

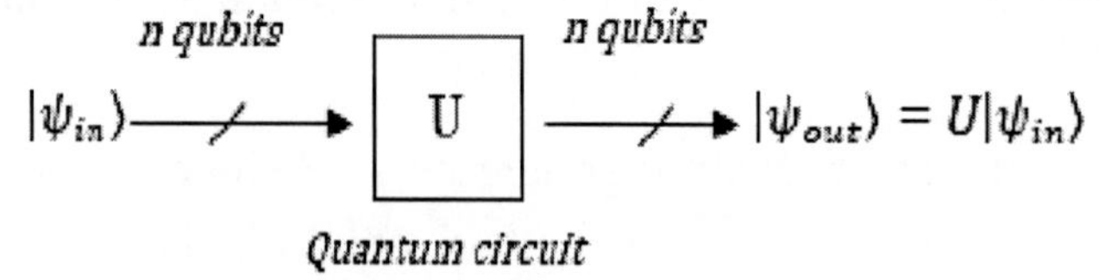

Fig.2.6 Quantum circuit with n qubits.

2.4 Measurement and Quantum Circuit

As was previously indicated, computation is the process of changing a physical system's states. A quantum computer uses a quantum state as its input and modifies it to improve the likelihood that the computation's output state will contain the solution. For example, Shor's approach modifies the quantum states in order to identify prime factors of a big integer. An important distinction between a quantum circuit and a classical (electronic) circuit is the presence of intermediate states in the circuits.

Since binary values, such as 0 and 5, are represented by voltages on circuit nodes, we may measure the intermediate state in a traditional electronic circuit. Thus, by measuring the voltage in the circuit, an error (such as 2.5 volts) can be found. On the other hand, the intermediate states in a quantum circuit are probably in a superposition state. The quantum state is distorted and turns into one of the two orthogonal base states (i.e., $|0\rangle$ or $|1\rangle$) at the moment of the measurement with the probabilities $|\alpha|2$ and $|\beta\rangle$ 2 if the superposition state is measured. When the photons in equation (6) are measured, for instance, one of the four states (e.g., $|\psi1\rangle|\psi2\rangle=|0\rangle|1\rangle$) is observed with an equal probability (i.e., 1/4), but the measurement eliminates all other information about the initial state (6). To put it another way, unlike classical one-way functions (like hashing), the measurement is a one-way operation that prevents us from deriving the original state from the measured result.

2.4 Quantum Gate and Reversibility

Quantum gates are the fundamental operations used to modify an input state for a quantum circuit. A matrix can be used to numerically represent each gate action. For example, the Filter-45° in the earlier mentioned Figure transforms from a superposition state (i.e., $1/\sqrt{2}|0\rangle+1/\sqrt{2}|1\rangle$) to one of the orthogonal base states (i.e., $|0\rangle$). The following matrix UH, referred to as the Hadamard gate, can be used to express this process.

$$U_H|0\rangle = \frac{1}{\sqrt{2}}\begin{bmatrix}1 & 1\\ 1 & -1\end{bmatrix}\begin{bmatrix}1\\ 0\end{bmatrix} = \frac{1}{\sqrt{2}}|0\rangle + \frac{1}{\sqrt{2}}|1\rangle| \tag{7}$$

The controlled-NOT (cNOT) gate (Below Figure), which functions similarly to a classical XOR gate as indicated in given below Table, is a further illustration of a quantum gate.

Table 2.1 A quantum XOR gate truth table with two inputs and two outputs

ψ_{in1}	ψ_{in2}	ψ_{out1}	ψ_{out2}
0	0	0	0
0	1	0	1
1	0	1	1
1	1	1	0

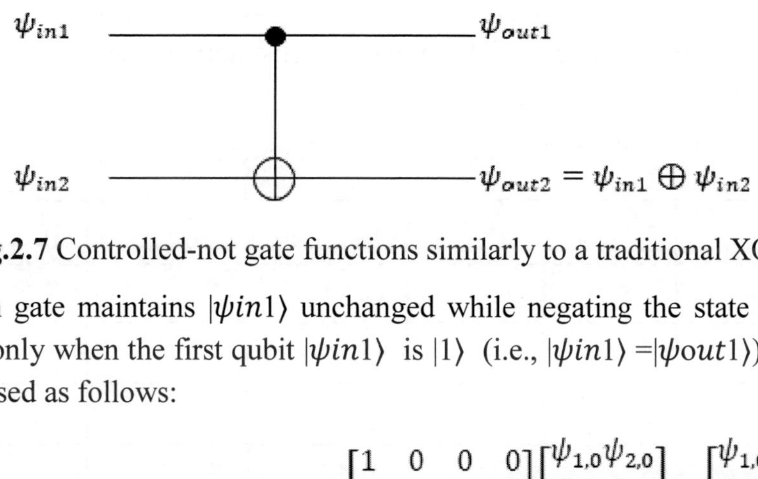

Fig.2.7 Controlled-not gate functions similarly to a traditional XOR.

This quantum gate maintains $|\psi in1\rangle$ unchanged while negating the state of the second qubit $|\psi in2\rangle$ only when the first qubit $|\psi in1\rangle$ is $|1\rangle$ (i.e., $|\psi in1\rangle = |\psi out1\rangle$). This process can be expressed as follows:

$$|\psi_{out1}\rangle|\psi_{out2}\rangle = U_{cNOT}|\psi_{in1}\rangle|\psi_{in2}\rangle = \begin{bmatrix}1 & 0 & 0 & 0\\ 0 & 1 & 0 & 0\\ 0 & 0 & 0 & 1\\ 0 & 0 & 1 & 0\end{bmatrix}\begin{bmatrix}\psi_{1,0}\psi_{2,0}\\ \psi_{1,0}\psi_{2,1}\\ \psi_{1,1}\psi_{2,0}\\ \psi_{1,1}\psi_{2,1}\end{bmatrix} = \begin{bmatrix}\psi_{1,0}\psi_{2,0}\\ \psi_{1,0}\psi_{2,1}\\ \psi_{1,1}\psi_{2,1}\\ \psi_{1,1}\psi_{2,0}\end{bmatrix} \tag{8}$$

Given the universality of the NAND gate, any logic gate, such as AND, OR, or NOT, can be constructed using quantum gates. The truth table for a conventional NAND gate is shown in the table below.

Table 2.2 A truth table with two inputs for the traditional NAND gate

IN_1	IN_2	Out
0	0	1
0	1	1
1	0	1
1	1	0

Given the truth table above and two qubit inputs, let's say that the NAND gate is constructed as follows: |0⟩|1⟩=[1,0]T⊗[0,1]T is equal to [0,1,0,0].T, according to Yanofsky and Mannucci, the operation can be expressed as follows.

$$NAND: \begin{bmatrix} 0 & 0 & 0 & 1 \\ 1 & 1 & 1 & 0 \end{bmatrix} \tag{9}$$

$$U_{NAND}|0\rangle|1\rangle = \begin{bmatrix} 0 & 0 & 0 & 1 \\ 1 & 1 & 1 & 0 \end{bmatrix}[0,1,0,0]^T = [0,1]^T = |1\rangle \tag{10}$$

However, because two-bit information becomes one bit after the gate in (10), this NAND gate cannot be achieved using quantum gates. A system (such as a quantum circuit) cannot lose information according to quantum physics unless its quantum states are measured. As a result, in order for a quantum gate to be reversible and not lose any information, it needs to have an equal number of inputs as outputs. On the other hand, all classical gates—aside from the NOT gate—are one-way functions that lose part of the incoming data as they escape. Another important distinction from classical computing is this necessity.

Table 2.3 Quantum NAND gate truth table.

ψ_{in1}	ψ_{in2}	ψ_{in3}	ψ_{out1}	ψ_{out2}	ψ_{out3}
0	0	1	0	0	1
0	1	1	0	1	1
1	0	1	1	0	1
1	1	1	1	1	0

A Toffoli gate, sometimes called a controlled-controlled-NOT (ccNOT) gate (see below figure and above table), can be used to create a quantum NAND gate. Table provides the updated truth table for the quantum NAND gate.

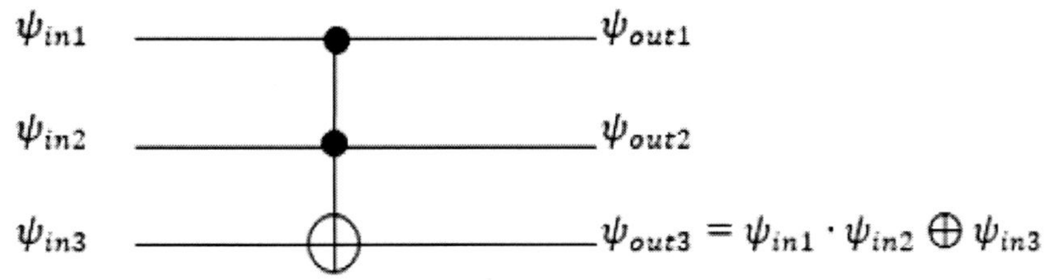

Fig.2.8 Controlled-Controlled-NOT (Toffoli gate).

Table 2.4 Truth table for Controlled-Controlled-NOT.

ψ_{in1}	ψ_{in2}	ψ_{in3}	ψ_{out1}	ψ_{out2}	ψ_{out3}
0	0	0	0	0	0
0	0	1	0	0	1
0	1	0	0	1	0
0	1	1	0	1	1
1	0	0	1	0	0
1	0	1	1	0	1
1	1	0	1	1	1
1	1	1	1	1	0

The ccNOT gate functions as a NAND gate when the Toffoli gate with ψ_{if3}=1 is used.

$$\psi_{out3} = \neg(\psi_{in1} \wedge \psi_{in2}) \tag{11}$$

Therefore, theoretically, we can use quantum gates to construct any kind of digital logic.

2.6 No-Cloning Theorem and Entangled State

In the above Table, when $\psi in2$ is zero, the cNOT gate maintains $\psi out2$ as zero for $\psi in1$=0 and modifies $\psi_{out}2$ to one for $\psi_{in}1$=1. Therefore, when $\psi_{in}2$=0, it appears like the cNOT gate replicates the classical bit information from $\psi_{in}1$=1 to $\psi_{out}2$.

$$\begin{aligned} |\psi_{out1}\rangle|\psi_{out2}\rangle &= cNOT|0\rangle|0\rangle = |0\rangle|0\rangle \\ |\psi_{out1}\rangle|\psi_{out2}\rangle &= cNOT|1\rangle|0\rangle = |1\rangle|1\rangle \end{aligned} \tag{12}$$

The cNOT gate ought to work for a superposition state if it can copy any arbitrary state from one qubit to the other. When the input $\psi in1$ is $\alpha|0\rangle+\beta|1\rangle$, the output $\psi out2$ should be $\alpha|0\rangle+\beta|1\rangle$.

$$\begin{aligned} |\psi_{out1}\rangle|\psi_{out2}\rangle &= \text{cNOT}(\alpha|0\rangle + \beta|1\rangle)|0\rangle \\ &\rightarrow (\alpha|0\rangle + \beta|1\rangle)(\alpha|0\rangle + \beta|1\rangle) \\ &= \alpha^2|0\rangle|0\rangle + \alpha\beta|1\rangle|0\rangle + \beta\alpha|0\rangle|1\rangle + \beta^2|1\rangle|1\rangle \end{aligned} \tag{13}$$

However, from (12), the output from the cNOT gate for the superposition state turns out to be $\alpha|0\rangle|0\rangle+\beta|1\rangle|1\rangle$.

$$\begin{aligned} |\psi_{out1}\rangle|\psi_{out2}\rangle &= cNOT(\alpha|0\rangle + \beta|1\rangle)|0\rangle \\ &= cNOT(\alpha|0\rangle|0\rangle + \beta|1\rangle|0\rangle) \\ &= \alpha|0\rangle|0\rangle + \beta|1\rangle|1\rangle \end{aligned} \tag{14}$$

It is evident that the equation (13) does not equal (14). It is impossible to replicate any given quantum state in quantum mechanics. The no-cloning theorem is the name given to this constraint (Nielsen & Chuang, 2010; Wootters & Zurek, 1982). This is not a classical definition of "copy," even though it appears that the cNOT gate is copying the classical bit information from $|\psi in1\rangle$ to $|\psi out2\rangle$, The outcomes in (12) represent the unique scenarios when α=1 or β=1 ($|\alpha|^2+|\beta|^2=1$).

Furthermore, the states that result in (14) are rather striking. According to the equation, if we measure 0 in $\psi_{out}1$, we may be certain that $\psi_{out}2$ is likewise zero without any further measurements. Comparably, without measuring $\psi_{out}2$, we know $\psi_{out}2$ is likewise one when we find one in $\psi_{out}1$. Put differently, the value observed in $|\psi_{out}1$ determines the quantum state in $\psi_{out}2$. It is therefore impossible to characterize the outputs $\psi_{out}1$ and $\psi_{out}2$ separately. The term "entangled state" refers to this strange situation in which qubits' separate states are closely connected to one another. The entangled states cannot be expressed as separable states in the same way as in equations (13), where $|\psi_{out}1\rangle=(\alpha|0\rangle+\beta|1\rangle)$ and $|\psi_{out}2\rangle=(\alpha|0\rangle+\beta|1\rangle)$ are the expressions. Another crucial component of quantum computing is the utilization of entangled states.

2.7 The quantum computing circuit model

The easiest way to characterize a classical computer is as a finite register of n bits. Simple operations like NOT and AND can be applied to individual bits or to pairs of bits, and they can be combined in a certain order to create any complicated logic function. It is possible to apply the circuit concept to quantum computing. One way to conceptualize the quantum computer is as a finite set of n qubits, or a quantum register of size n. In binary notation, an integer $i \in [0, 2^n - 1]$ represents the state of an n-bit classical computer.

$$i = i_{n-1}\, 2^{n-1} + \cdots + i_1\, 2 + i_0 \tag{a}$$

When an n-qubit quantum computer has $i_0, i_1, \ldots, i_{n-1} \in [0, 1]$ binary digits, its state is

$$|\psi\rangle = \sum_{i=0}^{2^n-1} c_i |i\rangle$$
$$= \sum_{i_{n-1}=0}^{1} \cdots \sum_{i_1=0}^{1} \sum_{i_0=0}^{1} c_{i_{n-1},\ldots,i_1,i_0} |i_{n-1}\rangle \otimes \cdots \otimes |i_1\rangle \otimes |i_0\rangle \qquad \text{(b)}$$

with the normalization criterion limiting the complex numbers Ci

$$\sum_{i=0}^{2^n-1} |c_i|^2 = 1 \qquad \text{(c)}$$

Consequently, a wave function that resides in a 2^n-dimensional Hilbert space—which is the tensor product of n 2 -dimensional Hilbert spaces, one for each qubit—is the state of an n-qubit quantum computer. The state of the quantum computer is determined by $2(2^n— 1)$ independent real parameters, taking into consideration the normalization condition (c) and the fact that the state of any quantum system is only denned up to a global phase of little physical consequence. Take the scenario with n = 2 qubits as an illustration. The generic state of a quantum computer with two qubits is expressed as

$$|\psi\rangle = c_0|0\rangle + c_1|1\rangle + c_2|2\rangle + c_3|3\rangle$$
$$= c_{0,0}|0\rangle \otimes |0\rangle + c_{0,1}|0\rangle \otimes |1\rangle + c_{1,0}|1\rangle \otimes |0\rangle + c_{1,1}|1\rangle \otimes |1\rangle$$
$$= c_{00}|00\rangle + c_{01}|01\rangle + c_{10}|10\rangle + c_{11}|11\rangle, \qquad \text{(d)}$$

where the shorthand notation $|i_1 i_0\rangle = |i_1\rangle \otimes |i_0\rangle$ is used in the final line. We can more easily write the state (b) using this notation as

$$|\psi\rangle = \sum_{i_{n-1},\ldots,i_1,i_0=0}^{1} c_{i_{n-1}\cdots i_1 i_0} |i_{n-1}\cdots i_1 i_0\rangle \qquad \text{(e)}$$

The superposition principle is evident in Eq. (b): the n-qubit quantum register can be prepared in both a superposition and the corresponding state $|i\rangle$ of the computational basis, but n conventional bits can only store a single integer i. We emphasize that the computing basis's number of states in this superposition can reach up to 2^n, which increases exponentially with the number of qubits. The superposition principle creates new computational opportunities. A classical computer requires distinct runs for different inputs when we do a computation. A quantum computer, on the other hand, can execute a calculation for an exponentially large number of inputs in a single run. The power of quantum computation is based on this enormous parallelism.

It is emphasized that the superposition principle is not a characteristic that is specific to quantum mechanics. There are, in fact, classical waves that meet the superposition principle. The wave equation for a vibrating string with fixed ends, for example, may be examined. The most general state $|\varphi\rangle$ of a vibrating string can be expressed as a linear superposition of its solutions $|\varphi_i\rangle$ that fulfill the superposition principle, similar to Eq. (b):

$$|\varphi\rangle = \sum_{i=0}^{2^n-1} c_i |\varphi_i\rangle \qquad \text{(f)}$$

Given that quantum computation is more powerful than any classical computation, it is crucial to emphasize the significance of entanglement. Let's talk about the resources required in conventional versus quantum physics to represent the superposition (f). The superposition of 2^n levels must be members of the same system in order to be represented traditionally. In fact, classical states of distinct systems can never be superposed since there is no entanglement in classical physics. Therefore, a number of layers that increases exponentially with n is required.

The energy needed for this calculation is determined by $\Delta 2^n$, where Δ is the usual energy separation between two successive levels. The physical resources required for the computation therefore increase exponentially with n.[2]. On the other hand, a general superposition of 2^n quantum mechanics may be represented by n qubits because of entanglement. As a result, the quantity of energy or physical resources only increases linearly with n. To carry out a quantum computation, one must be able to:

1. Set up the quantum computer in a clearly defined starting state $|\psi_i\rangle$, which we refer to as the computer's fiducial state (for example, state I0---00);
2. Drive any given unitary transformation U to produce $|\psi_f\rangle = U|\psi_i\rangle$ by manipulating the quantum-computer wave function;
3. Carry out a standard measurement in the computational basis at the conclusion of the algorithm, i.e., measure the polarization σ_z of each qubit.

Since the quantum computer is an n-body (-qubit) quantum system, the Schrodinger equation controls how the wave function (b) evolves over time. The evolution of the quantum-computer wave function is thus described by a unitary operator, according to the postulates of quantum mechanics. Non-unitary decoherence effects resulting from an undesirable interaction between the quantum computer and the environment are ignored here.

Despite the fact that a $2^n \times 2^n$ unitary matrix describes the evolution of an n-qubit wave function, this matrix can always be broken down into a product of unitary operations that only affect one or two qubits. The circuit model of quantum computation uses these operations as its basic quantum gates. Lastly, it can be demonstrated that, as long as a sufficient unitary transformation is performed beforehand, any complex collective many-qubit measurement may always be carried out in the computational basis.

2.8 Single-qubit gates

Because qubit operations need to maintain the normalization requirement, they are represented by 2 x 2 unitary matrices. In the next section, we will examine the Hadamard and phase-shift gates and demonstrate their sufficiency in carrying out any unitary operation on a single qubit.

The Hadamard gate is described as

$$H = \frac{1}{\sqrt{2}}\begin{bmatrix} 1 & 1 \\ 1 & -1 \end{bmatrix} \tag{1}$$

The computational basis $\{|0\rangle, |1\rangle\}$ is transformed by this gate into the new basis $\{|+\rangle, |-\rangle\}$, whose states are a superposition of the computational basis's states:

$$\begin{aligned} H|0\rangle &= \frac{1}{\sqrt{2}}(|0\rangle + |1\rangle) \equiv |+\rangle, \\ H|1\rangle &= \frac{1}{\sqrt{2}}(|0\rangle - |1\rangle) \equiv |-\rangle. \end{aligned} \tag{2}$$

Since $H^2 = I$, $H^{-1} = H$ is the inverse transformation. Be aware that H is Hermitian. In fact, $(H^T)^* = H$. is clearly seen from the matrix representation (1).

The phase-shift gate is described as

$$R_z(\delta) = \begin{bmatrix} 1 & 0 \\ 0 & e^{i\delta} \end{bmatrix}. \tag{3}$$

With this gate, $|0\rangle$ becomes $|0\rangle$ and $|1\rangle$ becomes $e^{i\delta}|1\rangle$. The states of the computational basis, $|0\rangle$ and $|1\rangle$, remain unaltered since global phases have no physical significance. But the phase-shift gate's effect on a generic single-qubit state $|\psi\rangle$.

$$R_z(\delta)\,|\psi\rangle = \begin{bmatrix} 1 & 0 \\ 0 & e^{i\delta} \end{bmatrix} \begin{bmatrix} \cos\frac{\theta}{2} \\ e^{i\phi}\sin\frac{\theta}{2} \end{bmatrix} = \begin{bmatrix} \cos\frac{\theta}{2} \\ e^{i(\phi+\delta)}\sin\frac{\theta}{2} \end{bmatrix} \quad (4)$$

The use of the phase-shift gate has altered the qubit's state because relative phases are observable. Eq. (4) makes it clear that this gate rotates counterclockwise through an angle δ with respect to the Bloch sphere's z axis.

It is crucial to understand that Hadamard and phase-shift gates alone are sufficient to construct any unitary operation on a single qubit. The qubit state is really moved from one point of the Bloch sphere to another point by a unitary transformation, which can be accomplished with just these two quantum gates. Specifically, the generic state can be accessed as follows, beginning at $|0\rangle$.

$$R_z(\tfrac{\pi}{2}+\phi)\,H\,R_z(\theta)\,H\,|0\rangle = e^{i\frac{\theta}{2}}\left(\cos\tfrac{\theta}{2}\,|0\rangle + e^{i\phi}\sin\tfrac{\theta}{2}\,|1\rangle\right) \quad (5)$$

2.8.1 Sphere of Bloch rotations

The rotations of the Bloch sphere about an arbitrary axis are an important class of unitary transformations. Initially, it require the following outcome: Since O is an operator, let $O^2 = I$. As a result, $O^k = O$ for k odd and $O^k = I$ for k even. Consequently, one can obtain from a Taylor expansion of the operator O's exponential

$$\begin{aligned} e^{-i\alpha O} &= \left[1 - \tfrac{1}{2!}\alpha^2 + \cdots\right] I - i\left[\alpha - \tfrac{1}{3!}\alpha^3 + \cdots\right] O \\ &= \cos(\alpha)\, I - i\sin(\alpha)\, O\,. \end{aligned} \quad (a)$$

For exponentials of σ_x, σ_y and σ_z, we can use Eq. (a) since the Pauli operators meet the condition $\sigma_x^2 = \sigma_y^2 = \sigma_z^2 = I$. With regard to σ_z, we have

$$\begin{aligned} e^{-i\frac{\delta}{2}\sigma_z} &= \cos\tfrac{\delta}{2}\, I - i\sin\tfrac{\delta}{2}\,\sigma_z \\ &= e^{-i\frac{\delta}{2}} \begin{bmatrix} 1 & 0 \\ 0 & e^{i\delta} \end{bmatrix} \equiv R_z(\delta) \end{aligned} \quad (b)$$

The sole difference between the definitions of $R_z(\delta)$ above is a global phase factor that has no physical meaning. When a generic vector $|\psi\rangle$ is subjected to the phase-shift gate, the state

$$R_z(\delta)\,|\psi\rangle = \cos\tfrac{\theta}{2}\,|0\rangle + e^{i(\phi+\delta)}\,\sin\tfrac{\theta}{2}\,|1\rangle \tag{c}$$

Thus, we obtain the following coordinate transformation if (x,y,z) represent the Cartesian coordinates of the vector $|\psi\rangle$ and (x',y',z') represent the coordinates of $R_z(\delta)\,|\psi\rangle$ (calculated from the Bloch-sphere coordinates):

$$\begin{cases} x' = x\cos\delta - y\sin\delta\,, \\ y' = x\sin\delta + y\cos\delta\,, \\ z' = z\,. \end{cases} \tag{d}$$

As a result, $R_z(\delta)$ represents a counterclockwise rotation about the Bloch sphere's z-axis at an angle of δ. Naturally, we might also argue that the Bloch sphere itself is turned clockwise via an angle δ or that the vector $|\psi\rangle$ is rotated counterclockwise through an angle δ. Consider a fixed vector and moving axis in the latter image, and visualize the motion of the vector on a fixed Bloch sphere in the first. The unitary matrices corresponding to counterclockwise rotations about the z-axis can be obtained in an analogous manner:

$$e^{-i\frac{\delta}{2}\sigma_x} = \begin{bmatrix} \cos\frac{\delta}{2} & -i\sin\frac{\delta}{2} \\ -i\sin\frac{\delta}{2} & \cos\frac{\delta}{2} \end{bmatrix} \equiv R_x(\delta) \tag{e}$$

Or the *y*-axis:

$$e^{-i\frac{\delta}{2}\sigma_y} = \begin{bmatrix} \cos\frac{\delta}{2} & -\sin\frac{\delta}{2} \\ \sin\frac{\delta}{2} & \cos\frac{\delta}{2} \end{bmatrix} \equiv R_y(\delta) \tag{f}$$

2.9 Controlled gates and entanglement generation

The most fascinating feature of quantum mechanics, entanglement, is already present with two qubits. Actually, the computational basis for a generic two-qubit state can be expressed as follows: α, β, γ and δ complex coefficients. There are still six real degrees of freedom after accounting for the normalization condition, $|\alpha|^2 + |\beta|^2 + |\gamma|^2 + |\delta|^2 = 1$, and the fact that the state is only defined up to an overall phase factor.

$$|\psi\rangle = \alpha\,|00\rangle + \beta\,|01\rangle + \gamma\,|10\rangle + \delta\,|11\rangle \tag{1}$$

As a result, the state (1) cannot generally be regarded as a separate state. In fact, when $|\psi\rangle = |\psi_1\rangle \otimes |\psi_0\rangle$ can be written using $|\psi_1\rangle$ and $|\psi_0\rangle$ wave functions for the two subsystems, a state $|\psi\rangle$ of a bipartite quantum system is considered separable. Since we may take the two parameters of each qubit's Bloch sphere, for example, a separable two-qubit state has just four degrees of freedom. As the number of qubits increases, the problem gets more complicated. The most generic (entangled) state has $2(2^n - 1)$ degrees of freedom, whereas a separable state of n qubits depends only on real parameters, suggesting that the complexity of entanglement increases exponentially with the number of qubits.

It is evident that in an n-qubit system, entanglement cannot be produced using single-qubit gates. Since $|\psi\rangle = |\psi_{n-1}\rangle \otimes |\psi_{n-2}\rangle \otimes \cdots \otimes |\psi_0\rangle$ is a separable state, we can move any qubit on its Bloch sphere at will to get $|\psi'\rangle = |\psi'_{n-1}\rangle \otimes |\psi'_{n-2}\rangle \otimes \cdots \otimes |\psi'_0\rangle$- In this case, any state of the type $|\psi_i\rangle$ can be changed by gates acting on the qubit i in any superposition of the states $|0\rangle$ and $|1\rangle$ but the n-qubit state remains separable.

A two-qubit gate, or inter-qubit interactions, are required to prepare an entangled state. The controlled-NOT gate is a classic example of a two-qubit gate that can produce entanglement. Similar to the traditional XOR gate, this gate operates on the states of the computational basis, $\{|i_1 i_0\rangle = |00\rangle, |01\rangle, |10\rangle, |11\rangle\}$: When x, y = 0,1, and © denote addition modulo 2, $\text{CNOT}(|x\rangle|y\rangle) = |x\rangle|x \oplus y\rangle$. The CNOT gate uses its first qubit as a control and its second as a target. If the control qubit is in the state $|0\rangle$, the gate does nothing; if the control qubit is in the state $|1\rangle$, it flips the target qubit's state. Note that the basis vectors can be shown as column vectors:

$$|0\rangle = |00\rangle = \begin{bmatrix} 1 \\ 0 \\ 0 \\ 0 \end{bmatrix}, \qquad |1\rangle = |01\rangle = \begin{bmatrix} 0 \\ 1 \\ 0 \\ 0 \end{bmatrix}$$

$$|2\rangle = |10\rangle = \begin{bmatrix} 0 \\ 0 \\ 1 \\ 0 \end{bmatrix}, \qquad |3\rangle = |11\rangle = \begin{bmatrix} 0 \\ 0 \\ 0 \\ 1 \end{bmatrix} \qquad (2)$$

where all other components of the vector $|i\rangle$ are equal to zero and the component *i* is equal to one. $|i\rangle = |i_1 i_0\rangle$ and $|j\rangle = |j_1 j_0\rangle$ are expressed in binary notation. As a result, we can determine the CNOT gate's matrix representation:

$$\text{CNOT} = \begin{bmatrix} 1 & 0 & 0 & 0 \\ 0 & 1 & 0 & 0 \\ 0 & 0 & 0 & 1 \\ 0 & 0 & 1 & 0 \end{bmatrix} \tag{3}$$

where $(\text{CNOT})_{ij} = \langle i|\,\text{CNOT}\,|j\rangle$ yields the components $(\text{CNOT})_{ij}$ of this matrix (Note that i,j = 0,..., 3). As an illustration, we have

$$(\text{CNOT})_{23} = \langle 2|\,\text{CNOT}\,|3\rangle = \langle 10|\,\text{CNOT}\,|11\rangle = 1 \tag{4}$$

Naturally, the CNOT gate can be used with any superposition of the computational basis states, unlike the traditional XOR gate. Because $(\text{CNOT})^2 = I$, CNOT is self-inverse. The ability of CNOT to produce entangled states is readily apparent. For instance,

$$\text{CNOT}\,(\alpha|0\rangle + \beta|1\rangle)\,|0\rangle = \alpha|00\rangle + \beta|11\rangle \tag{5}$$

Hence, insofar as $\alpha, \beta \neq 0$, cannot be separated.

2.9.1 Bell's foundation

Entanglement can be produced via the CNOT gate. Specifically, the Bell basis's entangled states, which are defined by

$$\begin{aligned} |\phi^+\rangle &= \tfrac{1}{\sqrt{2}}\left(|00\rangle + |11\rangle\right), \\ |\phi^-\rangle &= \tfrac{1}{\sqrt{2}}\left(|00\rangle - |11\rangle\right), \\ |\psi^+\rangle &= \tfrac{1}{\sqrt{2}}\left(|01\rangle + |10\rangle\right), \\ |\psi^-\rangle &= \tfrac{1}{\sqrt{2}}\left(|01\rangle - |10\rangle\right), \end{aligned}$$

can be obtained using the circuit shown in the figure below, beginning with the computational basis. Verifying that this circuit generates the following conversions is simple.

$$\begin{aligned} |00\rangle &\to |\phi^+\rangle, & |01\rangle &\to |\psi^+\rangle, \\ |10\rangle &\to |\phi^-\rangle, & |11\rangle &\to |\psi^-\rangle. \end{aligned}$$

Since both CNOT and Hadamard gates are self-inverse, we observe that this transformation can be reversed by simply looping the circuit of the figure below from right to left. Because we utilized a two-qubit gate, any state of the Bell basis is subsequently converted into a separable state. Using a standard measurement in the computational basis, it is now possible to determine which of the four Bell states existed initially.

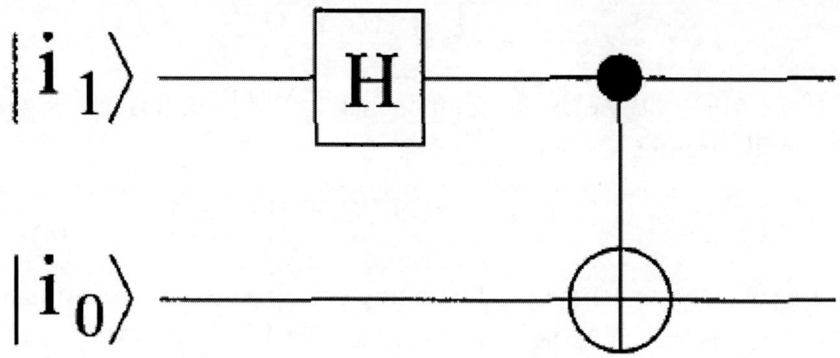

Fig.2.9 A circuit that converts the computational basis states $|i_1 i_0\rangle$ to the Bell states.

2.10 All-purpose quantum gates

The circuit model is useful in classical computation because it enables the construction of arbitrarily complicated computations from a series of simple operations (such as NAND and COPY). We will demonstrate that a similar outcome is true for quantum computation, namely that each unitary operation in the Hilbert space of n qubits may be broken down into CNOT gates with one and two qubits. To familiarize the reader with quantum logic gate operations, a thorough proof of this result will be provided.

Define the controlled- U operation first. Controlled- U indicates that if U is an arbitrary single qubit unitary transformation, it only affects the target qubit when the control qubit is set to $|1\rangle$.

$$|i_1\rangle|i_0\rangle \rightarrow |i_1\rangle U^{i_1}|i_0\rangle \tag{a}$$

Only single-qubit gates and CNOT are needed to build the controlled-U gate. Any 2 x 2 unitary matrix can be expressed as follows since a matrix U is unitary if and only if its rows and columns are orthonormal.

$$U = \begin{bmatrix} e^{i(\delta-\alpha/2-\beta/2)}\cos\frac{\theta}{2} & -e^{i(\delta-\alpha/2+\beta/2)}\sin\frac{\theta}{2} \\ e^{i(\delta+\alpha/2-\beta/2)}\sin\frac{\theta}{2} & e^{i(\delta+\alpha/2+\beta/2)}\cos\frac{\theta}{2} \end{bmatrix} \tag{b}$$

where the real parameters are δ, α, β and θ. Consequently, U can be broken down in the manner shown below:

$$U = \Phi(\delta)\, R_z(\alpha)\, R_y(\theta)\, R_z(\beta)$$

(c)

Where

$$\Phi(\delta) = \begin{bmatrix} e^{i\delta} & 0 \\ 0 & e^{i\delta} \end{bmatrix}$$

(d)

where Ry and Rz are the rotation matrices about the y and z axes. In fact, there are three unitary matrices, A, B, and C, for every U expressed as in Eq. (b):

$$A = R_z(\alpha)\, R_y\left(\tfrac{\theta}{2}\right),$$
$$B = R_y\left(-\tfrac{\theta}{2}\right) R_z\left(-\tfrac{\alpha+\beta}{2}\right),$$
$$C = R_z\left(\tfrac{\beta-\alpha}{2}\right),$$

(e)

Such that

$$ABC = I \qquad \text{and} \qquad \Phi(\delta)\, A\,\sigma_x\, B\,\sigma_x\, C = U.$$

(f)

In Eq. (f), the first equality is obvious, and the second may be readily verified using the following properties: $\sigma_x^2 = I$, $\sigma_x R_y(\xi)\sigma_x = R_y(-\xi)$ and $\sigma_x R_z(\xi)\sigma_x = R_z(-\xi)$.

The controlled-U operation can therefore be implemented as shown in the figure below. In fact, ABC = I is applied to the target qubit if the control qubit's value is zero. The target qubit receives the application of $A\sigma_x B\sigma_x C = \Phi(-\delta)U$ if the value of the control qubit is set to 1. Thus, the controlled-U transformation is almost ready to be implemented, with the exception of the phase factor $\Phi(-\delta) = e^{-i\delta}I$, which manifests when the control is set to 1. The circuit's final gate eliminates this undesirable phase component in the figure below. It only has non-trivial effects on the control qubit, and its matrix form is as follows:

$$R_z(\delta) \otimes I = \begin{bmatrix} 1 & 0 \\ 0 & e^{i\delta} \end{bmatrix} \otimes I = \begin{bmatrix} 1\cdot I & 0\cdot I \\ 0\cdot I & e^{i\delta}\cdot I \end{bmatrix} = \begin{bmatrix} 1 & 0 & 0 & 0 \\ 0 & 1 & 0 & 0 \\ 0 & 0 & e^{i\delta} & 0 \\ 0 & 0 & 0 & e^{i\delta} \end{bmatrix}$$

(g)

where matrices' tensor product has been carried out. The undesirable phase factor $\Phi(-\delta)$ is eliminated by this gate since it is trivially equal to the controlled-$\Phi(\delta)$ gate (as shown, this phase factor exists only when the control is set to 1). This completes the demonstration that the controlled-[/ operation is implemented by the circuit in Figure below.

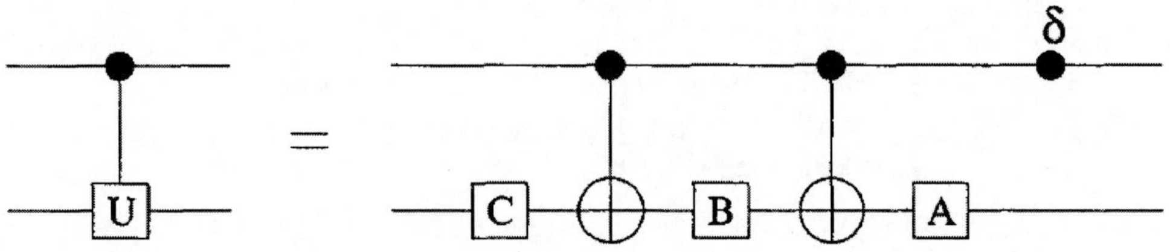

Fig.2.10 An implementation of the controlled-U gate circuit.

If all k control qubits are set to 1, the gate $C^k\text{-}U$, which we now examine, performs a unitary transformation U on the target qubit. The implementation of these gates using elementary gates, specifically single-qubit and CNOT gates, will be demonstrated. The Toffoli gate, also known as C^2-NOT, is of special significance because it only applies a NOT operation to the target qubit when both control qubits are set to 1. The figure below illustrates how the Toffoli gate is constructed. This is the matrix V.

$$V = \begin{bmatrix} 1 & 0 \\ 0 & i \end{bmatrix} \tag{h}$$

As seen above, the operations controlled V and controlled $V^\dagger$ can be performed with just single-qubit gates and CNOT since V and $V^\dagger$are unitary. Therefore, these simple gates serve as the foundation for the Toffoli gate. The following factors make this outcome especially significant:

1. Quantum circuits with single-qubit and CNOT gates as building blocks comprise classical computation because the Toffoli gate is universal for classical computation;
2. Reversible gates with one or two bits are not universal in classical computation, in contrast to quantum computation.

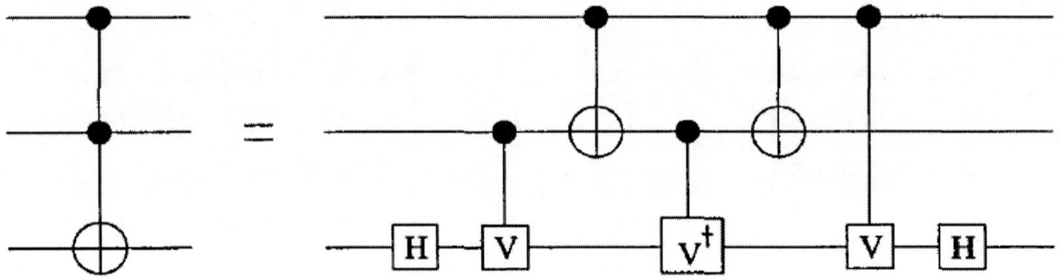

Fig.2.11 An implementation of the Toffoli gate circuit.

2.10.1 The initial state's preparation

The creation of a generic state for the quantum computer is covered in this subsection. It turns out that because this preparation calls for an exponential number of gates in relation to the number of qubits, it cannot be completed efficiently in general. Assume for the moment prepare the quantum computer from its starting fiducial state $|0\rangle$.

$$|\psi\rangle = \sum_{i=0}^{7} a_i |i\rangle \tag{1}$$

where we examine the specific scenario that corresponds to n = 3 qubits for the sake of clarity. The amplitudes $|a_i|$ $(a_i = |a_i|e^{i\gamma_i})$ should be set first. It is simple to verify that this is achieved by the circuit of the state $|000\rangle$ shown in Fig. below. In fact, the state $|000\rangle$ is changed by the first gate $(R_y(-2\theta_1))^3$ into

$$\left(\cos\theta_1 |0\rangle + \sin\theta_1 |1\rangle\right)|00\rangle \tag{2}$$

The state is then reached via the two generalized C-R*y* gates.

$$\Big(\cos\theta_1 \cos\theta_2|00\rangle + \cos\theta_1 \sin\theta_2|01\rangle + \sin\theta_1 \cos\theta_3|10\rangle + \sin\theta_1 \sin\theta_3|11\rangle\Big)|0\rangle \tag{3}$$

Lastly, the state is produced by the four generalized C2-R*y* gates.

$$\begin{aligned}&\cos\theta_1 \cos\theta_2 \cos\theta_4 |000\rangle + \cos\theta_1 \cos\theta_2 \sin\theta_4 |001\rangle \\ &+ \cos\theta_1 \sin\theta_2 \cos\theta_5 |010\rangle + \cos\theta_1 \sin\theta_2 \sin\theta_5 |011\rangle \\ &+ \sin\theta_1 \cos\theta_3 \cos\theta_6 |100\rangle + \sin\theta_1 \cos\theta_3 \sin\theta_6 |101\rangle \\ &+ \sin\theta_1 \sin\theta_3 \cos\theta_7 |110\rangle + \sin\theta_1 \sin\theta_3 \sin\theta_7 |111\rangle .\end{aligned} \tag{4}$$

The amplitudes $|a_i|$ are reproduced in this intervel $[0, \frac{\pi}{2}]$ if we adjust the angles θ_i as follows:

The circuit shown in Fig. below necessitates 2^n — 1 = 7 (controlled) single-qubit rotations about the y-axis. This is in line with the requirement to set 2^n — 1 degrees of freedom in order to compute the 2^n wave-function amplitudes due to the normalizing constraint. Phases γ_i. are now set. A unitary transformation (UD) must be carried out, with a diagonal matrix representation in the computational basis {|000>, |001), |010), |011), |100), |101), |110), |111»}:

$$U_D = \mathrm{diag}[e^{i\gamma_0}, e^{i\gamma_1}, e^{i\gamma_2}, e^{i\gamma_3}, e^{i\gamma_4}, e^{i\gamma_5}, e^{i\gamma_6}, e^{i\gamma_7}] \quad (5)$$

It is simple to verify that the operator UD is explicitly constructed using $2^n/2$ controlled operations in the following figure.

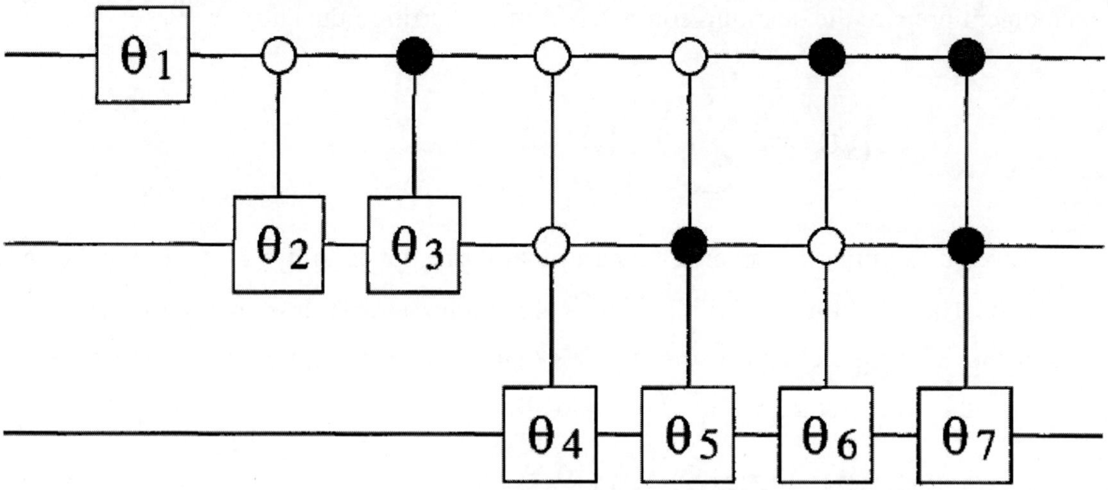

Fig.2.12 The amplitudes of a general three-qubit state are set by a circuit. To represent the rotation matrices, use the θ_i-symbols. $R_y(-2\theta_i)$.

Γ_k is a single-qubit gate used in these operations, and its matrix representation in the computational basis $\{|0\rangle, |1\rangle\}$ is provided by

$$\Gamma_k = \begin{bmatrix} e^{i\gamma_{2k}} & 0 \\ 0 & e^{i\gamma_{2k+1}} \end{bmatrix} \quad (6)$$

We require $2^N/2$ gates Γ_k, where k is between 0 and $2^n/2$ - 1. The phases $e^{i\gamma_0}$ and $e^{i\gamma_1}$ are placed in front of the basis vectors $|000\rangle$ and $|001\rangle$ respectively, because Γ_0 only works when the first two qubits are in the state |00), as shown in Fig. Similarly, Γ_1 only puts the phase $e^{i\gamma_2}$ and $e^{i\gamma_3}$ in front of the basis vectors $|010\rangle$ and $|011\rangle$ and so on, when the first two qubits are in the state $|01\rangle$.

Quantum computer has an exponential advantage in memory requirements, even if state preparation generally calls for an exponential number of operations, similar to those in classical computation: The coefficients of a wave vector's expansion over the computational basis, which are 2^n complex numbers, determine a wave vector loaded in n qubits. To load 2" complex numbers, the classical computer requires $O(2^n)$ bits; more specifically, we need $m2^n$ bits, where m is the number of bits needed to store a complex number with a specific accuracy. The fact that the quantum computer can complete this work with just n qubits makes its enormous memory capacities evident.

It is crucial to understand that a specific wave function can be effectively prepared in certain situations. If a quantum computer operation calls for a number of elementary gates that are polynomial in the number of qubits, it can be completed effectively. The equal superposition of every state in the computational basis, for example,

$$|\psi\rangle = \sum_{i=0}^{2^n-1} \frac{1}{\sqrt{2^n}} |i\rangle \tag{7}$$

is the result of applying n Hadamard gates to the state $|0\rangle$, one for each qubit.

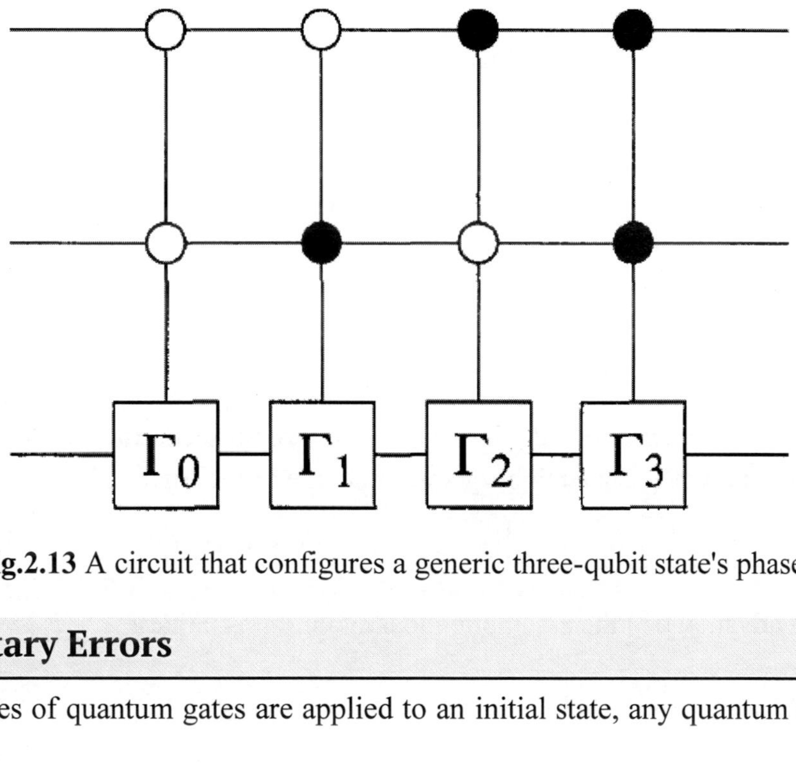

Fig.2.13 A circuit that configures a generic three-qubit state's phases.

2.11 Unitary Errors

When a series of quantum gates are applied to an initial state, any quantum computation is produced:

$$|\psi_n\rangle = \prod_{i=1}^{n} U_i |\psi_0\rangle \tag{a}$$

Any practical implementation will contain some inaccuracy since unitary operations constitute a continuous set. For the time being, let's assume that errors are unitary. Will discuss about non-unitary errors because of the inescapable coupling to the environment.

Use somewhat different unitary operators V_i ; in place of the operators U_i. After i stages, if we call $|\psi_i\rangle$ the ideal state, we have

$$|\psi_i\rangle = U_i\,|\psi_{i-1}\rangle \tag{b}$$

But when we use the real imperfect operation Vi, we get

$$V_i\,|\psi_{i-1}\rangle = |\psi_i\rangle + |E_i\rangle \tag{c}$$

Where,

$$|E_i\rangle = (V_i - U_i)\,|\psi_{i-1}\rangle \tag{d}$$

If $|\tilde{\psi}_i\rangle$ represents the quantum-computer wave function following the application of i imperfect unitary transformations, then we get

$$\begin{aligned} |\tilde{\psi}_1\rangle &= |\psi_1\rangle + |E_1\rangle\,, \\ |\tilde{\psi}_2\rangle &= V_2|\tilde{\psi}_1\rangle = |\psi_2\rangle + |E_2\rangle + V_2|E_1\rangle \end{aligned} \tag{e}$$

and so forth. Consequently, following n iterations, we get

$$\begin{aligned} |\tilde{\psi}_n\rangle &= |\psi_n\rangle + |E_n\rangle + V_n|E_{n-1}\rangle \\ &\quad + V_n V_{n-1}\,|E_{n-2}\rangle + \cdots + V_n V_{n-1} \ldots V_2\,|E_1\rangle \end{aligned} \tag{f}$$

The errors are aligned and add linearly in the worst scenario. This results in the following bound, which is a straightforward outcome of the triangle inequality.

$$\left\| |\tilde{\psi}_n\rangle - |\psi_n\rangle \right\| \leq \left\| |E_n\rangle \right\| + \left\| |E_{n-1}\rangle \right\| + \cdots + \left\| |E_1\rangle \right\| \tag{g}$$

where made advantage of the assumption that evolution is unitary.

$$\left\| V_i\,|E_{i-1}\rangle \right\| = \left\| |E_{i-1}\rangle \right\| \tag{h}$$

The error vector's Euclidean norm $|E_i\rangle$ can be restricted in this way:

$$\left\| |E_i\rangle \right\| = \left\| (V_i - U_i)\,|\psi_{i-1}\rangle \right\| \leq \left\| V_i - U_i \right\|_{\mathbf{sup}} \tag{i}$$

where the operator $V_i - U_i$'s sup norm, or its eigenvalue of maximum modulus, $\|V_i - U_i\|_{\mathrm{sup}}$ Considering that the mistake is consistently bound at every stage,

$$\left\| V_i - U_i \right\|_{\mathbf{sup}} < \epsilon \tag{j}$$

Following the application of *n* imperfect operators, we obtain

$$\left\| |\tilde{\psi}_n\rangle - |\psi_n\rangle \right\| < n\epsilon \tag{k}$$

Unitary errors so increase, at worst, linearly with the quantum computation's duration. This growth occurs for systematic errors that align in the same direction, but stochastic errors have a more favorable $\sqrt{n}$ growth because they are randomly directed.

The discrete set mentioned in the preceding section (Hadamard, $R_z(\frac{\pi}{4})$ and CNOT) contains $O(n\log^c(1/(\epsilon/n)))$ gates that can be used to approximate a quantum computation to accuracy e if it requires n elementary gates (single-qubit and CNOT gates). It is true that any single-qubit rotation can be roughly represented with an accuracy of ϵ/n in $O(\log^c(1/(\epsilon/n)))$ gates from the discrete set above, and the bound of Eq. (k) suggests that it is adequate to increase the accuracy of the gates linearly with the length *n* of the quantum computation.

The precision of the outcomes of a quantum computation and the precision of the quantum-computer wave function (measured by $\| |\tilde{\psi}_n\rangle - |\psi_n\rangle \|$) must be connected. The projective measurement that results from quantum computation in the computational basis is outcome i with probability $p_i = |\langle i|\psi_n\rangle|^2$. The true probability becomes $\tilde{p}_i = |\langle i|\tilde{\psi}_n\rangle|^2$ when unitary errors are present. Two, it can be demonstrated that $\sum_i |p_i - \tilde{p}_i| \leq 2\| |\tilde{\psi}_n\rangle - |\psi_n\rangle \|$.

Lastly, it is noticed that unable to ascertain how mistakes scale with the number of qubits in the quantum computer using thc reasoning presented above

2.12 Evaluation of functions

The evaluation of a binary (logic) function with an n-bit input and a one-bit output is the fundamental function carried out by a classical computer:

$$f : \{0,1\}^n \rightarrow \{0,1\}$$

The output $f(x_{n-1},\ldots,x_1,x_0)$ can be equal to 0 or 1. This indicates that / takes the input $(x_{n-1},\ldots,x_1,x_0)$ with $x_{n-1},\ldots,x_1,x_0$ binary digits. These binary functions can be assembled to evaluate any complex function by a computer.

The creation of the binary functions for n = 2 bits will be covered first. Displayed the $2^{2^n} = 16$ two-bit logic functions in the table below. In general, these functions cannot be inverted. For example, $f_1(x_1,x_0) = x_1 \wedge x_0$, where ($\wedge$ denotes the logic AND), equals 0 for three distinct inputs. The addition of an auxiliary bit allows evaluation of these functions in reversible computing. On a quantum computer, the proper unitary transformation that evaluates the function / uses the supplementary qubit $|y\rangle$ and is provided by

$$U_f|x_{n-1}, x_{n-2}, \ldots, x_0\rangle|y\rangle$$
$$= |x_{n-1}, x_{n-2}, \ldots, x_0\rangle|y \oplus f(x_{n-1}, x_{n-2}, \ldots, x_0)\rangle$$

wherein there is a distinct input for a specific output.

Table 2.5 Logic functions with two bits.

x_1x_0	f_0	f_1	f_2	f_3	f_4	f_5	f_6	f_7	f_8	f_9	f_{10}	f_{11}	f_{12}	f_{13}	f_{14}	f_{15}
0 0	0	0	0	0	0	0	0	0	1	1	1	1	1	1	1	1
0 1	0	0	0	0	1	1	1	1	0	0	0	0	1	1	1	1
1 0	0	0	1	1	0	0	1	1	0	0	1	1	0	0	1	1
1 1	0	1	0	1	0	1	0	1	0	1	0	1	0	1	0	1

2.13 Quantum adder

Building quantum circuits to carry out simple elementary operations is crucial, much like in classical computation. Several operations, such as plain addition, modular addition, and modular exponentiation, have explicit constructions. In this case, detailed on the simple addition of two n-bit integers, a and b (in binary representation, $a = a_{n-1}2^{n-1} + a_{n-2}2^{n-2} + \cdots + a_0 \equiv a_{n-1}a_{n-2}\cdots a_0$, and similarly for $b \equiv b_{n-1}b_{n-2}\cdots b_0$) After reading the previous section, one could compute reversibly by taking into account n + 1 auxiliary qubits.

$$|a, b, 0\rangle \rightarrow |a, b, a + b\rangle \quad (1)$$

Since the output a + b requires n + 1 bits to be encoded without overflows and we have a 2n-qubit input (encoding a and b), we must evaluate n + 1 binary functions with a 2n-bit input. The process is inconvenient. It is more beneficial to calculate the following bit by bit:

$$|a, b\rangle \rightarrow |a, a + b\rangle \quad (2)$$

This calculation can be carried out in reverse since the input can be recreated from the outcome.

As is customary in classical calculation, the total is calculated beginning with the least significant qubit. We must calculate the sum $s_i = a_i \oplus b_i \oplus c_i$ and the new carry c_{i+1} for the qubit i given ai, bi, and the carry Ci. Consequently, it is necessary to evaluate two 3-bit input binary functions: SUM, which computes Si, and CARRY, which computes Ci+1. Below Table provides the corresponding truth tables. The SUM(ai,bi,Ci) function provides

$$s_i = a_i \oplus b_i \oplus c_i \quad (3)$$

whereas CARRY(ai,bi &;,ci), as is easily verified, generates

$$c_{i+1} = (a_i \wedge b_i) \vee (c_i \wedge a_i) \vee (c_i \wedge b_i) \quad (4)$$

Table 2.6 Truth tables for the SUM and CARRY functions.

c_i	a_i	b_i	s_i	c_{i+1}
0	0	0	0	0
0	0	1	1	0
0	1	0	1	0
0	1	1	0	1
1	0	0	1	0
1	0	1	0	1
1	1	0	0	1
1	1	1	1	1

When at least two of the input bits, ai, bi, and ci, are set to one, ci+1 = 1. Two CNOT gates can be used to compute the function SUM directly from the expression (3). The function CARRY, on the other hand, needs an auxiliary qubit since it uses irreversible logic operations (AND, OR). The figure below depicts the quantum circuits that implement SUM and CARRY.

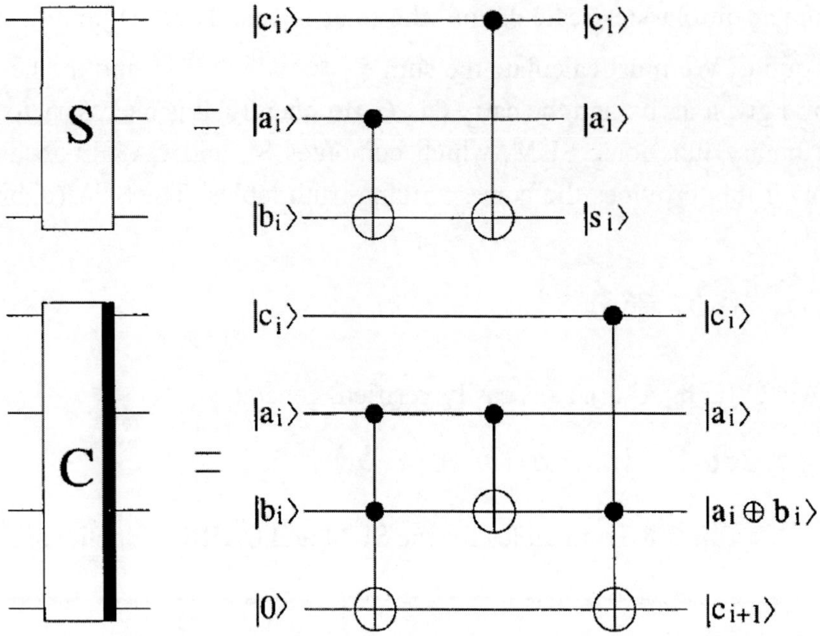

Fig.2.14 The quantum circuit that performs the operations CARRY and SUM (top).

The basic adder circuit, which computes the sum a + b, is represented in the figure below by the circuits implementing SUM and CARRY. Total three registers: the first (n qubits) with input and output $|a_{n-1}, a_{n-2}, \ldots, a_1, a_0\rangle$; the second (n + 1 qubits) with input $|0, b_{n-1}, b_{n-2}, \ldots, b_1, b_0\rangle$ and output $|(a+b)_n, (a+b)_{n-1}, (a+b)_{n-2}, \ldots, (a+b)_1, (a+b)_0\rangle$ and the third is made up of n — 1 qubits, initially in the state $|0\rangle$ to which the carries are temporarily written before being refreshed to the $|0\rangle$ state at completion. The circuit's first n CARRY'S each change $|c_i, a_i, b_i, 0\rangle$ into $|c_i, a_i, a_i \oplus b_i, c_{i+1}\rangle$.

The final carry yields (a + b)n, the sum's most significant digit. Next, $(a_{n-1}, a_{n-1} \oplus b_{n-1})$ is taken by a single CNOT gate into (a_{n-1}, b_{n-1}) is taken by an SUM operation $(c_{n-1}, a_{n-1}, b_{n-1})$ into $(c_{n-1}, a_{n-1}, a_{n-1} + b_{n-1})$. We then use CARRY and SUM n — 1 once. Consequently, all ancillary qubits are returned to their starting state $|0\rangle$. For each qubit i, the total ai + bi is calculated. Because it enables us to utilize these auxiliary qubits once more for other computations, this is significant.

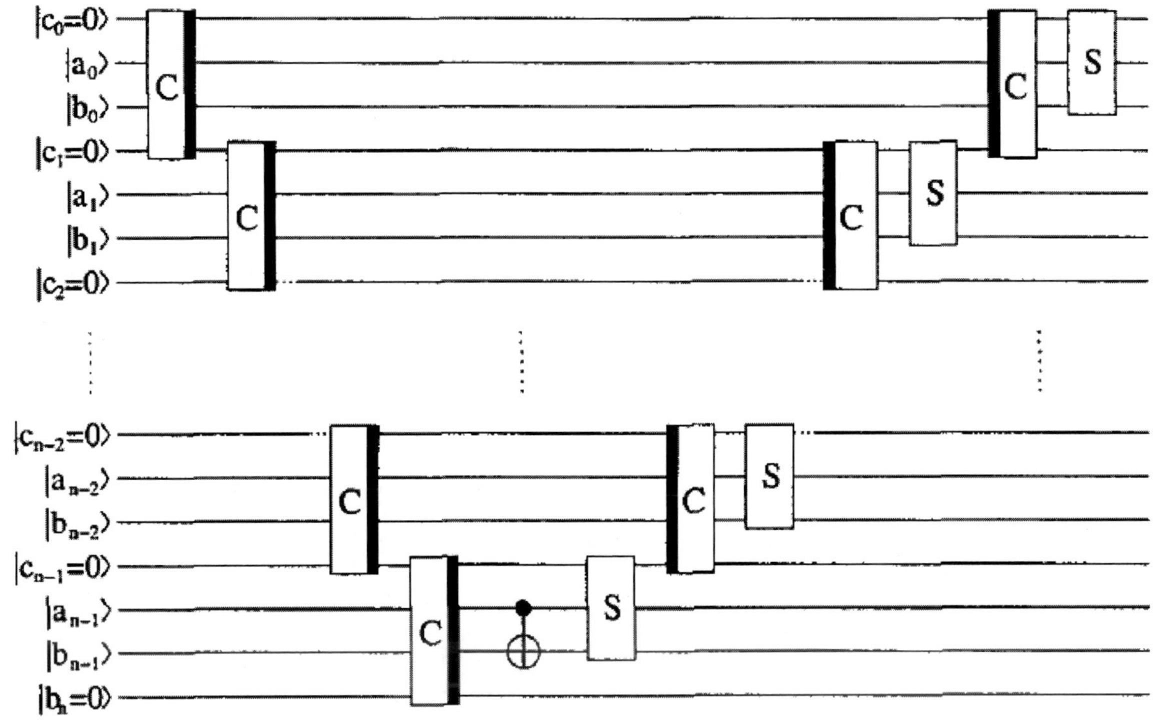

Fig.2.15 Two n-bit integers, a and b, are added using a quantum circuit. Take note of where the thick black bars on the CARRY circuits are located. In relation to a CARRY with the bar on the right, a CARRY with the bar on the left denotes the opposite sequence of elementary gates.

2.14 The Deutsch algorithm

Quantum interference's computational capacity is demonstrated by Deutsch's issue. A one-bit Boolean function $f:\{0,1\} \to \{0,1\}$ is evaluated by a black box known as the oracle. These four functions are listed in below given Table. One global trait that distinguishes them is that two of them are balanced (f_1 and f_2) and two are constant (f_0 and f_3). The challenge is to determine if a given function is balanced or constant. Two inquiries to the oracle in a traditional computer are required in order to solve this problem. Here, detailing how a quantum computer can use a single oracle query to answer the same problem.

Table 2.7 Logic functions with a single bit.

x	f_0	f_1	f_2	f_3
0	0	0	1	1
1	0	1	0	1

Deutsch's algorithm is implemented via the quantum circuit depicted in the figure below. Reversible computation uses an additional qubit $|y\rangle$ to evaluate the function f(x). $|x\rangle|y\rangle$ is changed into $|x\rangle|y \oplus f(x)\rangle$ it flips the second qubit by the unitary transformation U_f, provided that f(x) = 1. The qubits' starting state is $|x\rangle|y\rangle = |0\rangle|1\rangle$. Next, in the superposition $(|0\rangle + |1\rangle)/\sqrt{2}$, the first qubit is prepared via a Hadamard gate. In contrast to a classical computer, the quantum computer will be able to assess both $f(0)$ and $f(1)$ in a single run, as will be demonstrated below. The auxiliary qubit is prepared in $(|0\rangle - |1\rangle)/\sqrt{2}$ by another Hadamard gate. It is important to note that for any $x \in \{0,1\}$.

$$U_f|x\rangle \frac{1}{\sqrt{2}}(|0\rangle - |1\rangle) = (-1)^{f(x)}|x\rangle \frac{1}{\sqrt{2}}(|0\rangle - |1\rangle) \qquad \text{(a)}$$

In particular, in front of the first qubit, the phase factor $(-1)^{f(x)}$ is propagated backwards, or kicked back. Consequently, following the function evaluation, the quantum computer's state is

$$\frac{1}{\sqrt{2}}\left[(-1)^{f(0)}|0\rangle + (-1)^{f(1)}|1\rangle\right] \frac{1}{\sqrt{2}}(|0\rangle - |1\rangle) \qquad \text{(b)}$$

Since the second qubit is no longer in use, we will disregard it going forward. The state's first qubit is left behind by the last Hadamard gate.

$$\frac{1}{2}\left\{\left[(-)^{f(0)} + (-)^{f(1)}\right]|0\rangle + \left[(-)^{f(0)} - (-)^{f(1)}\right]|1\rangle\right\} \qquad \text{(c)}$$

This condition is equivalent to $|0\rangle = |f(0) \oplus f(1)\rangle$ if $f(0) = f(1)$. This state can be expressed as $|1\rangle = |f(0) \oplus f(1)\rangle$ if instead $f(0) \neq f(1)$ (in both circumstances up to an overall phase factor of negligible physical importance). In any event, the first qubit's final state can be expressed as

$$|f(0) \oplus f(1)\rangle \qquad \text{(d)}$$

Then, if the function is constant, a measurement of the first qubit yields the result 0 with unit probability, and if the function is balanced, the result 1. As a result, after a single call of *f*, a global property of the function f(x) has been encoded in a single qubit. This is due to the fact that a quantum computer is capable of simultaneously evaluating $f(0)$ and $f(1)$. The key idea is that the final Hadamard gate combines these two alternate "paths" to produce the intended interference pattern. For the outcome $f(0) \oplus f(1)$ the interference is constructive; for the alternative outcome, it is destructive.

2.14.1 The Deutsch-Jozsa issue

We will now look at a few Deutsch's problem generalizations. In just one Oracle query, the Deutsch-Jozsa technique resolves the following issue:

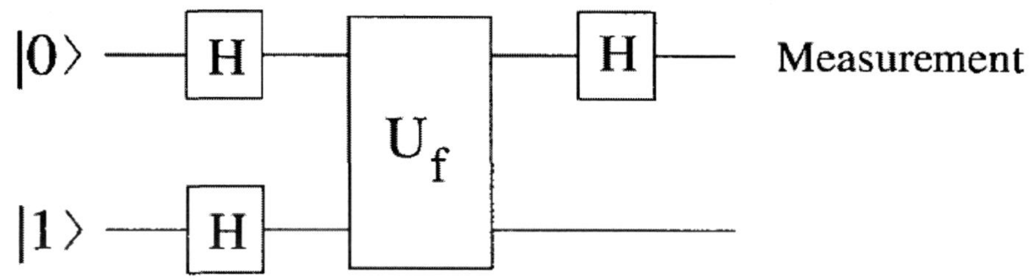

Fig.2.16 Deutsch's algorithm in a quantum circuit.

We want to know if the n-bit binary function $f : \{0,1\}^n \rightarrow \{0,1\}$ is balanced or constant, since it has been "promised" to be so (i.e., it has an equal number of output 0's and l's). With n qubits to store the input $x = (x_{n-1}, x_{n-2}, \ldots, x_0)$ the quantum circuit that resolves this issue is identical to that for Deutsch's algorithm (above Fig.). All n qubits are now subjected to parallel applications of the Hadamard gates,

$$H^{\otimes n} = H \otimes H \otimes \cdots \otimes H \qquad \text{(e)}$$

It is simple to verify that $H^{\otimes n}$ action on a state $|x\rangle$ of the computational basis results in

$$H^{\otimes n}|x\rangle = \prod_{i=0}^{n-1} \left(\frac{1}{\sqrt{2}} \sum_{y_i=0}^{1} (-1)^{x_i y_i} |y_i\rangle \right) = \frac{1}{2^{n/2}} \sum_{y=0}^{2^n-1} (-1)^{x \cdot y} |y\rangle \qquad \text{(f)}$$

where the inner product of x and y, modulo 2, is indicated by x * y:

$$x \cdot y = x_{n-1}y_{n-1} \oplus x_{n-2}y_{n-2} \oplus \cdots \oplus x_0 y_0 \qquad \text{(g)}$$

The circuit in the above figure applies the transformation and is generalized to n-bit input.

$$(H^{\otimes n} \otimes I)\, U_f\, (H^{\otimes n} \otimes H) \qquad \text{(h)}$$

to the input $|00\ldots0\rangle|1\rangle$ and produces the result

$$\left(\frac{1}{2^n} \sum_{x,y=0}^{2^n-1} (-1)^{f(x)+x\cdot y} |y\rangle \right) \frac{1}{\sqrt{2}} (|0\rangle - |1\rangle) \qquad \text{(i)}$$

This suggests that a measurement of the n qubits in the computational basis at the circuit's end yields the state $|00...0\rangle$ with zero probability if / is balanced and unit probability if *f* is constant. As a result, it is possible to ascertain if *f* is constant or balanced with a single execution of the algorithm and a single query of the function f(x). This is a remarkable outcome because, in classical computation, f(x) can only be guaranteed to be balanced after $2^n/2+1$ function inquiries. To assert that the quantum computer has an exponential advantage in this method would be unjust, though.

In fact, if *f* is balanced, there is $1/2^{k-1}$ chance of consistently receiving the same answer with k function inquiries. Given that this likelihood decreases exponentially with k, one can infer that *f* is constant in this scenario, with an exponentially decreasing probability of providing the incorrect response. The chance of mistake can therefore be decreased by a classical algorithm below a level e following a series of queries $k = O(\log(1/\epsilon))$. Furthermore, we observe that it is not feasible to expect the quantum computer to provide an answer with complete confidence due to physical limitations, as some degree of error will inevitably exist.

2.14.2 A variation of the Deutsch algorithm

Consider an additional generalization of the technique as an exercise, demonstrating that a quantum computer can be used to ascertain additional global features of a given function. To keep things simple, let's look at the scenario when n = 2 qubits. With the amplitudes ci displayed in the table below for the 16 two-qubit logic functions (omit the normalization factor to simplify writing), the state of the two qubits at the end of the Deutsch-Jozsa circuit can be expressed in the computational basis as $|\psi_f\rangle = c_0|00\rangle + c_1|01\rangle + c_2|10\rangle + c_3|11\rangle$.

Table 2.8 End-of-the-Deutsch-Jozsa circuit two-qubit states.

	f_0	f_1	f_2	f_3	f_4	f_5	f_6	f_7	f_8	f_9	f_{10}	f_{11}	f_{12}	f_{13}	f_{14}	f_{15}
c_0	4	2	2	0	2	0	0	−2	2	0	0	−2	0	−2	−2	−4
c_1	0	2	−2	0	2	4	0	2	−2	0	−4	−2	0	2	−2	0
c_2	0	2	2	4	−2	0	0	2	−2	0	0	2	−4	−2	−2	0
c_3	0	−2	2	0	2	0	4	2	−2	−4	0	−2	0	−2	2	0

With unit probability for the constant functions f_0 and f_{15} and zero probability for the balanced functions f_3, f_5, f_6, f_9, f_{10} and f_{12}, the measurement of the two qubits yields the result 00. - Additionally, if the function is balanced, the measurement enables differentiation between three subclasses: f_3 and f_{12} (outcome 10), f_5 and f_{10} (if the outcome is 01), and f_6 and f_9 (outcome 11). We see that since the global sign of the wave function cannot be observed, it is impossible to differentiate between f_i and f_{15-i}. Since the four alternative outputs of the two-qubit measurement have equal probability, the Deutsch-Jozsa circuit prevents learning anything about the remaining eight two-bit logic functions $(f_1, f_2, f_4, f_7, f_8, f_{11}, f_{13}$ and $f_{14})$

A permutation of the two-qubit binary functions f_i can also be used to distinguish between the other global features of the two-qubit binary functions. If the transformation (above eqn h) is significantly altered, these permutations can be easily achieved as follows:

$$\left(H^{\otimes 2} A_j \otimes I\right) U_f \left(H^{\otimes 2} \otimes H\right) \tag{j}$$

where the diagonal elements of the unitary diagonal matrices Aj equal ±1. These matrices, which have the same code as the Boolean function f*i*, have $2^{2^n} = 16$.

$$A_0 \equiv \text{diag}\{1,1,1,1\}, \qquad A_1 \equiv \text{diag}\{1,1,1,-1\}, \quad \ldots \tag{k}$$

It is simple to verify that the output wave function (i) changes f(x) for any unitary transformation Aj in the manner described below: where $(A_j)_{xx} = \langle x|A_j|x\rangle$ indicates a diagonal matrix element of Aj, and $f(x) \to f(x) \oplus (A_j)_{xx}$. Consequently, a permutation of the functions f_i is induced by each unitary transformation Aj. Consequently, the conventional Deutsch-Jozsa circuit $(i.e., A_j = I = A_0)$ enables us to definitively distinguish between

$$\{(f_0, f_{15}), (f_3, f_{12}), (f_5, f_{10}), (f_6, f_9)\} \tag{l}$$

In contrast, by using A1 we can distinguish between

$$\{(f_1, f_{14}), (f_2, f_{13}), (f_4, f_{11}), (f_7, f_8)\} \tag{m}$$

and so on.

2.15 Searching with Quantum Mechanics

The challenge of finding a single marked item inside an unstructured database of iV = 2™ items is one that a quantum computer can effectively handle. Let's use a straightforward example: we want to identify the name that corresponds to a phone number in a phone book. Using a traditional computer, our best option is to search the phone book until we discover the answer (the name). This indicates that while the solution is easy to identify, it is challenging to locate. This is a feature of the computational class N P issues, and in many instances, the best classical strategy for solving these problems is to search exhaustively through all potential solutions. This search is significantly sped up using quantum computing.

The search problem can be reformulated as an oracle problem: the oracle calculates the n-bit binary function after we label the database's objects as $\{0, 1, \ldots, N-1\}$ and x_o is the unknown marked item.

$$f : \{0,1\}^n \rightarrow \{0,1\} \tag{1}$$

defined as

$$f(x) = \begin{cases} 1 & \text{if } x = x_0 \\ 0 & \text{otherwise.} \end{cases} \tag{2}$$

Finding x_o with the fewest possible oracle *f* queries is the challenge. According to basic probability theory, there is a k/N chance of discovering x_o if one inputs A; items into the black-box function *f*. Therefore, each classical algorithm needs pN = O(N) oracle queries to find x_o with success probability p. Grover demonstrated that a quantum computer can solve the same issue in $O(\sqrt{N})$queries. Consequently, a quadratic speedup is possible with the quantum computer. There is a noticeable improvement even if the gain is not exponential and does not alter the problem's computational class.

It is enough to look at the fast Fourier transform algorithm as an example from classical computation to get a sense of the significance of a quadratic speedup. It is true that the fast Fourier transform has a quadratic gain over the regular Fourier transform, and it has greatly influenced signal analysis among many other uses.

2.15.1 Searching for one of four items

It is helpful to start by looking at the straightforward scenario of identifying one item from N = 4 items (two qubits). Below Fig. depicts the quantum circuit that goes with this straightforward use of Grover's technique. The necessary supplementary qubit is in the state $|y\rangle = |1\rangle$, whereas the two qubits are first produced in the state $|00\rangle$. The auxiliary in the state $\frac{1}{\sqrt{2}}(|0\rangle - |1\rangle)$ and the two qubits in the equal superposition state are prepared by the first Hadamard gates.

Consequently, the quantum-computer wave function turns into

$$\frac{1}{2}(|00\rangle + |01\rangle + |10\rangle + |11\rangle)\frac{1}{\sqrt{2}}(|0\rangle - |1\rangle) \tag{3}$$

After that, we evaluate the function f(x) and query the oracle. In fact, we have $|x\rangle|y\rangle \rightarrow |x\rangle|y \oplus f(x)\rangle$ following the oracle query. This indicates that the auxiliary qubit is loaded with the value f(x) that the oracle supplied. The auxiliary remains unchanged when f(x)=0 and changes its sign when f(x) — 1 since it was produced in the state $\frac{1}{\sqrt{2}}(|0\rangle - |1\rangle$ Take a look at the following specific situation, where the oracle only generates f(x) = 1 when x = x_o = (1,0). Since the other potential x_o values are handled equally, there is no loss of generality in this. Finding the four possible values of x_o - is resolved by the circuit shown in below Fig. Consequently, following the oracle query, the quantum-computer wave function is provided by

$$\frac{1}{2}(|00\rangle + |01\rangle - |10\rangle + |11\rangle)\frac{1}{\sqrt{2}}(|0\rangle - |1\rangle) \tag{4}$$

This, in terms of the sign of the coefficient in front of the indicated state, is different from the state (3). Observe that the sign has been kicked back in front of the register $|x\rangle$ just like in Deutsch's algorithm. We no longer take into consideration the second register, which remains unchanged.

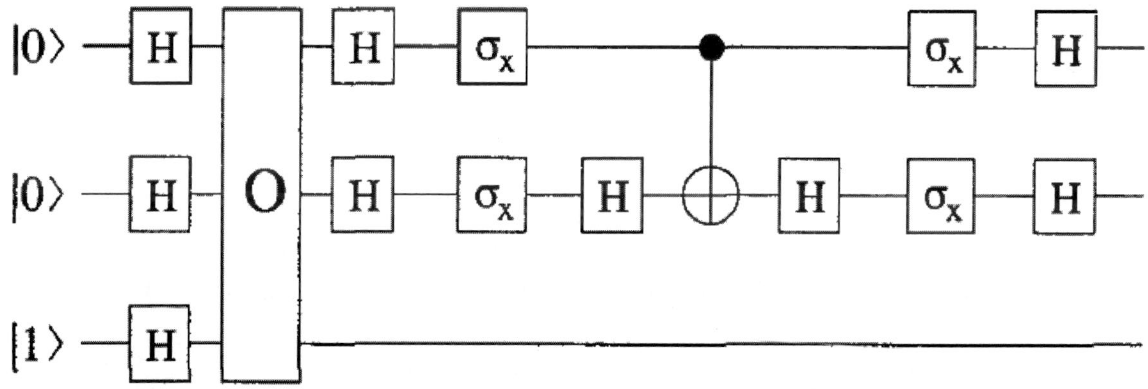

Fig.2.17 Grover's algorithm is implemented in a quantum circuit for N = 4. The NOT gate is carried out using the Pauli matrix σ_x. The oracle question is shown by the rectangle with the letter O inside.

A measurement of the $|x\rangle$ register following the oracle query would not differentiate between the various states of the computational basis since the amplitudes of the coefficients in front of them are all the same. Converting the phase difference that shows up in front of component $|10\rangle$ in (4) into an amplitude difference is the main goal of Grover's approach.

The following unitary transformation is utilized to accomplish this.

$$D_{ij} = -\delta_{ij} + \frac{2}{2^n} \tag{5}$$

Given n = 2, the matrix D in this instance is provided by

$$D = \frac{1}{2}\begin{bmatrix} -1 & 1 & 1 & 1 \\ 1 & -1 & 1 & 1 \\ 1 & 1 & -1 & 1 \\ 1 & 1 & 1 & -1 \end{bmatrix} \tag{6}$$

The portion of the circuit in the preceding figure that comes after the oracle query can be used to implement the transformation D. In fact, the following is a breakdown of this transformation:

$$D = H^{\otimes 2}\, D'\, H^{\otimes 2} \tag{7}$$

in which the diagonal matrix

$$D' = \begin{bmatrix} 1 & 0 & 0 & 0 \\ 0 & -1 & 0 & 0 \\ 0 & 0 & -1 & 0 \\ 0 & 0 & 0 & -1 \end{bmatrix} \tag{8}$$

provides a controlled phase shift by means of a negative angle π in the coefficient before the basis element $|00\rangle$. The following is a breakdown of matrix D' up to an overall phase:

$$D' = \sigma_x^{\otimes 2}\,(I \otimes H)\,\mathrm{CNOT}\,(I \otimes H)\,\sigma_x^{\otimes 2} \tag{9}$$

where af2 is equal to $\sigma_x^{\otimes 2} = \sigma_x \otimes \sigma_x$ $(I \otimes H)\,\mathrm{CNOT}\,(I \otimes H) = \mathrm{CMINUS}$, in fact. Furthermore, unlike a conventional controlled phase-shift gate, the NOT gates $\sigma_x^{\otimes 2}$ permit the phase factor to be positioned in front of the state $|00\rangle$ rather than the state $|11\rangle$.

When the transformation D is applied to the state of Equation (4), the result is

$$\mathbf{D}\,\frac{1}{2}\begin{bmatrix} 1 \\ 1 \\ -1 \\ 1 \end{bmatrix} = \frac{1}{4}\begin{bmatrix} -1 & 1 & 1 & 1 \\ 1 & -1 & 1 & 1 \\ 1 & 1 & -1 & 1 \\ 1 & 1 & 1 & -1 \end{bmatrix}\begin{bmatrix} 1 \\ 1 \\ -1 \\ 1 \end{bmatrix} = \begin{bmatrix} 0 \\ 0 \\ 1 \\ 0 \end{bmatrix} \tag{10}$$

Consequently, outcome 10 may now be determined with certainty using a standard measurement of the two qubits. One query of the function *f* has thus resolved the issue, whereas a classical computer typically needs Nc = 2.25 queries (the marked item can be located after the first, second, or third query, with probability $\frac{1}{4}$ each time); the fourth query is pointless after the third function evaluation since we know that there is only one marked item and $N_c = \frac{1}{4}\times 1 + \frac{1}{4}\times 2 + \frac{1}{2}\times 3 = 2.25$.

2.15.2 Searching a single item out of N

Grover's approach for a general number of items N = 2^n is now described. We prepare the quantum computer wave function in the state $|x\rangle|y\rangle = |00\ldots0\rangle|1\rangle$, and once more we require a single auxiliary qubit $|y\rangle$. The equal superposition of all foundation states for the $|x\rangle$ register and the state $\frac{1}{\sqrt{2}}(|0\rangle-|1\rangle)$for the supplementary qubit are then obtained by using n + 1 Hadamard gates, one for each qubit. The oracle function, $|x\rangle|y\rangle \rightarrow |x\rangle|y\oplus f(x)\rangle$ is then evaluated. This function evaluation kicks the sign back in front of the $|x\rangle$ register in the case of n = 2 qubits:

$$\begin{aligned} &\frac{1}{\sqrt{2^n}}\sum_{x=0}^{2^n-1}|x\rangle\frac{1}{\sqrt{2}}(|0\rangle-|1\rangle) \\ &\qquad\rightarrow \frac{1}{\sqrt{2^n}}\sum_{x=0}^{2^n-1}|x\rangle\frac{1}{\sqrt{2}}(|0\oplus f(x)\rangle-|1\oplus f(x)\rangle) \\ &\qquad= \frac{1}{\sqrt{2^n}}\sum_{x=0}^{2^n-1}|x\rangle\frac{1}{\sqrt{2}}(-1)^{f(x)}(|0\rangle-|1\rangle) \\ &\qquad= \frac{1}{\sqrt{2^n}}\sum_{x=0}^{2^n-1}(-1)^{f(x)}|x\rangle\frac{1}{\sqrt{2}}(|0\rangle-|1\rangle). \end{aligned} \tag{11}$$

But unlike the prior elementary example with n = 2 qubits, it is noted that finding the marked item X_0 requires more than one evaluation of the function f(x). Several iterations of the Oracle query that evaluates the function f(x) are required. More specifically, it is necessary to repeatedly perform the so-called Grover iteration G, which is defined as G=DO, where O represents the Oracle query and

$$D = H^{\otimes n}(-I + 2|0\rangle\langle 0|)H^{\otimes n} \tag{12}$$

The conditional phase shift that occurs between the two n-qubit Hadamard gates in (12) places a phase shift of —1 in front of every state of the computational basis, with the exception of the state $|00\ldots0\rangle$. Applying G repeatedly until the state of the register $|x\rangle$ is such that a standard measurement yields the result xo with high probability is how the quantum search method is carried out.

2.15.3 Visualization in geometry

A straightforward geometric representation aids in comprehending how many times Grover's iteration G must be used. Because the supplementary qubit's state is constant and factorized, we can disregard it for this purpose. First, it is evident from above Eq. (11) that the oracle O's action on an n-qubit state vector $|x\rangle$ is provided by

$$O : |x\rangle \to (-)^{f(x)}|x\rangle \tag{13}$$

As a result, we may write

$$O = I - 2|x_0\rangle\langle x_0| \equiv R_{|0\rangle} \tag{14}$$

The reflection about the hyperplane perpendicular to $|x_0\rangle$ is represented by this. For example, we have $O|\psi\rangle = -\alpha|x_0\rangle + \beta|x_0^{\perp}\rangle$ if we take a bi-dimensional space spanned by the vectors $\{|x_0\rangle, |x_0^{\perp}\rangle\}$ and a generic vector $|\psi\rangle = \alpha|x_0\rangle + \beta|x_0^{\perp}\rangle$. Therefore, as can be seen in the figure below, O causes the vector $|\psi\rangle$ to reflect about the axis $|x_0^{\perp}\rangle$ or about the hyperplane perpendicular to $|x_0\rangle$.

We then look at transformation D. Take note that

$$(H^{\otimes n})^{\dagger}(-I + 2|0\rangle\langle 0|)H^{\otimes n} = -I + 2|S\rangle\langle S| \tag{15}$$

where $|S\rangle$ is the equal superposition state and we have taken advantage of the fact that $(H^{\otimes n})^{\dagger} = H^{\otimes n}$

$$|S\rangle \equiv H^{\otimes n}|0\rangle = \frac{1}{\sqrt{2^n}} \sum_{x=0}^{2^n-1} |x\rangle \tag{16}$$

Eq. (12) can therefore be expressed as minus the reflection about the orthogonal hyperplane to $|S\rangle$:

$$D = -(I - 2|S\rangle\langle S|) \equiv -R_{|S\rangle} \tag{17}$$

Hence,

$$G = DO = -R_{|S\rangle} R_{|0\rangle} \tag{18}$$

The corresponding perpendicular unit vectors $\{|x_0\rangle, |S\rangle\}$ are drawn in the two-dimensional plane covered by $\{|x_0\rangle, |S\rangle\}$ (see Fig. below). It is simple to demonstrate that

$$G = -R_{|S\rangle} R_{|0\rangle} = R_{|S^{\perp}\rangle} R_{|0\rangle} \tag{19}$$

Therefore, G rotates a generic vector $|\psi\rangle$ in this plane by an angle 2θ if 6 represents the angle between the vectors $|x_0^{\perp}\rangle$ and $|S\rangle$ (see below Fig). Because the n-qubit state is the equal superposition state before the initial Oracle query

$$|\psi_0\rangle \equiv |S\rangle = \sin\theta|x_0\rangle + \cos\theta|x_0^{\perp}\rangle \tag{20}$$

and G rotates any vector in the plane spanned by $\{|x_0\rangle, |S\rangle\}$ by an angle of 2θ. The n-qubit state is then obtained after j Grover's iteration cycles.

$$|\psi_j\rangle \equiv G^j|\psi_0\rangle = \sin\left((2j+1)\,\theta\right)|x_0\rangle + \cos\left((2j+1)\,\theta\right)|x_0^{\perp}\rangle \tag{21}$$

It should be noted that this state is always found in the plane below Fig. After k steps, where k is such that $|\psi_k\rangle$ is extremely close to the marked state $|x_0\rangle$, the process must end. When $|\sin(2k+1)\,\theta| \approx 1$, this occurs. The following relation determines the smallest number k that satisfies this requirement:

$$(2k+1)\,\theta \approx \frac{\pi}{2} \tag{22}$$

which implies

$$k = \text{round}\left(\frac{\pi}{4\theta} - \frac{1}{2}\right) \tag{23}$$

where the nearest integer is indicated by round. Given that one begins in the situation of equal superposition,

$$\sin\theta = \langle x_0|\psi_0\rangle = \frac{1}{\sqrt{N}} \tag{24}$$

Consequently, for large $N, \theta \approx \frac{1}{\sqrt{N}}$ The number of iterations needed in Grover's algorithm is

$$k = \text{round}\left(\frac{\pi}{4}\sqrt{N} - \frac{1}{2}\right) = O(\sqrt{N}) \tag{25}$$

The algorithm yields the result $x = \bar{x}$ after a standard measurement in the computational base. Then, just like with any probabilistic method, we use the oracle to determine whether the solution is accurate. This occurs when $f(\bar{x}) = 1$, meaning that $\bar{x} = x_0$. We redo the quantum computation from the beginning if this is not the case, that is, $f(\bar{x}) = 0$, which implies $\bar{x} \neq x_0$. Therefore, the Grover method succeeds with a probability that is not equal to one, in contrast to the particular situation with N = 4. Nonetheless, the likelihood of success is really near to one. Given that $\theta = \frac{\pi}{6}$ in the specific instance N = 4, which is compatible with the geometric meaning of Grover's method, condition (22) is satisfied after k = 1 step.

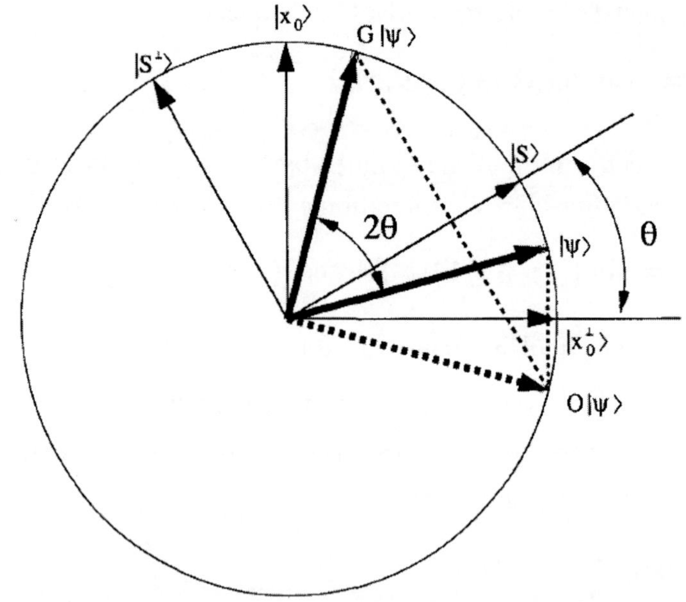

Fig.2.18 Grover's iteration in geometric form.

2.16 Determination of Eigenvalue and Eigenvector

We outline a quantum algorithm in this section that determines the eigenvalues and eigenvectors of a given unitary operator U. To be specific, we look at the instance where

$$U(\bar{t}) = \exp(-iH\bar{t}/\hbar) \tag{1}$$

is the evolution operator associated with a time-independent Hamiltonian H up to time t. The matching Schrodinger formula is

$$i\hbar \frac{\partial}{\partial t} \psi(x,t) = H(x)\,\psi(x,t) \tag{2}$$

where we have only looked at the one-dimensional situation for simplicity's sake (it is straightforward to extend what follows to higher dimensions). It can be observed that an eigenvector $\phi_\alpha(x)$ of H with eigenvalue E_α $(i.e.,\ H\phi_\alpha(x) = E_\alpha\phi_\alpha(x))$ is also an eigenvector of $U(\bar{t})$ with eigenvalue $e^{-iE_\alpha\bar{t}/\hbar}$, as well. With a classical computer, the eigenvalues and eigenvectors of the Hamiltonian operator H can be calculated as follows. We evolve a starting point.

$$\psi_0(x) \equiv \psi(x, t=0) \tag{3}$$

figuring out that $\psi(x,\bar{t}) = U(x,\bar{t})\psi_0(x)$. If $\psi_0(x)$ is expanded over the basis of H's Eigen functions,

$$\psi_0(x) = \sum_\alpha a_\alpha \, \phi_\alpha(x) \tag{4}$$

we can write

$$\psi(x,t) = \sum_\alpha a_\alpha \, e^{-i\omega_\alpha t} \, \phi_\alpha(x) \qquad (\omega_\alpha \equiv E_\alpha/\hbar) \tag{5}$$

Next, the Fourier transform is calculated.

$$\bar{\psi}(x_0, \omega) = F\,[\psi(x_0, t)] \tag{6}$$

provided that $x = x_0$. (5) makes it clear that the Fourier transform $\bar{\psi}$ has peaks that match the motion ω_α. frequencies. If the temporal evolution is calculated up to time $\bar{t}$ considerably longer, a specific peak is resolved. Compared to the frequency of interest's inverse. The Eigen functions $\phi_\alpha(x)$ can be obtained from the relative amplitudes of the peaks corresponding to the frequency ω_α by repeating the Fourier transform ip for various XQ values. The extension (5) makes this latter point clear by implying

$$\frac{\bar{\psi}(x_1, \omega_\alpha)}{\bar{\psi}(x_2, \omega_\alpha)} = \frac{\phi_\alpha(x_1)}{\phi_\alpha(x_2)} \tag{7}$$

Now let's use a quantum computer to carry out the same process. Using a grid of 2" points spaced by an interval $\Delta x = 2L/(2^n - 1)$, the wave function is coded inside some interval $x \in [-L, L]$ of interest for the physical motion.

$$|\psi\rangle = \sum_{i=0}^{2^n-1} \psi(i)\,|i\rangle \tag{8}$$

where $\psi(i) = \psi(-L + i\Delta x)$. We remark that the quantum computer has an exponential advantage in memory requirements, since one requires n qubits to store the 2^n complex numbers of the wave function (8). The unitary operator provides the evolution in a time step Δt.

$$U = \exp(-i\,H\,\Delta\,t/\hbar). \tag{9}$$

This can be effectively simulated by a quantum computer for a wide class of physically important Hamiltonians. The circuit presented for the phase estimation problem is the proper one to use in order to calculate the eigenvalues and eigenvectors of the operator U. The wave function, initially created in the state $|\psi_0\rangle = \sum_i \psi_0(i)|i\rangle$ is stored in the second (target) register (n qubits). In certain situations, such a preparation can be carried out effectively, such as when the wave function is confined at a point, $|\psi_0\rangle = |\bar{i}\rangle$.

Having non-zero projections over $|\psi_0\rangle$, that is, a non-zero component $\phi_\alpha(\bar{i})$. It is observed that this selection is sufficient to search for all eigenstates $|\phi_\alpha\rangle = \sum_i \phi_\alpha(i)|i\rangle$ (and corresponding eigenvalues). In order to store the wave function at various times $0, \Delta t, 2\Delta t, 3\Delta t, \ldots, 2^{l-1}\Delta t$ concurrently, the control register (/ qubits) must be prepared in the uniform superposition state $\sum_j |j\rangle/\sqrt{2^l}$. Following the operation of the controlled $-U^{2^0}$, controlled-U^{2^1},..., controlled-$U^{2^{l-1}}$ gates, the quantum computer's state is determined by

$$|\Psi\rangle = \frac{1}{\sqrt{2^l}} \sum_{j=0}^{2^l-1} |j\rangle\, U^j\, |\psi_0\rangle \tag{10}$$

Where we have

$$|\psi(j\Delta t)\rangle = U^j\,|\psi_0\rangle \tag{11}$$

The expansion (4) allows us to write

$$|\Psi\rangle = \frac{1}{\sqrt{2^l}} \sum_j |j\rangle \sum_{\alpha=0}^{2^n-1} a_\alpha\, e^{-i\omega_\alpha\, j\Delta t}\, |\phi_\alpha\rangle \tag{12}$$

It can be demonstrated that the frequencies ω_α correspond to the peaks in the Fourier transform of the state $|\Psi\rangle$ with respect to the $|j\rangle$ register. The frequency spectrum of the Hamiltonian operator could be obtained by doing a standard measurement of the $|j\rangle$ register after a suitably large number of computer runs. It can be verified that the other quantum register collapses upon an eigenstate $|\phi_{\bar{\alpha}}\rangle$ - following any such measurement. Standard measurements of this register can theoretically be used to recreate the eigenstates.

With regard to the classical algorithm mentioned above, there is an exponential advantage if the desired eigenvalues ω_α and eigenvectors are obtained after a polynomial number of trials. The method's drawback is that each computer run singles out different eigenvalues uia, with probability $|a_\alpha|^2$. For example, this occurs when the desired eigenstate, usually the ground state of a complicated system, is not exponentially tiny over the initial state $|\psi_0\rangle$.

2.17 Dynamical System Computation At The Quantum Level

The dynamical evolution of quantum systems could be simulated with the help of a quantum computer. Quantum many-body issues are challenging to simulate on a classical computer because the Hilbert space size increases exponentially with the number of particles. The Hilbert space is 2^n in size, for example, if we want to model a chain of n spin-$\frac{1}{2}$ particles. Specifically, two-dimensional complex numbers determine the state of this system.

According to Feynman (1982), on a quantum computer—which is a many-body quantum system in and of itself—the increase in memory requirements is merely linear. For instance, n qubits are all that are required to simulate n spin-$\frac{1}{2}$ particles. As a result, a quantum computer that uses just a few tens of qubits can perform better than a classical computer. This is only true, of course, if we can effectively extract valuable information from the quantum computer and discover an effective quantum algorithm.

2.17.1 Simulation of the Schrodinger equation at quantum level

As a concrete example, let's look at a particle's quantum-mechanical motion in one dimension; the extension to higher dimensions is simple.

Additionally, the Schrodinger equation governs it.

$$i\hbar \frac{d}{dt}\psi(x,t) = H\,\psi(x,t) \tag{1}$$

where the Hamiltonian H can be found using

$$H = H_0 + V(x) = -\frac{\hbar^2}{2m}\frac{d^2}{dx^2} + V(x) \tag{2}$$

The particle's free motion is controlled by the Hamiltonian $H_0 = -(\hbar^2/2m)\, d^2/dx^2$, whereas V(x) is a one-dimensional potential. We must first discretize the continuous variables x and t in order to solve Eq. (1) on a quantum computer with finite resources (a finite number of qubits and a finite series of quantum gates). The discretization step decreases exponentially with the number of qubits if the motion essentially occurs inside a finite region, say $-d \le x \le d$, we do this by decomposing the region into 2^n intervals of length $\Delta = 2d/2^n$, which we then represent using the Hilbert space of an n-qubit quantum register. As a result, the wave function $|\psi(t)\rangle$ can be roughly represented as follows:

$$|\tilde{\psi}(t)\rangle = \sum_{i=0}^{2^n-1} c_i(t)\,|i\rangle = \frac{1}{\mathcal{N}} \sum_{i=0}^{2^n-1} \psi(x_i, t)\,|i\rangle \tag{3}$$

Where

$$x_i \equiv -d + \left(i + \tfrac{1}{2}\right) \Delta, \tag{4}$$

$|i\rangle = |i_{n-1}\rangle \otimes |i_{n-2}\rangle \otimes \cdots \otimes |i_0\rangle$ represents a state of the n-qubit quantum register's computational foundation and

$$\mathcal{N} \equiv \sqrt{\sum_{i=0}^{2^n-1} |\psi(x_i, t)|^2} \tag{5}$$

is a component that guarantees the wave function is correctly normalized. When the discretization step Δ is significantly lower than the shortest length scale pertinent to the system's motion, it makes sense that $|\tilde{\psi}\rangle$ offers a decent approximation to $|\psi\rangle$.

By propagating the starting wave function if $\psi(x, 0)$ at every time-step ϵ, the Schrodinger equation (1) can be formally integrated as follows:

$$\psi(x, t + \epsilon) = e^{-\frac{i}{\hbar}[H_0 + V(x)]\epsilon}\, \psi(x, t) \tag{6}$$

If the time-step ϵ is sufficiently small to allow for the ignoring of terms of order ϵ^2, it is feasible to write

$$e^{-\frac{i}{\hbar}[H_0 + V(x)]\,\epsilon} \approx e^{-\frac{i}{\hbar}H_0\,\epsilon} e^{-\frac{i}{\hbar}V(x)\,\epsilon} \tag{7}$$

Because the operators H0 and V do not commute, this equation—also referred to as the Trotter decomposition—is only precise up to terms of order ϵ^2. In many intriguing physical issues, the operator on the right side of Eq. (7) can be effectively implemented on a quantum computer because it is still unitary and simpler than the operator on the left. We make use of the efficiency with which a quantum computer can perform the Fourier transform $-i(d/dx) = F^{-1}kF$, where F is the Fourier transform, is what we refer to as k, the variable conjugate to x.

As a result, the first operator on the right side of (7) can be written as

$$e^{-\frac{i}{\hbar}H_0\,\epsilon} = F^{-1}\, e^{+\frac{i}{\hbar}\left(\frac{\hbar^2 k^2}{2m}\right)\epsilon}\, F \tag{8}$$

This operator is diagonal in this expression, which we move from the x-representation to the k-representation via the Fourier transform F.

We then return to the x-representation, where the operator exp $(-iV(x)\epsilon/\hbar)$ is diagonal, using the Fourier transform F^{-1}. *l* times the unitary operator is applied to the initial wave function $\psi(x,t)$ to get the wave function $\psi(x,0)$ at time $t = l\epsilon$.

$$F^{-1} e^{+\frac{i}{\hbar}\left(\frac{\hbar^2 k^2}{2m}\right)\epsilon} F e^{-\frac{i}{\hbar}V(x)\epsilon}. \tag{9}$$

Thus, the application of the Fourier transform plus diagonal operators of the type is now all that is needed to simulate the Schrodinger equation.

$$|x\rangle \rightarrow e^{icf(x)}|x\rangle \tag{10}$$

In this case, c is a real constant. It should be noted that when the latter operator is expressed in the fc-representation, an operator of the type (10) appears in both the computation of exp$(-iV(x)\epsilon/\hbar)$ and of exp$(-iH_0\epsilon/\hbar)$. It takes $0(n^2)$ elementary quantum gates (Hadamard and controlled phase-shift gates) to build the Fourier transform.

The following procedures enable the quantum computation of (10) utilizing an ancillary quantum register $|y\rangle_a$.

$$\begin{aligned}|0\rangle_a \otimes |x\rangle &\rightarrow |f(x)\rangle_a \otimes |x\rangle \rightarrow e^{icf(x)}|f(x)\rangle_a \otimes |x\rangle \\ &\rightarrow e^{icf(x)}|0\rangle_a \otimes |x\rangle = |0\rangle_a \otimes e^{icf(x)}|x\rangle\end{aligned} \tag{11}$$

A normal function evaluation is the first stage, and $0(2^n)$ generalized C^n-NOT gates can be used to implement it. Of course, when the function f(x) has some structure, more effective implementations (polynomial in n) are conceivable. This is true for the potentials V(x), which are typically taken into account in quantum-mechanical difficulties.

The transformation $|y\rangle_a \rightarrow e^{icy}|y\rangle_a$, which is the second step in (11), can be carried out in m single-qubit phase-shift gates, where m is the number of qubits in the supplementary register. In fact, the binary decomposition of an integer $y \in [0, 2^m - 1]$ can be expressed as follows $y = \sum_{j=0}^{m-1} y_j 2^j$, with $y_j \in \{0,1\}$:

Therefore,

$$\exp(iy) = \exp\left(\sum_{j=0}^{m-1} icy_j 2^j\right) = \prod_{j=0}^{m+1} \exp(icy_j 2^j) \tag{12}$$

This results from multiplying m single-qubit gates, each of which acts on a single qubit in a non-trivial way (different from the identity). The transformation

$|y_j\rangle_a \to \exp(icy_j 2^j)|y_j\rangle_a$, with $|y_j\rangle_a \in \{|0\rangle, |1\rangle\}$ is carried out by the j-th gate vectors of the computational basis for the j-th ancillary

$$R_z(c2^j) = \begin{bmatrix} 1 & 0 \\ 0 & \exp(ic2^j) \end{bmatrix} \tag{13}$$

Using the identical set of gates as the first step but applied in the opposite sequence, the third step in (11) is simply the opposite of the first. Using the same ancillary qubits for each time-step is possible since the ancillary qubits are returned to their regular configuration $|0\rangle_a$ after this step.

When calculating the diagonal operator (10), keep in mind that the resolution is determined by the number of ancillary qubits, m. It is true that the function f(x) in equation (10) is discretized and has a range of 2^m values. The unidimensional harmonic and anharmonic oscillator, the transmission and reflection of a Gaussian wave packet by different barriers, and other common quantum-mechanical problems can be sufficiently resolved by simulating them with just a few qubits $(n \approx 10)$ to discretize the coordinate x and a few ancillary qubits $(m \approx 10)$.

Two intriguing dynamical systems that can be emulated on a quantum computer without supplementary qubits are the saw tooth map and the baker's map, which will be covered in the next subsections. Three to ten qubits and a few tens of hundreds of quantum gates can already be used in these models to study intriguing physical processes.

2.17.2 The quantum baker's map

This portion demonstrates the very easy and effective method of simulating the quantum baker's map on a quantum computer. Schack's quantum algorithm for the quantum baker's map calculates this system's dynamical evolution tenfold quicker than any known classical calculation.

According to the traditional baker's transformation, the unit square $0 < q, p < 1$ is mapped onto itself.

$$(q,p) \to (\bar{q},\bar{p}) = \begin{cases} (2q, \frac{1}{2}p), & \text{if } 0 \le q \le \frac{1}{2} \\ (2q-1, \frac{1}{2}p + \frac{1}{2}), & \text{if } \frac{1}{2} < q < 1 \end{cases} \tag{14}$$

Accordingly, the unit square is compressed in the p direction, stretched in the q direction, sliced along the p direction, and then stacked one piece on top of the other (much as when a baker kneads bread). Take note that map (14) preserves the area. The baker's map is a classic example of chaos theory. The characteristic that sets classical chaos apart is its sensitive dependence on beginning conditions, so even a slight mistake in establishing the original conditions is magnified over time. Stated differently, the maximum Lyapunov exponent λ, which is defined as follows, provides the rate at which two adjacent trajectories split exponentially:

$$\lambda = \lim_{|t|\to\infty} \frac{1}{t} \ln\left(\frac{\delta(t)}{\delta(0)}\right) \tag{15}$$

The number of map iterations is measured by the discrete time t, and $\delta(t) = \sqrt{(\delta q(t))^2 + (\delta p(t))^2}$. In order to calculate $\delta q(t)$ and $\delta p(t)$, we differentiate map (14) to get

$$\begin{bmatrix} \delta\bar{q} \\ \delta\bar{p} \end{bmatrix} = M \begin{bmatrix} \delta q \\ \delta p \end{bmatrix} = \begin{bmatrix} 2 & 0 \\ 0 & \frac{1}{2} \end{bmatrix} \begin{bmatrix} \delta q \\ \delta p \end{bmatrix} \tag{16}$$

As a function of $\delta q(0)$ and $\delta p(0)$ map (16) iteration yields $\delta q(t)$ and $\delta p(t)$. The eigenvalues $\mu_1 = 2$ and $\mu_2 = \frac{1}{2}$ of matrix M, often known as the stability matrix, are independent of the coordinates q and p. In this instance, $\lambda = \ln \mu_1 = \ln 2$ provides the greatest Lyapunov exponent.

The dynamics, which causes stretching in the q direction and contraction in the p direction, is universally unstable. The baker's map can be quantized in accordance with Saraceno, Balazs, and Voros. The position (q) and momentum (p) operators are introduced, and their eigenstates are indicated by $|q_j\rangle$ and $|p_k\rangle$, respectively. $p_k = k/N$ and $q_j = j/N$ provide the corresponding eigenvalues, where N is the Hilbert space's dimension and j, k — 0,...,N — 1. Keep in mind that we need to set $2\pi\hbar = 1/N$ in order to fit N levels onto the unit square. In order to simulate the quantum baker's map on a quantum computer, we utilize N = 2^n, where n is the number of qubits. A discrete Fourier transform Fn, determined by the matrix elements, is used to convert the position basis $\{|q_0\rangle, \ldots, |q_{N-1}\rangle\}$ and the momentum basis $\{|p_0\rangle, \ldots, |p_{N-1}\rangle\}$.

$$\langle q_k|F_n|q_j\rangle \equiv \frac{1}{\sqrt{2^n}} \exp\left(\frac{2\pi ikj}{2^n}\right) \tag{17}$$

It can be demonstrated that the transformation may define the quantized baker's map.

$$|\psi\rangle \to |\bar{\psi}\rangle = T|\psi\rangle \tag{18}$$

The unitary transformation T defining the quantum baker's map is given by where $|\bar{\psi}\rangle$ indicates the system's wave vector following the application of one map step to state $|\psi\rangle$.

$$T = F_n^{-1} \begin{bmatrix} F_{n-1} & 0 \\ 0 & F_{n-1} \end{bmatrix} \tag{19}$$

where F_{n-1} is the discrete Fourier transform specified by Eq. (17), and the matrix components are to be interpreted in relation to the position basis $\{|q_j\rangle\}$.

A quantum computer with n qubits may perform the unitary transformation T. We've

$$T = F_n^{-1}(I \otimes F_{n-1}) \tag{20}$$

The identity operator I acts on the most significant qubit, while F_{n-1} acts on the $n-1$ least significant qubits. Given that a quantum computer with $0(n^2)$ elementary gates can effectively perform the Fourier transform F_n, a quantum computer with $0(n^2)$ elementary gates may likewise efficiently mimic the quantum baker's map for each map iteration.

It should be noted that $0(n2^n)$ elementary operations are needed for the fast Fourier transform, the most well-known classical approach for simulating the Fourier transform.

As a result, a quantum computer may simulate the dynamics of the baker's map with exponential gain compared to any known classical calculation.

2.17.3 The map of quantum sawtooth

A prototypical model for studying both classical and quantum-dynamical systems, the sawtooth map displays a wide range of intriguing physical phenomena, including dynamical localization, cantori localization, normal and anomalous diffusion, and complete chaos and complete integrability. Additionally, the motion of a particle bouncing inside a stadium billiard—a well-known model of both classical and quantum chaos—is effectively approximated by the sawtooth map. We demonstrate in this subsection that a quantum computer may effectively simulate this map.

The sawtooth map is a dynamical system that is regularly driven and controlled by the Hamiltonian.

$$H(\theta, I; \tau) = \frac{I^2}{2} + V(\theta) \sum_{j=-\infty}^{+\infty} \delta(\tau - jT) \tag{21}$$

Conjugate action-angle variables $(0 \leq \theta < 2\pi)$ are represented as (I, θ). Since $H_0(I) = I^2/2$ is just the kinetic energy of a free rotator (a particle traveling on a circle parametrized by the coordinate θ), this Hamiltonian is the sum of two parts $H(\theta, I; \tau) = H_0(I) + U(\theta; t)$.

$$U(\theta; t) = V(\theta) \sum_j \delta(\tau - jT) \tag{22}$$

symbolizes a force that is applied to the particle that is changed on and off instantly at intervals of time T. Consequently, we declare that the dynamics outlined by Hamiltonian (21) are kicked. The matching Hamiltonian motion equations are

$$\begin{cases} \dot{I} = -\dfrac{\partial H}{\partial \theta} = -\dfrac{dV(\theta)}{d\theta} \displaystyle\sum_{j=-\infty}^{+\infty} \delta(\tau - jT) \\ \dot{\theta} = \dfrac{\partial H}{\partial I} = I\,. \end{cases} \tag{23}$$

These equations are easily integrated, and the map describes the evolution from time lT^- (before the Z-th kick) to time $(l+1)T^-$ (before the $(l+1)$-th kick).

$$\begin{cases} \bar{I} = I + F(\theta)\,, \\ \bar{\theta} = \theta + T\bar{I}\,, \end{cases} \tag{24}$$

while the force acting on the particle is expressed as $F(\theta) = -dV(\theta)/d\theta$.

The special situation $V(\theta) = -k(\theta - \pi)^2/2$. will be examined the next.

Given the sawtooth shape of the force $F(\theta) = -dV(\theta)/d\theta = k(\theta - \pi)$ and the discontinuity at $\theta = 0$ this map is known as the sawtooth map. It can be observed that the classical dynamics solely rely on the parameter $K = kT$ by rescaling $I \to J = TI$. The variables (J, θ) do, in fact, make map (24)

$$\begin{cases} \bar{J} = J + K(\theta - \pi) \\ \bar{\theta} = \theta + \bar{J}\,. \end{cases} \tag{25}$$

Similar to the situation of the baker's map, which was covered in the previous part, a stability study of the sawtooth map can be carried out. Following the differentiation of the map (25), we have

$$\begin{bmatrix} \delta\bar{J} \\ \delta\bar{\theta} \end{bmatrix} = M \begin{bmatrix} \delta J \\ \delta\theta \end{bmatrix} = \begin{bmatrix} 1 & K \\ 1 & 1+K \end{bmatrix} \begin{bmatrix} \delta J \\ \delta\theta \end{bmatrix} \tag{26}$$

Eigenvalues $\mu_\pm = \frac{1}{2}(2 + K \pm \sqrt{K^2 + 4K})$, which are complex conjugate for $-4 \le K \le 0$ and real for $K < -4$ and $K > 0$., are included in the stability matrix M.

Therefore, for $K < -4$ and $K > 0$, the classical motion is totally chaotic, and for $-4 \le K \le 0$, it is stable.

To ensure that no discontinuities are formed in the second equation of (25) when J is taken modulo $2\pi L$, the sawtooth map can be analyzed on the cylinder $(J \in (-\infty, +\infty))$ which can also be closed to produce a torus of length $2\pi L$ (L is an integer). The action (momentum) variable has normal diffusion for every K > 0. In practice, the velocity of a trajectory along the momentum direction is identical to that of a random walk, despite the sawtooth map being a deterministic system.

$$\frac{\partial f}{\partial t} = \frac{\partial}{\partial J}\left(\frac{1}{2}D\frac{\partial f}{\partial J}\right) \qquad (27)$$

In this case, the discrete time expressed in map iterations is denoted by $t \equiv \tau/T$, and the diffusion coefficient D is defined by

$$D = \lim_{t\to\infty} \frac{\langle(\Delta J(t))^2\rangle}{t} \qquad (28)$$

where (...) indicates the average across an ensemble of trajectories and . $\Delta J \equiv J - \langle J\rangle$ and $\langle\ldots\rangle$. If a phase space distribution with initial momentum J_0 and random phases $0 \leq \theta < 2\pi$ is taken at time t = 0, the Fokker-Planck equation (27) can be solved as follows:

$$f(J,t) = \frac{1}{\sqrt{2\pi Dt}} \exp\left(-\frac{(J-J_0)^2}{2Dt}\right) \qquad (29)$$

As time passes, the width of this Gaussian distribution increases, as per

$$\langle(\Delta J(t))^2\rangle \approx D(K)\,t \qquad (30)$$

The random phase approximation, which assumes that there are no correlations between the angles (phases) θ at different times, provides a good approximation of the diffusion coefficient for K > 1. Thus, we have

$$D(K) \approx \frac{1}{2\pi}\int_0^{2\pi} d\theta\,(\Delta J_1)^2 = \frac{1}{2\pi}\int_0^{2\pi} d\theta\, K^2(\theta-\pi)^2 = \frac{\pi^2}{3}K^2 \qquad (30)$$

Consequently, following one map step, the change in action is denoted by $\Delta J_1 = \bar{J} - J$. Because of the sticking of trajectories near broken tori (also called cantori), diffusion is delayed for 0 < K < 1, giving us $D(K) \approx 3.3\,K^{5/2}$. For -4 < K < 0, the motion is stable, anomalous diffusion, or $\langle(\Delta J)^2\rangle \propto t^{\alpha}$, with $\alpha \neq 1$ (for example, α = 0.57 when K = -0.1) is visible, and the phase space has a complicated structure of elliptic islands down to smaller and smaller scales. Cases K -1, -2, and -3 are integrable.

The standard quantization rules, $\theta \to \theta$ and $I \to I = -i\partial/\partial\theta$ (we set h = 1), are used to generate the quantum form of the sawtooth map. A unitary operator U acting on the wave function ψ describes the quantum development in a single map iteration:

$$\bar{\psi} = U\psi = \exp\left(-i\int_{lT^-}^{(l+1)T^-} d\tau\, H(\theta, I; \tau)\right)\psi \quad (31)$$

H stands for Hamiltonian. Given that the potential V(8) is only activated during specific lT times, it is simple to acquire

$$\bar{\psi} = e^{-iTI^2/2} e^{-iV(\theta)}\psi = e^{-iTI^2/2} e^{ik(\theta-\pi)^2/2}\psi \quad (32)$$

The classical limit corresponds to $k \to \infty$ and $T \to 0$ while maintaining K = kT constant, and the effective Planck constant is given by $\hbar_{\text{eff}} = \hbar/k$.

Here, we outline a quantum algorithm that simulates the map (33) with exponential efficiency. Its foundation is the forward/backward quantum Fourier transform between the bases of angle and momentum. The operator U, which is introduced in Eq. (32), is the product of two operators, $U_k = e^{ik(\theta-\pi)^2/2}$ and $U_T = e^{-iTI^2/2}$, diagonal in the θ and I representations, respectively, making this method convenient. The following actions are necessary for one map iteration of this quantum algorithm:

1. The wave function $\psi(\theta)$ is subjected to U_k. First, we write θ in binary notation to break down the operator U_k into one- and two-qubit gates:

$$\theta = 2\pi\sum_{j=1}^{n}\alpha_j 2^{-j} \quad (33)$$

using $\alpha_i \in \{0,1\}$. Since n is the number of qubits in this case, $N = 2^n$ is the total number of levels in the quantum sawtooth map. Because of this expansion, we get

$$(\theta-\pi)^2 = 4\pi^2\sum_{j_1,j_2=1}^{n}\left(\frac{\alpha_{j_1}}{2^{j_1}} - \frac{1}{2n}\right)\left(\frac{\alpha_{j_2}}{2^{j_2}} - \frac{1}{2n}\right) \quad (34)$$

The decomposition can be obtained by inserting this word into the unitary operator U_k.

$$e^{ik(\theta-\pi)^2/2} = \prod_{j_1,j_2=1}^{n}\exp\left[i2\pi^2 k\left(\frac{\alpha_{j_1}}{2^{j_1}} - \frac{1}{2n}\right)\left(\frac{\alpha_{j_2}}{2^{j_2}} - \frac{1}{2n}\right)\right] \quad (35)$$

This results from n^2 controlled phase-shift gates (two-qubit gates) working non-trivially solely on the qubits j_1 and j_2. The formula for each $\{|\alpha_{j_1}\alpha_{j_2}\rangle = |00\rangle, |01\rangle, |10\rangle, |11\rangle\}$ two-qubit gate in the computational basis written as $\exp(i2\pi^2 k D_{j_1,j_2})$, where D_{j_1,j_2} is a diagonal matrix:

$$D_{j_1,j_2} = \begin{bmatrix} \frac{1}{4n^2} & 0 & 0 & 0 \\ 0 & -\frac{1}{2n}\left(\frac{1}{2^{j_2}} - \frac{1}{2n}\right) & 0 & 0 \\ 0 & 0 & -\frac{1}{2n}\left(\frac{1}{2^{j_1}} - \frac{1}{2n}\right) & 0 \\ 0 & 0 & 0 & \left(\frac{1}{2^{j_1}} - \frac{1}{2n}\right)\left(\frac{1}{2^{j_2}} - \frac{1}{2n}\right) \end{bmatrix} \quad (36)$$

2. Using the quantum Fourier transform, which as we all know necessitates n Hadamard gates and $\frac{1}{2}n(n-1)$ controlled phase-shift gates, the representation is changed from θ to the I.
3. The operator U_T in the I representation can be broken down into n^2 controlled phase-shift gates, much like in Eq. (36), since it essentially has the same form as the operator U_k in the θ representation.
4. We use the inverse quantum Fourier transform to go back to the original θ representation.

Therefore, $3n^2 + n$ gates are needed overall for each map iteration of this quantum process ($3n^2 - n$ controlled phase-shifts and 2n Hadamard gates). This figure should be contrasted with the $0(n2^n)$ operations needed by a traditional computer to use a quick Fourier transform to approximate one map iteration. As a result, no known classical technique can match the exponential speed of the quantum simulation of the quantum sawtooth map dynamics. Keep in mind that the quantum computer only needs logarithmic resources for system size N in order to replicate the sawtooth map's evolution. Naturally, the challenge of deriving meaningful information from the quantum-computer wave function still exists.

2.17.4 Dynamical localization computing at the quantum level

One of the most intriguing features of the quantum behavior of classically chaotic systems is dynamical localization, which results in exponentially localized wave functions due to the suppression of chaotic diffusion in momentum by quantum interference effects. The Anderson localization of electronic transport in disordered materials bears significant similarities to this phenomena, which was initially discovered and investigated in the quantum kicked-rotator model. In tests involving cold atoms and the microwave ionization of Rydberg atoms, dynamical localization has been seen.

The sawtooth map model allows for the study of dynamic localization. The cylinder $(I \in (-\infty, +\infty))$, which is cut-off at a finite number N of levels because of the finite quantum (or conventional) computer memory, is used in this instance to study map (33) on. After a break time, quantum interference in the sawtooth map suppresses classical chaotic diffusion, just like in other models of quantum chaos.

$$t^* \approx D \approx (\pi^2/3)k^2 \tag{37}$$

where the index m separates out the eigenstates of I, that is, $I|m\rangle = m|m\rangle)$; and D is the classical diffusion coefficient, expressed in terms of the number of levels $(\langle(\Delta m)^2\rangle \approx Dt$. The probability distribution across the momentum eigenbasis decays exponentially after the break time t*:

$$W_m \equiv |\langle m|\psi\rangle|^2 \approx \frac{1}{\ell} \exp\left[-\frac{2|m-m_0|}{\ell}\right] \tag{38}$$

with m_o being the momentum's original value. Consequently, the localization length l for the average probability distribution is about equivalent to the classical diffusion coefficient, and only $\sqrt{\langle(\Delta m)^2\rangle} \sim \ell$ levels are populated for t > t*:

$$\ell \approx D \tag{39}$$

Therefore, if l is less than the system size N, the quantum localization can be identified. We demonstrate that exponential localization is already evident with n = 6 qubits in the below Fig.

Reiterating that a quantum computer's memory capacity increases exponentially with the number of qubits (the number of levels N is equal to 2^n) is helpful. Therefore, simulations could be rendered unusable by today's supercomputers even with fewer than 40 qubits. The probability distribution does, in fact, degrade exponentially over the momentum eigenbasis after the break time t*. Aside from quantum fluctuations, which we partially smooth out by averaging over a few map steps, Fig. below demonstrates that the exponentially confined distribution, which appears at $t \approx t^\star$ is locked in time.

A comparison of the probability distributions collected at a considerably larger $t = 300 \approx 25t^\star$ (the dotted curve in the same figure) and immediately after t* (the full curve in the figure below) demonstrates the freezing of the localized distribution. According to estimates, the localization length in this case is $\ell \approx 12$, and classical diffusion is reduced following a break time $t^\star \approx \ell \approx D$ (the diffusion coefficient is $D \approx (\pi^2/3)k^2 \approx 9.9$).

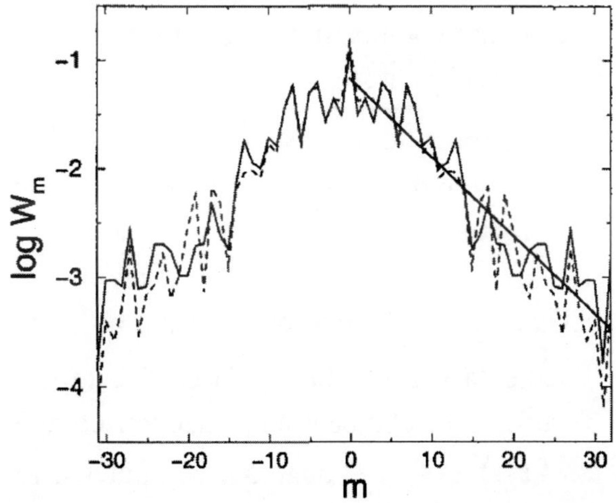

Fig.2.19 The sawtooth map's probability distribution over the momentum basis, with n = 6 qubits, $k = \sqrt{3}$, $K = \sqrt{2}$, and initial momentum m_o = 0, is calculated by taking a temporal average between 10 < t < 20 (complete curve) and 290 < t < 300 (dashed curve).

$W_m \propto \exp(-2|m|/\ell)$, the straight line fit, yields a localization length $\ell \approx 12$. The logarithm is base ten, as you can see.

The number of one- or two-qubit quantum gates needed for this quantum computation up to times of the order of *l* is $N_g \approx 3n^2\ell \sim 10^3$.

$$|\psi(t)\rangle = \sum_m \hat{\psi}(m,t)\,|m\rangle \tag{40}$$

Such a measurement yields outcome $\bar{m}$ with probability associated with $|m\rangle$ momentum eigenstates.

$$W_{\bar{m}} = \left|\langle \bar{m}|\psi(t)\rangle\right|^2 = \left|\hat{\psi}(\bar{m},t)\right|^2 \tag{41}$$

A preliminary set of data would enable us to provide a ballpark estimate of the distribution W_m's variance $\langle(\Delta m)^2\rangle$. The localization length *l* is then estimated first by $\sqrt{\langle(\Delta m)^2\rangle}$. A histogram bin of width $\delta m \propto \ell \approx \sqrt{\langle(\Delta m)^2\rangle}$ can then be used to store the measurement findings.

Ultimately, the localization length is derived from a fit of this coarse-grained distribution's exponential decay across the momentum basis. This allows us to determine the localization length with accuracy *v* after $1/\nu^2$ computer runs, according to basic statistical theory. Interestingly, all that is needed to produce a coarse-grained distribution is a coarse-grained measurement. This implies that measuring the most important qubits and ignoring those that would provide a measurement precision below the coarse graining δm will be adequate. As a result, *l* has no bearing on the quantity of runs and measurements.

Estimating the gain of quantum computation of the localization length in comparison to classical computation is now a critical step.

First, we remember that in order to achieve the localized distribution, approximately $t^\star \sim \ell$ map iterations are required (see Eqs. (38) and (40). Both the current quantum algorithm and classical computation can attest to this. It makes sense to detect localization using a base size of $N \propto \ell$, where *N* is a few times the localization length. To determine the localization length in such a scenario $(N \sim \ell)$ a quantum computer would use $O(\ell(\log \ell)^2)$ elementary gates, but a classical computer would need $O(\ell^2 \log \ell)$ operations. This is because both classical and quantum computers execute O(N) map iterations, therefore for $\ell \sim N = 2^n$ the quantum computer offers a quadratic speedup. For a given number of repetitions t, however, the quantum computation yields an exponential gain since, in this scenario, $O(t(\log N)^2)$ gates (quantum computation) should be compared to $O(tN \log N)$ gates (classical calculation).

Quantum dynamics simulation up to a specified time *t*. For example, it can be used to quantify dynamical correlation functions of the following type:

$$C(t) \equiv \langle\psi| A^{\dagger}(t)\, B(0)\, |\psi\rangle = \langle\psi|\, (U^{\dagger})^{t}\, A^{\dagger}(0)\, U^{t}\, B(0)\, |\psi\rangle \tag{42}$$

where U is the sawtooth map's time-evolution operator. The fidelity of quantum motion, a measure of primary interest in the investigation of the stability of quantum motion under disturbances, can also be computed effectively. The precision with which a quantum state can be retrieved by inverting the dynamics with a perturbed Hamiltonian at time *t* is measured by the fidelity f(t), also known as the Loschmidt echo. It is described as

$$f(t) = \langle\psi|\, (U_{\epsilon}^{\dagger})^{t}\, U^{t}\, |\psi\rangle \tag{43}$$

With U_{ϵ} as the appropriate time-evolution operator, the wave vector $|\psi\rangle$ evolves backward in time with a perturbed Hamiltonian H_{ϵ} after evolving forward in time with the Hamiltonian H of Eq. up to time *t*. For example, the sawtooth map's parameter *k* can be perturbed as follows: $k \to k' = k + \epsilon$. The fidelity of quantum motion can be assessed with exponential speedup in comparison to known classical computations if the evolution operators U and U_{ϵ} can be efficiently emulated on a quantum computer, as is the case in the majority of physically interesting scenarios.

For the correlation functions(43), the same conclusion holds true.

Chapter - 3
Quantum Communication

This section demonstrate how the fundamental ideas of quantum physics can be applied to information transfer. The most impressive use is in the art of secret communication, or cryptography. Following a brief introduction to conventional cryptography, we go into quantum physics' special contribution to cryptography. Two communicating parties, Alice (the sender) and Bob (the recipient), can determine whether Eve (an eavesdropper) has intercepted the given message thanks to quantum cryptography.

This is a result of the "no-cloning theorem," a fundamental property of quantum mechanics that states that an unknown quantum state cannot be replicated. Next, we demonstrate two amazing uses of quantum mechanics: dense coding and quantum teleportation. In dense coding, entanglement is used to improve the transmission of classical information; if Alice and Bob share an entangled EPR pair of qubits, Alice can operate on one of the qubits and then send it to Bob; this single qubit carries two bits of classical information. In quantum teleportation, entanglement is once more utilized to enable Alice to send Bob a quantum bit by sending him only classical bits.

3.1 Traditional cryptography

Since the necessity for covert communication has grown in importance, cryptography has roots that date back before the time of Christ. Julius Caesar's employment of the Cdssar cipher during the Gallic War more than 2,000 years ago is a notable example. This type of code employs an alphabet where every letter is moved by a predetermined number of steps. The alphabet has k — 1 = 25 potential codes if, for example, there are k = 26 letters. If the letters are labeled 1,2,..., k, then i —> i + j (mod A:) yields the code number j for i = 1,2,..., k. We state that Alice, the sender, uses a secret key to encrypt her plain text into a cypher text.

J serves as the key in the Caesar cypher. With j = 1,..., k - 1, it is evident that there are k—1 distinct codes, each identified by the number j. Since the original letters remain the same, the case j = k is unacceptable. In Caesar's day, it was challenging to crack this code, but it is obviously simple to do it now. It should be noted that Alice must first provide Bob the key via a secure route that Eve, the eavesdropper, is presumed to be unable to access. Alice then uses an unsecure route to send Bob the cipher text.

An intriguing variation of the Caesar cipher substitutes one of the alphabet's $k!$ potential permutations for the k letters. However, as the letters of an alphabet appear in texts at varying rates, even this code is today easily cracked. Therefore, all that is needed to crack the code is a basic statistical examination of the cypher text.

3.1.1 The Vernam cypher

Gilbert Vernam created the first unbreakable code, the Vernam cipher, in 1917, despite Shannon proving its unbreakability mathematically just over 30 years later. The following is Vernam's protocol.

1. A binary sequence of 0s and ls is used to represent the plain text.
2. A totally random binary sequence of the same length as the plain text serves as the secret key.
3. The secret key is added bitwise modulo 2 to the plain text to produce the cypher text.

The cypher text {CI,C2,…,CN} is obtained as follows if {p1, p2, …, pN } represents the plain text (with pi, p2,..., PN binary digits) and {k1,k2,..., kN} the secret key.

$$c_i = p_i \oplus k_i \qquad (i = 1, 2, \ldots, N) \tag{1}$$

Let's look at a basic example:

$$\begin{array}{ll} 001010011 & \text{plain text,} \\ 100111010 & \text{secret key,} \\ 101101001 & \text{cypher text.} \end{array} \tag{2}$$

Since the cypher text in this instance is also entirely random, the code cannot be broken as long as the key is also entirely random. It provides absolutely no details about the simple text. Alice and Bob share the secret key, so Bob can quickly piece together the plain text. He merely appends the secret key to the cipher text bitwise modulo 2:

$$p_i = c_i \oplus k_i \qquad (i = 1, 2, \ldots, N) \tag{3}$$

The Vernam cypher, also called the one-time pad, requires that the secret key be used just once. The bitwise addition of the two cypher texts, if they are reused and the eavesdropper can see them, is identical to the bitwise addition of the two matching plain texts. The code becomes breakable because simple texts inevitably have redundancy (they are not random binary sequences). Consequently, the distribution of the secret key rather than the transmission of the cypher text is the primary issue in cryptography. In other words, the issue of communication secrecy is simply moved to the issue of key secrecy, necessitating some sort of "trusted courier" for this distribution.

3.1.2 Public-key cryptosystem

Nowadays, only critical diplomatic communications employ the Vernam cypher because it is impossible to provide new random keys for each transmission. Public-key cryptography methods, whose concepts were developed by Dime and Hellman in the mid-1970s, are used in place of it for less sensitive operations.

The following are the main distinctions between the more modern public-key cryptosystem and the more conventional secret-key cryptosystem.

1. Alice uses a secret key to encrypt her message in the secret-key cryptosystem. Bob receives the encrypted communication from her; as he has the same secret key, he can decrypt it. The secret key is where the message's security lies. There is always a chance that the secret key will be intercepted because Alice and Bob will eventually need to share it.

2. There is no hidden key exchange between Alice and Bob in a public-key cryptosystem. Bob releases the public key, which Alice uses to encrypt the communication. Bob alone possesses the private key, which is the only key that can decrypt the message in place of this one. The key-distribution issue is thus avoided. The way the public-key cryptosystem operates is like Bob had built a safe and put the message inside. A public key is used to lock the safe, while a private key is used to open it. Only Bob has the ability to unlock the safe and remove the message, even though anyone can put a message inside.

A trap-door function f, which is simple to compute, is necessary for the public-key cryptosystem, whereas the inverse function f^{-1} is more difficult to compute. The notion of computational complexity must be applied in this context to understand the terms "easy" and "hard": f may be calculated with polynomial resources in the input size, however f^{-1} cannot be computed with polynomial resources (resources indicate processing time, hardware size, etc.). In theory, any issue that has a difficult-to-find solution but is simple to validate can be helpful for cryptography. These issues are classified under the computational class NP. Alice encrypts her text using the public key *f*, and Bob is the only one with the secret key f^{-1}, which he uses to decrypt the message.

3.1.3 The RSA protocol

Rivest, Shamir, and Adleman created the RSA cryptosystem in 1977, which is a well-known illustration of a public-key cryptosystem. This is how the RSA protocol operates:

1. Bob determines that two "large enough" prime numbers, p and q, equal N.

2. Bob selects at random a number d that is co-prime with (p — l)(q — 1), meaning that their greatest common divisor is equal to 1.

3. Bob calculates e, which is d's inverse modulo (p — 1){q — 1):

$$e\, d|_{\text{mod}(p-1)(q-1)} = 1 \qquad (4)$$

Note that p and q are no longer relevant.

4. Bob makes the pair (e,N) public. It is the public key that allows anyone to communicate with Bob.
5. The private decryption key, which only Bob has, is the pair (d, N).

Consequently, the only person who can decode the messages that were encrypted using the public key is Bob.

6. Alice separates her message into discrete blocks, each of which can be represented by a number. With $m_i < N.$ the number for the i-th block is m_i. Alice uses the following encryption for each block:

$$m_i \rightarrow m'_i = m_i^e|_{\text{mod}\, N}. \qquad (5)$$

7. Bob computes to decode the message.

$$m_i = m'^d_i|_{\text{mod}\, N} \qquad (6)$$

Indeed, $m_i^{ed}|_{\text{mod}\, N} = m_i$ according to basic number theory.

The following are some benefits of the Vernam cypher:

1. Distributing a secret key over a purportedly secure channel is unnecessary because anyone wishing to connect with Bob can use the public key, while Bob alone has the secret key;
2. Public key can be reused as often as needed.

Exercise

An important issue in cryptography is authentication: Bob must ascertain whether Alice sent the message and not someone else. Learn how to use a public-key cryptography system to verify Alice's message.

If one finds the prime factors p and q of N, they can crack the RSA code. After this, since e is known, d may be calculated with ease. Thus, the method's dependability is predicated on the fact that there are currently no effective (polynomial time) algorithms for determining an integer N's factors: $\exp(O(n^{1/3}(\log n)^{2/3}))$ operations are necessary for the number field sieve, the best classical algorithm currently available for integer factorization, where n = logN is the input size.

The factorization of a number with 250 digits would take roughly 10 million years on a computer with 200 MIPS (million instructions per second) to provide a tangible sense of the problem's difficulty. This indicates that using the technology available today to tackle the issue is practically impossible. More specifically, we should state that the number field sieve algorithm's optimality for integer factorization has not been demonstrated.

Additionally, just as it cannot be ruled out for any other NP issue, the potential that a polynomial time approach can be found is not ruled out either. In any case, we should emphasize that a quantum computer is capable of running such a polynomial time algorithm, as we have already observed. Therefore, the RSA encryption system would be broken if a large-scale quantum computer were built. This demonstrates unequivocally that public-key cryptosystem security is insufficient for messages that need to remain secret for an extended period of time.

3.2 The No-Cloning Theorem

One characteristic of the classical bit that we take for granted is its copyability. This section will demonstrate, however, that a qubit's generic state cannot be replicated. This is what Dieks, Wootters, and Zurek's so-called no-cloning theorem is all about. We'll start with a specific example, where the qubit is a photon's polarization state. If a photon is horizontally polarized, we call its state $|0\rangle$ (or $|\leftrightarrow\rangle$) and if it is vertically polarized, we call it $|1\rangle$ (or $|\updownarrow\rangle$).

As shown in below Fig., where x represents the horizontal axis, y the vertical axis, and z the photon's path of propagation, a photon can also be polarized along a direction that forms an angle β with regard to the horizontal. In this instance, the wave function describes it.

$$|\psi\rangle = \cos\beta\,|\leftrightarrow\rangle + \sin\beta\,|\updownarrow\rangle \tag{7}$$

Assume now that a polarization analyzer (a birefringent crystal like calcite) receives such a photon. Both horizontally and vertically polarized photons exit the analyzer (see below Fig., where vertically polarized photons are deflected while horizontally polarized photons pass through the crystal directly). The probabilities for these two mutually exclusive possibilities, which we refer to as 0 and 1, are $p_0 = |\langle\leftrightarrow|\psi\rangle|^2 = \cos^2\beta$ and $p_1 = |\langle\updownarrow|\psi\rangle|^2 = \sin^2\beta$ respectively. As a result, a measurement of a single photon's polarization state yields a single bit of information that represents the detected photon's polarization state. We see that this is entirely consistent with the measurement postulate, which is the second postulate of quantum mechanics.

Let's say there is a cloning machine. A disproportionately high quantity of copies of the state $|\psi\rangle$ provided by Eq. (7) could then be produced. Consequently, it would be feasible to measure each of these clones and determine the angle β with any level of precision. The cloning machine would go against the measuring postulate because it can be considered a component of the measurement instrument.

According to this assumption, we can discover only one piece of information by measuring a photon's polarization state. Probability $p_0 = \cos^2 \beta$ yields 0 and probability $p_1 = \sin^2 \beta.$ yields 1. On the other hand, we could calculate the parameter β with any level of precision if a cloning machine existed based on this measurement.

Thus, an infinitely huge quantity of information (the bits required to represent β to the acceptable accuracy) might be extracted from the straightforward measurement of the polarization state of a single photon. The measurement postulate of quantum mechanics leads us to the conclusion that there is no such thing as a quantum cloning machine.

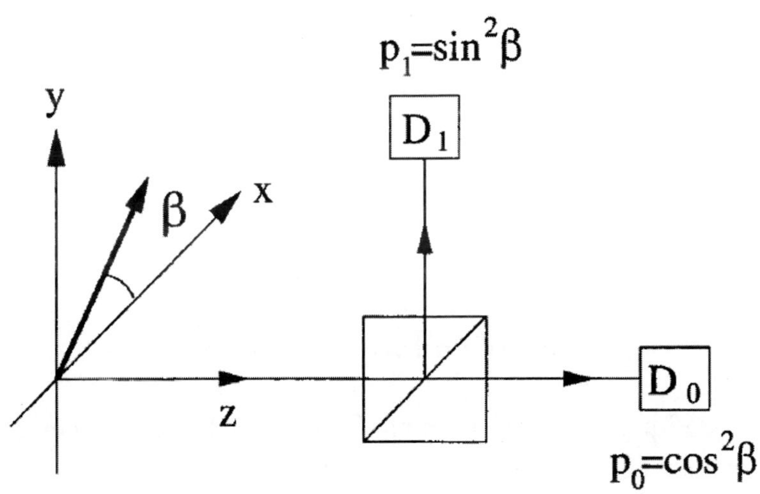

Fig.3.1 Measurement of a single photon's polarization. D1 and D0 stand for the two photodetectors.

The no-cloning theorem is now proved in a more formal way. Because it exploits the linearity of quantum mechanics, this demonstration must be seen as weaker than the prior one.

Theorem

A machine that can replicate a qubit's generic state and perform unitary transformations cannot be constructed.

Proof

Consider a system that consists of the cloning machine, a second qubit, and the qubit that has to be copied. A generic state is used to prepare the initial qubit.

$$|\psi\rangle = \alpha|0\rangle + \beta|1\rangle \tag{8}$$

restricted by the normalizing constraint $|\alpha|^2 + |\beta|^2 = 1$ with a and 0 complex numbers. The cloning machine and the second qubit are first set up in reference states, such as $|\phi\rangle$ and $|A_i\rangle$, respectively.

It should be possible for the cloning machine to carry out a unitary transformation U so that

$$U(|\psi\rangle|\phi\rangle|A_i\rangle) = |\psi\rangle|\psi\rangle|A_{f\psi}\rangle = (\alpha|0\rangle + \beta|1\rangle)(\alpha|0\rangle + \beta|1\rangle)|A_{f\psi}\rangle \tag{9}$$

where the $|\psi\rangle$ state to be replicated will typically determine the machine's final state. We now demonstrate that there is no such unitary transformation. When the initial qubit is in the state $|0\rangle$, the cloning machine's action needs to be

$$U(|0\rangle|\phi\rangle|A_i\rangle) = |0\rangle|0\rangle|A_{f0}\rangle \tag{10a}$$

Likewise, if the state $|1\rangle$ is used to prepare the first qubit,

$$U(|1\rangle|\phi\rangle|A_i\rangle) = |1\rangle|1\rangle|A_{f1}\rangle \tag{10b}$$

Consequently, the cloning machine's operation on a generic state, $|\psi\rangle = \alpha|0\rangle + \beta|1\rangle$, is provided by

$$U((\alpha|0\rangle + \beta|1\rangle)|\phi\rangle|A_i\rangle) = \alpha U(|0\rangle|\phi\rangle|A_i\rangle) + \beta U(|1\rangle|\phi\rangle|A_i\rangle) \tag{11}$$

when the linearity of quantum mechanics has been evoked. Now, we enter Equations 10a and 10b into Equation (11), yielding the state

$$\alpha|0\rangle|0\rangle|A_{f0}\rangle + \beta|1\rangle|1\rangle|A_{f1}\rangle \tag{12}$$

It is obviously not the intended cloned state of Eq. (9).

We emphasize the need of taking a generic state into account. We can measure the qubit's state with certainty and create as many copies of it as we want if we know right away that the qubit's quantum state is prepared in one of two orthogonal states, such as $|0\rangle$ or $|1\rangle$. The qubit functions as a classical bit in this instance, and we are aware that there are classical cloning devices.

3.2.1 Transmission of information faster than light?

It's intriguing to demonstrate how the presence of a doner would go against a fundamental tenet of relativity, namely that data may travel faster than light. Suppose that in the Bell state, a source generates EPR pairs.

$$|\phi^+\rangle = \frac{1}{\sqrt{2}}(|0\rangle|0\rangle + |1\rangle|1\rangle) \tag{13a}$$

Another way to express this situation is as

$$|\phi^+\rangle = \frac{1}{\sqrt{2}}(|0\rangle_x|0\rangle_x + |1\rangle_x|1\rangle_x) \tag{13b}$$

where the Pauli matrix σ_x eigenstates with eigenvalues of + 1 and —1 are represented by $|0\rangle_x$ and $|1\rangle_x$, respectively. Examining the equality of expressions (13a) and (13b) is simple given that

$$\begin{cases} |0\rangle_x = \frac{1}{\sqrt{2}}\begin{bmatrix} 1 \\ 1 \end{bmatrix} = \frac{1}{\sqrt{2}}(|0\rangle + |1\rangle) \\ |1\rangle_x = \frac{1}{\sqrt{2}}\begin{bmatrix} 1 \\ -1 \end{bmatrix} = \frac{1}{\sqrt{2}}(|0\rangle - |1\rangle) \end{cases} \tag{14}$$

Alice receives one member of each EPR pair, while Bob receives the other. Keep in mind that Alice and Bob could theoretically be anywhere from one another. Alice uses a binary string to encode a message that she wishes to deliver to Bob. Then, based on whether the accompanying digit is 0 or 1, she measures her member of each EPR pair, selecting to measure σ_x or σ_z(we assume that Alice and Bob share at least as many EPR pairs as digits in their message). Following this, Bob's member of the EPR pair collapses upon an σ_x or σ_z eigenstate.

Bob can't use his measurements to learn anything about Alice's message, though, because these states are not orthogonal. In contrast, Bob could create an infinite number of copies of his EPR qubits and differentiate between the σ_x or σ_z eigenstates with any level of precision he wished if a cloning machine didn't exist.

Bob could, in fact, estimate α and β from measuring these qubits as long as he had a large number of copies of the qubit with the generic state $|\psi\rangle = \alpha|0\rangle + \beta|1\rangle$. Therefore, he was able to ascertain whether this state was an eigenstate of σ_x or σ_z. As a result, superluminal information transfer would be feasible, which runs counter to a fundamental tenet of relativity theory.

3.3 Quantum cryptography

In classical physics, it is difficult to determine with precision whether Eve is listening in on a transmission. Classical information may be replicated without altering the original meaning, which is the reason. A physical system (a sheet of paper, radio transmissions, etc.) that can theoretically have its attributes passively monitored must, in fact, encode information. The system can be modified as little as is possible given the technologies at hand. On the other hand, for basic reasons, the measuring procedure in quantum mechanics generally disrupts the system. This results from the Heisenberg uncertainty principle.

When two non-commuting observables are taken into consideration, measuring one of them inevitably disrupts (randomizes) the other. This section will demonstrate how this intrinsic quantum feature enables intrusion detection, enabling Alice and Bob to determine whether Eve is listening in on their conversations. Two parties can use this possibility to generate a secret key. With the use of traditional cryptosystems like the Vernam cypher, Alice and Bob can converse covertly thanks to the generated key. The BB84 protocol and the E91 protocol are two quantum-key distribution protocols that are described here.

3.3.1 The BB84 protocol

Bennett and Brassard discovered the protocol BB84 in 1984. It requires two binary alphabets (the z-alphabet, $|0\rangle$ and $|1\rangle$, as well as four states: $|+\rangle \equiv |0\rangle_x = \frac{1}{\sqrt{2}}(|0\rangle + |1\rangle)$, $|-\rangle \equiv |1\rangle_x = \frac{1}{\sqrt{2}}(|0\rangle - |1\rangle)$. The eigenstates of the Pauli matrices σ_z and σ_x are linked to the letters of the z- and x-alphabets, respectively. The BB84 protocol is described below, with a basic example provided in the below Table.

1. Alice creates an arbitrary series of Os and ls.
2. Alice encodes every bit of data in a qubit, so that $|0\rangle$ or $|+\rangle = |0\rangle_x$ if the bit is 0, $|1\rangle$ or $|-\rangle = |1\rangle_x$ if the bit is 1. Alice uses a fair coin to select the x-alphabet and the z-alphabet at random for each bit (for example, if the coin lands heads, Alice selects the ar-alphabet, and if the coin lands tails, she selects the 2-alphabet).
3. Alice sends and Bob receives the resultant string of qubits.
4. Bob chooses at random which axis (alphabet) to employ for the measurement—x or z—for each qubit. He measures the spin polarization along the x axis in the first instance and the z axis in the second. Observe that Bob selects the same axis as Alice half of the time. Alice and Bob share the same bit in this instance, provided that there are no eavesdroppers or noise effects. Here, we define noise effects as things like faulty state preparation or detection, interactions of the transmitted qubit with the environment, etc. The bit that results from Bob's measurement, on the other hand, only coincides with Alice's bit half the time if he choose a different axis. For example, the probabilities of outcomes 0 and 1 are identical if Bob measures σ_z and obtains the qubit $|-\rangle$. Alice and Bob will now only communicate classically through a public channel.
5. Bob uses a traditional public channel to tell Alice the alphabet he used for each qubit measurement. Naturally, he keeps the results of these measurements to himself.

6. Over a traditional public channel, Alice tells Bob which alphabet she used for each qubit that was communicated (again, not the outcomes of these measurements).

7. Bob and Alice remove every bit that corresponds to the instances where they employed distinct alphabets. The so-called raw key is then shared. Since Eve and noise were not present, this key applies to Alice and Bob as well. Alice and Bob begin with the raw key and proceed to distill the secret key using the subsequent procedures.

8. Alice and Bob share a portion of their raw key and compare it over a public communication channel. They can calculate the error rate R caused by noise or eavesdroppers based on this comparison. They repeat the protocol from the beginning if this rate is too high. If not, they use the remaining bits of their raw key to accomplish privacy amplification and information reconciliation.

9. Just traditional error correction over a public transmission channel is what information reconciliation is.Here, we are restricted to illustrating a basic information reconciliation technique. Bob and Alice create subsets of length *I* from the remaining bits of their raw key. With R being the previously predicted error rate, this length is selected to make it improbable that there would be more than one error per subgroup ($Rl \ll 1$). The parity P of a binary string $\{b_1, b_2, \dots, b_l\}$ is defined as $P = b_1 \oplus b_2 \oplus \cdots \oplus b_l)$. Alice and Bob perform parity tests for each subset, discarding each time the last bit. The following is how they use binary search to find and remove the incorrect bit if Alice and Bob have different parities of a given subset. In order to verify the parities of the new blocks, they bisect the subset $(P_1 = b_1 \oplus b_2 \oplus \cdots \oplus b_{(l-1)/2}$ and $P_2 = b_{(l-1)/2+1} \oplus b_{(l-1)/2+2} \oplus \cdots \oplus b_{l-1})$. They repeat the bisection for the block where Alice's and Bob's parities differ, and so on. The final portion of the blocks whose parity is publicly declared is always deleted by Alice and Bob. They steer clear of Eve learning anything from their parity checks in this way. The same string of bits is most likely shared by Alice and Bob in the end.

10. Eve's knowledge of the final secret key is reduced to arbitrary small values by privacy amplification. Let's demonstrate a basic privacy amplification technique. Bob and Alice's estimation based on the error rate R. Previously, Eve knew the maximum amount of bits, k. Let s be a parameter for security. After that, Alice and Bob select n—k—s subsets of their key at random, where *n* is the number of bits in the key. The final secret key is formed by the parities of these subsets. Since Eve needs to know something about every bit of a subset in order to determine its parity, this key is more secure than the last one. Eve's residual information can be demonstrated to be $O(2^{-s})$.

Take note of the various eavesdropping techniques Eve has at her disposal:

1. Intercept and Resend: Eve measures and resends the qubits Alice sent after intercepting them;
2. Translucent attack: Eve uses probes, or ancillary qubits, to interact with Alice's qubits and determines their current state;
3. Collective attack: Eve manipulates a block of qubits rather than one at a time.

It is possible to demonstrate that quantum-key distribution is safe, regardless of the eavesdropping technique, by ensuring that Eve's knowledge of the final key is arbitrarily limited.

Table 3.1 The BB84 protocol in action.

Alice's data bits	1	0	0	0	1	1	0	1	0	1
Alice's alphabet	x	z	x	z	x	x	x	z	z	x
Transmitted qubits	$\|1\rangle_x$	$\|0\rangle$	$\|0\rangle_x$	$\|0\rangle$	$\|1\rangle_x$	$\|1\rangle_x$	$\|0\rangle_x$	$\|1\rangle$	$\|0\rangle$	$\|1\rangle_x$
Bob's alphabet	x	z	x	x	z	x	z	x	z	z
Measurement outcomes	1	0	0	0	0	1	0	0	0	1
Bob's data bits	1	0	0	0	0	1	0	0	0	1
Raw key	1	0	0			1			0	

Here, the Heisenberg principle serves as the foundation for the legitimacy of the BB84 protocol. σ_x and σ_z, two non-commuting observables, are linked to the two alphabets. Eve is unable to measure the same qubit's polarization along both x and z. She has an equal chance of getting the results 0 or 1, for example, if she measures σ_z for the qubit $|0\rangle_x$. She has thereby permanently randomized the polarization that Alice first sent.

The no-cloning theorem, which ensures that Eve cannot definitively discriminate between non-orthogonal quantum states, is also emphasized for its significance. If there was a quantum cloning machine, Eve could create a lot of copies of every qubit Alice sent and differentiate between the σ_x and σ_z eigenstates with arbitrary precision. Assume, for example, that Eve measures az for the qubit and each of its replicas. Every time she receives $|1\rangle$, she gets outcome 1. However, if she were to acquire $|1\rangle_x$, she would have equal odds of obtaining outcomes 0 and 1. Eve might then transmit Bob a copy of the qubit that was intercepted again. As a result, Eve might intercept Alice's qubits and deliver them to Bob again without anybody noticing her breach if the no cloning theorem could be broken.

3.3.2 E91 protocol

Now we discuss the protocol E91, a quantum cryptosystem that uses entangled EPR pairs.

1. A source S emits a pair of qubits (spin $\frac{1}{2}$ particles) in the EPR state

$$|\psi^-\rangle = \frac{1}{\sqrt{2}}(|01\rangle - |10\rangle) \quad (15)$$

Alice receives the first qubit, whereas Bob receives the second (see Fig. below). The qubits are transferred in opposite directions. Because Alice might create EPR pairings and then send a member of each pair to Bob, a third party is not strictly required.

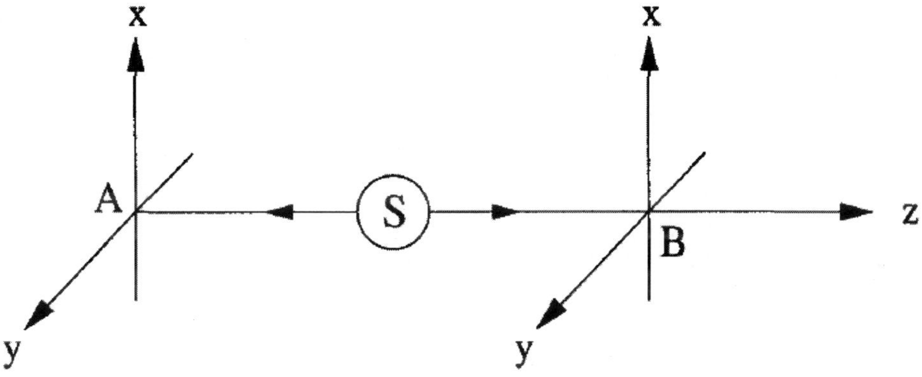

Fig.3.2 An illustration of the E91 protocol diagram. A, B and S stands for Alice, Bob, and the EPR source.

2. By taking advantage of the quantum correlations between EPR pairs, Alice and Bob may determine whether Eve has intercepted the transmission of the EPR pairs. They use one of the three directions $\hat{a}_1, \hat{a}_2, \hat{a}_3$ (Alice), $\hat{b}_1, \hat{b}_2, \hat{b}_3$ (Bob)—to measure the spin polarization (see below Fig.). Alice and Bob randomly select the measurement axes for each EPR pair from $\hat{a}_1, \hat{a}_2, \hat{a}_3$, and $\hat{b}_1, \hat{b}_2, \hat{b}_3$, respectively. Let's write $p_{\pm\pm}(\hat{a}_i, \hat{b}_j)$ to represent the likelihood that Bob's measurement along $\hat{b}_i$ yields ±1 and Alice's measurement along $\hat{a}_i$ yields ±1. The correlation coefficients are defined as follows:

$$E(\hat{a}_i, \hat{b}_j) = p_{++}(\hat{a}_i, \hat{b}_j) + p_{--}(\hat{a}_i, \hat{b}_j) - p_{+-}(\hat{a}_i, \hat{b}_j) - p_{-+}(\hat{a}_i, \hat{b}_j) \quad (16)$$

We can infer from the Bell's inequality that

$$C \equiv E(\hat{a}_1, \hat{b}_1) - E(\hat{a}_1, \hat{b}_3) + E(\hat{a}_3, \hat{b}_1) + E(\hat{a}_3, \hat{b}_3) = -2\sqrt{2} \quad (17)$$

In other words, the CHSH inequality, which states that $|C| \leq 2$, is broken by quantum mechanics.

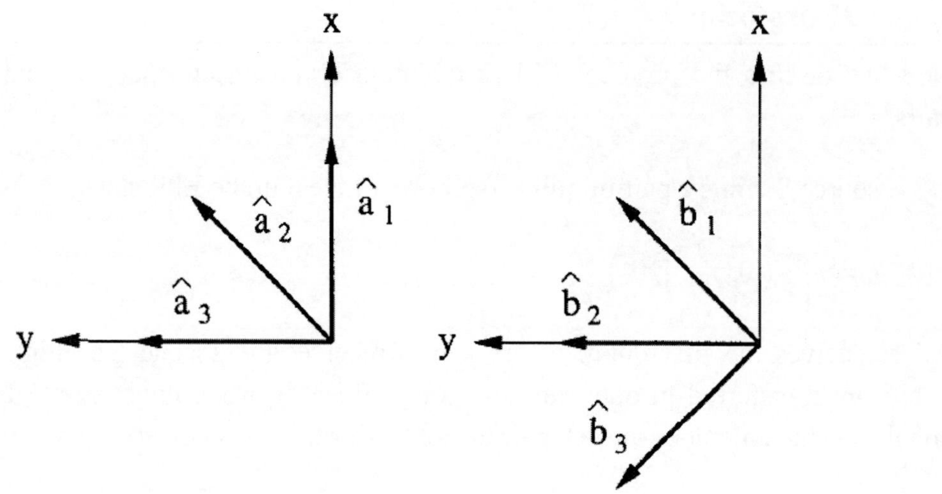

Fig.3.3 Alice's (left) and Bob's (right) measuring axis directions. These directions and the x axis have the following angles: $0, \frac{\pi}{4}, \frac{\pi}{2}$ for $\hat{a}_1, \hat{a}_2, \hat{a}_3$ and $\frac{\pi}{4}, \frac{\pi}{2}, \frac{3\pi}{4}$ for $\hat{b}_1, \hat{b}_2, \hat{b}_3$.

3. The axis selected for every measurement is announced by Alice and Bob via a public channel. The results of the measurements in the situations when their polarization axes did not coincide are then made public. Bob and Alice are able to verify the equality as a result (17). It is possible to demonstrate that $|C|$ cannot be greater than $2\sqrt{2}$; for an example of this, if $C > -2\sqrt{2}$, then Eve attacked the EPR pairs or there were noise effects. Alice and Bob's measurements along the same axis are entirely anticorrelated when these effects are absent, or when $C = -2\sqrt{2}$.

$$E(\hat{a}_2, \hat{b}_1) = E(\hat{a}_3, \hat{b}_2) = -1 \quad (18)$$

The raw key that Bob and Alice share is the result of these measurements; if Bob negates his results, the keys agree, 0 -> 1 and 1 -> 0. Following this, Alice and Bob can carry out privacy amplification and key reconciliation using the BB84 protocol.

It is observed that testing the relationship is not required (17). Bob and Alice may just measure along x or z. Every choice has a probability $\frac{1}{2}$ of happening, and the decision is random. Following the measurement procedure, Alice and Bob reveal on a public channel the observables they measured for every pair of EPRs. The results are completely anticorrelated when their measurement axes coincide. Bob and Alice keep the same raw key after discarding the other pieces. They then carry out the BB84 protocol. Interestingly, neither Alice nor Bob created the secret key. Until Bob and Alice measure their parts of the shared EPR pairs, the key remains unknown.

The secret key then emerges from the quantum measurement, which is essentially a random process. Lastly, we emphasize that key storage may find the E91 protocol intriguing. The issue is that Alice and Bob have to keep the secret key in their safes until they need it after it has been determined. Nonetheless, the key is a series of classical bits that can theoretically be replicated. Cracking the safe may be extremely challenging, but it is always achievable. This possibility is not excluded for any basic reasons. Alice and Bob might postpone establishing the secret key until they were required, though, if they could store EPR pairings.

Naturally, one must be able to shield the EPR pairs from noise effects resulting from interactions with their surroundings for extended periods of time, which makes the implementation of such key storage challenging. The current state of technology cannot accommodate this possibility.

3.4 Dense coding

The most basic example of using quantum entanglement in communication is dense coding. By sending Bob merely one qubit, it enables Alice to transmit him two bits of classical information. The dense coding protocol operates as follows (refer to the first schematic image below and the subsequent figure for the quantum circuit that implements the protocol).

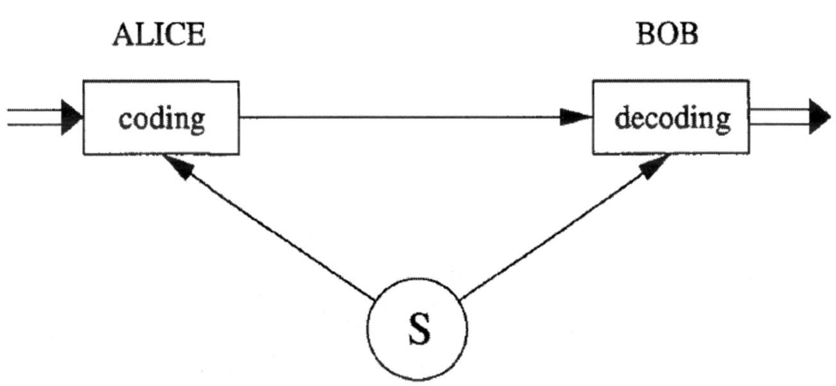

Fig.3.4 A schematic representation of the dense coding procedure. A single line indicates a quantum bit, while two double lines indicate two classical bits.

It should be noted that, as illustrated in the figure above, a source S generates the EPR pair before sending one of its members to Alice and the other to Bob. It is crucial to emphasize that Alice and Bob could be anywhere in the world.

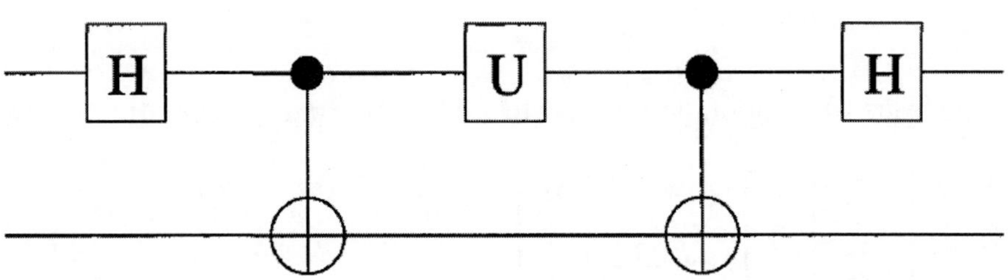

Fig.3.5 The dense coding technique is implemented via a quantum circuit.

An EPR pair shared by Alice and Bob is generated by a source S. The state, for example, prepares the EPR pair.

$$|\phi^+\rangle = \frac{1}{\sqrt{2}}(|00\rangle + |11\rangle) \tag{19}$$

A Hadamard gate and a CNOT gate are applied to the state $|00\rangle$ to produce the Bell state $|\phi^+\rangle$:

$$\text{CNOT}(H \otimes I)|00\rangle = |\phi^+\rangle \tag{20}$$

The transformation (20) in the computational basis with basis vectors $|00\rangle$, $|01\rangle$, $|10\rangle$ and $|11\rangle$ has the following matrix representation (take note that the first label corresponds to Alice's half of the EPR pair, and the second to Bob's half):

$$\begin{bmatrix} 1 & 0 & 0 & 0 \\ 0 & 1 & 0 & 0 \\ 0 & 0 & 0 & 1 \\ 0 & 0 & 1 & 0 \end{bmatrix} \frac{1}{\sqrt{2}} \begin{bmatrix} 1 & 0 & 1 & 0 \\ 0 & 1 & 0 & 1 \\ 1 & 0 & -1 & 0 \\ 0 & 1 & 0 & -1 \end{bmatrix} \begin{bmatrix} 1 \\ 0 \\ 0 \\ 0 \end{bmatrix} = \frac{1}{\sqrt{2}} \begin{bmatrix} 1 \\ 0 \\ 0 \\ 1 \end{bmatrix} \tag{21}$$

The two classical bits Alice wants to send to Bob can have any of the following four values: 00, 01, 10, and 11. $U = I, \sigma_x, \sigma_z$ or $i\sigma_y$ (where I stands for the identity and $\sigma_x, \sigma_y, \sigma_z$ for the Pauli matrices) is the unitary operation U that they identify Alice doing on her half of the EPR pair. In the following, the rationale behind selecting one of these four unitary transformations will be explained.

As previously stated, Alice wants to tell Bob the value of the two classical bits, which determines the operator U in the circuit shown in the above figure. She uses the identification on her half of the EPR pair to communicate 00 if she wants to. This provides the simple change.

$$I \otimes I|\phi^+\rangle = |\phi^+\rangle \tag{22}$$

She manipulates the Pauli matrix ax on her side of the EPR pair to obtain 01 if she wants to converse.

$$\sigma_x \otimes I|\phi^+\rangle = |\psi^+\rangle \tag{23}$$

which, on the basis of computation, translates to the matrix representation below:

$$\begin{bmatrix} 0 & 0 & 1 & 0 \\ 0 & 0 & 0 & 1 \\ 1 & 0 & 0 & 0 \\ 0 & 1 & 0 & 0 \end{bmatrix} \frac{1}{\sqrt{2}} \begin{bmatrix} 1 \\ 0 \\ 0 \\ 1 \end{bmatrix} = \frac{1}{\sqrt{2}} \begin{bmatrix} 0 \\ 1 \\ 1 \\ 0 \end{bmatrix} \tag{24}$$

In order to communicate 10, she uses σ_z, acquiring

$$\sigma_z \otimes I\,|\phi^+\rangle = |\phi^-\rangle \tag{25}$$

having a matrix representation

$$\begin{bmatrix} 1 & 0 & 0 & 0 \\ 0 & 1 & 0 & 0 \\ 0 & 0 & -1 & 0 \\ 0 & 0 & 0 & -1 \end{bmatrix} \frac{1}{\sqrt{2}} \begin{bmatrix} 1 \\ 0 \\ 0 \\ 1 \end{bmatrix} = \frac{1}{\sqrt{2}} \begin{bmatrix} 1 \\ 0 \\ 0 \\ -1 \end{bmatrix} \tag{26}$$

In conclusion, if she wants to convey 11, she uses $i\sigma_y$, acquiring

$$i\sigma_y \otimes I\,|\phi^+\rangle = |\psi^-\rangle \tag{27}$$

with matrix representation

$$\begin{bmatrix} 0 & 0 & 1 & 0 \\ 0 & 0 & 0 & 1 \\ -1 & 0 & 0 & 0 \\ 0 & -1 & 0 & 0 \end{bmatrix} \frac{1}{\sqrt{2}} \begin{bmatrix} 1 \\ 0 \\ 0 \\ 1 \end{bmatrix} = \frac{1}{\sqrt{2}} \begin{bmatrix} 0 \\ 1 \\ -1 \\ 0 \end{bmatrix} \tag{28}$$

The circuit in Figure has so far created one of the four Bell states listed in earlier Section $(|\phi^+\rangle, |\psi^+\rangle, |\phi^-\rangle$ and $|\psi^-\rangle)$.

Bob receives half of Alice's EPR pair.

Bob obtains the two classical bits by measuring the two qubits and applying the proper unitary operations to the EPR pair. Bob converts the Bell states into states of the computational basis first. As previously mentioned, the inverse of the circuit, which is also the first segment of the dense-coding circuit shown in the preceding Fig., is the proper circuit for this operation. Given that the CNOT and Hadamard gates are self-inverse, Bob functions

$$(\text{CNOT}\,(H \otimes I))^{-1} = (H \otimes I)\ \text{CNOT} \tag{29}$$

It is represented by a matrix

$$B = \frac{1}{\sqrt{2}} \begin{bmatrix} 1 & 0 & 0 & 1 \\ 0 & 1 & 1 & 0 \\ 1 & 0 & 0 & -1 \\ 0 & 1 & -1 & 0 \end{bmatrix} \tag{30}$$

It is simple to verify that

$$\begin{aligned} B|\phi^+\rangle &= |00\rangle, & B|\psi^+\rangle &= |01\rangle \\ B|\phi^-\rangle &= |10\rangle, & B|\psi^-\rangle &= |11\rangle \end{aligned} \tag{31}$$

Bob eventually determines the two desired classical bits with unit probability by measuring the two qubits in the computational basis.

In classical physics, dense coding is impossible because a classical bit also has a value that is known before it is measured. Entanglement is a concept in quantum mechanics. Alice acts on an entangled two-qubit system rather than an isolated qubit when she manipulates her side of the EPR pair.

3.5 Teleportation at the quantum realm

One of the most remarkable ways that quantum physics has been used to information theory is through quantum teleportation, which enables Alice to send Bob quantum information even while Alice only provides Bob classical information. For instance, the transfer of quantum information across various components of a quantum computer may be a useful application of this potential. Let's look at the most basic teleportation example: Alice is the owner of a two-level system in an unidentified state.

$$|\psi\rangle = \alpha|0\rangle + \beta|1\rangle \tag{32}$$

She can only send classical bits, not quantum ones, if she wants to communicate this qubit to Bob over a classical communication channel. The mission first appears desperate because Alice can only gather a single piece of information from the system's measurement, which would wildly alter its state. Given that this quantum state exists in a continuous space and is parametrized by two complex parameters, α and β) , it is observed that characterizing $|\psi\rangle$ necessitates an infinite quantity of classical information. The issue is resolved by quantum teleportation, though, if Alice and Bob have an entangled pair of qubits in common. The following describes the quantum teleportation procedure (the quantum circuit that enables teleportation is seen in Fig. below).

1. The Bell state is produced by the circuit's first two gates in below Fig.

$$|\psi^+\rangle = \frac{1}{\sqrt{2}}(|01\rangle + |10\rangle) \tag{33}$$

In fact,

$$\text{CNOT}\,(H \otimes I)\,|01\rangle = |\psi^+\rangle \tag{34}$$

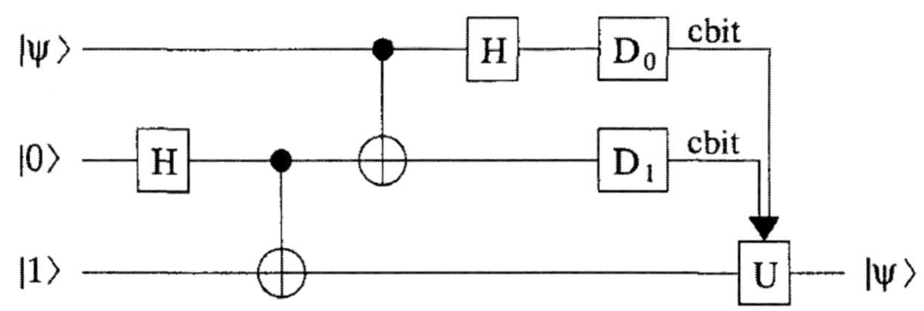

Fig.3.6 A teleportation quantum circuit.

Alice's qubit is shown in the second line, Bob's qubit is shown in the third, and the qubit to be transported is shown in the first line. The two cbits (classical bits) of information obtained from Alice's measurement (by means of the detectors D_0 and D_1) govern Bob's unitary transformation U.

The source S that produces the EPR pair is in charge of them. After that, Alice and Bob receive the first and second halves of the EPR pair, respectively. As a result, Bob owns one qubit (the second half of the EPR pair) while Alice owns two qubits (the state $|\psi\rangle$) and half of the EPR pair. Keep in mind that Alice and Bob may be extremely far apart, as is customary. The direct product yields the three-qubit state.

$$\begin{aligned} |\psi\rangle \otimes |\psi^+\rangle &= (\alpha|0\rangle + \beta|1\rangle) \otimes \tfrac{1}{\sqrt{2}}(|01\rangle + |10\rangle) \\ &= \tfrac{\alpha}{\sqrt{2}}(|001\rangle + |010\rangle) + \tfrac{\beta}{\sqrt{2}}(|101\rangle + |110\rangle) \end{aligned} \tag{35}$$

2. Alice lets her side of the EPR pair interact with the qubit $|\psi\rangle$. This step is essential. In fact, the quantum state $|\psi\rangle$ would collapse onto $|0\rangle$ or $|1\rangle$ if Alice just made a measurement in the computational basis, and she wouldn't have enough data to reconstruct it.

As seen by the states $|\phi^+\rangle$, $|\phi^-\rangle$, $|\psi^+\rangle$ and $|\psi^-\rangle$ the way out is a measurement in the Bell basis. Since these states make up a whole orthonormal set, the computational basis's states can be expanded over it. This provides

$$\begin{cases} |00\rangle = \tfrac{1}{\sqrt{2}}(|\phi^+\rangle + |\phi^-\rangle)\,, \\ |11\rangle = \tfrac{1}{\sqrt{2}}(|\phi^+\rangle - |\phi^-\rangle)\,, \\ |01\rangle = \tfrac{1}{\sqrt{2}}(|\psi^+\rangle + |\psi^-\rangle)\,, \\ |10\rangle = \tfrac{1}{\sqrt{2}}(|\psi^+\rangle - |\psi^-\rangle)\,. \end{cases} \tag{36}$$

By adding these relations to Eq. (35), we get

$$\begin{aligned} |\psi\rangle \otimes |\psi^+\rangle &= \tfrac{\alpha}{2}(|\phi^+\rangle + |\phi^-\rangle)|1\rangle + \tfrac{\alpha}{2}(|\psi^+\rangle + |\psi^-\rangle)|0\rangle \\ &\quad + \tfrac{\beta}{2}(|\psi^+\rangle - |\psi^-\rangle)|1\rangle + \tfrac{\beta}{2}(|\phi^+\rangle - |\phi^-\rangle)|0\rangle \\ &= \tfrac{1}{2}|\psi^+\rangle(\alpha|0\rangle + \beta|1\rangle) + \tfrac{1}{2}|\psi^-\rangle(\alpha|0\rangle - \beta|1\rangle) \\ &\quad + \tfrac{1}{2}|\phi^+\rangle(\alpha|1\rangle + \beta|0\rangle) + \tfrac{1}{2}|\phi^-\rangle(\alpha|1\rangle - \beta|0\rangle) \end{aligned} \tag{37}$$

Alice must thus execute a Bell measurement in order to get one of the four states $|\psi^{\pm}\rangle$ or $|\phi^{\pm}\rangle$ with an equal chance of $p = \frac{1}{4}$ In the computational basis, the Bell measurement can be converted into a standard measurement by using the unitary transformation, as we have already seen.

$$(H \otimes I)\ \mathrm{CNOT} \tag{38}$$

prior to the measurement. As a result, $|\phi^{+}\rangle$ to $|00\rangle$, $|\psi^{+}\rangle$ to $|01\rangle$, $|\phi^{-}\rangle$ to $|10\rangle$ and $|\psi^{-}\rangle$ to $|11\rangle$. Alice thus uses her two qubits and the unitary transformation (38) on them.

As a result, the three qubits reach the following global state:

$$\begin{aligned}&\tfrac{1}{2}|01\rangle(\alpha|0\rangle + \beta|1\rangle) + \tfrac{1}{2}|11\rangle(\alpha|0\rangle - \beta|1\rangle)\\ &+ \tfrac{1}{2}|00\rangle(\alpha|1\rangle + \beta|0\rangle) + \tfrac{1}{2}|10\rangle(\alpha|1\rangle - \beta|0\rangle)\end{aligned} \tag{39}$$

3. The two qubits that Alice possesses are measured in the computational basis. Each of the four possible outcomes—00, 01, 10, and 11—provides two pieces of classical data. As demonstrated by Eq. (37), Bob's particle's state collapses onto $\alpha|1\rangle + \beta|0\rangle$ if Alice's measurement yields 00. Similarly, results 01, 10, and 11 each depart from the post measurement state of Bob's particle in a $\alpha|0\rangle + \beta|1\rangle$, $\alpha|1\rangle - \beta|0\rangle$ and $\alpha|0\rangle - \beta|1\rangle$, respectively.
4. Bob receives these two classical bits from Alice.
5. These two pieces of classical information are given to Bob, indicating which of the four possible results Alice's measurement could have produced. Bob recovers the state $|\psi\rangle$ by performing one of four potential unitary operations U on his qubit, depending on this classical message. In the event that Alice received 00, Bob executes $U = \sigma_x$. The same is true for 01, 10, and 11; they drive $U = I$, $U = i\sigma_y$ and $U = \sigma_z$, respectively.

Quantum information cannot be communicated faster than light using teleportation. In fact, Alice needs to transmit two pieces of classical data so that Bob can rebuild the state $|\psi\rangle$. At a speed of no more than light, this information is conveyed through conventional means. Additionally, take note of the fact that Alice and Bob exchange information about the quantum state, or qubit, rather than the actual physical system.

Alice's and Bob's labs may have rather different physical systems that use the qubit.

The nocloning theorem is completely compatible with teleportation. At the end of the teleportation operation, Bob has the quantum state $|\psi\rangle$, but depending on Alice's measurement result, the original state is left in $|0\rangle$ or $|1\rangle$. In one location, the unknown quantum state $|\psi\rangle$ disappears, while in another, it resurfaces.

Interestingly, the same quantum circuit can be "cut" in different places to provide both dense coding and quantum teleportation (See Below Fig.).

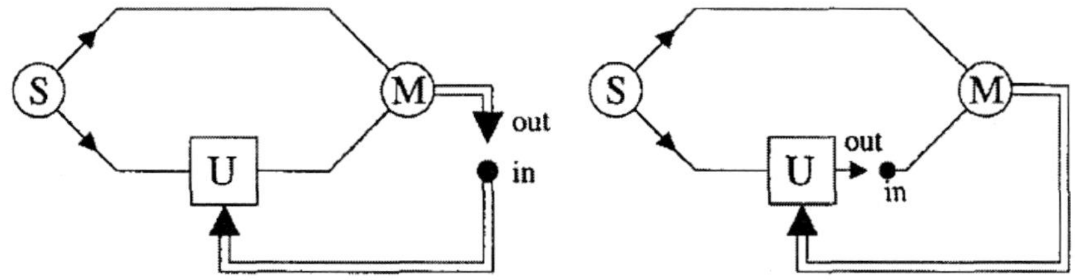

Fig.3.7 Diagrams showing teleportation (right) and dense coding (left).

S stands for the EPR source, M for the measurement procedure, U for the unitary transformation powered by the two classical bits, "in" and "out" for the circuits' input and output, and double lines for two classical bits and single lines for a quantum bit.

A key component of several quantum processing methods is teleportation. As would be necessary in a quantum computer composed of multiple independent units, it is an effective instrument for transferring quantum states from one system to another. Specifically, it has been demonstrated that teleportation and single-qubit operations are adequate to accomplish universal quantum processing.

3.6 Quantum Computing Security in 6G

Building an Open and Collaborative Ecosystem for Quantum Machine Learning

The rapid progress in machine learning (ML) over the past decade has been largely driven by a vibrant ecosystem of open-source software, freely available benchmark datasets, shared model repositories, and community-led challenges. Drawing on this success, we propose creating a similar infrastructure to accelerate research and collaboration at the interface of quantum science and machine learning.

To realize this vision, the standardization of quantum physics problems is a critical step. By developing interoperable, structured interfaces and common data formats, quantum challenges can be translated into a machine-learning-ready framework. This will allow the seamless sharing of experimental and simulated data, and ensure that ML models are reusable, comparable, and reproducible across both theoretical and experimental quantum physics contexts.

In addition to technical standardization, community-driven open projects should be launched to foster knowledge exchange. These projects can serve as hubs for collaborative tool development, shared interfaces, comprehensive tutorials, and thorough documentation—lowering the barrier to entry for newcomers, and strengthening cohesion across disciplines. They will also provide an essential resource for teaching, benchmarking, and developing best practices in the field.

To ensure sustained progress, it is essential to train a new generation of interdisciplinary researchers. Dedicated doctoral networks, cross-disciplinary symposia, and online training platforms will prepare young scientists to work at the interface of quantum science and AI. These initiatives will help bridge the gap between theory and experiment, enabling more integrated and data-informed quantum research.

Importantly, this talent pipeline will also benefit industry. Graduates of such programs will bring cross-functional expertise into the innovation ecosystem, driving the development of competitive products, technological breakthroughs, and industry-ready solutions in quantum computing, simulation, and sensing.

Engagement and communication are equally critical. Strategic science communication efforts, in collaboration with content creators, industry partners, and policymakers, can make the progress and promise of quantum machine learning accessible to wider audiences.

The creation of an open, standardized, and community-driven ecosystem, coupled with interdisciplinary training and public engagement, is essential for unlocking the full potential of machine learning in quantum science—and ensuring its benefits are shared broadly across research, industry, and society.

Recent breakthroughs in quantum technologies are accelerating a transformative shift in science and technology, with far-reaching implications for economies, security, and defense. Quantum innovations promise to revolutionize critical domains such as sensing, imaging, precise positioning, navigation and timing (PNT), secure communications, high-performance computing, modelling and simulation, and advanced information science.

Among these advances, the advent of the quantum computer stands out as a milestone in information processing—enabling operations far beyond the reach of classical computers. This surge in quantum capabilities has drawn significant interest from the telecommunications sector, particularly in the context of emerging 6G networks. The quantum internet concept, with its promise of ultra-secure, high-speed, and fundamentally new modes of communication, further amplifies this interest.

The future generation of 6G networks, expected to emerge around 2030, aligns closely with the global agenda of achieving the United Nations Sustainable Development Goals (SDGs). These 17 goals, with 169 specific targets, outline a comprehensive framework for global progress—addressing priorities such as eradicating poverty, ending hunger, advancing quality education, reducing inequalities, and combating climate change.

Launched in 2016, the SDGs provide a 15-year roadmap for all nations, building upon the momentum of the Millennium Development Goals (MDGs) that preceded them. Unlike the MDGs, the SDGs are universal—applying to all countries, all communities, and all individuals, ensuring that no one is excluded and no one is left behind on the path toward global sustainability.

The convergence of quantum technology deployment with the rollout of 6G creates a unique opportunity to leverage cutting-edge innovations in the service of these shared global objectives—fostering sustainability, resilience, and inclusivity in a digitally connected future.

3.6.1 Existing Perspectives on Providing Strategies for Digital Sovereignty

Traditionally, sovereignty refers to the authority of an independent state, recognized by the international community, to exercise administrative and jurisdictional power within its borders. When transposed to the digital sphere, however, this concept becomes more complex to define and enforce.

Broadly speaking, Digital Sovereignty signifies the capacity of a state or an organization to assert authority and exercise prerogatives within cyberspace. Beyond the theoretical dimension, it responds to very practical challenges such as technological dependence, control over critical infrastructures, and the management of citizens' personal data.

The World Economic Forum (WEF) defines Digital Sovereignty as the ability to control one's digital destiny—including the data, hardware, and software that societies and economies depend on and produce. This ability is not merely a matter of technological competitiveness but also a precondition for data security and cyber resilience, ensuring that both citizens and businesses are safeguarded from potential threats in the increasingly interconnected digital world.

Consequently, policy makers across the globe have grown increasingly concerned that:

- Too much control is concentrated in the hands of a small number of powerful technology companies.
- There is insufficient choice and diversity in the technology marketplace.
- Nations and organizations risk becoming overly dependent on foreign technologies for critical services and infrastructures.

As a result, digital sovereignty is no longer framed solely as a strategic autonomy issue, but as a multidimensional priority that spans cybersecurity, economic independence, citizen protection, and democratic governance.

Towards Digital Sovereignty through Quantum Technology Regulation

To achieve Digital Sovereignty, it is essential that each state develops and shares a Regulatory Strategy on Quantum Technologies. At present, only a limited number of countries have formalized such strategies, given the nascent and fast-evolving nature of quantum technologies and the inherent difficulty for legislators to formulate a long-term vision in this domain.

A notable example comes from Ireland, where the Department of Further and Higher Education, Research, Innovation and Science published, in November 2023, a comprehensive National Quantum Technologies Strategy. The Irish framework seeks to position the country as an internationally competitive hub for quantum science and engineering, leveraging research, talent development, collaboration, and innovation.

The strategy is structured around five interconnected pillars:

Excellence in Research (Pillar 1):

Focus on advancing both fundamental and applied quantum research.

Build on Ireland's strong track record to foster breakthrough discoveries that can feed the pipeline of future innovations.

Talent Development (Pillar 2):

Circulating knowledge into the economy and society through the cultivation of world-class talent in science and engineering.

Ensure Ireland has the skilled workforce needed to drive and sustain leadership in quantum technologies.

Collaboration and Partnerships (Pillar 3):

Strengthen national and international collaborations, involving multiple sectors.

Expand Ireland's active participation in European quantum research networks and projects.

Innovation and Economic Competitiveness (Pillar 4):

Promote entrepreneurship and commercial applications of quantum technologies.

Encourage the growth of indigenous SMEs and foster stronger ties between academia and industry.

Societal Awareness and Literacy (Pillar 5):

Enhance public understanding of quantum technologies and their benefits.

Work toward building a quantum-literate society to ensure the broad adoption of quantum-enabled innovations.

The strategy emphasizes that Pillar 5 (awareness and literacy) is critical to the realization of the first four pillars, as widespread understanding and engagement will be required for the successful deployment of quantum technologies across society.

As quantum technologies mature, several states have begun articulating national strategies to secure leadership, safeguard sovereignty, and ensure long-term competitiveness. While still a developing field, early strategies highlight the varied priorities of different governments.

Ireland (2023)

Vision: Establish Ireland as an internationally competitive hub for quantum technologies, grounded in excellence in science, talent, and innovation.

Key Pillars:

Fundamental & Applied Research – advancing internationally excellent science.

Talent Development – training the next generation of quantum scientists and engineers.

Collaboration – strengthening national and international partnerships.

Innovation & Entrepreneurship – fostering SMEs and academia-industry links.

Awareness & Literacy – building a quantum-literate society to ensure broad societal benefits.

Approach: Strong focus on academic research and talent, while also laying the foundation for economic competitiveness.

United Kingdom (2023)

Vision: Become a leading quantum technology-based economy by 2033, embedding quantum technologies into digital infrastructure and advanced manufacturing.

Commitment: £2.5 billion over 10 years (2023–2033) for research, innovation, skills, and industrial growth.

Strategic Priorities:

Investment in quantum facilities and infrastructure to host and operate quantum computers.

Support for the skills pipeline and training to ensure workforce readiness.

Development of a robust industrial ecosystem, with strong emphasis on commercialization.

Approach: Clear industrial and economic framing, building on the earlier National Quantum Technologies Program, with strong continuity in policy.

Canada (2023)

Vision: Maintain and expand Canada's position as a global leader in quantum innovation, with strong emphasis on sovereignty and security.

Three Key Missions

Quantum Computing Leadership – develop and deploy hardware and software for Canadian industry, governments, and citizens.

Quantum Security & Privacy – establish a secure national quantum communications network and roll out post-quantum cryptography.

Quantum Sensing Innovation – position government and key industries as developers and early adopters of advanced quantum sensing technologies.

Approach: Heavy emphasis on sovereignty and security, with a dual focus on innovation and national resilience.

Comparative Insights

Ireland leans towards research-driven growth and building societal literacy, preparing the foundations for a competitive ecosystem.

The UK places quantum technologies at the heart of its economic and industrial policy, committing significant funding to infrastructure and commercialization.

Canada emphasizes security, privacy, and sovereignty, while also ensuring adoption in critical sectors such as government and industry.

Together, these strategies reveal different interpretations of digital sovereignty in a quantum era:

Ireland → Knowledge sovereignty (research, skills, awareness).

UK → Economic sovereignty (industrial ecosystem, global competitiveness).

Canada → Security sovereignty (communications, cryptography, sensing).

National Quantum Technology Strategies: Expanding the Landscape

Australia (2023)

Vision: Position Australia as a leading, trusted hub for quantum technologies by fostering research, industry, and inclusive governance.

Five Central Themes (7-year roadmap)

Research & Development – strengthen R&D through sustained investment.

Infrastructure & Materials – secure access to critical quantum infrastructure and rare materials.

Workforce Development – build and expand a skilled, diverse quantum workforce.

Standards & Frameworks – align regulation and technical standards with national interests.

Ethics & Inclusion – ensure a trusted, ethical, and inclusive quantum ecosystem.

Approach: Shared responsibility: the government leads, but academia, industry, and international partners co-drive implementation.

Future-oriented: signals potential investment opportunities to stimulate ecosystem growth.

Sovereignty Framing: Balances innovation with ethics and inclusion, ensuring both competitiveness and public trust.

United States (2022–present)

Vision: Ensure quantum advantage and security resilience, particularly in cryptography and national security systems.

Presidential Memorandum (2022)

All federal agencies (civilian, military, and government corporations) mandated to prepare for the quantum transition.

Key Actions

By May 2023: Agencies submitted inventories of systems containing cryptographic components vulnerable to quantum attacks.

By May 2024: Agencies delivered cost estimates and transition plans for migrating cryptographic systems to post-quantum standards.

Approach: Highly security-centric; coordinated through the White House and National Institute of Standards and Technology (NIST).

Builds on the National Quantum Initiative Act (2018) and significant investment in both fundamental research and commercialization.

Sovereignty Framing: Anchored in cybersecurity and defense resilience, ensuring US leadership in post-quantum cryptography and secure digital infrastructure.

Together, these strategies show that digital sovereignty in the quantum era is multi-dimensional:

Knowledge (Ireland),

Economic competitiveness (UK),

Security and resilience (Canada, US),

Trust, inclusion, and ethics (Australia).

The United States has anchored its quantum-readiness agenda in statute. Public Law 117-260 (21 December 2022)—the Quantum Computing Cybersecurity Preparedness Act—formalizes the federal transition to post-quantum cryptography (PQC), reiterating prior executive guidance and setting the target of completing migration by 2035. This law both validates the urgency of quantum-resilient cybersecurity and provides the governance mandate to inventory vulnerable systems, plan upgrades, and fund the transition at scale.

In parallel, the transatlantic security community has moved in lockstep. NATO's first Quantum Technology Strategy, approved by Foreign Ministers on 28 November and published January 2024, positions quantum as a core arena of strategic competition with dual-use implications across computing, communications, and sensing/detection. The strategy's aims are to:

Accelerate responsible adoption to preclude adversary advantage.

Build a secure, resilient, and competitive allied quantum ecosystem, emphasizing coherent investment, allied cooperation, workforce development and protection, and enhanced situational awareness and information sharing.

Establish NATO as the principal transatlantic forum for quantum in defense and security—advancing shared understanding while protecting critical technologies from hostile exploitation.

Operationally, NATO adopts a "learn-by-doing" approach—embedding quantum considerations into operational concepts, defense planning, capability development, and standardization. As DIANA and the NATO Innovation Fund (NIF) become fully operational, their deep-tech pipelines will inform NATO's strategic posture and tighten links to the allied quantum industrial base.

Net effect: With the U.S. legislating PQC timelines and NATO institutionalizing quantum across defense planning, the Euro-Atlantic community has moved from aspiration to implementation, creating clear mandates, milestones, and mechanisms to achieve digital sovereignty in a quantum era.

Asian Perspectives on Quantum Strategies

On the Asian continent, several countries have begun to take early measures to anticipate quantum threats and opportunities.

China remains one of the most active nations in quantum cryptography and communications. In 2011, the National Space Science Center of the Chinese Academy of Sciences launched the Strategic Priority Programme on Space Science, with objectives that included:

Conducting large-scale experiments on entanglement and quantum transport.

Developing a wide-area quantum communication network to underpin long-distance, secure communications.

This program led to major milestones, including the Micius satellite, which enabled the first space-to-ground quantum-encrypted communications.

Russia, in 2023, collaborated with China to extend this progress, demonstrating quantum-secured communication between two earth stations 3,800 km apart—a step toward a wider Eurasian quantum communication infrastructure.

While national strategies across Asia vary in scope and focus, most emphasize technological sovereignty, communications security, and scientific leadership. However, it is notable that only Australia, in its National Quantum Strategy, explicitly articulates a central theme of building a trusted, ethical, and inclusive quantum ecosystem. This highlights a divergence between strategies centered on geopolitical competition and security imperatives (as in China and Russia) and those incorporating societal, ethical, and inclusive dimensions (as in Australia).

3.6.2 Ethical Responsibility of the Quantum Computing Service Provider towards the Consumer

The ethical implications of responsible research and innovation (RRI) provide an initial framework for developing a responsible quantum ecosystem. Such a framework establishes guidelines for researchers, industry, and policymakers to proactively address future challenges linked to:

Economic security – preventing monopolistic control or weaponization of quantum services.

Dual-use risks – ensuring quantum technologies are not exploited for malicious purposes.

Privacy – protecting consumers against vulnerabilities in the transition to post-quantum cryptography.

Product safety and liability – clarifying responsibility when quantum services fail or produce unforeseen consequences.

Fair competition – avoiding dominance by a small number of actors and ensuring accessibility.

Equality and inclusion – ensuring that the benefits of quantum technologies are not restricted to a privileged minority.

These challenges are closely intertwined with the broader concept of digital sovereignty, as already discussed. Digital sovereignty ensures that consumers, states, and organizations can retain control over data, infrastructure, and decision-making in a quantum-enabled world, fostering trustworthiness and resilience.

Quantum Computing, Trustworthiness, and Digital Sovereignty

For consumers to adopt quantum services with confidence, providers must embed trustworthiness at every level of design and delivery. This includes:

Transparency in algorithms, processes, and intended uses.

Accountability mechanisms that assign responsibility for errors, misuse, or bias.

Interoperability standards to prevent vendor lock-in and facilitate global cooperation.

In this sense, trustworthiness becomes the bridge between ethical responsibility and digital sovereignty, ensuring that sovereignty does not come at the cost of trust, and trust is not reduced to blind reliance on corporate or state promises.

Quantum Computing and the UN SDGs

Achieving these ethical objectives aligns closely with the United Nations Sustainable Development Goals (SDGs). Quantum computing offers potential contributions to several SDGs:

SDG 3 (Good Health and Well-being): accelerating drug discovery and medical simulations.

SDG 7 (Affordable and Clean Energy): optimizing energy grids and advancing material discovery for sustainable batteries.

SDG 9 (Industry, Innovation and Infrastructure): driving innovation in secure communications and computational science.

SDG 13 (Climate Action): enhancing climate modeling and mitigation strategies.

Trade-offs Between SDGs: An Example

Despite these benefits, trade-offs may arise. For instance, pursuing SDG 9 (Industry, Innovation and Infrastructure) by rapidly commercializing quantum computing could exacerbate inequalities (SDG 10) if access remains limited to wealthy corporations or nations. Similarly, prioritizing national security through quantum technologies may reinforce sovereignty (SDG 16: Peace, Justice, and Strong Institutions) but also risk curbing global collaboration needed for climate action (SDG 13).

Thus, quantum computing service providers carry a dual ethical responsibility: not only to their immediate consumers but also to society at large, ensuring that their practices advance sustainable development without undermining fairness, inclusivity, and trust.

3.6.2.1 Trustworthiness and Digital Sovereignty as a Requirement for Future Deployment of Quantum Computing in 6G

Big data is inherently correlated with unique patterns of individual behavior, meaning that even if personal identifiers are removed, privacy may not be fully safeguarded. Individuals or groups can often be re-identified through reconstituted datasets, exposing them to risks of surveillance, discrimination, or exploitation. Such risks arise primarily from weak data sovereignty (control) and digital sovereignty (ownership).

In the quantum domain, this issue is amplified. Most companies currently provide quantum computing services via the cloud, as the technology remains prohibitively expensive for individual ownership or widespread deployment. This creates a dual challenge:

Dependence on providers – individuals and organizations have little or no control over the governance of infrastructure.

Data exposure – users lack sovereignty over the collection, storage, and processing of their private data, mirroring the vulnerabilities of classical cloud computing but at higher stakes.

This results in a trustworthiness problem. As defined, trust in a network context refers to the "expected outcomes of communicating with a remote party in a session. The possible outcomes are either the positive value of the communication or being hacked or cheated in some way." In this sense, trustworthiness can be understood as the assurance that a system will perform as expected, without misuse, breach, or unintended harms. Without this assurance, scientific and technological progress may yield unintended negative consequences.

At the current stage, quantum computers remain far from their full potential. They are still subject to errors, instability, and scalability limitations. This transitional phase, however, provides a unique opportunity: to establish common responsibility and robust frameworks that ensure the deployment of quantum computing in 6G is both ethical and socially beneficial.

Embedding trustworthiness and digital sovereignty as requirements from the outset will help avoid repeating the mistakes of earlier technological revolutions, where progress often outpaced governance and ethical foresight. By doing so, quantum computing within 6G networks can evolve into a secure, transparent, and sovereign digital ecosystem that benefits all stakeholders rather than reinforcing existing vulnerabilities.

3.6.2.2 Impact of Quantum Computing on Sustainable Development Goals and Trade-offs

Quantum computing holds the potential to accelerate progress toward the 17 United Nations Sustainable Development Goals (SDGs), creating a more secure, equitable, and sustainable world for present and future generations. Although quantum technologies were not explicitly referenced in the 2015 SDG agenda, their rapid development positions them as possible catalysts to achieve major breakthroughs before the 2030 deadline.

Potential Contributions to SDGs

Quantum computing is expected to generate significant environmental and societal benefits in several domains, including:

Molecular simulation and materials discovery – supporting the development of sustainable materials, renewable energy technologies, and innovative drugs (aligned with SDG 3, SDG 7, and SDG 12).

Biological research – enabling advances in healthcare, food systems, and sustainable agriculture (aligned with SDG 2 and SDG 3).

Optimization and risk management in complex systems – improving efficiency in logistics, energy grids, and urban infrastructure (aligned with SDG 9, SDG 11, and SDG 13).

For example, Ford Motors explored quantum-inspired strategies to alleviate traffic congestion in Seattle, a major source of urban emissions. The study demonstrated that, compared to conventional "selfish" routing strategies, optimal routing powered by quantum algorithms reduced congestion by 73%, directly contributing to SDG 11 (Sustainable Cities and Communities) and SDG 13 (Climate Action).

SDG Trade-offs

As with all disruptive technologies, quantum computing may also exacerbate tensions between competing sustainability goals:

A well-known trade-off exists between SDG 2 (Zero Hunger) and SDG 15 (Life on Land). Increasing food production to eradicate hunger can intensify greenhouse gas emissions, expand land and water use, and threaten biodiversity. Quantum solutions may help optimize agricultural practices, but they cannot fully eliminate this fundamental tension.

The cloud-based availability of quantum computing supports SDG 9 (Industry, Innovation, and Infrastructure) and SDG 10 (Reduced Inequalities) by enabling global access to advanced computation without requiring local ownership of expensive infrastructure. However, this comes at the expense of digital sovereignty, raising concerns about dependence on a small number of technology providers and the potential exploitation of user data.

The Need for Proactive Regulation

If regulation lags behind technological deployment, societies risk repeating the mistakes made with previous digital revolutions, where governance was reactive rather than anticipatory. To avoid this, states must adopt proactive regulatory frameworks for quantum technologies, embedding principles of digital sovereignty, ethical responsibility, and sustainability from the outset. This approach will ensure that quantum computing becomes a force for equitable development, rather than reinforcing existing global inequalities or undermining fundamental rights.

3.6.3 Solutions and Regulations

Ensuring that quantum computing remains accessible while protecting users requires a combination of technical solutions and regulatory frameworks. At the European level, several initiatives are already laying the foundation for secure and trustworthy quantum cloud computing.

1. Quantum Internet Alliance (QIA) and Quantum Blind Computing

The Quantum Internet Alliance (QIA) is working toward building a quantum internet network that integrates security and privacy into its design. One of the core approaches under development is quantum blind computing, a method that ensures that the server performing the computation cannot access the client's private data.

The protocol operates in four main steps:

Preparation of quantum states (client-side) – The client prepares and transmits qubits securely to the quantum server.

Server-side circuit construction – The quantum server arranges these qubits into a quantum circuit without knowledge of the client's input or intended computation.

Execution and measurement – The server executes the computation, performs measurements, and generates results.

Feedback and decoding (client-side) – The server sends back only classical information, which the client decodes to obtain the final output, ensuring data confidentiality.

This approach directly addresses trustworthiness and digital sovereignty concerns, as the server is mathematically prevented from learning about the client's computation or sensitive data.

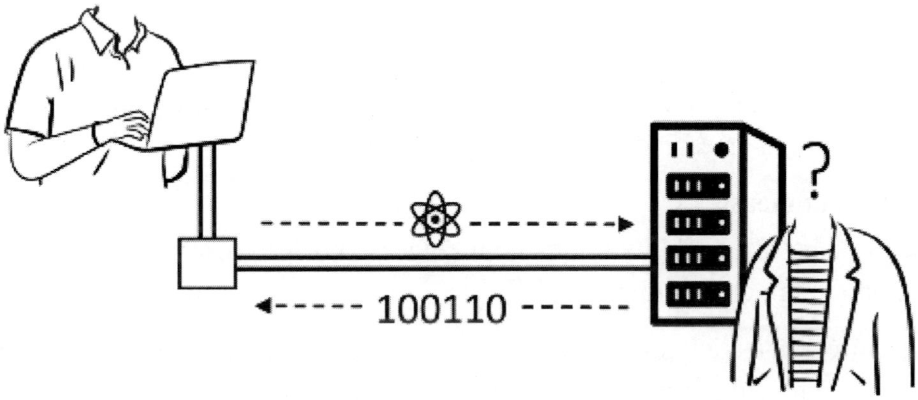

Fig.3.8 The blind quantum computing basic scheme. The malicious server is on the right, and the client is on the left.

2. Schirmprojekt Quantenkommunikation Deutschland (SQuaD)

In Germany, the SQuaD project (Schirmprojekt Quantenkommunikation Deutschland) plays a critical role in bridging basic research and industrial deployment of quantum communication technologies. Its long-term aim is to transfer quantum communication from the laboratory to real-world applications, enabling secure integration into industries and critical infrastructures.

Through its standardization workshops, SQuaD has identified several regulatory and technical gaps and proposed potential solutions. A key focus is on:

Protection profiles for quantum communication systems.

Hardware authentication and validation standards.

Implementation guidelines to ensure interoperability and security.

By filling these gaps, SQuaD contributes to establishing a trustworthy regulatory framework that aligns industrial practices with the highest standards of cybersecurity, while promoting digital sovereignty at both the national and European levels.

3. Toward a European Framework

Together, initiatives like QIA and SQuaD provide a blueprint for a European regulatory strategy that balances user protection, accessibility, and innovation. They also highlight the importance of cross-border collaboration, ensuring that Europe can compete globally in the quantum era while safeguarding ethical responsibility, privacy, and security.

This is a strong addition to your regulatory mapping. What you've built here is essentially a panorama of national and regional quantum strategies, and Italy's 2024 bill fits neatly into that global context—though with some key gaps.

Here's last point (the seventh measure) so it ties directly back to digital sovereignty and ethical responsibility:

Positioning: Italy's six macro-areas cover the technological, economic, and talent pipeline well, but they lack explicit provisions for user protection and trustworthiness, which are central themes in digital sovereignty.

Extension (7th measure)

Ensure consumer accessibility to quantum devices and services without disproportionate reliance on foreign cloud providers.

Introduce user-protection protocols against malicious or negligent service providers (e.g., obligations for transparency, explainability of algorithms, liability mechanisms).

Encourage open standards and certification schemes (possibly modeled after QIA/SQuaD) to guarantee trustworthiness and ethical alignment.

Implication: This seventh measure doesn't just close a gap; it reframes Italy's quantum bill from being infrastructure- and innovation-heavy to being sovereignty- and society-ready.

☞ In short: Without this layer, Italy risks advancing quantum R&D and commercialization while leaving unresolved the core issue of trust, privacy, and accountability that will determine user adoption.

3.6.4 Virtuous Governance and Global Coordination

The technical solutions and regulations outlined above can only be effective if different partners at the global level accomplish **cooperation, collaboration, and coordination**. A virtuous governance model for cloud quantum computing in 6G should be based on the **3C framework**:

Cooperation – Cloud quantum computing in future 6G can serve as a structural tool to foster cooperation between allied countries, thereby strengthening digital sovereignty and avoiding dependency on non-aligned actors.

Collaboration – Strengthening global networks through public–private partnerships ensures that innovation is distributed across research centers, industry, and governments, with shared accountability and mutual benefit.

Coordination – Efficient strategic coordination, particularly in organizing and protecting critical infrastructures, is a prerequisite to achieving digital sovereignty and building resilience against systemic risks.

Only by pursuing these three objectives in a balanced manner will it be possible to foster a **trusted, ethical, and inclusive quantum ecosystem**, one that integrates security, sovereignty, and societal well-being.

3.6.5 Post-Quantum Cryptography Standards

In parallel with this governance vision, **cryptographic preparedness** has reached a milestone. In September 2024, the U.S. Department of Commerce's National Institute of Standards and Technology (NIST) finalized its **principal set of encryption algorithms** designed to withstand cyberattacks from quantum computers. These algorithms, developed under NIST's post-quantum cryptography (PQC) standardization project, mark the first completed standards that are now ready for immediate deployment.

This development addresses the imminent risk that quantum computers—operating in radically different ways from classical machines—could break the cryptographic systems underpinning the privacy and security of virtually all online communications. The adoption of PQC standards represents not only a **technical safeguard** but also a **geopolitical necessity**, ensuring that service providers and users alike are protected in the emerging quantum era.

3.6.6 Implications for the SDGs

However, these measures also carry **societal implications**. On one hand, robust PQC standards promote **trust, equality, and secure digital participation** (aligned with SDGs 9 and 10). On the other hand, their implementation requires global harmonization of standards and equitable access, otherwise risks of technological asymmetry could **reinforce inequalities** between advanced and developing nations. This underlines the importance of embedding PQC adoption within the **3C governance model**, ensuring that cryptographic resilience contributes not only to digital sovereignty but also to the achievement of the UN's SDGs.

3.6.7 Ensuring Trustworthy Quantum Service Providers

Ensuring a trustworthy service provider for quantum computing is essential for the deployment of future 6G communication networks. Quantum technologies can only generate societal benefits if service providers act with ethical responsibility and build transparent, trustworthy connections with their users.

In the worst-case scenario—where providers fail to uphold this responsibility—a trade-off emerges between digital sovereignty and accessibility. Such a trade-off would not only weaken user trust but also risk undermining compliance with the Sustainable Development Goals (SDGs) by deepening technological inequalities and security vulnerabilities.

To address this, technological regulations based on methods such as blind quantum computing and Quantum Physical Unclonable Functions (QuPUFs) are indispensable. However, technical safeguards alone are not enough: a corresponding political commitment is required to ensure that regulation, standardization, and governance mechanisms uphold both digital sovereignty and equitable access. Only through this dual approach—technological and political—can quantum computing be integrated into society in a manner that is secure, ethical, and sustainable.

Chapter - 4
Quantum Algorithm

A unitary transformation, which embodies the correct logic of the algorithm, is the fundamental building block of a quantum algorithm. In a separate process (which turns out to be rather difficult), its input register $|r\rangle$ is constructed. The output $|s\rangle$ is obtained from the unitary transformation, and its result is determined in a separate measurement step.

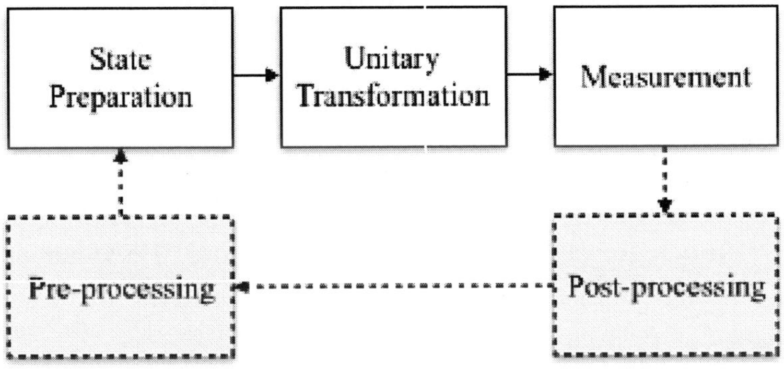

Fig.4.1 The fundamental framework of a quantum algorithm.

The total algorithm can become hybrid by choosing to do some pre- or post-processing in a classical context.

Especially, many effective algorithms in a NISQ environment make use of conventional processing to reduce the execution time on a quantum computer: the idea is to minimize decoherence and gate errors by spending just a small amount of time on a noisy quantum machine.

Variational Quantum Eigensolver, a hybrid approach for calculating eigenvalues, is one example. This may be accomplished by computing and measuring expectation values using a parameterized quantum algorithm, which is then post-processed on a classical computer. A traditional optimization phase is included in the postprocessing to calculate new parameters and minimize the measured expectation values. The algorithm's importance stems from the understanding of eigenvalues in resolving several real-world issues.

The Quantum Approximate Optimization Algorithm, which is employed to address combinatorial optimization issues, provides an additional illustration. It computes a quantum machine state, the values of which are related to the values of the cost function that has to be maximized. A parameterized quantum method is used to calculate the state, and as previously, classical algorithms are used in a post-processing stage to optimize these parameters. The significance of this approach is also evident given that many machine learning algorithms necessitate tackling optimization issues.

Problems with Integer Factorization and Hidden Subgroups

Because they have the ability to crack traditional crypto systems, quantum algorithms for polynomial time integer factorization are arguably the most well-known and frequently discussed quantum algorithms. Given a summary of the integer factorization process along with justifications and evidence for its accuracy.

Grover's quantum search algorithm

Another well-known quantum algorithm is Grover's algorithm. Grover's algorithm is a method for figuring out a function's properties given a quantum black-box representation of the function; it basically involves "searching" for a specific element within the function's domain.

Adiabatic quantum algorithms

In quantum adiabatic algorithms, computation is accomplished by developing a quantum system whose Schrodinger equation governs its behavior. Provided an example of a quantum adiabatic algorithm together with a summary of the mathematical model of quantum adiabatic computation.

4.1 The Quantum Software Stack

A software stack that supports quantum computer programming is depicted below in its typical configuration. The figure details how this stack has been adapted by significant suppliers.

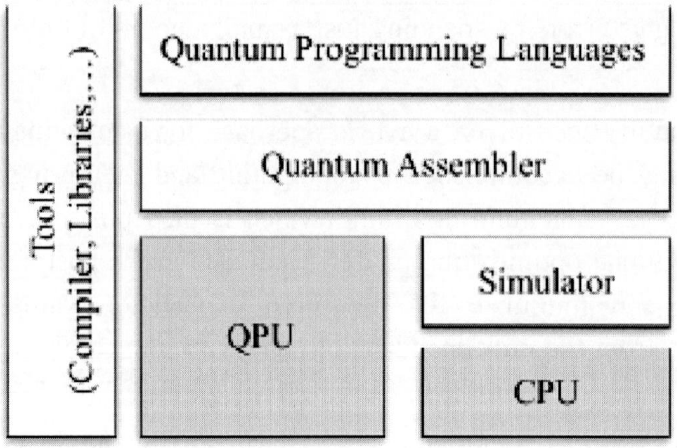

Fig.4.2 The fundamental design of the quantum software stack of today.

The core component of the stack is a quantum assembler, which offers a textual representation of the essential unitary transformations needed to define a quantum algorithm.

Quantum programming languages are available that house the components of the quantum assembler in a manner more recognizable to conventional programmers due to the extremely low level of a quantum assembler; yet, the assembler flavor still predominates. Additionally, there are features to connect to simulators, quantum machines (also known as quantum processing units, or QPUs), etc.

Additionally, libraries for quantum programming languages offer subroutine implementations of frequently used quantum algorithms.

An executable program that can operate on a specific QPU is created from a quantum assembler program by a compiler. Another option is for the compiler to convert the quantum assembler into a format that a simulator on a traditional CPU can use.

4.2 Characterization of Quantum Integers

4.2.1 The problem of integer factorization

To put it simply, the integer factorization issue is: given a composite N, find m prime numbers p1,..., pm such that p1 ×.. × pm = N. Particularly noteworthy is the situation where m = 2 (the composite is a multiple of only two primes), since the RSA public-key cryptosystem uses a composite number with these characteristics, allowing untrusted parties to encrypt using A public key, however this encrypted data can only be decrypted by entities who possess a private key. The difficulty of factoring the composite into two primes is the foundation of RSA's security. Data encoded with RSA can be decoded without a private key if such a factorization feat is achievable (efficiently, of course), which would compromise the cryptosystem's security. There is currently no known polynomial time classical factoring algorithm;

4.2.2 Algorithm for A quantum integer Factorization

By presenting a quantum method for integer factorization, Peter Shor's seminal work "Algorithms for quantum computation: Discrete logarithms and factoring" from 1994 rocked the computer science community. It is widely acknowledged that Shor's groundbreaking work sparked a broader interest in quantum computing, primarily due to the intriguing (and perhaps dangerous) possibility of an algorithm that may perfectly solve the issues upon which many cryptosystems are based. We will examine Shor's original algorithm in this text by applying the eigenvalue/phase estimation analysis method.

The factors of a given number are not directly generated by the quantum algorithms that are actually employed in "quantum" methods for integer factorization. Instead, order finding is a related problem that is resolved by the quantum techniques used. Finding a function f (x) such that f (x) = f (x + r) with the lowest period r is known as order finding. By using the function f (x) = a^x mod N to solve the order-finding problem for some a ∈ Z, a < N, we are able to solve the integer factorization problem.

The following is how quantum integer factorization techniques typically appear:

1. A series of effective classical steps reduces the problem to the order-finding problem given the input information (a huge composite). In particular, we start by selecting a random number a < N given an integer N. Next, calculate gcd(a,N). If $gcd(a, N) \neq 1$, then We're done when a and gcd(a,N) are factors of N.
2. A quantum algorithm solves the order finding problem (with high probability) in conjunction with an effective classical approach that uses continuous fractions. For f (x) = a^x mod N, the order-finding problem is resolved by a quantum method. Later sections will cover this algorithm (as well as its classical component) in greater detail.
3. The quantum algorithm's output is efficiently verified by a second series of classical steps. We now determine whether r is odd or $a^{r/2} = -1$ mod N. We return to step 1 in each scenario. We are finished if the factors of N are $gcd(a^{r/2} \pm 1, N)$.

Naturally, the astute reader has several concerns about such a process. In particular, how can the integer factorization problem be reduced to an order-finding problem, and how can we determine that the numbers generated in the final step are factors of N? A proof of the traditional components of steps 1 and 3 of this algorithm can be found in the subsection that follows.

4.2.3 Proof of the Classical Part in Quantum-Inger Factorization

The factorization algorithm's initial step involves choosing a random integer, a, and determining the function f (x) = a^x mod N's minimum period, r. Given that r is the period of f (x) = a^x mod N, we obtain

$a^r \equiv 1 \mod N$

By step 3, if r is even, as it will be, this turns into

$$\begin{aligned} a^r &\equiv 1 \mod N \\ a^r - 1 &\equiv 0 \mod N \\ (a^{r/2} - 1)(a^{r/2} + 1) &\equiv 0 \mod N. \end{aligned}$$

$a_0 = a^{r/2} - 1$and $a_1 = a^{r/2} + 1$ are assumed. $N|(a^{r/2} - 1)(a^{r/2} + 1)$ or $N|a_0 a_1$ is implied by this. Keep in mind that the algorithm

N cannot divide a0 since r is the lowest integer such that $a^r = 1$.

We make sure that N does not divide a1 by checking for this and restarting if it does.

N has a non-trivial factor in common with both a0 and a1, if we can demonstrate that N does not divide any of them. Accordingly, N must have the factors $(N, a^{r/2} - 1)$and $(N, a^{r/2} + 1)$.

Here is a contradiction-based evidence of thisa_1 $(gcd(N, a_0) = gcd(N, a_1 = 1)$. First, assume that N does not split either a0 or a1. We have kN = a0a1 for some integer k since N|a0a1 (as previously demonstrated). According to this, there are numbers m, n such that $ma_0 + nN = 1$. But take aware that

$$\begin{aligned} ma_0 + nN &= 1 \\ ma_1a_0 + nNa_1 &= a_1 \\ mkN + na_1N &= a_1 \end{aligned}$$

This defies our original assumption by implying N|a1.

4.3 Order Identification

Through the use of quantum algorithms and classical algorithms utilizing continuing fractions, it is possible to determine the order of the function f (x) as previously mentioned. Below figure provides a high-level summary. Comprising a quantum circuit for this method and the required classical steps that follow. The circuit is made up of an inverse quantum Fourier transform, a controlled operator that performs a function (sometimes called modular exponentiation), and a quantum Fourier transform.

This quantum algorithm can be conceptually understood in relation to two other problems for which we have quantum algorithms: phase estimation and eigenvalue estimation. In particular,

1. One way to conceptualize order finding is as an application of eigenvalue estimation.
2. Eigenvalue estimation can be thought of as a phase estimation application.
3. The inverse quantum Fourier transform can be used to frame phase estimation.

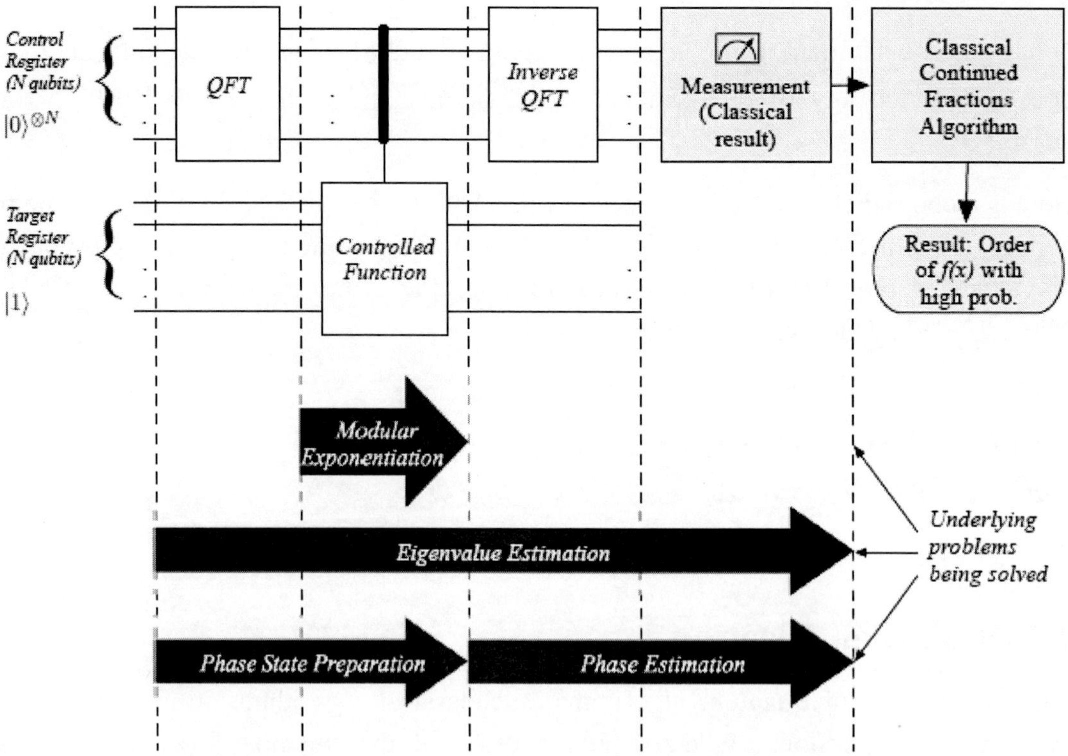

Fig.4.3 Overview of high level order-finding algorithm.

The fundamental connection between phase and eigenvalue estimation issues and the quantum circuit's stages is also depicted in the above graphic. The phase estimation analysis was initially presented shortly after Shor's original publication. Analyzing the algorithm in this way is not required (Shor's article does it differently from Kitaev's), but it does introduce practical primitives that can be applied to other algorithms.

The primary concepts underlying the reduction of order discovery to eigenvalue estimation and the classical continuous fractions approach needed to finish the process will be illustrated in the next two subsections, respectively. We must first introduce the phase and eigenvalues estimation problems in order to start explaining these ideas.

- Finding a reliable estimate of the phase parameter ω given the quantum state is the phase estimation problem. The inverse quantum Fourier transform is used for this phase estimation procedure.

$$|\psi\rangle = \frac{1}{2^n}\sum_{y=0}^{2^n-1} e^{2\pi i\omega y}|y\rangle,$$

The eigenvalue estimation problem is the challenge of obtaining a fair estimate of ω given a quantum operator U with eigenstate $|\psi\rangle$and eigenvalue $e^{2\pi i\omega}$. The first step in the quantum algorithm for eigenvalue estimation is to create a target register with the relevant eigenstate (in this case $|\psi\rangle$)and a control register with the value $|0\rangle^{\otimes n}$. We can now measure the first register to obtain an estimate ˜ω of ω after the algorithm executes the map $|0\rangle^{\otimes n}|\psi\rangle \rightarrow |\tilde{\omega}\rangle|\psi\rangle$. It is crucial to remember that the eigenvalue estimation procedure can be thought of as a two-stage algorithm consisting of the subsequent stages:

1. The eigenvalue in question is a phase term in a state that is created during the state preparation stage.
2. A use of the phase estimation procedure to identify the phase term in the recently generated state and, consequently, the desired eigenvalue.

4.3.1 Finding the order as an estimate of the quantum Eigen value

The order finding process can be deduced given effective strategies for resolving the eigenvalue and phase estimation issues. Think about an operator *U*a that is defined as

$$U_a : |s\rangle \rightarrow |sa \mod N\rangle$$

in which 0 ≤ s < N. Note that the state

$$|u_k\rangle = \frac{1}{\sqrt{r}} \sum_{s=0}^{r-1} e^{-2\pi i \frac{k}{r} s} |a^s \mod N\rangle$$

is an *U*a eigenstate with the matching eigenvalue $e^{2\pi i \frac{k}{r} s}$. This is demonstrated as follows:

$$\begin{aligned} U_a|u_k\rangle &= U_a\left[\frac{1}{\sqrt{r}} \sum_{s=0}^{r-1} e^{-2\pi i \frac{k}{r} s} |a^s \mod N\rangle\right] \\ &= \frac{1}{\sqrt{r}} \sum_{s=0}^{r-1} e^{-2\pi i \frac{k}{r} s} U_a |a^s \mod N\rangle \\ &= \frac{1}{\sqrt{r}} \sum_{s=0}^{r-1} \left[e^{2\pi i \frac{k}{r}} e^{-2\pi i \frac{k}{r}}\right] e^{-2\pi i \frac{k}{r} s} |a^{s+1} \mod N\rangle \\ &= e^{2\pi i \frac{k}{r}} \frac{1}{\sqrt{r}} \sum_{s=0}^{r-1} e^{-2\pi i \frac{k}{r}(s+1)} |a^{s+1} \mod N\rangle. \end{aligned}$$

The following equation's sum can be made simpler as

$$\begin{aligned} &\sum_{s=0}^{r-1} e^{-2\pi i \frac{k}{r}(s+1)}|a^{s+1} \mod N\rangle \\ =& \sum_{s=1}^{r-1} e^{-2\pi i \frac{k}{r}s}|a^s \mod N\rangle + e^{-2\pi i \frac{k}{r}r}|a^r \mod N\rangle \\ =& \sum_{s=1}^{r-1} e^{-2\pi i \frac{k}{r}s}|a^s \mod N\rangle + e^{-2\pi i \frac{k}{r}0}|a^0 \mod N\rangle \\ =& \sum_{s=0}^{r-1} e^{-2\pi i \frac{k}{r}s}|a^s \mod N\rangle. \end{aligned}$$

Thus, we have

$$\begin{aligned} U_a|u_k\rangle &= e^{2\pi i \frac{k}{r}} \frac{1}{\sqrt{r}} \sum_{s=0}^{r-1} e^{-2\pi i \frac{k}{r}(s+1)}|a^{s+1} \mod N\rangle \\ &= e^{2\pi i \frac{k}{r}}|u_k\rangle, \end{aligned}$$

This demonstrates that Ua's eigenstate is UK.

By calculating the eigenvalue $e^{2\pi i \frac{k}{r}}$ of an eigenstate u_k, we may ascertain r and, using a continuous fractions procedure, calculate the period (as seen in the following subsection). To obtain this eigenvalue, we can apply the eigenvalue estimation procedure. To prepare the state $|\widetilde{k/r}\rangle|u_k\rangle$, we need to know r, thus we cannot just apply the eigenvalue estimation procedure to a random state $|0\rangle|u_k\rangle$ for $0 \le k < r-1$. But, as we will demonstrate in a moment, we may apply the technique to $\frac{1}{\sqrt{r}}\sum_{k=0}^{r-1}|u_k\rangle$ without knowing r (the eigenvectors superposed uniformly). Using this state and the eigenvalue estimation process, the map will be completed:

$$|0\rangle\left[\frac{1}{\sqrt{r}}\sum_{k=0}^{r-1}|u_k\rangle\right] \mapsto \frac{1}{\sqrt{r}}\sum_{k=0}^{r-1}|\widetilde{k/r}\rangle|u_k\rangle.$$

Here, we may estimate k/r by measuring the first register, where k is a random integer between 0 and r − 1.

Since it is possible to demonstrate that $\left[\frac{1}{\sqrt{r}}\sum_{k=0}^{r-1}|u_k\rangle\right]=1$, we can accomplish this without knowing r by using the state $|0\rangle|1\rangle$ rather than $|0\rangle \frac{1}{\sqrt{r}}\sum_{k=0}^{r-1}|u_k\rangle$. Examine the amplitude of the state $|1\rangle$ in the superposition $\frac{1}{\sqrt{r}}\sum_{k=0}^{r-1}|u_k\rangle$ to illustrate this. Let $a_{|m\rangle}$ represent the amplitude in this superposition that corresponds to $|m\rangle$. Given that

$$\frac{1}{\sqrt{r}}\sum_{k=0}^{r-1}|u_k\rangle = \frac{1}{\sqrt{r}}\sum_{k=0}^{r-1}\frac{1}{\sqrt{r}}\sum_{s=0}^{r-1}e^{-2\pi i\frac{k}{r}s}|a^s \mod N\rangle$$
$$= \frac{1}{r}\sum_{k=0}^{r-1}\sum_{s=0}^{r-1}e^{-2\pi i\frac{k}{r}s}|a^s \mod N\rangle.$$

Clearly,

$$a_{|m\rangle} = \frac{1}{r}\sum_{k=0}^{r-1}\left[\sum_{\{s|a^s \mod N=m,\ s\leq r-1\}} e^{-2\pi i\frac{k}{r}s}\right].$$

Use the fact that s ≡ 0 mod $r \iff |a^s \mod N\rangle = |1\rangle$ to calculate the amplitude of $|1\rangle$. With this, we have

$$a_{|1\rangle} = \frac{1}{r}\sum_{k=0}^{r-1}\left[\sum_{\{s=0\}} e^{-2\pi i\frac{k}{r}s}\right] = \frac{1}{r}\sum_{k=0}^{r-1}e^{-2\pi i\frac{k}{r}0} = \frac{1}{r}r = 1.$$

Given that $\sum_{m=0}^{r-1}a_{|m\rangle} = 1$, we may deduce that $a_{|m\rangle} = 0$ for all $m \neq 1$, meaning that $\frac{1}{\sqrt{r}}\sum_{k=0}^{r-1}|u_k\rangle = |1\rangle$ as required.

4.3.2 Finding the Order: Persistent Fractions

We have seen how the eigenvalue estimation algorithm's measurement at the end provided us with an estimate of k/r. We will discover later that this estimate is actually a number x, so that $x/2^n$ is an estimate of k/r. Using this estimate, we now go over how to truly determine the function's ranking in inquiry.

Let's start by going over the idea of a continuing fraction. The form of a continuing fraction [a0,..., aM] is

$$[a_0, ..., a_M] = a_0 + \frac{1}{a_1 + \frac{1}{a_2 + \frac{1}{... + \frac{1}{a a_M}}}}$$

where, for any k, ak is an integer. The definition of a continuing fraction pn/qn's n-th convergent is

$$[a_0, ..., a_n] = \frac{p_n}{q_n}$$

Continued fractions can be used to express any rational number in terms of integers. The continuous fractions algorithm can be used to create such a representation. The following is the algorithm:

1. Let a/b be a rational number.
2. Split a/b is first divided into its fractional and integer components. Let c be the outcome of dividing a by b using an integer. Thus, we have:

$$\frac{a}{b} = c + \frac{a \mod b}{b}$$

3. Reverse, the next step is to invert the fractional component. This provides:

$$\frac{a}{b} = c + \frac{1}{\frac{b}{a \mod b}}$$

4. The following step repeats the process using the fraction $\frac{b}{a \mod b}$

In a/b in $O(L)$, if a and b are L-bit integers, doing this repeatedly yields the continuing fraction representation of a/b.

Why are the convergents produced during the computation of continuing fraction representations of importance to us? The rationale is that if a fraction k/r equals

$$\left| \frac{x}{2^n} - \frac{k}{r} \right| \leq \frac{1}{2r^2}$$

Therefore the list of convergents of $\frac{x}{2^n}$ contains k/r. This will enable us to calculate the period r at last.

Two iterations of the eigenvalue estimation procedure are sufficient to accomplish this. We will measure a value $\frac{x_1}{2^n}$ on the first run of the eigenvalue estimation technique, and then utilize the continuing fractions algorithm to obtain a value

$$\frac{k_1}{r} = \frac{c_1}{r_1} \text{ where } GCD(c_1, r_1) = 1$$

Because k1 and r may have a same factor, we might not be able to calculate r by looking at the resulting fraction. Because of this, the procedure must be run a second time in order to compute another fraction by measuring a different number, $\frac{x_2}{2^n}$.

$$\frac{k_2}{r} = \frac{c_2}{r_2} \text{ where } GCD(c_2, r_2) = 1$$

We can now calculate r = LCM (r1, r2) since both r1 and r2 divide r.

4.4 Estimation of the Quantum Phase

Producing a decent estimate of the phase parameter ω given the quantum state $|\psi\rangle = \frac{1}{2^n}\sum_{y=0}^{2^n-1} e^{2\pi i\omega y}|y\rangle$. is the aim of the phase estimation technique. The quantum Fourier transform (QFT) and the inverse quantum Fourier transform (iQFT) are two quantum operators that should be reviewed before moving on to the quantum phase estimation algorithm:

$$QFT \;:\; |x\rangle \mapsto \frac{1}{\sqrt{2^n}} \sum_{y=0}^{2^n-1} e^{2\pi i \frac{x}{2^n} y}|y\rangle$$

$$iQFT \;:\; \|x\rangle \mapsto \frac{1}{\sqrt{2^n}} \sum_{y=0}^{2^n-1} -e^{2\pi i \frac{x}{2^n} y}|y\rangle$$

The inverse QFT applied to the input state is all that makes up the quantum phase estimation technique. We can approximate the phase term by measuring the quantum state following this procedure. The proof that this works will be summarized in this section.

4.4.1 Overview of the phase estimation circuit's accuracy

Hadamard gates and controlled inverse rotation gates are the two types of gates. The following matrix defines the single qubit Hadamard gate:

$$H = \frac{1}{\sqrt{2}}\begin{bmatrix} 1 & 1 \\ 1 & -1 \end{bmatrix}$$

The definitions of a single qubit rotation gate R_k and its inverse R_k^{-1} are as follows:

$$R_k = \begin{bmatrix} 1 & 0 \\ 0 & e^{\frac{2\pi i}{2^k}} \end{bmatrix}, \quad R_k^{-1} = \begin{bmatrix} 1 & 0 \\ 0 & e^{\frac{-2\pi i}{2^k}} \end{bmatrix}$$

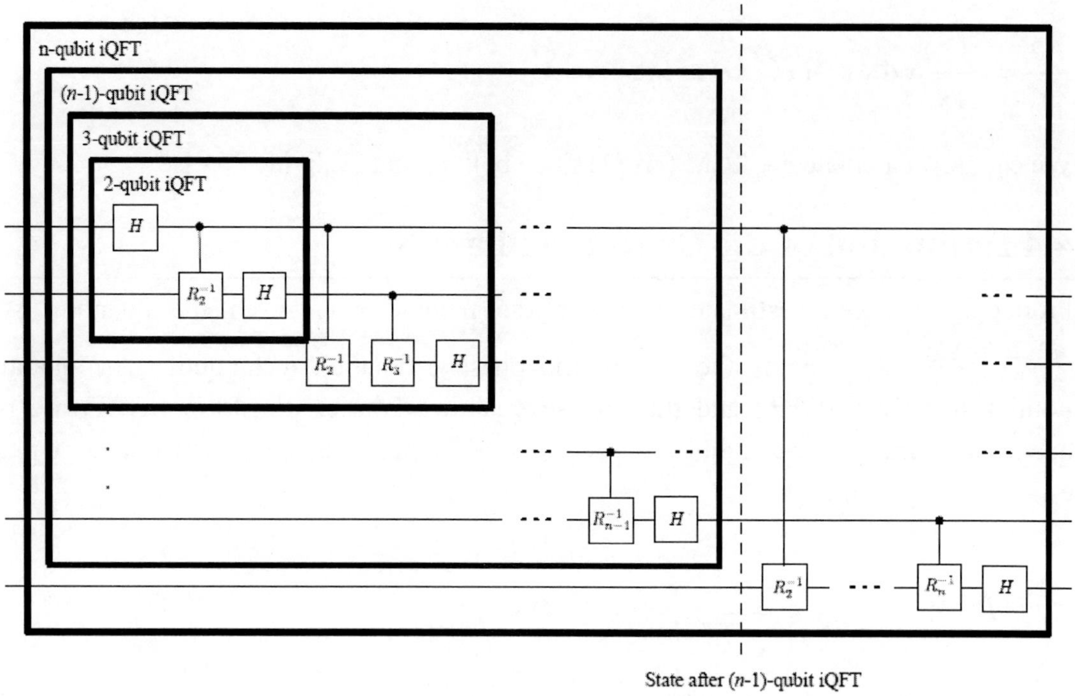

Fig.4.4 Circuit diagram for the Inverse Quantum Fourier Transform (iQFT).

The definition of the n + 1-qubit controlled gate controlled − G is as follows, given an n-qubit gate G operating on an n-qubit state |ψ}:

$$\text{controlled}-G : \begin{cases} |0\rangle|\psi\rangle & \mapsto & |0\rangle|\psi\rangle \\ |1\rangle|\psi\rangle & \mapsto & |1\rangle G|\psi\rangle \end{cases}$$

where G is a gate with one qubit. Now that we have these concepts, we can illustrate how the circuit in the image above uses the phase estimation process. The phase term ω = 0.x1x2... will be represented in binary in this sketch, with x1, x2,... being binary numbers. For clarity, divide this proof into two main sections, both of which can be completed using induction. The descriptions of these two compositions follow.

1. Lemma of state decomposition. An n-qubit quantum state of the type $|\psi\rangle = \frac{1}{2^n}\sum_{y=0}^{2^n-1} e^{2\pi i\omega y}|y\rangle$ is started at the start of the phase estimation process. To evaluate the circuit in the above given figure, it is helpful to obtain the expression for the state of each individual qubit. The state |ψ} can be expressed as the tensor product of n 1-qubit states using the connection below:

$$\frac{1}{\sqrt{2^n}}\sum_{y=0}^{2^n-1} e^{2\pi i\omega y}|y\rangle$$
$$= \left(\frac{|0\rangle + e^{2\pi i(2^{n-1}\omega)}|1\rangle}{\sqrt{2}}\right)$$
$$\otimes \left(\frac{|0\rangle + e^{2\pi i(2^{n-2}\omega)}|1\rangle}{\sqrt{2}}\right) \otimes \ldots \otimes \left(\frac{|0\rangle + e^{2\pi i(\omega)}|1\rangle}{\sqrt{2}}\right)$$

Induction makes it simple to demonstrate this relationship. We only need to re-form the sum on the right side of the equation and expand the tensor representation on the left to demonstrate the base case (for n = 1). We begin the induction phase by tensoring both sides of the equation with the state of the n + 1-th qubit and using the relation for n-qubits. This phase is finished by simplification of the resultant total.

2. Formulation of recursive iQFT circuits

The shaded portions of the diagram in the preceding figure show how the circuit can be defined recursively. This plus the first step's lemma allow us to inductively illustrate how the circuit works. We begin by looking at the n = 2 qubit basic case. The first qubit undergoes a Hadamard operation, the second qubit undergoes a controlled rotation operation (using the first qubit as the "control" line), and the second qubit undergoes a second Hadamard operation. The system's condition at the start of this circuit is:

$$\text{Initial state (2 qubits)} = \left(\frac{|0\rangle + e^{2\pi i(0.x_2)}|1\rangle}{\sqrt{2}}\right) \otimes \left(\frac{|0\rangle + e^{2\pi i(0.x_1x_2)}|1\rangle}{\sqrt{2}}\right)$$

As demonstrated below, we can now demonstrate that applying the previously specified set of operations to this initial state produces the intended result:

$$\text{Initial state} \xrightarrow{H\ applied\ to\ qubit\ 1} |x_2\rangle\left(\frac{|0\rangle + e^{2\pi i(0.x_1x_2)}|1\rangle}{\sqrt{2}}\right)$$
$$\xrightarrow{Controlled\ rotation\ on\ qubit\ 2} |x_2\rangle\left(\frac{|0\rangle + e^{2\pi i(0.x_1)}|1\rangle}{\sqrt{2}}\right)$$
$$\xrightarrow{H\ applied\ to\ qubit\ 2} |x_2\rangle|x_1\rangle.$$

Assume that the circuit operates for n qubits and then proceed to demonstrate its operation for n + 1 qubits, leaving just the induction step to complete. The n-qubit iQFT estimates the phase parameter (in binary) to be $\omega_n = 0.x_2 \ldots x_{n+1}$, which will simplify the subsequent manipulations.

In this n + 1-qubit iQFT will enable us to estimate the phase parameter $\omega_{n+1} = 0.x_1 \ldots x_{n+1}$. Think about the system's condition following the n-qubit QFT (designated as "State after (n − 1)-qubit iQFT") in Figure

$$|x_2\rangle \ldots |x_{n+1}\rangle \left(\frac{|0\rangle + e^{2\pi i (0.x_1 \ldots x_{n+1})}|1\rangle}{\sqrt{2}} \right)$$

We can calculate the final state by applying the remaining circuit operations, which include a Hadamard gate and a series of controlled rotation gates:

$$\text{State after } (n-1)\text{–qubit iQFT}$$
$$\xrightarrow{R_n^{-1} \ldots R_2^{-1} \text{ on qubit } n+1} |x_{n+1}\rangle \ldots |x_2\rangle \left(\frac{|0\rangle + e^{2\pi i (0.x_1)}|1\rangle}{\sqrt{2}} \right)$$
$$\xrightarrow{H \text{ applied to qubit } n+1} |x_{n+1}\rangle \ldots |x_2\rangle |x_1\rangle.$$

Since this phase state is what we needed, the proof is finished.

We shall measure the state encoding the phase parameter ω with probability 1 if ω is of the form $0.x_1 \ldots x_n$, if we measure the quantum state at the end of the phase estimation circuit depicted in this section. Although it is less accurate, the circuit can still be used to estimate various values of ω. It can be demonstrated that if $\frac{x}{2^n} \leq \omega \leq \frac{x+1}{2^n}$, Next, with probability $\frac{8}{\pi^2}$, we shall measure the states that correspond to the binary representations of x or x + 1.

4.5 Eigenvalue Assessment

We can now develop an algorithm for eigenvalue estimation since we have seen an effective technique for phase estimation. The following is the eigenvalue estimation problem: Given a quantum operator U with eigenstate |ψ} and eigenvalue $e^{2\pi i \omega}$. calculate the parameter ω. The remedy. The solution to this issue is to construct a quantum state using a series of controlled operators, after which we can calculate ω using the phase estimation procedure.

Let's start by looking at a controlled version of operator U. Dial c − U to reach this operator. Let's examine the results of applying this operation to a control qubit in the state $\frac{|0\rangle+|1\rangle}{\sqrt{2}}$ and the target state |ψ}:

$$
\begin{aligned}
c\text{–}U\left[\left(\frac{|0\rangle+|1\rangle}{\sqrt{2}}\right)|\psi\rangle\right] &= c\text{–}U\left(\frac{|0\rangle|\psi\rangle}{\sqrt{2}}\right)+c\text{–}U\left(\frac{|1\rangle|\psi\rangle}{\sqrt{2}}\right)\\
&= \frac{|0\rangle|\psi\rangle}{\sqrt{2}}+\frac{e^{2\pi i\omega}|1\rangle|\psi\rangle}{\sqrt{2}}\\
&= \left(\frac{|0\rangle+e^{2\pi i\omega}|1\rangle}{\sqrt{2}}\right)|\psi\rangle
\end{aligned}
$$

The eigenvalue $e^{2\pi i\omega}$ has been added to the control register's state, as can be seen above. The status of the control register would have been as follows if we had selected operator U^{2^j} rather than U:

$$\frac{|0\rangle+e^{2\pi i(2^j\omega)}|1\rangle}{\sqrt{2}}$$

Because the eigenvalue of U^{2^j} is $(e^{2\pi i\omega})^{2^j}=e^{2\pi i(2^j\omega)}$. At the start of the phase estimation method, the states of the individual qubits should remarkably resemble the state of this control register. The state of the m-th qubit at the beginning of the phase estimation process is actually the state that results from the controlled operations if we set j = n − m. An n-qubit state that we may use as input to the phase estimation method to obtain an estimate of the parameter ω can be created by preparing n control registers in the state $\frac{|0\rangle+|1\rangle}{\sqrt{2}}$ and applying U^{n-m} to the m-th qubit. A circuit for doing this is shown in the image below. Keep in mind that we can get the state's n control registers ready.

$$\left(\frac{|0\rangle+|1\rangle}{\sqrt{2}}\right)^{\otimes n}$$

Using the state $|0\rangle^{\otimes n}$and the QFT.

This type of circuit with U = Ua = |sa mod N} can be used to discover the eigenvalues of Ua in the order-finding procedure previously discussed. Modular exponentiation refers to the series of regulated applications of $U_a^{2^j}$ an in that context. Modular exponentiation is frequently defined as the mapping rather than a series of controlled functions.

$$|z\rangle|y\rangle \mapsto |z\rangle|ya^z \mod N\rangle$$

How does this mapping result from the series of controlled actions that just observed? Using the controlled sequence of operations on the state vector $|y\rangle|z\rangle$, we may analyze the results. `

$$
\begin{aligned}
|z\rangle|y\rangle &\xrightarrow{\text{Controlled operations}} |z\rangle U^{z_n 2^{n-1}} \ldots U^{z_1 2^0}|y\rangle \\
&= |z\rangle U^{z_n 2^{n-1}} \ldots U^{z_2 2}|y a^{z_1 2^0} \mod N\rangle \\
&= |z\rangle U^{z_n 2^{n-1}} \ldots U^{z_3 2^2}|y a^{z_2 2^1} a^{z_1 2^0} \mod N\rangle
\end{aligned}
$$

By carrying on in this manner for every controlled function, we obtain

$$
\begin{aligned}
|z\rangle|y\rangle &\xrightarrow{\text{Controlled operations}} |z\rangle|y a^{z_n 2^{n-1}} \ldots a^{z_1 2^0} \mod N\rangle \\
&= |z\rangle|y a^{z} \mod N\rangle.
\end{aligned}
$$

Depending on how the operation is carried out using quantum adders and other components, a modular exponentiation circuit's real structure can change.

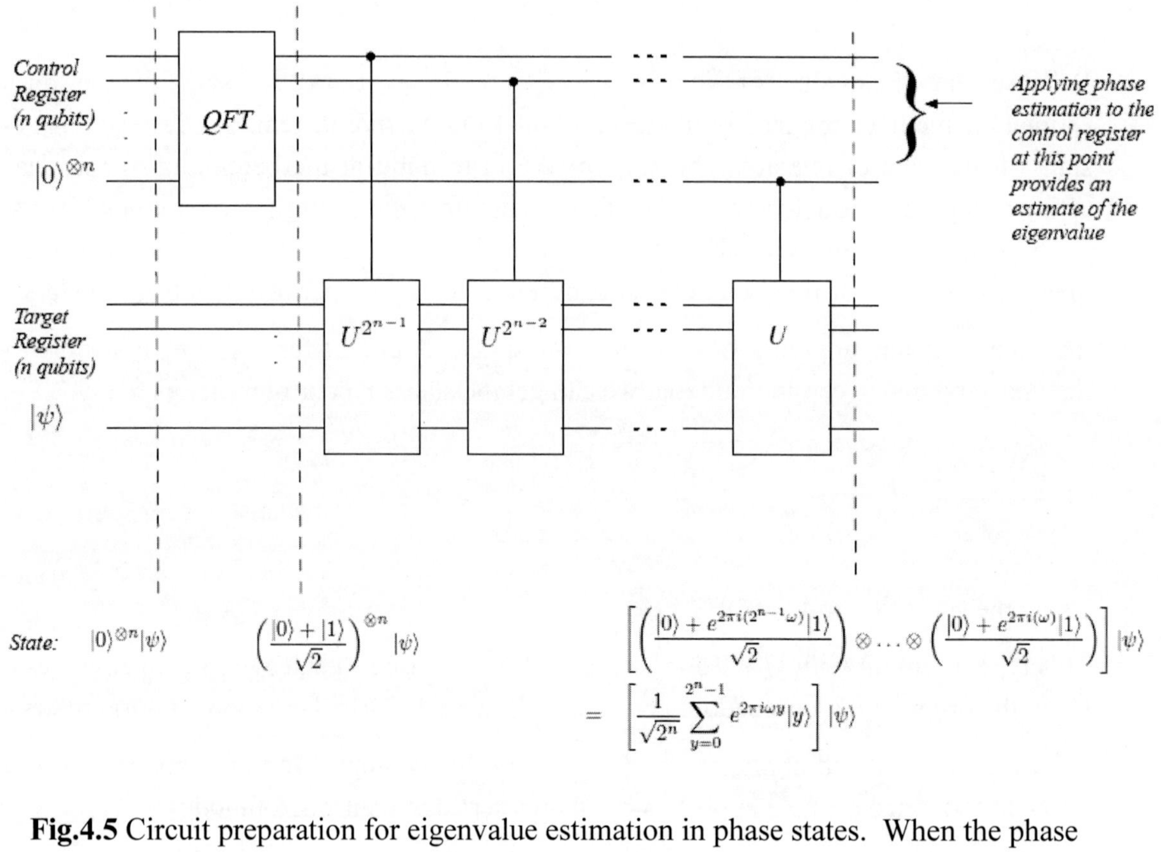

Fig.4.5 Circuit preparation for eigenvalue estimation in phase states. When the phase estimation procedure is applied to this circuit's output, an estimate of the operator U's eigenvalue is obtained.

4.6 The Hidden Subgroup Issue

As previously stated, the period-finding problem is an illustration of what group theory refers to as a Hidden Subgroup Problem (HSP). A number of other hidden subgroup issues, though not all of them, have effective quantum techniques. Indeed, whether or whether there are effective quantum algorithms for specific hidden subgroup problems is one of the largest unresolved issues in the theory of quantum processing.

The definition of the hidden subgroup problem requires a basic understanding of group theory. If a set G meets the following criteria, it is referred to as a group over a binary group operation.

- **Finalization** For every $x, y \in G$, $x \cdot y \in G$, the outcome of the group operation on any two elements is also in the group.
- **Associativity** The group operation is associative: $(x \cdot y) \cdot z = x \cdot (y \cdot z)$ for any x, y, and $z \in G$.
- **Identity** There is an identity element $I \in G$ such that the element in the group is produced by the group operation with any element in the group and identity element: $x \cdot I = I \cdot x = x$ for all $x \in G$.
- **Inverse** Every element x in G has an inverse x^{-1} in G, so that when any element is group operated with its inverse, the identity is produced: $I = x \cdot x^{-1} = x^{-1} \cdot x$

If, for all $x, y \in G$, $x \cdot y = y \cdot x$, then the group is abelian. A subset of a group that is also a group is called a subgroup H of a group G. To indicate that H is a subgroup of G, we can use the $\leq$ symbol: G: $H \leq G$.

The sets $x \cdot H = \{x \cdot y : y \in H\}$ and $H \cdot x = \{y \cdot x : y \in H\}$ are referred to as left and right cosets of H, respectively, given any subgroup $H \leq G$ and any element $x \in G$.

Take Z8, the additive group of the integers modulo 8, as an example. The components of this group are displayed in a table. The components in the table that are bolded belong to the Z8 subgroup 2Z8. The multiples of two in the group are represented by the integers in this subgroup. The diagonal symmetry of the group table in this case shows that both the group and the subgroup are abelian.

Table 4.1 Subgroup and example group (bolded subgroup elements).

Column element · Row element	0	1	2	3	4	5	6	7
0	0	1	2	3	4	5	6	7
1	1	2	3	4	5	6	7	0
2	2	3	4	5	6	7	0	1
3	3	4	5	6	7	0	1	2
4	4	5	6	7	0	1	2	3
5	5	6	7	0	1	2	3	4
6	6	7	0	1	2	3	4	5
7	7	0	1	2	3	4	5	6

Given a group G, a set X, and a map f: G → X, such that for any x, y ∈ G, f (x) = f (y) ⇐⇒ xS = yS, there exists a "hidden subgroup" S ≤ G, find the subgroup S. The characteristics of the subgroup S are illustrated in the below fig. When comparing the cosets of S corresponding to the elements of G that map to various elements of X under f, the cosets of S corresponding to the elements of G that map to the same element of X under f are all different and constant.

An HSP for the problem of figuring out the order of the previously defined function $f(x) = a^x$ mod N looks like this:

- The group of integers modulo N under addition (ZN) is called group G.
- ZN is also the set X.

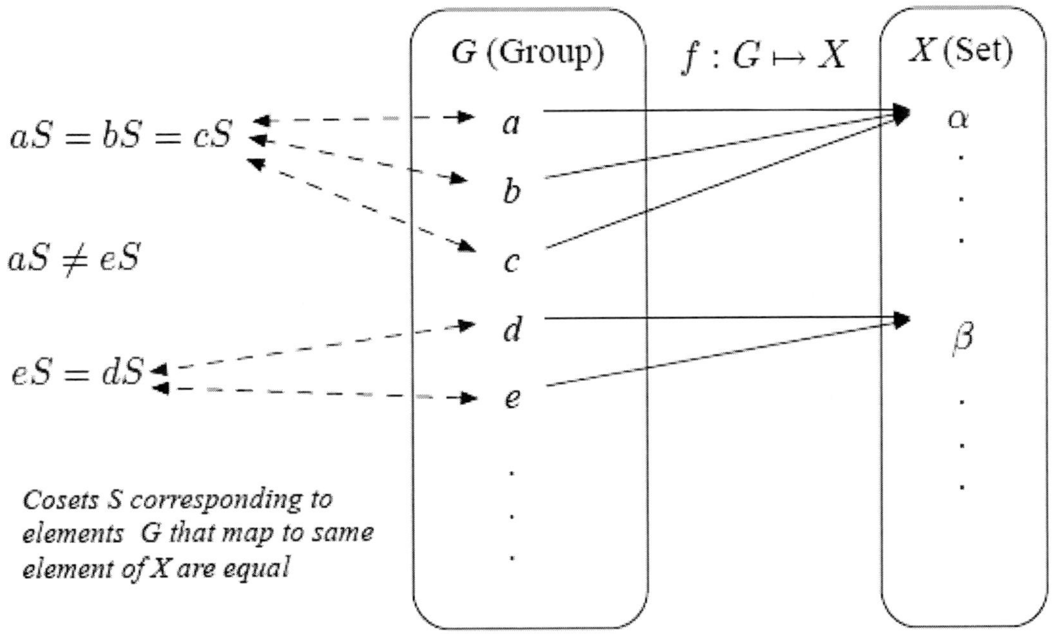

Fig.4.6 Properties of the subgroup S in the hidden subgroup problem.

- The function f (x) = a^x mod N is the map f: G → X.
- rZN, where r is the order of f (x), is the hidden subgroup S.

Let's explore the problem of computing the period of f (x) = 3^x mod 8. S = 2Z8 since G and X are Z8 and r = 2 (which we can determine by evaluating f(x) for 0,..., 7).

Keep in mind that the group and subgroup in question are identical to those in our basic group example. f (0) = f (2) = f (4) = f (6) = 1, 0 + 2Z8 = 2 + 2Z8 = 4 + 2Z8 = 6 + 2Z8 = {0, 2, 4, 6}, f (1) = f (3) = f (5) = f (6) = 3, and 1 + 2Z8 = 3 + 2Z8 = 5 + 2Z8 = 7 + 2Z8 = {1, 3, 5, 7} are all readily apparent.

This order-finding problem was previously solved using an effective quantum algorithm. It can be demonstrated that an effective quantum algorithm can solve any HSP on an Abelian group.

The structure of these algorithms is presumably similar to that of the period finding algorithm; it involves applying a black-box function, a quantum Fourier transform (defined appropriately for the group in question), an inverse quantum Fourier transform, and then classical steps to try and compute the generators of the hidden subgroup. While there are now effective quantum algorithms for tackling specific particular circumstances, there are no known efficient algorithms for solving arbitrary instances of the non-Abelian HSP. Since non-Abelian HSPs can be used to address a variety of computational issues, such as graph automorphism, it would be particularly intriguing to show whether or not such an algorithm exists from the standpoint of quantum complexity theory.

4.7 Grover's algorithm

An item in an unordered list is intended to be found using this database search algorithm. For instance, it can be applied to symmetric key encryption, like AES, to expedite the brute force key search process (Bernstein, 2010). It is known that in order to search an unsorted array of size N, this technique needs $O(\sqrt{N})$ operations, whereas classical approaches require (N) operations.

The following is the concept behind Grover's algorithm. In an extensive unsorted database, the qubits are first put to a superposition state of all conceivable ID numbers $\{x=0,1,2,\ldots,N-1\}$ when the number x_a that fulfills $f(x_a)=1$. The n-qubit is expressed using decimal notation to make it simpler. For instance, $|4\rangle$ is expressed as $|1\rangle|0\rangle|0\rangle$. The starting point (Below Figure) can be expressed as

$$|\psi\rangle = \sum_{x=0}^{N-1} \rho_x|x\rangle = \rho_0|0\rangle + \rho_1|1\rangle + \rho_2|2\rangle + \cdots \rho_{N-1}|N-1\rangle \qquad (1)$$

where the initial values of ρx are $1/\sqrt{2n}$ when $N=2^n$. Thus, $\sum_{x=0}^{N-1} \rho_x^2 = 1$.

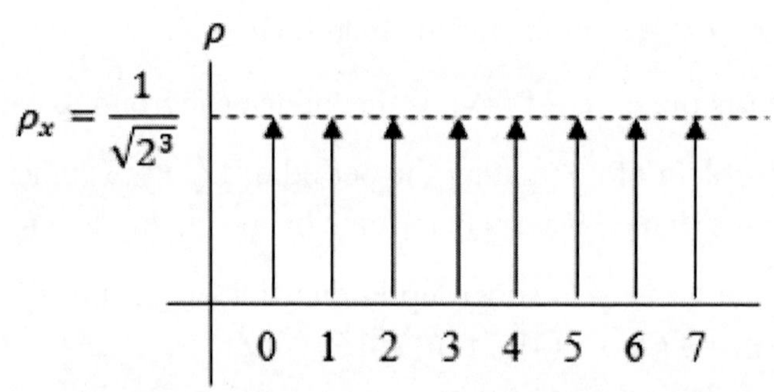

Fig.4.7 Initial States for N = 8 (n = 3).

Next, the state's phase is reversed using a quantum circuit, where x is equal to x_a (below figure)

$$\begin{aligned} |\psi'\rangle &= (-1)^{f(x)} \sum_{x=0}^{N-1} \rho_x|x\rangle \\ &= \rho_0|0\rangle + \rho_1|1\rangle + \cdots + (-1)\rho_{x_a}|x_a\rangle + \cdots + \rho_{N-1}|N-1\rangle \end{aligned} \qquad (2)$$

where $f(x) = \begin{bmatrix} 0 & x \neq x_a \\ 1 & x = x_a \end{bmatrix}$

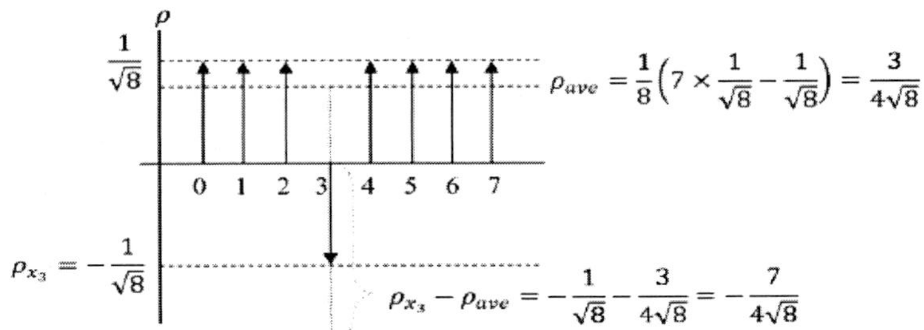

Fig.4.8 For N = 8 (n = 3), flip the phase of the state x_a, assuming that in this case $(x_a=3)=1$.

Next, the amplitude ρ_{ave} is subtracted from the difference between the average of the probability amplitudes ρ_{ave} and the amplitude ρ_x. (Below Figure).

$$|\psi''\rangle = \sum_{x=0}^{N-1} \{\rho_{ave} - (\rho_x - \rho_{ave})\}|x\rangle = \sum_{x=0}^{N-1} (2\rho_{ave} - \rho_x)|x\rangle \tag{3}$$

where $\rho_{ave} = \frac{1}{N}\sum_{x=0}^{N-1} \rho_x$.

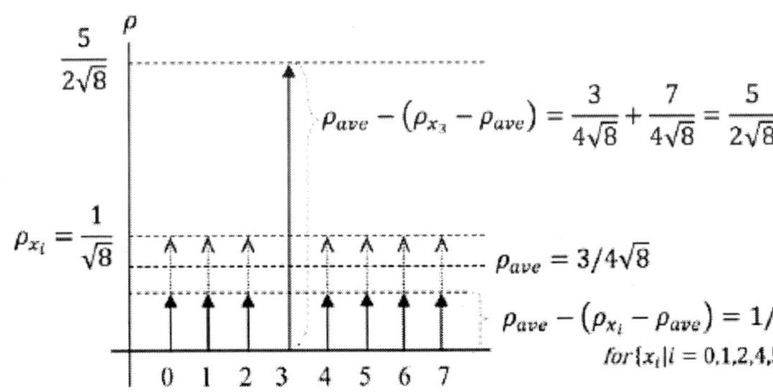

Fig.4.9 For N = 8 (n = 3), the difference between $\boldsymbol{\rho ave}$ **and** $\boldsymbol{\rho x}$ is deducted from $\boldsymbol{\rho ave}$.

We refer to this process as inversion about the average. The probability amplitude of the target state $|3\rangle$ increases to $5/2\sqrt{8}$ from $1/\sqrt{8}$ following the operation, as demonstrated in the example with N = 8 (n = 3), while the amplitudes for the remaining states decrease to $1/2\sqrt{8}$. This result still satisfies $\sum_{x=0}^{N-1} \rho_x^2 = (5/2\sqrt{8})^2 + 7 \times (1/2\sqrt{8})^2 = 1$.

As a result, there is a 78.1% increase in the likelihood of identifying the target state $|3\rangle$ by measurement, up from 12.5%. A further repetition of the operation yields $\rho_{ave}=1/8\sqrt{8}$ and $2\rho_{ave}-\rho_{x3}=11/4\sqrt{8}$. As a result, the likelihood $(2\rho_{ave}-\rho_{x3})^2$ is raised to 94.5%. The likelihood of generating the targeted ID xa by measurement can be increased from the starting probability of $1/N$ by repeatedly conducting inversion about the average. The quantum algorithm does not outperform classical algorithms significantly when N is small because, on average, identifying an item from N items requires $N/2$ operations.

$$O(\sqrt{N}) < O(N/2) \tag{4}$$

The benefit is noticeable, though, when *N* is high. For instance, Grover's technique requires just 1000 steps to find an item in a database of 106 entries (for biometric authentications, for instance), but a traditional algorithm requires 50,000 steps.

The following describes the algorithm, which operates on a n + 1-qubit register made up of a 1-qubit control register and an n-qubit target register.

1. **Initial State Configuration** Commence with the state within the intended register

$$|\psi\rangle = \frac{1}{\sqrt{2^n}} \sum_{x=0}^{2^n-1} |x\rangle$$

As demonstrated below, an n-qubit Hadmard gate, whose action is the same as the QFT we observed when we examined the phase estimation procedure, makes it simple to generate $|\psi\rangle$ from the state |00... 0}:

$$|\psi\rangle = H|00\ldots0\rangle = \frac{1}{\sqrt{2^n}} \sum_{x=0}^{2^n-1} e^{2\pi \frac{0}{2^n} x}|x\rangle = \frac{1}{\sqrt{2^n}} \sum_{x=0}^{2^n-1} |x\rangle$$

2. **The Grover Iteration** Use the subsequent procedure $\lfloor \frac{\pi}{4}\sqrt{2^n} \rfloor$ times:

   a) Apply the black-box function U_f, set the control register to $\frac{|0\rangle-|1\rangle}{\sqrt{2}}$, and then discard the control register to cause the previously described map |x} U_f —→ (−1)f (x) $|\psi\rangle$ on the target register.

   b) Use a Hadmard gate with n qubits

   c) Use the operator $U_{0\perp}$, which has the following definition:

$$U_{0\perp} : \begin{cases} |x\rangle \mapsto -|x\rangle, & x \neq 0 \\ |0\rangle \mapsto |0\rangle \end{cases}$$

   d) Use the Hadmard gate with n qubits once more.

3. **Measurement** The target register is to be measured. The state that corresponds to the element in the domain of f (x) that yields a nonzero result should be the state that we measure, with a high probability.

The relevant quantum circuit for this algorithm is depicted in Figure.

4.7.1 Verification of the accuracy of the Grover iteration

Trace the state of the quantum register through the various iteration steps to show that repeated applications of the Grover iteration result in the state that (when measured) has a high probability of obtaining the desired result.

Applying the operator $U_f(HU_{0^\perp}H)$ on the quantum state repeatedly is all that makes up the Grover iteration process. Establish a number of states and subspaces first to facilitate the analysis of the use of $U_f(HU_{0^\perp}H)$. In particular, two 2-dimensional subspaces of the n-qubit state space (whose dimension is 2^n) will be defined. The influence of U_f will be understood in the first subspace, while the effect of $HU_{0^\perp}H$ will be understood in the second. The bases of these subspaces are described in the list below:

Knowing U_f: Assume that w is the value of x such that f (x) = 1. In this case, $|w\rangle$ is the quantum state that we wish to measure at the algorithm's conclusion.

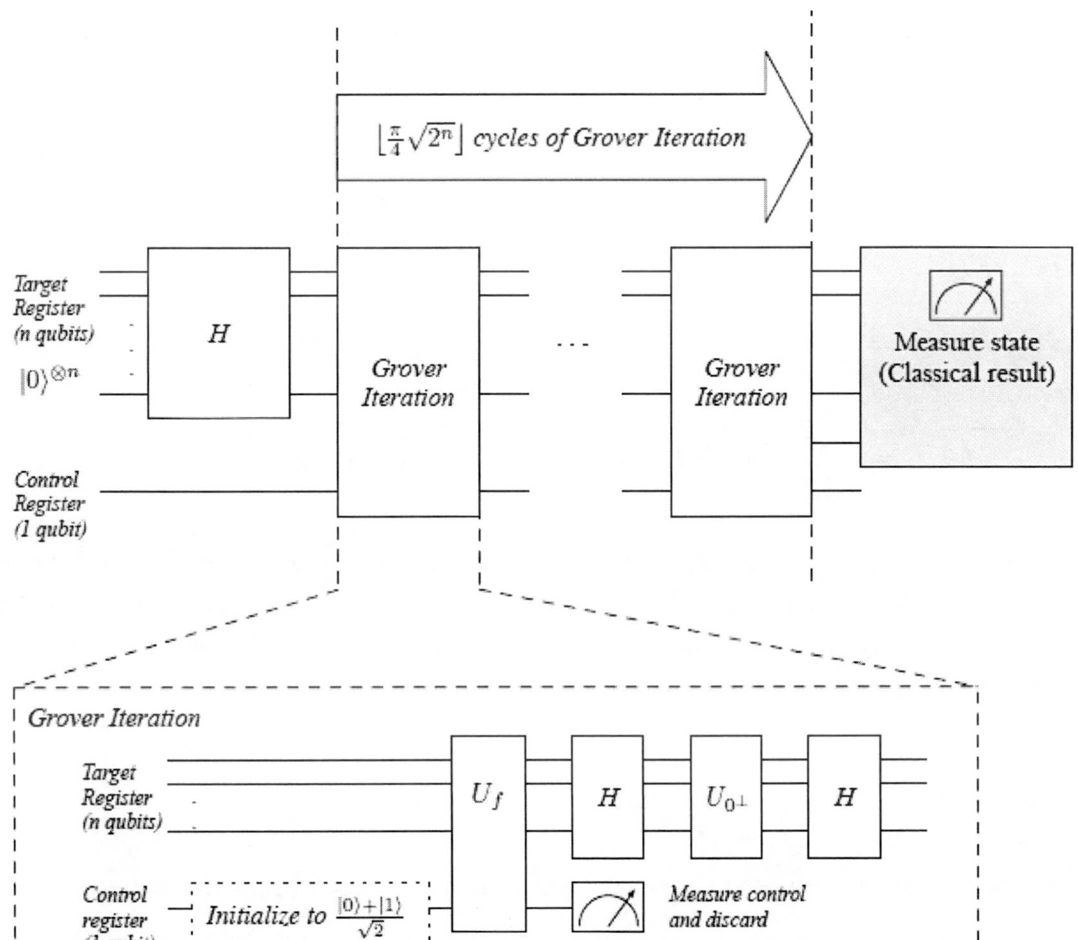

Fig.4.10 An algorithm for Grover's quantum circuit.

Establish that the states $|\psi_{good}\rangle = |w\rangle$ and $|\psi_{bad}\rangle = \frac{1}{\sqrt{2^n-1}}\sum_{x\neq w}|x\rangle$ so that the state $|\psi\rangle$ at the conclusion of the first step may be expressed as follows:

$$|\psi\rangle = \frac{1}{\sqrt{2^n}}|\psi_{good}\rangle + \sqrt{\frac{2^n-1}{2^n}}|\psi_{bad}\rangle$$

Since the mapping operation of U_f is specified in terms of $|\psi_{good}\rangle$ and $|\psi_{bad}\rangle$, it is simple to observe the effect of applying U_f to an element of the subspace spanned by $\{|\psi_{good}\rangle = |w\rangle, |\psi_{bad}\rangle\}$.

- **Comprehending** $HU_{0^\perp}H$: Let $|\bar{\psi}\rangle$: Assume that the state orthogonal to $|\psi\rangle$ is $|\bar{\psi}\rangle$ When x = 0, we can express $|\bar{\psi}\rangle$ as a linear combination of states of the type $H|x\rangle$. (where $x \neq 0$)

$$|\bar{\psi}\rangle = \sum_{k=1}^{2^n-1} a_k H|k\rangle, \; a_k \in \mathbb{R}.$$

Observe the outcome of applying the operator $HU_{0^\perp}H$ to $|\psi\rangle$ and $|\bar{\psi}\rangle$, which takes place in the final three Grover iteration steps:

$$\begin{aligned}
HU_{0^\perp}H|\psi\rangle &= HU_{0^\perp}H[H|00\ldots0\rangle] = H|00\ldots0\rangle = |\psi\rangle \\
HU_{0^\perp}H|\bar{\psi}\rangle &= HU_{0^\perp}H\left[\sum_{k=1}^{2^n-1} a_k H|k\rangle\right] = \sum_{k=1}^{2^n-1} a_k HU_{0^\perp}H[H|k\rangle] \\
&= \sum_{k=1}^{2^n-1} a_k(-H|k\rangle) = -\sum_{k=1}^{2^n-1} a_k H|k\rangle = -|\bar{\psi}\rangle.
\end{aligned}$$

The impact of applying $HU_{0^\perp}H$ to an element of the subspace spanned by $\{|\psi\rangle, |\bar{\psi}\rangle\}$ can be readily quantified using these identities. The Grover iteration procedure will now be examined. The Groover iteration process should begin with the state ψ, represented by |ψgood } and |ψbad } (because U_f applied to this state first):

$$|\psi\rangle = \frac{1}{\sqrt{2^n}}|\psi_{good}\rangle + \sqrt{\frac{2^n-1}{2^n}}|\psi_{bad}\rangle$$

Sine and cosine can be used to express the coefficients of each of the basis states. Make sure that $\sin(\theta) = \frac{1}{\sqrt{2^n}}$ for the chosen angle θ. This yields $\cos(\theta) = \sqrt{\frac{2^n-1}{2^n}}$, which is conveniently the coefficient of |ψbad } in the preceding equation according to the identity $\sin^2\theta + \cos^2\theta = 1$. As a result, |ψ} becomes

$$||\psi\rangle = \sin(\theta)|\psi_{good}\rangle + \cos(\theta)|\psi_{bad}\rangle.$$

When Uf is applied to this state, we obtain

$$\begin{aligned} U_f|\psi\rangle &= U_f[\sin(\theta)|\psi_{good}\rangle + \cos(\theta)|\psi_{bad}\rangle] \\ &= -\sin(\theta)|\psi_{good}\rangle + \cos(\theta)|\psi_{bad}\rangle. \end{aligned}$$

Applying $HU_{0^\perp}H$ to this state is now possible. We shall first express this state in terms of the states $\{|\psi\rangle$ and $|\bar{\psi}\rangle$ before proceeding. A set of expressions for switching bases between the two sets we previously specified is displayed in Table.

Table 4.2 Basis identities for the proof sketch demonstrating Grover's algorithm's accuracy.

State	Representation in other basis
$\|\psi\rangle$	$\sin(\theta)\|\psi_{good}\rangle + \cos(\theta)\|\psi_{bad}\rangle$
$\|\bar{\psi}\rangle$	$\cos(\theta)\|\psi_{good}\rangle - \sin(\theta)\|\psi_{bad}\rangle$
$\|\psi_{good}\rangle$	$\sin(\theta)\|\psi\rangle + \cos(\theta)\|\bar{\psi}\rangle$
$\|\psi_{bad}\rangle$	$\cos(\theta)\|\psi\rangle - \sin(\theta)\|\bar{\psi}\rangle$

The basic product-to-sum trigonometric identities and the basis identities in Table are applied to obtain

$$\begin{aligned} U_f|\psi\rangle &= -\sin(\theta)|\psi_{good}\rangle + \cos(\theta)|\psi_{bad}\rangle \\ &= -\sin(\theta)\sin(\theta)|\psi\rangle - \sin(\theta)\cos(\theta)|\bar{\psi}\rangle \\ &\quad + \cos(\theta)\cos(\theta)|\psi\rangle - \cos(\theta)\sin(\theta)|\bar{\psi}\rangle \\ &= \cos(2\theta)|\psi\rangle - \sin(2\theta)|\bar{\psi}\rangle. \end{aligned}$$

$HU_{0^\perp}H$ can now be applied to obtain

$$\begin{aligned} HU_{0^\perp}HU_f|\psi\rangle &= HU_{0^\perp}H\left[\cos(2\theta)|\psi\rangle - \sin(2\theta)|\bar{\psi}\rangle\right] \\ &= \cos(2\theta)|\psi\rangle + \sin(2\theta)|\bar{\psi}\rangle \\ &= \cos(2\theta)\left[\sin(\theta)|\psi_{good}\rangle + \cos(\theta)|\psi_{bad}\rangle\right] \\ &\quad + \sin(2\theta)\left[\cos(\theta)|\psi_{good}\rangle - \sin(\theta)|\psi_{bad}\rangle\right] \\ &= \left[\frac{\sin(2\theta+\theta) - \sin(2\theta-\theta)}{2}\right]|\psi_{good}\rangle \\ &\quad + \left[\frac{\cos(2\theta-\theta) + \cos(2\theta+\theta)}{2}\right]|\psi_{bad}\rangle \\ &\quad + \left[\frac{\sin(2\theta+\theta) + \sin(2\theta-\theta)}{2}\right]|\psi_{good}\rangle \\ &\quad - \left[\frac{\cos(2\theta-\theta) - \cos(2\theta+\theta)}{2}\right]|\psi_{bad}\rangle \\ &= \sin(3\theta)|\psi_{good}\rangle + \cos(3\theta)|\psi_{bad}\rangle. \end{aligned}$$

This provides us with a formula for $HU_{0^\perp}HU_f|\psi\rangle$ in both base states, which is the state following a single Grover iteration. However, particularly it is curious about the system's condition following several Grover iterations. Fortunately, it is simple to demonstrate that the following relationship is true for any integer k > 1:

$$\begin{aligned}(HU_{0^\perp}HU_f)^k|\psi\rangle &= \cos(2k\theta)|\psi\rangle + \sin(2k\theta)|\bar{\psi}\rangle \\ &= \sin((2k+1)\theta)|\psi_{good}\rangle + \cos((2k+1)\theta)|\psi_{bad}\rangle\end{aligned}$$

We can accomplish this by using induction. Since the base case (for k = 1) has already been completed, we must concentrate on the induction stage, which involves demonstrating the equality for k + 1 given that it is true for k. It is pretty similar to the base case to do this: Applying U_f first, we begin with the prior equation:

$$\begin{aligned}U_f(HU_{0^\perp}HU_f)^k|\psi\rangle &= U_f\left[\sin((2k+1)\theta)|\psi_{good}\rangle + \cos((2k+1)\theta)|\psi_{bad}\rangle\right] \\ &= -\sin((2k+1)\theta)|\psi_{good}\rangle + \cos((2k+1)\theta)|\psi_{bad}\rangle.\end{aligned}$$

Next, using HU0⊥H, we obtain

$$\begin{aligned}&(HU_{0^\perp}H)[U_f(HU_{0^\perp}HU_f)^k|\psi\rangle] \\ =\;& HU_{0^\perp}H\left[-\sin((2k+1)\theta)|\psi_{good}\rangle + \cos((2k+1)\theta)|\psi_{bad}\rangle\right] \\ =\;& HU_{0^\perp}H\left\{-\sin((2k+1)\theta)\left[\sin(\theta)|\psi\rangle + \cos(\theta)|\bar{\psi}\rangle\right]\right. \\ &\left.+\cos((2k+1)\theta)\left[\cos(\theta)|\psi\rangle - \sin(\theta)|\bar{\psi}\rangle\right]\right\} \\ =\;& -\sin((2k+1)\theta)\left[\sin(\theta)|\psi\rangle - \cos(\theta)|\bar{\psi}\rangle\right] \\ &+\cos((2k+1)\theta)\left[\cos(\theta)|\psi\rangle + \sin(\theta)|\bar{\psi}\rangle\right] \\ =\;& -\left[\frac{\cos((2k+1)\theta-\theta) - \cos((2k+1)\theta+\theta)}{2}\right]|\psi\rangle \\ &-\left[\frac{\sin((2k+1)\theta+\theta) + \sin((2k+1)\theta-\theta)}{2}\right]|\bar{\psi}\rangle \\ &+\left[\frac{\cos((2k+1)\theta-\theta) + \cos((2k+1)\theta+\theta)}{2}\right]|\psi\rangle \\ &-\left[\frac{\sin((2k+1)\theta+\theta) - \sin((2k+1)\theta-\theta)}{2}\right]|\bar{\psi}\rangle \\ =\;& \cos(2(k+1)\theta)|\psi\rangle + \sin(2(k+1)\theta)|\bar{\psi}\rangle.\end{aligned}$$

When bases are switched, this can be demonstrated to be equal to sin((2(k + 1) + 1)θ)|\ψ good} + cos((2(k + 1) + 1)θ)|\ ψbad}. Thus, the induction phase is over, and the proof is finished.

A graphic depiction of the link between the quantum system's state and the basis states {|ψgood }, |ψbad }} throughout multiple Grover iterations cycles is shown in below figure. We can visualize the state of the system after k iterations (sin((2k + 1)θ)|ψgood} + cos((2k + 1)θ)|ψbad }) as a vector with phase (2k + 1)θ) if we label the x and y axes of an R2 plot with |ψbad } and |ψgood }, respectively.

Grover subsequently "rotates" this vector at each repetition step. Objective is to measure the state |\ψgood}, hence we want to rotate the state vector to get as close to |\ψgood} as possible. This happens when both sin((2k + 1)θ) and cos((2k + 1)θ) are near 1. By calculating the likelihood of obtaining the right answer and solving for k, it can be demonstrated that k = {π4 √ 2n} inquiries are needed to measure the state |ψgood } with probability $1 - O(\frac{1}{2^n})$.

4.7.2 Using a Quantum Black Box for Searching

Consider a quantum black boxUf that implements a function f (x): {0, 1}^{n} {→ {0, 1}. An n + 1-qubit operator is working on a n + 1 qubit state; the last qubit can be viewed as a control register, and the first n-qubits as a target register $|x\rangle|y\rangle$. It's operation is displayed below, with $|x\rangle$representing an n-qubit basis state and $|y\rangle$ representing a 1-qubit basis state:

$$U_f : |x\rangle|y\rangle \mapsto |x\rangle|f(x) \oplus y\rangle$$

As we can see, Uf encodes information about the values of the function f (x) by mapping an input state to an output state. Note that

$$\begin{array}{lll} f(x) = 0 & \Longrightarrow & |f(x) \oplus 0\rangle = |0\rangle, |f(x) \oplus 1\rangle = |1\rangle \\ f(x) = 1 & \Longrightarrow & |f(x) \oplus 0\rangle = |1\rangle, |f(x) \oplus 1\rangle = |0\rangle \end{array}$$

Applying U_f after preparing the control register to the state $\frac{|0\rangle - |1\rangle}{\sqrt{2}}$ has the following effect:

$$\begin{aligned} |x\rangle \left(\frac{|0\rangle - |1\rangle}{\sqrt{2}} \right) & \xrightarrow{U_f} \left(\frac{|x\rangle|f(x) \oplus 0\rangle - |x\rangle|f(x) \oplus 1\rangle}{\sqrt{2}} \right) \\ & = \left(\frac{(-1)^{f(x)}|x\rangle|0\rangle - (-1)^{f(x)}|x\rangle|1\rangle}{\sqrt{2}} \right) \\ & = (-1)^{f(x)}|x\rangle \left(\frac{|0\rangle - |1\rangle}{\sqrt{2}} \right) \end{aligned}$$

The map can be induced if the control register is discarded after applying U_f.

$$|x\rangle \xrightarrow{U_f} (-1)^{f(x)}|x\rangle$$

The Grover issue assumes that, with the exception of one value, the function f (x) evaluates to 0 for every x ∈ {0, 1}^{n}. The objective is to identify the unique element x that belongs to {0, 1}^{n} such that f (x) = 1.

4.8 Algorithms for Quantum Adiabatics

The evolution model of quantum systems is one of the key components of the theory of quantum mechanics. According to the Schrodinger equation, a quantum state |ψ(t)} behaves as follows over time:

$$i\frac{d}{dt}|\psi(t)\rangle = H(t)|\psi(t)\rangle.$$

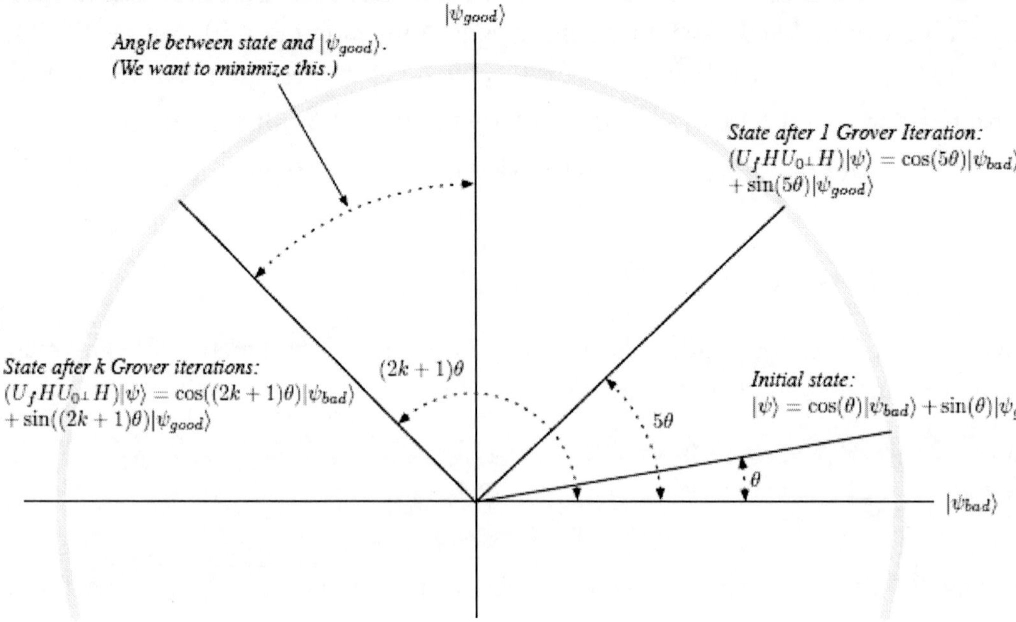

Fig.4.11 Grover Iterations' impact on |ψ} is shown graphically.

where the time-dependent Hamiltonian is denoted by H(t). Conduct "computation" in quantum adiabatic computation by using the Schrodinger equation to control the Hamiltonian's transition from one state (H_{start}) to another (H_{end}). We are specifically interested in each operator's ground states, or the eigenvectors that correspond to the least eigenvalue. According to the quantum adiabatic theorem, the ground state of H_{start} will change into the ground state of H_{end} if the system is evolved for a long enough period of time. Assume that we choose Hstart so that its ground state is simple to locate and Hend such that its ground state encodes the problem solution.

We may now use the ground state of the final operator to find the solution to the issue if we develop the system for the proper length of time. A graphic representation of the idea underlying quantum adiabatic algorithms may be found in the figure below.

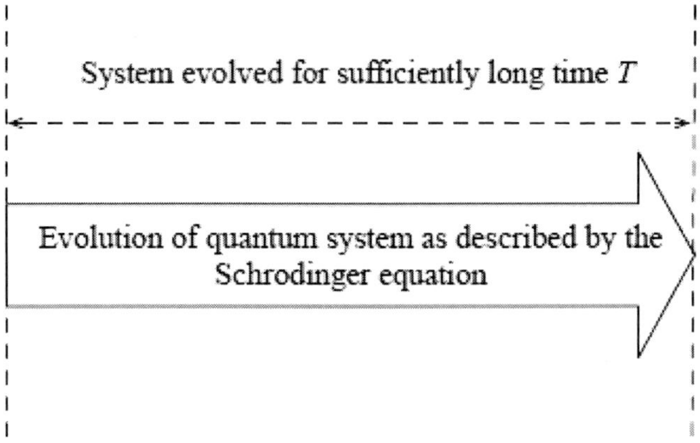

Fig.4.12 An overview of adiabatic quantum processing at a high level.

A number of findings make an effort to exactly estimate how long T will take for the system to evolve in order to tackle problems in this way. Here is an example of such a bound. Assume that ˜ H(0) = H_{start} and ˜ H(1) = H_{end}, and that ˜ H(s) is the state of the Hamiltonian at time s, where $0 \leq s < 1$. In this case, we suppose that the first and second derivatives are bounded and exist. Choose now

$$H(t) = \tilde{H}(\frac{t}{T}), t \in [0, 1].$$

for every $\delta > 0$, if we choose

$$T \geq \frac{10^5}{\delta^2} \max \left\{ \frac{||H'||^3}{\lambda^4}, \frac{||H||'||H||''}{\lambda^3} \right\}$$

The final state is at most δ away from the end Hamiltonian's ground state, where λ is the minimal eigenvalue gap of $\tilde{H}$.

4.8.1 3-Sat: A Quantum Adiabatic Algorithm Application

Finding a valid set of assignments to N Boolean variables x1,..., xN that fulfill a collection of M Boolean clauses is the problem known as 3-SAT. The form of each phrase in C is as follows:

$$C = y_{C1} \vee y_{C2} \vee y_{C3}$$

where yCk $\in \{x_1, \ldots, x_n, \neg x_1, \ldots, \neg x_n\}$. Since the Boolean function $f(x_1, \ldots, x_n) = C_1 \wedge \ldots \wedge C_k$ evaluates to true, we may alternatively state 3-SAT as the issue of finding x1,..., xN. 3-SAT is a fascinating computer science issue for many reasons. Its membership in the NP-complete complexity class is crucial among these. It is presently unknown whether polynomial time techniques exist for addressing NP-complete problems on both classical and quantum computers.

A single unique solution to the 3-SAT instance was ensured using another adiabatic quantum technique for solving unique 3-SAT, computer simulations on arbitrary 3-SAT cases. It was eventually shown that this is not the true for all instances of the issue, despite the initial polynomial relationship between the number N of Boolean variables in the problem and the time T needed to evolve the system. For NP-complete algorithms, this does not preclude the development of quantum adiabatic algorithms with polynomial time. The structure of the Hamiltonians H_{start} and H_{end} in the adiabatic quantum algorithm will be examined in order to further clarify the idea of adiabatic quantum algorithms.

- **Ending Hamiltonian**

First, let's examine Farhi's algorithm's final Hamiltonian H_{end}. A solution to the 3-SAT issue should be encoded in the ground state of this Hamiltonian. Assume that the system's basis states |x1.. xn} correspond to the 2n possible assignments of the variables x1,..., xn. Define to be the operator Hk that the 3-SAT formula's clause C corresponds to as

$$H_k|x_1 \ldots x_n\rangle = h_C|x_1 \ldots x_n\rangle$$

where hC is 0 else and 1 if (x1... xn) does not satisfy clause C. Let H_{end} represent the total of all operators H_k.

$$H_{end} = \sum_C H_C$$

Take into consideration how this operator affects a basis vector |x1... xn}:

$$H_{end}|x_1 \ldots x_n\rangle = \sum_C H_C|x_1 \ldots x_n\rangle.$$

The number of clauses that |x1... xn} violates is the sum's value. This integer should be called λ|x1...xn}. Thus, H_{end} is now

$$H_{end}|x_1 \ldots x_n\rangle = \lambda_{|x_1 \ldots x_n\rangle}|x_1 \ldots x_n\rangle$$

Every basis state |x1... xn} is an eigenvector of H_{end} with a corresponding eigenvalue λ|x1...xn}, as can be seen from this. The basis vector that represents the assignment of Boolean variables that fulfills each sentence is the operator's ground state, and its ground state energy is 0. Since all of the other eigenvectors match assignments of the Boolean variables that break one or more clauses, this is assured to be the ground state.

- **Beginning Hamiltonian**

Let di be the number of times bit i occurs in the clauses of the 3-SAT instance under consideration, and let $H_B^{(i)}$ be an operator acting on the i-th bit of the base state. The definition of $H_B^{(i)}$ is

$$H_B^{(i)} = I^{\otimes(i-1)} \otimes \frac{1}{2}\begin{bmatrix} 1 & -1 \\ -1 & 1 \end{bmatrix} \otimes I^{\otimes(N-i)}.$$

This allows us to define H_{start} as

$$H_{start} = \sum_{i=1}^{N} d_i H_B^{(i)}$$

Making use of the eigenvalues and eigenvectors of

$$\frac{1}{2}\begin{bmatrix} 1 & -1 \\ -1 & 1 \end{bmatrix}$$

Given the identity operators' eigenvalues and eigenvectors, we may conclude that the sole eigenvector of Hstart with eigenvalue 0 is

$$\left[\frac{1}{\sqrt{2}}|0\rangle + \frac{1}{\sqrt{2}}|1\rangle\right]^{\otimes N} = \frac{1}{\sqrt{2^n}} \sum_{x_1=0}^{1} \sum_{x_2=0}^{1} \cdots \sum_{x_n=0}^{1} |x_1 \ldots x_n\rangle$$

and the eigenvalues of every other eigenvector are positive. Thus, this is the system's initial Hamiltonian's ground state.

4.9 The Shor Algorithm

Peter Shor demonstrated in 1994 that a big integer may be factored in polynomial time using a quantum computer (Shor, 1994). His approach caught the interest of security organizations because it might potentially break the most popular public-key encryption algorithm, RSA, in the event that a quantum computer is constructed.

There are quantum and classical components to Shor's algorithm. After a brief introduction to the RSA algorithm, this section describes how quantum computation is used with the classical computation in Shor's algorithm.

An overview of the RSA encryption technique

Alice, the recipient of a covert message, determines that $N=pq$ by taking two huge prime numbers, P and q. Furthermore, she selects at random the number e, which is coprime to $(p-1)(q-1)$. (that is, $\gcd\{e,(p-1)(q-1)\}\equiv 1$) and determines the value d, which fulfills

$$ed\equiv 1 \ \{(p-1)(q-1)\} \quad (1)$$

She maintains the number d as her private key and makes those two numbers $(N,)$ available as her public key. A sender, Bob, computes $C=M^e \ mod \ N$ in order to encrypt a message M. Alice does the decryption by computing $M=C^d mod \ N$. Eve, the eavesdropper, needs to locate the private key d in order to defeat the RSA's security.

Since N and e are in the open, all she needs to do to compute (1) is locate p and q from N. However, factoring a huge integer in polynomial time is not possible with any classical approach. The difficulty of factoring a large number (such as 200 digits) is what gives rise to the security of the RSA encryption.

4.9.1 Shor's algorithm's classical computations

Number theory (Stallings, 1999) states that if an integer a is coprime to N and randomly selected such that $0 < a < N$, then the function

$$f_{a,}(m) = a^m \ mod\ N \tag{2}$$

is periodic, and the condition is satisfied by at least one integer m

$$a^m \equiv 1\ mod\ N \tag{3}$$

For instance, if a=7 and N=15,

$f_{7,15}(1)=7^1\ mod\ 15=7$

$f_{7,15}(2)=7^2\ mod\ 15=4$

$f_{7,15}(3)=7^3\ mod\ 15=13$

$f_{7,15}(4)=7^4\ mod\ 15=1$

$f_{7,15}(5)=7^5\ mod\ 15=7$

$f_{7,15}(6)=7^6\ mod\ 15=4$

$$f_{7,15}(7)=7^7\ mod\ 15=13 \tag{4}$$

Thus, the function $f_{7,15}(m)$ equals 1 when m=4,8,12,…. The period produced by $f_{a,}(m)$ has the least positive exponent. The period r in this instance is 4. One can modify condition (3) by deducting one from each side of the equivalence.

$$a^r - 1 \equiv 0\ mod\ N \tag{5}$$

When the period r is an even number,

$$(a^{r/2} - 1)(a^{r/2} + 1) \equiv 0\ mod\ N \tag{6}$$

Therefore, the residual is zero when the number N is a divisor of $(a^{r/2} - 1)(a^{r/2}+1)$. One of the two variables $(a^{r/2} - 1)(a^{r/2}+1)$ is most likely a factor for N. With the exception of the situation when $ar/2=\pm 1\ mod\ N$, a factor for N can be discovered using the conventional Euclidean approach with $gcd\ \{\ ^{/2} - 1, N\}$ and $gcd\ \{\ a^{r/2} + 1, N\}$. In the example, if m=4, then $gcd\{7^2 - 1, 15\} = gcd\{48, 15\} = 3$ and $gcd\{7^2 + 1, 15\} = gcd\{50, 15\} = 5$ may be found by computing the factors 3 and 5.

4.9.2 Equations of state in Shor's algorithm

Finding the period of $f_{a,N}(m)$ on a classical computer (if possible) is exceedingly time-consuming when the integer N is large (e.g., 200 digits). Therefore, by computing $f_{a,N}(m)$ for m=0 to, at least, m=N^2, the period is found using a quantum superposition state.

Grover's approach increases the likelihood that the targeted index will be found by measuring just one set of qubits that are in the superposition state. Two qubit sets are employed in Shor's algorithm: $|\psi 1\rangle$ for the input m and $|\psi 2\rangle$ for the output of $f_{a,N}(m)$. Since $f_{a,N}(m)$ is always smaller than N, the number of qubits for $|\psi 2\rangle$ is k=log$N$, but the number of qubits for $|\psi 1\rangle$ is, at the very least, logN^2=2k. The qubits' starting state for m is

$$|\psi_1\rangle = \sum_{m=0}^{N^2-1} \rho_m |m\rangle = \rho_0|0\rangle + \rho_1|1\rangle + \rho_2|2\rangle + \cdots + \rho_{N^2-1}|N^2-1\rangle \quad (1)$$

where the initial values of ρm are 1/√22k. The initial state of the qubits for $fa,(m)$ is

$$|\psi 2\rangle=|000\ldots0\rangle=|0\rangle \quad (2)$$

As seen in the picture below, $|\psi 1\rangle$ and $|\psi 2\rangle$ are inserted into a quantum circuit that computes $fa,(m)$.

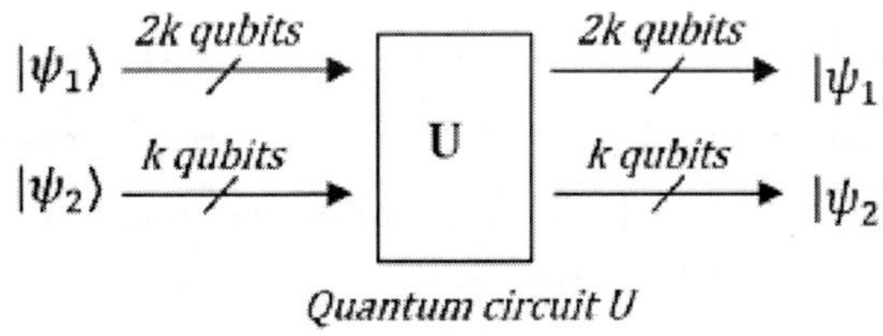

Fig.4.13 In Shor's algorithm, quantum computation.

The quantum circuit's output states can be expressed as

$$U|\psi_1\rangle|\psi_2\rangle = U|m\rangle|0\rangle = |m\rangle|f_{a,N}(m)\rangle = |\psi_1\rangle|\psi_2'\rangle \quad (3)$$

$|\psi 1'\rangle$ and $|\psi 2'\rangle$ are intertwined. For instance, when Y=7 and Z=15 (where Y=4), this can be written as

$$|\psi_1\rangle|\psi_2'\rangle = \frac{1}{\sqrt{256}}(|0\rangle|1\rangle + |1\rangle|7\rangle + \|2\rangle|4\rangle + |3\rangle|13\rangle + |4\rangle|1\rangle + |5\rangle|7\rangle + \cdots + |254\rangle|1\rangle + |255\rangle|7\rangle) \quad (4)$$

It goes without saying that, unlike their initial states, $|\psi 1\rangle$ and $|\psi 2'\rangle$ cannot be stated as separable states.

One of four states (i.e., $\psi 2$=1,7,4,13) is detected on $|\psi 2'\rangle$ when the superposition state of the second set of qubits, $|\psi 2'\rangle$, is corrupted during measurement. However, the initial qubit set $|\psi 1\rangle$remains in a superposition state. As soon as the measurement on $|\psi 2\rangle$ yields 4, the state (4) will be

$$|\psi_1\rangle|\psi_2{}'\rangle = \frac{1}{\sqrt{64}}(|2\rangle|4\rangle + |6\rangle|4\rangle + |10\rangle|4\rangle + \cdots + |254\rangle|4\rangle)$$
$$= \frac{1}{\sqrt{64}}(|2\rangle + |6\rangle + |10\rangle + \cdots + |254\rangle)|4\rangle \quad (5)$$

Therefore, in the next picture, the period r of $f_{a,}(m)$ can be detected as the gap Δt between successive potential states of $|\psi 1\rangle$.

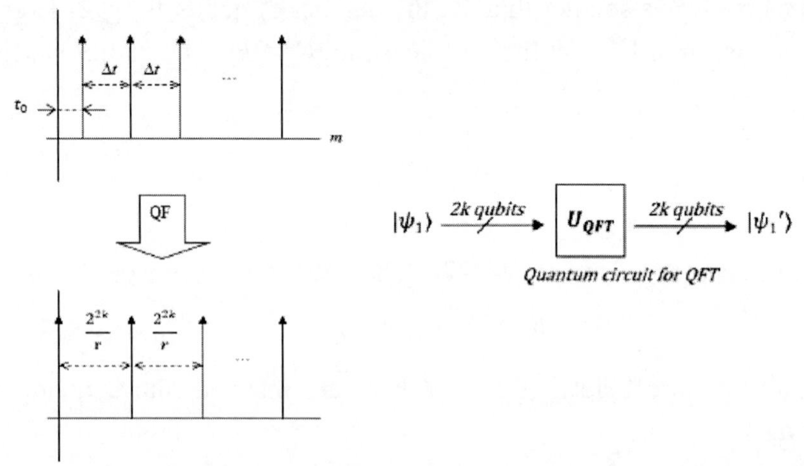

Fig.4.14 Fourier Transform in Discrete.

Finding r cannot be accomplished by a simple measurement on $|\psi 1\rangle$ since the measurement result is $m=l\Delta t+t_0$, where $f0$ is unknown and l=0,1,2,3,... It is necessary to remove the offset t_0 before to taking the measurement. The goal of the quantum Fourier Transform (QFT), a quantum circuit for the Discrete Fourier Transform for qubits, is to transform Δt to $2^{2k}/r$ and remove the offset in $|\psi 1\rangle$. Following the QFT procedure, a number $c=[2^{2k}/r]$ (j=1,2,3,...) is obtained from the measurement on the state $|\psi 1'\rangle$. The result value c can be divided by 2^{2k} since 2^{2k} is known.

$$\frac{c}{2^{2k}} = \frac{j}{r} \quad (6)$$

The nearest rational to j/r can be found by applying the continuing fraction expansion. The period r can be determined by doing this quantum operation multiple times.

An overview of Shor's algorithm

In order to factor a huge integer N,

1. Select an integer a at random that satisfies both $\gcd\{a,N\}=1$ and $0<a<N$.

2. Using the quantum computing with the classical continuous fraction expansion, find the period r for $a^m \ mod \ N$ (0< m <N^2)
3. Compute gcd {$a^{r/2}$−1,} and gcd {$a^{r/2}$+1,} when r is an even number.

a. Go back and do steps 1 and 2 if r is an odd number.

4. Verify if the factor of N is one of the outcomes from step 3. Repeat each step if not.

4.9.3 Finding periods and Shor's algorithm

Shor's algorithm, the most remarkable quantum computing discovery, effectively resolves the prime factorization problem, which is to determine the prime factors of a composite odd positive integer N. It is hypothesized, but not confirmed, that this fundamental computer science problem belongs to the class NP but not P in classical computation: given the components, it is simple to determine if they solve the problem, but it is challenging to identify them. Cryptographic systems that are widely used today and are based on this theory include RSA.

The number field sieve, the best classical approach now in use, requires exp $(O(n^{1/3}(\log n)^{2/3}))$ operations; in other words, it is super-polynomial in the input size n = log N, despite decades of efforts to discover a polynomial time factoring procedure. Shor found a quantum algorithm that uses $O(n^2 \log n \log\log n)$ basic gates to achieve the same result. As a result, this approach has an exponential speedup over all known classical algorithms and an input size that is polynomial.

Finding the period of the function f(x) = a^x mod N, where N is the number to be factorized and a < N is selected at random, is the problem's simplified form. We won't go over the procedures to run this reduction here because they can be completed effectively on a traditional computer.

The problem of determining the period r of a function f(x) with f{x + r) = f(x) is examined in the following. In order to make the topic easier, we will focus on the specific instance where r divides by m, an integer, the number of points N = 2^n over which the function f(x) is evaluated. Although the generic case introduces certain complexities, the essential concepts covered here remain unchanged. Two registers are required; the first is set up in the state of equal superposition, and the second has the function f(x), which builds the overall state.

$$\frac{1}{\sqrt{2^n}} \sum_{x=0}^{2^n-1} |x\rangle \, |f(x)\rangle \qquad \text{(a)}$$

It should be noted that both a quantum and a classical computer can effectively compute the modular exponentiation function needed for Shor's algorithm (for the quantum case).

Nonetheless, the function f(x) may be calculated for every a; in a single run because to quantum parallelism. Additionally, observe that the two registers are entangled following function evaluation. Sadly, we are unable to directly access every value of f(x). In contrast, it collapses upon a specific state $|f(x_0)\rangle$ following a measurement of the second register. Consequently, the wave function of a quantum computer becomes

$$\frac{1}{\sqrt{m}}\sum_{j=0}^{m-1}|x_0+jr\rangle|f(x_0)\rangle \qquad (0 \leq x_0 < r-1), \tag{b}$$

The number of x values such that f(x) = f(xo) is denoted by m = N/r. We obtain $f(x_0) = f(x_0+r) = f(x_0+2r) = \cdots = f(x_0+(m-1)r)$ as r is the period of f(x). The second register, which is factorized and no longer of importance to us, can now be ignored. It can be verified that the state is obtained via a quantum Fourier transform of the first register.

$$\frac{1}{\sqrt{r}}\sum_{k=0}^{r-1}\exp\left(\frac{2\pi i\, x_0\, k}{r}\right)\left|k\frac{N}{r}\right\rangle \tag{c}$$

As a result, certain frequencies have been chosen via quantum interference. In actuality, one of the r outcomes $kN/r\ (k = 0,1,\ldots,r-1)$ will be given with equal probability by a quantum measurement of the wave function (c). Therefore, if we represent the measured value by c, we obtain $c/N = \lambda/r$, where λ is an unknown integer. We can acquire both λ and r by reducing c/N to an irreducible fraction if λ and r do not share any factors. According to number theory, the likelihood that this will occur is at least $1/\log\log r$. If not, the algorithm breaks and has to be redone. It can be demonstrated that after an O(log logr) number of runs, the method succeeds with a probability that is arbitrarily near to one.

As a straightforward illustration, let's try to determine the period of the function $f(x) = \frac{1}{2}(\cos(\pi x)+1)$, presuming that x is loaded in a 3-qubit register, or N = 2^3 = 8. Since the function f(x) can have values of 0 or 1, it can be kept in a single-qubit register. Given that f{x) = 0 for odd x and f{x) = 1 for even x, we are unaware that the function has a period r= 2. The period-finding algorithm is what we want to use to find this period. To do this, we construct the state (a) from the fiducial state |000)|0) and read

$$\frac{1}{\sqrt{8}}\big(|0\rangle\,|f(0)\rangle+|1\rangle\,|f(1)\rangle+|2\rangle\,|f(2)\rangle+|3\rangle\,|f(3)\rangle \\ +|4\rangle\,|f(4)\rangle+|5\rangle\,|f(5)\rangle+|6\rangle\,|f(6)\rangle+|7\rangle\,|f(7)\rangle\big) \tag{d}$$

The second register is then measured, yielding, for instance, the result 0. Consequently, the state is collapsed by the whole wave function.

$$\frac{1}{2}\left(|1\rangle + |3\rangle + |5\rangle + |7\rangle\right)|0\rangle \tag{e}$$

where f(x) = 0 for the values x — 1, 3, 5, 7. Since the second register is no longer in use, we will disregard it from now on. The first register is then subjected to the quantum Fourier transform, which produces the following change:

$$|x\rangle \rightarrow \frac{1}{\sqrt{8}}\sum_{k=0}^{7} e^{2\pi i k x/8}|k\rangle \tag{f}$$

Thus, we derive the wave function.

$$\begin{aligned}|\psi\rangle = {} & \frac{1}{2\sqrt{8}}\left(|0\rangle + e^{i\pi/4}|1\rangle + e^{i2\pi/4}|2\rangle + \cdots + e^{i7\pi/4}|7\rangle\right) \\ & + \frac{1}{2\sqrt{8}}\left(|0\rangle + e^{i3\pi/4}|1\rangle + e^{i6\pi/4}|2\rangle + \cdots + e^{i21\pi/4}|7\rangle\right) \\ & + \frac{1}{2\sqrt{8}}\left(|0\rangle + e^{i5\pi/4}|1\rangle + e^{i10\pi/4}|2\rangle + \cdots + e^{i35\pi/4}|7\rangle\right) \\ & + \frac{1}{2\sqrt{8}}\left(|0\rangle + e^{i7\pi/4}|1\rangle + e^{i14\pi/4}|2\rangle + \cdots + e^{i49\pi/4}|7\rangle\right)\end{aligned} \tag{g}$$

Verification of the cancellation of the complex amplitudes in front of the states |1), |2), |3), |5), |6), and |7) is simple. Only for the phrases that come before the states |0) and |4) is the interference constructive. The wave function $|\psi\rangle$ can therefore be expressed as follows:

$$|\psi\rangle = \frac{1}{\sqrt{2}}\left(|0\rangle - |4\rangle\right). \tag{h}$$

The generic formula (c) agrees with this expression. Ultimately, we get outcomes 0 or 4 with equal probability from the measurement of the first register. The process must be repeated in the first scenario since we are unable to determine the period r of the function f(x). In the latter instance, the measured value is c = 4, and we write $c/N = \lambda/r$. The period r = 2 is eventually obtained by reducing c/N = 4/8 to an irreducible fraction $c/N = \lambda/r = 1/2$.

The question that naturally comes up when discussing the power of quantum computation is: Why is the speedup of quantum computation (in comparison to any known classical algorithm) quadratic for the searching problem and exponential for the factoring problem? Let's present an intuitive justification for this fact. A classic structure less problem is the seeking problem. Yes, we look for a certain object in an unstructured database. Thankfully, quantum mechanics provides a substantial quadratic speedup for this search. Regretfully, it appears that this gain is the highest that may be achieved. Conversely, the factoring problem has a structure that Shor's algorithm takes advantage of. Because of this structure, the integer-factoring problem can be reduced to the challenge of determining a function's period.

4.10 Quantum Fourier Transform (QFT)

Many quantum algorithms, such as Shor's algorithm for factoring huge numbers and quantum phase estimation techniques, rely heavily on the Quantum Fourier Transform (QFT). QFT can be helpful for tasks involving spectral analysis, data compression, and signal processing in the context of big data analytics. Large datasets' discrete Fourier transform can be computed quickly and effectively with QFT, facilitating quicker and more effective data processing and analysis. Additionally, it can be applied to dimensionality reduction and data compression techniques, which are crucial for managing complicated and high-dimensional data in big data analytics.

A new complex vector $\{\tilde{f}(0), \tilde{f}(1), \ldots, \tilde{f}(N-1)\}$ is created by the discrete Fourier transform of a vector with complex components $\{f(0), f(1), \ldots, f(N-1)\}$.

$$\tilde{f}(k) = \frac{1}{\sqrt{N}} \sum_{j=0}^{N-1} e^{2\pi i \frac{jk}{N}} f(j) \tag{1}$$

The same is true of the quantum Fourier transform. The unitary operator F, which acts on the states of the computational basis, is defined on a quantum register of n qubits (N = 2n) as follows:

$$F(|j\rangle) = \frac{1}{\sqrt{2^n}} \sum_{k=0}^{2^n-1} e^{2\pi i \frac{jk}{2^n}} |k\rangle \tag{2}$$

This allows an arbitrary state $|\psi\rangle = \sum_j f(j)|j\rangle$ to be changed into

$$|\tilde{\psi}\rangle = F|\psi\rangle = \sum_{k=0}^{2^n-1} \tilde{f}(k)|k\rangle \tag{3}$$

where the discrete Fourier transform of the coefficients $\{f(j)\}$ is represented by the coefficients $\{\tilde{f}(k)\}$ as per the relation (1)

The quantum circuit for calculating the quantum Fourier transform is now being built. The following notations for the binary representation of j are helpful to introduce:

$$j = j_{n-1}\, j_{n-2} \cdots j_0 = j_{n-1}\, 2^{n-1} + j_{n-2}\, 2^{n-2} + \cdots + j_0\, 2^0 \tag{4}$$

in addition to a binary fraction:

$$0.j_l\, j_{l+1} \cdots j_m = \frac{1}{2} j_l + \frac{1}{4} j_{l+1} + \cdots + \frac{1}{2^{m-l+1}} j_m \tag{5}$$

We may acquire the Fourier transform's product representation in a few easy steps.

$$\begin{aligned}
F(|j\rangle) &= \frac{1}{\sqrt{2^n}} \sum_{k=0}^{2^n-1} \exp\left(\frac{2\pi ijk}{2^n}\right) |k\rangle \\
&= \frac{1}{\sqrt{2^n}} \sum_{k_{n-1}=0}^{1} \cdots \sum_{k_0=0}^{1} \exp\left(2\pi ij \sum_{l=1}^{n} \frac{k_{n-l}}{2^l}\right) |k_{n-1} \ldots k_0\rangle \\
&= \frac{1}{\sqrt{2^n}} \sum_{k_{n-1}=0}^{1} \cdots \sum_{k_0=0}^{1} \otimes_{l=1}^{n} \exp\left(2\pi ij \frac{k_{n-l}}{2^l}\right) |k_{n-l}\rangle \\
&= \frac{1}{\sqrt{2^n}} \otimes_{l=1}^{n} \left[\sum_{k_{n-l}=0}^{1} \exp\left(2\pi ij \frac{k_{n-l}}{2^l}\right) |k_{n-l}\rangle \right] \\
&= \frac{1}{\sqrt{2^n}} \otimes_{l=1}^{n} \left[|0\rangle + \exp\left(2\pi ij \frac{1}{2^l}\right) |1\rangle \right] \\
&= \frac{1}{\sqrt{2^n}} \left(|0\rangle + e^{2\pi i\, 0.j_0}|1\rangle\right) \left(|0\rangle + e^{2\pi i\, 0.j_1 j_0}|1\rangle\right) \cdots \\
&\qquad \cdots \left(|0\rangle + e^{2\pi i\, 0.j_{n-1}j_{n-2}\cdots j_0}|1\rangle\right)
\end{aligned} \tag{6}$$

It is noteworthy that this product representation is factorized, indicating the absence of entanglement in the associated quantum state.

Building a quantum circuit that effectively computes the quantum Fourier transform is made simple by the product representation (6). Such a circuit is depicted in the figure below, where Rk stands for the operator.

$$R_k = \begin{bmatrix} 1 & 0 \\ 0 & \exp\left(\frac{2\pi i}{2^k}\right) \end{bmatrix} \tag{7}$$

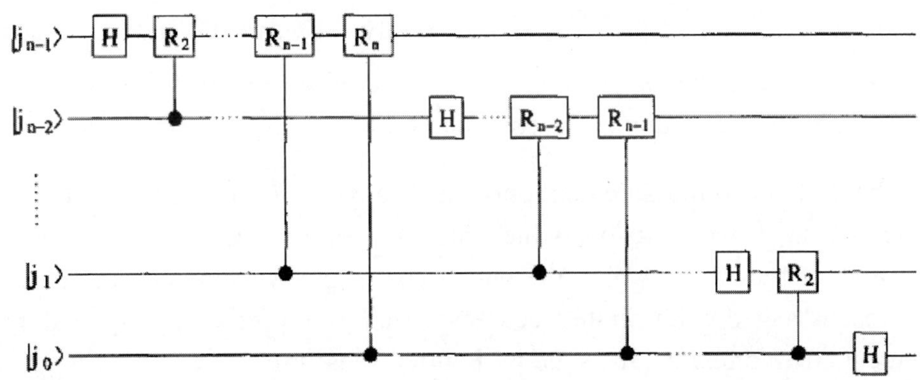

Fig.4.15 An implementation of the quantum Fourier transform on a circuit. The result is provided by below Eq.10.

It is sufficient to keep in mind that the Fourier transform is a linear operator when we examine the circuit's operation on a state $|j\rangle = |j_{n-1}j_{n-2}\cdots j_0\rangle$ of the computational basis (for a generic state $|\psi\rangle = \sum_j c_j|j\rangle$. The state is produced by the first Hamamard gate acting on the most important qubit.

$$\frac{1}{\sqrt{2}}\left(|0\rangle + e^{2\pi i\, 0.j_{n-1}}|1\rangle\right)|j_{n-2}\,\ldots\, j_0\rangle \tag{8}$$

If the associated control qubit is set to one, the ensuing controlled phase rotations, controlled-R_2 to controlled-R_n, add phases from $\pi/2$ to $\pi/2^{n-1}$. Following these n — 1 two-qubit gates, the state of the quantum-computer wave function remains

$$\frac{1}{\sqrt{2}}\left(|0\rangle + e^{2\pi i\, 0.j_{n-1}j_{n-2}\cdots j_0}|1\rangle\right)|j_{n-2}\,\ldots\, j_0\rangle \tag{9}$$

The output is produced by the quantum circuit in below Fig. after a similar process is repeated for the remaining qubits.

$$\frac{1}{\sqrt{2^n}}\left(|0\rangle + e^{2\pi i\, 0.j_{n-1}j_{n-2}\cdots j_0}|1\rangle\right)\left(|0\rangle + e^{2\pi i\, 0.j_{n-2}\cdots j_0}|1\rangle\right)\cdots \\ \cdots\left(|0\rangle + e^{2\pi i\, 0.j_0}|1\rangle\right). \tag{10}$$

With the exception of the qubits' reversible order, this state corresponds to the product representation (6). The 0(n) SWAP gates (see Fig. 3.4) can be used to acquire the right order, or qubits can be relabeled. The circuit demonstrates how n Hadamard and n(n — 1) /2 controlled phase-shift gates can be used to effectively implement the discrete Fourier transform of a complex vector of size N = 2^n on a quantum record of n qubits. Consequently, 0(n^2) elementary quantum gates are needed to calculate the quantum Fourier transform, while 0(2^nn) elementary operations are needed to compute the discrete Fourier transform using the fastest classical approach, the fast Fourier transform.

The final state $|\tilde{\psi}\rangle = \sum_k \tilde{f}(k)|k\rangle$ is not easily accessible, and a generic state $|\psi\rangle = \sum_j f(j)|j\rangle$ cannot be prepared efficiently, therefore we stress that we cannot really discuss an exponential speedup in the computation of the Fourier transform.

It is true that a standard measurement only yields a result $\bar{k}$ with probability $|\tilde{f}(\bar{k})|^2$. The amplitudes of the wave function, which are not readily accessible, are used for the quantum Fourier transform, which presents a challenge. After numerous runs, they can only be reconstructed with finite accuracy (each run produces a typical projective measurement after computing the state $|\psi\rangle$ Fourier transform).

We can estimate $\tilde{f}(k)$ as N_k/N, where Nk is the number of times the measurement yields outcome k, where N is the number of runs. This problem is actually a common challenge of quantum processing, and we already ran into it in regard to function evaluation. The quantum-computer wave function can be efficiently used to extract relevant information using quantum algorithms.

The quantum Fourier transform is a crucial component of exponentially efficient quantum algorithms, as we will see in the sections that follow.

4.11 Quantum Annealing Algorithms

The goal of quantum annealing methods is to discover the global minimum of an objective function in order to solve optimization problems. Combinatorial optimization issues that come up in a variety of big data analytics jobs, including resource allocation, scheduling, routing, and logistics, are especially well-suited for these techniques. Compared to classical methods, quantum annealing algorithms are more efficient in exploring the energy landscape of a problem and converge to the ideal solution by utilizing quantum fluctuations and tunneling processes. They have demonstrated encouraging outcomes when tackling challenging optimization issues, such as the job-shop scheduling problem and the traveling salesman challenge.

4.12 Quantum Cryptography Algorithms

Quantum cryptography algorithms are essential for protecting data security and privacy in the context of big data analytics, even though they have nothing to do with data processing or analysis. To enable safe data transmission and storage, these algorithms take advantage of quantum phenomena including quantum secure direct communication and quantum key distribution. Because quantum cryptography methods can withstand attacks from both classical and quantum computers, they have the potential to offer complete security. Sensitive information can be shielded from future quantum cryptanalytic assaults and unwanted access by integrating these techniques into big data analytics frameworks.

4.13 Quantum Key Distribution

Currently, one of the most useful uses of quantum information technology is quantum cryptography. The quantum key distribution (QKD) protocol (Bennett & Brassard, 1984), which has been used and made commercially available for more than ten years, is the most well-known example of quantum cryptography. The OKD with the one-time pad can use quantum mechanical features in a classical cryptography protocol to achieve theoretically unbreakable end-to-end security.

In this context, "unbreakable" refers to a physical characteristic that forbids decryptions without the key, rather than the algorithm's complexity, as the source of the cryptography's security. Classical cryptography's one-time pad is regarded as the ideal encryption method. These are the basic steps of the protocol. Before the transmission, a sender named Alice creates a one-time shared key called K, an n-bit random number, and sends it to a recipient named Bob.

$K=\{ki=0,1 \mid i=1,2,3,\ldots n\}$

For each bit in M and K, Alice executes exclusive OR operations in order to convey the n-bit secret message M to Bob. She then discards the K and sends Bob the resultant bit sequence, C.

$$M = \{m_i = 0,1 \mid i = 1,2,3,\ldots,n\}$$
$$C = \{c_i = m_i \oplus k_i \mid i = 1,2,3,\ldots,n\}$$

Bob uses the shared key K to conduct exclusive OR operations on the ciphertext C, then discards the K. There is complete security in this protocol. An entirely random bit sequence is produced when the message is supplemented with a random bit sequence. The sole feasible attack, since the key is only used once, is to guess the n-bit random bit sequence for an n-bit message. The issue with this approach is that there isn't a completely safe way to provide Bob the key, or K, before the transmission. The one-time pad protocol's strength depends on the strength of classical cryptography, which is not a perfect encryption technique, if RSA or AES were utilized.

When it comes to providing the keys for the one-time pad, QKD is crucial. C.H. Bennett and G. Brassard proposed the BB84 protocol in 1984, which was the first instance of QKD. After the procedure is finished, BB84 will employ photons to deliver a random bit sequence that Alice and Bob will use as a shared key. In the sections that follow, we present the application of BB84 with photon polarization.

Below figure provides a basic example of BB84. The distinction lies in the fact that Filters have changeable polarization angles.

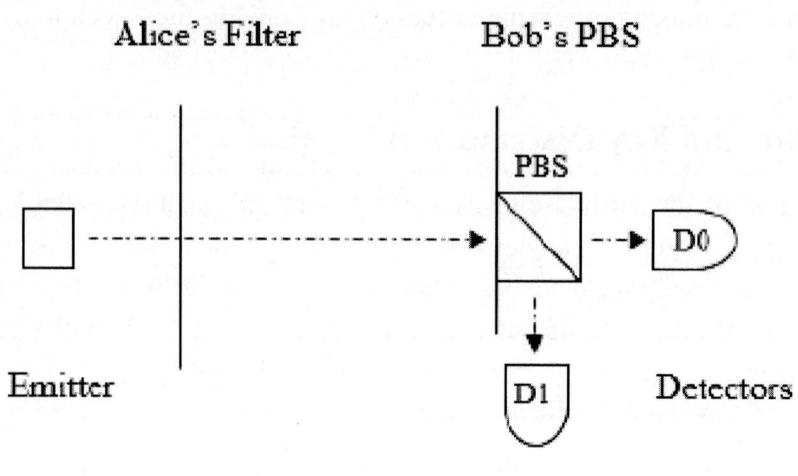

Fig.4.16 Basic example of BB84.

Bob can adjust the base angle (PBS) orientation to 0° or 45° degrees, while Alice can set her filter to four different angles: 0°, 45°, 90°, and 135° (see below figure).

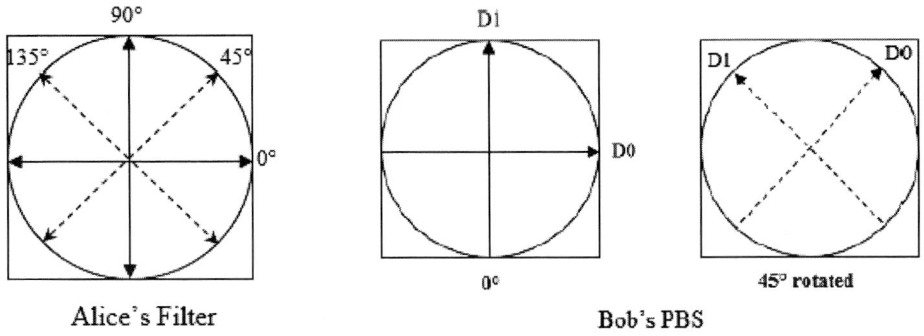

Fig.4.17 The angles of Bob's and Alice's filters.

In the BB84 protocol,

1. Alice creates a t-bit random bit sequence, R. $R=\{ri=0,1 \mid i=1,2,3,\ldots t,$.
2. Before sending each photon, Alice selects at random a diagonal base (D) or a horizontal-vertical base (H-V). Alice sets her filter to the 0° position when she selects a horizontal-vertical base and ri =0, causing Bob to receive a photon that is horizontally polarized. Alice sets her filter to 90° position when she selects a horizontal-vertical base and ri =1, causing Bob to receive a photon that is vertically polarized. Similarly, Alice positions her filter at 45° to send Bob a photon that has been polarized by 45° when she selects the diagonal base and ri=0. Alice sets her filter to 135° position when she selects the diagonal base and ri=1, causing a photon to be delivered to Bob with a 135° polarization.
3. Prior to receiving each photon at his PBS, Bob furthermore autonomously selects a diagonal base or a horizontal-vertical foundation.
4. After Alice sends Bob all t photons for R, Bob and Alice communicate over a public channel (such as the phone) regarding the base they selected for each transmission and reception. As a shared bit sequence K, only the bits whose bases match are retained. Table displays each transition's outcome.

Table 4.3 Bob's measuring results for every transmission made by Alice.

Alice				Bob		
Chosen Base	Random Bit r_i	Rotation Angle	Photon State	Chosen Base	Photon State after PBS	Measured Result
Horizontal -Vertical (H-V)	0	0°	↔	H-V	↔	0
				D	⤢ or ⤡	?
	1	90°	↕	H-V	↕	1
				D	⤢ or ⤡	?
Diagonal (D)	0	45°	⤢	H-V	↔ or ↕	?
				D	⤢	0
	1	135°	⤡	H-V	↔ or ↕	?
				D	⤡	1

If Alice and Bob coincidentally selected the same base, they can share the same classical bit information. However, since Bob's measurement result is unreliable, the bit information is deleted when Alice and Bob utilize separate bases.

For instance, the polarization is rotated by 45 degrees when Alice selects the D base and ri=0. Thus, Jones matrix for a rotator can be used by utilizing a rotation operator.

$$U_{R(\theta)} = \begin{bmatrix} cos\theta & -sin\theta \\ sin\theta & cos\theta \end{bmatrix} \tag{1}$$

The photon's state can be expressed as

$$|\psi_i\rangle = U_{R(45°)}|0\rangle = \frac{1}{\sqrt{2}}|0\rangle + \frac{1}{\sqrt{2}}|1\rangle. \tag{2}$$

Comparable to the illustration in above figure, Bob will receive $|0\rangle$ or $|1\rangle$ with a chance of 1/2 if he selects the H-V base. When Bob's base orientation and Alice's rotation angle differ in temperature, Bob's measurement result is either 0 or 1, with a chance of 1/2.

Eve, the eavesdropper, applies the same rule to the measurements. Eve can intercept photons from Alice and retransmit the same state of a photon to Bob if she has the same equipment as Alice and Bob. However, 25% of the measurement findings are incorrect because Eve is unsure about which basis to employ. In addition, 25% of Bob's measurement results are erroneous if Eve encodes additional photons depending on her measurement results and sends them to Bob. Therefore, the error rate is greatly increased when there is an eavesdropper. By examining a few bits in K to determine the error rate, Alice and Bob are able to identify Eve's attack. The no-cloning theorem prohibits the replication of any random unknown quantum state, even though Eve might want to replicate Alice's photon in order to prevent growing mistakes.

Limitations of Quantum Key Distribution Protocols that use the principles of quantum mechanics to securely exchange encryption are known as quantum key distribution (QKD) protocols. However, issues with scalability, distance restrictions, and susceptibility to specific attack types, such Trojan horse and side-channel attacks, still exist.

4.14 A New View on the Linear Superposition Principle

4.14.1 Wave function modification required for quantum teleportation

In this instance, modifying the Expansion Theorem for correlated terms in an EPR scenario. A correlation term in the definition of wave function (Ψ) provided by the Linear Superposition Principle in this section. The following word equation can be used to express the wave function (y) in general:

Wave Function (Ψ) = sum of the uncorrelated components + the related state term (δ).

The following is a numerical expression for this word equation:

$$\psi = \delta + \Sigma\, a_n\, \psi_n$$

where n ε allowed un-correlated states & Ψ (n) are eigen states.

Therefore, after providing an overview of our wave function formalism, we can now broadly classify wave function into three types, which are as follows:

1. Quantum Systems with $\text{Corr.} = \bar{0} \Rightarrow \psi = \Sigma\, a_n\, \psi_n$ where n ε (1,2,3,4..) & Ψ (n) are eigen states.
2. Quantum Systems with $0 < \text{Corr.} < 1 \Rightarrow \psi = \delta + \Sigma\, a_n\, \psi_n$ where n ε allowed uncorrelated states & Ψ (n) are eigen states.
3. Quantum Systems with $\text{Corr.} = 1 \Rightarrow \psi = \delta$ and $\Sigma\, a_n\, \psi_n = 0$ $\psi(n)$ are eigen states.

Therefore, the explanation of the Expansion Theorem in Quantum Systems above indicates that the wave function definition should be changed to allow for the representation of EPR states and that more research be done to ascertain the value of δ in the wave function definition. I have used the Schrodinger Wave Equation, both time dependent and time independent, to verify and reinforce the aforementioned formalism and see whether the Expansion Theorem's form changes.

We have Schrodinger Wave Eq. in the conventional formulation of quantum mechanics, which is provided by:

$\nabla^2\psi + 2m/h'\,(E-V)\,\psi = 0$ ------(1) Schrodinger time independent Eq.

In this eq. Ψ: wave function, m is effective mass of the system, E is total energy, V is potential energy of the system and $h' = h^2/4\pi^2$ (h: Plank Constant) and Schrodinger Time dependent wave eq. is given by:

$$ih/2\pi\,(\partial/\partial t)\,\psi = H\,\psi \text{ ---------(2)}$$

where Ψ: wave function of the system, H is Hamiltonian of the system.

Now that we have incorporated all three definitions of Ψ into these foundational wave equations of quantum mechanics, we can conclude that the updated definition of Ψ is accurate since the predicted outcomes are obtained.

4.14.2 Appropriateness of Quantum Bits for Quantum Processing

As covered in earlier parts, there are three different kinds of wave function systems. The relationship between these systems and qubits is as follows:

1. The Linear Superposition Principle gives the wave function of a quantum system with entirely unentangled states, or Corr. = 0.

$\psi = \Sigma\, a_n \psi_n \;\&\; \Sigma\, |a_n|^2 = 1$ where n ε(1,2,3,4……) and $\psi(n)$ are Eigen states.

Quantum algorithms can be implemented "efficiently" in these kinds of qubit systems because, in this instance, the Bloch Sphere theory permits parallel computing and massive information storage because each state □n is independent of the others and can therefore be utilized for information processing and storing.

2. In a quantum system with mixed entangled states, or 0< Corr. < 1, the wave function is as follows: $\psi = \delta + \Sigma\, a_n \psi_n \;\&\; \Sigma\, |a_n|^2 \neq 1$ where n ε permitted un-correlated states and $\psi(n)$ are Eigen states. Since separating entangled and unentangled states would result in an interaction with the system that would cause information loss and wave function collapse, it is not possible to do so in this situation. Therefore, this kind of situation is unsuitable for calculation as it might provide erroneous outcomes.

3. The wave function of a quantum system with entirely entangled states, or Corr. = 1, is given by: $\psi = \delta$ and $\Sigma\, a_n \psi_n = 0$ $\psi(n)$ are Eigen states. These states are not appropriate for computing or information storage; instead, they are useful for teleporting information utilizing EPR states. Therefore, scenario 3 is only appropriate for information sharing while maintaining the validity of the Quantum No Cloning Theorem.

4.14.3 A different take on the Quantum No Cloning Theorem.

The following is the definition of the Quantum No Cloning Theorem: "Quantum bits of an unknown quantum state cannot be copied."

Alternatively, "It is not possible to replicate information of arbitrary qubits."

The following is Heisenberg's Uncertainty Principle, which brings forth this basic limit:

$$\Delta x . \Delta p >= h/2\pi$$

The location measurement uncertainty is represented by Δx.

The uncertainty in the momentum measurement is denoted by Δp.

The Uncertainty Principle, which states that an act of observation causes the wave function to collapse and information held by a quantum system to be lost, therefore gives rise to the measurement issue in quantum mechanics.

$$\psi = \alpha|0> + \beta|1> \xrightarrow{\text{observation}} \text{either } |0> \text{ or } |1>$$

The 2nd Law of Thermodynamics provides a further reason for the information loss related to qubit measurement: energy exchange results in irreversibility being introduced into the system. Measuring or making observations has itself introduced an irreversibility component to the system, which is further explained by the existence of the notion of canonically conjugate variables in quantum mechanics. That is, in a quantum system with two canonically conjugate observables, let's say A and B, they satisfy the inequality $AB \neq BA$, which is expressed in quantum mechanics as commutator brackets $[A, B] = h/2\pi \Rightarrow AB\text{-}BA=h/2\pi$.

The Heisenberg Uncertainty Principle states that uncertainty seeps in during the measurement of a quantum system due to the varied fact that $AB \neq BA$ implies that some irreversibility was introduced. This raises several crucial queries, such as:

1. Does the idea of a quantum of action h (h, 2h, 3h, etc.) cause the measurement process to become irreversible since ½ h or any fraction value of h cannot occur?
2. Since entropy is a statistical phenomena, does the introduction of irreversibility into the system have any bearing on the statistical behavior of quantum probabilities?
3. Does the irreversibility of a quantum measurement explain the necessity of the Uncertainty Principle by causing uncertainty in the measurement process and ultimately in the system?

Accordingly, entropy (S) in classical mechanics refers to the information lost in a system as a result of energy interaction and the second law of thermodynamics. However, the idea of choice of information in Quantum Mechanics is a result of wave function collapse, which allows us to construct a new parameter for quantum systems that is connected to the choice of information and is equivalent to entropy. As a result, we raise the possibility that a new parameter—analogous to entropy—is required to represent the idea of information choice. More study may be conducted in the domain of the new parameter. Another explanation for the Quantum No Cloning Theorem is the idea of irreversibility in the system as a result of the measurement process leading to non-replication of information on a qubit.

Chapter - 5
Quantum Computing Architecture

Quantum computing will require compilers and computer-aided design tools. A high-level language program that represents a quantum computing algorithm is converted into a computer-aided design flow that implementation that is customized to a given technology. Show the changes to the quantum program's representation by following the important steps in this flow. The languages and conversions required to represent and optimize a quantum algorithm along the design flow are the main topic. For those who design algorithms, create tools, and conduct experiments, this software architecture offers substantial advantages. The accuracy and performance trade-offs that can be achieved by comparing various optimization and error-correction techniques at specific design hierarchy levels are of special interest.

Compilers and design tools will be essential for quantum computing, just as they are for classical computing. A four-phase computer-aided design pipeline with a layered software architecture that maps a high-level language source program that represents a quantum algorithm to a technology-specific implementation. The sequence of actions in this flow and demonstrate the accompanying changes in the quantum algorithm's intermediate representations. To demonstrate the general design flow and specific design changes, use the outcomes of the optimization and simulation tool work.

This section discusses the languages and notational representations required to facilitate this design flow. Specifically, the high-level programming language used to define quantum algorithms is crucial. Compilers for the quantum programming language must be optimized in order to translate the programs into reliable and effective low-level programs that can run on a quantum device or be replicated on conventional computers with the aid of high-performance tools.

The toolsuite, the advantages of the layered software architecture, and the design flow are covered in detail in the next section. then the characteristics required for a simulator with layout tools, a quantum computer compiler, a quantum assembly language, a quantum programming language, and a quantum physical operations language. Ion-trap computer design processes provide as examples of what is now feasible. It highlights areas where software help may soon be needed and highlights the difficulties in developing software structures for quantum design automation.

5.1 Tools for Quantum Design

5.1.1 The Tool Suite

Here, a layered hierarchy of tools and notations is envisioned, comprising layout tools, compilers, optimizers, simulators, and programming languages. As our understanding of new quantum technologies advances, the programming languages and compilers at the top of our toolsuite must support the abstractions used to design quantum algorithms and adapt to changes in technology-independent and dependent optimizations.

Details of the new quantum technologies that will eventually be used to implement the algorithms outlined in the high-level programming language must be incorporated into the simulation and layout tools at the bottom end. Performance, qubit reduction, and fault-tolerant implementation tradeoffs must all be balanced by the tools. These factors led to the implementation of a tiered hierarchy of design tools with straightforward interfaces at each level.

5.1.2 Advantages of open software architecture

For quantum computing, a layered software architecture with clearly defined interfaces has various advantages. Technically speaking, adding new tools to an existing toolkit is made simpler and tool interoperability is facilitated by a layered architecture. It also makes it simpler to update and manage already-existing tools. The current state of quantum circuit optimization for noise avoidance is confined to maximizing speed and minimizing errors. A layered design would enable researchers to test novel algorithms and assess their advantages with specific quantum technologies through simulation before building the real physical components of the device. The enormous software development costs necessary to create all the tools required to create quantum devices are beyond the financial means of any one entity.

The open software design, which enables broader community participation in the development and usage of necessary tools, would be advantageous to all parties involved in quantum computing. Designers of quantum algorithms can test novel algorithms in more realistic environments with real-world resource limitations and noise.

When creating quantum circuit improvements, researchers can assess tradeoffs by accounting for physical characteristics and quantum noise. Before conducting costly lab tests, experimentalists and device designers can simulate key quantum algorithms on emerging technology. Designers of tools can test out new algorithms and assess how they affect the design process as a whole. For customized-correction processes, researchers can also create more accurate noise models.

5.1.3 Flow of Design

The design flow, which is a four-step procedure shown in the figure below, converts a high-level program that represents a quantum algorithm into an implementation or simulation tailored to a particular technology. In the quantum computer compiler (QCC), the initial three stages of the design flow are included. The final stage consists of simulating or implementing the quantum algorithm on a quantum gadget.

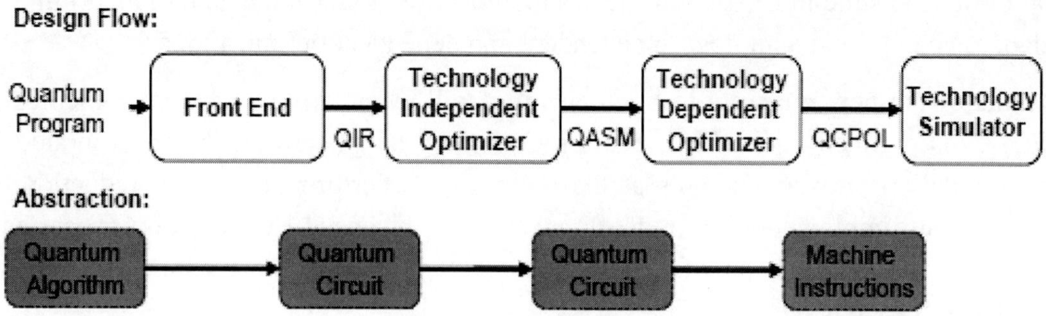

Fig.5.1 Design flow.

The secret to a hierarchy of interoperable tools is the representations of the quantum algorithm between the phases. A high-level specification of a quantum algorithm is mapped into a quantum intermediate representation (QIR) via the compiler's front end in the first stage. An encoding of quantum circuits with gates taken from a universal basis set is the most widely used option for the quantum intermediate representation.

The quantum algorithm's QIR representation is mapped into a corresponding lower-level circuit representation of single-qubit and CNOT gates by a technology-independent optimizer in the second phase. For quantum assembly language, take a look at the lower-level notation, QASM. Using a variety of goodness metrics, including circuit size, depth, accuracy, and fault tolerance, the second phase aims to provide the best possible QASM representation.

In order to simulate or execute the quantum algorithm, the third phase carries out optimizations appropriate for the quantum computing technology. It produces QCPOL, a physical language representation for quantum computing physical operations language with technology-specific features. There are multiple sub phases within the third phase. Using a fault-tolerant discrete universal set of gates, the first sub phase converts the QASM representation of single qubit and CNOT gates into a QASM representation. Use the Solovay-Kitaev approach to approximate the original gate set when mapping the gates to a discrete set. These gates are mapped into a QCPOL representation in the second sub phase, which also includes the necessary movements and the physical instructions for the fault-tolerant processes. This is where knowledge of the physical arrangement comes in.

Technology-dependent tools like layout modules and circuit or physical operations simulators, as well as execution on a real quantum device, are part of the last stage. Real designs are probably going to be iterative in nature, requiring multiple iterations through one or more of these stages. Furthermore, it is essential that a quantum algorithm be physically implemented in a fault-tolerant manner. Error-correction circuitry can be incorporated into this design flow at any level of the hierarchy, although the ideal location for its introduction is still unknown. It is particularly intriguing to find out if the compiler can create a fault-tolerant QASM or QCPOL representation and automatically add error-correction.

5.2 Code Sources for Quantum Programming

Since the present repertory of quantum algorithms is small, creating a quantum programming language is a challenging endeavor. According to the QRAM model, communication between the quantum device and the classical processor occurs. For any quantum processing to be carried out, the high-level quantum programming language must provide the abstractions required by algorithm designers and experimental physicists. The majority of these languages provide abstractions derived from Dirac notation or the quantum circuit model.

A quantum programming environment should have a few essential features. First and foremost, the environment requires a quantum programming language that is comprehensive in the sense that it can be used to write and express all quantum algorithms, both present and future. In essence, the language should be able to describe the traditional pre- and post-processing computations, support complex numbers, and express and compose unitary transforms and measurements. To create a quantum algorithm, the environment needs also have gate libraries or reusable subroutines that the programmer can call.

Second, if the surroundings and language are founded on well-known ideas and constructions, that is beneficial. It will be simpler to learn how to write, debug, and execute a quantum program in this manner as opposed to using a whole different environment.

Third, it should be simple to distinguish between quantum and classical computations in the environment. Given the noise and restricted coherence time of a quantum computer, the separation can be used to estimate and constrain the amount of time required to execute the quantum operations on the quantum device. It should be possible for a quantum programming language's compiler to convert a source program into a reliable and effective quantum circuit or physical implementation; Using straightforward, effective, and efficient methods, it should be simple to translate into various gate sets or optimize with regard to a particular cost function.

Fourth, since the source code shouldn't depend on hardware, the high-level programming language should be compatible with various quantum technologies.

However, technology-specific modules should be able to be included due to the language and environment. The last benefit would be having a language that allows high-level abstractions, which would make it simple to create new algorithms that make use of quantum mechanical concepts like superposition and entanglement. The abstractions contained in the various quantum programming languages that are currently in use, including QCL, Q, and others, do not fully utilize the quantum-mechanical concepts that underlie quantum calculations.

An interpreted language like QCL, for instance, has several common programming elements like arrays and subroutines. It gives the programmer the ability to create new processes and offers a universal set of gates. But as the operators' and states' descriptions rely on matrices and vectors, they offer no further information beyond the standard Dirac notation. Q is a C++ extension that distinguishes between quantum and classical processes clearly. It constructs a quantum operator as a data object instead of a function to facilitate simple compositions and run-time optimizations. However, once more, this language lacks further information and is based on Dirac notation.

By integrating suitable abstractions into a quantum computing language and environment, create a setting that facilitates the creation and programming of quantum algorithms. Moreover, anticipating a language that makes it simple to develop reliable, optimized target programs.

5.3 Quantum Computer Compiler (QCC)

A classical machine's generic compiler for a classical language is made up of several stages, each of which changes the source program's representation. The original software is tokenized into logical character sequences by the lexical analyzer. The syntax analyzer receives the tokens and converts them into a syntax tree. The semantic analyzer receives this representation and proceeds to examine it for compatible type operations and semantic mistakes. To produce an intermediate representation for the program being compiled, the output is thereafter routed to the intermediate code generator.

To increase the code's performance, potential machine-independent improvements are sought after during the intermediate code optimization step. The code generation phase generates the target code for the machine to run using these optimizations. Optimizations based on machine dependencies are carried out prior to generating a target program.

The compilation process has been divided into several stages, which has prompted the creation of effective tools and algorithms for creating components for each stage. The techniques and tools for creating lexical, syntactic, and semantic analyzers for QCCs can be applied to quantum compilers because their front-end procedures are comparable to those of classical compilers. However, compared to conventional compilers, QCCs' intermediate representations, optimization, and code generation stages necessitate new strategies, like a method for integrating error-correction functions into the target language program. This section outlines the state of the art in terms of optimization, code generation, and intermediate representations.

5.3.1 The Quantum Intermediate Representation and the Front End

A quantum algorithm's high-level specification is converted into a quantum intermediate representation (QIR) based on the quantum circuit model during the first stage of QCC. This approach is useful since the quantum circuit model can be used to express alternative forms of quantum computation, such as adiabatic quantum computing. Specifically, we can take into account fault-tolerant constructs at different stages of our design flow by selecting the circuit formalization. Additionally, we may apply circuit synthesis and optimization methods to both the technology-dependent and technology-independent stages of the design flow by utilizing the quantum circuit model.

5.3.2 Optimization and Synthesis of Circuits

A quantum circuit's QASM representation is created and optimized in the second and third stages of QCC. This section provides specifics on potential synthesis and optimization processes that, in analogy with traditional chip design methods, can be used in these two stages. Classical logic circuit synthesis algorithms translate a Boolean function into a circuit that uses gates from a specified gate library to implement the function. Usually, these methods are used in conjunction with compilers in conventional chip design methodologies or following high-level synthesis. Likewise, quantum circuit synthesis is the process of creating a quantum circuit that "computes" a given unitary matrix up to a specified quantum measurement or relative phase.

When a Boolean function's truth table is available, a two-level circuit that is linear in the truth table's size can be built right away. However, the circuit structure optimization is not simple. In comparison, it is difficult to even identify a suitable quantum circuit to implement a 2^n X 2^n unitary matrix. For a 2^n X 2^n unitary matrix, constructive methods that produce an asymptotically optimal circuit with 4^n gates have only recently been created. The constant numerical factor between the lower and upper bounds, however, stays high, with the exception of certain exceptional circumstances, including diagonal circuits and two-qubit circuits. In addition to up to three CNOT gates, an arbitrary two-qubit operator needs either fifteen more elementary single-qubit gates or six more generic single-qubit gates.

Of special interest is the distinction between basic and elementary gates. By using the Euler-angles formula, basic gates can be broken down, up to phase, into a product of one-parameter rotations. As a result, we consider one-parameter rotations to be elementary.

Although some outcomes in terms of elementary gates can be restated in terms of coarser gates, the costs of physical implementations are not necessarily reflected in coarser gates. As a result, depending on the specific technology selected, the third phase requires mapping the representation into a universal set of gates. In many NMR implementations, for instance, single-qubit basic gates seem to be just as inexpensive. However, Rz gates are far simpler to design than Rx and Ry gates when working with ion traps.

Some degree of avoidance of this basic reliance on technology is desirable when creating reusable software for automating the design of quantum circuits. It's true that this issue is not new. In the 19th century, Boole proposed the traditional selection of elementary logic gates in classical computing (AND-OR-NOT) for purely abstract reasons rather than because of particular technological considerations. CMOS-based integrated circuits now make it simpler to implement the NAND gate than the AND gate. Libraryless logic synthesis and technology mapping are separated in commercial circuit synthesis tools to overcome this problem. An abstract gate library, like AND-OR-NOT, is used in the former, which highlights the scalability of synthesis algorithms that capture the global structure of the supplied computation.

Based on local optimizations, the final stage transfers logic circuits to a technology-specific gate library, frequently provided by a semiconductor vendor. AOI (AND/OR/INVERTER) gates and other composite multi-input gates with optimal layouts may be found in technology-specific libraries. According to theory, re-expressing circuits using a new set of universal gates could result in a maximum increase in circuit size of a constant, provided that certain fair assumptions regarding the gate libraries in question are made.

It is anticipated that quantum circuits will also be distinguished from technology-independent circuit creation and technology mapping. To do this, basic-gate circuits can be made simpler by applying handy circuit identities by momentarily breaking down basic gates into elementary gates. The lower bounds for the number of CNOTS in an n-qubit circuit $(\lceil (4^n - 3n - 1)/4 \rceil)$ and all lower bounds for two-qubit circuits do, in fact, depend on these circuit identities. The autonomous instantiation of error-correction, a potentially crucial component for scalable quantum computing, is a continuous endeavor in the synthesis and optimization of quantum circuits. The technology-dependent optimization phase also requires circuit synthesis and optimization using discrete gate libraries, which is yet mostly unexplored.

In light of this, it is noted that the Gottesman-Knill theorem postulates a correspondence between classical reversible circuits made up of CNOT and Toffoli gates and stabilizer circuits, which are essential to quantum error correction. Stabilizer circuits may be optimized by optimizing the latter. Partitioning stabilizer circuits into eight groups of Phase, Hadamard, and CNOT gates (H-P-C-P-H-P-C-P) is an alternate method of optimizing stabilizer circuits. After cancellations, the Phase and Hadamard groups can only have linear sizes (in terms of qubits) since they are single-qubit gates.

The asymptotically optimal technique can therefore be used to find circuits with a maximum of cn2= log2(n) gates, as all the complexity is concentrated in two CNOT groups. Such universal circuit partitions could yield canonical forms that could aid in compiler optimization. Circuit partitions can also inspire novel reprogrammable circuit architectures and circuit layouts. To create acceptable circuits for implementation on a quantum device, the second and third phases of QCC will require techniques like those covered above.

5.4 Quantum Assembly Language

The QCC's technology-independent phase converts a quantum algorithm representation into a corresponding set of instructions in quantum assembly language (QASM). With a set of quantum instructions derived from the quantum circuit model of quantum computation and the traditional RISC instruction sets, QASM is an expansion of a RISC assembly language. QASM employs qubits and classical bits (cbits) as the fundamental information units, just as the quantum circuit model does. The storage of each cbit in a distinct classical register guarantees the usability of the classical RISC instruction set. Nevertheless, QASM does not have any quantum registers. As static resources, every qubit and classical register used in a QASM program needs to be declared at the outset.

Only unitary operations and measurements make up quantum operations. Each unitary operator in QASM is represented by an equivalent series of CNOT and single-qubit gates. Because they can precisely express any quantum circuit, these gates are known as the universal gate set. Since single-qubit operations are defined by three Euler-angles, they are stored as a triple of rationals. Every rational number in the triple is assumed to be implicitly multiplied by π. By first zeroing out the classical register and then copying the measurement result into it, the non-reversible measurement operation on a single qubit replicates the measurement result to a classical register. Additionally, the measurement's result is put to the qubit. QASM uses an OR of the bit values to condition off of the classical register in order to achieve classical control of a qubit. It is therefore necessary to mask and shift the bits into a single register in order to properly deal with the outcome of many measurements.

5.5 Quantum Physical Operations Language (QCPOL)

A specific quantum circuit's exact execution on a given physical system is specified by the quantum physical operations language (QCPOL). The target system-specific instruction set of a physical operations language includes sufficient low-level details to clearly execute the quantum circuit. After providing an overview of the general characteristics of a QCPOL, we move on to a particular illustration of a physical language for the trapped-ion quantum processor.

5.5.1 Characteristics of a QCPOL

Physical operations were categorized as system-specific instructions, communication, computation, initialization, and classical control. This classification is broad enough to include future devices as well as those that have so far achieved quantum information processing. Instructions for initialization outline how to get the system ready for use. These consist of loading qubits into the system and putting them in a recognized, legitimate initial state. In actuality, this calls for adjusting the degrees of freedom of the physical qubit carriers that could influence an internal qubit or the capacity to govern an internal qubit.

Measurements and gates are both part of computation instructions. Gates for the majority of physical systems are equivalent to regulated electromagnetic pulses. Only a small number of gates are allowed in ordinary systems because gate types and speeds are highly dependent on the interaction that binds qubits. In addition to being restricted to specific operators in practice, measurement techniques depend on connection to a measurement device.

In order for groups of qubits to participate in local gates, movement instructions regulate the relative distance between them. Swap gates are the primary function of certain systems with stationary qubit carriers. There are mobile qubit carriers in other systems, or possibly a combination of immobile and mobile carriers. The movement instructions for these systems will be machine-specific.

At least a portion of conventional logic processes will be present in quantum information processors. In the most basic scenario, quantum processors will have access to the entire conventional instruction set and be managed by external computers. However, it's possible that future quantum processors will combine particular low-level functionality and interfaces with classical logic.

Lastly, system-specific commands that might not fit into broad categories are included in a physical operations language. These commands most likely regulate additional qubit carrier degrees of freedom or nondestructively identify whether carriers are present or absent.

By defining each instruction's start time and duration, QCPOL instructions are arranged into a logical program. If the machine is capable of parallel operation, then commands can be arranged into groups or streams that run concurrently. In essence, more semantic restrictions are produced by physical limitations.

5.5.2 QCPOL Illustration: Trapped-ion QCPOL

The languages used for physical operations might differ significantly among various physical systems. The functioning of a trapped-ion quantum computer system is demonstrated by one example of a physical operations language in this section.

Qubit carriers in trapped-ion devices are charged, electromagnetically trapped atoms. The intrinsic electronic and nuclear states of a single ion serve as the representation for each qubit. Laser pulses with particular frequencies that target one or more ions use both single-qubit and multi-qubit quantum gates. Ions in the $|0\rangle$ state can glow when laser pulses are calibrated properly, which allows for measurement as well.

By coupling to one another via Coulomb repulsion, two or more ions can be held in a single trap. This allows for a qubit-qubit interaction through their aggregate vibrational modes. If ion temperatures are maintained at low levels and vibrational states are managed, these modes can function as a "bus" qubit. If two ion qubits are near enough to each other to communicate with the bus qubit, they are linked.

There is a lot of promise for trapped-ion systems as a quantum information processing technique in the future. Numerous teams have shown a universal set of gates and measurements for trapped-ion quantum information processing, which includes quantum teleportation more recently and simple multi-qubit quantum algorithms. Static voltages can also transfer ion-qubits between traps, as shown by tests. When combined, these studies provide a path toward a scalable technology that could be set up in a sizable microarray similar to charge-coupled devices.

Designed a QCPOL instance dedicated to ion traps that included system-specific instructions, initialization, computation, movement, and classical control. The loading of several ions into a designated loading zone and laser cooling to lower ion temperatures are the two steps involved in initializing an ion trap processor. After that, conditional rotations are carried out to place every qubit in the $|0\rangle$ state, followed by measurement. A controlled-phase gate between ions in the same trap, done with three sideband pulses, and single qubit rotations in the $\hat{x} - \hat{y}$ plane, accomplished with pulsed laser excitation, are the natural descriptions of computation using quantum gates. A multiply-controlled phase gate, which is helpful for producing massive entangled states, may also involve chained ions. The qubit readout is characterized by a projective measurement using a readout laser pulse.

Ions are moved into and out of traps (and chains) by means of electrostatic fields. With "T" and "X" connections, assume that there are enough movement instructions for a planar rectangular trap setup. Further instructions for splitting and joining split and re-join chains. It is assumed that classical control of ions is universal and is carried out by a quick external classical processor. Either a local microprocessor chip fitted close to the trap or a remote control PC can be used in practice.

The decoherence and heating of ion-qubits and bus qubits during a computation, in the movement, splitting, and joining operations, require system-specific instructions for trapped ions. High temperatures have the potential to expel ions from the trap in the worst situation. Therefore, a system-specific technique for reinitializing the bus qubit utilizing recooling pulses is included in the instruction set. Similar to sideband pulses used in multi-qubit gates, these are handled differently and require particular handling from the design tools.

5.6 High-throughput Quantum Circuit Simulation

Richard Feynman noted in the 1980s the inherent computational challenge of emulating quantum computation on conventional computers. Furthermore, as a result, he proposed using quantum-mechanical effects to accelerate classical computing. Theoretically, Shor and Grover have found these speedups, but for engineering purposes, numerical simulation of quantum computers on classical computers is still appealing. Similarly, before expensive manufacture, chip designers in traditional Electronic Design Automation always simulate individual modules and entire systems on test vectors. Numerical simulations can also be used to assess "quantum heuristics" that only function well for a small percentage of inputs or that defy formal worst-case analysis.

For a number of reasons, the quantum circuit formalism appears to be the most appropriate for the numerical simulation stage. Quantum state and circuit mathematical models use linear algebra: gates can be represented by square matrices of different sizes, and n-qubit quantum states by 2^n-dimensional vectors. Gates with serial composition match the conventional matrix product, whereas those with parallel composition match the tensor (Kronecker) product. Applying a series of 2^n X 2^n matrices consecutively to a state vector can naively approximate a quantum circuit. This reduces quantum simulation to normal linear algebraic operations using vectors and matrices of exponential dimension. Additionally, linear algebra is used to simulate quantum measurement.

Utilizing the structure that quantum circuits may provide in matrices and vectors is a crucial realization for effective simulation. Polynomial-time simulation methods designed for "slightly entangled" quantum computation and circuits with limited gate types were developed in order to achieve this. Circuits used for quantum error-correction and the states that these circuits can produce (stabilizer states) are the focus of the Gottesman-Knill approach. Two simulation tools that could be used in the fourth stage of our design flow are described in the following sections.

5.6.1 QuIDDPro: All-purpose Graph-Based Simulator

Using the QuIDD data structure, a general simulation method based on data compression exists. In the worst situation, its performance is no better than that of simple linear algebra, but it can significantly reduce the size of structured vectors and matrices, including small gates, all basis states, and some tensor products. A directed acyclic graph with one source and several sinks that are each assigned a complex integer is called a QuIDD. Any given vector or matrix can be represented as a QuIDD, and vice versa (subject to memory limits). The graph's directed paths represent matrix and vector elements. It is surprising to see that, when considering compressed data representations, all linear-algebraic operations can then be expressed as graph algorithms.

QuIDDs use time and memory that scale polynomially with the number of qubits to simulate a practical class of quantum circuits. For instance, this class includes every element in Grover's algorithm, with the exception of the application-dependent oracle. Moreover, the time and memory resources needed for the QuIDD-based simulation of Grover's technique are polynomial in the size of the oracle p(}) function that is represented by a QuIDD. Therefore, Grover's algorithm can be simulated classically almost as quickly as an ideal quantum circuit if a given p(}) for a search problem can be represented as a QuIDD using polynomial time and memory resources (including converting an original specification into a QuIDD). This is due to the fact that Grover's algorithm's complexity is mostly determined by the quantity of iterations.

A formal data structure for compressed linear algebra operations used in quantum computing, QuIDDs are distinct from other simulation methods and are connected to the state-vector representation. All that is needed to extend QuIDDs to simulate density matrices is the implementation of a few extra graph traversal operations, like trace-overs. These extensions, together with empirical performance results on a variety of circuit types up to 24 qubits, have been detailed. 64TB of memory would be needed for the simple modeling of any 16-qubit density matrix, for example. With CNOT and Toffoli gates, the QuIDDPro package consumes less than 2MB of memory for a reversible 16-qubit adder circuit. The authors are presently offering this software, which has an ASCII front end and Matlab-like input language capabilities.

5.6.2 The Trapped-Ion Simulator, Scheduling Tools, and Layout Tools

The first tools used to study trapped ion systems are covered in this section. Large-scale device or component design and testing can be facilitated by the use of layout, scheduling, and simulation technologies. The topology of a quantum network is used by layout tools to determine the initial geometric configuration of qubits as well as the acceptable places for qubit relocation during computing.

Scheduling tools identify movement patterns during a calculation and incorporate movement-related machine-specific activities. Lastly, the arrangement and movement sequence are assessed by simulation tools.

An arbitrary quantum circuit is mapped onto a Turing machine with a single head and a circular tape using a general layout tool that we have developed (see figure below).

Scheduling operations are made especially easy by the single-headed Turing machine's straightforward structure. Prior to each multi-qubit gate, qubits are transferred into the head, and following the gate, they are returned to the tape. An H-tree is mapped onto circuits built from concatenated quantum codes using a more specialized layout tool. Similar to a Koch curve or other fractal, an H-tree is built recursively. Because the qubits for the inner codes are kept close to one another, concatenated quantum codes have a self-similar structure, requiring fewer movement operations per gate. Employed the pathways for simple operations to schedule operations onto the H-tree, but we anticipate that more advanced methods will be able to automate this process.

The physical operation sequences produced by these two layout and scheduling techniques can be simulated to confirm accuracy, dependability, and overall running time. A simulation tool that uses the model of a trapped-ion quantum computer was created here for large-scale trapped ion systems. Both a layout and a QCPOL program that implements a quantum circuit, produced by scheduling and layout tools, are accepted by the simulator. The final quantum state, single-shot measurement and failure histories, total execution time, and overall circuit reliability are all included in the simulator output. Furthermore, the QCPOL instructions as they are emulated can be shown graphically by the simulator. An illustration of this output may be found in the below figure.

Deeper comprehension of the structure seen in practical quantum circuits and improved algorithms will lead to advances in the performance of quantum-circuit simulators and designing tools. One especially intriguing method is to automatically reorganize a given quantum circuit so that the new circuit has fewer gates and generates the same output but is simpler to mimic. Another way that simulation and synthesis are related is that only a limited number of universal quantum gates are directly supported by optimized simulation primitives.

More complex gates must be broken down into low-level primitives in order to be simulated. From a physics standpoint, these decompositions also seem essential, since a given Hamiltonian can be numerically simulated after being broken down into a quantum circuit.

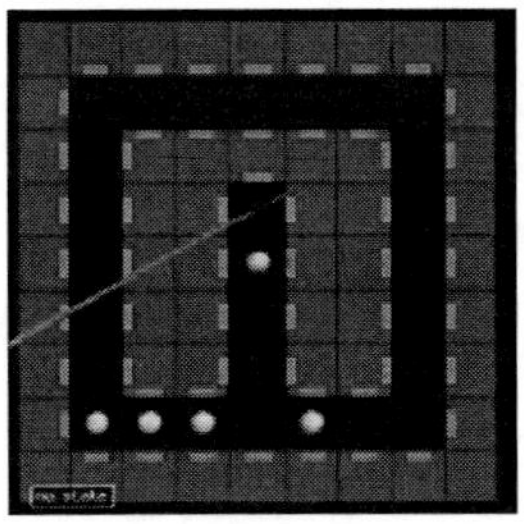

(a)

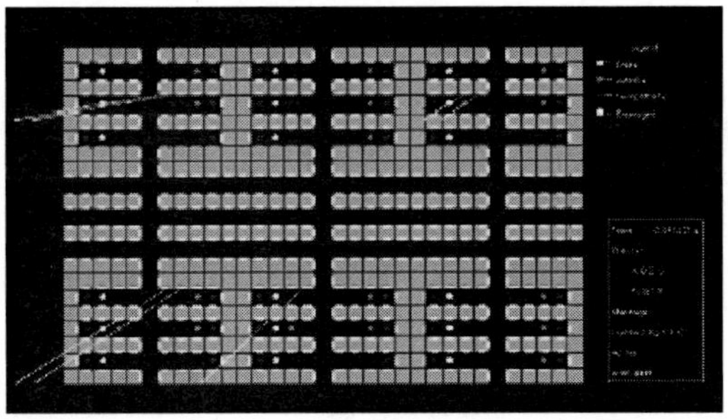

(b)

Fig.5.2 (a) An automatic layout tool creates the Turing machine layout for a trapped ion processor. (b) A screenshot displaying an H-tree layout from the simulator's graphical display.

Ions, depicted as spheres, are qubits, and lines, or laser pulses, are used to apply gates. The qubits can travel inside the black areas of the image, but they are not allowed to enter the substrate, which is depicted by light squares. The simulator shows current operations, noise-induced failures, and predicted execution time in the right pane.

5.7 Design Process for an Ion-trap Architecture with Fault Tolerance

This section explains how to incorporate fault-tolerant components and presents the idea of fault-tolerance. In a hardware-driven design flow, a system architect can apply the procedure manually; in a software-driven design flow, a compiler can apply it automatically. Although the concepts may apply to other devices, both of these design procedures are being applied especially for trapped-ion systems. Ensuring fault-tolerant execution of the final stream of physical operations is the primary objective of both design approaches. The usefulness and generality of the high-level design flow for systematic research of quantum device design methodologies are illustrated by these examples.

5.7.1 Traditional Fault-Tolerant Elements

Let's start by going over triple modular redundancy (TMR), which is the standard technique for integrating fault-tolerant processing into contemporary digital computers. This construction would be a common feature of computer architectures if the fundamental gates of digital computers weren't inherently error-rejecting. The TMR code is used to encode the inputs, which are then fed into three simple gates to create a fault-tolerant gate. Three majority voting gates are formed by the fanout of each logic gate's output lines. The encoded calculation result is output via the majority gates.

Fault-tolerant components can be designed to fail with probability $(cp)^{2^k}/c$ by executing this fault-tolerant technique recursively k times, as shown in the figure below. The number of ways fundamental gates in the component can fail is the constant c. Since there are six possible ways for two fundamental gate failures to result in a component failure, c = 6 for the NAND gate. In theory, the fault-tolerant NAND can be made arbitrarily reliable if each fundamental gate fails with probability $p < 1/6$. We state that the fault-tolerance threshold for this construction is $p_{th} = 1/6$. Next, the fault-tolerant NAND component needs to be positioned on a layout so that cross-talk doesn't add too much more noise and wire delays aren't too long.

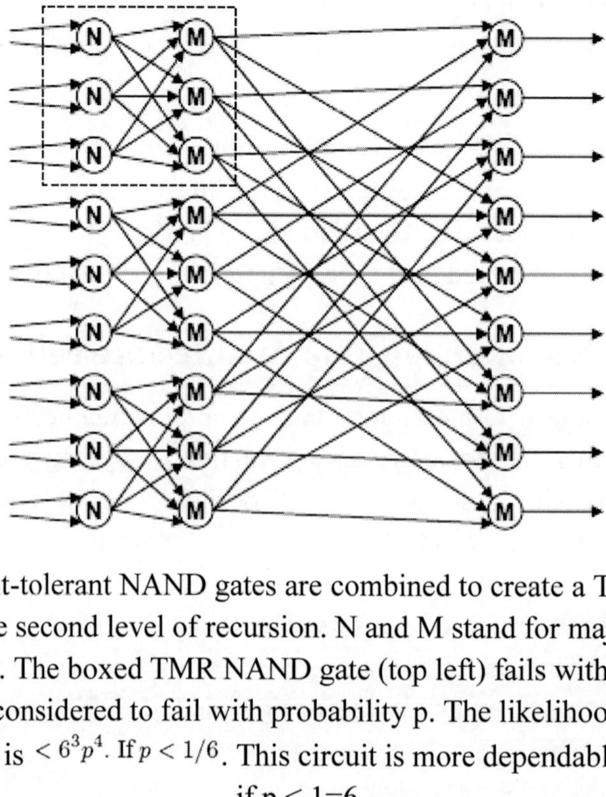

Fig.5.3 Three fault-tolerant NAND gates are combined to create a TMR fault-tolerant NAND gate at the second level of recursion. N and M stand for majority and NAND gates, respectively. The boxed TMR NAND gate (top left) fails with probability < $6p^2$, since all gates are considered to fail with probability p. The likelihood of the full circuit in this figure failing is $< 6^3 p^4$. If $p < 1/6$. This circuit is more dependable than a simple gate if p < 1=6.

5.8 Design Process for an Ion-trap Architecture with Fault Tolerance

Defining fault-tolerance and outlining a procedure for adding fault-tolerant components. The procedure can be used automatically or by a system architect manually in a hardware-driven design cycle by a compiler in a design cycle that is driven by software. Although the ideas behind both of these design approaches may be applied to other devices, they are being implemented especially for trapped-ion systems. The primary objective of both design methodologies is to ensure fault-tolerant execution of the final stream of physical activities. These illustrations show how useful and universal the high-level design flow is for systematic research into quantum device design methodologies.

5.8.1 Traditional Fault-Tolerant Elements

Let's start by going over triple modular redundancy (TMR), which is the standard technique for integrating fault-tolerant processing into contemporary digital computers. This construction would be a common feature of computer architectures if the fundamental gates of digital computers weren't inherently error-rejecting. The TMR code is used to encode the inputs, which are then fed into three simple gates to create a fault-tolerant gate. Three majority voting gates are formed by the fanout of each logic gate's output lines. The encoded calculation result is output via the majority gates.

By using this fault-tolerant technique recursively k times, as depicted in Figure, fault-tolerant components can be made to fail with probability $(cp)^{2^k}/c$ for a constant c specified by the number of ways fundamental gates in the component can fail. Since there are six possible ways for two fundamental gate failures to result in a component failure, c = 6 for the NAND gate. In theory, the fault-tolerant NAND can be made arbitrarily reliable if each fundamental gate fails with probability p < 1=6. We state that the fault-tolerance threshold for this construction is pth = 1=6. Next, the fault-tolerant NAND component needs to be positioned on a layout so that cross-talk doesn't add too much more noise and wire delays aren't too long.

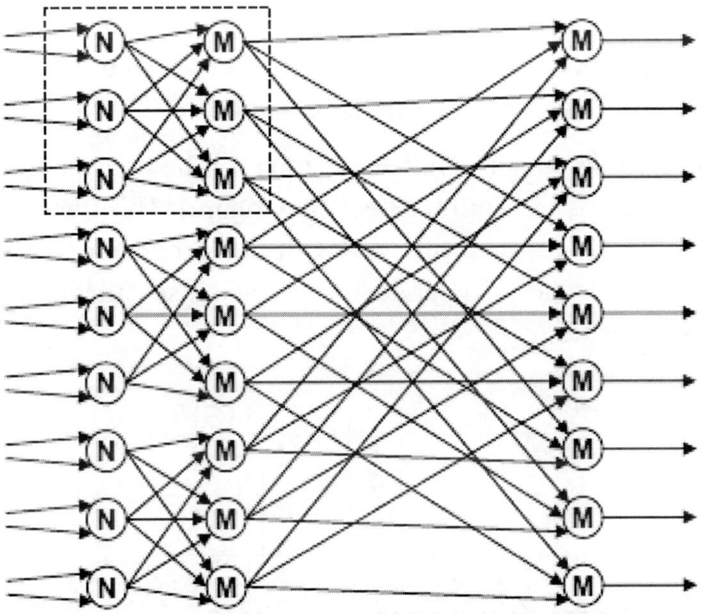

Fig.5.4 Three fault-tolerant NAND gates are combined to create a TMR fault-tolerant NAND gate at the second level of recursion. N and M stand for majority and NAND gates, respectively. The boxed TMR NAND gate (top left) fails with probability $< 6p^2$, since all gates are considered to fail with probability p. The likelihood of the full circuit in this figure failing is less than $< 6^3p^4$. This circuit is more dependable than a simple gate if $p < 1/6$.

5.8.2 Fault-Resilient Quantum Elements

Like conventional fault-tolerance, fault-tolerant quantum components are built using comparable techniques. Using a discrete universal set of gates, quantum computation codes that enable fault-tolerant computation can be used to encode quantum information. Transversal application of CNOT gates is a useful feature of the CSS codes, one family of quantum computation codes. Because they are implemented bitwise, transversal gates are always fault resilient. Hadamard and CNOT transverse gates are shown in the figure below.

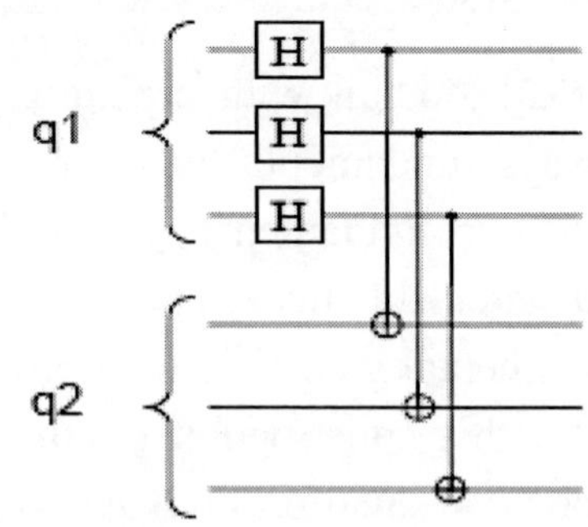

Fig.5.5 Three physical qubits working on two logical qubits via CNOT and Hadamard gates. As long as the quantum code is a CSS code, transversal CNOT is an acceptable operation. For a doubly even self-dual CSS code, the transversal Hadamard operation is valid.

A broad technique based on quantum teleportation can be used to build nontrivial fault-tolerant quantum gates, as the Toffoli gate (below figure). This type of fault-tolerant gate construction uses only measurements and Clifford group gates, both of which are transversal. A tensor product of input qubit states and a specifically created ancilla state are subjected to these gates.

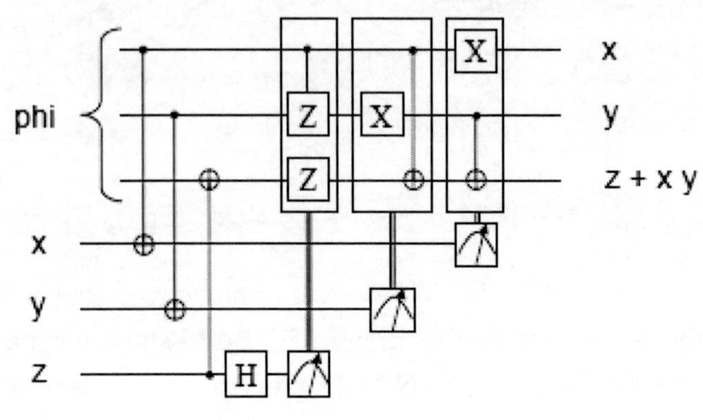

Fig.5.6 Tolerant of faults Quantum teleportation was used to construct the Toffoli gate.

This circuit's gates can all be applied transversally when a punctured, self-dual, doubly-even CSS code is used. Clifford group operators and fault-tolerant measurements of Clifford group operators can be used to prepare the ancilla $|\phi\rangle$ that the gate demands in a fault-tolerant manner.

Several types of ancilla must be prepared in a fault-tolerant manner in order to implement these gates in practice. For every nontrivial gate, such as the Toffoli gate or the $\pi/8$ gate., a specifically prepared ancilla state must first be created. Measurement can be used to prepare these states in a fault-tolerant manner. Every nontrivial gate must be followed by a recovery operation on each qubit. The image below depicts the general layout of a recovery effort. For each syndrome bit recovered, recovery operations use a syndrome extraction ancilla. Additionally, this ancilla needs to be readily available and prepared to withstand errors.

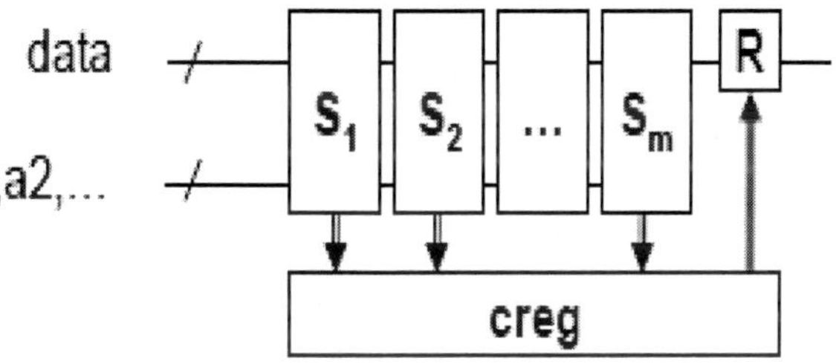

Fig.5.7 This network is a network for recuperation.

Through syndrome bit extraction networks S_i, a recovery operation communicates with the data in a fault-tolerant manner. Every syndrome bit is stored in a classical register after potentially several measurements. The register is processed by a traditional computer, which then applies the proper error correction R to the data. Every fault-tolerant gate must be followed by recovery procedures in order to fix any mistakes that the gate may have introduced.

The generic structure of a single syndrome bit extraction is also depicted in the figure below. To check for crucial mistakes, each extraction ancilla has to have access to the last ancilla, a cold verification qubit. When qubits can only interact locally, all of these activities need to continue to be fault resilient. Movement faults can be fixed at every stage of code concatenation before they get out of hand if the target computer supports a geometry that frequently allows intermediate error-correction. For a device with a designed arrangement, like the "quantum CCD" concept for a trapped ion quantum device, this may be the case.

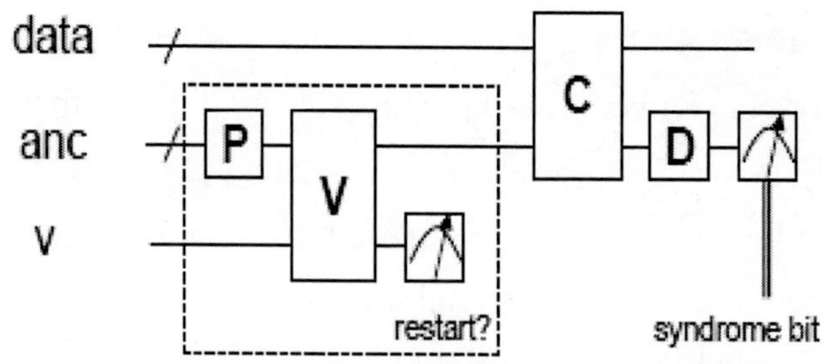

Fig.5.8 This network is used to extract syndromes.

An ancilla state $|anc\rangle$ is necessary before extracting a single syndrome bit fault-tolerantly. The network prepares and verifies the ancilla in the box that is indicated. If the verification was unsuccessful, it is indicated by a verification qubit. Following the successful preparation of an ancilla, the C network engages in fault-tolerant data interaction to gather a syndrome bit. D decodes and measures this bit. The quantum network D may be replaced by some traditional post processing.

5.8.3 Design processes

The hardware and software-driven design flows are thoroughly explained here. Both strategies utilize the conceptual separation of the logical and physical machine to apply the identical replacement rules that are outlined in this section.

The replacement criteria we have outlined are used in a software-driven design cycle to introduce fault-tolerance prior to the generation of technology-dependent code. In order to maintain fault tolerance, scheduling algorithms and layout tools reduce movement and include machine-specific instructions. At the lowest layers of the design cycle, the software approach depends on precise substitutions and modifications. Because moving qubits may frequently use device-dependent details, these tools must eventually provide physical operations in the QCPOL language, even though they may function in several phases.

A system architect uses a combination of replacement rules and heuristic techniques to produce universal, fault-tolerant, technology-specific components in a hardware-driven design flow. The collection of parts and the design guidelines for joining them are published together. The machine architecture, not the actual device, is then the focus of the lowest stages of the design flow. The hardware method provides rough component placement criteria and isolates the technical aspects of fault-tolerance into a machine architecture.

5.9 Developing Scalable and Dependable Quantum Architectures

It is desirable to design computer architectures that are both quicker and physically smaller in both the conventional and quantum computing worlds. However, in the realm of quantum mechanics, the influence of these two design characteristics is particularly significant. A more dependable semiconductor that is less prone to faults is typically implied by slower clock speeds and larger gate sizes in classical computing. In contrast, increased clock speeds in quantum computing reduce the amount of time it takes for each qubit to decohere, potentially increasing the architecture's dependability. The underlying qubit registers in the architecture may become less error-prone if the quantum computer chip area is minimized because this also lowers the physical distances that the quantum information must traverse.

The graphic that follows displays a high-level schematic of an example quantum computer architecture that uses the Quantum Random Access Machine paradigm for quantum computing. An expansion of the traditional Random Access Machine paradigm, the QRAM model is made up of a classical subsystem that generates the quantum operations that are carried out on a quantum subsystem. The architecture depicted in the image below is the quantum subsystem and is made up of several processing elements (PE), each of which is intended to carry out a specific localized portion of the overall application.

The interconnect makes it possible for individual qubits to be teleported or physically moved between various PEs, facilitating dependable PE-to-PE communication. Direct physical qubit movement (permitted by the underlying technology) can be used to facilitate communication between qubits within each PE if the PEs are small enough (in terms of area). The scheduling of quantum operations is coordinated by classical control processors, and measurement results are the only channel of communication between the classical and quantum hardware. Each PE and the interconnect design may use quantum error correction codes to reduce the impact of decoherence on the individual qubits. After physical qubits and quantum gates have been successfully implemented, a set of hardware requirements has been established that, if satisfied by a particular device technology, might theoretically be used to construct a functional computer.

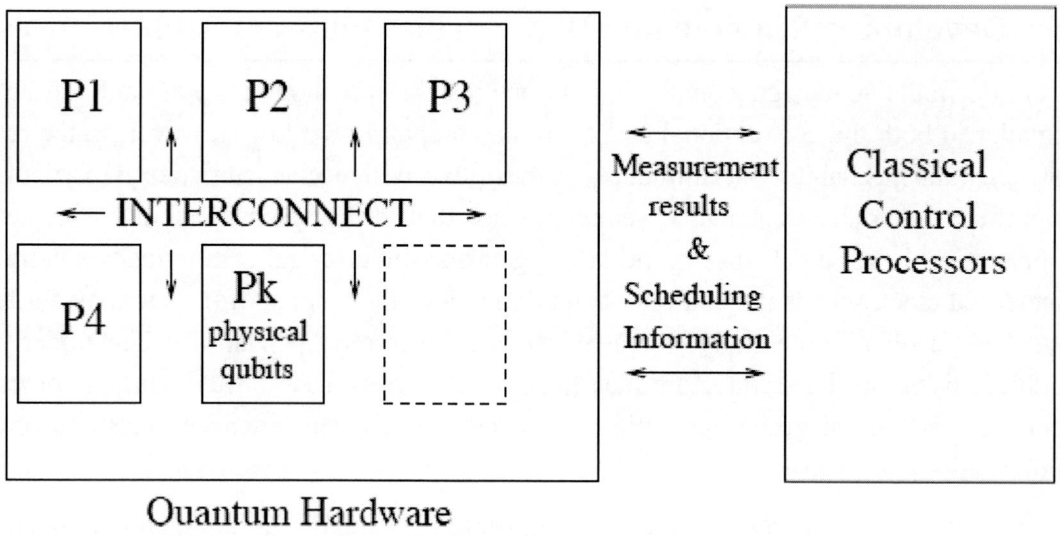

Fig.5.9 A quantum computer architecture based on the quantum random access machine model.

The following four bullet points provide a summary of the set of criteria:

A well-known beginning state, such |00... 0}, must be used to set up a quantum register, which is defined as a collection of distinct single-qubit states.

- There must be a "universal" set of quantum logic gates with gate cycle times significantly less than the corresponding quantum register decoherence time cycle.
- Any single-qubit condition must be subjected to accurate measurements.
- The capacity to transfer quantum data between designated locations, either by means of the qubit's direct physical movement or by sending the data to "flying" qubits, which can then relay it back to "stationary" qubits for processing.

However, there is a distinction between being able to physically put together the parts required for a quantum computer and creating a comprehensive, expansive quantum architecture meant to run computationally significant applications. Three primary areas where there are major obstacles to creating scalable architectures have been identified by prior work in large-scale quantum architecture design, which is based on the circuit model:

1. Implementation technique that is dependable and practical while meeting the requirements for quantum computation.
2. Sturdy, resilient structures that are encoded with effective error correcting methods. In order to execute an arbitrary lengthy series of universal quantum logic operations within the architecture decoherence time, this requirement offers system-level fault-tolerance.

3. Effective allocation of quantum resources that permits the greatest amount of processing and error correction overlap at the physical qubit level as well as the application level.

In the following subsections of this chapter, each of the three difficulty areas is examined in greater detail. This section examines the current technology for achieving large-scale quantum computation and provides a summary of some of the elements of optical quantum computers and trapped ion quantum computation. The next part will explain the application of quantum error correcting codes in the construction of fault-tolerant, scalable structures. An overview of quantum data distribution techniques is given in the final section.

5.9.1 Reliable Implementation techniques

The idea of quantum computing is now a realistic possibility thanks to the development of practical technologies and the physical realization of the fundamental elements required for universal quantum computation. Physical systems employing trapped atomic ions are now proven to have all of the essential low-level architectural elements required for scalable computing. Plans are being developed for large-scale systems that use superconductors, polar molecules, and quantum dots. Most recently, superconducting qubits were used to experimentally demonstrate the cnot gate, and photonic quantum circuits were used to demonstrate a basic version of Shor's quantum factoring algorithm. However, the engineering challenges of current QIP technologies are substantial, and the technological models differ so much that a definitive winner at this early stage could have a negative impact on future advancements in the construction of quantum computers.

Two primary constraints exist for technologies that can be utilized to construct quantum hardware for a large-scale computer.

- In order to shield several qubits from outside influences that lead to decoherence, they must be ready and isolated from the outside world. There is a finite coherence time before a physical qubit loses its quantum state since it is impossible to fully isolate qubits.
- When a quantum state maintains its superposition, it is said to have a coherence time. Along with the requirement to conduct logic operations and measurements on any arbitrary qubit, the basic impossibility to replicate a quantum state represents the second significant challenge for developing quantum technologies.

Overcoming the second restriction is especially challenging. From the memory components to the processing units, classical data can be sent via wires and reproduced using a FANOUT gate. Parts of the classical state may be impacted by an imprecise classical gate or a leaking wire, but typically not enough to offset the number of electrons required to encode a single bit of information. However, to work with many qubits, we need to be able to construct them in a way that makes them firmly connected to external gate devices and to each other throughout the life of a quantum logic gate, in addition to being extremely weakly coupled to external decoherence effects. The information must also be properly safeguarded during physical movement in order to send quantum data undetected.

Two highly incompatible ideas are represented by physical qubit implementations that facilitate easy state manipulation and those that facilitate easy movement of quantum information. A qubit, for instance, which is characterized by the polarization states of photons, is perfect for movement since it moves quickly and does not readily interact with its surroundings. However, due to their poor interaction with everything, including one another, photons are challenging to confine and implement in two-qubit gates. Heavy atoms, on the other hand, are perfect for computation since they are challenging to move but relatively simple to slow down and manipulate (sometimes using lasers).

A middle ground qubit is one that can move relatively easily and quickly in addition to being exposed to the computation environment. Any decision involving a qubit has essentially limited dependability and decoherence time since, regrettably, the qubit's computational availability also exposes it to uncontrollable factors during computation and movement.

Physical implementations of the circuit model of quantum computation include a number of experimental proposals from a wide range of physical science domains, including cavity quantum electro-dynamic (QED) computation [206], optical quantum computation, solid state spin-based quantum computation, quantum dots, nuclear magnetic resonance (NMR) quantum computation, ion trap quantum computation [53], optically through the coupling of neutral atoms with photons and physical segmented traps, and "unique" qubits like electrons floating on liquid helium, the quantum Hall effect, and qubits encoded in the charge distribution of a single electron on two donors. The qubit's implementation, which in turn directs the computer's control infrastructure and speed, is what sets apart all of the suggested technologies.

Every strategy has advantages and disadvantages when it comes to building a computer that is really scalable. One advantage of the Kane technology method, for instance, is that it expands on previous investments in silicon fabrication techniques by leveraging the electronic states of phosphorus atoms buried in a silicon substrate to realize qubits. However, there is currently no experimental implementation of logic gates, and current measurement techniques can take up to 4 days, which is significantly longer than the qubit coherence period of less than 60 ms.

The electric potentials of metal electrodes hold qubits in pairs of energy levels of ions trapped in space in another well-developed work. The ion-trap method is the only technology that offers a clear, scalable communication paradigm and all of the universal components for quantum computation. The ion-trap technique has a drawback in that it requires the coordination of millions of ions that are addressed separately by laser pulses, making it spatially costly in terms of area. As a result, it is uncertain if this technology will continue to be a viable option for universal quantum processing in the far future. Because of this, it's critical to understand that a technology's worth must be assessed based on both its present experimental condition and its potential promise. The optical quantum computer and the trapped-ion quantum computer, two of the most effective experimental methods to date, are briefly described here.

5.9.1.1 Optical Quantum Computation: Qubits As Photons

The use of photons as qubits in the experimental and commercial realization of quantum cryptography protocols demonstrates its significance. Furthermore, entanglement, teleportation, several small-scale quantum algorithms, and even tiny instances of quantum factoring have all been experimentally shown for the first time using photon-based qubits. Additionally, existing quantum architecture concepts based on the cluster-state paradigm of quantum computation use photonic qubits as their underlying device technology.

When using single-qubit gates, the photon, the smallest unit of quantum information, has the benefit of being almost decoherent. Because quantum information is frequently "trapped" in the photon, making two-qubit gates extremely challenging to use with a high enough success rate, this stability is also the source of a significant experimental problem. This indicates that photons are appropriate for quantum key distribution but challenging to implement for scalable quantum processing due to their problematic interactions with one another.

In 2001, Knill, Laflamme, and Milburn devised a plan that shows that, in theory, linear optical components consisting of phase shifters, beam splitters, single photons, and photo detectors can be used to build highly effective scalable quantum computers with a polynomial resource overhead. It was demonstrated that any unitary operator may be realized using linear optical components prior to the proposal of this approach. Beam splitters and phase shifters, which are theoretically represented as 2×2 operators along the Z and Y axes of the qubit state representation, are relatively simple single qubit operators.

Linear optics is not enough for two-qubit gates. Measurement is done with photo detectors, and when paired with teleportation, two qubit processes can be implemented. Single-qubit operations are almost noiseless, and the most dependable cnot implementation with linear optics has a success rate of over 7%. At the expense of exponential photon resources, the teleportation procedure's success can be brought nearly to unity by combining the Fourier transform with a generalized beam splitter. When two-qubit gates' teleportation reliability is decreased enough to allow for the use of quantum error correction, scalable quantum computation becomes feasible.

For distributed quantum computation, photon-based qubits provide the perfect setting. In processors made of qubits that enable effective quantum computation, such ion-traps, photons are a desirable medium for transporting quantum information between different parts of the processor. By employing a shared laser beam as a quantum bus, optical qubits provide by far the most sophisticated experimental design for entangling two distant ions or generating qubit-qubit interactions between solid-state qubits. The teleportation process, which involves entangling two distant qubits, enables the movement of quantum information between locations.

The advent of cluster-state quantum computation, which creates initially entangled states that reflect all required qubit resources in the architecture, has recently significantly advanced linear optics quantum computation. It is possible to mimic arbitrary quantum circuits using single-qubit measurements on the entangled states.

5.9.1.2 Quantum Computation of Trapped Ions: Ions As qubits

Recent studies using trapped atomic ions have shown that all of the quantum hardware elements required to construct massive quantum computers are present. The concept of employing trapped ions, in which many atomic ions are worked upon by lasers to implement quantum logic, was first put up by Cirac and Zoller in 1995. The internal nuclear and electronic states of the ions retain quantum information, and the segmented metal traps (also known as electrodes) that make up the traps themselves enable the treatment of individual ions.

Usually, the electrodes and the necessary electronics for controlling the trapping potentials are positioned on a 2D alumina substrate. The qubit-qubit interactions required by multi-qubit quantum gates are provided by the vibrational modes of a linear chain of ions that can couple to one another in nearby traps. This results in a universal set of quantum logic when combined with single bit rotations. Lasers are applied to the target ions to carry out all quantum logic operations, including measuring the quantum state. Focusing lasers by MEMS mirror arrays allows for the parallel control of many ions in various trap arrays. After data ions are muted by laser manipulation, undesired vibrations are absorbed by additional sympathetic cooling ions.

The physical layout of a trap element in an ion-trap computer is schematically depicted in the image below. In figure below, we observe that one ion-group is trapped in the center trapping zone. An inseparable pair of data ions and sympathetic cooling ions that constantly travel together will be abstracted as an ion-group. In practice, the cooling ions between the data ions may need to be supplied separately since it may not be technically possible to conduct dependable two-qubit quantum operations with them. The areas known as "trapping regions" are where ions can be primed for the application of a logical gate operation, which is essentially an external laser beam beaming on the ion group.

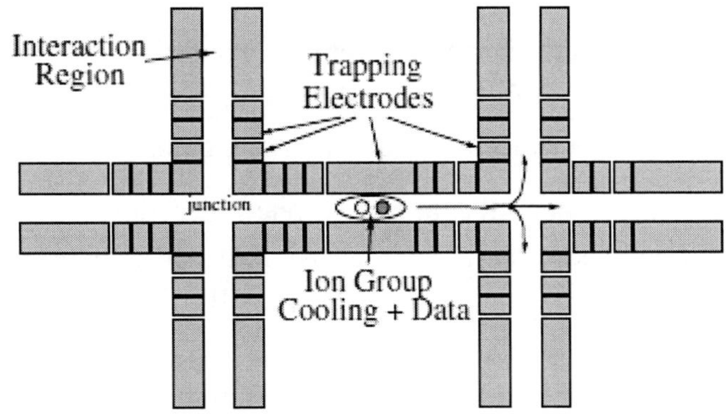

Fig.5.10 The center trapping zone contains a trapped single ion-group.

An ion-group transitioning from the upper left trapping zone to the center region, where a two-bit logical operation is to be carried out, is shown in the figure below. Any one-bit or two-bit logical operation, a simple move operation from one trapping region to another, and measurement are considered to be part of an ion-trap computer's fundamental time-step, also known as a clock cycle. Optimistic projections for the typical physical cycle time of roughly 10 μs and the likelihood of failure for basic operations in ion-traps have been proposed to be in the range of 10^{-7}. It has been demonstrated that cooling and the extra join and split operations required for each basic operation may be completed in this cycle time.

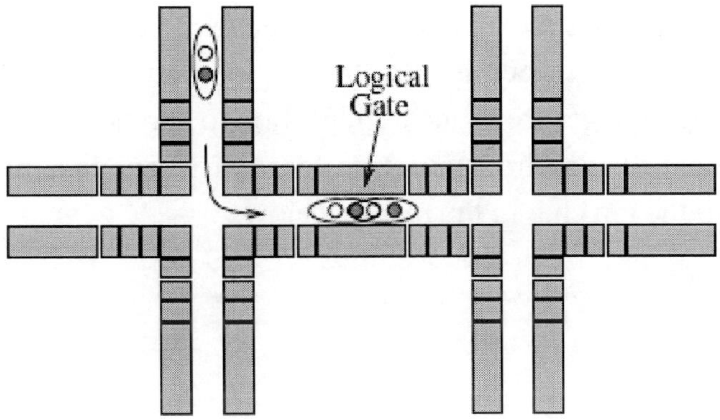

Fig.5.11 shows how to move an ion-group from the upper left trapping zone to the center region.

The fundamental elements required to construct a large-scale ion-trap processor have been shown in recent experiments that achieve quantum teleportation using trapped ions. These include ions trapped in segmented electrode structures, laser-induced ion cooling and manipulation, measurement using a pump laser that causes a state-dependent scattering of photons from the ion, and, lastly, the ability to move ions around by varying the trapping potentials. The trapping electrodes should be around tens of micrometers in size. A cooling ion holds the data ion together, and it is cooled both before and after each logic gate or movement step. In order to connect with another ion-group, the ion-group may relocate to any one of the six nearby trapping zones. The ion-group in the upper left junction of a two-qubit gate shifts to the middle in this sequence. An external laser beam acting on the two ion groups is used to implement the gate.

An experimentally viable natural ion-trap model that does not overlook any major technological obstacles is described using laser-controlled trapped ions with the quantum error correction needs for a scalable, computationally useful quantum computer. The computer is built using the quantum charge coupled device (QCCD) architecture, which creates a linear array of ion traps (like the ones in Figure above) and is scalable.

In order to avoid the technological challenges of maintaining and working with huge chains of ions, the QCCD structure aims to minimize the amount of ions linked together in a single trapping zone. By altering the electrodes' trapping potentials, ions in various interconnected trap arrays can be ballistically shuttled—that is, physically moved—from trap to trap. This implies that any two randomly chosen ions could interact as long as the state of the qubit that is stored in each ion is not destroyed by the accumulation of mistakes that takes place during ion shuttling.

The graphic below depicts a schematic of Steane's ion-trap computer. Ions are trapped between segmented gold electrodes that are placed on an aluminum substrate in his model of an ion chip. Planar ion-traps, in which ions are trapped above a group of separately addressable electrodes in a plane, are electrode architectures that provide more scalability. Because the ions are able to "float" above the electrode surface thanks to the planar traps, the lasers can impact the ions from a wider range of angles. It is possible to regulate the trapping voltages from one trap location to another, which in turn permits the controlled movement of ions from one trap location to another, thanks to the ion-trap electronics beneath the ion chip in the picture below.

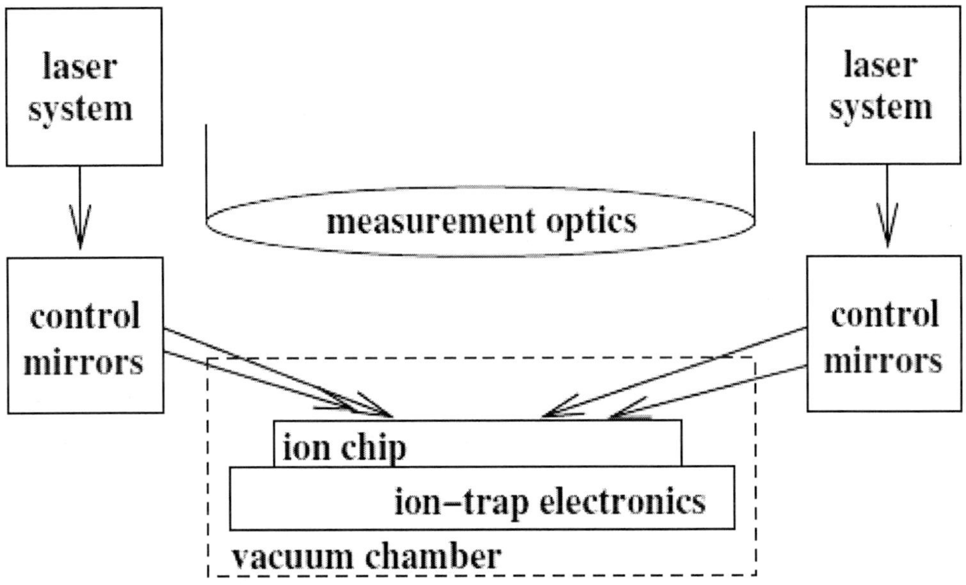

Fig.5.12 Diagram for an ion-trap scalable computer.

Developing high-density control electrode interconnects that enable the individual control of millions of trap locations is a major technological problem. Presently available via technologies can be used to provide control voltages to the trapping electrodes vertically at the densities and sizes needed by an ion-trap computer. It is obvious that one of the main optimization objectives for system designers is to develop scalable ion trap shapes that reduce the extent of laser resource distribution and required electronics infrastructure.

For tasks like qubit preparation, logic gate operations, measurement, and cooling of ions following logic operations or movement, the laser systems depicted in the above diagram supply the various laser pulses required for ion-qubit manipulation. Sympathetic ions are employed to absorb the heat that accumulates from ion movement and gate operations, as seen in the previous picture. The laser beams used to initialize the data ions are also utilized to chill the sympathetic ions. Gate operations require a variety of laser beams with a range of wavelengths. The dependable implementation of single- and two-qubit gates requires that these laser beams precisely target individual ions. Together with doing logic operations, the computer must have the speed and dependability to read out qubit states.

Error-correcting code-based fault-tolerant system designs necessitate repeated measurements of individual qubits throughout application execution. This calls for the usage of measurement pump lasers, which scatter photons from the ions in a state-dependent manner. Photo-electric light sensors that count the amount of photons released are able to detect the scattered photons. System designers may be forced to develop ion-trap geometries that split the ion chip into an ion interaction/storage region and a distinct measurement zone due to the measurement optics region's extreme size and required precision.

Lastly, the selection of ion species for computing will have a significant impact on the system-level parameters, control settings, and optimization strategies of the ion-trap computer architecture. At this level of research, it is challenging to make a firm decision regarding a general ion-trap computer because there are substantial tradeoffs between various system needs for various ion types.

5.9.2 Fault Tolerant Structures and Robust Error Correction

The most important prerequisite for a genuinely usable scalable machine is probably the presence of "good" error correcting codes that enable the building of effective fault-tolerant structures that overcome decoherence. Since quantum data is highly volatile, one of the most resource-intensive processes that takes place throughout the quantum algorithm's execution is actively stabilizing the system's state through error correction (EC). In contrast to classical computation, which depends on the idea that failures are so infrequent that it is preferable to take longer to recover rather than use more resources for error correction, quantum computing involves errors so frequently that the application run-time depends on how quickly the error correction technique is implemented.

Perhaps the most crucial ability required of computer architects interested in quantum computing is the ability to create large-scale quantum architectures that use quantum fault-tolerance and quantum error correction. An important area of study that has yielded some extremely potent quantum error-correcting codes that are comparable to yet fundamentally distinct from their classical counterparts is quantum error correction and quantum fault-tolerance. The Threshold Theorem, which states that an arbitrarily reliable quantum gate can be implemented using only imperfect gates as long as the failure probability of the imperfect gates is less than a specific threshold value, is the most significant finding in terms of scalable quantum computing.

Using quantum error-correction codes, conducting all computations on encoded data, employing fault-tolerant techniques, and iteratively encoding until the required dependability is attained are the methods used to achieve this amazing outcome. Recursive error correction overhead must be kept to a minimum and some of the most effective error correcting codes must be supported by a well-designed architecture.

Fault-tolerant quantum error correction's primary objective is to eliminate mistakes from an unknown n-qubit state $|\Psi\rangle$ from accumulated decoherence by means of a series of operations. A random unitary error operator acting on $|\Psi\rangle$can be used to abstract the amount of decoherence that exists.

Since the physical qubits themselves are constructed via various quantum control protocols, we assume that additional kinds of noise that cannot be characterized as a random unitary operator are handled by them. In order to prevent direct measurement of the data qubits, error correction offers recovery algorithms that can correct t mistakes on a register of n qubits by transferring the errors to a set of ancillary qubits, provided that the error operator works non-trivially ont < nqubits. Following transfer, the supplementary qubits are either disposed of or set to $|0\rangle$ so they can be used again.

We provide a concise introduction to quantum error correction and the error correction codes utilized in the designs we cover in the sections that follow in this chapter. Without having to decode the encoded states, Shor-Steane Codes enable comparatively simple quantum computation utilizing the circuit model. The quantum error correction is to highlight the factors that make it the application that distinguishes quantum architectures.

5.9.3 Model Assumptions for Noise

Both classical and quantum systems use two common noise assumptions when modeling faults that can be fixed with fault-tolerant quantum ϵ error correction codes: The noise is stochastic, meaning that each position has an equal chance of an error occurring; and mistakes are uncorrelated, meaning they happen separately. Even while errors aren't always totally uncorrelated in practice, underlying control techniques can reduce any correlations.

If a classical circuit has A possible error locations and an error occurs at each location with probability ϵ, then the chance that t errors occur is provided by these noise assumptions.

$$\binom{A}{t}\epsilon^t(1-\epsilon)^{A-t}$$

It is the number of ways that t sites might fail and (A – t) locations could succeed. Let a bit be in the classical states of "0" with probability p0 and "1" with probability p1. A noise operator that flips the bit with the transition probability ϵ will cause it to be in the states of 0 with probability q0 and 1 with probability q1 after it occurs. Next, the following model can be used to represent the evolution of the classical system for each independently occurring noise operation:

$$\begin{bmatrix} q_0 \\ q_1 \end{bmatrix} = \begin{bmatrix} 1-\epsilon & \epsilon \\ \epsilon & 1-\epsilon \end{bmatrix} \begin{bmatrix} p_0 \\ p_1 \end{bmatrix}, \quad or \quad \vec{q} = E\vec{p}$$

where the transition probability matrix is denoted by E. The evolution of a quantum system can be similarly modeled in quantum computation. Let's say we want to use the gate U on a quantum register with n qubits $|\Psi\rangle$. Because the possible unitary operators that can be applied to a state $|\Psi\rangle$ form a continuum, the physical mechanism used to implement the gate will introduce an error (with some probability ϵ) to our original state even if the technology permits the state to be completely isolated from the environment. After applying gate U, the final state can be expressed as follows:

$$|\Psi\rangle \quad \rightarrow \quad \sum_{a} E_a U|\Psi\rangle \otimes |a\rangle$$

where E_a is the sum of 2^{2n} potential error operators that act on our state after the gate has been applied, and $|a\rangle$ are environmental states (untangled from the data register). The string of n Pauli matrices {I,X,Y,Z} represents each error operator.

$$I = \begin{bmatrix} 1 & 0 \\ 0 & 1 \end{bmatrix}, \quad X = \begin{bmatrix} 0 & 1 \\ 1 & 0 \end{bmatrix}, \quad Z = \begin{bmatrix} 1 & 0 \\ 0 & -1 \end{bmatrix}, \quad Y = -iZX = \begin{bmatrix} 0 & -we \\ we & 0 \end{bmatrix}$$

For instance, the error on the three qubits following a three-qubit operation on a three-qubit register could be any of the following combinations:

$$\{I, X, Y, Z\}^{\otimes 3} = \{X \otimes I \otimes I\}, \ \{Z \otimes I \otimes Y\}$$

where the i'th element in each n-bit Pauli operator acts on the i'th qubit (the $\oplus$ signs within each n-qubit Pauli operator will be deleted in the material that follows). Depolarizing noise is the type of noise that the Pauli matrices describe. Depolarizing noise is corrected by all error correcting codes, and generally speaking, devices can be designed so that the depolarizing channel is the dominant noise channel.

The majority of error-correcting protocols depend on the low weight of the n-bit Pauli operators and the extremely uncommon occurrence of highly correlated mistakes that impact many qubits at each step. It is quite improbable, nevertheless, that the technologies will enable the total eradication of associated mistakes. For instance, qubits are stored in the electronic spins of silicon-embedded phosphorous atoms using the Kane technology. Metallic control structures erected on the silicon substrate's surface govern qubit interactions. The electron that holds the qubit from one atom is moved to the other atom in order to carry out a two-qubit operation. The largest obstacle to physically implementing dependable quantum operations with Kane technology is really the interaction between the charge fields produced by the control structures and the qubit states contained in the data electrons during the transfer procedure.

When an operation on a single qubit fails while it is being executed, that qubit has an error. A quantum circuit may experience two errors—one on the control qubit and one on the target qubit—if the two-qubit cnot gate fails. Employ the following noise model to examine the behavior of quantum structures based on this supposition:

- Failures are stochastic and uncorrelated. This indicates that, absent explicit entanglement between the two qubits in the quantum circuit, a mistake on qubit q_i will not lead to an error on qubit q_j.
- A single qubit error can be expressed as a superposition of the Pauli operators, where a single timestep failure causes the density operator of our initial system state $|\Psi\rangle$ to go to:

$$|\Psi\rangle_{new} = (1-\epsilon)we|\Psi\rangle + \frac{\epsilon}{3}(X|\Psi\rangle + Z|\Psi\rangle + Y|\Psi\rangle)$$

Put differently, the qubit rotates by X, Z, or Y with probability ϵ prior to a gate being executed, and it stays the same with probability $(1 - \epsilon)$.

- For every two qubits, there are 15 potential error patterns: {IX,XI, IZ,ZI, IY, YI,XY, YX,XZ,ZX,ZY, YZ,XX,ZZ, YY}, each with probability $\epsilon/15$. A two-qubit gate introduces two errors with probability ϵ on the input qubits. An error with probability $\epsilon/3$ (any of the three options between {X, Y, Z}) is introduced by single qubit gates. The only exception to this rule is the single-qubit T gate, which adds an error that can be expressed as a superposition of the Z and X gates.
- Unit operations for memory and movement have a well-defined failure rate. Each qubit in a certain technological model can travel a certain distance in a single gate cycle, with a specific failure rate at which an error will be introduced by the move gate. Likewise, a memory cycle is similar to a single gate cycle during which the qubit is idle, with a particular failure rate ϵ at which the qubit will decohere.
- Steane makes the crucial supposition that qubits involved in a gate at a particular cycle only experience gate noise, not memory noise. In a similar vein, moving qubits experience channel-introduced movement noise rather than memory noise.

Errors are not entirely uncorrelated, as was previously stated. A quantum computer's initial state is set up to be as environment-independent as possible given the technology used to construct it. The degree of entanglement between the computer state and its environment determines the strength of the error correlations between individual qubits in the quantum computer. Furthermore, an unknown error operator is applied to the environment's state when a logic gate is applied to a qubit; as a result, the computer system and the environment share the noise at each timestep. The reliability scale attained through error correction is not asymptotically impacted by correlated errors if the entanglement between the two systems is minimal in comparison to uncorrelated gate failure rates ϵ. For instance, the varying global electric and magnetic fields on the ion-trap device cause phase shifts in the qubit states in the ion-trap technology. By utilizing two actual ions to fix a single ion-qubit so that

$$|0\rangle \rightarrow |01\rangle; \quad |1\rangle \rightarrow |10\rangle; \quad |+\rangle \rightarrow \frac{1}{\sqrt{2}}(|01\rangle + |10\rangle)$$

By shielding the qubits from a phase rotation on both qubits, the correlation between them and the environment can be greatly decreased (referred to as a decoherence free subspace, or DFS). The sign of the encoded $|0\rangle$ and $|1\rangle$ states will be flipped by any phase mistake on both qubits, making the error universal and factorable out.

Small rotations in each qubit, which are brought about by the traditional control mechanisms at each gate, are an example of non-stochastic errors in the computer. These rotations may occur randomly at each gate or as a continuous phase shift. The overall angle of rotation following m operations will be around $\sqrt{m}\theta$ with probability $m\theta^2$ if the state is randomly rotated by a relatively tiny angle θ. We must assume as system designers that coherent non-stochastic mistakes would eventually accumulate to sufficiently big rotations such that, as in the incoherent noise model, they can be discretized into a superposition of the Pauli operators.

Identifying faults without fixing them is arguably the most straightforward approach to handling them. Error-detecting codes, which are used in memory systems, Arithmetic Logic Units (ALU), and classical computation in the transmission of data packets over noisy channels, are used to identify errors. It might be less expensive to retransmit the information packet upon error detection rather than pinpointing the precise error location if error detecting codes are computationally cheap enough and the traditional transmission channel causes a sufficiently small number of errors. The two parameters n and k, where n is the number of bits utilized to encode a piece of information and k is the minimum number of bits required to represent the information, generally constitute an error detecting code C (C is denoted as a [[n, k]] error detecting code).

A typical error-detecting code that only adds one bit of overhead is the [[n, n − 1]] parity check code. Parity check codes can be constructed in a variety of ways. Counting how many times the bit 1 occurs in the original n-bit binary message string is one easy method. An additional bit of 0 is added to the string if the number of 1s is even; if not, a 1.

Since the original message codeword 101, for instance, contains an even number of 1s, the extra check digit should be 0. This changes the codeword to 1010, which is now a codeword in a [[4, 3]] code. The example codeword's parity will shift from even to odd with a single fault on any of the original bits (two flaws won't be noticed, though). In order to ascertain whether the parity bit corresponds to the parity of the received codeword, a parity check is performed after receiving the codeword by counting the number of 1s. The message is rejected and a request to resend the data is sent if the parity bits are not the same. Keep in mind that any odd number of faults can be detected by the parity check algorithm. Regarding the precise location of any problem that has happened, the code gives absolutely no information.

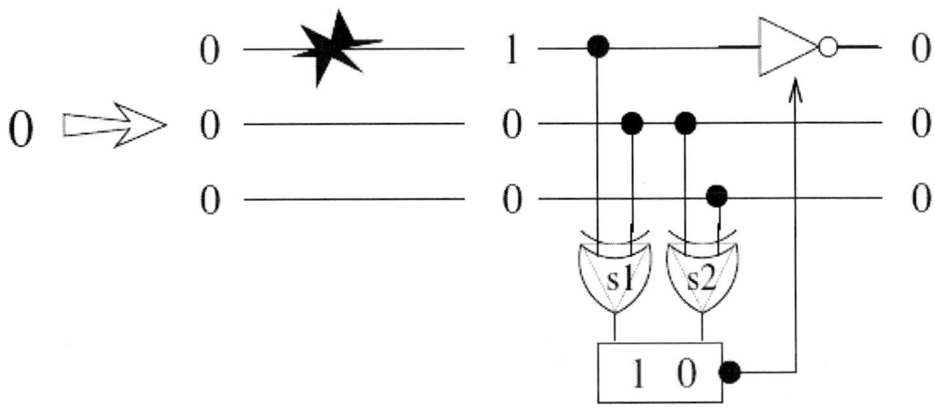

Fig.5.13 Using the 3-bit classical repetition code for correction. The syndrome bits (s1, s2) are set by calculating the parity between bits (1,2) and (2,3) following the error on the first bit. A NOT gate on the bit where the error occurred serves as the corrective operation.

Data must be encoded in a way that makes it possible to identify errors' presence and location in order to be corrected. The 3-bit repetition code using the codewords "000" and "111" is among the most basic error-correcting codes. Three redundant encodings are performed on each bit in the original information bitstring, changing the bit "0" to "000" and the bit "1" to "111." A majority vote is used to identify the fault's position if a mistake results in one of the bits being flipped (the three-bit repetition code is a [[3, 1]] code that can fix up to one error in any codeword). For instance, it is reasonable to presume that the string encodes the bit "1" if the received bitstring is "110" and the error probability ϵ is low enough. The original value can be readily recovered, or the error can be fixed by switching the value of the third bit to "1."

In order to demonstrate the error correction process, the bit "0" is first delivered across a noisy channel three times as 000, where an error on the first bit causes its value to change to 1. The parity between the first and second bits, as well as the second and third bits, is measured concurrently (i.e., using the XOR gate) to determine the majority vote. The outcome is saved in the syndrome string (s1, s2). The measured syndrome in the preceding figure is (1, 0), indicating that the first bit contains the error. The fault is in the second and third bits, respectively, according to the syndromes (1, 1) and (0, 1). It is obvious that if multiple errors occur, the 3-bit repetition code is of no assistance.

Actually, if there are two errors, the error correction will fix the incorrect bit, which will throw off our calculation. A majority vote for a 5-bit repetition code (i.e., $0 \rightarrow 00000$, and $1 \rightarrow 11111$) can be used to identify and fix two faults. Actually, the distance between good codewords needs to be t + 1 in order to identify t mistakes. The gap between valid code words must be at least 2t + 1 in order to fix t faults.

A bit more is required for a quantum error correcting code. The states of several physical qubits, which are not duplicated but are entangled with one another, are encoded into a logical qubit state. We also have to be concerned about sign problems because of the phase-flip Z operator. Nine physical qubits are used to encode a single qubit of information as three blocks of three qubits each in an example quantum error correcting code that is comparable to classical repetition codes and capable of correcting both kinds of errors.

$$|0\rangle \quad \longrightarrow \quad |\bar{0}\rangle = \frac{1}{\sqrt{8}}(|000\rangle + |111\rangle)(|000\rangle + |111\rangle)(|000\rangle + |111\rangle)$$
$$|1\rangle \quad \longrightarrow \quad |\bar{1}\rangle = \frac{1}{\sqrt{8}}(|000\rangle - |111\rangle)(|000\rangle - |111\rangle)(|000\rangle - |111\rangle)$$

An arbitrarily encoded one-qubit superposition state can be expressed as follows, where the logical $|0\rangle$ and $|1\rangle$ states are written as $|\bar{0}\rangle$ and $|\bar{1}\rangle$..

$$|\Psi\rangle \quad = \quad \alpha|\bar{0}\rangle + \beta|\bar{1}\rangle$$

Phase-flip mistakes can be identified and fixed by comparing the signs of the three blocks, whereas bit-flip errors can be identified and fixed by comparing the values of qubits within blocks. This code can fix any arbitrary single-qubit error on any of the nine qubits utilized in the encoding as all defects are a combination of X and Z errors.

In the below given figure, the arbitrary single qubit $|Q\rangle = \alpha|0\rangle + \beta|1\rangle$is encoded to $\alpha|\bar{0}\rangle + \beta|\bar{1}\rangle$. This circuit encodes nine qubits to represent a single encoded qubit as a superposition of the $|\bar{0}\rangle$ and $|\bar{1}\rangle$.states. Qubit q1 contains the data that must be encrypted and safeguarded as Eight extra qubits, {q2 − q9}, are entangled with the arbitrary state $|Q\rangle$, which is initially set to the $|0\rangle$state. Like the 3-bit repetition code, the first two cnot gates divide the state of qubit q1 among qubits q4 and q7: $|q1, q4, q7\rangle \longrightarrow \alpha|000\rangle + \beta|111\rangle$. The three qubit states are changed by the three Hadamard gates into:

$$|q1, q4, q7\rangle \longrightarrow \frac{\alpha}{\sqrt{8}}|+++\rangle + \frac{\beta}{\sqrt{8}}|---\rangle$$

where the well-known $(|0\rangle + |1\rangle)/\sqrt{2}$ state is represented by $|+\rangle$. If the signs of qubits (q1, q4) and (q4, q7) are compared, the state the three qubits are in following the Hadamard gates permits the correction of a phase-flip Z error on any of the three qubits. Using the remaining six qubits, {q2, q3, q5, q6, q8, q9}, the three qubits are encoded using the 3-bit repetition code to allow for the correction of bit-flip errors. Each $|+\rangle$ and $|-\rangle$ become:

$$|+\rangle \longrightarrow \frac{1}{\sqrt{2}}(|000\rangle + |111\rangle)$$
$$|-\rangle \longrightarrow \frac{1}{\sqrt{2}}(|000\rangle - |111\rangle)$$

The encoded arbitrary single qubit state $(\alpha|\bar{0}\rangle + \beta|\bar{1}\rangle)$, as indicated by the equation above, is the outcome. The classical 3-bit repetition code and the technique for identifying the symptoms of a bit-flip error in any of the three qubits within each group of three are the same. The state contains each of the three blocks of three qubits:

$$|q_1q_2q_3\rangle = |000\rangle + |111\rangle$$

where the $\frac{1}{\sqrt{8}}$ global phase factor has been left out. The parity checks (q1 ⊕ q2) and (q2 ⊕ q3) can be used to obtain the 2-bit syndrome string that would indicate which qubit was flipped. For instance, if qubit q3 experiences a bit-flip error:

$$|q_1q_2q_3\rangle = |000\rangle + |111\rangle \rightarrow |001\rangle + |110\rangle$$

The syndrome bitstring (0, 1) should be produced by the syndrome measurement. After that, an X gate is applied to the flipped qubit to complete the rectification phase. For the remaining two blocks of three qubits, |q4q5q6} and |q7q8q9}, bit-flip errors are calculated similarly.

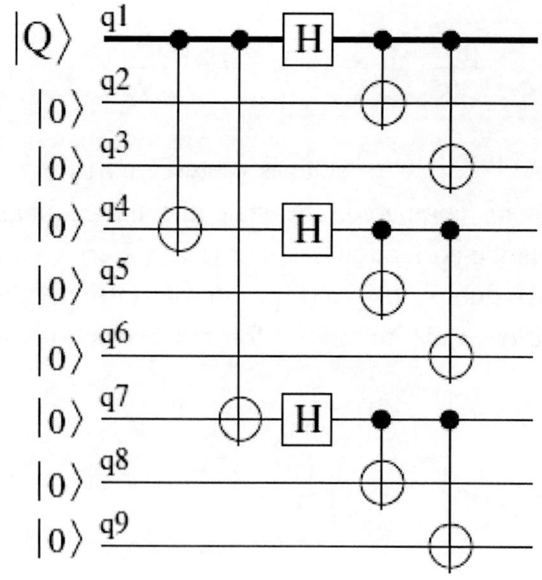

Fig.5.14 Quantum 9-bit code encoding process. The first step is to create a 3-qubit state that enables Z error detection and rectification. Six extra qubits are used to encode each of the three qubits using the quantum 3-bit repetition code, which guards against bit-flip mistakes.

By comparing the signs of the three blocks, the phase-flip Z faults are found and fixed on any one of the nine qubits. For instance, if qubit q6 has a phase-flip mistake, the middle block's sign will be reversed as illustrated below:

$$|\bar{0}\rangle = \frac{1}{\sqrt{8}}(|000\rangle + |111\rangle)(|000\rangle - |111\rangle)(|000\rangle + |111\rangle)$$

$$|\bar{1}\rangle = \frac{1}{\sqrt{8}}(|000\rangle - |111\rangle)(|000\rangle + |111\rangle)(|000\rangle - |111\rangle)$$

Therefore, the syndrome (1, 1) that results from measuring the parity between blocks 1 and 2 as well as the parity between blocks 2 and 3 should show that there was a Z mistake in the middle block. Interestingly, the sign will be reversed back to its initial condition if the correction is applied to any one of the three qubits in the middle block (q4, q5, or q6). Any one X or Z fault in any of the state's nine qubits will be fixed by the 9-qubit code. It might fix certain higher weight X errors, but it won't fix more than one Z fault. For instance, when there is an X fault on qubits q3, q6, and q9, the error operator "IIXIIXIIX" with weight w = 3 results in all three defects being in distinct blocks, enabling the 9-qubit to identify and fix the mistakes. However, the first block will incorrectly fix qubit q3 due to the error operator "XXIIIIIII," removing the entire encoding from the codespace and erasing the data we are attempting to safeguard.

Perhaps the most basic true quantum error-correcting code that can fix both bit-flip and phase-flip mistakes is the 9-qubit code, which is merely one form of an error-correcting code. Although there are many more quantum error correcting codes, a quantum error code C may generally correct errors on up to t qubits and encode k qubits into the state of n lower-level qubits. Usually, the three parameters [[n, k, d]] are used to identify codes, where d is the code distance so that t = (d − 1)/2. It is possible to think of the 9-qubit Shor code as a [[9, 1, 3]] code with distance d equal to 3. It will have a distance of 5 if it fixes any two faults in its encoded codewords.

However, merely storing error-free quantum information is insufficient; we also need a method for processing it consistently throughout the procedure. Decoding a qubit before processing will be lethal if it is encoded and protected with some [[n, k, d]] error correcting code. Every time a gate is applied in quantum computation, a mistake with probability ϵ is introduced. By running each gate several times and accepting the majority of agreed gates as the proper gate function, a classical computer with noisy gates may be made more dependable. Multiple copies of the data would need to be made in order to be sent through the same gate type, which is not possible with quantum processing. Performing operations on states that are encoded is the answer. Fault-tolerant operations must be carried out, meaning that more faults cannot be introduced than can be fixed.

Protecting the encoded data from a single error, which occurs with probability ϵ , is ensured by a 9-qubit encoded state that constitutes a single logical qubit. If multiple uncorrectable faults arise, the data will be destroyed; however, if we never decode, the likelihood of larger errors occurring is exponentially reduced.

The functional difference between computing with physical qubit registers and performing quantum computation on registers made up of n logical qubits {Q1,Q2,·Qn}, where the qubits are encoded with well-defined logical computational states $|\overline{0}\rangle$ and $|\overline{1}\rangle$, generally identical. A logical gate $\overline{U}$ is made up of several physical gates so that when applied to an arbitrary logical qubit state, its function $\overline{U}$ is identical to that of a corresponding physical gate U on the same arbitrary physical qubit state.

To flip the value of the logical qubit from $|\overline{0}\rangle$ to $|\overline{1}\rangle$ or $|\overline{1}\rangle$ to $|\overline{0}\rangle$, for instance, the operator "IIZIIZIIZ" applied to an arbitrary 9-qubit logical qubit state encoded with the 9-qubit code will alter the sign of each of the three blocks that comprise the logical states $|\overline{0}\rangle$ and $|\overline{1}\rangle$.. Therefore, a Z gate is applied to qubits q3, q6, and q9 in order to create the logical bit-flip operator $\overline{X}$ using the 9-qubit encoding discussed in this section. Similarly, applying a logical $\overline{Z}$ gate to change the state $\alpha|\overline{0}\rangle + \beta|\overline{1}\rangle$ to the state $\alpha|\overline{0}\rangle - \beta|\overline{1}\rangle$ is identical to applying the 9-qubit operator "XXXXXXXXX" (i.e., applying an X gate on all 9 qubits). Unfortunately, using the 9-qubit code to build other logical gates is more difficult. Consequently, while selecting an error-correcting code for a particular application, it is crucial to take the universal gate implementation circuits into account. Every logical gate that is implemented during computation may be followed by a syndrome extraction process that fixes any mistakes (X, Z, or both) that may have arisen during the series of operations that implement the gate.

Performing error correction on encoded qubit states presents three main challenges:

- Quantum states, which are distinguished by the probability amplitudes of the state vector, exist in a continuous space. This indicates that errors are continuous and that, in theory, identifying the precise error that has occurred should require an endless amount of resources (a single qubit may contain any combination of bit-flip X errors, phase-flip Z errors, and bit-flip and phase-flip Y errors).
- Quantum data superposition is destroyed by measurement; however, the error syndrome can only be extracted by measuring an encoded qubit. In order to preserve the qubit's quantum information, we must measure it indirectly.
- Compared to classical data, quantum data is inherently more flawed. For instance, it might not be feasible to produce fewer than one error for every 108 operations for ion-traps, even if implementation technology becomes really dependable. Quantum data is entangled as well. This implies that in addition to preventing decoherence at higher than classical error rates, quantum error correcting codes also need to be made to minimize the impact of entanglement on the propagation of errors through the error correcting circuits following each underlying operation.

One of the most amazing features of the theory of quantum error correction (QEC) is that the first barrier is resolved when a quantum error correcting code is used, which discretizes data mistakes. In contrast to classical analog systems, a limited discrete set of mistakes, specifically X, Z, and the combined X and Z errors, can be rectified to fix any arbitrary error on one or more qubits. The data state $|\Psi\rangle$ can be expressed as a superposition of the original state $|\Psi\rangle, X_i|\Psi\rangle, Z_i|\Psi\rangle,$ and $Z_i X_i|\Psi\rangle$ following an arbitrary mistake, the operator E_i applied to the *we*'th qubit in the encoded logical qubit.

The data state is collapsed into one of the four elements of the superposition by the error syndrome extraction process, regardless of how minor the error is. This can then be fixed by applying an X, Z, or both. By extracting a syndrome for X errors and then a syndrome for Z errors, followed by the appropriate corrective operation, one may easily extract the error within a logical qubit. This is a great feature of error discretization.

The second challenge is that the error syndrome cannot be immediately extracted by measuring an encoded qubit. It's interesting to note that this barrier is also not lethal, but it does add a significant overhead auxiliary qubit. The error information is moved from the encoded qubit to several specially encoded ancillary qubits, which are subsequently decoded and measured to identify the error's position. This allows for the measurement of the error syndrome without compressing the data. The Steane Method for syndrome extraction, depicted in the picture below, is a common technique used in the QEC codes we cover here to extract the error syndrome for a [[n, k, d]] code through interaction between the encoded data and the ancilla.

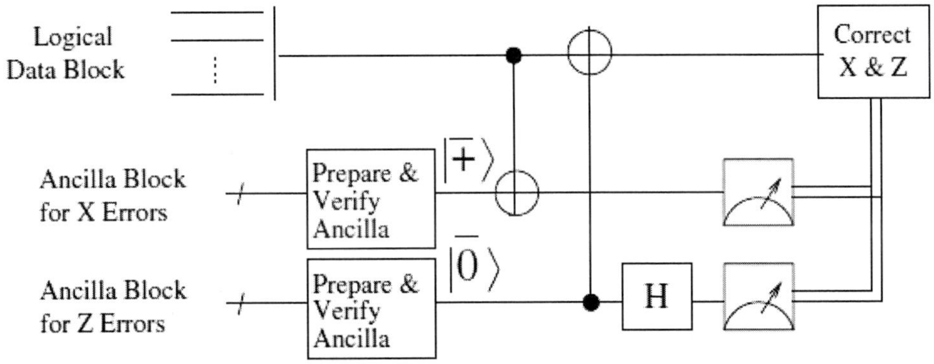

Fig.5.15 Error correction using the Steane method and syndrome extraction.

Calderbank-Shor-Steane (CSS) quantum error correcting codes are frequently extracted using the Steane approach for X and Z syndrome. Two sets of n ancilla qubits are encoded using the same error code as the data, as seen in Figure. The ancilla is prepared in the logical $|\bar{+}\rangle = \frac{1}{\sqrt{2}}(|\bar{0}\rangle + |\bar{1}\rangle)$ state, and a logical cnot gate is applied between the ancilla block as target and the data block of n qubits as control in order to measure X errors. The bit-flip X errors from the data block will be passed to the ancilla because a cnot gate propagates bit-flip errors forward (control → target).

By measuring the ancilla in the computational basis, the mistake and its position can be determined. The ancilla is set up in the logical $|\bar{0}\rangle$ state and serves as the control block while interacting with the data in order to identify and fix phase-flip Z errors (Z errors propagate backwards in a cnot gate). The Z errors are transformed into bit-flip errors by applying a logical Hadamard gate to the ancilla; these mistakes can be measured in the computational basis. When measuring an encoded block of qubits, the process is essentially the same as measuring a physical qubit with its state compressed to the logical $|\bar{0}\rangle$ or $|\bar{1}\rangle$ base states. Measuring a state with any weight errors $w \leq t$ present will produce the right measurement if the encoded block is meant for a code that corrects up to t errors (unless some of the measurement gates fail themselves).

The Ancilla Factory Concept: Two n-qubit ancillary blocks, one for X errors syndrome and one for Z errors syndrome, are depicted in the above image. In order to make sure that errors made during ancilla encoding either (1) do not propagate to the data, causing errors of higher than correctable weight, or (2) do not result in an incorrect syndrome being measured, it is necessary to check the ancilla blocks themselves for the presence of X and Z errors after encoding. By creating extra ancilla blocks and utilizing them to check one another, ancilla blocks can be confirmed (much like the mistake correction procedure).

Improving verification structures is essential for reducing computation delay. By re-preparing the ancilla for each type of mistake, we may execute the syndrome extraction sequentially using a single ancilla block for both X and Z errors. While using a single ancilla lowers the overhead of physical resources, it lengthens the error correction time cycle. Alternatively, it is possible to prepare many ancilla blocks at once, ensuring that there is always a prepared and confirmed ancilla block available for syndrome extraction for both X and Z errors concurrently.

5.9.4 Quantum computation with logical qubits

In our discussion of large-scale quantum architecture design, we introduce the logical qubit tile as the primary architectural abstraction. From the standpoint of a computer architect, iteratively constructing logical qubit tiles (or blocks) in order to stabilize an n-qubit quantum state is comparable to rate per logical operation, after mistake correction, drops below a predetermined threshold that will enable the necessary computation to continue.

At Level L recursion, every logical qubit tile needs to be designed so that the failure rate per tile scales as $\bar{O}(\epsilon^{t+1})$, where ϵ is the failure rate of each Level (L − 1) tile that encodes the higher-level qubit. Put differently, each Level L logical qubit's physical layout and construction need to be fault-tolerant.

A number of non-orthogonal design decisions can affect how well a fault-tolerant logical qubit tile is designed:

1. Considering the qubit tile's functioning in connection to the processor architecture as a whole, the fault-tolerant error-correcting code is the first and most crucial design decision.

2. To increase the reliability of the underlying error correcting process, the lower-level qubits into which each higher-level qubit is encoded must be structured as efficiently as possible after a suitable code has been selected.

3. The total number of lower-level qubits allotted for error correction is another crucial design decision. We are assured that at least one ancilla block will have passed verification for the syndrome extraction when several ancilla blocks are assigned for a single error correction procedure and generated in simultaneously. As an alternative, we might assign qubits to just one ancilla block and hold off on extracting the syndrome until the ancilla has been ready and verified.

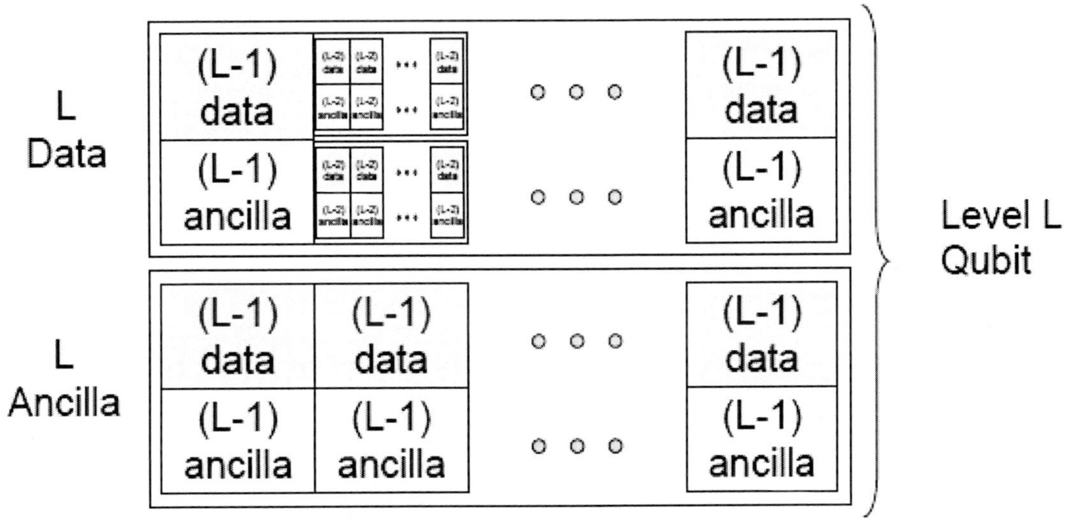

Fig.5.16 Tile-Based Logical Qubit Structure.

Without any particular low-level constructs, the above graphic depicts a possible schematic of a logical qubit tile that is created recursively. A logical qubit at Level L, made up of a Level L data block and a Level L ancilla block, is depicted in the entire figure. (The Steane syndrome extraction method requires the ancilla block.) According to the illustration, each qubit block at level L is made up of 2n Level (L − 1) blocks, which are made up of Level (L − 2) blocks.

A Level L data block must be close to the Level L ancilla block utilized for syndrome extraction in order for there to be a threshold value (and consequently, the capacity to boost reliability with each higher level building). Furthermore, none of the extra ancilla blocks required for the simultaneous extraction of the X and Z syndromes or for the validation of the ancilla blocks employed in the syndrome extraction procedure are depicted in the above image.

5.9.5 Fault-Tolerance and Quantumerrorcorrection: The Outcome

The QEC hypothesis is far more profound and potent than we could reasonably cover here. However, a method to address the exponential propagation of mistakes in an entangled quantum system during algorithm execution is required for scaled computationally relevant quantum information processing to be really beneficial. This is particularly crucial as the gates engaged in error correction are flawed in addition to the gates the application uses.

The threshold result and the development of fault-tolerant quantum circuits have enabled all discussions regarding scalable, dependable quantum computation using the circuit model. As long as the failure rate of each physical gate is less than a specific accuracy threshold number, the threshold result asserts that an arbitrary length of quantum computation can be carried out with arbitrary reliability employing defective physical gates. In order for the threshold values to exist, they must:

- Each place in a quantum circuit experiences noise separately on the quantum hardware. Any activity on a qubit, such as a gate, or even an idle cycle in which the qubit awaits the completion of a gate on another qubit, is referred to as a location in a quantum circuit. A move gate and an await gate are two abstractions for qubit movement operations and idle cycles, respectively. It is not strictly necessary for errors to be independent.
- A quantum circuit must function flawlessly with probability (1 − ϵ) and introduce an error on the qubit with probability { at each site. Stated otherwise, the failure probability ϵ is only dependent on the type of operation, and the noise is stochastic.
- Logical circuit topologies for gates and error correction procedures, such as encoding networks and syndrome extraction networks, must be fault-tolerant if n qubits are encoded to create a single logical qubit. When a single error on any lower-level physical qubit does not propagate to (t + 1) or more errors elsewhere in the circuit, the circuit is said to be fault-tolerant. (It is assumed that we have an error-correcting code that can fix up to t errors.).

The graphic below depicts the abstraction for a fault-tolerant cnot gate. The figure's left-hand side displays the physical cnot gate, where both the control and target qubits are actual qubits. In a [[n, k, d]] code for the data and the extra ancilla required for error correction, the control and target are both logical qubit structures of n qubits at the encoded logical level. Seven physical cnot gates are applied in simultaneously to create the code's transversal logical cnot gate. Each logical gate in a logical circuit is essentially followed by an error correction step since the error correction step for one logical gate serves as the initial error correction step for the subsequent logical gate.

As long as the gate construction and error correction processes are built fault-tolerantly (where the probability of errors of weight greater than t is a second order event), the main premise is that the error correction procedure that comes after the logical gate construction network will correct the number of errors that slip through it.

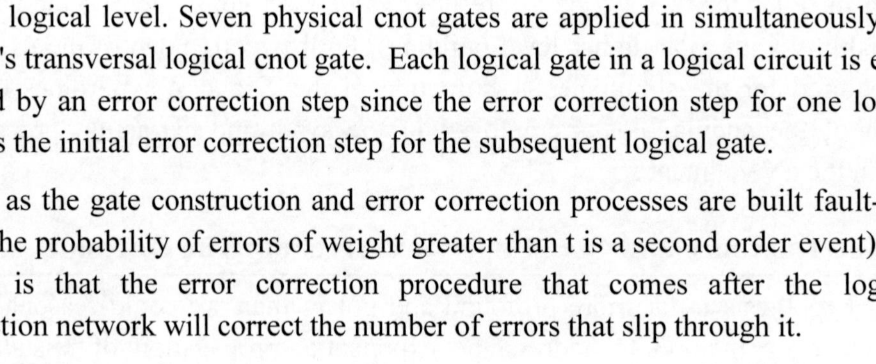

Fig.5.17 Physical → logical gate construction, in which error correction comes after a fault-tolerant logical gate.

Each logical operation that error correction precedes and follows has a failure rate that can be limited as

$$\epsilon_1 \leq A\epsilon^{(t+1)}.$$

In the gate and error correction circuits, A is the number of places where mistakes larger than (t + 1) show up at the circuit's output. Whereas ` without a subscript indicates the failure rate of a physical gate, which is at level 0 encoding, the "1" subscript on ` indicates a single level of encoding. When a logical qubit is encoded in a block of n qubits, an m-qubit code can be used to encode each of those n qubits once more, creating a mn encoding. Concatenation, or recursion, of codes can further lower the failure rates of logical operations as long as the physical failure rates fall below the threshold.

The cost of concatenated error correcting increases exponentially as the level of recursion increases. Each line in the above image contains at least n^L physical qubits if each logical qubit block or line is constructed using a [[n, k, d]] code concatenatedL times. The structure of a logical qubit at level L encoding is depicted in the picture below. Level 1 encoding is the encoding of n physical qubits. Again, encoding, we have a logical qubit at Level 2 for a cost of n^2 physical qubits.

The same fault-tolerance guidelines that apply to the physical circuit described above also apply to logical circuits made up of logical gates, which are made up of self-similar lower-level logical gates. A level L logical gate's failure rate upper bound can be expressed as follows:

$$\epsilon_L \leq A(\epsilon_{L-1})^{(t+1)} = \frac{1}{A}(A\epsilon)^{(t+1)^L}$$

where ϵ_L represents a logical gate's failure rate at level L encoding. Observe that if the physical component failure rate ϵ is higher than A^{-1}, the "≤" sign will not hold for ϵ_L As a result, for a [[n, k, d]] error correcting code, the accuracy threshold value e_{th} is given as 1/A, where A is directly impacted by the error correcting code employed. If the physical component failure rate for a given error correcting code is less than $\epsilon_{th} = 1/A$, we can increase the recursion level until we get the required computation dependability, or even one that is sufficient to continue computation until the application is finished.

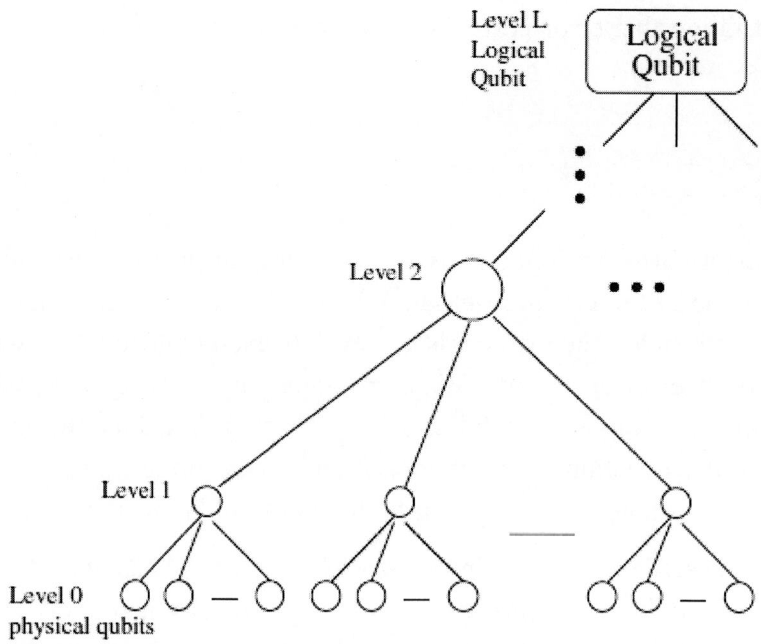

Fig.5.18 A logical qubit's tree structure employing concatenated error-correcting codes.

Finding the threshold value for a selected error correction code will assist in figuring out how reliable the code can be at various recursion levels. The Steane code's $\epsilon_{th} = 10^{-4}$ is the most often mentioned threshold number. This value, however, is predicated on quick and accurate measurement processes as well as noiseless and instantaneous qubit communication.

5.9.6 The Price of Quantum Error Remedial

While dealing with decoherence adds a time and space overhead that is likewise exponential in the number of qubits and the algorithm's running duration, quantum computing offers processing that may be exponentially powerful in the number of qubits. We look at this "contest of two exponentials" in this part and describe how to create systems that win while maintaining the computational benefits of quantum systems.

The cost of the physical resources and the time required to implement single logical gates increase dramatically as the level of concatenation increases when employing quantum error correction. As we recurse, the increase in physical resource can end up being the most expensive parameter because each logical qubit needs ancillary qubits in order to execute quantum error correction following each logical operation. Prior to error correcting the data, level L auxiliary qubits must also be inspected and repaired.

But as processing power increases, the likelihood of each logical operation failing drops by a super-exponential amount. The use of concatenated error correction improves the reliability of logical quantum circuits as $(t + 1)^L$. For distance 3 quantum codes, such the Steane code, on the other hand, the likelihood of failure ϵ_L per logical operation drops doubly exponentially with L. Because of this, a particular program may only need a few layers of recursion to provide the required level of reliability, maintaining the exponential improvement over the application's execution on traditional computers.

5.9.7 System scalability increase as a result of error correction

The product of Q logical qubits and K timesteps is the system size S for a certain application. The time required to complete the logical operation, which comprises error correcting the n lower level qubits stored in the logical qubit and then error correcting each logical qubit, is considered the duration of a timestep. Desired = 1/KQ = 1/S is the failure rate required to reach a system size S = KQ per logical operation. In order to obtain the required degree of reliability for a given system size, a quantum computer with adequate computational resources may use as many of these resources as required for each application to encode data at the desired level of encoding (using a well selected error correcting code). Numerous qubit resources would be left underutilized for applications with modest KQparameters according to this. In the hopes that the acquired dependability per operation is adequate for the available set of desired applications, another approach would be to assume a fixed error correcting code and level of recursion.

In contrast to the Steane code, which uses a significantly higher number of encoded lower level qubits for each logical qubit and the number of locations A that may produce a fault has not been clearly identified, it is evident that a lower failure rate could be achieved faster with [[n, k, d]] error correcting codes with t > 1. This is especially true when qubit communication is taken into account within the error correction procedure. Furthermore, for k > 1, larger error-correcting codes that suggest far more resource- and latency-efficient logical circuit designs. Block codes are codes that encode n qubits in k > 1 qubits; often, n is rather large. However, because the error correction processes are so intricate, it is still uncertain if these codes are effective for large-scale quantum architecture.

Gottesman's estimate for local architectures, which is displayed below, can be used to calculate the predicted logical gate failure rate for quantum codes where k = t = 1 at a certain degree of recursion L.

$$\epsilon_L = \frac{1}{Ar^2 r^L}(Ar^2\epsilon)^{2^L} = \frac{\epsilon_{th}}{r^L}(\epsilon_{th}^{-1}\epsilon)^{2^L}$$

where the average number of move operations per physical qubit, or the communication distance within Level 1 encoded blocks, is represented by the value for r. The above equation is a pretty gloomy approximation, assuming that the recursion level L causes the qubits' trip distance before they need to be corrected to increase exponentially. Although this is true, the idea of teleportation could be applied to alter the movement model and enable lower failure rate ϵ_L estimations for sufficiently long distances.

5.9.8 Delay in Error correction

Even with qubit tiles of only a few levels of recursion, the exponential slowness caused by error correction appears to be prohibitive when the system size S grows significantly. However, in certain situations, the exponential speedup provided by the quantum algorithm structure in comparison to its classical equivalent balances the exponential delay from error correction.

Shor's quantum factoring technique, which is intended to crack the popular RSA public-key cryptosystem, is one example of such an application. Since the RSA system and cryptography in general have garnered a lot of attention, so too has the factoring issue, which is the foundation of RSA's security: Determine p and q given a big number M with two prime components p and q such that $M = p \times q$.

Numerous academics' efforts have made it simpler to solve this classical factoring problem for numbers of any size, regardless of hardware speed. Factoring is still an extremely challenging problem, though. The complexity of the best classical algorithm available now is

$$\exp\left((1.923 + o(1))(log\ N)^{1/3}(log\ log\ N)^{2/3}\right)$$

For an integer with N bits. Base our comparison on the most recent achievements in factoring with traditional computers. On 80 2.2 GHz classical computers, a 663-bit number was factored using traditional methods over the course of nearly two years.

Large numbers can be factored in polynomial time using Shor's quantum factoring algorithm. The algorithm uses a reduction of the factoring problem to determine the period r of the periodic function $f(x) = a^x \bmod M$, where M is the number being factored, an is a randomly selected number co-prime to M, and x is an integer such that $M^2 \leq x < 2M^2$. M's factors, p and q, can be discovered with some postprocessing since the period r splits the integer M equally. Period r splits the number $M' = (p - 1) \times (q - 1)$ evenly; hence, M's factors p and q can be obtained with a little postprocessing. Three main steps may be distinguished in the algorithm:

- The most prominent component is the Modular Exponentiation (quantum portion), which calculates f (x) in superposition over all values of x. A sequence of quantum multiplication stages, which are further subdivided into a number of quantum adders, comprise the modular exponentiation process.

- The Quantum Fourier Transform (quantum portion) modifies the superposition so that, upon measurement, the states with the period of f (x) have the highest probability.
- Classical Postprocessing — finds the factors p and q from the discovered period r of f (x).

The Draper Quantum Carry Lookahead Adder, which has the shortest known predicted runtime, has been used to mimic the modular exponentiation routine in the QLA architecture's performance predictions.

Table 5.1 Some of the Algorithm's parameters.

Modulus	Minimum Operation Failure Rate	Logical Qubits	Timesteps	QFT Timestep Ratio
128	$O(10^{-11})$	37,971	9×10^5	$O(10^{-4})$
512	$O(10^{-12})$	150,771	6×10^6	$O(10^{-4})$
1024	$O(10^{-13})$	301,251	1×10^7	$O(10^{-5})$
2048	$O(10^{-14})$	602,259	3×10^7	$O(10^{-5})$

Below image plots the necessary degree of recursion against the issue size N for factoring an N-bit integer using Shor's approach. The Steane code and optimistic ion-trap technology assumptions are the system parameters that are employed; yet, they remain within the basic bounds of the technology and are not unattainable in the future. aforementioned the aforementioned architecture design, we can observe that Level 2 recursion using the Steane code may be adequate for factoring a 1024-bit (or perhaps a 2048-bit) integer. The current estimate for the accuracy threshold value of roughly 10−5 for the Steane code is nearly three orders of magnitude higher than the optimistic error rates for the ion-trap technique.

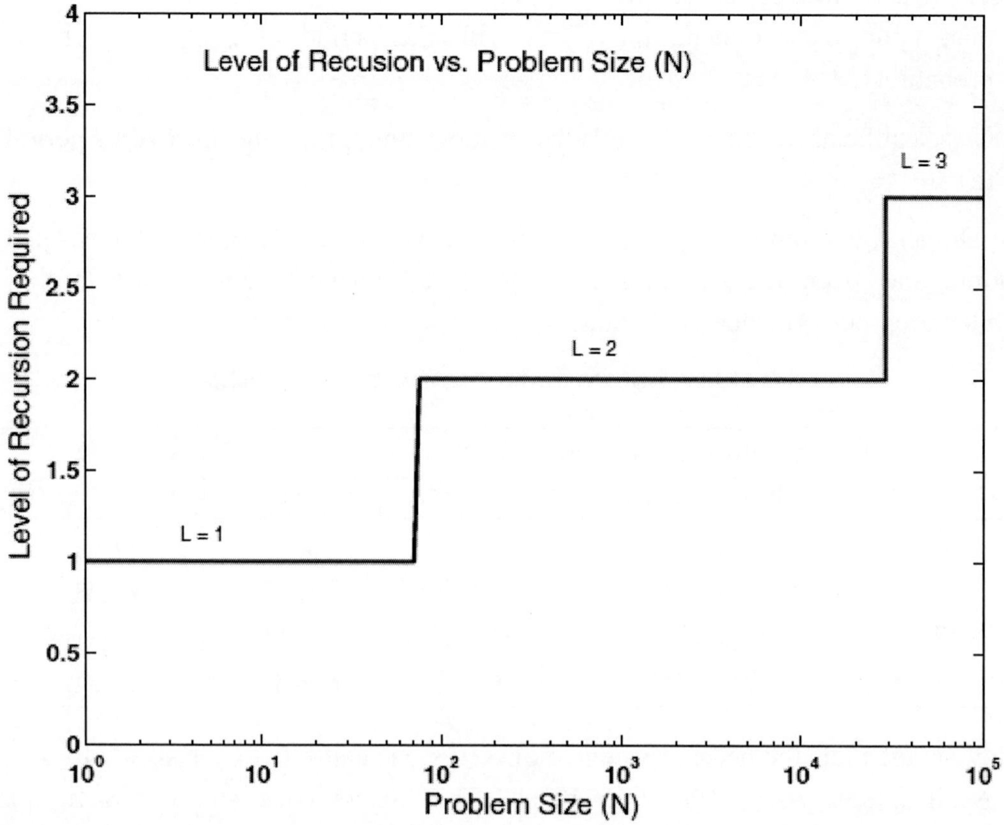

Fig.5.19 The required level of recursion for Shor's algorithm in relation to the issue size N, which is stated in terms of an N-bit number that is being factored.

The logarithmic scale plot in the image below, where the ˆy-axis indicates the speedup of the quantum algorithm from its classical equivalent, illustrates the slowing caused by error correction. The speedup is computed by dividing the number of days spent utilizing quantum computing by the number of days spent conventionally. The speedup without error correction is shown in the top line. The speedup with optimistic ion-trap parameters is shown in the center line, and the speedup with technological error rates at the threshold value of around 10^{-5} is shown in the bottom line. The amount of recursion is increased by one unit for every "blip" on the speedup lines with error correction. At N = 700, the smallest issue size displayed, Level 2 encoding is necessary. In the event that the technology parameters reach the threshold value, Level 3 encoding is necessary for the same problem size.

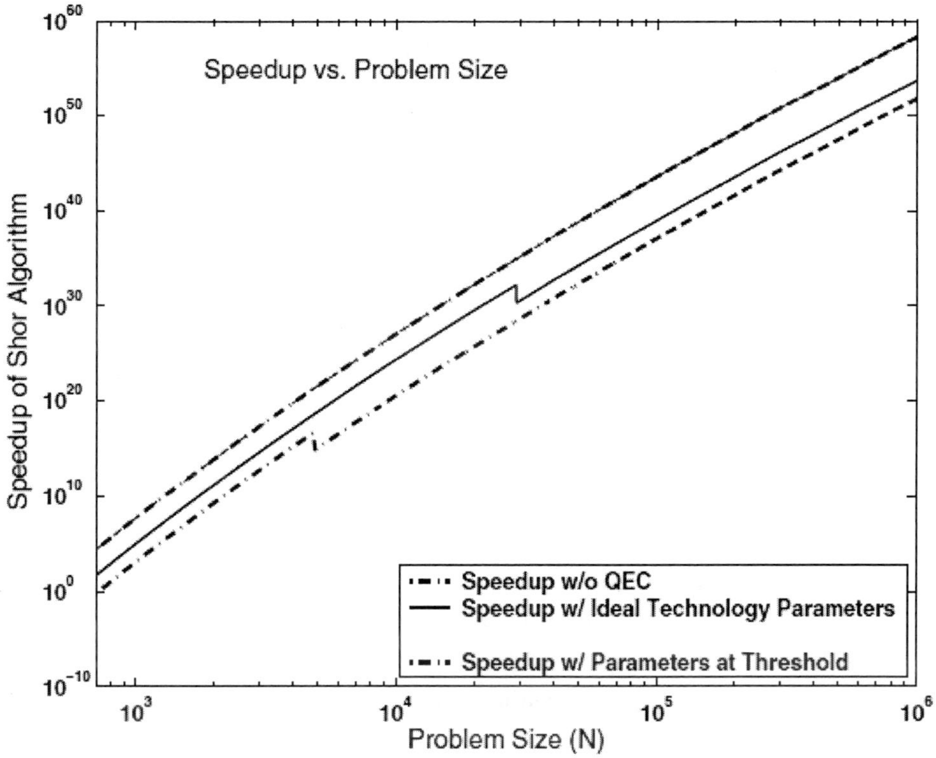

Fig.5.20 Shor's algorithm speedup in relation to problem size N.

The speedup without error correction is displayed in the top line, the speedup with error correction is displayed in the middle line, but at error parameters that are roughly three orders of magnitude below the Steane code's accuracy threshold, and the error parameters are at the code's threshold value in the bottom line. The degree of recursion rises with each "glitch" in the two lower lines.

The exponential speedup over classical calculation is maintained, as we can observe, even with error correction. The departure of the speedup lines from being completely exponential (see the slight curve) is caused by the polynomial cost incurred by the computation, which is also the asymptotic cost of Shor's algorithm. The speedup computed is predicated on a KHz quantum computer at the physical level since an ion-trap quantum computer requires an order of 10 μs for a physical operation.

5.10 Distribution of Quantum Resources

The realization of scalable quantum computers is significantly hampered by the third key scalability issue that must be taken into account while developing the quantum architecture: quantum resource distribution. Each qubit is essentially a carrier of quantum information that needs to be physically moved from one location to another and cannot be replicated. This restricts our communication options to two: Either (1) each qubit physically transmits quantum information by moving the qubit itself, or (2) operations are used to send the information over a predetermined distance.

Both approaches severely limit the speed and dependability of the distribution of quantum data. Using more error correction resources to continuously error correct along the channel is one way to prevent data corruption during transmission. Implementing a long-range wire using the purely quantum idea of teleportation—which has been shown experimentally on a very tiny scale—is an additional option. With teleportation, a quantum state is sent between two locations using two bits of classical information for each qubit on both ends rather than any actual quantum data. It is also possible to use photon interactions to couple distant atomic qubits, which are ideal for computation.

One of the main areas in which computer architects will contribute is the design and optimization of a quantum architecture that supports effective data communication scalable to arbitrarily large applications. The two forms of data distribution—physical qubit movement and teleportation movement—are now briefly explained.

5.10.1 Mechanical Qubit Transaction

The most common operation that necessitates qubit-qubit contact and, hence, data transport is the cnot gate. To enable two qubits to interact, the existing technologies use a wide range of physical qubit communication techniques. The communication methods that are available for engaging with two or more qubits actually play a major role in the classification of the different types of qubits.

Certain qubit implementations fall under the category of flying qubits, including photons, which are always moving, and gates, which are physical objects that are immovable but have an impact on the photon-qubits as they "fly" through them. Photons are often transmitted by fiber optic cables, and the primary. Photon absorption is the cause of decoherence during conveyance.

The solid-state qubit proposals and other physical qubit implementations are referred to as stationary qubits because they occupy a defined qubit container or a specified physical region where qubit-qubit interactions are restricted to nearest neighbor only. Until two particular qubit states reside in adjoining qubit containers, it is entirely feasible to construct arbitrary one- and two-dimensional lattices for logical qubits utilizing stationary qubits by successfully exchanging two neighboring qubit states. External forces, such as lasers shining on the qubits or electrostatic forces produced by metal gates, apply gates. Although the core qubit-qubit gate in the majority of nearest-neighbor technology ideas is the $\sqrt{swap}$ gate, the dependability of the swap operation, which may be abstracted by applying three successive cnot gates, limits the nearest-neighbor communication channels.

A balance between "flying" and "stationary" qubits is provided by trapped atomic ions, which retain the qubit states in place between the segmented electrodes. Any previously specified interaction region can be used to execute a logic gate using lasers. In order to occupy the same trap, two ions interact by ballistically moving over the physical architecture. Since they provide the simplest route to reconfigurable quantum logic, nearest-neighbor and ballistic qubit communication techniques are most appropriate for implementing the circuit model for quantum processing. From the standpoint of a systems designer, there may be no difference between the two communication models: Moving the ions physically via a series of unit lengths in an empty ballistic channel is comparable to the expense of successive swap operations across a swapping channel.

System designers will face the difficulty of translating quantum circuits to physical layouts in a way that minimizes the impact of communication delay on circuit execution latency. A greater amount of swap operations, or move operations across a unit length channel, is also comparable to carrying out random defective operations on the carried qubit, which the physical arrangement designer must take into account. Therefore, it is crucial to plan quantum circuits carefully such that programs are optimized for reliability requirements in addition to latency limitations.

A significant amount of physical qubit movement may be necessary for the error correction processes for qubits encoded at comparatively low concatenation levels; However, it may be feasible to lessen the errors that data collects during transmission by employing astute optimization techniques. The execution of a transversal two-qubit gate between two logical qubits at level 3 concatenation is an example of a major issue that occurs when qubits encoded at a reasonably high level of recursion need to communicate with one another. With each new degree of recursion, the physical qubits' separation increases significantly, creating lengths that most known quantum device technologies cannot physically travel without losing all data. The idea of quantum teleportation as a dependable long-distance communication method in quantum structures is explained in the next section.

5.10.2 Quantum repeaters and communication based on teleportation

The image below shows the three-stage implementation of the idea of teleportation as a long-distance communication channel. In the initial phase, two qubits are entangled using the network to create an EPR pair. Then, the two qubits are moved—one near to the source qubit and the other to the point where the source qubit is transported—through a physical channel. The source qubit can be replicated at the destination once the source and EPR qubits have interacted and been measured.

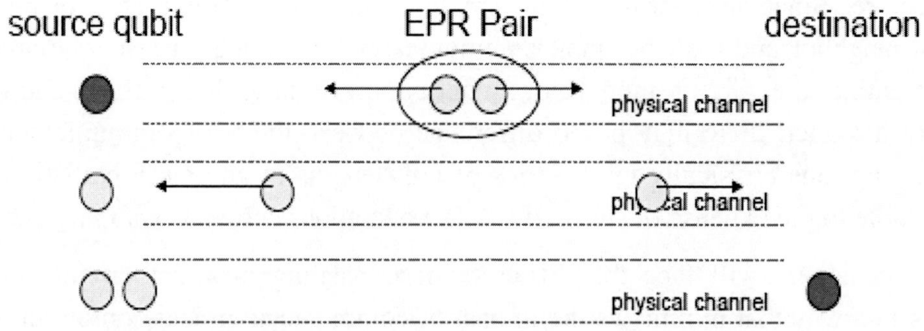

Fig.5.21 A representation of the several teleportation phases.

The entangled EPR qubits are still being physically moved, so take note. EPR qubits, however, can be swapped out, unlike the source qubit. A technique known as entanglement purification, which separates the good pairs from the poor pairings using supplementary EPR pairs, can repair the broken EPR pairs. The drawback of purification is that resources grow exponentially with the distance that the EPR pairs travel. In addition, if the EPR pair gets sufficiently tainted, it could not even be used for purification. When the EPR pairs' required physical distance becomes closer to the coherence length permitted by the implementation technology, two possibilities happen:

(1) The fidelity of each qubit transmitted over the channel drops exponentially, and (2) the number of extra EPR pairs needed to purify a single EPR pair rises exponentially. We will need to send qubits at distances significantly greater than the coherence length of the physical channels for large-scale quantum systems, and it would appear that a significant amount of resources will be required to do this. Because entanglement is maintained during teleportation, we can successfully teleport the physical qubits between any two logical qubits in the design at any distance. After part of the physical qubits have been transported to a different area of the architecture, for instance, a logical qubit encoded into the state of 49 physical qubits stays the same.

Likewise, in an EPR pair, the maximum entanglement between the two qubits remains intact when one of them is teleported. It is possible to build a quantum architecture's logical qubit connection so that, instead of physically transporting the EPR qubits, EPR pairs can be formed between the source and the destination by teleporting them. Following the creation of the EPR pairs (A1,A2) and (B1,B2), they can be split apart, extending the span of (A1,A2)'s entanglement once A2 is teleported over to B2. The entanglement swapping technique, depicted in the image below, involves transferring the entanglement of EPR pairs across a channel that is split up into several smaller sections called quantum repeaters. One EPR pair that covers the whole channel is the end outcome.

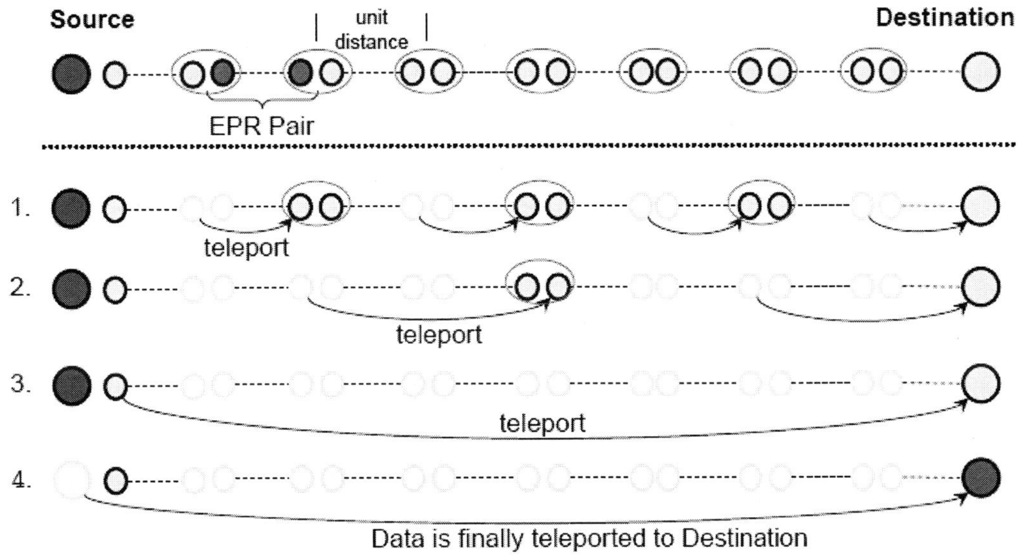

Fig.5.22 An Entanglement example switching method for teleporting the "S"-designated source qubit.

EPR pairs only go to two nearby repeater islands (shaded boxes) in the entanglement swapping protocol seen in the above diagram, where they can be effectively purified. We can generate (extend) a single entangled EPR pair between the source and the destination across the whole channel using this technique. Each protocol step, as depicted in the above picture, cuts the number of connected EPR pairs in half without severing the link between the source and the destination. Once a single EPR pair has been created to cover the full communication channel, the source qubit has finally been transported to the appropriate place. For each of the 49 ion-qubits of qubit Q1, an EPR pair must be allocated between the logical qubits Q1 and Q2 in such a manner that each of the Teleporting 49 qubits to qubit Q2's computational tile is possible.

The closest neighbor communication protocol, which is used by many promising technological implementations where the physical qubit containers are fixed in space, is another long-distance communication option for logical qubit structures. Furthermore, a scalable architecture model for flux qubit quantum computers—which rely on nearest-neighbor interactions at their lowest level—is presented. If the "hop" of an ion from one trapping region to the next is substituted by a "swap" operation of the data qubit with another qubit along the direction of movement, then nearest neighbor communication is comparable to the ion-trap ballistic movement model.

The nearest neighbor physical communication method is fault-tolerant, according to recent threshold research, and there is no compelling reason why quantum designs, like the QLA architecture, shouldn't be physically implemented using closest neighbor interaction technology. Furthermore, circuit synthesis has demonstrated that the asymptotic depth of quantum circuits is preserved by closest neighbor communication.

However, a nearest-neighbor-based connection will need to perform as many logical "swap" operations at the logical level as there are logical qubits separating the source and destination qubits. Error correction must come after each of these "swap" actions since they must be regarded as transversal logical gates in order to maintain fault-tolerance. The nearest neighbor logical interconnect adds a linear factor slowdown for the application execution equal to the average communication distance since the time to error correct determines the duration of a single timestep in the execution of a logical circuit with the QLA architecture.

For instance, factoring a 1024-bit Shor's method will necessitate 256 swap operations during the modular exponentiation part of the algorithm, and consequently 256 extra error correction steps, due to the maximum distance covered by logical qubits. We can "hide" the temporal cost of communication and separate it from any logical qubit subroutines by using a teleportation-based interconnect for the QLA architecture. Communication and computation overlap, which reduces the need for extra error correction when logical qubits are moving.

5.11 Quantum Computation Simulation

Simulating a quantum architecture may pose an extra and noteworthy obstacle to the three main ones for creating scalable quantum architectures. However, simulation is essential for validating and confirming various architectural concepts. This chapter covers the various approaches that can be used to simulate quantum computers. Specifically, outline a technique for tracking the mistakes generated by a wide subset of quantum processes in order to simulate their behavior. Additionally, outline the stabilizer formalism for modeling the same subset of operations.

The inability of a conventional computer to effectively imitate the execution of a quantum program presents a barrier for modeling quantum architectures. This can be understood by acknowledging that quantum information processing is an extension of the classical computational model, in which data is not represented as a single classical bitstring but rather as a superposition of classical bitstring states. A classical system is unlikely to be able to effectively imitate a quantum system as the classical computational model is a subset of the wider quantum information processing method. However, the necessity of precisely confirming and validating the designs of such systems will grow in importance and urgency as the overall structure of large-scale quantum computers becomes more apparent with each technological breakthrough.

$O(2^n)$ operations are needed to emulate a unitary operation on an n-qubit quantum register, or $O(2^n)$ data bitstring entries are needed to store the register's state. The reality that no quantum computer system is totally isolated from its surroundings, however, makes the simulation of quantum computers considerably more difficult. As time passes, the system becomes entangled with the environment, and unidentified forces acting on the environment cause the quantum computer itself to decohere. This is because quantum systems used for computation are inherently susceptible to external forces that apply the logic gates. This implies that more data must be stored than is required to track the superposition state of an isolated quantum register in order to precisely trace the evolution of a quantum computing system that is connected to the environment.

It is not feasible to simulate even a few hundred qubits because the cost of all current general-purpose simulators increases exponentially with each more qubit. As long as the circuits' functioning complies with certain restrictions, other simulators that place restrictions on the system's entanglement can replicate quantum circuits in polynomial time. However, a systems designer attempting to represent error correction—which necessitates highly entangled qubits for even a single logical codeword—cannot tolerate an entanglement restriction. When one takes into account the types of simulations that system designers require, the situation is not as dire. A system designer must monitor a quantum application's precise calculations as well as its behavior inside the architecture, including latency, fault tolerance, and impact on system size.

Two kinds of simulation techniques—error propagation simulation and the use of the special stabilizer representation of an n-qubit register—allow us to simulate the behavior of quantum circuits using techniques that are polynomial in time but do not place any restrictions on the entanglement generated by the simulated circuit. However, both approaches necessitate that the circuits consist solely of Clifford group gates. However, quantum error correction—which requires the majority of computational resources during application execution—can be simulated using just Clifford group operations.

The stabilizer formalism for quantum circuits, which is used to directly simulate stabilizer circuits, will be covered in full in the next section. Any n-qubit state $|\Psi\rangle$ that the Clifford group gates may completely create

$$\{H, \text{CNOT}, X, Z, Y = -iZX, S\}$$

A stabilizer state is one in which the qubits must begin in the starting state |0102... 0n}. Any stabilizer state $|\Psi\rangle$ may be uniquely characterized by the O(n^2) unitary one-qubit Pauli operators {I,X,Y,Z}. The stabilizer circuit is the circuit made up of the Clifford group gates that form |�`.

It is an effective representation of quantum states that was initially published by Gottesman, who also describes a particularly potent family of error-correcting codes called stabilizer codes. A subset of the class of stabilizer codes is the class of CSS codes, which includes the Steane code.

5.11.1 Error Propagation Simulation

If the failure rate of the system as a whole is more important to a system designer than the exact state of the system at any one time, error propagation can be used to effectively model the behavior of any system component that is implemented using a stabilizer circuit. Furthermore, stabilizer circuits are also used in long-distance communication systems that rely on teleportation. Accordingly, error propagation can be used to effectively replicate the dependability and effectiveness of a long-distance link on a traditional computer.

A qubit's state can be altered by an error at any one point in a circuit, which alters the behavior of all control gates that depend on it. This is the fundamental idea behind error propagation. As the program runs, the error spreads to further qubits after propagating through two-qubit gates. For this reason, fault-tolerant implementation of error-correcting circuits is crucial, ensuring that an error on any one to t qubits will never propagate to more than t qubits.

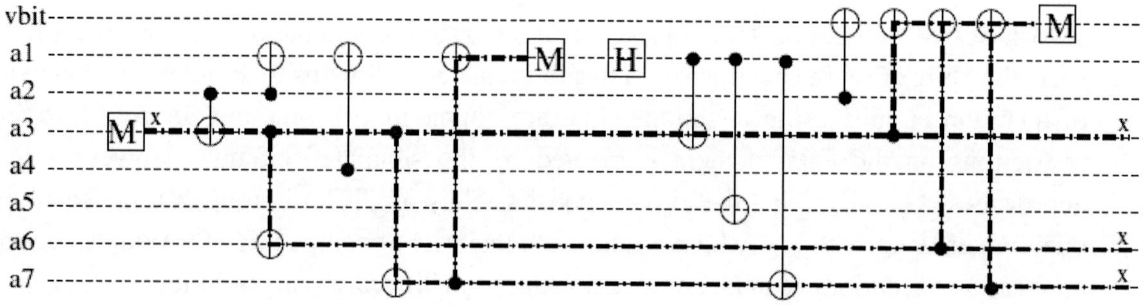

Fig.5.23 Propagation of X-error. A thicker dot-dashed line represents the qubit lines impacted by the error. The measurement activities at the network's middle and end are made to produce "0" otherwise and "1" in the event of error.

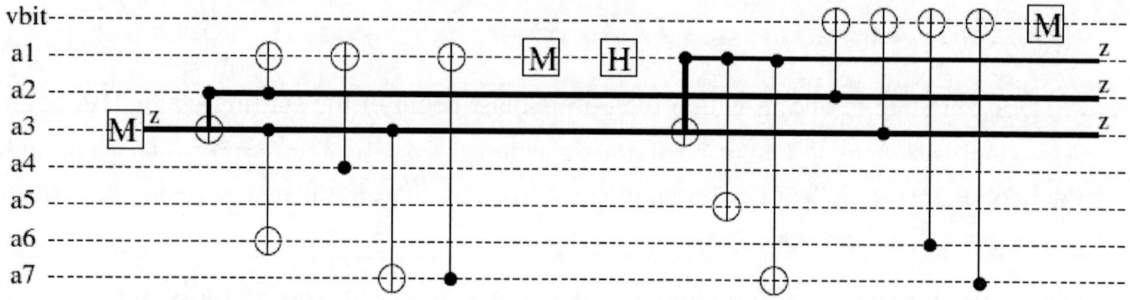

Fig.5.24 Propagation of Z-error. The error-affected qubit lines are displayed as thicker solid lines.

Remember that this network does not detect Z faults, and that a single Z error in the middle of the circuit has resulted in three Z errors in the output. Examine the basic circuit examples that illustrate the propagation of X and Z faults, respectively, in the images above. Although both networks begin with the first measurement operation, they are exact replicas of the Steane code's encoding network. Since the measurements are made on a computational basis, they will identify the states $|0\rangle$ or $|1\rangle$ and either measurement gate will identify the X error. In contrast, phase-flip mistakes can multiply into several faults as they go across the network, as seen in the above image. The extraction of the syndrome may produce the incorrect error syndrome, perhaps rectifying the incorrect data bit, if several Z errors occur in the network throughout the recovery process. Prior to applying actual error correction to the data block, the syndrome extraction is repeated because a single Z error can result in several errors and, ultimately, an inaccurate syndrome.

In practice, error propagation simulations can be used to track the impact of faults caused by all gates.. The universal set for computation would be completed by include the T gate in the group of gates whose mistakes to monitor. The issue is that we have to follow both error routes because the T gate's mistakes are characterized by a superposition of the X and Z gates. The number of paths in a quantum circuit doubles with each T gate, making the circuit simulation unmanageable very fast. The Toffoli gate, which may be made up of nearly all T gates, is essential to the majority of applications, including Shor's algorithm.

Take note of how the two-qubit cnot gates transmit X and Z mistakes in various ways. When bit-flip errors propagate "forward," that is, control → target, phase-flip errors propagate "backward," via a cnot gate. Bit-flip mistakes are easily visible since the target bit's state is flipped based on the control bit's state. Understanding phase-flips is made simpler if we assume that the input and target qubit states are $(|0\} + |1\}) \otimes (|0\} + |1\})$. The target qubit's state will change from $[0\}$ to $[1\})$ following a Z mistake. The system enters the state $(|00\} - |01\} + |11\} - |10\})$ upon applying the cnot gate, which is expressed as $(|0\} - |1\}) \otimes (|0\} - |1\})$.

Thus, we can observe that the Z error has now been transmitted to the control qubit as well as the target qubit after the cnot gate. The complexity of simulation increases exponentially with the number of T gates in the circuit while tracking the error behavior of the T gate using the error propagation methodology, which would enable us to simulate universal circuits. Rather than introducing a product of phase-flip and bit-flip defects, the T gate introduces a linear mixture of the two. This doubles the number of fault paths we are simulating at each T gate as both the phase-flip path and the bit-flip path must be followed independently at each gate instance.

The error propagation method is used by the large collection of quantum architecture tools called QUALE to confirm that the error correction networks they model have fault-tolerant characteristics. To facilitate the study of large-scale quantum hardware and applications, QUALE maps quantum circuits onto a realistic physical layout using conventional compiler techniques. Error correction, the most common use, is validated by simulating the propagation of mistakes, and the goal of the QUALE software tool chain is to make the creation of large-scale quantum applications easier.

Monte-Carlo simulation can be used to determine the failure probability of any stabilizer circuit because errors occur with related probabilities and the noise model is stochastic. The simulated failure probability of the complete circuit is calculated by dividing the number of registered failures by the number of registered successes per trial after the network behavior has been simulated enough times. Any time more faults have spread to the circuit's output than the error correction code can fix, it is considered a registered failure.

The application is marked as "failed" and restarted whenever one of two things occurs in a large-scale quantum computation made up of a series of logical gates, such as the gate in Figure 4.11: (1) more errors enter the recovery network than can be fixed, completely changing the meaning of the encoded codeword; or (2) either the recovery network or the logical gate circuitry is not fault-tolerant, causing a single fault at any location to propagate to more errors than the next recovery network can correct. However, the disadvantage of simulating error propagation is that, in contrast to statistical data derived from alternative simulation techniques, the failure probability results are gloomy.

It is hard to identify the kind of fault that will truly be a real fault without knowing the state of the quantum register. The phase-flip operator Z, for instance, has no effect on the $|0\rangle$ state, despite the fact that all Pauli operators are applied with equal probability ϵ. Therefore, it is basically a non-error since modeling the propagation of errors might occasionally produce failures on qubit states that are unaffected by the error operator. A logical $\overline{X}$ operator has no effect on a logical qubit in the encoded $|\overline{+}\rangle$ state; nevertheless, if enough X errors have spread to that logical qubit that they implement the $\overline{X}$ operator, this will be recorded as a logical error and cause the application to crash.

5.11.2 The Quantum Simulation Stabilizer Method

Using the stabilizer formalism is another way to effectively simulate stabilizer circuits. Assuming that every qubit in the register has been initialized to $|0\rangle$, any arbitrary n-qubit state $|\Psi\rangle$ that can be created using gates in the Clifford group is a stabilizer state. If U does not alter the state $|\Psi\rangle$, then an n-qubit operator U stabilizes it: $U|\Psi\rangle = |\Psi\rangle$. The Gottesman-Knill theorem, which asserts that if the n-qubit state $|\Psi\rangle$ is a stabilizer state, then: is the key to using the stabilizer formalism for simulating quantum circuits.

- A collection of n-qubit operators made up of the Pauli group matrices stabilizes $|\Psi\rangle$.

- Every stabilizer operator of the state $|\Psi\rangle$ may be expressed as a product of a small set of stabilizer operators for $|\Psi\rangle$, meaning that the stabilizer group can be created using $\Omega(n)$ n-qubit Pauli operators.
- The set of operators that produce all of the stabilizers of the state $|\Psi\rangle$ is unique. For $|\Psi\rangle$, these operators are referred to as stabilizer generators.

According to the final argument, representing a stabilizer state $|\Psi\rangle$ with its stabilizer generators is exponentially less expensive than describing the state explicitly. Take the stabilizer generators for the unknown three-qubit state {I I I, ZZI, IZZ, ZIZ}, for instance, where it is known that the i'th Pauli operator in a stabilizer string acts solely on the i'th qubit. Since the first operator III is simply the identity on all three qubits, it stabilizes anything. Four states are stabilized by the second operator ZZI: |000}, |001}, |110}, and |111}. Stabilizing the states |000}, |100}, |011}, and |111} is the third operator, IZZ. Finally, the states |000}, |101}, |010}, and |111} are stabilized by the final operator. Because the two states |000} and |111} are shared by all four operators, the state stabilized by the generators {I I I, ZZI, IZZ, ZIZ} is $|\Psi\rangle = \frac{1}{\sqrt{2}}(|000\rangle$ ± |111}).

To specify an n-qubit stabilizer state $|\Psi\rangle$, a total of (2n + 1) classical bits are required; the sign bit is responsible for the "1," and there are 2n X and Z operators to record. The action of these gates may be described in only O(n) time since Gottesman and Knill also demonstrated that unitary operations on the qubits that make up the Clifford group, such as the cnot, Hadamard, S-gate, and measurement, take each stabilizer state to a distinct stabilizer state. If the result is predictable and the stabilizer generators can be updated in O(n^3) time, the measurement costs a little more. Since then, Aaronson and Gottesman have shown how to create a stabilizer-based simulator that allows for O(n^2) time updates to measurements [1].

Although stabilizer circuits alone cannot be used to imitate Shor's algorithm, we may effectively simulate the most well-known type of quantum error correcting codes, which are stabilizer CSS codes like the Steane code. Furthermore, the stabilizer approach enables us to model several of the most significant quantum protocols, including superdense coding and teleportation. It is actually possible to explicitly design encoding and error-correction methods for stabilizer codes using the stabilizer formalism. The six operators {gl, g2, g3, g4, g5, g6}, for instance, supply the set of n-qubit Pauli operators that produce the stabilizers for the encoded logical states $|\bar{0}\rangle$ and $|\bar{1}\rangle$for the Steane, where:

$$\begin{aligned}\{g1, g2, g3, g4, g5, g6\} = \{&XXXXIII,\ XXIIXXI,\ XIXIXIX,\\ &ZZZZIII,\ ZZIIZZI,\ ZIZIZIZ\}\end{aligned}$$

The reader can confirm that the two codewords will remain unchanged if any of the aforementioned operators are applied to the code's encoded $|\bar{0}\rangle$ and $|\bar{1}\rangle$ states. However, the stabilizers for the two codewords will be altered if a Pauli error occurs on any one of the seven qubits. Therefore, another method of establishing an error syndrome for the code is to measure each stabilizer generator to see which ones continue to stabilize the codeword states. Using Monte Carlo simulations, stabilizer circuits' functionality and fault tolerance can also be confirmed. The tool chain that is compatible Aaronson's enhanced stabilizer simulator CHP is used to functionally verify stabilizer circuits, while QASM-TOOLS use the assembly language QASM as an input language to model and investigate fault-tolerant quantum circuits by predicting depolarizing noise thresholds using Monte-Carlo simulation. The Steane code and other distance 3 codes can also have their accuracy thresholds lowered by QASMTOOLS employing general malignant set counting, which keeps track of every possible combination of locations in a logical gate circuit that can lead to a network failure.

5.12 Architectural Components

A broad quantum architecture's components are covered in this section. Two main components are assumed to be present in a quantum architecture:

1. Using self-contained computational tiles, logical qubits enable gates to be executed. Immediately after a logical gate is executed, directly on the encoded data, and with the resources required for error correction.

2. Communication channels that use teleportation and maybe the idea of quantum repeaters to transfer data between any two points in the architecture.

Since error correction would likely be the primary application carried out by a large-scale quantum computer and may be necessary after each logical gate, self-contained logical qubit tiles make sense. To prevent the states of the logical qubits from decohering, error correction must really be provided continually to those qubits that are not involved in any quantum gates.

Logical qubit tiles can be classified into two categories by an architecture designer: those that store logical qubits that take part in the execution of logical gates and those that only store quantum information through memory gates or multiple execution cycles.

Another obvious option would be to simply use the same encoding and error-correcting code for all logical qubit tiles, regardless of whether the logical qubits stored in each tile are subjected to memory gates or logical gates.

Similar to classical applications, quantum applications naturally display serialization. Designing logical qubit tiles optimized for computation and logical qubit tiles optimized for quantum data storage allows for the reduction of area requirements while increasing performance by taking advantage of the limited parallelism of a quantum computer at both the application and physical microarchitecture levels. The main takeaway from this is that, when taking into account the amount of parallelism that is possible in quantum applications, we find that restricting processing to a particular area can yield significant benefits. It is possible to optimize the remaining space for quantum data storage.

The Draper carry-lookahead quantum adder, a fundamental part of Shor's quantum factoring algorithm, is a good illustration of the advantages of specialization in quantum applications. Below figure demonstrates that limiting the computation to 15 locations does not improve performance when giving a 64-bit adder unrestricted computational resources. By supplying only 15 compute sites rather than 64, we can cut the area used by each adder by around half without affecting performance if there are twice as many ancillary qubits as there are data qubits.

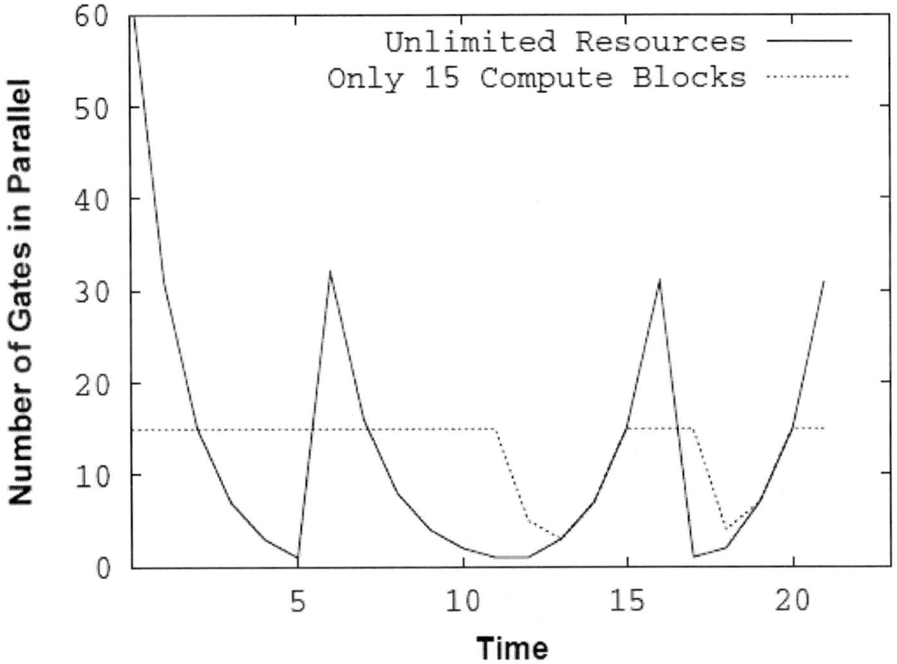

Fig.5.25 The amount of parallelism that can be obtained from a 64-qubit adder with limits on the number of gates per cycle and unbounded resources.

The graphic below depicts the high-level specialized architecture concept that we are discussing here. Regardless of the actual implementation technology, the model is built from a number of specialized architectural pieces, much like a classical architecture. Each element is made up of several "tiles," each of which stands for one or more logical qubits, which are made up of several physical qubits that have been encoded with a predetermined error-correcting code. Logical data qubits are represented by the colored tiles in the above image, while logical ancilla blocks—which are employed for error correction at the highest level of recursion—are represented by the transparent tiles.

Any particular quantum memory would just use a wait gate (also known as a memory gate), which is essentially doing nothing. If the implementation technology makes a wait gate significantly more dependable than other gates, then altering the memory and computational areas' proportion of logical data blocks to logical ancilla blocks can decrease the total computer space. For instance, the memory tile depicted in the below figure is primarily used to store and error-correct encoded data qubits. For every logical qubit, the time between two consecutive error correction operations lowers as the number of ancillary qubits required to error correct a particular set of logical data qubits drops.

However, more auxiliary qubits will guarantee faster computational speeds at the cost of greater physical resources because error correction is required after each gate in the computing zone is executed. Additionally, by specifying a specific compute code (CC) for the processing elements and memory code (MC) for data storage, we might be able to combine space reductions with enhanced performance. A sophisticated transmission network between the various tiles will be necessary when different encodings are employed by tiles that can compute and tiles that can merely store qubits. Additionally, the data must not be decoded during the transfer process. The transfer network is sluggish because it consists of several gates and measurement operations on the encoded data, each of which is followed by error correction, as we will see later in this section.

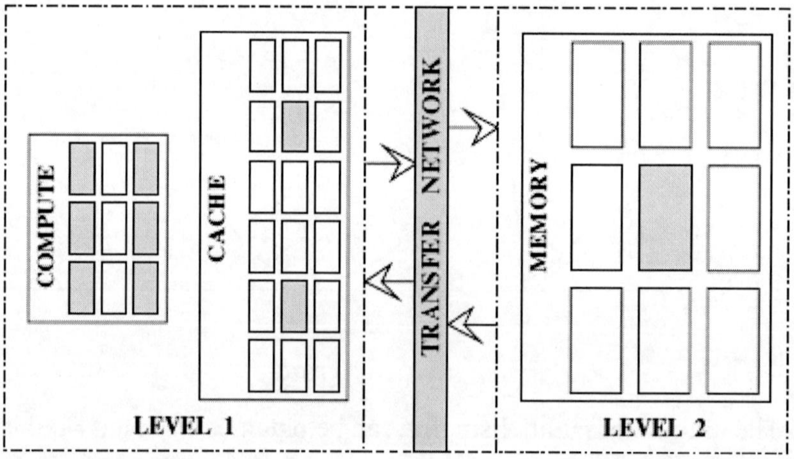

Fig.5.26 High-level overview of a tailored quantum architecture.

Following its transfer from memory, the data encoded with the computational code is buffered in the additional cache region depicted in the above picture. The memory hierarchy that we outline in this part is somewhat similar to a code hierarchy, where the hierarchical structure is required to get around the latency discrepancies between code transfer between encodings and state stability. The hierarchy's structure and optimization may be the most intricate part of the architecture since it offers the transition operations required to move data encoded at the top of the hierarchy to the encoding required for computation without causing the algorithm to execute more slowly.

5.12.1 Components: Quantum Processing

The processing element (PE) tiles are where all logical quantum processes occur. Figure displays a schematic of a fictitious PE tile. A logical qubit is encoded using the compute code (CC), which is selected because it is quick and reasonably priced in terms of the quantity of physical qubits required for encoding and error correcting a single logical qubit, and it is stored in either of the two accumulators when it is teleported to an available PE. Using the closer of the two supplementary blocks, error correction is carried out both before and after a single logical gate is applied to the data kept in either of the two accumulators.

The logical qubit can be teleported straight from main memory if an accumulator is accessible in some Processing Element (PE) units, or it can be located waiting in the quantum cache encoded with the same CC. Because the physical qubits of each of the two participating logical qubits must interact with one another, a two qubit gate necessitates the usage of both accumulators. Enough CC ancilla are available in each accumulator to correct both logical qubits. The boundaries between each PE's several regions are not as distinct in practice as they appear in the figure. For instance, with the ion-trap technology, 49 pairs of ions must be inserted in the same trap in order to execute a two-qubit gate using the Steane code. Therefore, both accumulators can be built with 49 traps that enable the execution of physical two-qubit gates.

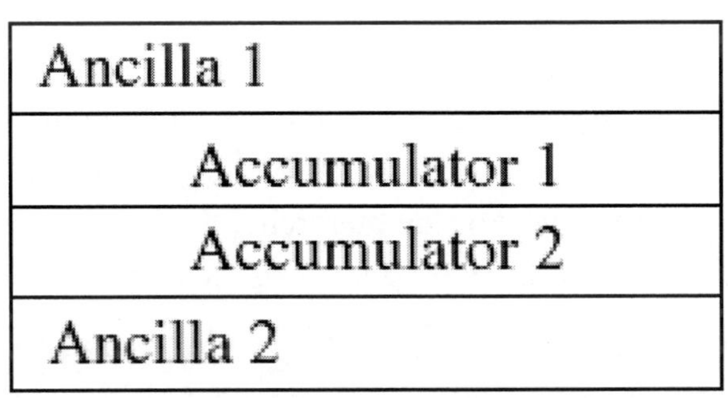

Fig.5.27 A hypothetical Schematic of a Processing Element (PE) tile.

In order to prevent a single defect on one of the lower-level logical qubits from propagating to more lower-level qubits than the CC can fix, gates working on logical qubits must maintain fault-tolerance. A compiler that optimizes each gate's fault-tolerant structure must have precisely defined transformation rules that maintain fault-tolerance since the gates operate on logical qubits without decoding the states.

The best CCs allow for "easy" design of fault-tolerant gates and use very little overhead in physical qubit resources. The Steane code and the recently improved Bacon-Shor code are both excellent choices for CC codes. Based on the well-known Shor 9-bit code, the Bacon-Shor code enables incredibly quick and effective error correcting processes. The T gate, however, is more challenging to use. In essence, the T gate is a two-qubit gate since it necessitates the interaction of the logical qubit with a specifically prepared encoded Aπ/8 ancilla (also in CC). Upon executing a T gate, the logical qubit and a ready Aπ/8 qubit are transferred to two accumulators in an empty Processing Element (PE) since many of the tiles in the processing region must be used to prepare the Aπ/8 logical qubits.

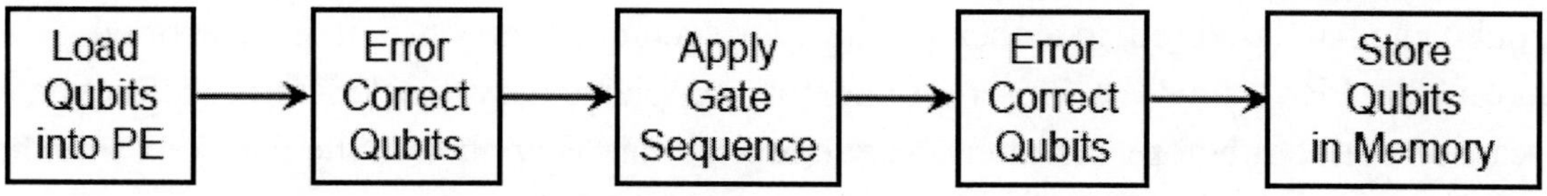

Fig.5.28 The five steps a processing element takes to execute an instruction.

An instruction is carried out in five steps, as depicted in the above diagram, from the viewpoint of each PE: First, the logical qubits are loaded into a PE that is available; next, they undergo error correction; third, the gate implementation sequence is performed to the logical qubits; fourth, error correction is applied once again; and lastly, 5) the logical qubits are delivered to a cache address that is accessible.

5.12.2 Hierarchy of Quantum Memory

With varying performance and cost technologies (e.g., SRAM and DRAM), traditional memory hierarchies optimize for speed. This section talks about a quantum memory hierarchy that instead optimizes for error correcting codes, which might increase store density or make computing easier. The purpose of the quantum memory hierarchy is to offer the dependability required to encode and store quantum data in a fault-tolerant manner over the duration of an application. By accepting and storing differentially encoded data from the upper levels of the hierarchy, the lowest level structures are made to satisfy the processing components' demands for speed and efficiency.

Due to its modest size and the fact that most operations can be done transversally, the Steane error correcting code is ideally suited for computing. On the other hand, more effective block codes that fix many errors and have a code scale-up ratio (which is calculated by dividing the number of logical qubits by the number of physical qubits) greater than 1/7 are worth taking into account for memory. Block codes are those that have [[n, k, d]] codes with $k > 1$. When moving a logical qubit that is resting in memory to an accumulator in the processing region, a significantly more intricate transfer network is required when employing distinct CC and MC codes. The simple repeater-based link utilized inside each architecture region is insufficient to transport a logical qubit to a different place with a different encoding state code. In addition to utilizing temporal and spatial locality to efficiently store data in the CC code, the transfer network must enable quick and effective conversion between the CC and MC codes. Figure provides an illustration of the memory hierarchy idea.

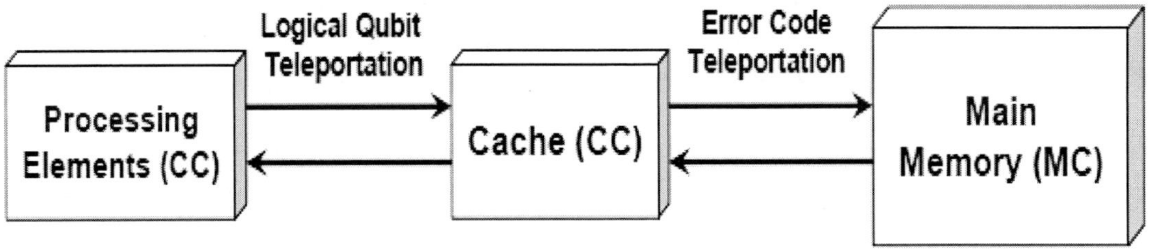

Fig.5.29 High-Level Concept of Quantum Memory Hierarchy.

One of the most intriguing aspects of the memory hierarchy is the transfer zone, which includes the cache, between memory and computation. Data encoded in code C1 is teleported to code C2 in this region without being decoded (decoding the data at any point throughout the computation exposes individual qubits to errors). This idea is depicted in the figure below. The data in C1 is teleported to C2 via the transfer network; C1 and C2 could be any two error-correcting codes. The process of code teleportation functions similarly to that of conventional data teleportation, which is employed in communication. To begin, a multi-qubit cat-state (i.e. (00...0 + 11...1)) is used to create an entangled auxiliary pair between C1 and C2.

Through a cnot gate, the data qubit communicates with the auxiliary qubit that is similarly encoded, and the two are measured. The C2 encoded auxiliary qubit recreates the data state after the measurement. Each time a qubit is moved from memory to the cache, this procedure is necessary. The transfer network's most crucial feature is that C1 and C2 don't have to be two distinct codes; they can be the same code at different recursion levels (for example, CC can be a level 1 code while MC can be a level 2 code).

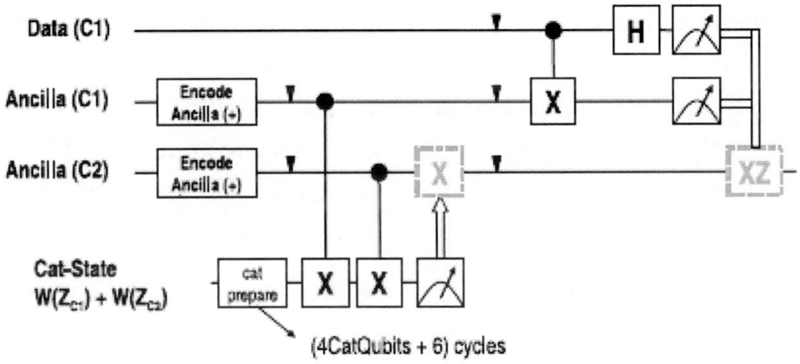

Fig.5.30 Code teleportation network from code 1 (C1) to code 2 (C2); the error-correcting codes C1 and C2 may even be identical, but they have different encoding levels. The stage for error correction is indicated by the solid triangles.

The processor elements, cache, main memory, and transfer area are all made up of logical qubit tiles coupled by programmable teleportation-based bus lines in the high-level view of a customized quantum architecture. When there is a cache hit, the teleportation channels between the cache and the PE receive the majority of the classical control resources, with the transfer of more qubits to the cache taking second place. However, this is a scheduling decision, and there aren't any real schedulers for large-scale quantum computation at the moment.

To effectively utilize and parameterize the architectural design, the next step in the architecture development process is to put effective simulators into place. The design of the interconnect and the arrangement of the architectural components affect the parameterizations of the cache read time, memory access time, operation times, and qubit failure rates in addition to the error corrections we select. We must address a number of crucial issues, including the availability of classical resources, cache replacement guidelines, and error correction selections.

Making the choice for error correction codes for the computation (CC) and main memory (MC) tiles is a crucial step. Numerous factors are dependent on the parameters and characteristics of an error correcting code, including the size of each tile, the time it takes for logical operations to execute, the size of the application being run, and—above all—the high-level coupling between communication and computation. Furthermore, there are significant differences in the data transfer patterns of various error-correcting codes, which could have an impact on the code's overall effectiveness. For instance, during encoded state preparation and error correction processes at the first level of encoding, the Bacon-Shor code, a recently optimized version of the code, requires virtually no physical qubit movement between the two-qubit physical gates. Using a different smaller code at the next encoding level in conjunction with the Bacon-Shor code could potentially provide a computational tile that is far more dependable and efficient than utilizing the same CC code throughout all encoding levels.

Cache Replacement Guidelines: It's critical to comprehend the replacement guidelines when the cache is full. Although compiler can statically schedule the operations and cache consumption at compile time because the program being executed is known ahead of time, it can only forecast with limited precision the time to error correct and the preparation of the interconnect channels on demand. The likelihood of failure, which results in stalling, is always present.

Availability of Classical Resources: What are the classical resources that are available? For ion traps, there are infinite classical control signals that are represented by lasers. The replacement criteria in the cache and the PE units, however, will become crucial if we only have a limited quantity of lasers available. Currently, a qubit is sent straight to memory upon completion of the computation and only sent to the cache if necessary prior to the cache storage failure rates. It is intended to hold qubits for extended periods of time using a very little number of laser resources, therefore sending it to memory might be beneficial. The cost of transferring code from memory to memory storage must be carefully balanced, though.

5.12.3 Assessing Quantum for Classical Memory

When optimizing an architectural design for particular quantum applications, a computer architect can use the system-level division between memory and computation zones that has been covered thus far. By using the quantum search method, also called Groover's method, to search an unsorted database of N entries, a novel and intriguing division between memory and computation is provided. Quantum mechanically, the cost is $O(\sqrt{N})$, but traditionally, the search would need O(N) operations.

All data entries are stored in a long-term memory unit in a naive classical database search design, which executes a maximum of N load operations from the memory to the processor for every database entry. A solution string that has been stored in the processor is then compared to the newly loaded entry string.

The oracle operator O, whose behavior can be expressed as follows, is the primary driver of the quantum searching process.

$$|x\rangle \rightarrow (-1)^{f(x)}|x\rangle$$

where x is the index register that directs the user to the database entry. If x is a solution to the search problem, the input x into the search function f returns 1; if not, it returns 0. Each bitstring state $|x_i\rangle$ in the superposition indexes a data entry, and the index register $|x\rangle$ is made up of logN qubits. Therefore, if a solution is identified, the oracle's job is to flip the index register's sign. The search algorithm's processing unit has a l-qubit register to contain a l-bit data entry initialized to $|0\rangle$ and a l-qubit register to store the solution string in addition to the n-qubit index register (where n = logN).

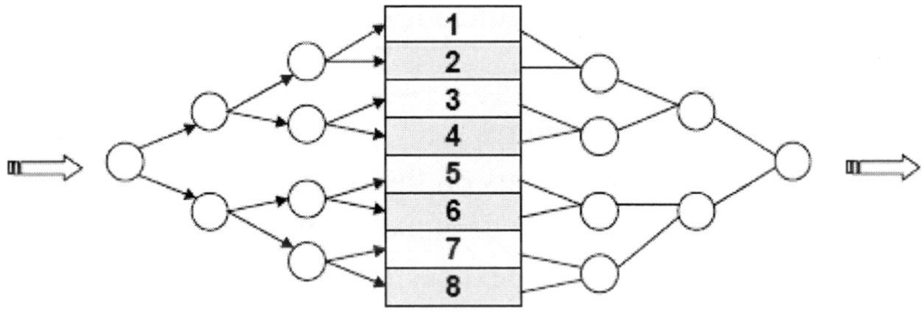

Fig.5.31 Qubit-based schematic for classical memory. A 3-qubit address memory with eight data entries is used in the figure to demonstrate the idea. An auxiliary qubit that serves as a switch to direct the input index register to the appropriate data entry is represented by each circle.

An N-entry memory must be addressed quantum mechanically by logN qubits in order to achieve the polynomial speedup. The architecture of the quantum search implementation is interesting because it allows data to be stored in quantum bits that only accept values of

0 or 1, which reduces the concern for reliable database storage. The above figure shows the concept with a 3-qubit address memory of 8 data entries, where each circle represents an ancillary qubit that serves as a switch to route the input index register to the correct data entry. Each data register qubit is routed to the corresponding entries in the memory based on the state of each qubit-switch, which is dictated by the processor's index register.

In the above figure, the data register qubits enter at the left and depart at the right. A switch is said to be routed in both directions if it is in the superposition state $\frac{1}{\sqrt{2}}(|0\rangle + |1\rangle)$. The load procedure thus yields a superposition of data entries that are comparable to the solution string stored in the l-qubit register. The l-qubit solution stores a solution string that must be matched with one of the data strings from memory using $O(\sqrt{N})$ load operations.

In practice, quantum mechanically searching an unsorted database is not any more effective than conventionally storing and searching the database. Once the data is loaded into memory, the quantum addressed classical memory needs O(N log N) auxiliary qubit swaps in addition to the overhead of operations. The slowness brought on by error correction may outweigh the slightly polynomial advantage over classical searching if error correction is required for both storing and searching over big databases. However, the implementation of quantum accessible memory can become intriguing if qubits are made as simple and affordable as classical logic transistors.

Prefetching classical registers in the classical memory hierarchy is one application of a quantum addressing method. A whole superposition of classical registers at any point in the memory can be retrieved by the quantum address in a single clock step.

5.12.4 Quantum architecture design and error correction

In order to ensure dependable operation from a somewhat unstable collection of primitives, quantum computer architectures heavily rely on quantum error correction. Quantum architects must base their systems on the concepts of quantum error correction as it is such an essential component of the design of a quantum system. We will examine some prominent quantum designs in the next sections, whose organization and structure are largely impacted by error correction (specifically, the abstraction of a logical qubit). In order to try to create more efficient quantum structures, we will first examine a variety of works that consider the impact of various error correction strategies and optimizations (measured using mathematical models). These examples, while by no means comprehensive, serve to highlight the kind of enhancements that can be made to an architecture when error correction is taken into consideration.

5.12.4.1 Implications Of Ancilla Design And Preparation

Kreger-Stickles offers a domain space investigation of an ion-trap quantum computer's architecture. The performance of various design variations using an error correcting system based on the Steane code on a Òsea of trapsÓ layout is assessed in this investigation. The ancilla/verification qubit arrangement and ancilla preparation method vary between these variations. These test cases are evaluated using potential fault point counting, which counts all possible faults in the system and uses them in combination with component operation fidelity to calculate the system fidelity.

Kreger-Stickles presents the first case study, which focuses on two algorithms for preparing and using ancilla qubits. In addition to a compact version of the 7-qubit technique (which uses fewer verification qubits) and a nearest neighbor version of the 4-qubit technique (where all preparation is done via interactions with neighboring qubits on a linear array), ancilla preparation techniques employing 7-qubits and 4-qubits are also taken into consideration. For these four ancilla preparation methods, three hardware configurations are taken into account:

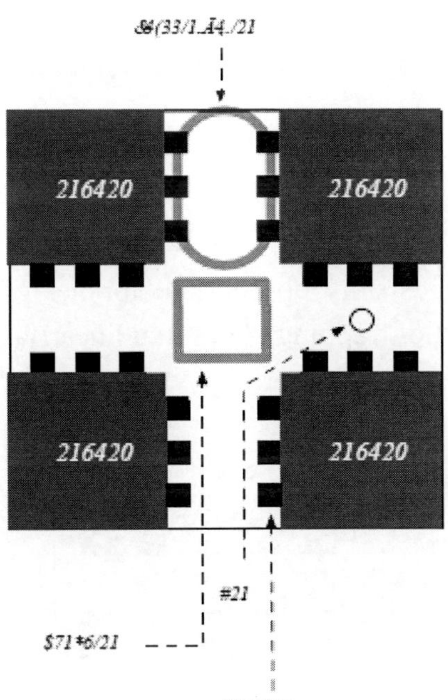

Fig.5.32 Sea of traps ion-trap configuration.

- Vector: The ancilla bits are laid out in a linear sequence of traps next to unallocated communication and routing traps.

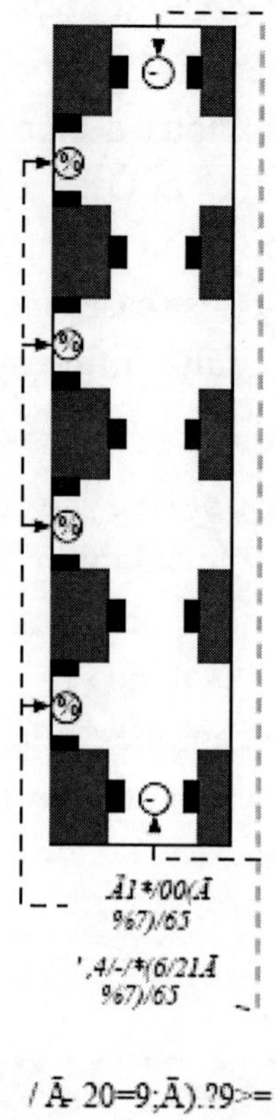

Fig.5.33 Vector layout.

- Linear: This design is only appropriate for nearest neighbour designs since it arranges a collection of trapping zones in a linear fashion, making it impossible to route arbitrary bits to one another.

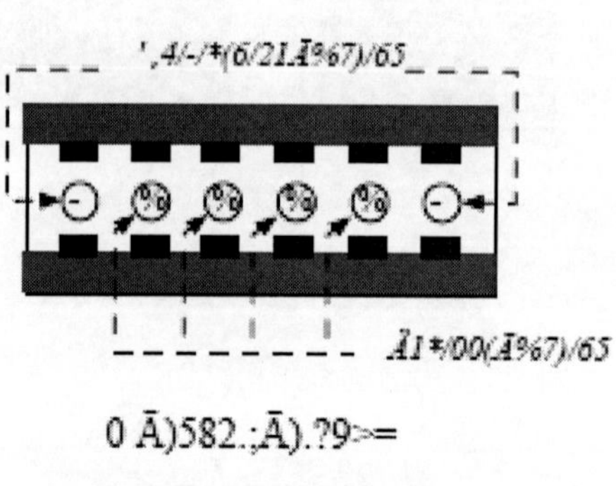

Fig.5.34 Linear layout.

- Folded: A crossbar is used to hold the verification and ancilla qubits. Although this method produces a greater size, the arrangement lowers the communication requirements and latency.

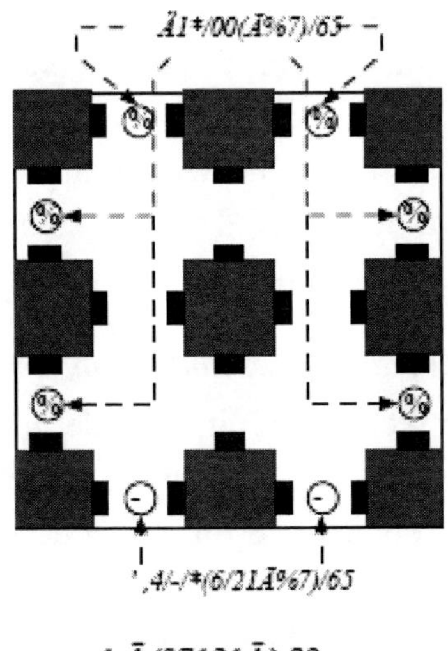

Fig.5.35 Folded layout.

For each of these hardware layouts and preparation methods, two scheduling layouts are taken into account: early verification and late verification. Early verification verifies qubits as soon as possible, while late verification verifies qubits only when the ancilla qubits are adjacent to the data qubits with which they will interact.

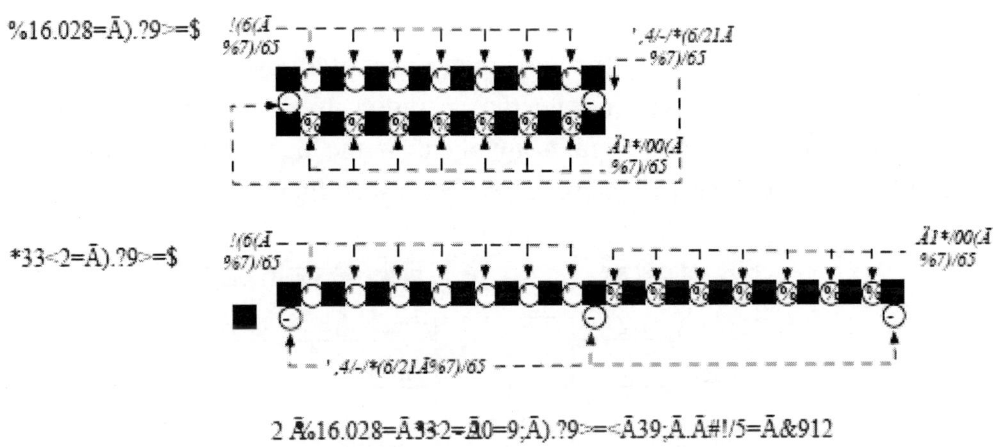

Fig.5.36 vector layouts that are adjacent and optimal for a 7-bit code.

According to Kreger-Stickles' calculations of circuit run time and probable fault locations, the 4-bit linear closest neighbour approaches outperform the other approaches in both verification scenarios. The 4-qubit code is more appealing for a system with multiple levels of recursive error correction because calculations on the number of potential faults in a given communication scenario show that the 7-qubit code has a significantly higher incidence of storage-related potential faults than the 4-qubit code.

Simulations of a small level 1 operation on the resulting design permutations reveal that the offset linear nearest neighbour 4-qubit codes deliver the fastest performance, smallest size, and highest reliability of all the designs tested. Prior to doing this, the authors add two more design attributes to the mix: whether the ancilla qubits are arranged adjacent to the data qubits or offset from the qubits. The previous figure illustrates an example of these layouts for a 7-bit vector arrangement.

5.12.4.2 Critical Path Error correction Optimisation

Building a faster and more effective circuit is made possible by optimizing where and when error correction takes place, as it is a typical operation in a fault-tolerant datapath. One method for maximizing quantum error correction in an architecture intended to perform Shor's algorithm was mentioned by Mr. Whitney. It is a reasonable assumption that qubits that interact with other "dirty" qubits—which might have encountered an error—are more prone to develop mistakes of their own. Consequently, it might be more economical to do error correction only after a qubit has experienced multiple "dirty" interactions rather than after each operation. Nevertheless, this kind of error correction removal may make the circuit more likely to fail. We must decide between circuit size and reliability in order to perform such an optimization.

The image below shows the fundamental idea underlying this optimization technique. For each qubit, Mr. Whitney established an EDist metric to determine when error correction should be carried out. Each time a qubit undergoes an operation, EDist is updated. A qubit's EDist is set to the maximum EDist of all the qubits participating in the operation plus one (which accounts for the operation itself) in order to account for the mistakes collected in the other qubits involved in the operation. Error correction is carried out and EDist is reset whenever it reaches a specific value.

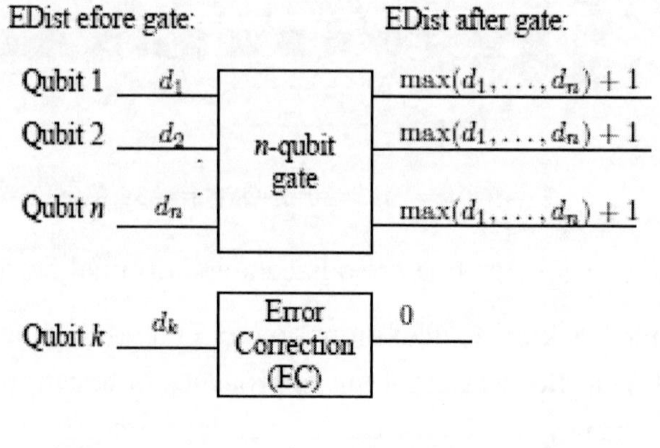

Fig.5.37 Guidelines for updating EDist.

Below image provides an illustration of how to use EDist for mistake correction. According to Mr.Whitney, improving an unmapped 1000-bit random circuit in this way yields extremely encouraging outcomes. When error correction is carried out with EDist

= 6, the circuit's success probability drops from 0.987 (in the unoptimized scenario) to 0.956, and the number of operations is reduced by nearly an order of magnitude, from 3,105,611 to 366,411.

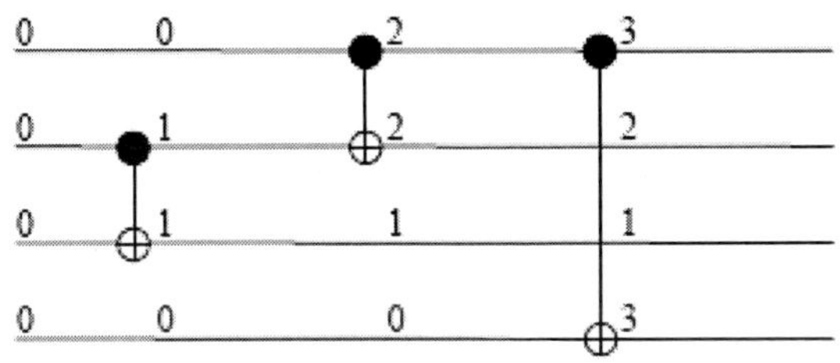

Fig.5.38 Nil error correction.

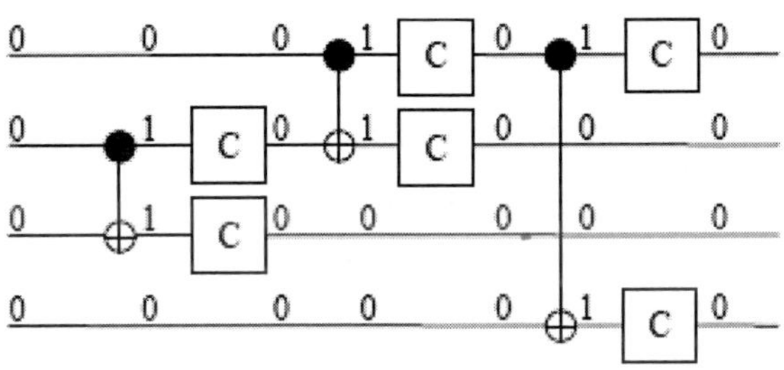

Fig.5.39 Correcting errors following each operation.

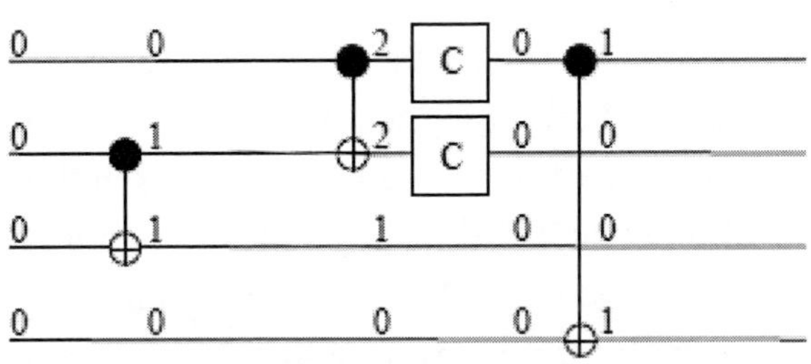

Fig.5.40 Correcting errors when EDist = 2.

By using EDist = 9 for error correction, the circuit's success probability is further decreased to 0.87 and the number of operations is reduced by an additional order of magnitude to 24,011. Because faster execution times result from fewer error correction steps, this optimization can also lower the circuit's latency.

5.13 Quantum Architecture Programming

The programming of a quantum architecture (like the QLA) is covered in this section. The notion that each logical qubit tile can be thought of as a distinct processing device that is intended to carry out a specific localized portion of the broader application—a single logical gate followed by error correction—guides the programming model for the

QLA architecture. The architecture of QLA is made up of reconfigurable processing units, each of which is a separate logical qubit tile.

When communication and processing are separated, the QLA is reduced to an architecture made up of reconfigurable computational units, each of which is a separate logical qubit tile. Therefore, the classical GALS model is followed for creating the timed physical pulse sequences for a quantum application subroutine: At the application level, the error correction processes are both locally synchronous (using the same pulse-sequence of operations within each logical qubit tile) and globally asynchronous.

The bridge that connects a quantum compiler to quantum hardware is called the Instruction Set Architecture (ISA). Logical instructions acting on logical qubits make up the application level, while measurement operations inform the control processors about how the algorithm is being executed. The physical layout, which is below the application level, is where simple logical gates are broken down into a fault-tolerant series of fundamental, assembly-like, technology-dependent instructions. The compiler can coordinate the available architectural resources thanks to the high-level instruction set architecture, which is separate from the physical implementation technology.

Both quantum data (logical qubits) and classical data (logical qubit addresses, measurement results, and classical control bits) are used by the machine instructions that will be discussed. The classical control processors store and manipulate all classical data. The execution of measurement instructions, which incorporate both classical and quantum arguments, is the only way that the classical processors can communicate with the quantum hardware. Below table provides a summary of some of the recommended instruction types. The majority of a quantum computer's architecture-level instructions fall under the category of procedure call instructions. A simple quantum gate instruction would be "gate_cnot," for instance. Q1,Q2," where Q2 is the target and Q1 is the control logical qubit. If the gates are logical gates, a fault-tolerant series of operations on lower-level qubits is used in the hardware to implement them. As a result, every logical gate is an independent computer program that is integrated into the bigger application and optimized independently. The entire set of lower-level actions required to complete a logical block is directed to be carried out by the control processors.

Table 5.2 Instruction types.

Instruction	Arguments	Type	Function
GATE_A	Q1, [Q2]	Quantum	Single or Two-Qubit Operations
MEASURE	Q1, cbit	Quantum	Measurement, result stored in the classical cbit
PREPARE	Q1	Quantum	Prepare an initial qubit state
FETCH	Q1, PE_i, AC_j	Classical	Fetch qubit Q1 into PE_i and accumulator j
SEND	Q1, memory_address	Classical	Send Q1 from a PE into memory (cache or main)
LOAD/STORE	Q1, memory_address	Classical	Load/Store Q1 to the specified address
REFRESH	Q1	Classical	Error correct qubit Q1

A single logical qubit is used as a parameter in error correction processes, which are also implemented as a single instruction. Although the decision to branch or not is always determined by a classical bit set by the outcome of a quantum measurement, branching instructions accomplish the same goal as classical branches.

The low-level quantum assembly language (QASM) provides a comparable ISA. It is composed of a series of physical qubit declarations and commands, much like the logical processes displayed in Table. The first declarations include qubits, classical bits, gate names, and classical functions.

The two physical gates, xprepare and zprepare, indicate the preparation process. They place a qubit in the eigenstate of the X or Z operator, respectively, and may be broken down into a measurement operation and a matching single-qubit gate. Applying a measurement gate first, then a bit-flip gate if the measurement result returns a "1," is how the zprepare process is carried out. In this manner, the |0> state is used to initialize the qubit. By performing a Hadamard operation on a qubit prepared in the |0> state, the xprepare gate puts the qubit in either the $| + \}$ or $| - \}$ state.

5.13.1 Scheduling instruction at the physical level

Regardless of the technology used to implement a circuit-model based quantum system, one of the main challenges of accurately modelling the physical components of a large-scale architecture is scheduling and mapping a quantum application onto a physical layout while accounting for the maximum amount of parallelism that can be exploited, the cost of communication, and the classical resources. Physical schedulers that employ conventional, classical scheduling methods could be helpful in this regard. The output of a quantum physical operations scheduler can be a QASM file, similar to that of classical superblock schedulers, but with communication instructions added and the file fully parallelized.

A physical operations scheduler can determine the exploitable instruction-level parallelism (ILP) in quantum circuits and produce two-dimensional information about the communication pathways for a particular quantum circuit. Hardware designers can save money by researching the limitations of ILP rather than investing in traditional control features that will be underutilized during computation. Additionally, one fundamental prerequisite for reaching the best feasible schedule in quantum error correction is the availability of huge ILP. The capacity to accurately forecast the quantity of communication during mistake correction is essential for figuring out how high the threshold value can actually be, even if it has been demonstrated that there is a threshold value when movement is taken into account. Furthermore, evaluating the available ILP and communication requirements can help us pinpoint the precise hardware resources required for error correction.

The University of Washington's QUALE toolchain maps a quantum circuit instruction onto a physical layout using the traditional Path-Finder package, assuming that the qubits that are intended to move are known in advance. Instead, without assuming a specific technology implementation, the physical scheduler QPOS was created. It is a quantum physical operations scheduler that is based on conventional classical instruction scheduling heuristics and carefully calculates priorities at the circuit and physical layout levels. QPOS is intended to produce, given a particular geometrical arrangement, the precise transmission pattern for quantum data. Instruction priority at the circuit level are determined by how many instructions are dependent on each operation. Once the source and destination qubits have been de-ambiguated, the priorities are used to select the desired communication pathways. Paths are ranked according to shortest path and least path interference if instructions have the same priorities. The movement activities are attempted to be as parallel as possible.

At the hardware design level, QPOS makes use of the general layout abstraction for quantum devices. Ions are transported through the shared junction resources indicated by the regions where the lines cross after being deposited on any of the lines, also referred to as interaction regions. Two qubits must be positioned in the same interaction zone in order for two-qubit gates to accept data. Although no gates are permitted at any junction, the junctions must be specified to prevent qubit data-path overlap. An application description in the form of a quantum assembly language file and a physical layout description are fed into the scheduler, a heuristic that generates a series of operations that include the available Instruction Level Parallelism (ILP) that can be extracted based on each qubit's communication paths.

Even though recent advances in error correction algorithms and astute large-scale quantum architecture design (like the specialization of the QLA architecture) give us hope for the implementation of applications like Shor's quantum factoring algorithm, the design and optimization of realistic device implementations will surely require the precise hardware orchestration of millions of interacting physical qubits. For instance, modeling and engineering the interfaces between the computer's many physical ions (qubits) and the classical equipment that governs them is one of the key obstacles still standing in the way of the development of a large-scale ion trap quantum computer. It is described in the next part how QPOS can help with the design of effective ion-trap systems to expedite their development and preserve the threshold value required to enable fault-tolerant quantum processing.

5.13.2 Design of High-Level Compiler

One level of algorithm optimization/compilation is the coupling of computation and communication, where the cost of a given high-level is considered when the circuit is mapped to a specific set of logical hardware resources. A third level of optimization is when error correction and communication methods at the logical level of application execution are used to aid in the synthesis of logical quantum circuits. These are the various levels of "reordering rules" that a quantum compiler may use at any stage of the compilation process. On the first level, circuit optimizations independent of the underlying architecture are used (i.e., communication cost is not considered, and each gate has a unit cost). Logical circuit synthesis may be impacted. One makes use of established methods that enable the teleportation protocol to execute one and two-qubit gates.

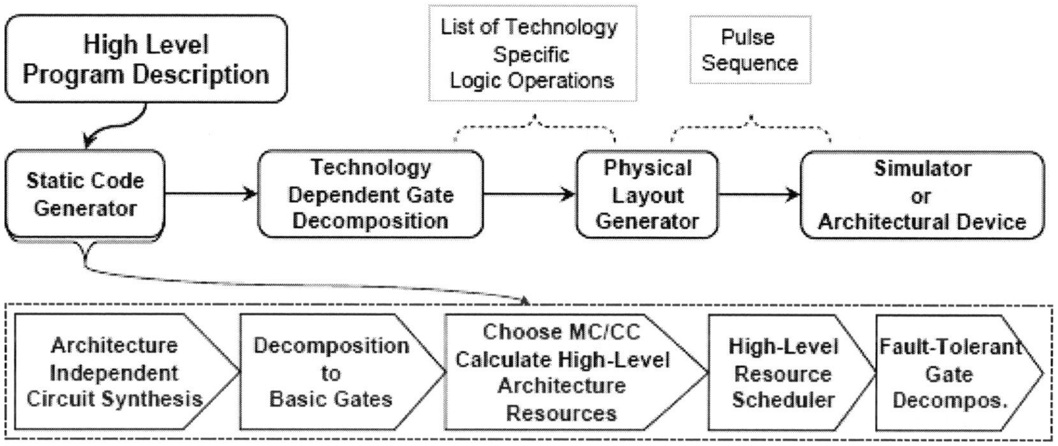

Fig.5.41 Compilation Layers.

The components of an example quantum architecture compiler are depicted in the above diagram. An input to the Static Code Generator (SCG) is a description of the program in a very general high-level format, like a big unitary matrix, or a high level C-like language, like QCL, that is independent of layout and technology. The SCG component's steps are displayed at the bottom of the figure.

The algorithm is divided into a practical, distinguishable set of quantum operations by the first SCG stage, which carries out technology and architecture agnostic circuit synthesis. The SCG further breaks down the circuit into one and two-qubit gates after identifying a universal set of basic gates, revealing all high-level qubit resources required for the application. Based on the high-level structures and architectural resource restrictions, the SCG then chooses the proper error-correcting codes for the memory and computation. As shown in previous Table, the program is now made up of instructions that resemble assembly language, fully exposing the hardware resources and prepared for high-level scheduling. Lastly, by breaking down each logical gate and LOAD/STORE operation into a fault-tolerant list of lower level quantum/classical instructions based on the selections for MC and CC, the SCG adds fault-tolerance to every operation.

A high-level quantum assembly language program that explains a fault-tolerant, error-correction-enabled quantum algorithm and provides a detailed explanation of the system-level quantum and classical resources that are accessible is the result of the Static Code Generator. The next step is the Technology Dependent Compiler (TDC), which breaks down the quantum operations into the corresponding elementary operations that are available for the specific technology, while having no knowledge of the geometrical arrangement of individual tiles. A list of ion-trap logic gates, including controlled-Z gates and single qubit rotations, is the output in the case of ion-traps.

The Physical Layout Generator (LG), which comes last, assigns physical locations and data-paths for every physical qubit in the system based on a description of the resources that are available.

Even if this modifies the initial sequence supplied by the SCG, the LG organizes the elementary qubit operations in accordance with its complete understanding of each tile's physical arrangement. The LG aims to 1) reduce the physical communication costs for multi-qubit gates and 2) optimize the distribution of physical resources, assuming that maximal parallelism has been applied at earlier phases. A series of control pulses that have been input into the device and are prepared for execution make up the LG's output.

5.13.3 Design-Independent Circuit Synthesis

The design and optimization of classical integrated circuits, where technology independent synthesis is carried out using abstract logic gates, is comparable to architecture-independent circuit synthesis. Next, as explained in the previous section, the circuit is mapped to the technology by changing the gates to the ones that are most appropriate for the designated technology. Given a broad logical circuit, a compiler can find distinct sub circuit architectures that lend themselves to different optimization approaches at any point in the compilation pipeline (possibly with the exception of the layout generator).

The action of a quantum algorithm on n logical qubits is represented as a 2n × 2n unitary matrix at the highest level of the algorithm. This is comparable to describing a program in classical computation using a boolean function. Decomposing an arbitrary n-qubit unitary operator into fundamental quantum logic gates is as simple as translating a boolean function into a comparable circuit of operations. Additionally, optimizing the resulting circuit is a challenging endeavor, just like in classical computation. The transformation rules for a quantum circuit might be the most significant difference.

A substantial amount of work is still being done in the area of architecture-independent quantum circuit synthesis. Circuits made solely of controlled-NOT gates are the first sub circuits that a compiler may detect. The synthesis of universal classical reversible circuits and controlled k-NOT circuits has been the subject of extensive research. For controlled k-NOT circuits, which are NOT gates that are managed by the AND of k bits, there are transformation rules. Using a heuristic whose cost function is the minimal average number of control qubits, every controlledk-NOT circuit can be transformed into an equivalent circuit in its canonical form.

A regulated k-NOT circuit can be used to express quantum modular exponentiation, the priciest part of Shor's factoring method. Aaronson and Gottesman also give a method for reorganizing stabilizer circuits, which are utilized in all error correction procedures. With only $O(n^2/\log n)$ gates, Aaronson and Gottesman demonstrate that any stabilizer circuit has an equivalent circuit in canonical form, raising the question of whether an ideal structure exists. Since cnot gates and one-qubit gates make up the universal gate library, it is generally preferable to break down any two-qubit operator into a number of controlled-NOT gates, or cnot. Song and Klappenecker have developed a technique for optimizing two-qubit operators with arbitrary controls. An method that simulates arbitrary two-qubit unitary operators is implemented by Shende, Bullock, and Markov. With three cnot gates as the worst case scenario, they more precisely offer a way to identify which two-qubit operators are cnot optimal. In other circuit synthesis projects, random n-qubit diagonal operators and even two-qubit operators with insufficient specifications have been used. In the initial phase of the quantum compiler example depicted in the preceding figure, all of the circuit optimizations previously mentioned are implemented.

Despite the fact that architecture-independent circuit synthesis has seen a great deal of foundational work, these optimizations can be expanded, improved, and unified with a well-designed quantum compiler. Specifically:

- To offer stabilizer circuits a better canonical form, a set of specific transformation rules can be provided. Heuristics that optimize error correcting circuits can be developed using the canonical form.
- The implications of combining various transformation rules have not been thoroughly investigated before; fault-tolerance preserving transformation rules were created to enable designers to alter the universal set of basic gates while keeping the maximum time to failure in a high-level algorithm. For instance, once the rules are put into practice in a shared optimization tool, it is unknown how they would influence one another.

5.13.4 Mapping Architecture with Circuits

The biggest possibility for optimization may lie in translating these idealized circuits to a real machine, even though circuit synthesis is a crucial first step. In addition to being impractical due to machine size limitations, the traditional method of direct circuit synthesis to hardware is unappealing in the quantum domain because it requires teleportation, technology-dependent elementary operations, and high fault-tolerance overheads. One of the main contributions of computer architects will be the development of schedulers that leverage the tradeoffs associated with quantum hardware and the capabilities at the systems level to transfer quantum circuits onto similar fault-tolerant procedures.

An example that illustrates a portion of the mapping and optimization procedure for a controlled k-NOT circuit will be discussed. The image below depicts three analogous controlled k NOT-based circuits to demonstrate this. Schematically, the necessary communication between qubits during the execution of multi-qubit gates, such as controlled operations, may be "seen."

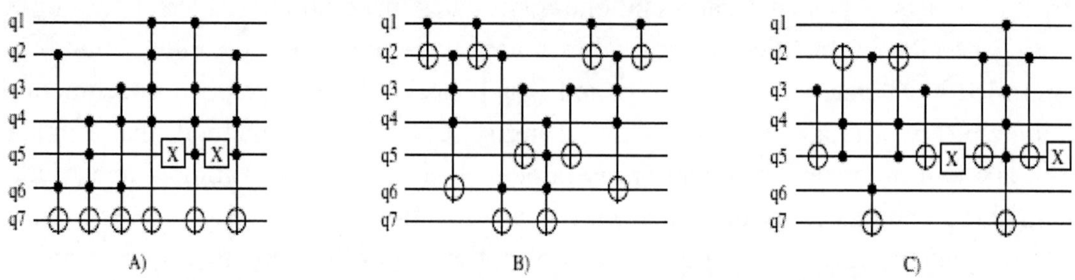

Fig.5.42 Circuit optimization to reduce the number of control bits. On the vertical lines, the circles represent NOTgates, which are managed by the AND of the qubits joined by solid dots. Bit-flip gates are indicated by the "X"-marked boxes. Reduce the quantity of solid dots per gate while keeping the total number of gates somewhat constant. The standard version of an unoptimized Controlled-Not based circuit (A). (B) Using the transformation rules, each gate's control qubit count is decreased to 1.7. To get to 1.4 control qubits per gate, (C) simplifies the circuit in (A) using boolean algebra.

Using the transformation principles of an initial unoptimized cnot-based circuit, the circuit in Figure (a) represents the derived canonical form. Because it enables all NOT operations to be focused on the final qubit (q7), the canonical form is a helpful place to start when optimizing any boolean cnot-based circuit. This implies that the gates can be operated in any sequence, therefore applying the simplification of boolean algebra would be simple. Reducing the number of control qubits per gate is a good cnot-based circuit cost metric. Figure (b) displays the outcome.

Since any controlled k-NOT gate with k > 2 needs to be split into (2 ∗ {log k} + 1) Toffoli gates (a three-input, three-output reversible NAND gate, implemented as a NOT with two control bits), employing {log k} extra logical ancilla qubits to increase the total resources required from the architecture, this is a reasonable assumption. Furthermore, it is somewhat costly to synthesize each Toffoli gate into one and two qubit operations. Two Hadamard gates, one S gate, six cnot gates, and seven T gates are separated by a Toffoli gate. Since the T gates need both accumulators in a PE and must interact with the specialized ancilla qubits, they are effectively two-qubit gates. We used boolean algebra-derived simplification techniques to construct Figure (c), which shows an even better circuit in terms of the control-qubit cost (i.e., $A \oplus BA = A\overline{B}$).

Quantum researchers hope to develop a compiler that can identify previous Figure's ideal circuit topology given the given architectural restrictions. The compiler will select the MC and CC encodings, break down the fundamental circuit gates into fault-tolerant processes, and optimize each one separately across the architecture to minimize communication, computation, and traditional resource overhead during the high-level circuit execution. The most costly operation in a circuit of one and two-qubit gates is moving a logical qubit from the MC-encoded memory to the PE (CC-encoded cache).

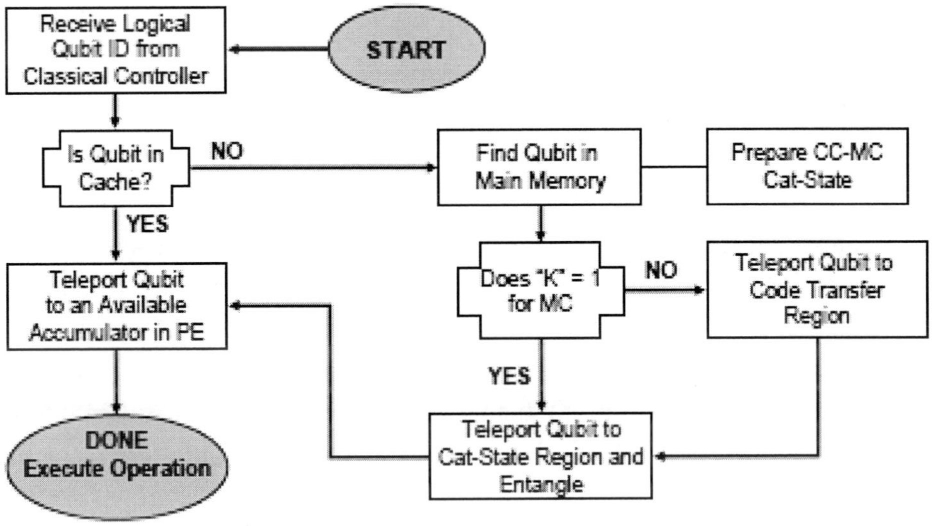

Fig.5.43 Cache read operation overview for memory read time estimation.

According to the above figure, the memory read time (MRt) is approximately equal to one error correction step over CC, five MC error corrections, five logical gate times over MC (whose sequence diagram is illustrated in the figure below), and two MC teleportation steps. A cache-hit is merely a single teleportation step from the cache to the processing unit over the CC encoding, whereas a cache-miss is equivalent to MRt. Consequently, the cache read time (CRt) is

$$CR_t \quad = \quad X(t_{tel,CC}) + Y(MR_t)$$

This represents a weighted average of the anticipated cache-hit and cache-miss rates. The trade-off is that the logical qubits saved over MC are far more dependable. The CC is selected so that the time required for a logical operation following the recovery of the data should be significantly less than the time required for an operation over an MC encoded qubit.

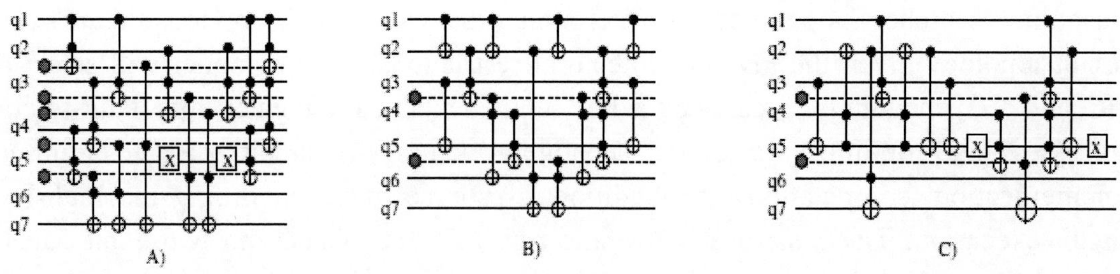

Fig.5.44. Similar circuits to that in previous Figure, but with all gates broken down into Toffoli gates and all necessary logical qubit resources fully exposed. When mapped to the architecture, the dotted horizontal lines stand for ancilla qubits, which are introduced to lower overall communication costs. Using the most logical qubits, network (a) is the least preferred. Since it breaks down into fewer basic activities, network (c) is the most preferred.

Using a number of auxiliary logical qubits initialized in the "0" encoded state (dashed lines), the circuits controlledk>2-NOT gates are broken into cnot and Toffoli's alone in the image above. Each Toffoli gate is not yet broken down into one- and two-qubit gates, but the gates are rearranged to reveal the potential parallelism at this level. The choice of CC determines the physical circuit depth and size of each fault-tolerant logical gate, which is made up of several physical operations across the PE tile. Even for such a little circuit, the size of the computation is conceivable. The circuit in Figure (a) requires three more logical qubits than the other two circuits, as can be seen without explicitly calculating the schedule for each circuit across simple single and two-qubit operations. It also needs ten Toffoli gate time-steps out of a total of fifteen Toffoli gates. In Figures (b) and (c), just seven and six Toffoli time-steps and eight and seven total Toffoli gates are needed, respectively.

The circuit in Figure (a) is the least ideal even with infinite resources and parallelism because of the number of Toffoli timesteps that restrict the circuit's overall performance. Without further analysis, the aforementioned information does not give us much insight into the communication costs of the circuit. Two PE units and two logical qubit cache tiles are needed for a Toffoli gate in order to prevent cache misses. A Toffoli gate will take about the same amount of time as 14 logical operations via CC plus the initial expense of loading the three data qubits from memory.

Only a component of the compiler design flow—the static code generator—is implemented in the controlled^k-NOT circuit example, giving a general idea of the complexity involved. The most crucial initial steps in implementing a quantum compiler must be determining the special components of quantum computing circuits and characteristics of quantum computation that enable the development of the suitable intermediate compiler data structures. We can pinpoint a number of significant difficulties for system designers when creating a compiler for the creation of extensive quantum applications, in addition to outlining the essential intermediate processes of a quantum compiler.

Some of these are as follows:

- The creation of modeling and simulation methods for the quantum circuits used in the high-level architectural parts' implementation.
- Identifying appropriate compiler optimization cost criteria that enable us to produce and assess effective fault-tolerant circuits for a given quantum application at both the architecture and physical execution levels.
- Finding methods that optimize, maintain, and add low-level, fault-tolerant circuits that carry out high-level calculations.
- Developing architectural plans that can take advantage of special quantum communication and computation capabilities, like teleportation-based error correction and different logically universal sets of quantum operations.

5.13.5 Logical Qubit Tiles Optimization

The QLA architecture and other system-level studies provide particular design elements that demonstrate high-level organization and effective worldwide communication. Although these are essential to a quantum computer's scalability, the fundamental components of the microarchitecture must also be carefully designed. Examine how a quantum computer compiler affects the logical qubit tiles' performance characteristics. The trade-offs involved in the interaction between the quantum and classical components of a quantum computer are examined, along with the answers to two important questions: (1) is the low-level device architecture practical when considering a more realistic technology model, and (2) how does the necessary control circuitry impact the fault-tolerance and execution of quantum circuits?

5.13.5.1 Estimates of the fault-tolerant threshold

The scheduler QPOS is used to take into account the communication needs of the logical not gate quantum circuit mapped onto an ion-trap device. Utilize the circuit designs and threshold calculation methods, and think about a two-dimensional nearest-neighbor lattice architecture that works well with technologies that have fixed qubits and nearest-neighbor only interactions. A MOVE operation from one zone to the next can be used in place of each SWAP gate in the ion-trap ballistic communication model to make it comparable to nearest-neighbor communication.

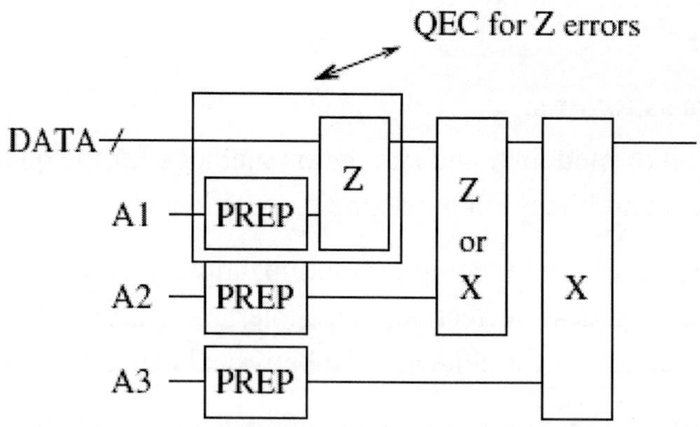

Fig.5.45 A schematic of the Steane's single deterministic QEC process.

Define an adversarial stochastic noise model in which each physical gate location in the logical cnot circuit (i.e., each of the cnot gates, wait gates, movement gates, and measurement gates) can fail with a probability related to the gate type. Then, use the Steane error correcting code to calculate a lower-bound for the physical threshold failure rate for the logical cnot gate to be on the order of $O(10^{-5})$. The threshold for the logical cnot circuit, assuming that all gates are treated equally, is roughly 3.1×10^{-6}. Examine the threshold further as it affects the failure rates of each location type in relation to the failure rates of the other location types.

Since it necessitates moving either the logical control qubit or the logical target qubit to allow for interaction, followed by error correction on both qubits, the logical cnot gate is the most computationally demanding gate in logical quantum circuits. As a result, other logical gates will inevitably have a greater component threshold failure rate than the logical cnot gate. Use the methodology that counts the number M of cancerous pairings of places in the circuit to estimate the threshold value of the cnot circuit.

Any pair of gates that results in several errors at the output is considered malignant in a fault-tolerant circuit. A circuit that is fault-tolerant won't fail due to a single gate, but it might if there are numerous gate pairs. Errors can sometimes cancel one other out.

Then, $p_{th} > M^{-1}$ lower-boundeds the threshold value, p_{th}; this is a tight lower bound and, as a result, a rather accurate estimate.

Deterministic syndrome extraction is necessary for the pair counting procedure for the QEC circuit depicted in the preceding figure. To enable interaction with the data, the circuit is used to prepare three ancilla qubits, designated {A1,A2,A3}. X and Z syndromes can be extracted if at least two ancilla pass the preparation process. It takes the Z syndrome with it if the initial ancilla passes. The second ancilla is used to extract the Z syndrome if the first one fails but the second one passes. Likewise, the second and third ancilla blocks are used in X syndrome.

Since there wouldn't be any good ancilla remaining to fix it, it is presumed that logical errors are communicated to the data if two or more ancilla blocks are not prepared. The fact that a single mistake in the ancilla preparation could result in the preparation failing but still leaving us with two functional ancillas is what makes this QEC circuit fault-tolerant. Two faults must occur in two distinct ancilla blocks, which is a second order event, in order for an error from a flawed preparation step to be transferred to the data.

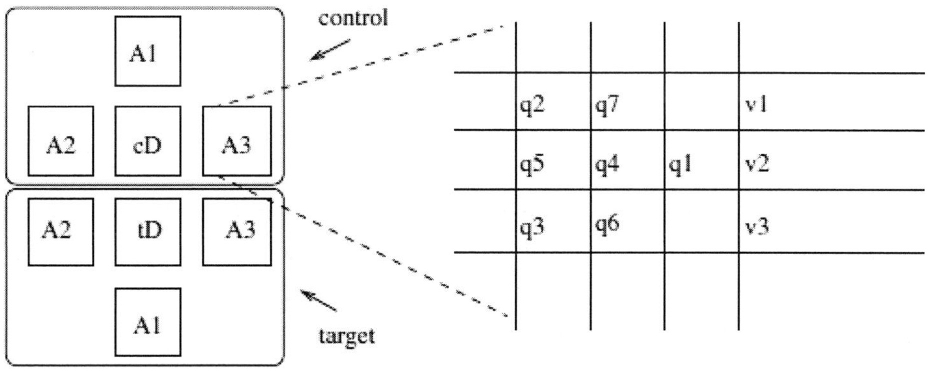

Fig.5.46 Physical layout for the logical cnot gate.

The full logical cnot gate's layout is depicted in the above figure. Each of the seven lower-level qubits that make up the control and target data blocks, designated cD and tD, are encoded using the Steane error correcting code. For a deterministic circuit architecture, three ancilla blocks are assigned to each data block. The physical qubit configuration for each logical sub-block in the cnot gate is displayed on the right side of the diagram. The arrangement of ions {q1 to q7} permits the gates required to prepare the ancilla to move as little as possible. The following general guideline is used to create an effective 2-D encoder layout: For every circuit, first manually design a communication density graph (CDG) in which every ion represents a vertex and every physical cnot gate indicates an edge connecting two vertices. Next, we produce a 2-D CDG visual description with the fewest possible intersecting edges.

Create 1000 random mappings using the scheduler to guarantee that each qubit block's physical architecture is genuinely efficient. Put the qubits on the encoder's 2-D ion trap grid at random for each one. The schedule generated when starting with the designated ion positions in the above figure had less cycles than any of the 1000 random schedules, it was discovered. To ensure that each qubit moves on just one or two junctions during the whole ancilla preparation process, arrange the ions on the 2-D grid that is displayed on the right-hand side of the above figure.

5.13.5.2 Circuit Scheduling and the Limitation of Failure Tolerance

The cnot circuit was scheduled using the QPOS scheduling strategy. Using the trap abstraction depicted in the figure below, the original QPOS implementation is altered to provide a more precise scheduling of the pulse sequences required for the ion-trap technology. As shown in recent ion-trap literature, Figure (a) shows a single trap zone made up of three electrodes arranged planerly on either side of the trapping region.

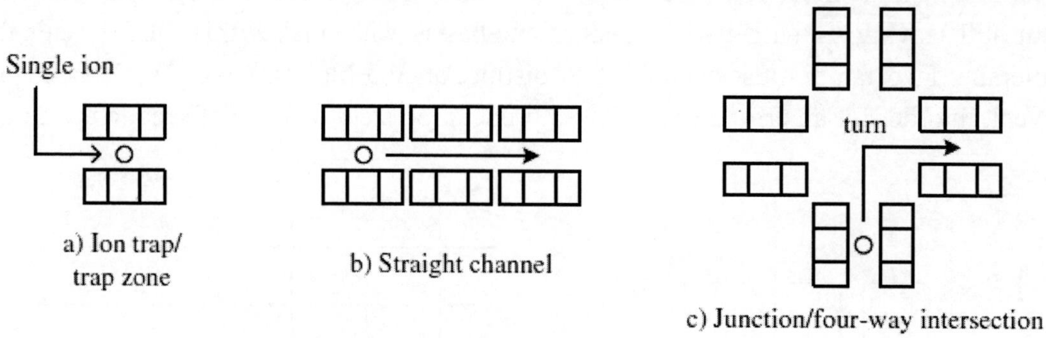

Fig.5.47 a) Three electrodes on either side of a vacuum make up our abstract trap zone, which can produce the potential well needed to trap an ion. b) To create a straight path for ballistic movement, trap zones can be arranged sequentially. c) Four adjacent trap zones make up a junction. To go past the junction, all four electrodes must be present.

As seen in Figure (b), a series of these trap zones are aligned to form a straight route for qubit migration. Then, by decreasing the potential of the electrodes "in front" of it and increasing the potential of the electrodes "behind," a positively charged ion is ballistically carried. To more precisely control the potential well's progression, the specifics of the pulse sequences must be more intricate than this. We can, however, abstract away the intricacy of the complete sequences by defining our trap zones as having three electrodes on each side and assuming that just the electrodes in these two zones are used when moving between adjacent trapping zones. Lastly, junctions are required to enable two-dimensional qubit routing. An abstraction of a four-way intersection with potential communication between four trap zones is shown in Figure (c). The application of particular pulse sequences to electrodes in each of the four neighboring trap zones is necessary for a qubit to travel through such a junction.

Each action in the assembly-level circuit description is broken down into the necessary cycles of operation that match the gate's duration in the ion-trap technology in order to assess the resource needs for fault-tolerant logical blocks like the logical not gate. The time of each gate in the planned circuit program is fixed in relation to the duration of a single qubit operation, or 1 μs, which is equivalent to one clock cycle. The physical circuit locations and their breakdown in the calculated timetable are as follows:

- MOVE ION Z1 -> Z2: for two neighboring trap zones, Z1 and Z2. The MOVE operation takes seven cycles to finish in a straight line and fourteen cycles to finish across a junction at an ion speed of around 30 m/s and ≈ 100 μm per trap zone of three control electrodes.

- **MEASURE ION:** A measuring procedure that, based on our estimation, will take ten cycles. The measuring duration is now around 100 μs, but it might be as short as 10 μs.
- **JOIN/SPLIT ION1,ION2:** According to the literature, it shouldn't take more than a few microseconds to join and split two ions in nearby trap zones, assumed that each would last for one cycle.
- **CNOT ION1, ION2:** With a total assumed lifetime of 23 cycles, the cnot gate has been applied in recent ion-trap experiments using the following sequence: 1-qubit gate, join, Controlled-Phase Gate (8 cycles), split, 1-qubit gate, join, Controlled-Phase Gate (8 cycles), split, 1-qubit gate.
- **WAIT ION:** When an ion is left idle (does not undergo any operation during a cycle), it may develop memory problems. Although 14.3 seconds is the experimentally confirmed decoherence period of ions, 50–100 seconds is the anticipated decoherence time.

The nine cnot gates in the 7-bit encoder circuit can be operated in any order without compromising the circuit's performance, which makes it an especially intriguing circuit. However, faults propagate differently depending on the gate order, which could lead to the failure of the verification circuit component. We refer to this restriction as the fault-tolerance constraint. We have designated the nine encoding cnot gates in the figure below as "a" through "i" in order to illustrate the fault-tolerance restriction for scheduling quantum algorithms.

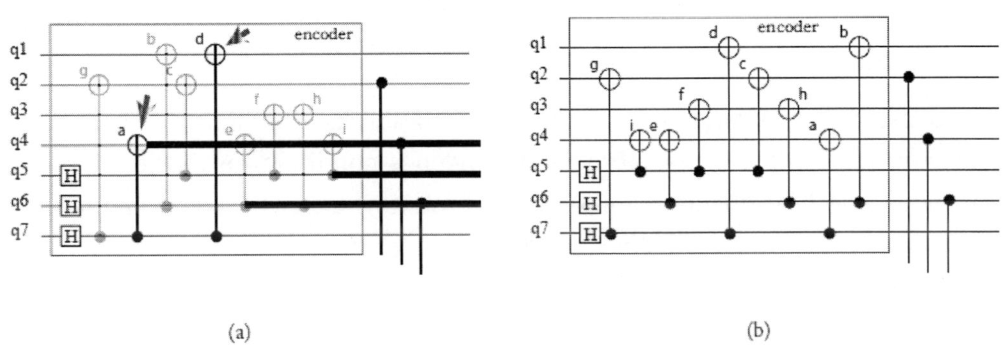

Fig.5.48 (a) shows the pattern of error propagation in the event that gate "a's" control bit fails. We observe that the output error passes through two of the three verification gates, resulting in equal parity in the measurement of the verification qubits and a "no-error" outcome for the verifier. (b) A fully rearranged encoder circuit that is still fault-tolerant (incidentally, gate "g" is still scheduled first). Any combination of the indicated gates maintains the encoding circuit's functionality in an error-free setting.

The encoder circuit's original gate order permits bit-flip mistakes to spread, making it possible to identify any non-trivial error pattern—that is, two or more defects—by looking at the parity of the bits acquired by measuring just qubits q2, q4, and q6. The encoding circuit with gate "g" scheduled first is depicted in Figure (a). In this way, even though the encoded data contains numerous errors, a single failure at either gate "a" or "d" will result in multiple errors passing through the verification circuit and the verifier returning an equal parity result, or "no-error." Both qubits q4 and q6 at the circuit's output will experience the error in the example. Therefore, a schedule that violates the fault-tolerance restriction mandated by the Steane error correcting code occurs when a single circuit failure results in more than one error at the output. Only one error can be fixed by the Steane error-correcting code. A fault-tolerant encoder must therefore make sure that any given circuit error results in no more than one output error, and if it does, the verification circuit must be able to identify it.

Although the circuit in Figure (b) appears to be identical to the one in Figure (a) at first glance, with gate "g" still scheduled first, there is no place in the circuit where a single mistake will result in an inaccurate result from the verifier. The evaluation of error propagation at each stage of the QPOS scheduler was found to be prohibitive when calculating gate dependencies based on the fault-tolerance constraint. Consequently, the scheduler should be dynamically linked to the QASM-TOOLS suite, which indicates the existence of any single error in a given circuit that causes more than one error at the output, in order to satisfy the dependency constraint. The input circuit program indicate whether a fault-tolerance requirement is required for universal quantum circuits by means of a flag. For instance, the conventional encoder and verifier for the Steane code does not have to adhere to the fault-tolerance restriction, but it also needs 14 qubits rather than 10 and more gates.

Nowhere else in the literature on quantum compilation has the fault-tolerance restriction been examined, despite it being a crucial dependency condition for quantum processes. It draws attention to how quantum and classical programs differ in their compilation: Data dependencies may not exist between two activities, but fault-tolerant error correction requirements can introduce dependencies.

Accurate research into fault-tolerant LCBs and the interactions of each LCB component requires a scheduler that both schedules quantum operations and guarantees that the constraint is met. Entanglement facilitates the rapid spread of mistakes, so that no amount of higher-level error correction can increase the dependability of quantum operations (and prevent practical quantum computing) even if the smallest, most harmless low-level LCB is not fault-tolerant.

The challenge posed by the quantum computing paradigm in determining the best geometrical arrangement for maximum SIMD gate execution is another obstacle to implementing the scheduling mechanism for the iontrap technology. By forcing each electric pulse to apply to as many gates as possible during a program cycle, optimizing SIMD execution will reduce some of the classical resource overhead (which has been identified as a bottleneck) in ion-trap chips. However, when such an opportunity is found, it is impossible to allocate various ions to separate activities. Because the scheduler is unable to track how each qubit is entangled with other qubits throughout earlier program stages, it is unable to dynamically recognize that the three verification qubits {v1, v2, v3} can be assigned to any of the three data qubits {q2, q4, q6} and prioritize the communication resources accordingly. To put it another way, due of entanglement, $A \neq C$, making register renaming impossible for quantum programs where $A = B$, $B = C$.

5.13.6 Threshold Computations

Assuming that every position of any sort of gate is handled as a single location that requires exactly one cycle of execution and that there is a chance that it will introduce an error on the qubits it operates on, we approximated the threshold value for a logical CNOT block. The results are displayed in the figure below. The circuit statistics, which are separated into three separate subroutines—encoding, logical cnot gate, and error correction procedure—are displayed in Figure (a). The circuit is intrinsically serial after the communication routes have been mapped, and there is a lot more idling (like WAIT gates) than any other process. Given that the circuit for the logical cnot gate has 73 total time cycles, the overall period of a logical cnot gate at a single level of recursion can reach 500 microseconds (for an ion-trap device) if a single time cycle is upper constrained by the duration of a two-qubit gate, or 7 µs. This is well within the 14.3-second decoherence duration for individual ions.

Since every location (or logic gate) in a quantum device needs its own physical calibration (and even procedures), we take into account how the threshold changes when each gate's relative dependability varies in comparison to other gate types. Figure (b) displays the results, demonstrating that the "WAIT" and "MOVE" gates in the circuit had the greatest impact on the threshold value.

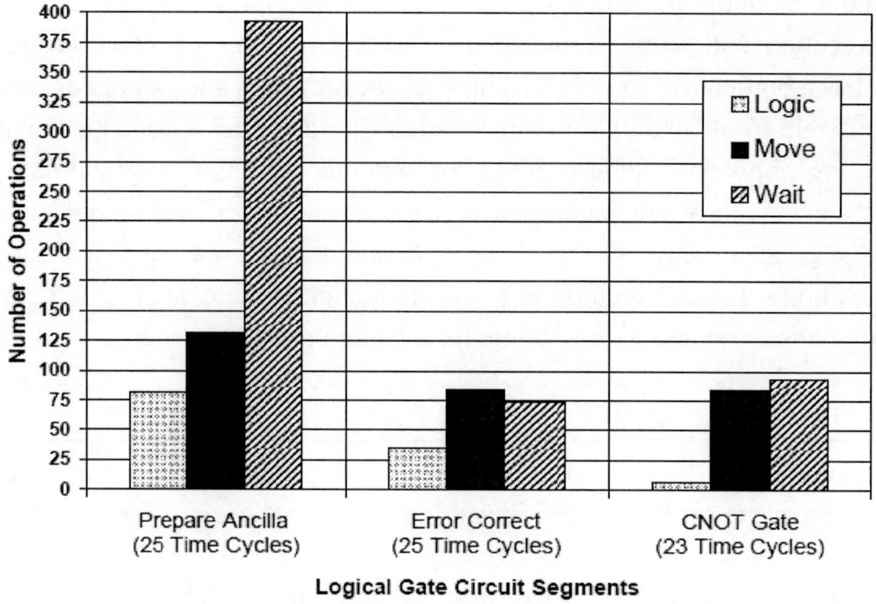

(a)

Fig.5.49 (a) shows the logical cnot circuit's total number of operations when the QPOS heuristic scheduler is used. Every operation is thought to take precisely one cycle, therefore the name "logic" has been used to refer to all logic gates, including cnot gates, single-qubit gates, and measurement gates.

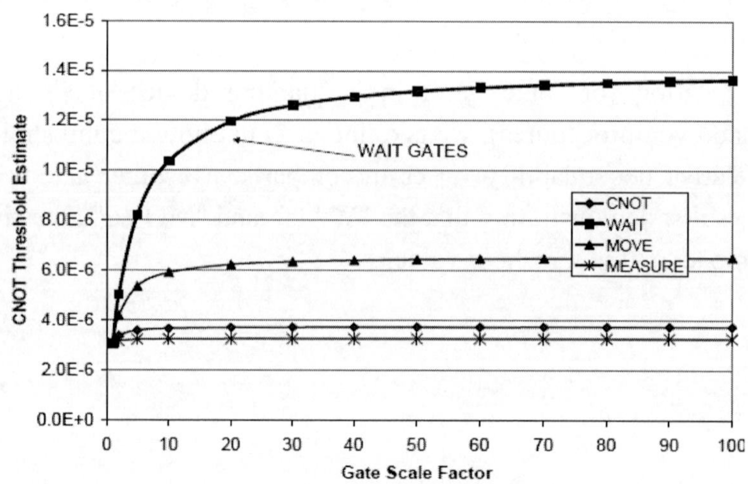

(b)

Fig.5.49 (b) The logical cnot circuit's threshold variation in relation to the other gate types as a function of the likelihood of gate failure. When WAIT gates are 100 times more dependable than the other gates in the circuit, the threshold increases by an order of magnitude (to 1.36 × 10−5). Changing the relative weight of the other gate types to the remaining locations has a significantly less impact on the threshold.

The threshold really increases by nearly an order of magnitude (to about 1.4 × 10−5) when "WAIT" gates are configured to be 100 times more dependable than the other gates in the circuit. Figure (b) shows that there are 58700 malignant pairings with a cnot gate as one of the pairs, 19792 pairs of locations with a measurement operation as one of the pairs, 174076 pairs with a "MOVE" action, and 254909 pairs with a "WAIT" operation.

The ion-trap technology's scalability is severely limited by the communication latencies inherent in a 2-D physical device, as the analysis above shows. This is because a lower threshold value necessitates an increase in recursion level in order to achieve the desired system reliability. For lengthy calculations that involve manipulating millions of logical qubits through millions of logical gates, optimistic ion-trap values may need to be considerably lower than the bottom-bound threshold estimate of 3.1×10^{-6}.

Moreover, this model is at best optimistic for ion-trap technology because it assumes a single time cycle for every action. The pulse sequences required for each type of gate are taken into account in a more realistic model. For instance, it takes around 7 μs to traverse directly between adjacent trap zones because moving between them requires traveling over 200 micrometers. A measurement operation takes 10 μs, and a cnot gate takes roughly 23 μs per cnot gate, which consists of two controlled-phase gates, three single-qubit gates, and the joining and splitting of the ions. Lastly, it costs more to move through a junction than it does to move between two nearby trap zones; according to our conversations with NIST researchers, the latter is thought to be twice as sluggish. Consequently, the lower-bound of the threshold value for ion-traps significantly drops if the circuit schedule is remapped to reflect the different length for each gate type and a single cycle is taken as the duration of the quickest gate, such as single-qubit gates.

Adjusting the scheduling heuristic to account for the different gate latencies produced the initial estimations of the impact on the threshold. The duration of a single-qubit gate, 1 μs, was specified as the basic program cycle. Therefore, for a single movement operation, the ions must pass through seven WAIT gates, and for a single cnot action, the impacted ion must pass through two two-qubit gates and three single-qubit gates. This more realistic ion-trap model's revised threshold estimations are displayed in the figure below. This is not the threshold, but it is the threshold for just one QEC circuit—a very little part of the logical cnot circuit—out of the entire circuit.

The cnot circuit's threshold value is therefore even lower. Memory mistakes significantly affect the device's scalability, as demonstrated by our approximate estimation of the single QEC circuit using the revised device assumptions. Almost eliminating the impact of memory failures, the QLA architecture was modeled assuming an ion lifetime of 50 seconds or more; however, experimental lifetimes of 14.3 seconds are taken into account in the research presented here.

According to estimates, the threshold is 1.8×10^{-8} when all gate cycles are handled identically, and it increases by two orders of magnitude to 1.7×10^{-6} when WAIT gates are 100 times more dependable than other gates. Counting wait gates, it appears that none of the other gate types have a significant impact on the threshold.

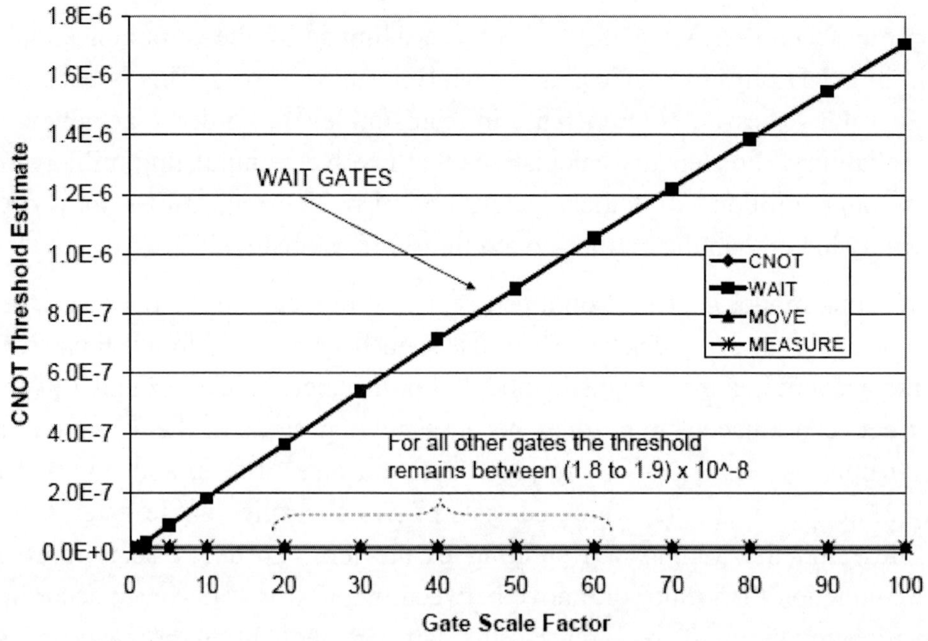

Fig.5.50 Threshold for the logical cnot circuit varies with the likelihood of gate failure in comparison to the other gate types using the more practical ion-trap model.

The threshold, which is unaffected by improving any of the other gates, is estimated to be 1.8×10^{-8} when all gate cycles are handled identically and improves to 1.7×10^{-6} when WAIT gates are 100 times better.

Our abstraction of the ion-trap devices itself reflects the estimation of their threshold value. However, the abstractions are broad enough to imply that substantial technological advancements are necessary to achieve genuine scalability. However, our ability to estimate the technology's scalability is greatly influenced by the abstractions created for any high-level ion-trap device. It is crucial to develop a simulation and device optimization infrastructure that considers both the impact of the interaction between the classical and quantum components in the devices on the failure rate of the logical operations, in addition to a theoretical estimate of the threshold value, in order to design a large-scale quantum computing system that accurately reflects the capabilities of an assumed technology.

Improvements not taken into account in the error correction circuits themselves, in addition to technological advancements, will raise the threshold value estimate even more. For instance, the fact that the schedule only consisted of legal gate reordering that maintained the preparation circuit's fault-tolerant characteristics placed restrictions on the schedule generated by QPOS for the preparation circuits. To make the entire circuit fault-tolerant, it would be more intriguing if we could determine the ideal gate arrangement that provides the optimum communication pathways and automatically creates the verification circuit. Additionally, the controlled-phase gate is the natural two-qubit gate for ion-traps, and upgrading all of the gates to controlled-phase gates will significantly enhance circuit implementation.

5.13.7 Applying the QLA to Quantum Simulation: The Transverse Ising Model

Quantum simulation is a significant non-factoring quantum application that is implemented using the QLA. In particular, it incorporates the fault-tolerant quantum error correction methods used by the QLA to estimate the resource needs for a quantum simulation of the ground state energy for the 1-D quantum Transverse Ising Model.

5.13.7.1 Compilation of Transverse Ising Model

At zero temperature, one of the most basic models that exhibits a quantum phase shift is the 1-D Transverse Ising Model. For frustrated 2-D lattices, the computation of the TIM's ground state energy is computationally inefficient, although it can be solved analytically in the linear case. Monte-Carlo simulations, for instance, are computationally demanding when calculating the magnetic behavior of frustrated Ising anti-ferromagnets. An excellent benchmark model for quantum computation is the TIM, which is crucial to investigations of quantum phase transitions and quantum annealing, and the generic problem is challenging.

N-spin-1/2 particles with nearest-neighbor spin-spin interactions along the z-axis and an external magnetic field along the x-axis make up the Transverse Ising Model. For this system, the Hamiltonian, or HI, is

$$H_I = \sum_i \Gamma \sigma_i^x + \sum_{\langle i,j \rangle} J_{ij} \sigma_i^z \sigma_j^z.$$

where {i, j } denotes a sum exclusively over nearest-neighbors, J is the spin-spin interaction energy, and Γ is the energy of a spin in the external magnetic field. In this section, we set $\hbar = 1$ and use σ^x i and σ^z i as the Pauli spin operators for the ith spin.

With constant Ising interaction energy Jij = −J, the 1-D linear chain TIM of N-spins is the main topic of this chapter. $g = \Gamma/J$ is the ratio that determines the system's ground state. There are two degenerate ferromagnetic ground states in the limit of small magnetic field, $g >> 1$. These are parallel and anti-parallel to the $\hat{z}$ axis. In the case of strong magnetic field, $g >> 1$, the system is paramagnetic, with all the spins aligned along the $\hat{x}$ axis. A quantum phase transition is observed in the linear 1-D TIM at g = 1 in the intermediate range of magnetic field strength.

For the 1-D situation with constant coupling, the TIM Hamiltonian in the preceding equation can be expressed as follows:

$$H_I = -J\left(\sum_{j=1}^{N} gX_j + \sum_{j=1}^{N-1} Z_j Z_{j+1}\right)$$

When the corresponding matrix operators, Xj and Zj, are used in place of the Pauli spin operators, σx j and σzj. In the limit of largeN, the ground state energy for the 1-D TIM may be computed analytically. Either the density matrix renormalization group approach or the Monte-Carlo method can effectively mimic the TIM when there are a finite number of spins with non-uniform spin-spin interactions (J not constant). The 2-D TIM on a frustrated lattice, where the simulation expands exponentially with N, is a difficulty for classical computers. Physical qubit resources, which scale polynomially with N, are needed to use the quantum phase estimation circuit to determine the ground state energy of the TIM. The number of computational time steps is likewise polynomial in N, albeit exponential in numerical accuracy M. Furthermore, the resources needed to implement the quantum phase estimation circuit are mostly independent of the dimensionality of the TIM Hamiltonian, much as the problem's complexity is independent of the lattice dimension and layout when using classical brute force diagonalization.

5.13.8 Estimates of Time Quantum Simulation Resources

There are two steps in Clark's method for determining the resources needed for the TIM ground-state energy calculation using Hamiltonian HI. The authors first transplant the challenge of calculating the TIM Hamiltonian's eigenvalues in the preceding equation onto a phase estimation quantum circuit, adopting the methodology of Abrams and Lloyd. Second, within the framework of the QLA architecture, the authors break down every action in the phase estimation circuit into a collection of universal gates that may be implemented fault-tolerantly. This makes it possible to calculate the resources in a fault-tolerant environment with accuracy.

5.13.8.1 Circuit for Phase Estimation

Using an eigenvector of HI.φ < 1 and a binary fraction 0.x1... xM, the phase estimation technique computes an M-bit estimate of the phase φ of the eigenvalue $e^{-i2\pi\phi}$ of the time evolution unitary operator $U(\tau) = e^{-iH_I\tau}$ for fixed τ. When $E\tau < 2\pi$, the energy eigenvalue $E = \frac{2\pi\phi}{\tau}$. For the ground state energy |Eg| to be calculated, τ must be less than

$2\pi/|Eg|$. The ground-state energy |Eg| magnitude for the 1-D TIM is constrained by NJ(1+ g). We select $\tau=(10JN)^{-1}$ in the vicinity of the phase transition $g \approx 1$.

The figure below depicts the quantum circuit used to implement the phase estimation technique. Two quantum registers make up the circuit: an output quantum register with a single qubit recycled M times, and an N-qubit input quantum register setup in an initial quantum state $|\Psi\rangle$. In the TIM model, one of the N spin-1/2 particles is represented by each of the N qubits in the input register. A Hadamard (H) gate is used to arrange the output qubit into the state $\frac{1}{\sqrt{2}}(|0\rangle + |1\rangle)$ at the start of each of the algorithm's M steps. A regulated power of U(τ), represented by $U(2^m\tau)$, applied to the input register after the H gate, where $0 \leq m < M - 1$, comes next.

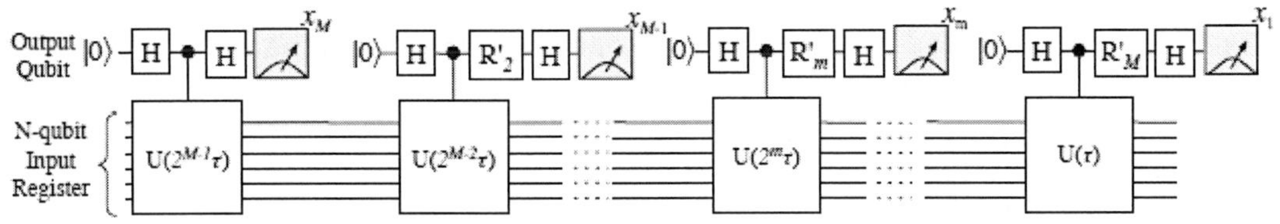

Fig.5.51 The circuit that uses a single continuously recycled control qubit to accomplish the phase estimation technique.

Using j to represent the jth step in the circuit, the output qubit is rotated via the gate and the result is in the mth bit in the estimate of φ each time it is measured (meter symbols):

$$R_j = |0\rangle\langle 0| + \exp\left(i\pi \sum_{m=M+2-j}^{M} \frac{2^{M+1}x_m}{2^{m+j}}\right)|1\rangle\langle 1|$$

The application of the Quantum Fourier Transform to the output qubit at each step is represented by the gate Rj. Following each M measurement, the output is an M-bit binary string {x1x2... xM}, which is equivalent to the M-bit approximation of φ provided by 0.x1... xM. Since $|\Psi_g\rangle$ is the ground eigenstate of HI, the corresponding energy eigenvalue $E = \frac{2\pi\phi}{\tau}$ will be the ground-state energy Eg with probability equal to $|\langle\Psi|\Psi_g\rangle|^2$ using this estimate of φ.

The initial quantum state $|\Psi\rangle$` should approximate the ground state $|\Psi_g\rangle$ in order to increase the likelihood of success $|\langle\Psi|\Psi_g\rangle|^2$. It is typically computationally challenging to prepare an approximation to $|\Psi_g\rangle$ for arbitrary Hamiltonians. In some situations, the preparation can be carried out via adiabatic quantum state preparation methods or by calculating an estimated wavefunction using classical approximation techniques. The resources needed to prepare $|\Psi\rangle$ are similar in complexity to those needed to create the circuit for the phase estimation technique depicted in the above figure if the state can be prepared adiabatically. Assuming that the input register has already been constructed in the N-qubit quantum state, emphasis is placed on determining the number of computational time steps and qubits needed to build the circuit $|\Psi\rangle$.

5.13.8.2 Breakdown of the equivalency circuit into fault-tolerant gates

The high-level TIM circuit with N + 1 unitary operators is depicted in the above figure. The circuit's unitary operations are broken down into a collection of simple one- and two-qubit gates, which the QLA architecture allows for fault-tolerant implementation. The controlled-$U(2^m\tau)$ gates and each Rj gate are the high-level circuit operations that need to be broken down.

The second-order Trotter formula can be used to deconstruct the Controlled -$U(2^m\tau)$ gate. First, HI is divided into two terms: $H_{ZZ} = \sum_{j=0}^{N-1} Z_j Z_{j+1}$, which represents the Ising interactions, and $H_X = \sum_{j=0}^{N} gX_j$ which represents the transverse magnetic field. Taking into account the associated unitary operators

$$
\begin{aligned}
U_x(2\tau) &= \prod_{j=1}^{N} \exp(-ig\tau X_j) \\
U_{zz}(2\tau) &= \prod_{j=1}^{N-1} \exp(-i\tau Z_j Z_{j+1}).
\end{aligned}
$$

The Totter approximation of $U(2^m\tau)$ represented by $\tilde{U}(2^m\tau)$, can be constructed as follows, with g = 1.

$$
\begin{aligned}
U(2^m\tau) &= \left[U_x(\theta)\, U_{zz}(2\theta)\, U_x(\theta)\right]^k + \epsilon_T \\
&= \tilde{U}(2^m\tau) + \epsilon_T,
\end{aligned}
$$

where the Trotter approximation error, which grows as $\mathcal{O}\left(\frac{(2^m\tau)^3}{k^2}\right)$, is represented by ϵ_T and $\theta = (2^m\tau/k)$. The integer Trotter parameter k can be increased to make the Trotter approximation error arbitrarily small. The precision of the (M − m)th measured bit in the binary fraction for the phaseφ is $1/2^{M-m}$, and since the controlled -$U(2^m\tau)$ corresponds to the (M − m)th bit, ϵ_T must be smaller than $1/2^{M-m}$.

Consequently, k is raised until ϵ_T is smaller than $1/2^{M-m}$ while approximation $U(2^m\tau)$. With the restriction that $\epsilon_T < 1/2^M$, provide a numerical value for the Trotter parameter k(m = 0) = k0 as a function of N ≤ 10 for a given M. For fixed M, k0 scales as 1/N, and for larger N, k0 is extrapolated based on a power-law fit of N ≤ 10. In order to satisfy the error bound based on the scaling of ϵ_T with k, set $k = 2^m k_0$: with Form > 0.

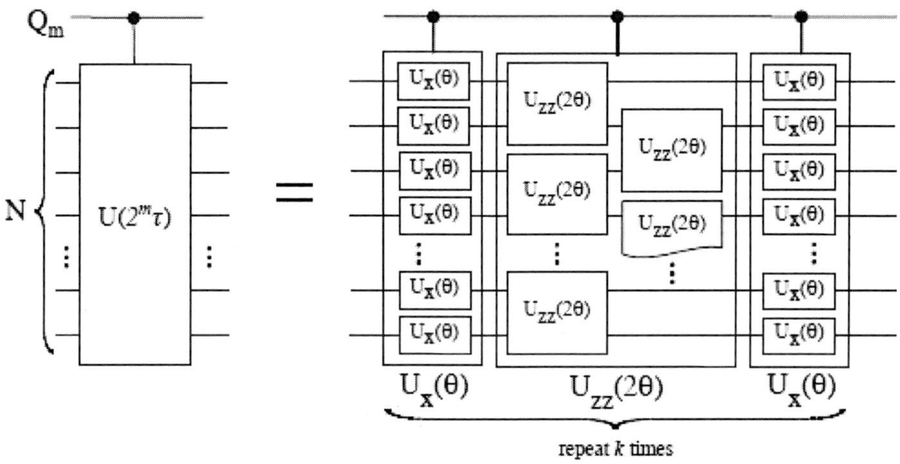

Fig.5.52 The Trotter formula is used to estimate the circuit for the controlled unitary operation $U(2^m \tau)$.

The circuit that corresponds to the Trotter approximation of $U(2^m \tau)$ is depicted in the above figure. It is evident that the controlled $-U(2^m \tau)$ is made up of two controlled $-U_x(\theta)$ operations and one controlled$-U_{zz}(\theta)$ operation. These operations are repeated k times, and the output qubit, denoted by Q_m, is controlled on the tenth instance. Extending the circuit in the figure above demonstrates that $\tilde{U}(2^m \tau)$ can be written as follows:

$$\tilde{U}(2^m \tau) = U_x(\theta)\left[U_{zz}(2\theta)U_x(2\theta)\right]^{k-1} U_{zz}(2\theta)\, U_x(\theta)$$

This indicates that k controlled $U_{zz}(2\theta)$ gates, (k − 1) controlled $-U_x(2\theta)$ gates, and two instances of controlled$-U_x(\theta)$ gates, all controlled on the mth instance of the output qubit, must be implemented sequentially in order to approximate $U(2^m \tau)$.

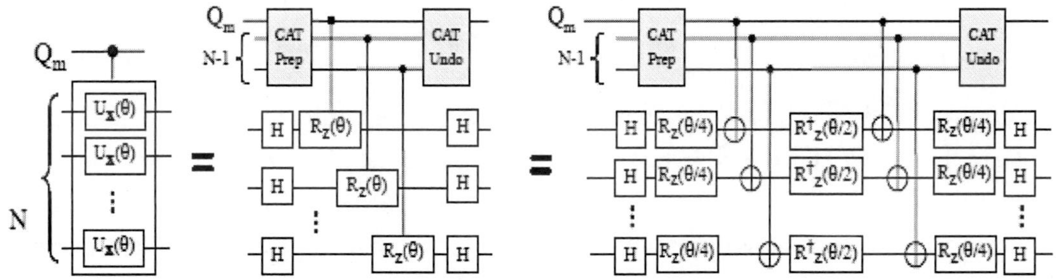

Fig.5.53 The breakdown of the controlled unitary operation $U_x(\theta)$ into cnot gates and single-qubit Rz gates.

Figures above and below depict the quantum circuits for the controlled$-U_x(2\theta)$ and controlled-$-U_{zz}(2\theta)$ gate decomposition, respectively. The gates are broken down into cnot gates, $R_z(\theta) = \exp(-i\frac{\theta}{2}Z)$, and rotations on the $\hat{z}$-axis.

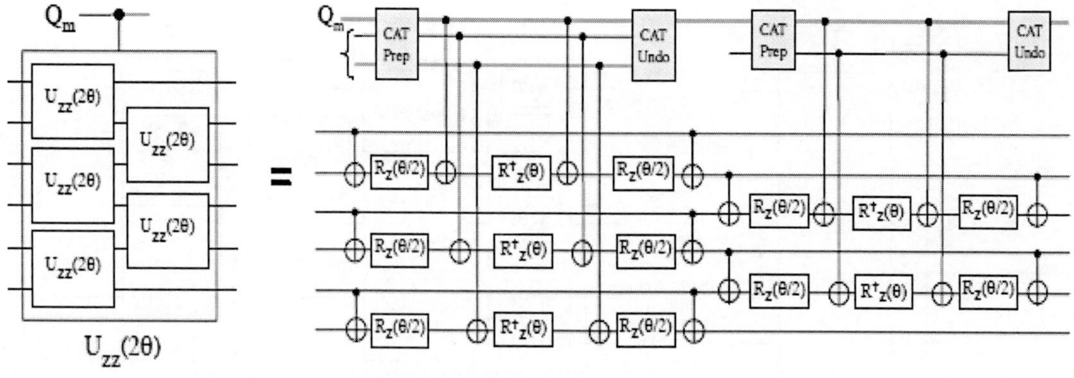

Fig.5.54 The controlled unitary operation $U_{zz}(2\theta)$ gate is broken down into Rz and cnot single-qubit gates.

The cnot gates, the $\hat{z}$-axis, and $R_z(\theta) = \exp(-i\frac{\theta}{2}Z)$, To parallelize each of the N Rz(θ) gates, an N-qubit cat state is prepared using (N − 1) extra qubits. One can implement (N−1) cnot gates in $\mathcal{O}(N)$ time steps in parallel with the Rz(θ/4) gates in prior to last Figure and in parallel with the Rz(θ/2) gates in last Figure to prepare an N-qubit cat state.

The Solovay-Kitaev theory allows us to approximate the three single-qubit Rz gates (Rz(θ), Rz(θ/2), and Rz(θ/4)) using $\mathcal{O}(\log^{3.97}(1/\epsilon_{sk}))$ basic gates (H, T, S). A slight spin imparted to the qubit is equivalent to the Solovay-Kitaev error (ϵ_{sk}). The sequence of H, T, and S gates needed to approximate each of the three Rz gates for $\theta = \frac{2^m\tau}{k}$ is calculated using the Dawson and Nielsen technique.

The length of the longest of these three sequences is what Clark defines as SR. For instance, SR = 4 × 105 for M=30, necessitating a sixth order Solovay-Kitaev approximation. The computation's findings demonstrate that when the authors estimate $U(2^m\tau)$ the Solovay-Kitaev error $\epsilon_{sk} < \frac{\epsilon_T}{k}$, so that the total error, ϵ_T, is less than the necessary pre cision (1/2M−m). SR scales as $\mathcal{O}(\log^{3.97}(k/\epsilon_T)) = \mathcal{O}(M^{3.97})$ as a result.

The controlled $-U(2^m\tau)$ has now been fully decomposed into the fundamental gate set {X,Z,H, T, S,CNOT,MEASURE}. The time steps needed to implement controlled $-U_x(\theta)$ and $U_{zz}(\theta)$ are equivalent to (3SR + 4) and (6SR + 7) as a function of SR. According to the following equation, k(9SR + 11) + 3SR + 4 time steps are needed to perform the full controlled $-U(2^m\tau)$, where k = $2^m k_0$. Each Rj gate takes less than an SR gate and is comparable to a rotation by $R_z(\theta)$.

Combining everything mentioned above, the total number of time steps (K) needed to implement the TIM circuit as a function of SR, k₀, and M may be found using the formula:

$$K = \sum_{m=0}^{M-1} [2^m k_0(9S_R + 11) + 3S_R + 4 + S_R]$$
$$= \mathcal{O}(2^M) \times S_R.$$

The exponential reliance on the accuracy (M) dominates the total number of time steps since SR scales as $O(M^{3.97})$. N qubits are needed for the input register $|\Psi\rangle$, one qubit is needed for the output register, and N − 1 qubits are needed for the cat state, so 2N qubits are needed to implement the circuit. Then, using the QLA design, the authors incorporate fault-tolerant QEC into the TIM circuit and calculate the corresponding resource requirements, K and Q. Considering the underlying physical implementation of each gate and qubit within the framework of the QLA architecture, an estimate of the potential time required to address the TIM problem in real-time is also given.

5.13.9 The QLA architecture's metric circuit

We may estimate the size of the physical system needed for quantum simulation by comparing the number of computational tiles needed by the QLA to the number of logical qubits Q for the TIM issue. Similarly, as the QLA architecture defines the duration of a single time step as the time needed to execute error correction, the number of time steps K closely correlates to the time needed to construct the application.

In previous Section, evaluated the parameters K and Q for the TIM issue, and the results showed that K is O(2M) × SR and Q is 2N. However, the fault-tolerant implementation of the T gate necessitates the preparation of an auxiliary logical qubit into the state T | + } for one time step, which is followed by four time steps made up of measurement gates, H, cnot, and S. As a result, K and Q rise. Since many of the gates in the Solovay-Kitaev sequences that approximate the Rz gates are T gates, the value of SR must account for the increased number of cycles for each T gate when calculating K using Equation. Every other fundamental gate is transversally implemented and only needs a single time step.

The figure below displays the final functional arrangement for the QLA architecture for the TIM problem. There are 4N logical qubit tiles in the architecture. The logical qubits utilized in the N-qubit input register $|\Psi\rangle$ are stored in the data tiles designated Q1 through QN, whereas the output register is represented by the "OUT" tile. The N − 1 qubit tiles for the cat state are those that have the labels C1 through CN−1. In the event that T gates are applied to any of the data qubits, the $T|+\rangle$ tiles are used to prepare the auxiliary states. In order to reduce the amount of communication needed for each logical cnot gate between the control and target qubits, all tiles are aligned precisely as seen in the figure below.

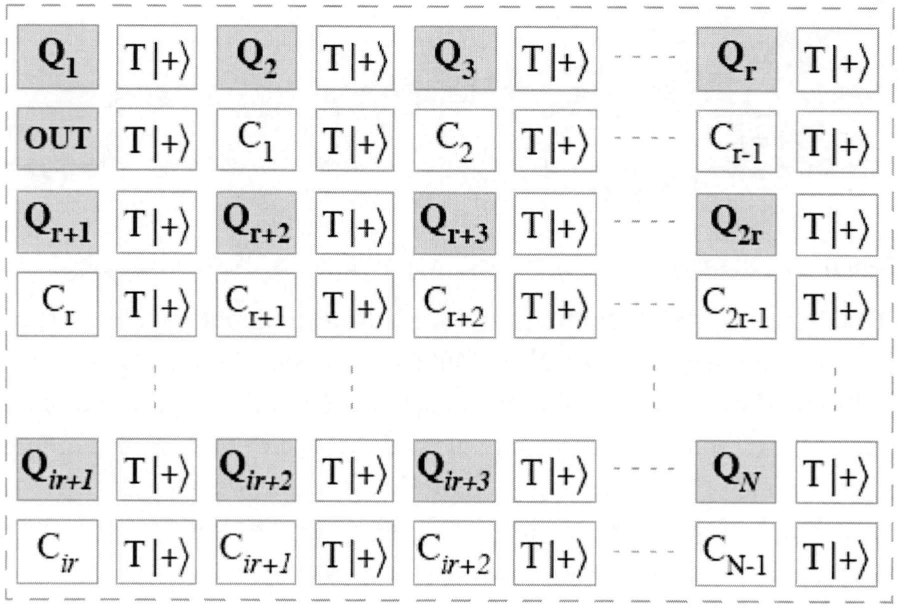

Fig.5.55 QLA framework for the TIM issue.

For instance, cnot gates are only needed between the "OUT" tile, C1, and Cr when creating the cat state with all Ci tiles and the "OUT" tile. In a similar manner, during the cat state preparation, C1 only interacts with C2 via a cnot gate, whereas C2 only interacts with Q3.

5.13.9.1 Estimates of Resources for the 1-DTIM Issue

The figure below, which assumes N = 100 and displays a logarithmic plot of the number of time steps K as a function of the energy precision M < 20, provides the resource needs for implementing the 1-D TIM problem using the QLA architecture. The exponential dependence of K on M is evident in the figure below. Only the k0 part in the previous equation, O(1/N), shows the slight dependence of K on the number of spins (N). The value of the entire problem size KQ is really predicted to increase relatively little as N increases because Q = 4N.

It is evident that no error correction is necessary when $M \leq 8$. This is due to the fact that the physical ion-trap gate reliability of 1×10^{-7} is still higher than the required dependability per gate of 1/KQ. The architecture is made up of only physical qubits and all gates are physical gates in the absence of error correction. As a result, SR = 1 in the previous equation and the total number of qubits becomes 2N rather than 4N. This indicates that each single-qubit Rz gate can be implemented directly without the need to approximate it using the Solvay-Kitaev theorem. Error correction is necessary for M > 9, which causes a sharp increase in the number of timesteps at M = 9 and an extra scaling factor of O(M4) in K because of SR's reliance on M. Actually, K rises so fast that level 2 error correction is needed at M = 9 rather than level 1. Level 3 error correction is needed at M > 18, and although K does not grow, the number of computation days increases since each time step is substantially longer. For M = 9, the Solovay-Kitaev order is three, and for M = 20, it rises to order five.

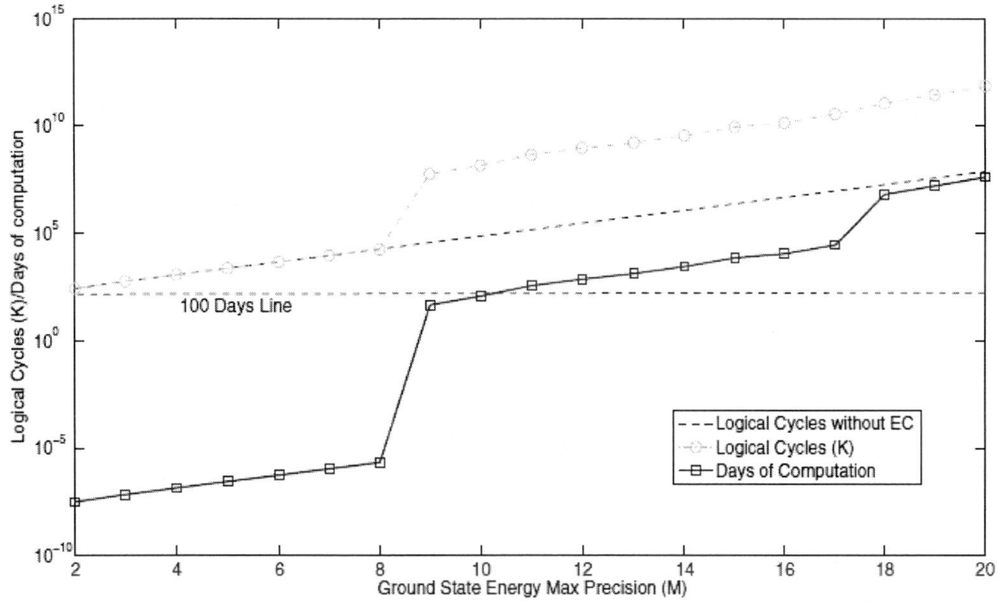

Fig.5.56 The number of logical cycles K (solid line) and computing days required are calculated numerically, assuming that N = 100 spin TIM issue as a function of the desired maximum accuracy M ≤ 20.

5.14 Quantum Architectures Using Teleportation

The physical implementation of quantum logic gates should ideally be approached with a particular technology in mind, such as the way the QLA handles ion-traps. The issue is that there are a plethora of options for building conceptually universal circuits, just as many options exist for the physical implementation of gates. In order to create logic gates through teleportation circuits that are more appropriate for other quantum computation technologies, this section presents architectures that utilize teleportation as a computational primitive.

The quantum computation circuit model that uses universal quantum logic as a series of unitary matrices acting on the probability amplitude vector to describe a group of quantum data units called qubits. The single-qubit T gate and Clifford group operations were also introduced as a basic foundation for universal quantum computation. Relatively simple, fault-tolerant methods for applying quantum logic to encoded qubits are provided by the selected basis of gates. A number of ideas for building a universal set of quantum operations that is fault-tolerant and incorporates the Clifford group are compiled by Steane.

As an elementary operation, some proposals use the three-qubit Toffoli gate, while others use the controlled-S gate. When creating a quantum architecture or modeling software for one, a system designer might need to give the program some leeway in selecting the right universal set of gates that enable generalization to all [[n, k, d]] error correcting codes. The possibility that universal quantum computation can be accomplished without the direct use of gates is perhaps even more intriguing. All that is required is a mechanism or circuit structure that carries out the functions of universal gates. More precisely, a method that permits a quantum state $|\Psi\rangle$ to undergo a unitary transformation without the unitary operation itself being physically applied. Teleportation is one of these mechanisms. Teleportation was demonstrated by Gottesman and Chuang in 1998 as a universal quantum logic primitive that may be applied to any quantum computation.

Optical quantum computers employ the teleportation gate method to enable two-qubit operations. This can be further developed by examining the potential trade-offs involved in developing an architecture that applies universal quantum logic to teleportation-encoded data. The structure of the entire quantum system, as specified by the QLA architecture case study, could be significantly altered by such investigations.

The ability to coordinate universal quantum logic, which is often made up of single-qubit gates, two-qubit gates, and measurement in the circuit model of quantum processing, is one of DiVincenzo's main demands for quantum technologies. The majority of technologies permit quite simple arbitrary single-qubit rotations, with the exception of superconducting qubits. Thus, the most important prerequisite for a particular technology is the capacity to execute two-qubit gates or qubit-qubit interactions. Especially since the capacity to exchange quantum information between the two qubits is an implicit presumption in any qubit-qubit interaction.

Many of the circuit synthesis articles discussed in Section 8.3 synthesize circuits that are cnot-optimal and assume that the cnot gate is the typical elementary two-qubit gate. Perhaps untruely, a common misconception is that DiVincenzo's criteria require a technology to be able to demonstrate a dependable cnot gate; however, this is not always the case. For instance, the controlled-Z rotation is the basic two-qubit gate in ion-trap technology, and it may be utilized to effectively build a cnot gate as illustrated in the below Figure.

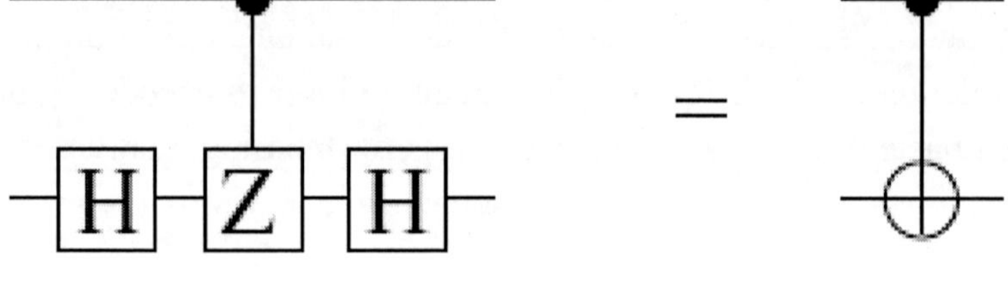

Fig.5.57 Two Hadamard gates and a controlled-Z gate can be combined to create a cnot gate.

Two qubits must interact in order for any two-qubit gate to implement a cnot operation. This interaction can be either direct, which requires that the quantum data for both qubits be placed in the same spatial location through teleportation or direct physical movement of the qubit carriers, or indirect, which involves the use of a shared medium that enables the coupling of the two-qubit states without requiring the data to be spatially close together.

There are disadvantages to both kinds of engagement. Direct interaction between qubits necessitates either information exchange between nearest neighbors or the movement of qubits through empty channels, which introduces errors proportional to the channel length. Complex low-level schedulers like QPOS or the inner workings of QUALE are required for the transfer of quantum information; both of these involve technologies that require direct physical qubit connection. Furthermore, combining the states of two qubits makes it harder to tell them apart and increases the possibility of correlated errors.

Although leaving the qubits in place may initially appear to make the indirect qubit-qubit interaction more effective, it still necessitates a common medium for coupling the qubits and may create correlated errors. This can be accomplished in a number of ways: One method relates qubits via a common quantum field mode, which can be conceptualized as a shared quantum "bus" and is achievable with a laser beam. Another method use single photons to create multi-qubit gates between trapped atoms.

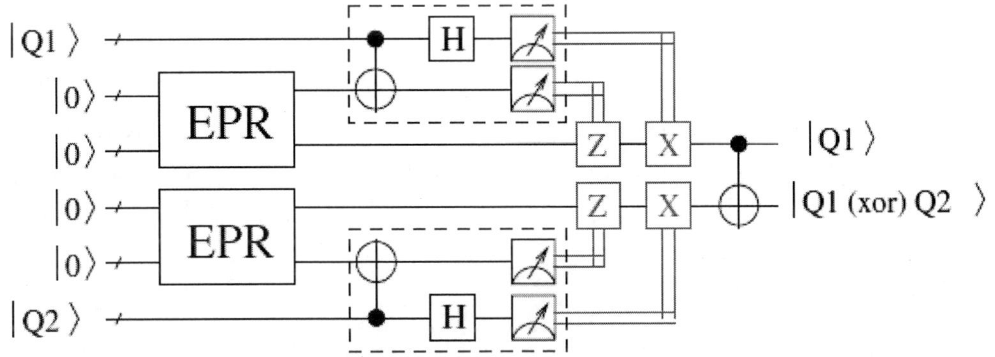

Fig.5.58 Normal cnot operation between two distant logical qubits. The qubits interact with a cnot gate after being teleported to a shared location, like two nearby accumulators in a processing element.

5.14.1 Teleportation of Cnot Gate and Single-Qubit Gates

The QLA design already makes use of the most straightforward method for thinking about implementing a cnot gate utilizing teleportation. The figure above shows a schematic. Through EPR pairs formed between each individual memory address and the PE, qubits Q1 and Q2, which are located in the memory region, are transported to the PE.

A Bell Measurement between any two qubits is implemented by the gates in the dashed boxes in the circuit of the preceding figure. Remember the four Bell states with two qubits $\{|\Psi_+\rangle, |\Psi_-\rangle, |\Phi_+\rangle, |\Phi_-\rangle\}$. The state with two qubits, $|\Psi_+\rangle$, is the well-known two-qubit EPR state. A two-qubit state can be expressed as a superposition of the four Bell states, just as a single-qubit state can be expressed as a superposition of two basis states like $|+\rangle$ and $|-\rangle$ or $|0\rangle$ and $|1\rangle$.

$$|q_1, q_2\rangle = c_0|\Psi_+\rangle + c_1|\Psi_-\rangle + c_2|\Phi_+\rangle + c_3|\Phi_-\rangle$$

Which of the four Bell states the two qubits are in is determined by a Bell measurement, like the circuit in the dashed boxes of the preceding figure. The two qubits collapse into one of the Bell states as a result of the measurement. If the two qubits were initially untangled, the Bell measurement also acts as an entangling operation between them. As with the EPR pair formation, extract the Bell measurement process as a box since every technology has a unique way of putting a Bell measurement on two qubits into practice:

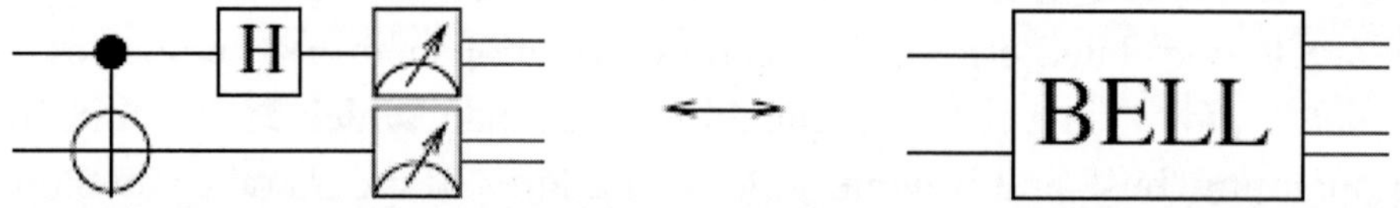

Fig.5.59 The Bell measuring circuit is abstracted as a box labeled "Bell."

Between qubits Q1 and Q2, the long-distance communication channel functions as a repeater-based link that generates 49 pure elementary EPR pairs that cover the whole channel. Their 49-qubit encoded states are transferred to the 49 elementary EPR pair qubits in the two destination accumulators via the teleportation process. Once they are in adjacent accumulators, the logical qubit transfer is followed by the direct application of a transversal cnot gate.

By altering their order, we may shift the cnot gate through the single-qubit X and Z operations without compromising the circuit's functionality and avoiding the direct contact between the two logical qubits. The outcome is displayed in the figure below. Qubits Q1 and Q2 do not directly interact, but the EPR blocks do have a direct cnot gate. Only when the four EPR blocks are originally encoded as logical qubits in the logical $|\overline{0}\rangle$ states, as depicted in the picture, can the blocks interact with one another. Thus, the cnot gate implementation breaks down into encoding four qubits initialized to $|\overline{0}\rangle$ into a predetermined 4-qubit state, represented as the state $|\overline{M}\rangle$ where:

$$|\overline{M}\rangle = \frac{(|\overline{00}\rangle + |\overline{11}\rangle)|\overline{00}\rangle + (|\overline{01}\rangle + |\overline{10}\rangle)|\overline{11}\rangle}{\sqrt{2}}$$

Furthermore, by performing a Bell measurement between two of the qubits in each GHZ state, followed by single-qubit gates controlled by the outcome of the Bell measurement, the $|\overline{M}\rangle$ state may be created utilizing two 3-qubit cat-states $(|000\rangle + |111\rangle)$ also referred to as GHZ states. The four qubits that aren't used in the Bell measurement will still be in the M state and can be applied to the cnot gate. This provides us with a cnot gate mechanism that only needs two Bell basis measurements, a specially designed 4-qubit entangled state, and classically controlled single-qubit gates. Without any direct qubit-qubit interaction, the cnot gate between two logical qubits may be achieved since the construction of the $|\overline{M}\rangle$ state may be done offline and deterministically, much like the creation of EPR qubits.

Two qubits can be remotely entangled to create an EPR pair. Furthermore, it might be feasible to remotely entangle three qubits into a GHZ state or even develop a black-box mechanism that, like in the QLA model, generates GHZ states of encoded qubits and distributes them across the architecture via a repeater-based channel. The black-box can be confined to a particular state "factory" zone where the distances are low in comparison to the application-level system, even if it uses conventional data shuttling to generate qubit-qubit interactions for the encoded special states.

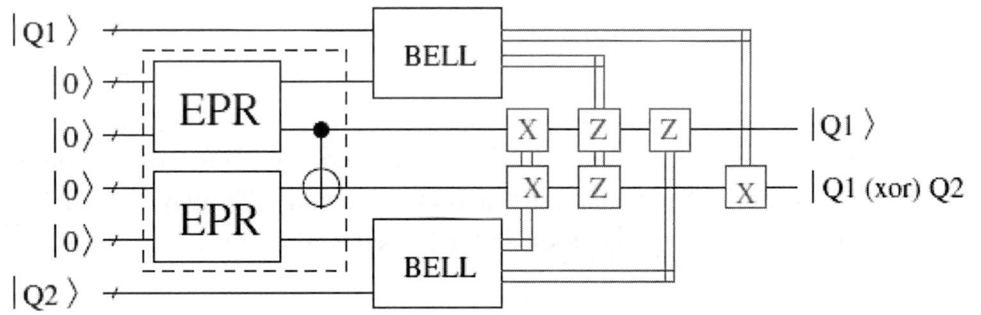

Fig.5.60 Using only single-qubit rotations, Bell measurements, and a unique 4-qubit state |M}—which can be made up of two EPR pairs or two GHZ states—two qubits can be teleported through a controlled-not gate. A Bell measurement between the two GHZ states will take the role of the cnot gate between the two EPR pairs if two GHZ states are employed.

Gottesman and Chuang also demonstrate how any encoded single-qubit logical operation may be built using the same process to create a teleportation-based mechanism. Figure following displays a schematic for creating an arbitrary single-qubit operator $\overline{U}$.

Any other single-qubit gate is transversal and applicable locally, while the universal gate-set under consideration just needs a teleportation implementation for the T gate. The T gate circuit, which uses the one-bit teleportation principle and is far simpler than the network shown in the figure below, needs a cnot gate to connect the data state to the specifically created $|A_{\pi/8}\rangle$ ancilla state. With the resource cost of four extra qubits for the formation of the $|M\rangle$ state, the necessary cnot gate can be built using the teleportation circuit to circumvent direct qubit-qubit contact.

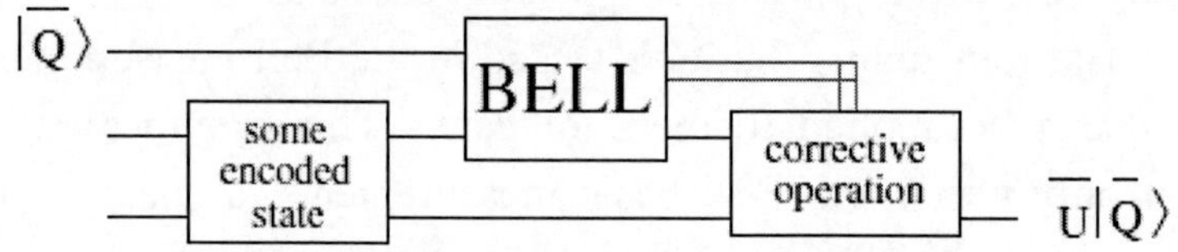

Fig.5.61 Teleportation is used to implement a single-qubit operator U. For the implementation, a Bell measurement and two logical auxiliary qubits must be used to prepare an encoded state, after which the correction operation must be performed.

5.14.2 Design Structure

There are two options for implementing gates. The first option is to use the repeater-based connection to teleport data to a processing zone. The second option is to teleport gates through auxiliary states that have been specially designed. The difference between the two options for allocating quantum computing in the two-bit adder is depicted in the figure below. The first two timesteps of the adder's computation are initially carried out in parallel by its two primary processing zones. A Toffoli gate between the ancilla qubit in the first region and two qubits from the lower (second) region is necessary for the third timestep. In the dashed box on each half of the figure below, the Toffoli gate has been broken down into simple one- and two-qubit gates. We can either teleport the data or the qubits through the gates used in the Toffoli gate's breakdown if the two 3-qubit areas are substantially separated. The schematic distinction depicted in the image below introduces the tradeoffs between teleporting gates and teleporting data on a distributed quantum computer.

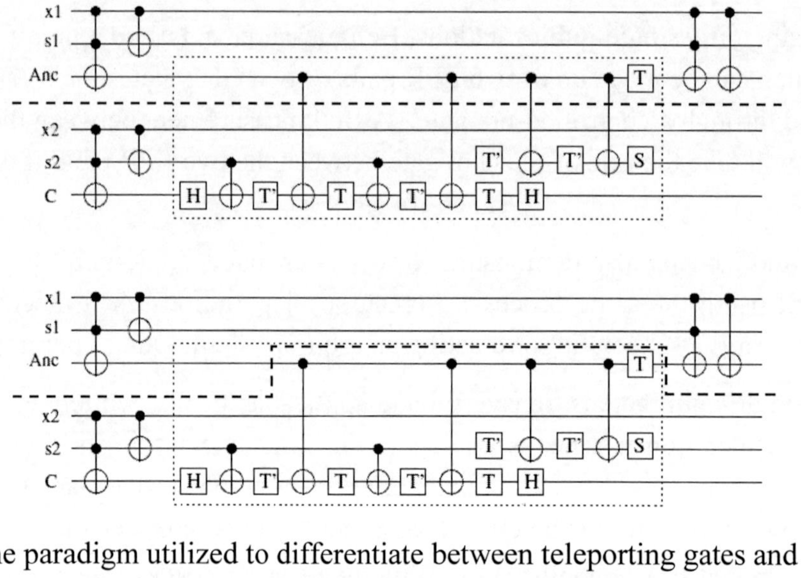

Fig.5.62 The paradigm utilized to differentiate between teleporting gates and teleporting data in a distributed quantum computer.

The figure's north half depicts a 6-qubit 2-bit adder with the middle Toffoli gate enlarged into its one- and two-qubit gate decomposition. The thick dashed line, which is meant to show that gates are transported from one processing zone to the other while the data stays in place, evenly divides the two processing regions. Data teleportation as defined by the QLA architecture is depicted in the south portion of the picture.

Given the preceding figure, it makes intuitive sense to conclude that teleporting gates are less effective than teleporting data. The sequence of gates can be carried out straight to finish the Toffoli process with minimal communication overhead once the data has been transported to a particular area, making it local to that area.

Based on multiple implementations of the adders used for Shor's factoring algorithm, the authors' investigation reveals that, on a large scale, teleporting gates is more costly than teleporting data due to the amount of elementary operations vying for the same resources. The authors employ a smart architecture of the teleported cnot gate that leaves the implementation of the cnot gate in the encoded data qubits instead of the EPR qubits and eliminates the need for the four auxiliary qubits to be in the |M} state. The figure below illustrates how they are constructed.

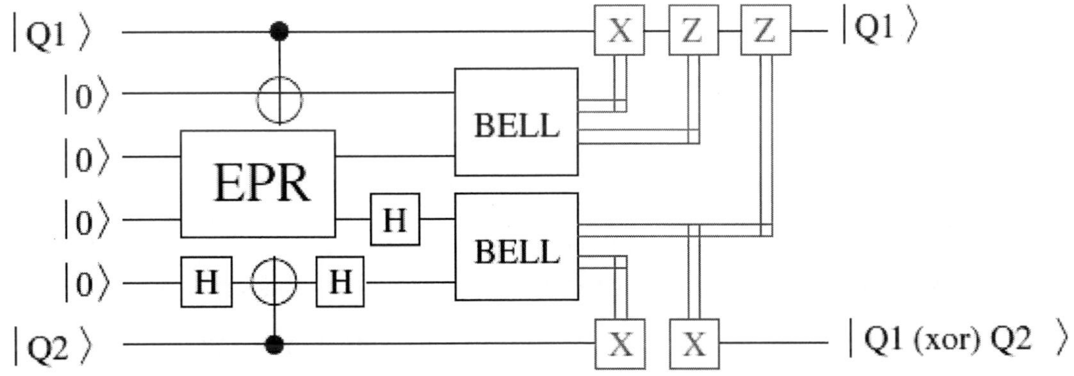

Fig.5.63 A controlled-not gate that requires four auxiliary qubits but only requires two to be encoded as an EPR pair is used to teleport two qubits.

Prior to the Bell measurement process, the data is coupled with the other two.

Solid-state qubits that are indirectly connected via a universal quantum bus form the foundation of the underlying architecture. By linking two ions via optical detector stations and beam splitters, the ion-trap technology can achieve a similar distributed architecture. The application level system's dispersed components are connected by a quantum bus, to which each component links via transceiver qubits. The transceiver qubits can be used as EPR pairs for teleportation in this way, transferring data or gates between several dispersed areas. The quantum bus allows for the distant entanglement of two transceiver qubits located in different locations. The contention for the transceiver qubits rises when gates are teleported, necessitating frequent use of the quantum bus.

However, large-scale applications will surely require fault-tolerantly created logical qubit states with encoded gates. Since the Bell measurement process necessitates two local cnot operations between the data qubits and the auxiliary qubits, the cnot gate structure in the above figure is not a fully teleported cnot gate. When data is exchanged between the control and target qubits, we can employ the more simpler teleportation-based cnot gate structure described in Reference if locally run cnot gates are permitted.

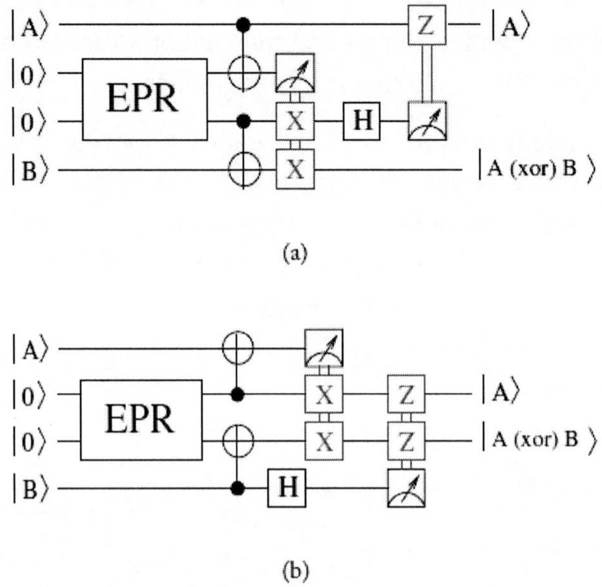

Fig.5.64 Two simplified "remote" cnot gate variations.

As an encoded EPR pair between the control and target qubits, Above Figure illustrates two variants of a teleported cnot gate that require just two auxiliary qubits.

Examining the ideal logical distances for conventional direct interaction cnot gates versus the greater distances for teleportation processes using distant data coupling would be an intriguing tradeoff. The N regions designated {R1,R2,...RN} in this architecture, which can be a distributed logical architecture, contain logical data qubits as well as logical accessory qubits that are used to create specialized states for gate teleportation. By doing this, the application's dependability might be greatly increased. Each section uses standard logical cnot gates for direct interaction. Inter-region cnot gates are implemented using the specific auxiliary qubits in each area, but the logical data never leaves to another region.

Because inter-region gates are teleported and logical gate distances between regions are comparatively short, this technique has the potential to greatly increase the architecture's reliability. Independent of the application's execution, the specialized states between areas can be created and their accuracy checked. By leveraging the shared quantum bus or entangling trapped ions via fiber optic cables, the individual qubits can be coupled remotely. For gate teleportation where Bell measurements are made, only specific states that successfully complete the verification processes will be employed. Naturally, this plan would necessitate a significant investment of resources in order to prepare the specialized ancillary states for gate teleportation.

The error correcting techniques required for each logical qubit tile would inevitably be included in the specialized ancillary qubits and logical data qubits, thus expanding the available error correction resources. To speed up quantum applications, gate teleportation would be an alternate construction. For instance, the first program operation can be carried out while teleporting the qubits to the processing zone if qubits Q1 and Q2 are needed for a specific series of operations and they are located in the memory region.

5.14.3 Errors Correction Using Teleportation

The potential error correction benefits of allocating enough network bandwidth to send encoded EPR pairs rather just elementary EPR pairs, as in the QLA architecture, are even more astounding. Take note of the connection between the closest EPR qubit and the control data qubit in Figure (a) above (lines 1 and 2). The series of operations between lines 1 and 2 is quite similar to the Steane method for error correction if the qubits are encoded using some CSS [[n, k, d]] code, such as the Steane code. In actuality, it is, and the measurement made when teleporting the gate is comparable to removing the data's error syndrome.

As a matter of fact, teleportation is error correction. Let's step back and look at the cnot gate, which is a conventional teleportation method that merely teleports quantum data. The logical measurement operation will accurately identify the qubit's encoded state if, by the time the Bell measurement is finished, there are less than $t = (d - 1)/2$ mistakes on the logical data. The destination EPR logical qubit will then recreate the right state. Another technique for fixing flaws in encoded data is teleportation, provided that the EPR qubit is sufficiently well distilled.

Knill has researched the fault-tolerance of linear optical structures employing teleportation as an error correction algorithm. He has developed comprehensive error-detecting coding algorithms and shown that scalable quantum computation can have an accuracy threshold of up to 1% error rate per physical gate. The logical states employed for computation are only accepted if no errors are found with a high enough probability, according to his post selected quantum computation approach. He demonstrates that the probability of error in his design may be arbitrarily decreased by post-selecting the output of the logical processes using straightforward four-and six-qubit concatenated quantum error detection codes. Teleportation of gates is the method used for all quantum logic.

Chapter - 6
Cloud Computing

Distributed computing refers to managing, accessing, and arranging online applications. It provides infrastructure, application, and a restriction on internet information.

Why is everyone staring at disjointed figures? Excessive, drawn-out IT expectations that are planned and executed with few core points for the exchange colleagues are typical. On the other hand, dispersed registration gives exchange clients the ability to instantly accept connections with use-based pricing that is customized to their needs, often without consulting the IT department. However, viewpoints verifying security, strategy, usability, and standards are frequently overlooked.

Purchasers of cloud services eventually become vulnerable to the cloud provider. Conditions that necessitate switching cloud providers in the event that one fails, as well as the associated transfer of data and extra apps, have not been sufficiently attempted. An important task should be recognized by business intelligibility right from the start of a cloud evaluation strategy. The integration of current knowledge and frameworks into the cloud strategy is most likely the best test in this case. Without negotiating across clouds and current frameworks, strategies should be implemented in segments, activating cloud-specific repositories of eliminated components.

Customers' basic data isn't accessible through various tactics and architectures. Problems that might have arisen inside the association's own IT department have been transferred to the cloud provider. Rebuilding "heritage hazes" or difficult-to-maintain blueprints requires proactive handling of the entire setup, particularly the cloud-based coordination. Cloud providers don't have to wait for us to notice something new; in other words, one strange piece of IT can be appropriated for cloud-based strategies.

As distributed computing continues to gain traction, structure heads are searching for more methods to manage control in order to integrate with their cloud appearance. All of the most obvious use cases for suitable enrollment are displayed here, necessitating further levels of modification. The state of the Cloud Programming Interface (API) has been influenced by the capacity to update cloud knowledge and have cross-cloud similarities. Specifically, heads may use these APIs to enable apps and unique professions that need to be carried out on the cloud. Focuses on being well-known for a while after recently engaging in conversation. i) Selecting the appropriate display from a natural standpoint, and ii) Integrating a programming interface into the cloud.

One way to think about the origins of distributed computing is as a series of advancements in matrix processing. From the outset, cloud computing is essentially built on modern system-based architecture, which uses grid organizations and integrates various innovations such as virtualization and action plans.

In summary, cloud computing is just a large number of individual PCs arranged in the same or distinct geographic areas, working together to provide different clients with varying needs and responsibilities on an as-needed basis through virtualization. Using a pay-per-use business model, cloud organizations are provided to cloud users as utility services like phone, internet, and water. These utility companies are commonly referred to as XaaS (X as a Service), where X can be software, a platform, a framework, and so forth. Cloud customers utilize these companies provided by cloud providers to create web applications, which they then present to their decision customers. Thus, cloud users don't need to be concerned about installing, maintaining, or upgrading any necessary PC software or hardware. They are also able to afford these services since they just have to pay for what they really utilize. Therefore, cloud users can use cloud organizations to reduce their usage and effort in their industry rather than establishing IT framework themselves.

In essence, widely distributed data communities provide cloud computing. The cloud is founded on the finest system administrators, and these server farms are frequently coordinated as a grid. Virtual images of the actual computers inside the server farms are provided to cloud clients. Since virtualization essentially creates a mirror over the actual structure, it is one of the fundamental concepts of distributed computing. A growing number of cloud apps are gaining recognition for their transparency, unwavering quality, adaptability, and usefulness. These programs made registration easier because the cloud provider handled all the important aspects.

Nowadays, distributed computing is becoming more and more popular among personal and professional groups, but it may also be useful for addressing societal concerns. E-Government is being implemented in modern nations to increase administrative appropriateness and effectiveness. By replacing traditional ICT with distributed computing, this technique can advance significantly. India's economy is centered on horticulture, and a sizable majority of the population lives in rural areas. When distributed computing is used properly, it may enhance rural proficiency, way of life, and other aspects of society. These two applications of distributed computing face equally formidable obstacles in their quest for survival.

6.1 Cloud Computing Fundamentals

One way to think about distributed computing is as a way to use spread processing to provide customers with utility-based figuring services that are available on demand. As a result, cloud users may provide their clients with more dependable, transparent, and up-to-date services. The cloud itself is made up of real computers housed in cloud providers' data centers. On the greatest of these real computers, virtualization is provided. The cloud clients receive these virtual computers. Cloud providers provide different levels of deliberation to their cloud enterprises. There are several types of cloud companies, such as Infrastructures as a Service, Platforms as a Service, and Software as a Service. These services are offered online throughout the whole virtual world, where the cloud serves as the only point of access for all clientele. Distributed computing architecture addresses large-scale data management issues.

6.2 Cloud Computing Regulations

Disseminated processing might be demonstrated for use-based structure admittance to a standard pool of quickly supplied and used customizable figure assets (e.g., workers, limit frameworks, applications, and associations). IP-based associations can be freely used online and requested via self-service. Principal for a broadband Web alliance that is typically idle. The IT resources are bundled into pools and distributed as needed. The associations that are used determine the charging.

6.3 Cloud Models

The following models in dispersed registering are divided according on smooth scaling: The cloud framework is managed, operated, and enabled by an outsider. Everyone can try their hand at anything being ascended to on the foundation. The organization is promoted to various clients via a standard structure. The untouchable provider who provides the assets and pays for their usage will grant the organizations access to the internet. Cloud computing suppliers and customers according to industry center and use case. Broad associations where IT recognizes a core function or confers with an advantage sometimes create "private clouds" in their worker farms to house secret association cloud techniques. Most small and medium-sized businesses employ open cloud associations.

6.4 Models for Cloud Deployment

Sending, displaying, organizing, limiting, and programming framework are provided in the cloud as associations that abruptly scale up or down based on user interest. Three rule association models are shown in the Cloud Computing presentation. These are:

Private Cloud

This type of cloud is maintained within an organization and is only used for internal analysis. Thus, given the current situation, the utility display is everything from a massive phrase. Many businesses are heading in this direction, and experts believe that a company's initial move onto the cloud should be made in this manner. Network throughput and security are not crucial problems for private clouds.

Public Cloud

Spread registering in the standard sense is portrayed by public or open clouds. This involves the powerful provisioning of resources on a fine-grained, self-Service prelude via the Web through web applications and web associations. These resources are provided by an off-website supplier who bills on a fine-grained utility basis. Compensation is routinely agreed upon for each usage delineate. Since public clouds place an additional burden on ensuring that all apps and data required on the basic people cloud are shielded from harmful attacks, they are less secure than alternative cloud models.

Hybrid Cloud

This type of cloud is composed of different external or inside clouds. This is usually the case when an organization transitions from its own private cloud to an external distributed computing environment. A half-and-half cloud is a private cloud that is connected to at least one external cloud association, half-managed, half-provisioned as a single entity, and enclosed by a secured framework. By combining an open and private cloak of haze, it provides virtual IT ways. Crossbreed Cloud allows many parties to originate data via the Web and provides safer control over the data and apps. Additionally, it has an open arrangement that facilitates integrating with various association frameworks.

Creamer Cloud can plan the connection of a nearby device, such as a Plug PC with cloud connections. It may also provide plans that connect virtual and physical resources in a coordinated way. For example, it can show a first segment virtualized state that needs real workers, switches, or other equipment, or it can show an outline of a system machine that serves as a firewall or spam channel.

Community Cloud

An unreachable managed expert center or a dispersed figuring solution for a certain number of individuals or affiliations that is handled, monitored, and obtained generally by all interested parties may be what is meant by a "people pack cloud."

Cloud Virtualization

A virtual private cloud (VPC) is a pool of shared recruiting assets that can be configured on demand and is allocated within an open cloud environment. It provides a precise estimate of separation between the obvious affiliations (perhaps future customers) that use the assets. In a virtual private cloud demonstration, the fundamental cultural foundation as-a-service (IaaS) provider is responsible for ensuring that each private cloud customer's data remains separate from each other's data both in transit and within the cloud provider's infrastructure.

6.5 Prerequisites

The criteria are divided into three sections. The first section consists of a set of general requirements on the IaaS for economically advantageous automated applications as distributed computing services; the second group consists of specific requirements on the robots that the IaaS facilitates; the third group consists of specific requirements on the algorithm to determine the best possible alliance for each assignment as a function of the robot network Level Virtualization carried out by the IaaS.

Given the circumstances, the robots don't belong in a business substance that is comparable, which suggests that there are a few IaaSs that are claimed by different company substances that employ these robots. Therefore, we have a look at a framework that consists of an IaaS and the crucial robots for the IaaS. After receiving a request for an errand from a PaaS, the IaaS contacts the robots—which are crucial to the IaaS—and sends them the request.

6.5.1 Requirement for the IaaS

The main prerequisite is the capacity to scale. It should be scalable, accommodating, and compatible with a large number of robots.

The next necessary condition is that the IaaS must have a generalized innovation for the connection interfaces, i.e., the interface that allows the connection between the IaaS and the robots that it facilitates, as well as the interface that connects the IaaS and the PaaS. For example, depending on each robot's supplier, the robots may support different interfaces in different scenarios. Regardless, the design ought to be able to communicate with the robots using a unified standard interface innovation.

Furthermore, a variety of interface-level improvements may be used by the Wildfire Suppression application, which requests that the IaaS use the PaaS to put out the fire. It should be possible for the IaaS and PaaS to communicate via standard interface innovation.

The third prerequisite is that the IaaS must provide confinement, which enables the operation of many automated applications on comparable IaaS. For example, two applications, such as the Degradation Location scenario and the Wildfire Suppression Application, may operate on comparable IaaS using different robot networks. One group of robots may be sent to continue putting out the fire somewhere in the forest, while another group of robots could be used to cover an area by keeping an eye out for the Subway Debasement Application.

Each application's execution should be completely independent of the other's operation; they shouldn't interfere in any way.

The ability for IaaS to support diverse robots is the fourth need. Owing to the diversity of robot vendors, the Infrastructure as a Service (IaaS) may comprise robots hosted by many vendors, each with a unique programming language and interface. Robots with a location with different merchants should be able to get assistance from the IaaS, which means the overall setup should be suitable for a variety of different types of robots.

Extensibility represents the fifth requirement. Future development should be considered in the arrangement; extensibility may be achieved by changing current practical parts or by introducing new practical substances, such as executive shortfalls that might improve the appearance of the IaaS. As a result, the solution should generally be expandable in order to include additional IaaS functions.

The ability for the IaaS to assign jobs to robots that can work with various clouds is another requirement. This is important in some situations, such as when there are too many or too few robots residing in one cloud to adequately complete a work, which might lead to an assignment being incomplete or completed in an inefficient manner. For example, in the Search and Salvage Robots scenario, the local cloud may not have a sufficient number of tiny robots (such as Snake Robots) that can reach areas that people or other machines cannot access. As a result, it may assign some tasks to small robots that are located in different clouds, allowing the task to be completed more successfully.

Finally, because we are handling dynamic situations, the IaaS must support Network Level Virtualization. Similarly, certain tasks that need to be completed collaboratively by several robots may be those that cannot be completed individually or that are resolved more successfully in groups. In an out-of-control fire suppression scenario, for example, one robot cannot perform the task of stifling the fire; instead, multiple robots must work together. As a result, a group of robots with the appropriate quantity and skill sets should be assembled and dedicated to the task of "smothering the fire" gradually.

6.5.2 Conditions for the Robots the IaaS Hosts

IaaS-integral robots ought to support Node Level Virtualization. This allows several apps to reside on and operate concurrently on a single robot, enabling the robot to run multiple applications concurrently without any interference. Instead of using different robots for each work in the Subway Degradation Detection scenario, a group of the same robots may be used to provide continuous recordings and cover an area by monitoring using different sensors for each task.

6.5.3 The Network Level Virtualization Algorithm's requirements

The calculation's key requirement is that it must be multi-measures, which means it must consider both static and dynamic standards: Robots' sensors and actuators are examples of static rules, whereas their location, battery, kind of administration, and other attributes are examples of dynamic rules or standards that may vary over time. The second need is that the computation should be able to streamline different destinations, meaning that it should be able to limit or extend several target tasks simultaneously while keeping an eye out for compromises between at least two competing objectives. For example, there are competing objectives when it comes to decreasing the amount of time needed to put out the fire and, at the same time, keeping the cost of the robot network low. The third requirement is that since the robots have limited communication capabilities, the algorithm should reduce or eliminate any communication between them as much as is reasonable.

When a single robot is unable to complete a job on its own, the algorithm must have the capability to select between an alliance or a group of robots for that assignment. This completes the fourth condition. In the Wildfire Concealment scenario, one robot is unable to put out a fire that is happening in a forest; therefore, a group of robots is needed. Additionally, the algorithm should use explicit filtering and placement techniques or capacity to choose the subset of robots for a certain job. These strategies help make different robots available for various tasks and restrict the number of robots the algorithm runs on, which reduces the algorithm's reaction time.

The method must also have a respectable reaction time, which implies that its processing time must be kept to a minimum and should not exceed reasonable bounds. In fact, the algorithm's assembly season need to be kept as short as possible, even on incredible real computers. Some situations are time-sensitive, and the algorithm should produce results quickly.

The program should also optimize the situation's assets, which are the robots. Overall, the algorithm should restrict the number of robots in a single group performing a comparable activity; this will enable robots to be utilized for various tasks. In order to fulfill the cost agreed upon with the customer, the algorithm should also cap the cost of sending a robot to do a work that is supplied.

The last prerequisite is that the algorithm should set a time restriction on how long a group of robots should be able to complete a task. It is evident that the final three conditions have been compromised. Reducing the amount of time needed to complete a job that requires more exceptional robots also necessitates having more robots in one group, which means increasing the cost of robot arrangement and the number of robots in one group.

6.6 Cloud AI

Cloud computing services have evolved beyond platforms like Google App Engine and Azure to infrastructure, which consists of setting up servers for capacity and registration. Additionally, cloud providers provide information stage services that cover a variety of available data types. The advancement of cloud computing and artificial intelligence is the main goal of this chain of improvements.

Cloud providers that have AI capabilities built into their systems include IBM, Amazon, Microsoft, and Google. They provide AI cloud services and cloud machine learning platforms, including PC vision, powerful text analysis, strong speech recognition, fast dynamic translation, intelligent search, intelligent language, and intelligent information. Artificial Intelligence is the power of a new generation of cloud computing. We cover the uses of AI in cloud computing in this book, specifically in relation to cloud machine learning platforms and cloud AI services.

The foundation of intelligent cloud computing is the union of cloud computing with artificial intelligence. Similar to cloud machine learning (ML) platforms and artificial intelligence cloud services, providers are also offering AI as a cloud service. It is a rapid, massively scalable, and easily navigable machine learning service. It provides modern AI services, including pre-made models and help in creating your own custom-fit models. The Google Cloud Vision API enables developers to easily integrate vision discovery features into applications, such as photo labeling, face and milestone recognition, optical character recognition (OCR), and unambiguous substance labeling.

Engineers of various skill levels may easily use AI innovation with the help of Amazon Machine Learning. Without needing to understand intricate AI computations and creativity, Amazon Machine Learning provides visualization tools and wizards that walk you through the process of creating AI models. Microsoft Azure Machine Learning is a fully managed cloud service that enables you to create, send, and share visionary research plans with ease. With only a few lines of code, Microsoft Cognitive Services provides an Intelligent Cloud Environment for developing applications with amazing computations. IBM Watson is a stage of innovation that extracts knowledge from vast amounts of unstructured data by using artificial intelligence and natural language processing.

1. Cloud-based machine learning

a. The Machine Learning Platform on Google Cloud

It is an easy-to-use, vastly expansive, and rapid machine learning solution. Several features of the Google Cloud Machine Learning Platform are explained below:

Mainstream Machine Learning:

The Google Cloud AI Platform provides modern AI services, including pre-made models and assistance in creating your own unique models. When compared to alternative massively expansive deep learning frameworks, their neural net-based machine learning stage exhibits improved accuracy and better preparation execution. Its administrations are easy to use, rapid, and versatile. Cloud Machine Picking up is used by important Google apps including Translate, Inbox, Voice Search, Photos (image search), and the Google application. Their base may now be accessed as a cloud administration, giving commercial applications unmatched speed and scale.

Large-Scale Machine Learning Service:

With Google Cloud Machine Learning, you can easily put together cutting-edge, very comprehensive AI models that address a variety of scenarios, from developing complex relapse models to characterizing images. You can definitely get your models ready because it is a flexible, fully managed, and integrated product with other Google Cloud Data Platform goods like Google Cloud Storage, Google Cloud Dataflow, and Google Cloud Data lab.

Strong Image Analysis:

By typifying amazing AI models in an easy-to-use REST API, the Google Cloud Vision Programming interface enables you to understand the content of an image. It quickly classifies images into several groups, identifies individual objects and appearances inside images, and locates and reads printed text embedded within images.

Strong Speech Recognition:

Using neural organization models in an easy-to-use programming interface, the Google Cloud Discourse API enables you to convert sound into message. The API can understand over 80 different languages and variants, which will benefit your global clientele. Among many other use cases, you may empower order and control by speech or interpret the content of clients directed to an application's recipient.

Robust Text Analysis:

With its incredible AI models in an easy-to-use REST API, Google Natural Language API reveals the structure and significance of text. It may be used to extract information on people, places, events, and much more that is mentioned in text reports, news articles, or blog posts. It may also be used to interpret customer conversations that take place in a contact center or informational application, or to understand the perspective of your product on social media.

Quick and Dynamic Translation:

The Google Cloud Decipher API provides a simple automated interface for interpreting a given text into any supported language using judgment. Because of the outstanding responsiveness of Interpret API, websites and applications may integrate it to interpret source text dynamically and quickly from a source language into an objective language.

b. Amazon Machine Learning:

This tool facilitates the use of AI innovation by engineers with varying degrees of expertise. Amazon Machine Learning provides visualization tools in addition to wizards that walk you through the process of creating AI models without requiring you to understand intricate AI computations and creativity. Once your models are ready, Amazon AI streamlines the process of obtaining predictions for your application using easy APIs, eliminating the need for proprietary expectation age code calculations or framework management.

Amazon Machine Learning is predicated on a similarly proven, incredibly adaptable AI invention that Amazon's internal information research team has been using for quite some time. It makes use of amazing computations to create Machine Language models by identifying patterns in the data we already have. At that moment, these models are used by Amazon Machine Learning to process fresh data and generate predictions for your application. With Amazon Machine Learning, you can start small and grow as your application grows. It is incredibly flexible and can create billions of expectations every day, all while serving those expectations continuously and at a high throughput. Additionally, there is no upfront equipment or programming required.

c. Microsoft Azure Machine Learning:

Currently included in the Cortana Intelligence package, this is an incredible cloud-based analysis tool. It is a fully managed cloud service that enables you to quickly create, distribute, and share vision assessment plans. Azure Machine Learning Studio has support for custom code and several implicit bundles. Applied machine learning was the planned use for it. Go from idea to organization in a matter of seconds by using advanced calculations and a simple drag-and-drop interface. Azure Machine Learning suggests a commercial endeavor. In just a few minutes, you can turn your model into a web application that can be accessed from anywhere, on any device, and with any information source.

2. Cloud Services for AI

a. Microsoft Cognitive Services:

With only a few lines of code, Microsoft Cognitive Administrations provides an intelligent cloud environment for developing applications with amazing computations. They are easy to set up, continue to improve, and function with iPhone, Android, and Windows devices and platforms.

Below, Microsoft Cognitive Services provide clarification:

- **Perception**
    - Computer Vision API: Extract important information from images.
    - Emotion API: Customize interactions by identifying emotions
    - Face API: Identify, separate, inspect, organize, and label faces in images.
    - Video API: Examine, modify, and gauge recordings within your program.

- **Oration**
    - Bing Speech API: Translate speech to message and back again, and understand its purpose.
    - Custom Recognition Intelligent Service (CRIS): Accurate discourse recognition for all users, anywhere.
    - Provide your application with the ability to identify who is speaking with the Speaker Recognition API.
- **Phonology**
    - Bing Spell Check API: Recognize and correct spelling errors inside your program.
    - Master the language your apps need to understand the orders that come in from your customers using Language Understanding Intelligent Service (LUIS).
    - Easy parsing of complicated information through linguistic study is possible with the Linguistic Analysis API.
    - Text Analytics API: Extract concepts, keywords, themes, and language from your text.
    - Web Language Model API: Utilize the power of language models built using data at web scale.
- **Expertise**
    - Academic information API: Examine the relationships between academic publications, diaries, and authors.
    - The Intelligence Service that links entities:
    - Logically expand knowledge about people, places, and events.
    - Knowledge Exploration Service: Enhance your project with a strategic search over well-organized data.
    - Recommendations API: Offer your customers personalized item recommendations.
- **Examine**
    - Give your application look-ahead alternatives based on Bing Autosuggest API.
    - Integrate advanced image and information search into your application using the Bing Image Search API.
    - Connect your clients to the best and most suitable news look using the Bing News Search API.

- The Bing Video Search API offers rich results, detailed metadata, and trending records.
- Integrate outstanding search into your apps using the Bing Web Search API.

b. API for Google Cloud Vision:

The Cloud Vision API enables application developers to integrate vision recognition features into their work efficiently. One such feature is the Face API, which can be used to detect, identify, analyze, and categorize faces in photos, locate faces and milestones, recognize optical character recognition (OCR), and label clear materials.

Google Cloud Vision API provides the following kinds of support, which are explained below:

Robust Image Analysis:

The Google Cloud Vision Programming interface, which embodies amazing machine learning models in an easy-to-use REST API, enables designers to understand the content of a photo. It quickly classifies images into several groups, identifies individual objects and appearances inside images, and locates and reads printed text embedded within images. You may add fake metadata to your photo library, control offensive content, or, conversely, create new exhibition scenarios by using photo end analysis. Examine images uploaded upon request or combine with your Google Cloud Storage photo collection.

Gain Understanding From Your Photos:

Recognize a broad range of objects in your photos, such as flowers, animals, cars, and many more item classes that are typically present inside photos. After some time, when new concepts are introduced and accuracy is increased, Vision API gets better.

Identify Unsuitable Content:

Use Google Safe Search to efficiently filter content from your publicly accessible images. The Vision API gives you the ability to recognize a wide range of inappropriate content, from mature to violent material.

Image Sentiment Analysis:

Vision API can analyze the intense facial expressions of people in your photos, including joy, anguish, and fury. Combine this with item and object logo identification so you can assess people's perceptions of your logo.

Excerpt:

Identify landmarks and man-made structures inside an image using landmark detection. Together with programmed language identification evidence, optical character recognition (OCR) enables you to discern text inside your images. A large array of languages is supported by Vision API. The following are some highlights provided by the Google Cloud Vision API:

Label detection: Find diverse groupings of classes inside an image, ranging from modes of transportation to animals.

Identify explicit material in an image, such as mature or violent content.

Identify popular product logos within an image using logo detection.

Identify the general attributes of the image, such as the predominant shade.

Integrated REST API: Use the REST API to request at least one kind of remark for each image. Images can be coordinated with Google Cloud Storage or shared in the request for proposals.

Optical Character Recognition: Locate and focus text inside an image, supporting a wide range of dialects in addition to preprogrammed language recognition evidence.

Face Detection: Identify several faces in an image together with the associated important facial features, such as a passionate expression or the wearing of a headpiece. Facial Recognition is not maintained.

c. Watson from IBM:

IBM Watson is a stage of innovation that leverages machine learning and natural language processing to extract experiences from vast amounts of unstructured data. A variety of language, discourse, vision, and information APIs are available through the Watson Developers Cloud to enhance your application's intellectual features.

6.6.1 Cloud Computing's AI-Powered Infrastructure

Creation of Machine Learning (ML) models: When a vast amount of data is required for certain computations, it becomes necessary to use the cloud for this. The different instances that are obtained from the available data might benefit the models.

The more data we feed this algorithm, the more accurate and precise the forecast becomes. For instance, a significant amount of radiology reports are used to construct the framework for machine learning models that identify cancers. Any industry can use this example since it can be modified to meet the specific demands of the enterprise. The required information is there, and it is available in a variety of formats, including unstructured and primitive information.

Owing to sophisticated computation techniques that need a combination of CPUs and GPUs, cloud providers now provide virtual machines with GPUs that are just impossibly powerful. Furthermore, AI projects are currently being automated with the use of services like serverless computing, compartment organization, and cluster preparation. Additionally, IaaS aids in the management of vision analysis.

6.6.2 Intelligence services based on computers for cloud computing

Indeed, it is possible to value services that are equivalent to those provided by AI frameworks even in the absence of creating an engaging machine learning model. Designers can use, for instance, text analysis, conversation, vision, and machine language interpretation. In a sense, they may integrate this into their programs for betterment.

Distributed computing vendors are managing to ensure that these services are continuously enhanced even though they are not exclusive or tailored to certain uses. A paradigm known as psychological processing enables clients to provide their unique information, which is then prepared to provide clear services. Finding the appropriate preparation model or fitting computation is therefore eliminated.

Benefits of Using Cloud Computing and AI

Cost-Effectiveness

The cloud application enhancement eliminates the need for expensive local programming and equipment purchases and arrangements by being accessible over the internet. It also eliminates the need for on-site server farms and the associated expenses of hiring staff, maintaining the servers, and providing constant electricity to run the servers' cooling systems and IT departments.

Expanded Productivity

Distributed computing is entirely web-based, therefore it doesn't require any IT executives to handle chores like programming, racking, and stacking, which are all necessary for a hard drive or local storage device. This allows the IT team to concentrate on achieving other business goals.

Steadfastness

There is more risk of damage when there is a hard drive or when the foundation is really exposed. One must deal with the risk of an accident, misplaced paperwork, and reinforcing disappointment, among other things. Distributed computing architectures, however, ensure information reinforcement, faster and easier disaster recovery, and business coherence.

Advanced Infrastructure Availability

Generally speaking, artificial intelligence applications perform better on workers with several, incredibly fast Graphics Processing Units (GPUs). In any case, these frameworks are extremely expensive and excessive for certain associations. These associations can access artificial intelligence (AI) for cloud application development at a lower cost.

Using AI to Power a Self-Managing Cloud

IT foundations are being equipped with artificial intelligence to automate tedious tasks and streamline workflows. Some have gone so far as to predict that when AI becomes more sophisticated, both private and public cloud scenarios would rely on these AI capabilities to monitor, screen, and, shockingly, self-repair when a problem arises. First, AI may be used to automate essential labor activities. Later, over time, intelligent capabilities can create superior, mostly autonomous cycles. The real framework has the ability to monitor routine cycles, which helps IT teams even more to realize the benefits of distributed computing and focus on more important but higher-value tasks.

Using AI to Improve Data Management

Artificial intelligence tools are also enhancing data management at the cloud level. Think about the massive information archives that today's enterprises create and amass, as well as the cycle of essentially managing that infrastructure—identifying data, consuming it, indexing it, and managing it over an extended period of time. Artificial intelligence (AI) devices are being used in distributed computing configurations to help with certain aspects of information interaction. For example, in the banking industry, even the smallest financial institution could need to review a significant volume of transactions every day.

Computer-based intelligence tools can facilitate the process of ingesting, updating, and managing data, allowing financial institutions to provide clients with accurate and up-to-date information more efficiently. An analogous interaction can also aid in identifying various danger zones or banner dishonest movement. Similar improvements can have a big impact on areas like client service, advertising, and shop network information for executives.

Finishing Up Additional AI-SaaS Integration

In order to provide greater value, automated reasoning devices are also being used as a component of larger Software-as-a-Service (SaaS) platforms. SaaS providers are gradually integrating AI tools into their larger programming suites to provide end users with greater utility and value. We ought to look into one well-known model: Salesforce's Einstein AI system for customer relationship management. A CRM's value lies in its ability to be anything except a copious amount of client data, while also simplifying client relationships and collaboration customization. But there is often too much information available.

Salesforce acquainted Einstein with assistance transform information into significant bits of knowledge organizations can use to sell more, improve their business methodologies, and draw in with clients. The instruments can help a business search for designs in client associations, for instance, to help exhort deals on what strategy like telephone, email, or an in-person meeting–is bound to drive a change. It can likewise be utilized to make "subsequent stage" suggestions dependent on the purchasing signals the apparatus is seeing.

Making Use of Dynamic Cloud Services

The employment of computer-based intelligence as a tool is also altering how businesses rely on their equipment. Think about a cloud-based retail module that streamlines the selling process for brands. The module has a valuation highlight that, when used, may alter the evaluation of an item that is being given to reflect factors such as interest, stock levels, competitor deals, and market trends. Organizations may get a far better order of their information through complex analysis that relies on presenting tugging on deep neural networks, with important ongoing implications. For example, an AI-managed estimating module ensures that an organization's valuation will constantly be improved. The challenging part of using information is initiating the study and then putting it into action without the need for human intervention.

Every aspect of business is evolving due to distributed computing and artificial intelligence. The prospect is encouraging from deeper understanding of how to tackle competing computerization of important cycles. Even if there are now a few examples of this on the market, a quick look suggests that more will continue to appear in the years to come. Investigate how distributed computing and AI may work together to help you communicate experiences, do tasks more efficiently, and extract the most value from the knowledge and insights you acquire while keeping an eye out.

6.6.3 Benefits and drawbacks of using AI infrastructure for cloud computing

Upsides

Progress in Information Technology Infrastructure: The competition is already fierce and will only get stronger as more projects aim to update and enhance their cycles. Blends of capacity and asset figures expedite the cycle and improve framework platform planning. However, artificial intelligence (AI) is a relatively recent development, and its application in the workplace is yielding notable advantages. A prime example of elevated consumption is Cortana.

Unbounded Data Accessibility: AI systems have been able to make better, more intelligent judgments by utilizing the vast amount of information that is currently available. Organizational dynamic cycles can be accelerated by making more thoughtful decisions. Regular information flow leads to a large-scale expansion of an organization's capacity quickly. A real example of how this is applied in significant ways, such as combating cybercrime, is IBM's Watson.

Cost-cutting: The desire for a certain blend is greatly influenced by economics. It is evident that a significant reduction in expenses will result from the innovation pair's acceleration measure and positive results. Organizations will ask for more and more of these procedures due to cost considerations. These days, on-site storage devices are costly and repetitious.

Benefits of Analytics: Specializations and a high level of preparation allow for effective research. Investigating pertinent facts might lead to improved outcomes. Above all, it is completed at a lesser cost. Various organizations working on related information gathering tasks might provide unique and important sources of data. Human effort can stray into more expansive and stimulating pursuits. Artificial intelligence provides insightful predictions to help increase adequacy and increase benefits.

Improved decision-making ability: By optimizing informational indices and streamlining organizational operations, individuals will be able to make more informed decisions based on flexible assumptions and documented information architectures. Visionaries in business always get the benefits of this extra advantage.

Encouraging Dynamism: AI offers clients a distinct learning advantage because of the way this discipline is always evolving, learning, and improving over time. Organizations may become more versatile and adaptive through planned changes and improved information organization. In this way, markets gain by using these interactions to support their operations.

Downsides:

Inaccuracy Probability: Artificial intelligence (AI) may seem exciting, but like other research, it isn't always successful in achieving goals. In a scenario from 2016, the AI tool attempted to learn and provided some hazy remarks on contentious topics in the process. Given the vast range of possible outcomes when dealing with AI, there is where errors are most likely to occur. We don't fully understand this interaction enough to let it guide decisions just yet. In a different scenario, the potential consequences were concerning when Facebook's AI program was terminated due to the language the AI started creating on its own. Creating a sense of control and trust is necessary before using this innovation.

Chapter - 7
Quantum Cloud Computing

By providing quantum-resistant encryption and decryption services, quantum cloud services can shield data from any dangers posed by quantum computers. By doing this, the long-term security of data processed and stored on the cloud is guaranteed. Complex quantum systems, such chemical reactions and material properties, can be simulated with previously unheard-of accuracy using quantum cloud computing. This has uses in quantum chemistry, materials science, and drug development. The underlying structure and materials that make it possible to offer quantum computing services via cloud platforms are referred to as quantum cloud infrastructure. It blends cloud computing's scalability, accessibility, and ease of use with the ideas of quantum computing.

By enabling academics, companies, and developers to access and use quantum hardware and software remotely via the internet, quantum cloud infrastructure seeks to make quantum computing resources accessible to a wider range of users. This includes the actual quantum devices that carry out quantum computing, such as qubit arrays and processors. Building and maintaining quantum technology can be costly, and its efficient operation necessitates very low temperatures. This hardware must be managed and maintained by quantum cloud providers. The software layer of quantum cloud infrastructure enables users to program and manage quantum devices. Typically, these consist of quantum software libraries, quantum development kits (QDKs), and quantum programming languages. Quipper, Cirq, and Qiskit are well-known examples.

Remote Access: The resources of quantum computing are accessible to users remotely thanks to quantum cloud infrastructure. The cloud service provider performs calculations on the available quantum hardware after receiving quantum tasks and algorithms from users. By using this remote access, customers can take use of quantum computing capability without needing to buy pricey quantum hardware. The management and optimization of quantum resource distribution to consumers falls under the purview of quantum cloud providers. They have to deal with things like scheduling, resource reserve, and queue management to guarantee that quantum processors are used effectively. Both conventional and quantum processing are used in many quantum computations. It must be possible for quantum cloud infrastructure to seamlessly integrate quantum and classical components so that users can run hybrid quantum-classical algorithms.

Strong security measures must be in place to safeguard user data and guarantee the security of quantum computations because quantum cloud computing deals with sensitive data and encryption. Quantum-resistant encryption techniques and defenses against quantum hacking might fall under this category. Large-scale quantum cloud infrastructure construction is a constant issue. The development of quantum computers is still in its infancy, and it is difficult to scale up quantum hardware while preserving qubit coherence durations. As their offerings grow, quantum cloud providers must deal with scalability concerns. User-friendly tools and interfaces are frequently offered by quantum cloud infrastructure to make quantum programming and task submission easier. The purpose of these interfaces is to enable a wider range of people, including those without substantial quantum knowledge, to access quantum computers.

Quantum computers are prone to faults and extremely sensitive to their surroundings. For dependable quantum cloud computing, effective quantum error correction codes must be developed. Large-scale quantum cloud infrastructure construction is a difficult and expensive undertaking. There are still issues with scaling quantum hardware and guaranteeing adequate qubit coherence times. Through quantum-resistant encryption, quantum cloud computing improves security, but it also presents new security threats. One of the top priorities is defending quantum systems from threats like quantum hacking. It is not easy to integrate quantum and conventional computing systems. For real-world uses, hybrid quantum-classical algorithms and interfaces must be created.

7.1 Cloud Computing Beneath Quantum

Although quantum technology has advanced quickly, the day when every household or business possesses a quantum computer is still a long way off. Early quantum computing will probably rely on a quantum "cloud," where consumers submit computation jobs and data to a cutting-edge quantum computer housed by Google, IBM, or another business. Is that strategy safe, though? Because quantum-based protocols provide unbreakable confidentiality, it is possible. Using trapped ions, a recent experiment illustrates a form of "blind quantum computing" [1]. Because the protocol is scalable, it has the ability to be integrated into ever-bigger quantum computing platforms.

In computationally demanding fields like drug discovery and material design, quantum computers might prove revolutionary. Using a cloud-based quantum computer would raise questions in these fiercely competitive industries. According to Peter Drmota of the University of Oxford in the UK, "a company looking for a new wonder drug or for a high-performance battery material wouldn't want to reveal confidential secrets." On the other hand, it has been demonstrated—in theory—that calculations may be carried out on a distant quantum computer while the data and the operations performed on it are concealed. According to Drmota, "a client could feel more confident using whoever's quantum computer with blind quantum computing."

Previous research on blind quantum computing with photonic methods has been conducted by several groups. The primary drawback of these configurations is their probabilistic nature, which necessitates repeated trials and post selection of the intended output since quantum entanglement processes occasionally succeed and sometimes fail. "It is difficult to perform blind quantum computing using only photons due to the lack of deterministic entangling operations," says Joe Fitzsimons of Horizon Quantum Computing, a firm that creates integrated software for quantum computers. The community has been waiting for a demonstration of blind quantum computing utilizing matter-based qubits, as opposed to photon-based qubits, according to Fitzsimons, who was not engaged in this work.

Drmota and associates have successfully shown this using a basic blind quantum computing setup consisting of two trapped ions, strontium and calcium. With its extended coherence durations, the calcium ion functions as a memory qubit, while the strontium ion serves as the network qubit that transmits photons to a "client." The two ions work together to form the quantum cloud system's "server."

The network qubit transmits a photon to the client over an optical fiber as the first step in the team's blind computing protocol. The two objects are quantum entangled as the polarization of the photon depends on the electronic state of the network ion. By measuring the state of the photon, the client use that entanglement to "steer" the ion's state. In particular, the customer selects the orientation of the polarization measuring equipment in secret while measuring the photon's polarization. The client prepares the network qubit's state using this measurement. "The entire system 'collapses' into a specific state that only the client is aware of," claims Dominik Leichtle, a team member from France's Sorbonne University. "The server does not know which state the network qubit ends up in because it is unaware of the measurement."

Nonetheless, the network qubit's information may be processed by the server using a laser-based procedure that entangles the network qubit and the memory qubit. Information that can be utilized in later protocol rounds is stored in the memory qubit. To proceed with the calculation, the client sends a message to the server via a standard communication line. The message instructs the server to measure the network qubit's spin along a certain axis and relay the results back to the client. The server then sends another photon to the client, and the entire process is repeated.

The group encrypts data via a technique known as "one-time-pad encryption" in order to better guarantee the protocol's security. Using this method, additional rotations are added to the instructions supplied to the server by the client, which creates a list of random integers. According to Drmota, "everything that leaves the client and everything that is brought back to the client is gibberish." The server is oblivious to the meaning of the data and the processes because of this encryption. However, the client's list of random numbers may be used to decode the gibberish.

Also, the client has a means of verifying that the computation is being performed accurately. According to Leichtle, this kind of verification is crucial to establishing confidence in a quantum computer that is uncontrollable or prone to mistakes. Verification techniques were developed in the past, but they usually needed a lot of computer power. A more effective approach was created by Leichtle and his associates, which entails testing these dummy inputs while alternating actual data with fake data. Using the two-ion setup, the researchers put this procedure into practice and demonstrated how a client could confirm the accuracy of the quantum calculations.

The group's initial presentation revealed that the client may instruct the server to carry out a straightforward quantum operation known as a qubit rotation. The customer discovered a fringe pattern when the data was analyzed and decrypted, which was the anticipated outcome. By adding more memory qubits, the trapped-ion system may be made more powerful, capable of calculating more complex operations. It won't be easy to connect all these qubits together, but quantum information experts have demonstrated that they can do it with several tens of trapped ions, and systems with 1000 ions have been proposed. According to Drmota and Leichtle, their blind quantum computing method can "scale" in line with the advancement of this technology. "We define 'scalable' as the ability of the client apparatus and interface to remain unchanged regardless of the size of the server," Drmota explains.

According to Canadian quantum information specialist Anne Broadbent of the University of Ottawa, "the recent demonstration of blind quantum computing using trapped ions and photonic detection represents a significant milestone toward scalable and secure quantum communication." "These advancements open the door to a quantum Internet that guarantees privacy and verifiability as we approach practical deployment." Fitzsimons concurs, pointing out that in order to link matter qubits to a photon-based communication network, the researchers had to overcome considerable technological obstacles.

Process of cloud-based quantum computing

Imagine computing at seemingly unthinkable speeds, where bits can exist in numerous states at once, and where the rules of classical physics no longer apply. The rules of information processing are being rewritten by quantum computing. Welcome to the quantum universe. Moreover, cloud computing has made this remarkable technology more widely available than ever before. Examining its practical uses and the revolutionary possibilities it presents for our digital future, let's take an intriguing look into the realm of cloud-based quantum computing.

How does cloud computing for quantum computing operate?

The potential of cloud computing combined with the scalability and accessibility of quantum computing is known as cloud computing. Users don't require specialized hardware to conduct quantum algorithms or access quantum resources via the cloud.

Throughout a computation, these processes allow for the manipulation and modification of quantum information.

Cloud-Based Quantum Computing Applications

Researchers and companies may address challenging issues and open up new knowledge frontiers by utilizing the potential of quantum algorithms and resources. Let's examine a few of the most important cloud-based uses for quantum computing.

Research on Operations and Optimization

Complex optimization problems can be solved at a never-before-seen speed by quantum algorithms such as the Quantum Annealing Algorithm and the Quantum Approximate Optimization Algorithm (QAOA). Businesses can optimize their operations and make well-informed decisions based on quantum-optimized solutions by using cloud-based quantum computing platforms to test and develop these algorithms.

Machine Learning at Quantum Level

The capabilities of quantum computing with the ideas of machine learning are combined in the new field of quantum machine learning. In order to improve data analysis and pattern recognition tasks, researchers can investigate quantum machine learning algorithms in the cloud that take advantage of the special characteristics of quantum systems. In fields including natural language processing, quantum chemistry, cryptography, and financial modeling, QML algorithms may perform better than traditional machine learning methods, opening the door to fresh insights from intricate datasets.

Material Science and Drug Discovery

The fields of material science and drug research stand to benefit greatly from quantum computing. Molecular interactions, which are crucial for comprehending chemical events, forecasting the characteristics of materials, and creating novel medications, can be precisely modeled using quantum simulations. Researchers can drastically cut down on the time and expense associated with drug development and material science research by using the cloud's quantum computing capabilities to speed up the modeling of complicated molecules. This opens the door for ground-breaking developments in material engineering and healthcare by allowing researchers to investigate new chemicals, optimize medicine prospects, and find materials with specific qualities.

Cloud Computing's Prospects for Quantum Computing

As long as hardware, software, and algorithmic developments continue, quantum computing has enormous potential for breakthroughs and advancements. It will have an impact on a number of businesses and sectors, spurring creativity, facilitating breakthroughs, and changing how we approach challenging challenges. By taking advantage of opportunities and overcoming obstacles, we may fully utilize cloud-based quantum computing and usher in a new era of technological advancement.

Quantum Computing Developments

The future of quantum computing is being shaped by a number of new trends as the science develops further:

a) **Growing Qubit Counts:** The goal of increasing the number of qubits in quantum computers is driving the rapid advancement of quantum technology. Quantum computers will grow more potent and able to tackle bigger and more challenging tasks as the number of qubits increases.

b) **Error Correction and Noise Mitigation:** To increase the stability and dependability of quantum calculations, research into error correction methods and noise mitigation is essential. Quantum computers will produce more accurate and dependable results because to developments in mistake mitigation techniques and error correction codes.

c) **Hybrid Quantum-Classical Architectures:** These architectures effectively tackle complicated problems by combining the advantages of quantum and classical computing. These designs transfer computationally demanding jobs to quantum processors while using classical computers for preparation and post processing. This method creates new possibilities for resolving issues that traditional computing cannot handle.

Benefits of Quantum Computing

Users can use quantum computing systems hosted in the cloud, eliminating the need for large upfront infrastructure investments. All revolutionary technologies, however, have advantages and disadvantages. Let us examine the advantages and challenges of cloud-based quantum computing and see how quantum computing providers are tackling these issues.

Accessibility: Cloud-based quantum computing makes this state-of-the-art technology more widely available. Prior to now, only well-funded organizations and specialized research institutions could use quantum computing. Platforms for cloud-based quantum computing, like AWS Quantum Computing, Google Quantum Computing, IBM Quantum Experience, and Microsoft Azure Quantum, offer an easy-to-use interface and infrastructure for conducting quantum simulations and experimenting with quantum algorithms. Because of its accessibility, companies, developers, and researchers can investigate the possibilities of quantum computing without having to make significant infrastructure and hardware investments.

Scalability: To meet growing demand and new developments in quantum hardware, cloud providers can dynamically scale their quantum infrastructure. Cloud users can benefit from these developments without having to significantly alter their own infrastructure as quantum computers and qubit counts rise.

Flexibility and Experimentation: Users can test algorithms and model quantum circuits using cloud-based quantum simulators without requiring actual quantum hardware. Rapid prototyping, algorithm development, and the investigation of novel use cases are made possible by this flexibility, which promotes creativity and discovery.

Collaboration & Community: Cloud-based platforms for quantum computing make it easier for academics, developers, and enthusiasts to work together on quantum projects and exchange ideas and knowledge. By creating a dynamic community that pushes the limits of the new technology, this collaborative environment aids in the acceleration of quantum computing developments.

Quantum computing's ethical and societal ramifications

A number of ethical and societal issues are raised by the technology's enormous capability and promise. Examining the moral ramifications, mitigating possible hazards, and guaranteeing the appropriate and moral application of quantum computing technology are all vital as this technology develops.

Concerns regarding data security and privacy are raised by the possibility that quantum computing would defeat conventional cryptography algorithms. As encryption methods that are immune to quantum errors are created, it is critical to secure private rights and sensitive data.

Bias and Fairness: As quantum machine learning algorithms advance, it is critical to address concerns about transparency, bias, and fairness. It is important to make sure that quantum machine learning models are equitable, open, and responsible by preventing the spread of biases found in training data.

Intellectual Property and Patenting: The development of quantum computing may result in discoveries that have important ramifications for intellectual property. Ownership, patentability, and sharing of innovations in quantum computing are all questioned. To encourage innovation while preserving intellectual property rights, it is essential to create inclusive and equitable laws.

Regulations and Ethical Frameworks: It is crucial to establish rules, guidelines, and ethical frameworks for the creation, use, and usage of quantum computing. Concerns like responsibility, equity, privacy, and the prudent use of sensitive data should all be covered by these frameworks.

Global Cooperation: Addressing ethical and sociological ramifications on a global scale requires international cooperation and coordination between governments, organizations, and researchers. Best practices, regulations, and ethical standards that encourage the appropriate use of quantum computing technologies can be developed through cooperative initiatives.

Ethical Education and Public Awareness: It's critical to raise public knowledge and educate people about quantum computing and its moral ramifications. Promoting candid discussion and public involvement can aid in improving knowledge of the technology and its possible effects, enabling people to make morally sound choices and influence laws.

Cloud-based quantum computing is here to stay, and its revolutionary potential is set to completely change our digital future. You may open up new possibilities, resolve challenging issues, and start a new era of creativity by utilizing the potential of this remarkable technology. As the rules of information processing are being rewritten and the limits of what is conceivable are being pushed beyond comprehension, it is an exciting time to be in the vanguard of this quantum revolution.

7.2 Cutting Edge of Quantum Cloud Computing

Quantum Cloud Computing (QCC) is a new computational paradigm that combines cloud computing and quantum computing concepts to perform quantum calculations on cloud-based quantum platforms. This concept democratizes access to quantum computing capabilities by enabling quantum computational resources to be made available either privately within a particular business through a protected network or openly via the Internet (public quantum cloud). Without having to buy their own quantum gear, users may do tasks requiring quantum computing thanks to QCC. Users engage with these quantum computing resources via a cloud interface, as shown in the image below, and utilize APIs to obtain software as a service.

Large-scale quantum applications may be broken down into micro services and quantum functions using this paradigm, which makes it easier for them to be effectively deployed and maintained on cloud-based platforms. The cloud platform includes all the necessary parts to manage resource allocation, networking, storage, and the quantum runtime and execution environment. In the end, quantum computers handle the quantum workload, which is overseen from distant data centers.

The possible integration of QCC with the quantum Internet is a significant advance. By applying quantum principles to network communications, this paradigm has the potential to completely eliminate the requirement for classical intermediaries in quantum data transmission, therefore revolutionizing data communication. The creation of reliable quantum communication protocols and the fusion of quantum and classical systems are among the present obstacles that must be overcome before a fully developed quantum Internet can be realized. Hybrid quantum cloud computing solutions are emerging because cloud-based quantum computers and users are still primarily connected through traditional Internet and computing technologies. These hybrid models offer a practical step towards achieving the full promise of quantum cloud computing by combining quantum computational power with traditional networking and data processing.

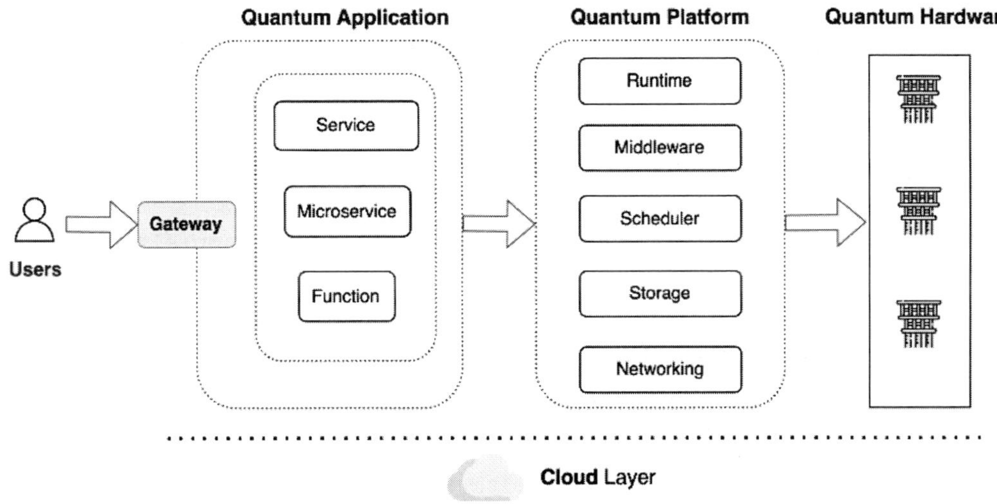

Fig.7.1 A panoramic perspective of modern quantum cloud computing.

Although quantum cloud computing is still in its infancy, companies and academic institutions working on creating and implementing these services are becoming more and more interested in it. Future quantum computing may use this combined approach, which combines the concepts of quantum computing with cloud integration. The University of Bristol's Center for Quantum Photonics (CQP) carried out one of the first experiments in early 2016 to introduce quantum resources to the cloud.

One of the first quantum resources to be deployed in the cloud is a two-qubit optical quantum computer that can be tested via the Internet. Then, as part of their cloud services offerings, industry heavyweights like IBM (IBM, 2023), Amazon Web Services (AWS), and Microsoft Azure (Microsoft, 2023) started to make quantum computing services available to the general public. These endeavors demonstrated the practicality and increasing availability of quantum computing resources using cloud computing platforms. The architecture of a typical quantum cloud computing platform is described in detail below, with four key parts identified:

1. A device that holds physical qubits;
2. A control system that operates the device;
3. An executor that manages the control system; and
4. A compiler that builds quantum circuits for the executor.

There's a middleware-based hybrid quantum cloud computing architecture that makes it easier to integrate and manage quantum and conventional calculations. Moreover, a number of proposals have been made to improve cloud-based quantum computer interfaces' error resilience. For instance, a significant improvement in the dependability and efficiency of quantum computations was made possible by the significant error reduction in quantum logic operations realized by the use of tailored pulses over a cloud quantum computing interface. In order to fully exploit the potential of quantum cloud computing, these innovations taken together constitute the first steps towards creating a uniform strategy for cloud-based quantum infrastructure across academics and industry.

Owing to the noisy intermediate-scale characteristics of currently accessible quantum machines, cloud-based high-performance quantum simulators are also required to provide the experimental setting for quantum-related investigations. Large-scale quantum simulators are available for use in prototyping quantum applications by the majority of quantum cloud providers. A number of simulators, including as the 32-qubit state vector simulator, the 32-qubit QASM simulator, and the Clifford simulator—which can accommodate up to 5,000 qubits for the Clifford circuit—are accessible through IBM Quantum (IBM, 2023) for instance. Similar to this, a variety of quantum simulators, including state vector, density matrix, and tensor network simulators, are accessible through Amazon Braket and Azure Quantum.

Moreover, Intel provides a cloud-ready quantum simulator that supports noise/error modeling, parallel quantum device emulation, and numerical investigations. It can simulate up to 42-qubit quantum circuits. It's also critical to remember that there are other metrics available for evaluating a quantum computer's performance in addition to its qubit count. A quantum computer's total performance is determined by a number of parameters, such as the qubits' quality, error rate, and connection. Scale, quality, and speed are three essential metrics that IBM researchers propose be used to assess the NISQ devices' performance. Scale is quantified in terms of qubit count, quality by quantum volume, and speed by Circuit Layer Operations Per Second (CLOPS).

Because of the high expenses of constructing and cooling quantum computers, using their resources can sometimes be more expensive than using those of a traditional computer. However, quantum computers naturally do some computationally challenging tasks far quicker than a conventional computer because they can handle the concurrent superposition of states. When the total cost of completing the operation is substantially less than that of completing it on a classical computer, it makes sense to carry out such activities on a quantum computer. In order to reach a quantum computer, latency limitations must be taken into account in addition to execution costs.

For instance, depending on the distance between these computers, the submission of a job from a classical computer to a quantum computer in a hybrid quantum-classical system may include an access delay on the order of 10 ms to 20 ms each way. The process of getting a job ready to be sent to a quantum computer may also add to the delay. Since the resources of a quantum computer are usually shared by several users, other factors like task compilation delay or job queuing latency would also need to be taken into account. Generally speaking, before selecting a quantum computer over a conventional computer to do a particular task, one must carefully examine a variety of limitations, such as the total cost for execution and the overall delay.

7.3 Models of Quantum Cloud Computing

7.3.1 Quantum Computing as a Service (QCaaS)

Within the dynamic environment of quantum cloud computing, Quantum Computing as a Service (QCaaS), also known as Quantum as a Service (QaaS), is a broad quantum cloud service paradigm. This concept makes it possible for users to explore and utilize quantum computing without having to acquire and maintain quantum hardware by giving them remote access to quantum computing resources. For hybrid quantum-classical applications, Quantum-Algorithms-as-a-Service (QAaaS) is a notion. By removing the components of quantum computing from the software development process, QAaaS allows developers to concentrate more on application logic and less on the nuances of quantum processing. This abstraction is essential for both making quantum resources more available to a wide variety of users, including those with little to no background in quantum physics, and integrating quantum computing into larger IT infrastructures. Therefore, QCaaS plays a critical role in democratizing access to cloud-based quantum computing resources, encouraging innovation, and hastening the creation of quantum applications for a variety of sectors.

7.3.2 Serverless Quantum

The growing usage of a serverless computing architecture to enable quantum computing and improve its usability and dependability by removing users from the deployment of applications and infrastructure configuration is known as serverless quantum computing. With this paradigm, users just have to concentrate on leveraging cloud-based services to construct quantum applications. Because serverless apps are extremely scalable and efficiently employ resources, the pay-per-use approach optimizes overall costs. The hybrid quantum-classical application deployment is a good fit for the serverless quantum computing paradigm. IBM presented the proof of concept for Quantum Serverless architecture in 2021. This architecture enables the integration of both conventional and quantum workloads into a single application. They assert that this is the way quantum programming will go in the future and want to launch quantum serverless with intelligent orchestration, a toolkit for circuit knitting, and circuit libraries.

A Minimum Viable Product (MVP) design has been created to show how serverless workflow may be integrated with quantum computing. This concept consists of three architectural layers that use IBM's quantum services together with certain cloud-native technologies. However, integrating a single vendor's services might result in data lock-in, a common issue with serverless computing. QFaaS is one of the first full-stack serverless function-as-a-service platforms that supports numerous quantum SDKs and quantum computing services, extending the notion of mixing standard serverless and cloud-native methodologies for quantum computing. The deployment of hybrid quantum-classical applications using a function-as-a-service serverless computing paradigm and DevOps methodologies is supported by QFaaS. The feasibility and promise of bringing serverless methodologies for speeding quantum software engineering, which has been used in industrial platforms, are demonstrated by the evaluation of QFaaS with real use cases on various quantum software kits and cloud suppliers.

7.3.3 Hybrid Quantum-Classical Computing

Almost all quantum cloud computing systems now under development still rely on classical architecture; this is known as the hybrid quantum-classical cloud (HQCC). According to this design, customers submit their quantum circuits to traditional cloud services (like IBM Cloud or Amazon Web Services) via web API. Before being sent to a quantum processor for execution, these circuits are queued. Ultimately, the outcomes will be sent back to the original user on the traditional cloud.

This hybrid architecture is being used by all of the major quantum cloud providers, including Amazon Braket, Azure Quantum, IBM Quantum, and others, for their quantum computing services. HQCC combines the advantages of both conventional and quantum computing to tackle particular problems more quickly by utilizing both types of computing resources in a cloud setting. By combining the strength and adaptability of conventional computing with the special powers of quantum computing, such as quantum parallelism and entanglement, the goal is to increase the system's performance. A middleware architecture is available to facilitate the orchestration of hybrid quantum-classical computing systems. In order to maximize cloud-based resource usage, this heterogeneous design emphasizes the advantages of integrating the capabilities of both quantum and conventional computing.

The programming approach known as Kernel-as-a-Service (KaaS) is designed to facilitate diverse workflows that incorporate both conventional and quantum processing workloads. This prototype demonstrates the HQCC architectural design's encouraging evolution.

7.4 Securing Dispersed Data Lakes by Using Quantum Key Distribution in a Multi-Cloud Environment

Advances in quantum computing have showed promise in addressing major data leakage issues, thanks to the availability of early cloud-based prototypes of quantum machines that can do workloads that would take a long time on traditional computers. An atom's state, electron, photon, or other constituent particle are typically used to represent a quantum bit, also known as a qubit, which is the smallest unit of quantum information. A quantum bit has additional properties than a conventional bit, allowing for new methods that are not achievable with classical processing. It can also exist in superposition states, which are both 0 and 1 simultaneously with differing probabilities.

Cloud data leak prevention employs quantum cryptography, which is also grounded in quantum physics. An unsafe link can be used to securely transmit data between two entities thanks to a particular quantum technique called the Quantum Key Distribution (QKD) protocol. They can use this protocol to identify if someone is attempting to measure or intercept data traveling over an unprotected channel.

In order to protect user connections with a single cloud provider, current research efforts are concentrated on incorporating the QKD protocol into cloud deployments. Multi-cloud deployments, on the other hand, have been used recently to provide services that access data from dispersed sources. The security concerns surrounding distributed data lake access have gained attention as a result of this trend. Slow multi-cloud distributed data lake transfer, vulnerability brought on by improper parameter setups, and third-party disruption in the event that improper techniques are employed are the main problems.

Although the cloud is becoming more and more popular as a first choice for businesses looking to deploy new resources, the amount of data saved there for analytics and preservation purposes is substantial enough to be referred to as big data or data lakes. On-premises, cloud, hybrid, and multi-cloud data lakes are the primary types that are examined, and their architectures are displayed. Various studies illustrate the applicability of working with massive data lakes. For instance, how the researchers were able to coordinate efforts across various international teams from NASA and ESA to design and oversee an open data lake on the cloud. Researchers have revealed the particular application of multi-cloud data lakes, where several CSPs partition data analysis to save costs and increase throughput.

As data volumes grow, it becomes more challenging to encrypt, decrypt, or confirm the legitimacy of the stored information, making big data security a critical concern. The present difficulties in storing, retrieving, processing, and implementing security requirements, for instance, as well as potential solutions for Big Data Security in cloud environments. Two algorithms that can be used to identify internal and external hackers and serve as frameworks for accessing large amounts of data. Additionally, a distributed method exists to divide large data files into segments and store them in numerous CSPs in order to improve security and reduce the significant risk of losing all data in the event that a CSP fails and goes down.

Based on quantum mechanics, quantum computing is a kind of computation. It derives findings that are not achievable using classical computation by utilizing the properties and behaviors of particular physical phenomena. Many quantum computers are currently housed on the major cloud service providers' and other private companies' servers. The experts (IDC, 2022) predict that this study sector would grow by 8.6 billion dollars in 2027, however they are still in the early phases. IBM, AWS, GCP, and Azure are the primary CSPs and providers of quantum computing services. There are currently 433 qubits on an Osprey chip, making IBM the largest quantum machine in terms of qubit quantity.

The smallest representation of information in classical computation is a bit. Only 0 or 1 can be a bit at any one time. Although a qubit in quantum computation will also produce 0 or 1 when measured, it may simultaneously be 0 and 1 with varying probabilities prior to the measurement procedure. This results directly from the application of quantum mechanics. The most popular representation for numerically expressing this behavior is the Dirac notation (Dirac, 1939). This allows the 0 and 1 qubits to be represented as vectors in the manner described below:

$$|0\rangle = \begin{bmatrix} 1 \\ 0 \end{bmatrix} \quad (1)$$

$$|1\rangle = \begin{bmatrix} 0 \\ 1 \end{bmatrix} \quad (2)$$

When the outcome is $|0\rangle$ in the zero state (1), it may be said that all of the probabilities are at vector point 0. Furthermore, in state (2), all of the probabilities are at position 1 of the vector when the outcome is $|1\rangle$.

A bit could be represented graphically by a switch that is switched to on or off, denoting 0 or 1. In the meanwhile, a bloch sphere (see below figure) is typically used to represent a qubit. The $|0\rangle$ is at the top, the $|1\rangle$ is at the bottom, and each point in between is a combination of the probabilities between these two values.

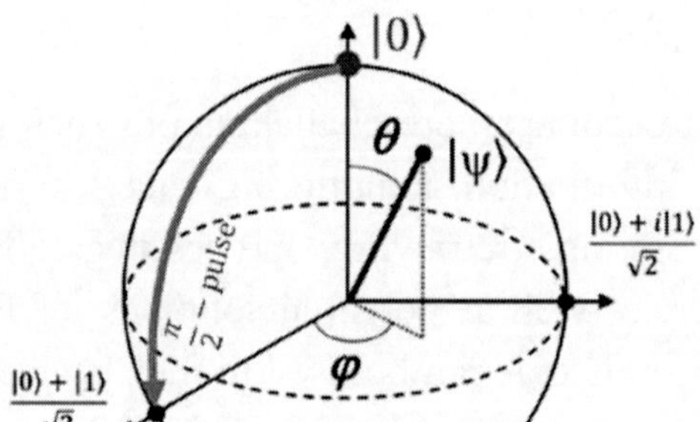

$$|\psi\rangle = cos\frac{\theta}{2}|0\rangle + e^{i\varphi}sin\frac{\theta}{2}|1\rangle$$

Fig.7.2 The Bloch Sphere.

The QKD protocol is among the most well-known quantum protocols in quantum cryptography. This protocol uses a quantum channel to transmit a one-pad secret message that, because of the physical characteristics of photons, will be distorted and visible to both the sender and the recipient if it is intercepted by a third party. The receiver will measure those and share portions of the results using the QKD, which entails delivering a number of random qubits and a number of operations. The results of the measures in the target endpoint will be inaccurate if the data has already been measured.

Prior to delving into the design, it is important to address the following major issues with dispersed data lakes:

- The permission and access mechanism for data across many clouds is insecure. Data transmissions between the CSP are susceptible to eavesdropping since they travel across the Internet and other unstable networks.
- The distributed multi-cloud data lakes are sluggish. The data undergoes an encryption and decryption procedure that involves every byte once it reaches the CSP.

The QKD protocol is widely recognized as a one-pad security procedure; an illustration of its elements and operational procedures can be found in the figure below.

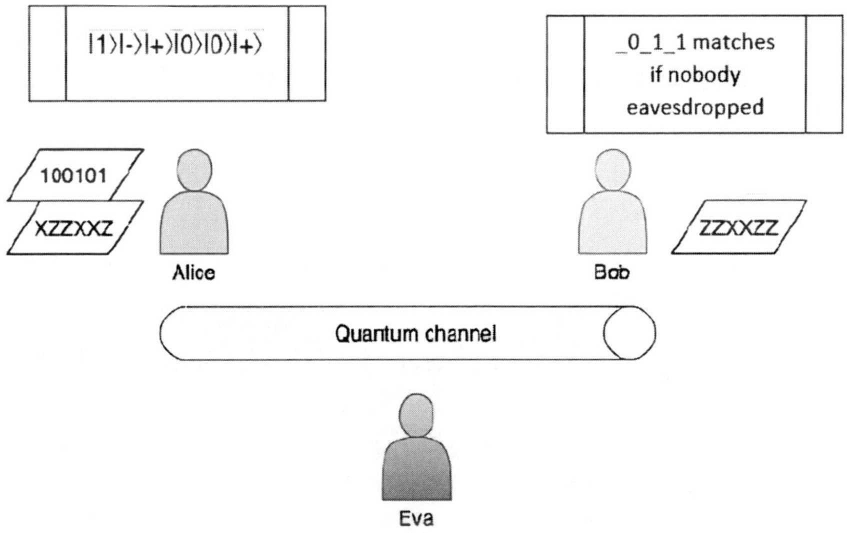

Fig.7.3 Elements and Operational Processes.

The steps are as follows:

- Step 1: Alice selects a string (the message) and a basis or set of operations at random. Alice has private access to those. As an illustration:

X denotes a bit, and Z denotes an operation;

string = 100101;

basis = XZZXXZ;

- Step 2: Using the selected basis, Alice encodes each bit onto a string of qubits and sends it to Bob.

This indicates that each qubit is randomly selected from one of the following states $|0\rangle, |1\rangle, |+\rangle$ or $|-\rangle$.

As an illustration:

$message = |1\rangle |-\rangle |+\rangle |0\rangle |0\rangle |+\rangle$

- Step 3: Bob uses a selected basis to randomly measure each qubit.

As an illustration:

$basis = ZZXXZZ$

- Step 4: Bob and Alice make their basis for each qubit publicly available. They utilize it to create a portion of the shared secret key if Bob measured a qubit using the same methodology that Alice had prepared it; else, the qubit is thrown away. Given that the bases in the second, fourth, and sixth locations (Z X Z) in this example are equal, the value in those positions should be the same for both (0 1 1) and will be included in the shared key.
- Step 5: Lastly, both exchange a random sample of their keys (which, following the preceding procedure, should be 011), and if the samples match, they can be extremely certain that a third party (Eva in the figure) did not intercept their message.

To verify the transmission, the speed should increase and the data distribution procedure might be completed more quickly if the first bytes of each file are extracted rather than the entire file. With the improved QKD protocol, security will win out. If eavesdropping occurs on the network, it will detect it.

Data lakes that are dispersed across several clouds (multi-cloud) might benefit from improved data authorization and transmission security thanks to the QKD protocol. By executing the quantum portions of the QKD protocol, the various quantum computers from each CSP might assist in achieving this.

As seen in the figure below, there are four primary layers: the user layer, cloud layer, quantum layer, and data layer.

The primary layers in the figure below communicate with one another, determining how data will move between them. The duties assigned to each stratum come next.

The User Layer.

The hardware and software that are run locally on the user's computer, as well as the system user, make up this layer.

The Cloud Layer.

This layer contains all of the resources that are part of any CSP. For instance, the network, computing, and identity resources that will be employed.

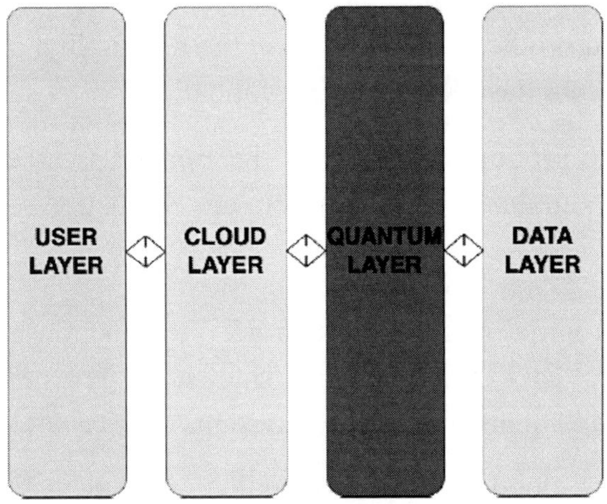

Fig.7.4 The Primary Layers.

The quantum layer.

All quantum computers (QC), simulators, and any hybrid or pure quantum software are included in this layer.

Data Layer.

The data layer can be considered separately even though the resources on this layer are also on the cloud because it is where the data files end up.

It is anticipated that the unusual components that will be divided among the CSPs would make up the distributed data files to be used. The complex numbers are extended by the quaternions. Large matrices derived from Hamilton's quaternion calculations will serve as the data source for the distributed data lake.

The formula below illustrates how the quaternions can be expressed as a linear combination.

$$H = \alpha + \beta i + \gamma j + \delta k$$

Software need the values for a, b, g, and d as inputs in order to represent quaternions. Both the user layer and the cloud layer ought to be capable of producing this data.

The multi-cloud architecture shown in the figure below is used to split the dispersed data and determine the data transfer between the many CSPs. Similar methods are applied to authorization and data access. However, the user data will be used to transmit the messages as quantum blocks rather than the data in the data lakes.

- Step 1: Involves generating quaternion data using a program and storing it in files up to 2GB in size.

- Step 2: A second software splits those files and distributes them to the other CSP. Before being saved on the native data lake, the data is first analyzed by the quantum computers to carry out the QKD tests and validations.
- Step 3: A separate program will record the times, assess each CSP's outputs, and verify the times in simultaneously. The primary evaluation results are as follows:

Generating Data

Data generation is the initial stage. This step need to function both locally and within a cloud virtual machine. This virtual machine shall serve as a central point of contact for users and the multi-cloud quantum data lake system.

It is anticipated that the cloud hub virtual machine components will have an auto scaling group (ASG). When the application generates the files, this will boost the processing power if necessary. Two Availability Zones (AZ) are also included in the architecture for high availability.

Distribution of Data

The following step is to distribute the data files after they have been made (if they were created locally, they must first be sent to the cloud hub virtual machine). All of the CSPs must be properly connected to the cloud hub ASG in order for this to happen. The three CSPs utilized for the implementation must be properly connected to the cloud hub ASG.

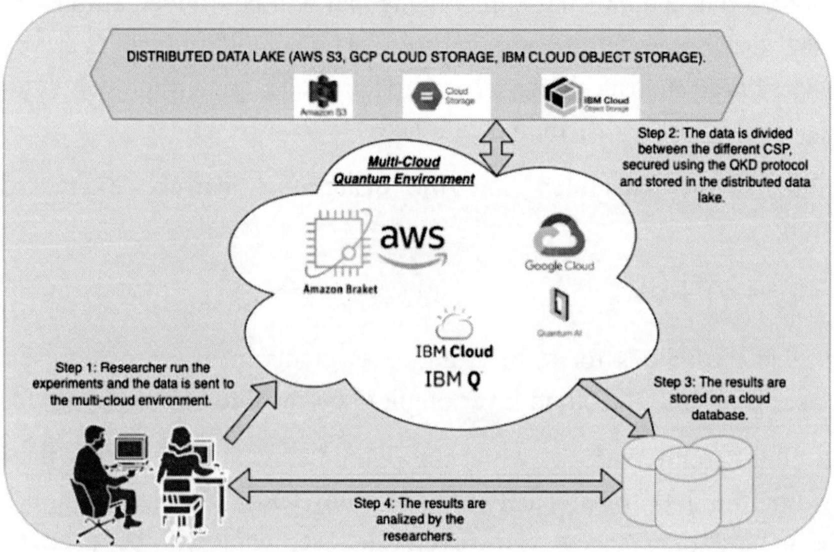

Fig.7.5 Architecture of a multi-cloud distributed data lake.

Furthermore, the cloud hub ASG and a cloud database (DB) need to be operating in the same VPC. The researcher will query all of the findings on this cloud database to obtain data about times and accuracy. As a result, each AZ should have one instance of the cloud database.

Multi-Cloud Quantum Infrastructure

Each CSP will handle the data files in parallel after they arrive at this stage. Each one uses a distinct quantum API (Cirq for GCP, Qiskit for IBM, and Braket for AWS) to run its native quantum code.

Comprehensive System Architecture

All of the previously listed components are part of the entire system. After being created locally or in the cloud virtual machine hub, the data files are sent to every CSP server via the internal network of every CSP. The ideal channel for it would be a quantum network. When the data reaches this point, each data file's header is checked using the QKD protocol and compared to the hub's header; if the check is successful, the data file is saved on the local data lake service.

Figure below shows the entire system design. On this figure, every component from before has been added. The way the data moves through the system is evident. It will travel from the user to the cloud hub ASG to the server on each CSP. From there, the QKD protocol on the quantum machines and simulators is used to do computations before approving the data files to be saved on each CSP's local data lake.

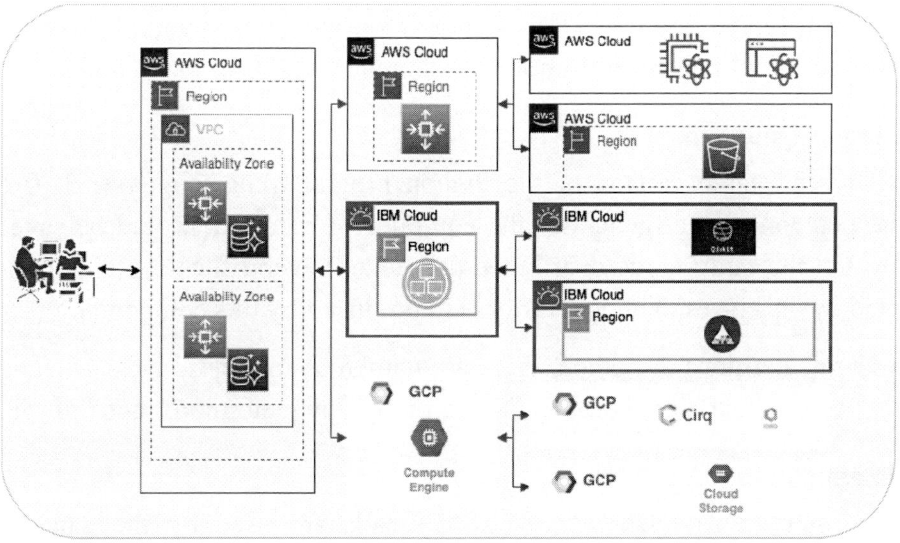

Fig.7.6 Comprehensive System Architecture.

Multiple Cloud Environment

For this implementation, the CSPs with the most developed quantum services are employed. These CSPs include GCP, IBM Cloud, and AWS. Because there are now no sophisticated procedures for a global quantum network, it is crucial to remember this when implementing the quantum layer. Quantum communication between the cloud hub virtual machine (VM) and the quantum machines occurs as planned (directly); however, communication between the various quantum machines is made via the cloud hub VM acting as a middleman (relayed).

The services utilized on AWS include Identity Access Management (IAM), the networking-related Virtual Private Cloud (VPC), the compute-related Elastic Compute Cloud (EC2), the storage-related Simple Storage Service (S3), and the quantum computing-related Braket. Furthermore, an Aurora cluster on AWS serves as the cloud database containing the test results. Virtual servers from the compute offers, IBM Cloud Object Storage for the data lake, and the IBM Quantum set from the quantum computing domain are the services utilized for the IBM Cloud.

The services utilized from GCP include object storage, compute engine virtual machines, and the IonQ Quantum machine, which is supplied by their partner IonQ. The distributed platform known as the multi-cloud quantum system needs to be operational on every CSP at the time of data delivery.

It consists of a Linux server listening on port 22 in each CSP, specifically running Ubuntu 20.04 LTS. It establishes a client/server private connection via SSH and exchanges the necessary files with the client whenever it receives a communication request. After the connection is made, it begins to receive data packets from the client and sends them to the data lake after undergoing a quantum validation process with the help of the local CSP's quantum computer or simulators and the QKD protocol.

Generation of Quaternions

The most recent stable version of the Python programming language, 3.10.2, used to create the component that generates the complicated data that would be saved on files divided to test the multi-cloud distributed data lake. Several files containing quaternions represented by the corresponding matrices are produced by this component.

To represent quaternions in Python, there are numerous modules, packages, and libraries available. As an illustration, consider "quaternion," "pyquaternion," and "rowan."

Data Dissemination

Each cloud storage data lake's various API calls are used by the data distribution component to distribute the files. This part serves as the Multi-Cloud Quantum system server's client.

Authorization of QKD

The user authorization component can receive user input and validate credentials by authorizing a file communication over the QKD protocol. The same node that runs the distribution component must also run this. After receiving each local data file from the distribution, it extracts the first two 16-bit quaternion data bytes and converts them to an initial state on qubits. It uses this bit sequence to carry out the QKD protocol, depending on the version, on both simulators and actual quantum machines. The constraints of the existing quantum simulators mean that it only requires 2 bytes (16 bits). There are fewer restrictions on quantum computers, which only have four bits. It makes the decision to send the file to the data lake or not based on this authorization step.

7.5 Quantum Cloud Platforms and Providers

7.5.1 Providers of quantum hardware enabled by the cloud

Recent innovations from well-known providers of quantum hardware with cloud capabilities. While some suppliers, like Amazon Braket and Azure Quantum, primarily work with outside hardware makers to deliver quantum computing services, other vendors, including IBM Quantum, Rigetti, and IonQ, provide cloud-based computing services to their quantum computers. Quantum chips, also known as quantum processing units, or QPUs, are the result of the application of a number of technologies, including superconducting, neutral atoms, trapped ions, and quantum annealing. Every method uses different physical systems to implement quantum operations and qubits.

The superconducting method uses qubit creation by taking use of the characteristics of superconducting circuits. This method allows the manipulation of quantum states by taking use of macroscopic quantum mechanical events through the use of Josephson junctions. Superconducting qubits are renowned for their potential for scalability and for being comparatively easier to integrate into electrical systems. Many top businesses, like IBM Quantum, believe this method to be the most popular for constructing quantum computers.

Rigetti, Google, and Oxford Quantum Circuits (OCQ). A major advancement in quantum computing was made in 2019 when Google asserted its quantum dominance with their Sycamore 54-qubit superconducting processor. The processor was able to complete a work in 200 seconds that would have taken the finest traditional supercomputer 10,000 years. But unlike other hardware makers, Google's quantum processor is still not widely available to the general public. From 5 qubits to 433 qubits, IBM Quantum provides a variety of quantum computers on its cloud-based platform. A major advancement in the development of quantum hardware was made in 2023 with the unveiling of the Condor processor, which has 1,121 superconducting qubits, and the Heron processor, a high-performance device with 133 qubits.

With their 127-qubit superconducting processor, IBM further illustrated the usefulness of quantum computing by demonstrating accurate expectation values measurement that goes beyond the capabilities of classical computation and by emphasizing the importance of developments in coherence, calibration, and noise management as prerequisites for pre-fault-tolerant quantum computing applications. Superconducting methods were also used by other businesses, as Rigetti, Oxford Quantum Circuits (OCQ), and Quantum Inspire (QuTech), to construct their quantum hardware that is cloud-based. Additionally, QuTech presents their second hardware approach for creating a silicon 2-qubit quantum processor based on single electron spin qubits.

Trapped ions, or charged atoms trapped in electromagnetic fields, are another well-liked quantum hardware method that uses them as qubits. Qubit measurement, manipulation, and initialization are done with lasers. Long coherence periods and high-fidelity operations are hallmarks of this approach. Prominent suppliers in this field include IonQ, Alpine Quantum Technologies (AQT) and Honeywell Quantum (now part of Quantinuum). All of these companies have created fully-connected qubit devices that showcase sophisticated quantum computing systems based on trapped ions. In addition, there was interest in neutral atom technology, which use lasers to cool and trap neutral atoms—atoms devoid of any net electric charge—in a 2D or 3D array. As Atom Computing said that they successfully constructed a 1,180-qubit quantum computer in 2023 and are getting ready to make their system available for cloud-based access, this technology offers scalability and large qubit numbers. Other noteworthy examples of businesses investigating quantum computing with neutral atoms to create their cloud-based hardware include Pasqal and QuEra.

Moreover, photonics presents a viable approach towards the development of quantum processors. In order to support higher-order interactions among qudits and leverage entropy and noise, Quantum Computing Inc. (QCI) introduced their Dirac-3 quantum system as a novel approach to quantum computing through Entropy Quantum Computing (EQC) (QCI, [n. d.]). This allowed for room temperature operation without the need for a cryogenic environment and promised increased computing speed and capacity. Through the use of photonics, QCI's technology implements multi-level qudits, which go beyond conventional two-level qubits. Each photon may enable up to 10,000 levels through different degrees of freedom, such as orbital angular momentum and polarization.

With this capacity, up to 949 photons/qudits may be managed. The degrees of freedom of each photon are utilized to represent various levels, so converting each variable into a qudit whose level corresponds to the value of the variable. By reducing the cooling needs of quantum computing systems, EQC research has the potential to greatly improve the energy efficiency of quantum cloud computing. Another business, Xanadu, has created a room-temperature Nano photonic quantum device that provides scalability and stability benefits.

Although gate-based quantum computers are being developed using superconducting, trapped ion, photonics, and neutral atom techniques, the goal of the quantum annealing approach is to solve optimization issues by naturally determining the ground state of a quantum system. It solves optimization issues by minimizing energy states using a quantum mechanical approach. The most well-known business using quantum annealing technology is D-Wave Systems, which provides quantum cloud computing services for certain optimization tasks. On the other hand, their roadmap for creating devices for universal quantum processing now includes the gate-based quantum model.

The efficiency and kind of calculations that may be performed are largely determined by the quantum hardware technology used, which also has an immediate impact on the scalability, coherence time, and error rates of quantum computing systems. The advancement of this sector will depend heavily on how these technologies are developed and interact in order to provide widely available and useful quantum cloud computing services. Moreover, the cloud-based supply of quantum computing resources streamlines the integration process with resources for high-performance computing (HPC), indicating improved computational capacities and wider potential applications.

7.5.2 Quantum cloud computing platforms and services.

In addition to commercial quantum computing as a service, the majority of cloud-based quantum computing systems provide cloud services straight from the hardware makers. There are now chances to integrate quantum compute activities with classical ones since major cloud platforms including Google Cloud, IBM Cloud, Microsoft Azure, Amazon Web Services (AWS), and IBM Cloud have begun to offer quantum computing services inside their cloud ecosystems. IBM provides cloud services and platforms to access various quantum hardware providers, including Rigetti, IonQ, and Quantinuum, OCQ, Pasqal, and QuEra. Meanwhile, IBM provides access to its in-house built quantum processing resources through IBM Cloud and IBM Quantum platform.

A variety of software development kits (SDKs) are also available for these quantum cloud platforms, which may be used to plan, create, and assess quantum applications. For instance, IBM Quantum offers a variety of tools, including IBM Quantum Composer and IBM Quantum Lab, to facilitate the creation, visualization, execution, and analysis of quantum applications. Additionally, Google Cloud, Azure Quantum, and Amazon Braket provide their quantum SDKs, which they refer to as Cirq, Microsoft Quantum SDKs (which include the Q# programming language), and Braket, respectively. In order to provide a complete cloud platform that gives customers access to practically all existing quantum hardware and other software platforms, Strangeworks works with nearly all major suppliers of quantum computing hardware and software.

In addition to a number of cloud-based frameworks focused on quantum software, the QuantumPath platform facilitates the creation of quantum applications. With the potential to develop into an agnostic software framework for quantum computing, this framework supports many SDKs and incorporates numerous visual editors to facilitate the creation of quantum circuits. Another open-source platform for quantum software, called QFaaS, facilitates the creation of serverless quantum function-as-a-service applications.

Several quantum SDKs and programming languages are integrated into QFaaS, and it may be expanded to integrate with several quantum cloud providers, including IBM

Quantum and Amazon Braket. In addition, PlanQK is a complete quantum platform and environment designed to facilitate the creation of quantum workflow applications, with the ultimate goal of creating a marketplace for quantum applications. The majority of quantum cloud platforms and frameworks offer simulation environments for creating and prototyping quantum applications in addition to providing quantum computing services. A number of cloud systems, like QEMIST and 1QCloud, are devoted to offering quantum simulation services for particular issues including quantum chemistry and optimization.

Table 7.1 Different cloud systems and models.

Platforms/ Framework	Type	Quantum Backends	Supported SDKs	Serverless Model	Quantum Computing Models		
					Simulation	Annea ling	Gate-based
1Qloud	CQS	1Qbit	1Qbit		Yes		
Amazon Braket	CQS	Rigetti, OCQ, IonQ, QuEra	Braket, Qiskit, Pennylane	Yes	Yes		Yes
Azure Quantum	CQS	Quantinuu m, Rigetti, IonQ, Pasqal	Q#, Qiskit, Cirq,		Yes		Yes
Google Cloud	CQS	Google, IonQ	Cirq		Yes		Yes
IBM Cloud	CQS	IBM Quantum	Qiskit	Yes	Yes		Yes
PlanQK	CQS	IBM Quantum, Amazon Braket, Azure Quantum	Qiskit, Pennylane	Yes	Yes	Yes	Yes
QEMIST	CQS	1Qbit	OpenQEMIS T		Yes		
QFaaS	OSF	IBM Quantum,	Qiskit, Cirq, Q#	Yes	Yes		Yes

		Strangeworks					
Quantum Path	CQS	IBM Quantum, Amazon Braket, D-Wave, QuTech	Qiskit, Ocean, Braket, Q#		Yes	Yes	Yes
Strange works	CQS	IBM Quantum, Amazon Braket, Azure Quantum, Hitachi, Toshiba, ...	Qiskit, Braket, Rigetti	Yes	Yes	Yes	Yes

7.6 Management of Quantum Cloud Resources

As quantum cloud computing develops further, resources must be distributed and managed effectively, just as in regular cloud computing. But managing resources in a quantum cloud is beset with more difficult problems. The first set of difficulties is brought about by the variability of quantum resources with respect to qubit counts, qubit connections, quantum processor speeds, and error rates. It is true that the performance and scalability of each quantum hardware technology varies, as do its benefits and drawbacks. For instance, trapped ion quantum devices struggle to reach high processing speeds (CLOPS) but can achieve greater quantum volumes (qubit quality).

On the other hand, spin-based quantum devices exhibit the reverse. Secondly, unlike conventional resources, quantum resources cannot be split or scaled freely. Instead, they are almost fixed. Within a single traditional host machine or a cluster of devices, we may establish numerous virtual machines, also known as containers, as separate environments for carrying out separate activities at the same time. On the other hand, no analogous methods for quantum resources have yet been put out. In addition, the criteria for each quantum work vary and are either unknown or unforeseen, making it difficult to assign a suitable quantum device for completion. The inaccuracy of quantum job specifications and the finite quantity of resources available on quantum computers cause the intricacy of quantum resource management issues to increase, leading to either an excess or under abundance of resources being allocated. Consequently, resource allocation (or work scheduling) and resource estimate of quantum jobs are two important sub-problems of quantum resource management that need to be taken into account.

7.6.1 Estimation of Quantum Resources

With regard to particular quantum activities, QuRE is a Quantum Resource Estimator that measures qubit count, execution duration, success probabilities, and gate operations. Its investigation to include several approaches to error correction, evaluating how differences in error rates affect the total resource estimates, leading to more effective quantum computing architectures.

A complete framework called ScaffCC was created with scalability and resource estimation—such as circuit breadth, depth, gate count, and qubit interactions—in mind when compiling and analyzing quantum circuits. By addressing the crucial elements of quantum circuit complexity and resource allocation, this framework improves the design of hardware-independent quantum circuits, making it optimal for both small- and large-scale applications.

NISQ Analyser is a new tool that assesses the particular needs of quantum jobs in order to optimize the quantum backend selection procedure. In order to maximize the practicality of quantum computing applications, it evaluates critical characteristics such as qubit requirements, circuit depth, and gate complexity. This allows for the most effective alignment of quantum algorithms with available quantum computing resources.

7.6.2 Quantum Scheduling and Resource Allocation

A number of aspects need to be taken into account when creating a complete resource allocation for the quantum cloud computing paradigm. Using IBM Quantum Cloud services, analyze various quantum workloads and resource utilization characteristics, assessing the importance of quantum circuit execution, waiting, and compilation times, fidelity, error rates, and quantum machine utilization. Based on previous IBM Quantum computer data, a prediction model is available to forecast the fidelity of quantum computers and the queueing time for each device. This work compiles and transpiles the matching quantum circuit for each quantum computer, extracts the circuit's essential features, and maps the circuit with the machine's characteristics in order to schedule incoming jobs to the right quantum computer. The optimal quantum computer will then be chosen for task execution utilizing correlation coefficient approaches.

Utilizing the Weighted Round Robin (WRR) algorithm, a different method of allocating resources for distributed quantum computing is designed to optimize network resource allocation for quantum applications. The main idea is to assign network resources using the round-robin technique after determining the weight of each traffic flow in each quantum application beforehand. The assessment was conducted using a quantum network provisioning simulator, which illustrated the trade-offs between the network resource allocation algorithm's temporal complexity and fairness.

Only quantum circuits with a finite number of qubits can be precisely implemented since NISQ devices are error-prone. Because only one circuit may be run at a time and more qubits are wasted, it results in the widespread issue of underutilizing quantum resources. Thus, multi-programming and parallel processing strategies are crucial for optimizing resource usage in quantum cloud computing.

The realm of quantum cloud resource management relies heavily on circuit transpilation and selective qubit allocation. A qubit mapping method is necessary for cloud-based quantum computing in order to maximize the use of quantum resources while minimizing error rates and fidelity degradation. QuCloud improves inter-program interactions by dividing physical qubit topologies and introducing the X-SWAP design to decrease SWAP overheads.

7.6.3 Simulation Toolboxes for Issues with Quantum Cloud Resource Management

The use of simulation toolkits such as CloudSim in the classical domain is essential for developing and assessing quantum cloud resource management algorithms in the rapidly changing field of quantum cloud computing, where physical quantum resources are not easily accessible. iQuantum is a toolset designed to model and simulate cloud-based resource scheduling methods. Specifically designed for job scheduling and hybrid quantum-classical task orchestration, this toolbox is especially useful for simulating scenarios involving cloud-based quantum resources and quantum computing. In the upcoming years, a simulator for quantum edge computing will be available. This idea will draw attention to how crucial it is to standardize, develop such simulators and toolkits for cloud-based quantum computing, and expand it to edge computing settings.

7.7 Quantum Technology's effect on the Cloud

Cloud Security

The cloud is a multi-tenant system where users can share computer resources and possibly live on the same host as hackers. Because of this, cloud security is largely dependent on the security of the Trusted Execution Environments (TEE) that underpin it, such as ARM TrustZone (TZ), AMD Secure Processor (SP), and Intel SGX. The development of a quantum-resistant TEE is therefore necessary to prepare for the quantum era, when a large-scale quantum computer becomes a reality, or else cloud security will be jeopardized.

The good news is that symmetric key-based algorithms, such as AES (FIPS-197), SHA-1/2/3 (FIPS-180/202), HMAC (FIPS-198), etc., are less affected by quantum computing. The Grover algorithm cuts their search space in half when they are subjected to a thorough key search brute force attack. Using AES-256 rather than AES-128 and doubling the key size for certain schemes could be a quick workaround. As a result, symmetric cryptography-based TEE solutions, like the Intel Advanced Encryption Standard New Instructions (AESNI), are still functional in the quantum age.

Asymmetric cryptosystems, on the other hand, do not operate in this manner. Since some form of Moore's law scaling is shown to be valid for quantum computers, and a 72 qubit quantum device was recently disclosed by Google, quantum technology will be able to break RSA-2048 with a 1/7 probability by 2026 and a 1/2 chance by 2031. A number of novel quantum-resistant cryptographic techniques, such as Post-Quantum Cryptography (PQC), are being actively researched as a result of the imminent development of scalable quantum computers. It alludes to a new generation of cryptographic algorithms that are thought to be impervious to both nuclear and classical attacks. To make sure they are reliable and effective, the suggested algorithms are thoroughly examined and tested. Given that it can crack a lot of the current cryptography techniques, this involves analyzing their performance in different contexts as well as their resistance to well-known quantum algorithms like Shor's algorithm. Some of the methods being standardized to guarantee long-term security in the age of quantum computing include hash-based cryptography, multivariate cryptography, and code-based encryption.

The digital signatures standard (FIPS 186) and key establishment schemes (800-56A/B/C), which are public key cryptographic algorithms that ensure the confidentiality and integrity of digital communications on the Internet and elsewhere today, must be completely abandoned and replaced with cryptographic systems that are safe from both quantum and classical computers and that can work with current networks and communications protocols. To encourage, assess, and ultimately standardize a suite of quantum-resistant public key cryptography algorithms, the National Institute of Standards and Technology (NIST) has launched a public competition.

Positive aspects of the post-quantum cryptography adaptation include the enhanced security measures it offers for the cloud. The following is a list of some of the security features that are included in lattice-based cryptographic structures:

The "Holy Grail" of cryptography, fully homomorphic encryption (FHE), protects data privacy throughout cloud storage and communication by enabling calculations on encrypted data.

Identity-based encryption (IBE), its extension hierarchical IBE (HIBE), and attribute-based encryption (ABE) are all included in functional encryption (FE), which has been demonstrated to be feasible with lattices. These structures offer an alternative to extensive cloud-based public key infrastructures by generating public keys from pre-existing user data, including identification or attributes. The pre-existing user attribute becomes the public key instead of tying a user to it through a certificate. This makes it possible to deliver messages without first requesting a certificate or even registering the recipient in the public key database. Additionally, it enables the incorporation of timestamps to assign life cycles to keys or encrypt messages that may eventually be decrypted. ABE limits decryption capabilities to individuals with specific attributes, while HIBE uses delegation to lighten the master key extractor's burden.

On the other hand, as quantum technology is going to disrupt a number of current cryptosystems, it creates the opportunity for new quantum-based security that does not rely on the computational hardness assumptions of classical cryptography, but rather on the special characteristics of quantum physics. Quantum entanglement, for instance, can function as an unbreakable technique for safe transmission. However, because quantum measurements have very unpredictable results and entanglement breaks if we test an entangled particle in a way that causes it to be in a specific state, scientists are unable to transmit information using this attribute. A key for the one-time pad, a cryptosystem that is completely safe from all forms of cryptanalysis, can nonetheless be generated and exchanged using it. E91 is a quantum entanglement-based quantum key distribution (QKD) technique. Similarly, another QKD procedure that makes use of the no-cloning theorem of quantum physics is the BB84 method. Secure key distribution across a 200 kilometer quantum channel has been successfully tested. Furthermore, because quantum mechanics is inherently unpredictable, quantum systems are an ideal source of entropy for random number generators, which are essential to encryption.

Thus, it is possible to view quantum computing as a two-edged sword. It builds increasingly complex asymmetric cryptosystems that are even more difficult to crack, even while it breaks a number of the ones that are currently in use. Therefore, we do not believe that cloud security will be threatened by quantum technology; on the contrary, we believe that it may be strengthened by its new suite of quantum-based security solutions.

Lookup Services

Finding the right element in a database of unsorted elements typically requires checking half of the elements. An O(N) complexity is this. O(√N) is a quantum-based search method that is quadratically quicker than the classical one. This greatly enhances performance. The quantum approach requires only 1,000 tests, while the classical approach requires an average of 500,000 checks if N=1,000,000.

However, it takes O(log N) time to locate the proper element in a traditional binary search. The quantum method is ten times less efficient than this. Nevertheless, the binary search is limited to sorted data. Therefore, before we can do a binary search on the database, it must be sorted. The most well-known sorting algorithm has a complexity of O(N log N). Since we will be sorting the data for the first time and searching through it indefinitely, this is still preferable. However, it is difficult to ensure that we would only work with sorted data in the unstructured big data environment we currently inhabit. As a result, we may anticipate that in the future, cloud database servers would use quantum-based search features to significantly reduce search times. Businesses and research communities may be encouraged to outsource their data to the cloud in order to take use of quantum search capabilities, which are typically too expensive to have on-site.

AI-Powered Services

AI systems pick up new skills by going through a lot of situations one at a time and searching for trends. However, by interfering with one another and avoiding examining each example separately, experts assert that quantum superpositions could accelerate the learning process. Actually, quantum computing has already shown its worth in the realm of artificial intelligence. The D-Wave system, a quantum annealer known for determining the global minimum of a given function over a given set of solutions, has demonstrated its effectiveness in its problem domain. It is not a universal quantum computer. According to Google, DWave outperforms traditional simulated annealing on a single core CPU by a factor of 100 million. Google discovered that the D-Wave quantum annealer was still 100 million times faster even after conducting the test with Quantum Monte Carlo, a method that mimics solving quantum problems on classical processors.

Quantum annealer has previously been used in a number of fields that need machine learning, modeling, and optimization services. NASA space research, material modeling, the financial industry, traffic flow optimization, medical science for the best radiation therapy, and even intrusion detection have all made use of it. Thus, in addition to other cutting-edge cloud-based AI solutions, quantum annealing is anticipated to be the first quantum service made available on public clouds.

7.8 The Cloud's Impact On Quantum Technology

A. Accessibility

The cost of quantum technology is high. In actuality, a quantum computer is anticipated to be more expensive than a supercomputer once it becomes a reality. The 2000Q quantum annealer from D-Wave is currently available for $15 million [45]. On the other hand, IBM also sells its universal quantum device with 50 qubits for $15 million. On average, SMBs spend 6.4% of their yearly revenue on IT. On the other hand, small enterprises' average income is not anticipated to surpass $50 million, resulting in a ceiling of $3.2 million for all IT expenditures related to software, communication, and infrastructure. It is obviously far from the potential cost of a quantum computer.

In contrast, the activation of the quantum state in quantum technology necessitates extremely particular operating circumstances. The D-Wave 2X processor, for example, runs at 15 milli-kelvin, or -273 degrees Celsius. Accordingly, people will not find contemporary quantum technology as practical or physically affordable as today's classical computing, which can function at 67 degrees Celsius. Thus, the cloud computing pay as you go service offering model is the only way for quantum technology to reach individuals and SMBs.

In fact, IBM's online platform, IBM Q Experience, has already made its 5-qubit and 16-qubit quantum processors available. Similarly, Google's online Quantum Computing Playground, which can currently simulate up to 22 qubit quantum registers, was introduced today. Furthermore, with just one minute of free QPU time per month, D-Wave has made its real-time QPU available through its web platform, Leap.

B. Effective Utility

Quantum technology has particular uses despite its strong computational prowess. It won't take the place of the deterministic classical computing approach in that regard. Rather, they will work side by side. Even if they can afford to buy a quantum computer, big companies won't use it to its full potential. It is anticipated that a quantum computer will remain inactive for most of the time. Therefore, the only way to maximize the effective use of quantum computing capacity is in a multi-tenant cloud environment.

Cloud computing and quantum technologies will work in tandem. The cloud's computing capabilities will be improved by the power of quantum computing, enabling it to provide more effective computing services. On the other hand, quantum technology will be fully unlocked by the cloud, which will make it accessible to individuals and more reasonably priced for SMEs.

7.9 Integration of Quantum Computing in the Cloud Quantum Cloud Computing

By integrating quantum as a service with cloud infrastructures, developers can access sophisticated quantum computing or clients can access quantum resources, all while concealing the difficulty of interacting with quantum computers. This is crucial because cutting-edge quantum computing experiments are conducted in quantum labs using a combination of analog, digital, and controlling equipment, producing ever-more complicated and large amounts of data.

Small and medium-sized businesses and other researchers can access quantum computing resources much more easily with a cloud-based architecture. Research can be done on a number of different facets of developing a quantum cloud computing service. Data storage, transmission, and management are all crucial components. The combination of cloud computing and quantum computing is known as quantum cloud computing. The network's resources are typically dispersed, diverse, and geographically dispersed in cloud computing. Managing data transit between quantum computers and storage, cloud, and well-understood network topologies is necessary for the integration of quantum computers in such environments.

Three operational models are being studied at the moment: Quantum as a Service, Virtual Laboratory, and Open Grid Service Architecture. In the cloud, the Quantum as a Service model will be able to operate as a decoupled classical service. Trials of quantum cloud computing have been carried out and documented in the following applications: quantum machine learning, search algorithms, and cryptography. The overall processing and solution performance in cloud computing environments that were tested. For clients of cloud and classical computing systems to communicate with quantum computing systems effectively, shared common services that are scalable and safe are necessary.

This unique setting might make it possible for more network experts to access the quantum computers with shared collaboration across the cloud and quantum systems. Security is the primary issue with quantum cloud computing. The quantum computer and its state will never come into direct contact with the client. The primary transmission, storing, and feeding of data into and out of the system should be the emphasis of security. The second difficulty is preserving qubit coherence, particularly when it comes to key storage and transit. As with HPC clusters today, future research, development, and deployment of quantum cloud systems may open the door for quantum computers that can be used in a wide range of fields and applications.

Cloud-based resources are necessary for quantum computing, and it is likely that programs in cloud computing and quantum computing will converge. This is where cloud computing and quantum computing meet. The significance and benefits of quantum computing in the cloud are further explored by combining the two computing paradigms into a synergistic platform.

Equ 1. Chemical dynamics modeling using analog quantum.

$$\begin{aligned}\hat{H}_1^{\mathrm{MQB}} &= \sum_n \sum_j \Theta'_{n,j} |n\rangle\langle n| \left(\hat{a}_j^\dagger e^{i\delta_j t} + \mathrm{h.c.}\right) \\ &+ \sum_{n \neq m} \sum_k \Omega'_{n,m,k} |n\rangle\langle m| \left(\hat{a}_k^\dagger e^{i\delta_k t} + \mathrm{h.c.}\right) \\ &+ \frac{1}{2} \sum_n \chi_n |n\rangle\langle n|.\end{aligned}$$

7.10 Dynamic Quantum Network

7.10.1 A Multitenancy-Enabled Quantum Network

Traditional data centers use technologies that allow different users and apps to share computing resources in order to support cloud computing. This idea is known as multitenancy. Flexible data center interconnection networks are a crucial technological enabler for multitenancy because they allow computer resources to be dynamically and on-demand clustered into several coexisting slices, similar to containers, each of which serves a distinct application. A quantum data center should use a quantum interconnection network, which enables clustering and the distribution of qubit processors among various users and applications, in order to replicate this idea. It is quite difficult to accomplish this while maintaining the quantum state amongst linked quantum computers; this calls for a dynamically reconfigurable quantum network that allows for teleportation and entanglement distribution.

7.10.2 Quantum Network Intra-Data Center

Two kinds of coexisting, interconnected networks are necessary for a quantum datacenter that houses several few-qubit quantum processors. One network facilitates classical communication between quantum computers and is a classically interconnected network. The execution of quantum algorithms requires the interchange of classical information between processors, such as measurement information between qubit processors, which is supported by such a network. The second network is a quantum network that allows for teleportation and entanglement distribution. At the quantum state level, this network links quantum computers. Entanglement distribution, qubit teleportation, or gate teleportation for remote operation between qubit processors must all be supported by such a network.

The interconnect networks' structure and architecture are additional crucial factors. They have a direct impact on the quantum data center's effectiveness and performance. Crucial elements consist of: 1) A network topology that uses on-demand connections between quantum computers to achieve the best possible execution of quantum algorithms. The placement of measurement modules within the network; for instance, several entanglement-based wavelength-division multiplexing (WDM) optical network topologies, including ring, star, semi-mesh, and full mesh. Bell state measurement, which is required for the creation of entanglement between quantum processors, is carried out via measurement modules. These modules can be shared throughout processors and incorporated in the network; 3) Finding the ratio of qubits to communication qubits. To connect to other quantum processors, each one needs to have a few flying or communication qubits. A greater number of qubits must be reserved as communication qubits within a quantum processor in order to increase the degree of connectivity between them. Moreover, each quantum link requires a quantum transducer that interfaces stationary communication qubits with flying qubits. This will further complicate the management and operation of the quantum network with a low ratio of communication qubits to computation qubits.

7.10.3 Inter-Data Center Quantum Network

A regulated atmosphere is beneficial for data center warehouses. This makes it possible to achieve the high level of accuracy needed for a dynamic entanglement intra data center network to function properly, such as phase and temperature stability. Yet, transferring quantum states across a large distance in an efficient and dependable manner with a high success rate is a difficult challenge for which there is yet no practical answer. Consequently, connecting two or more geographically separated quantum data centers at the quantum state level is not a feasible option. Connecting them at the classical information level is the only feasible way to do this.

7.10.4 Secure multi-tenant quantum cloud computing

In order to share quantum computing capacity in a data center at scale with several users and applications, security and isolation amongst tenants must be ensured both within the data center and at the access level. Because quantum entangled photons don't clone, the intra-data center quantum network is naturally safe. However, security is required for both the access network to the quantum data center and the classical network inside the data center. To secure classical information sharing across qubit processors, the intra-data center classical network can also use the quantum entangled interconnected network's entanglement photon resources to implement the QKD protocol. The QKD protocol or additional security measures like post-quantum cryptography or universal blind quantum computing can also be used to secure the access network.

7.10.5 Dynamic Networking Using Entanglements for Intra-Data Center

A potential method for establishing a dynamic entangled quantum network to link qubit processors in a data center and for supplying entangled images for the application of QKD to secure the classical information transmission is depicted in the below Fig. Through the spontaneous parametric down-conversion (SPDC) process, which frequently results in polarization entangled photons, such a network needs a broadband entangled photon source. Additionally, it needs an optical fiber switch (OFS) to dynamically distribute entangled pictures between qubit processors, a DEMUX to split the broadband entangled photon spectrum into many entangled channels.

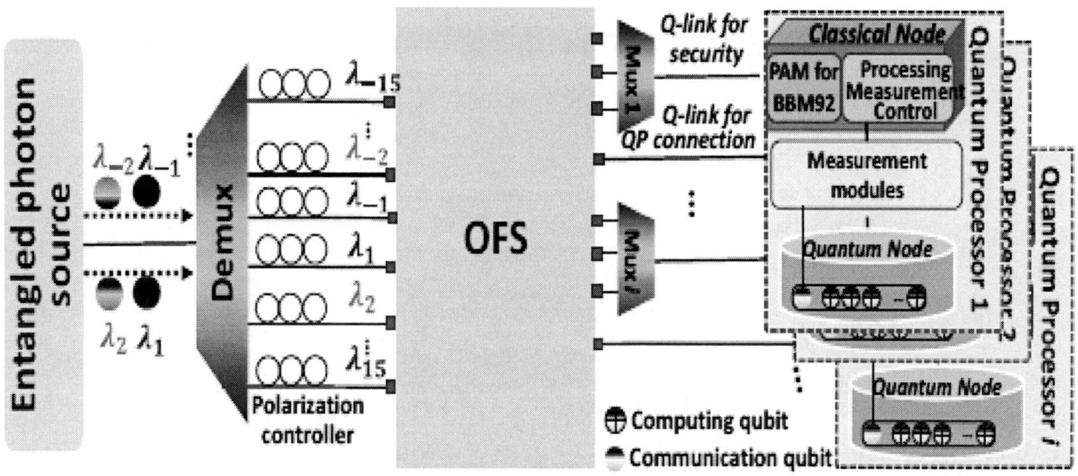

Fig.7.7 Dynamic intra-quantum datacenter network with SPDC for both distribution and entanglement generation between QPs and quantum-secured communications.

(Ref: Open access, University of Bristol, 2022)

With the help of classical measurement outcome information, the measurement modules will apply certain quantum gates to carry out the teleportation procedure when a pair of entangled photons successfully reach both QPs. In order for the polarization analysis module (PAM) at the classical component to measure in the required orthogonal bases to carry out the BBM92 QKD protocol, the entangled photons can also be used for QKD with MUX. The architecture enables a fully reconfigurable quantum network within the data center that may be set up in any topology with dynamic wavelength and time. Setting up bipartite entangled communication with low QBER for quantum-secured classical connections and high entangled fidelity for qubit processor interconnection is crucial to the functioning of such a dynamic network.

The figure below shows another method for realizing linkages between QPs. A Bell state measurement (BSM) module receives two flying qubits that are entangled with their own stationary communication qubits of quantum transduces in two QPs via OFS. The stationary qubit's state is projected into an entangled state via BSM. This makes it possible to switch entanglement between two stationary qubits at two different QPs. In contrast to the aforementioned technique, in this instance, the entangled photons from the broadband entangled source via SPDC process will solely supply as QKD for protected classical information transmission.

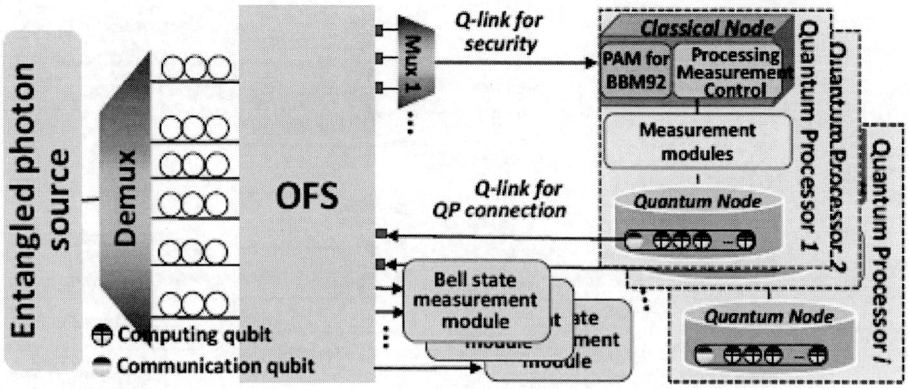

Fig.7.8 A dynamic intra-quantum datacenter network with BSM to enable QP and SPDC entanglement for safe quantum communications.

As the size of the data center and the number of its qubit processors expand, so does the complexity of controlling such a dynamic entangled quantum network. Using intelligent technologies like machine learning techniques is a useful way to manage such a network. A DNN model has been used to forecast the QBER of quantum links in a quantum network based on the coincidence window, beam splitter, and assigned wavelength. This will enable the quantum data center network's efficient routing and resource assignment techniques to be implemented by other technologies. For QP connectivity, comparable instruments will be needed to forecast the fidelity of quantum communications. Additional features and modules are needed to support the intra-quantum data center network's essential and effective operation as depicted in the below figure.

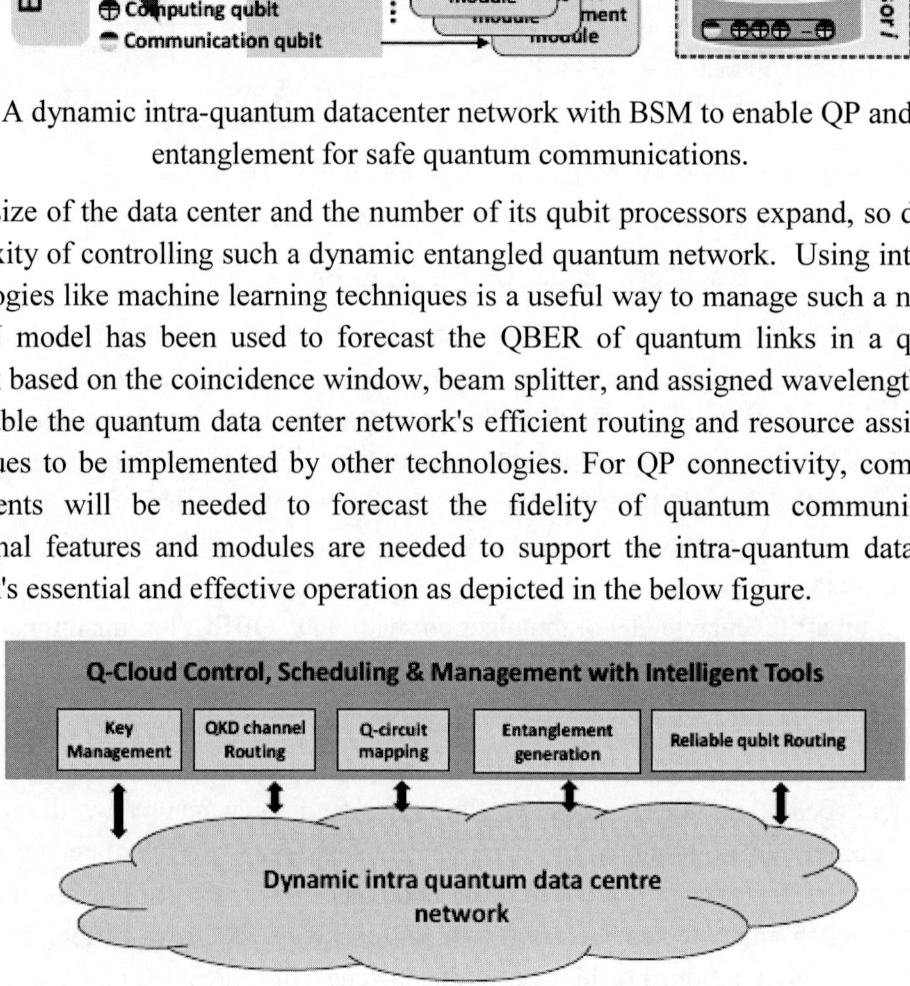

Fig.7.9 Management and control plane for quantum data center network.

The key technological enabler for building a scalable quantum data center with scalable quantum computing capability is a dynamic entangled quantum network driven by a machine learning control mechanism. These data centers are made up of a network of many qubit processors. The fundamental component needed to realize future quantum computing services in the form of quantum cloud computing is a quantum datacenter. Multiple users and applications can share the quantum data center's processing power thanks to quantum cloud computing.

Chapter - 8
Quantum Software Development Patterns

For some tasks, quantum algorithms may perform better than classical ones. New difficulties arise when incorporating quantum algorithms into applications and putting them into reusable implementations. Quantum algorithm implementations should be able to process various issue sizes, be processed by multiple quantum computers, and be utilized and integrated by non-quantum professionals in order to provide reusability and integrability. Many design concepts and best practices are well-known and documented as patterns in classical software engineering, where the goal is to achieve reusability of classical software components.

There are some best practices in quantum software engineering for building reusable quantum algorithm implementations. Below five patterns that outline and true methods for the translation, integration, and modularization of quantum algorithm implementations.

By taking advantage of entanglement and other quantum mechanical phenomena, quantum algorithms have the potential to perform better than their conventional counterparts. The majority of quantum algorithms are hybrid, meaning they combine quantum and conventional processing. This covers both variational quantum algorithms (VQAs), such as the Variational Quantum Eigensolver (VQE) and Quantum Approximate Optimization Algorithm (QAOA), as well as hybrid methods like Grover search and Shor's algorithm for prime factorization that call for classical pre and post-processing steps.

The intricate process of putting a quantum algorithm into practice calls for knowledge of both software engineering and quantum computing. Code representing quantum circuits and code outlining the quantum algorithm's classical logic make up implementations. Then, to address particular issues, these method implementations might be included into hybrid quantum-classical applications. Therefore, a key component of quantum software engineering is the reusability of quantum algorithm implementations and their integration into applications, where the hybrid nature of algorithms and applications presents extra hurdles.

In the context of implementing quantum algorithms, reusability encompasses several elements: Reusability of an implementation across several applications is one factor. The reusability of an implementation is greatly influenced by the programming language employed. For example, applications written in Python can effortlessly incorporate quantum algorithms created in a Python-based quantum programming language. Reusability for various problem cases is another factor. Reusable quantum algorithm implementations, such as those for solving the maximum cut issue [10], should be able to handle graphs of various widths, as this may have an impact on the quantity of qubits needed. Furthermore, implementations of reusable algorithms ought to run on various hardware, such as quantum computers made by various manufacturers.

Classical software engineering offers numerous well-known and well-documented best practices for organizing the code of classical systems, such as modularization to establish separation of concerns, in order to obtain a high degree of reusability. To the best of our knowledge, the developing discipline of quantum software engineering lacks both established and well-documented best practices for incorporating quantum algorithms into applications.

Patterns are a tried-and-true way to record best practices for handling recurrent issues. It offers a methodical approach to encoding architectural and design expertise in a comprehensible manner. Alexander was the one who first introduced patterns into the field of building architecture. These days, they are widely employed in many different fields, such as software engineering, where they are used, for example, in cloud computing, enterprise application integration, and object-oriented application design. Patterns within a given domain are usually arranged using a pattern language. Patterns in a pattern language are linked together to make it easier to combine relevant patterns and comprehend associated issues and their fixes.

A pattern language in the field of quantum computing that has subsequently undergone multiple extensions. The pattern language includes patterns belonging to several categories, such as classes of quantum algorithms or patterns associated with quantum operations. Nevertheless, the language does not currently include patterns that record recommended practices to increase the reusability of quantum algorithm implementations. Add five new patterns to the quantum computing pattern language that address various facets of the implementations' reusability in order to bridge this gap.

8.1 Engineering Quantum Software

The goal of the newly-emerging field of quantum software engineering is to use software engineering concepts to create apps that use quantum algorithm implementations. In particular, one of the primary objectives of quantum software engineering is the reusability of such implementations.

The capacity to incorporate quantum method implementations into many applications is one facet of reusability. While classical computers are used for general-purpose computation and data storage, quantum algorithm implementations are typically integrated into hybrid quantum-classical applications, or hybrid applications for short, to solve problems that can only be solved efficiently using a quantum computer.

The majority of quantum algorithms, including variational algorithms and all algorithms requiring pre- and post-processing using classical computing, are hybrid algorithms. Hence, a quantum part and a classical part make up an implementation of a quantum algorithm. While both classical and quantum components can be implemented in text-based programming languages that are comparable to each other, creating quantum components necessitates not only software engineering expertise but also in-depth knowledge of quantum computing and its mathematical underpinnings.

Specific instruction sets are used by quantum computers. In the gate-based quantum computing concept, quantum gates stand in for the operations carried out on qubits, and they combine with measurements to produce the quantum circuit that a quantum computer is able to process. However, when designing quantum algorithms, different vendors' quantum computers may support different gates natively, which could result in vendor lock-in. A quantum algorithm's inputs, such as the problem instance, need to be encoded into the quantum circuit. Consequently, dynamic quantum circuit synthesis based on the input is needed for reusable quantum algorithm implementations.

The goal of the two patterns, QUANTUM MODULE and QUANTUM MODULE TEMPLATE, is to encapsulate the quantum portion of a quantum algorithm's implementation as reusable sections. Quantum circuits can be produced by quantum modules. Whereas QUANTUM has a known structure and behavior. Modular templates enable the incorporation of any behavior into the quantum circuit that is produced. Conversely, Utilizing a hybrid module, a full quantum implementation of an algorithm that incorporates both the quantum and the traditional components, like the ongoing fraction expansion of the quantum algorithm and Shor's algorithm.

The distribution and deployment of a quantum algorithm implementation for hybrid application integration is its primary use case. Another way to modularize the implementation of a HYBRID MODULE is to use quantum modules or quantum module templates, for example. Experts in nonquantum computing can leverage quantum methods with the help of a CLASSICAL-QUANTUM INTERFACE. Finally, by converting the circuits into a format that is compatible, a QUANTUM CIRCUIT TRANSLATOR permits the execution of quantum circuits on quantum computers made by various suppliers. The details of these patterns are provided in the ensuing subsections.

A. The Quantum Module

Problem: How can the quantum portion of an algorithm's implementation be packed for reuse without relying on specific input values?

Context: All quantum algorithms are hybrid algorithms, meaning that although some parts of the algorithm must be executed on quantum computers, others must be executed on conventional computers.

A quantum circuit carrying out the necessary operations is required for the quantum portion to be executed. The problem instance or the starting values for parameterized quantum gates are two examples of the many inputs that quantum circuits rely on because they are problem-specific. These inputs are then optimized by a classical optimizer. For a quantum algorithm to be reusable, the quantum portion of the algorithm's implementation needs to be input-agnostic.

Forces:

A quantum computer can only process quantum circuits that already have all of the input values stored correctly. It is impossible to apply a static implementation of a quantum circuit—one that prevents the quantum circuit from changing in response to certain input values—to other problems. As a result, the ability to adjust the quantum circuit to various input values is necessary for a reusable implementation of the quantum portion of a quantum algorithm. First, the problem to be addressed (for example, the number to be factored into primes in an implementation of Shor's algorithm) and second, parameters used for optimization or machine learning (e.g., for QAOA) are the input values that must be encoded in a quantum circuit.

Moreover, a thorough understanding of quantum computing and the underlying mathematical ideas is necessary to execute the quantum portion of a quantum algorithm. Experts in quantum computing are thus needed in the development teams. Some algorithmic components, like classical optimizers, on the other hand, might not even require a working knowledge of quantum computing and might be developed by multiple teams without the need for a quantum computing specialist.

Solution:

One possible solution is to divide the quantum algorithm's implementation into one or more quantum modules. The code in these modules creates quantum circuits by using input values that are supplied to the module. Utilizing reusable quantum modules to build common components of a quantum circuit can also help reduce the amount of duplicate code. According to the solution sketch in the below figure, a QUANTUM MODULE accepts input values and builds quantum circuits based on these values using generative code.

Because the implementation can produce quantum circuits for various issue sizes and parameters, this guarantees the QUANTUM MODULE's reusability.

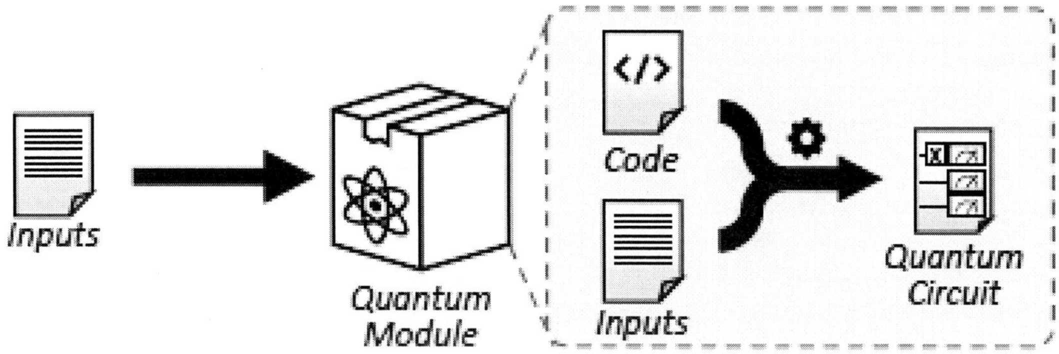

Fig.8.1 Sketch of the solution: Quantum Module.

Result:

An implementation of a quantum algorithm is divided into two parts: (i) QUANTUM MODULES, which include the implementations of the quantum component, and (ii) additional classical code needed for the algorithm's control flow and other classical operations. The reusability of the quantum modules for various quantum algorithm implementations is increased by their independence from the actual input values.

The division of code that results in quantum circuits into quantum modules can therefore be seen in the development teams' organizational structure as well. professionals in quantum computing are only required by the teams working on the quantum modules; professionals in classical software engineering are mostly needed by other teams.

Known Applications:

A number of libraries already contain quantum modules for the construction of quantum circuits. The Grover algorithm is available in Amazon Braket as a module that includes functions for creating the oracle and carrying out the Grover search. The PhaseOracle in Qiskit is an additional illustration of a QUANTUM MODULE for constructing oracles. The quantum fourier transformation utilized in Shor's algorithm is one example of a generic component used in several quantum algorithms. It may be found in Qiskit and Amazon Braket. Using the PhaseEstimation module in Qiskit, one may construct the quantum phase estimation, which is also a component of Shor's method.

Similar Patterns:

A HYBRID MODULE that combines the implementation of the overall quantum algorithm with its quantum and classical components can be employed inside a QUANTUM MODULE that generates particular quantum circuits for a quantum algorithm. If a quantum module only generates a portion of a quantum circuit, the quantum circuits it generates can be combined into a quantum module template to form a whole quantum circuit. A quantum module's border corresponds exactly to the quantum-classic split. According to the QUANTUM-CLASSIC SPLIT pattern, code run on classical computers and code run on quantum computers must necessarily be separated from one another. As a result, this design and the QUANTUM MODULE pattern are connected.

B. Template for Quantum Module

Problem: When some behavior is known later, how may the quantum portion of an algorithm's implementation be packaged for reuse?

Context: Certain quantum algorithms can be applied repeatedly, although how they behave will vary depending on the problem they are used to solve.

As an illustration, the Grover search algorithm has an unidentified oracle. It is possible that the data needed to define the specific behavior of this oracle won't be available for some time. Algorithms such as QAOA that do not provide a specific ansatz for use are examples of similar circumstances. Therefore, it is necessary to implement the quantum portion of these algorithms, where the behavior that is not yet known can be incorporated later.

Forces:

It is possible for quantum algorithms to purposefully omit certain aspects of the quantum part's behavior until a later time. For instance, the Grover search [5] makes use of an ambiguous placeholder gate since it is impossible to determine the precise function that indicates the right values before deciding what to look for. Selecting an appropriate ansatz in the QAOA scenario requires knowledge that is only available during runtime. But before the quantum circuits on a quantum computer are run, the missing behavior needs to be integrated in order for the algorithms to run. Be aware that if various teams work on different aspects of the creation of a quantum algorithm, similar scenarios may occur.

A definition of the conditions that an implementation must meet in order to be integrated and operate properly is necessary for integrating quantum behavior into an already-built circuit. This covers the details of the qubits that can be used as input, potential ancilla qubits, which qubits to use and what shape the output should take, as well as any additional specifications or limitations, like those pertaining to entanglement formation between quantum bits. A quantum computer with more qubits can assign more ancilla qubits if the total number of qubits used in the circuit remains constant. As such, some of the limits, such as the number of accessible ancilla qubits, may also depend on the quantum computer used for execution.

Solution:

In a QUANTUM MODULE TEMPLATE, implement the general behavior of the quantum portion of a quantum algorithm. Inputs defining the undefined behavior to be incorporated into the final quantum circuit are accepted by this module. Either a quantum circuit or a quantum module that creates the necessary quantum circuit can be used to describe the behavior. The primary quantum circuit representing the generic behavior is then integrated into this circuit by the quantum module thermostate. The QUANTUM MODULE TEMPLATE must include specifications in the documentation that can be used to construct a compatible quantum circuit, as outlined in the pattern forces, in order to guarantee that the behavior input, in the form of a quantum circuit, can be integrated to correctly perform the operations it contains. This specification is essentially an agreement that the quantum circuit that serves as the template's input must meet. Classical software engineering also makes use of contracts like plugin contracts.

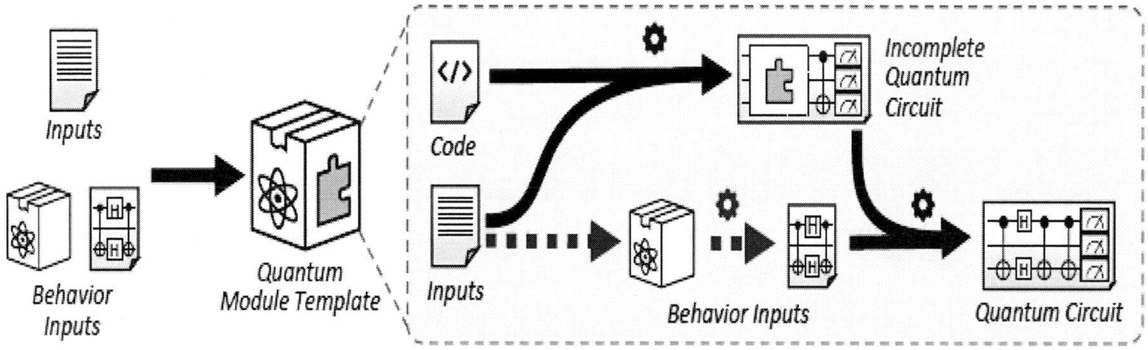

Fig.8.2 Solution sketch: Quantum Module Template.

Above figure illustrates the fundamental components of a Quantum Module Template. Two different types of inputs are needed by the template: (i) behavior inputs, which can be supplied in the form of a quantum circuit or a QUANTUM MODULE, and which partially specify the algorithm's behavior. These inputs represent the problem to be solved as well as parameters affecting the circuit generation.

Similar to the QUANTUM MODULE, the QUANTUM MODULE TEMPLATE generates a quantum circuit using the input values; however, the circuit is not yet complete since the behavior from the behavior inputs is not included. This module is used to create a quantum circuit from the behavior inputs if they are given in the form of a quantum module. The quantum circuit is finally included into the unfinished main circuit. Nonetheless, applications of the template are not restricted to the sample procedures displayed here.

Result:

A quantum algorithm's generic behavior is implemented as a quantum module template, which needs behavior inputs to create an executable, fully functional quantum circuit. The portions of the algorithm's behavior that are unknown in advance are specified by the behavior inputs. Consequently, compared to a QUANTUM MODULE, their influence on the final quantum circuit can be much greater. The behavior inputs have to match the template's necessary input definitions.

If the behavior is given as a quantum module, the integration of the behavior inputs can be completed during the design phase since the quantum module creates the circuit based on the input values. To create quantum circuits from quantum modules implementing higher level circuit functions, templates can be layered inside other templates. This makes it easier to change a portion of a quantum circuit if that portion needs to be produced by a new quantum module that uses an enhanced method, like a state preparation that is more effective.

Known Uses:

A number of quantum algorithms, including the Grover search and the Deutsch algorithm, employ an unidentified unitary gate as a placeholder. These algorithms' general behaviors have implementations in Qiskit and Amazon Braket. Oracle circuits, which are outlined in the ORACLE pattern, are required by these algorithms in order to substitute the placeholder gate. An Oracle Expansion Task for workflows utilizing the Quantum Modeling Extension describes the Oracle replacement. The implementation of generic components of QAOA, including the mixer operator and state preparation, is possible with Amazon Braket and Qiskit by supplying a quantum circuit that encodes the cost function.

Similar Patterns:

A unique form of quantum module known as a TEMPLATE takes behavior inputs as well and incorporates them into the quantum circuit that is created. Circuits can be constructed from smaller modules by integrating, for example, ORACLES and STATE PREPARATION circuits into an executable quantum circuit using quantum module templates.

C. Module Hybrid

Problem: How can a quantum method that requires both quantum and conventional computations be implemented and packaged for integration into applications?

Context: In order to pre- and post-process the outputs of quantum computation, algorithms frequently call on classical computation. Thus, nearly every quantum algorithm is a hybrid. Therefore, for a quantum algorithm to function, its implementation must include both the quantum and the classical components.

Forces: A classical computer is usually needed for some computations involved in quantum algorithms. This implies that they can have more than one quantum and classical component. VQAs, like VQE and QAOA, for instance, switch between quantum and conventional computations. For the algorithm to function properly, both the quantum and the classical parts are needed.

This also covers the algorithm's control flow, which is a component of the algorithm's classical element. The complete algorithm must be implemented in order to include a quantum algorithm into an application. For the integration into apps to be possible, a specialized interface is needed.

Implementing the algorithm on a runtime that is hybrid and capable of the algorithm's quantum and classical components, even demands that the two components be used in tandem.

Solution:

Assemble the complete quantum algorithm as a HYBRID MODULE, comprising both the quantum and classical components. It is possible for this module to be made up of smaller modules, like quantum modules. Moreover, it has the control flow logic needed to coordinate classical and quantum computation. An interface for the hybrid module should be included to make it easier to integrate into apps. The problem that has to be handled by the algorithm should be the primary input value that this interface takes. Furthermore, a hybrid module's interface can accept behavior inputs for both quantum and conventional computations, much like quantum module templates do.

Below figure displays an example of a HYBRID MODULE drawing. With a loop connecting quantum and classical computation, it incorporates the control flow logic and implementations of both classical and quantum components. A number of smaller modules can be used to construct a hybrid module of this kind. For example, the three classical and one quantum computation processes that are displayed can each be implemented in their own module.

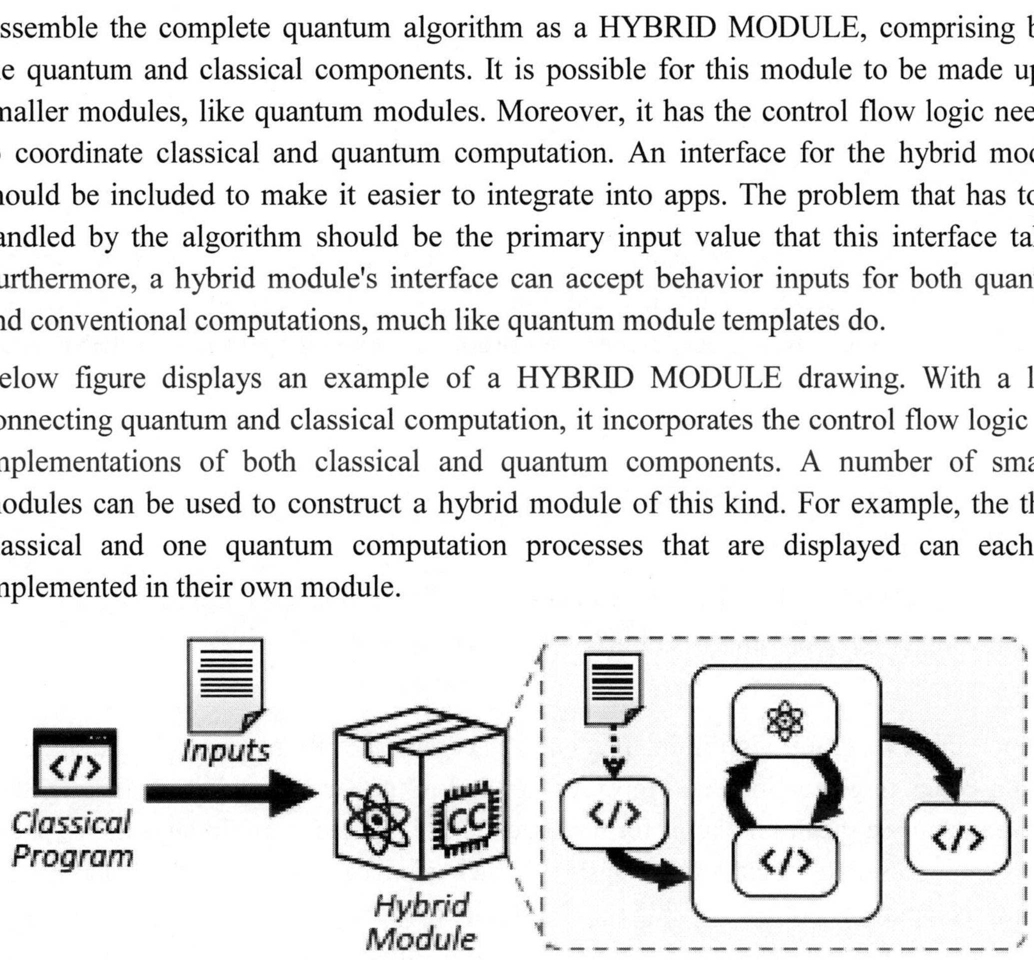

Fig.8.3 Hybrid Module Solution.

Result:

As a result, a HYBRID MODULE contains the whole implementation of the quantum algorithm. It includes the control flow logic as well as the quantum and classical components. The method can be implemented as a standalone service using HYBRID MODULES, for example, in a hybrid runtime environment that can execute both the quantum and the classical parts. Additionally, a library that implements the quantum method and may be included into classical applications is available for distribution as a HYBRID MODULE. It gives the application an interface to utilize. Experts in the problem domain can more easily integrate a hybrid module by using a classical quantum interface as the module's interface.

Known Uses:

Implementations of Shor's algorithm [3], which determines the input number's prime factors, are one specific example. Packaged as a HYBRID MODULE in Amazon Braket, the period-finding computed on the quantum computer and the classical post-processing carrying out the ongoing fraction expansion.

Additional instances of hybrid modules are VQA implementations, such as the Qiskit Runtime's QAOA and VQE implementations, which include the complete quantum algorithm implementation.

Similar Patterns:

There are two categories for the quantum portion of an algorithm's implementation inside a hybrid module: quantum modules and quantum module templates. The HYBRID MODULE has the ability to expose a problem domain-specific CLASSICAL-QUANTUM INTERFACE, making it easier for issue domain experts who are not knowledgeable in quantum computing to integrate them into applications.

D. Conventional-Quantum Interface

Problem:

How can developers who don't know anything about quantum computing use an implementation of a quantum algorithm?

Context:

Implementing a quantum algorithm frequently necessitates a thorough understanding of quantum computing. For instance, in order to employ the Grover search technique, the user must supply a quantum circuit for the oracle that is absent. Certain algorithms, such as QAOA, necessitate selecting an ansatz, which also calls on an understanding of quantum computing. Instead of having in-depth knowledge of quantum computing, software engineers who wish to include a quantum algorithm implementation into an application have a thorough understanding of the problem area.

Forces:

An appropriate interface is needed in order to include a quantum algorithm implementation into an application. Although a hybrid module now has an interface that makes it possible to integrate it into applications, employing this interface would still necessitate a deep understanding of quantum computing. For instance, the issue instance could need to be sent to the quantum portion of the algorithm as a behavior input, or it might contain parameters that affect the quantum portion in other ways, such activating specific error mitigation techniques. Without knowledge of quantum computers, estimating the implications of the changes, such as on runtime or resource requirements, is challenging. Therefore, such an interface is insufficient to enable problem-domain specialists without quantum computing skills to integrate quantum algorithms.

Solution:

Hide the specifics of the quantum implementation by using a CLASSICAL-QUANTUM INTERFACE. The interface can receive inputs in formats unique to the issue domain. The inputs specific to the issue area are internally transformed into the forms needed for the quantum part's implementation. Since comprehending their influence on algorithm execution is crucial knowledge when integrating the quantum algorithm implementation, the documentation of interface inputs that affect the quantum component needs special attention.

Thus, it is the interface developer's responsibility to clearly and concisely define how these inputs affect the algorithm. For instance, the following could be written in the documentation for a parameter that improves the accuracy of the result but also increases the number of gates in the generated circuits, which may lead to more errors with current quantum computers: "Increasing this parameter can increase the accuracy of the result." But it also raises the likelihood that computation errors would compound, thereby negating any accuracy gains.

Below figure illustrates how a CLASSICAL-QUANTUM INTERFACE connects a quantum algorithm built as a HYBRID MODULE with a classical application. It converts the inputs needed by the quantum algorithm from the issue domain-specific input of the classical program. It is also possible to incorporate this interface straight into the HYBRID MODULE.

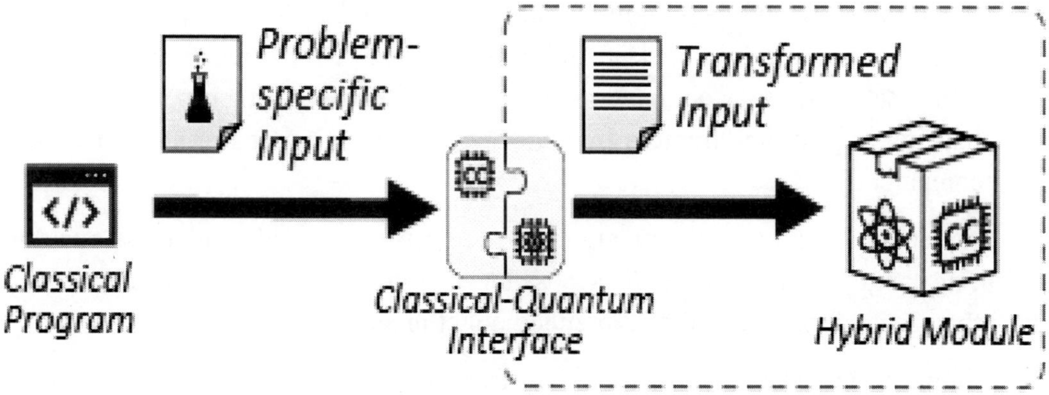

Fig.8.4 Sketch for the Classical-Quantum Interface solution.

Result:

A CLASSICAL-QUANTUM INTERFACE can be used to access the quantum algorithm implementation. Experts in certain problem domains can utilize this version of a quantum algorithm by utilizing the CLASSICAL-QUANTUM INTERFACE designed specifically for their domain. The documentation for the interface provides the information needed to use the algorithm implementation, and specialists in the issue domain are familiar with the format of the input parameters.

Known Uses:

Some of the earliest applications of this design were found in domain-specific libraries for quantum computing. Examples of CLASSICAL-QUANTUM INTERFACES that have already been put into practice may be found in the Qiskit and Amazon Braket chemical area. They provide transformation modules that convert molecules' electronic structures into qubits.

Similar Patterns:

Applications can now incorporate quantum method implementations thanks to the CLASSICAL-QUANTUM INTERFACE. It can function as an interface for a hybrid module that implements a quantum algorithm. The QUANTUMCLASSIC SPLIT separates the various programming paradigms; this interface acts as a bridge between them. For quantum algorithms, there is a unique type of FACADE that not only masks the algorithm's complexity but also bridges the gap between the issue domain and the quantum computing domain.

E. Translator of Quantum Circuits

Problem:

How are separate quantum computers with distinct instruction sets able to perform the same quantum circuit?

Context:

Various quantum gates and programming languages can be used to create quantum circuits. But as a result of vendor lock-in and limited support for particular circuit designs and instruction sets, quantum computers often pose a barrier to interoperability. As a result, translating a quantum circuit is frequently necessary in order to run it on various quantum computers.

For the implementation of quantum algorithms, there are a wide range of quantum programming languages accessible. It is possible to implement a quantum circuit in a language that isn't compatible with the intended quantum computer.

The circuit must be redesigned using an instruction set and quantum programming language that work together. However, a manual re-implementation is impractical for real-world problem sizes due to its error-proneness, time-consuming nature, and requirement for competence in quantum computing. In order to convert unsupported gates into gates that the quantum computer can support natively, an automatic translation is necessary.

Solution:

Replace unsupported gates with comparable gates from the target instruction set by transpiling the quantum circuit to the target instruction set using a translator to translate it into the target language. Figure's solution sketch depicts the use of a QUANTUM CIRCUIT TRANSLATOR, which converts a quantum circuit between two programming languages and instruction sets. The left target quantum circuit's SWAP gate, which linked the outside qubit wires, has been divided into three C-NOT gates in the right target quantum circuit.

The ability to automatically translate a quantum circuit into a target format is achieved by a QUANTUM CIRCUIT TRANSLATOR. This allows components with disparate circuit formats and instruction sets to utilize the same circuit. Because it allows them to be used with various quantum computers.

Result:

A QUANTUM CIRCUIT TRANSLATOR promotes the reusability of quantum modules. Alternatively, the translated circuits can be used as inputs for a QUANTUM MODULE TEMPLATE, negating the necessity for direct execution. The creation of quantum algorithms based on modules implemented in various computer languages is made possible by a QUANTUM CIRCUIT TRANSLATOR, thus. Consequently, the interoperability of quantum modules can be improved by using a QUANTUM CIRCUIT TRANSLATOR.

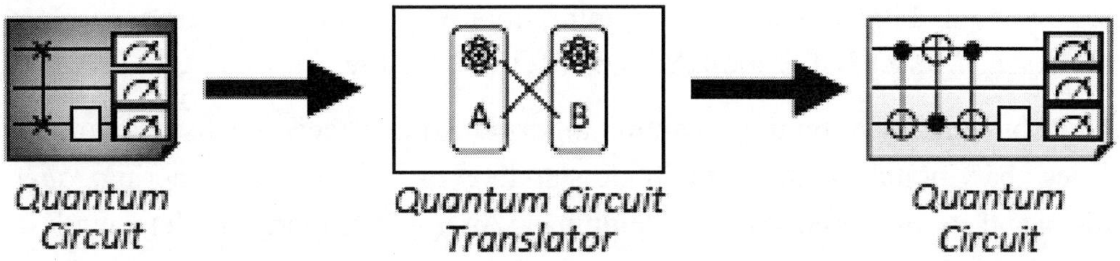

Fig.8.5 Quantum Circuit Translator Solution Sketch.

Known Uses:

OpenQASM, an open quantum assembly language, is a format that is frequently used to define quantum circuits. Numerous quantum software development kits (SDKs), including Amazon Braket, Qiskit, and Cirq, are capable of importing and exporting it. The transpiled circuit for the corresponding quantum device is required by the NISQ Analyzer in order to estimate if a quantum circuit may be implemented. There are several circuit translators in it. There is a plugin for the Python SDK Pennylane that makes it possible to handle IBM quantum computers without the need for further libraries.

Similar Patterns:

The MESSAGE TRANSLATOR pattern from the enterprise integration pattern language is connected to the QUANTUM CIRCUIT TRANSLATOR design. Quantum circuits in any language can be translated into any other language utilizing a CANONICAL DATA MODEL with a maximum of two translators for each language. Circuits created by a Quantum Module implemented in one programming language can be translated using a circuit translator before being utilized with a Quantum Module Template implemented in a different programming language.

The quantity of real-world applications of a software engineering pattern determines its validity. Every recently released pattern has several established actual applications listed in the section on known uses.

With the exception of quantum computing libraries like Qiskit, which are intended for a broader user base, the majority of quantum software development is currently done on an as-needed basis, for example, when implementing an experimental algorithm once without following best practices from traditional software engineering. A contributing factor in the prevalence of ad-hoc development is the fact that only the largest quantum computers available today can simulate more qubits than can be done on a classical computer.

These qubits' prospective uses are further limited by the fact that they are still noisy. Therefore, with today's quantum computers, most quantum algorithms are unable to demonstrate their quantum advantage for meaningful issue sizes. Because of this, current quantum algorithm implementations are frequently one-time uses, such as for proof-of-concepts, because the restricted technology available today can only handle simple issues. As such, the bigger quantum computing libraries contain the majority of examples of the QUANTUM MODULE and HYBRID MODULE patterns.

As previously mentioned, putting quantum algorithms into practice calls for a unique set of abilities that include a thorough understanding of software engineering, quantum computing, and its mathematical underpinnings. As a result, many implementations are made by physicists who have little experience with software engineering. Once they can tackle problems of a relevant size, quantum algorithms are predicted to play a crucial role in numerous applications across a wide range of areas. The HYBRID MODULE design, which can conceal all of this complexity inside the module, will be helpful in this situation since applications integrating quantum algorithms do not depend on the implementation specifics of the algorithms.

Dividing an algorithm's implementation into several modules is a well-known method for lowering implementation complexity. In order to adapt this well-established design approach to the unique needs of quantum computing, module patterns were introduced to the developing field of quantum software engineering. Implementations of quantum algorithms can be modularized using the two patterns, QUANTUM MODULE and QUANTUM MODULE TEMPLATE. Modularization has several applications. A HYBRID MODULE, for instance, can be constructed with QUANTUM MODULES.

Once they can tackle problems of a relevant size, quantum algorithms are predicted to play a crucial role in numerous applications across a wide range of areas.

The HYBRID MODULE design, which can conceal all of this complexity inside the module, will be helpful in this situation since applications integrating quantum algorithms do not depend on the implementation specifics of the algorithms. Modules must expose an interface that other modules can use in order for their compatibility to be guaranteed. The reusability of quantum algorithm implementations is enhanced and complexity is concealed by a well-defined interface, allowing for their use even by those lacking extensive expertise of quantum computing. When developing algorithm implementations that facilitate seamless integration into current applications, the CLASSICAL-QUANTUM INTERFACE design is essential.

On various quantum computers, the QUANTUM CIRCUIT TRANSLATOR pattern is primarily utilized for the execution of quantum circuits. Since hardware suppliers haven't decided on a common format for depicting quantum circuits, it's necessary. Right now, OpenQASM appears to be the most viable option for this kind of format. We will probably still have a variety of quantum programming languages with unique characteristics even if all current quantum computers are able to understand OpenQASM. When creating quantum algorithms, one can also employ a QUANTUM CIRCUIT TRANSLATOR, which converts quantum circuits between two of these languages.

It is possible to use quantum modules implemented in different computer languages using such a translator.

8.2 Quantum Applications: Execution Patterns

Outlined here is the language of quantum computing patterns and how the extension enhances it. The present patterns for quantum computing are depicted in the image below, with the goal of assisting developers in creating and executing quantum applications. Different categories of the language are used to handle different components of the quantum application lifecycle.

The Program Flow patterns, for instance, offer guidance on how to divide computational activities between quantum and classical resources. It describes methods to enhance hybrid quantum algorithms, such as the so-called Warm-Starting methodology, and explains algorithms like the Quantum Approximate Optimization Algorithm (QAOA). The majority of quantum algorithms add a subroutine that creates the relevant state to the circuit's start in order to encode classical data into the quantum circuit. The Data Encodings category collects many methods for encoding the data to make this work easier.

Error handling is another important factor to take into account. The category of the same name, which is seen in the image below, brings together a number of pertinent patterns. For example, as a post-processing method to address measurement mistakes, NISQ devices can benefit from using so-called readout error mitigation. Patterns that document quantum circuit and application execution solutions are shown here. These patterns were developed by examining the documentation of quantum cloud services that are currently in use.

The following figure illustrates the new execution patterns that are intended to make it easier for customers to select the quantum service offerings that best meet their needs in terms of execution requirements. When quantum circuits must be executed without the need for deployment or integration, the STANDALONE CIRCUIT EXECUTION pattern is designed to address the most fundamental execution circumstances. Therefore, quantum services that make interacting with quantum devices easier can be advantageous in such cases.

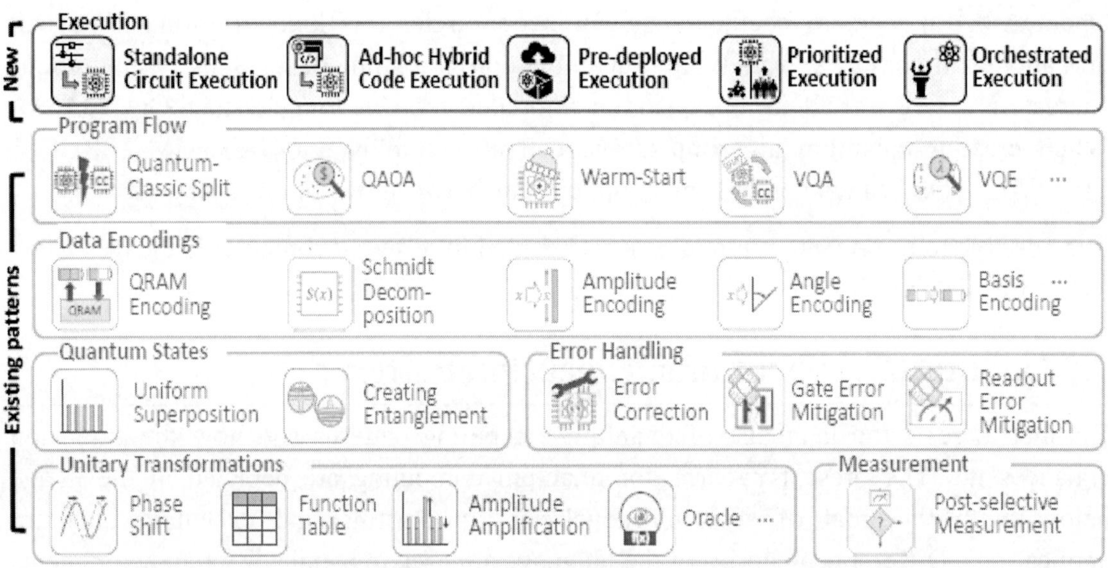

Fig.8.6 Summary of the Pattern Language for Quantum Computing.

On the other hand, the AD-HOC HYBRID CODE EXECUTION design concentrates on the ad-hoc execution of quantum circuits with classical pre- and post processing stages, i.e., without requiring deployment modification for both quantum and conventional code sections. The PRE-DEPLOYED EXECUTION pattern addresses more complex cases wherein components of quantum applications must be deployed in a certain manner, such as distributed to take advantage of diverse offerings or installed in close proximity to boost efficiency.

By cutting down on queuing times, the PRIORITIZED EXECUTION pattern outlines methods for efficiently executing several quantum circuits. It makes it possible to reserve a quantum device exclusively or to execute numerous quantum circuits with shorter wait durations after only one wait. The ORCHESTRATED EXECUTION pattern describes the execution of quantum circuits as a component of orchestrated quantum applications. Workflows can help these kinds of systems by guaranteeing data and control flow and offering benefits like robustness, scalability, or transactional processing. Depending on the needs of the particular application, one can select between the AD-HOC HYBRID CODE EXECUTION, PRE-DEPLOYED EXECUTION, ORCHESTRATED EXECUTION, and STANDALONE CIRCUIT EXECUTION patterns, which capture many execution variants for quantum applications.

The PRIORITIZED EXECUTION pattern, on the other hand, can be used with other execution patterns and is centered on enhancing execution efficiency.

8.2.1 Execution of Standalone Circuit

***Problem*:** How may standalone quantum circuits be implemented with no integration or deployment requirements?

Context:

In other cases, such as circuit design and testing or teaching, just isolated quantum circuits need to be implemented. Thus, it is advantageous to operate quantum circuits with little difficulty and understanding of various quantum offerings in addition to technology for deployment or integration.

Forces:

The capabilities and characteristics of quantum offerings differ. Using sophisticated solutions, such as deployment automation and integration technologies, for straightforward use cases might result in needless management overhead and even cause the task to get unfinished owing to a lack of technical knowledge. On the other hand, some quantum services, including those that generate execution requests automatically, lessen the amount of management work that is necessary.

Solution:

Use quantum offers to execute quantum circuits without having to integrate them with other services or build bespoke deployment logic. The solution sketch in the below figure, which uses products that may create and execute circuits, illustrates how various quantum circuits are carried out. This comprises text-based tools or specialized graphical circuit composers that transfer the quantum circuits to the offering. Most of the management work, such as circuit deployment and authentication to the underlying quantum service, is typically handled by providers.

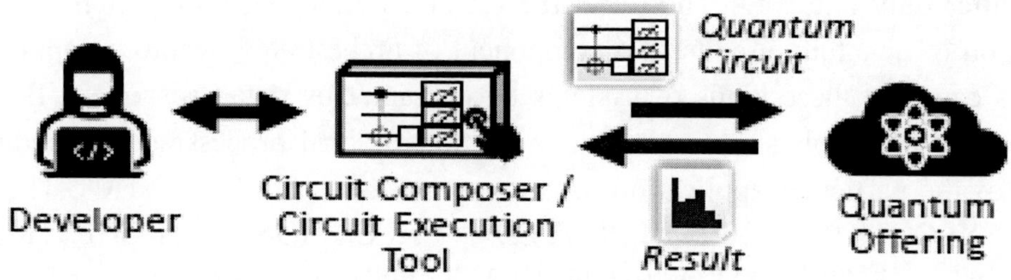

Fig.8.7 Execution of Standalone Circuit.

Result:

This pattern's quantum features offer a straightforward method of implementing quantum circuits. However, these products cannot be used to design traditional pre- and post-processing procedures. Larger quantum programs cannot be executed with this form of execution, and there is either no support for integration with external apps or very little support for it. Furthermore, this form of computing does not allow for the utilization of prioritized executions.

Known Uses:

This technique is supported by vendors like IBM through graphical circuit composer services, which allow users to graphically model and execute quantum circuits from a graphical user interface (GUI), abstracting away the authentication and invocation request building.

Similar Patterns:

The AD-HOC HYBRID CODE EXECUTION can be employed in situations where quantum circuits are tested and then need to be integrated with classical pre- and post processing procedures. Furthermore, when modeling quantum circuits, many quantum computing patterns, such as AMPLITUDE AMPLIFICATION or UNIFORM SUPERPOSITION, can be applied.

8.2.2 Ad-hoc Execution of Hybrid Code

Problem:

How may quantum circuits be implemented without the need for extra deployment or integration stages using traditional pre- and post processing steps?

Context:

Often, standalone quantum circuits with their traditional pre- and post-processing procedures must be implemented in order to avoid additional costs associated with their deployment, operation, and management in the cloud.

Forces:

Comparable to the execution of a standalone circuit. Nevertheless, merging the traditional pre- and post-processing phases is hindered by employing this approach. The use of provider-managed or local development environments minimizes management work, such as when executing both classical and quantum code with a single command.

Solution:

Use local editors with manually added token-based authentication or code editors handled by the supplier. The quantum circuits and classical code execution using AD-HOC HYBRID CODE EXECUTION are depicted in the figure below. Either a local or remote code editor is used for the traditional pre- and post-processing procedures. The quantum circuits are transmitted to the quantum cloud providing by function calls, which are frequently supplied by the quantum programming language or quantum SDK.

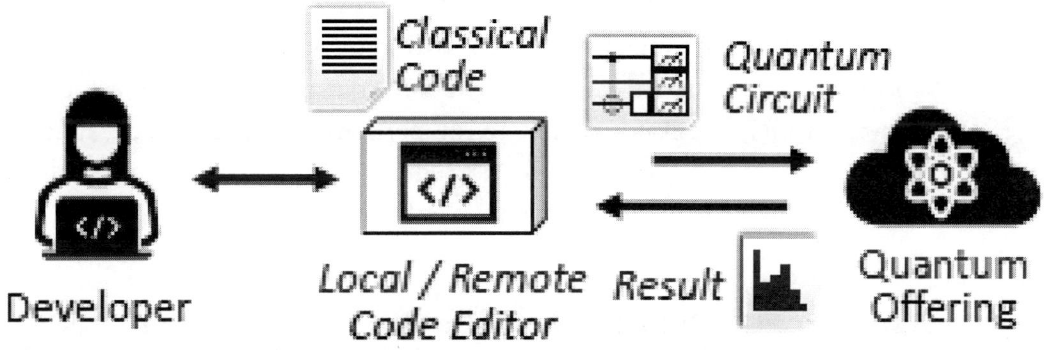

Fig.8.8 Ad-hoc Hybrid Code Runtime.

Result:

As a result, compared to the STANDALONE CIRCUIT EXECUTION paradigm, this pattern gives developers more control over the execution of quantum and classical components, such as token management or request building via SDKs. However, it is not appropriate for creating larger applications or doing multiple separate computations due to its frequently restricted integration with external programs. Once quantum circuits and associated classical pre- and post-processing stages have been successfully executed ad hoc, all artifacts can be published through application marketplaces or packaged and deployed to a compatible offering, making reuse easier.

Known Uses:

Numerous vendors support this design. For instance, Google with Cirq (Google, 2020), IBM with Qiskit (IBM, 2023b), and Amazon with Braket (AWS, 2023) all offer Python notebooks as remote code editors. Different languages are supported by local code editors with specialized packages, such as Rigettis pyQuil and Forest SDK. Then, manual access token configuration is used to authenticate to quantum services.

Similar Patterns:

STATE PREPARATION is one of the traditional pre-processing processes; this can be completed with tools like ANGLE or BASIS encoding. Among the post-processing processes are READOUT ERROR MITIGATION. To improve efficiency when executing many quantum circuits, PRIORITIZED EXECUTION can be employed.

8.2.3 Pre-deployed Implementation

Problem:

How may quantum circuits with specific deployment requirements be implemented using conventional pre- and post processing steps?

Context:

The majority of quantum algorithms are hybrid; for example, VQAs have a hybrid loop that consists of several parameterized quantum circuit executions carried out one after the other on classical hardware for optimization purposes. Moreover, quantum devices can be accessed through the cloud, and in order to run a circuit, it must be put in the task queue of the relevant service, which might not be able to run portions of classical code. It could be necessary to do pre- and post-processing procedures in a certain way, such as simultaneously or by utilizing particular combinations of cloud service providers.

Forces:

The features offered by Quantum service providers varies greatly, and they frequently rely on proprietary formats, SDKs, and distinct authentication techniques. For example, due to data processing requirements, more technical skills could be needed to correctly execute a given quantum circuit with its pre- and post-processing processes that can be hosted separately. There are situations where it makes more sense to run the application's quantum and classical components close to one another, such as when minimizing networking overhead.

Solution:

Either on (i) a single quantum offering that enables the execution of quantum and classical components, or (ii) a particular combination of quantum and cloud services that satisfies the specified deployment requirements, pre-deploy the quantum circuit with its pre- and post-processing stages. The pattern's solution sketch is displayed in the figure below: Step 1 involves the deployment of the classical and quantum components in accordance with deployment choices. Developers or client programs can execute and retrieve the findings displayed in Steps 2 and 3 on their own.

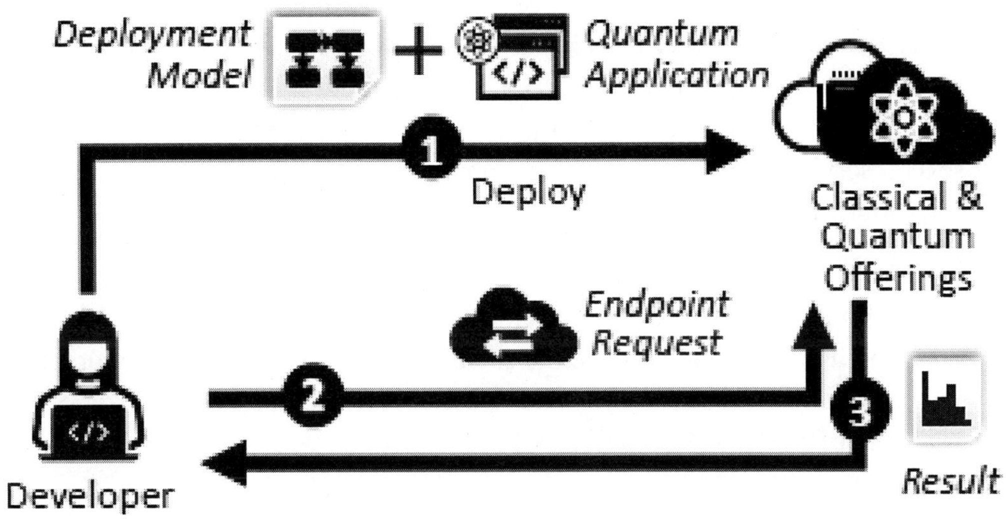

Fig.8.9 Pre-deployed Execution pattern's solution sketch involves running a quantum application across a variety of cloud providers.

Variants:

A Hybrid Execution Environment offering that can accelerate the interplay between quantum and conventional calculations is one deployment target choice in Step 1. As a result, they shorten wait times for numerous subsequent quantum circuit executions and lower network overhead. A Distributed Deployment is an additional variation wherein segments of the quantum application are set up across many cloud providers. The deployment models and methods for implementing both quantum and classical components vary depending on the technologies selected. For example, implementing QAOA for Qiskit Runtime would impose more deployment modeling and coding constraints than more general deployment scenarios like packaging the quantum application into one or more containers that can be deployed to a container orchestration engine like Kubernetes and then executed via client requests.

Result:

Quantum applications can be distributed and executed independently, allowing for integration with other apps or invocation by other users. For example, a VQA that has already been deployed can be integrated into another application. When using hybrid runtimes, the pre-deployed application is constrained by the specifications and features of the underlying offering but gains transparency in provider-managed execution. For some areas of the application, developers can combine various services in the Distributed Deployment version.

Known Uses:

IBM's Qiskit Runtime service provides a hybrid execution environment that may be used to launch a quantum application that is packaged as a Python file with a JSON metadata file and then run over an HTTP endpoint that is accessible to the public. Amazon Braket Hybrid Jobs is a comparable service (AWS, 2023). Additionally, Microsoft presented the hybrid execution environment and provided a usage sample (Frachon, 2023). Different cloud providers can be used for traditional jobs in distributed deployment settings. AWS provides several services, such as Lambda for running Python code, S3 for object storage, and Amazon Cloudwatch for monitoring.

Similar Patterns:

Pre-deployed hybrid application execution enhances the reusability of several methods, like VQA, as well as more tangible patterns, such VQE and QAOA. Furthermore, to run on preferred execution targets, pre- and post-processing processes like STATE PREPARATION or READOUT ERROR MITIGATION can be used.

8.2.4 Prioritized Execution

Problem:

How can several quantum circuits be executed consecutively with minimal waiting time?

Context:

Multiple quantum circuits must frequently be executed for quantum applications. This is particularly true when using VQAs on modern NISQ gadgets. Consequently, these quantum circuits ought to be used effectively by cutting down on wait times.

Forces:

In order to ensure equitable use of quantum devices, access is typically granted through lines. As a result, while running several quantum circuits independently of one another, the waiting periods add up. Using batch processing, which involves integrating several quantum circuits into a single task that is then done all at once, is one method. This method, however, cannot be used in situations where quantum circuits are dependent on the outcomes of earlier executions, such as VQAs.

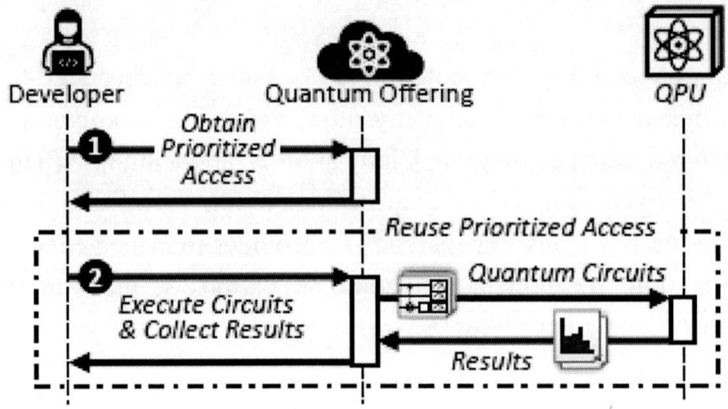

Fig.8.10 Prioritized Execution solution drawing: illustrates the use of prioritized access to execute several circuits.

Solution:

As seen in the solutions sketch in the above figure, employ quantum offerings that allow for prioritized access to quantum devices to cut down on or eliminate waiting times. Step 1 provides privileged access to quantum devices for this purpose. Through this prioritized access in Step 2, which limits the user base to shorten wait times for many circuit executions, the quantum device may then be reused.

Variants:

Using Session Reuse to enable prioritizing is one option. Therefore, the session created for the initial quantum circuit execution is used for several ensuing circuit runs. Specific Access is an additional version where a quantum gadget is set aside for exclusive use without requiring a prior line-up scheduling a time slot. But usually, this results in extra expenses.

Result:

This pattern reduces the amount of time spent waiting in extremely busy job queues. Cost and runtime are traded off when choosing between the two choices. Since the reservation of a quantum device is more expensive than other types of access, runtime is given first priority in the reserved time-slice scenario. There may still be concurrent executions from other users in the task queue even when sessions are being used for the execution.

Known Uses: At the moment, IBM and AWS support the Session Reuse version. Furthermore, providers like AWS, Azure, and IBM provide the Dedicated Access version. The possible options for the session are highlighted, together with data like the session duration restriction, in a practical example of a prioritized execution using Qiskit.

Similar Patterns:

Due to the quantity of consecutive quantum circuit executions, priority is strongly encouraged when utilizing the VQA, VQE, or QAOA patterns. In certain situations, it may be used in conjunction with the PRE-DEPLOYED EXECUTION pattern to meet specific deployment needs.

8.2.5 Synched Execution

Problem:

What measures may be taken to guarantee data flow and control for quantum applications that involve one or more quantum circuits and the accompanying classical pre- and post-processing stages?

Context:

According to Leymann and Barzen (2020), the majority of quantum algorithms are hybrid, meaning that certain portions are performed on quantum devices and some on classical hardware. Additionally, numerous quantum algorithms as well as extra classical components, such as user interaction or database loading, may be included into quantum applications. These components need to be coordinated, meaning that the data flow and control between them need to be guaranteed.

Forces:

There are significant differences between quantum devices and the associated quantum cloud services in terms of qubit availability, execution costs, and wait times. Without external orchestration tools, the orchestration of components operating in diverse environments may become unmanageable due to factors including lengthy invocation chains, intricate data transfers, data format conversions, and interactions with several heterogeneous APIs.

Solution:

As seen in the graphic below, use a workflow language to represent the classical and quantum components as jobs inside a workflow model. The workflow model may then be applied to a workflow engine, which ensures the necessary data flow and orchestrates the quantum and classical components by calling them in the prescribed order. Thus, the workflow engine provides capabilities like data format translation and the invocation of diverse services. Although there are workflow solutions designed for the quantum computing space, such as pre-implemented quantum algorithms, established workflow languages and matching workflow engines may also be used to take advantage of their broad feature sets and maturity.

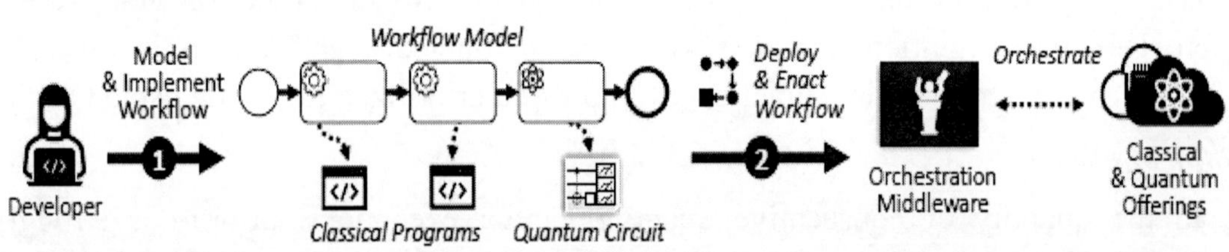

Fig.8.11 A schematic solution for a coordinated implementation: With the aid of orchestration middleware, actions that are implemented in both the quantum and classical domains are carried out in the designated sequence and setting.

Solution:

The workflow model outlining their integration is divided from the classical code and the quantum circuitry needed to execute a quantum application. As a result, development time and expense are reduced and modularity is increased and existing code may be reused. Quantum applications can also profit from the robustness, scalability, and dependability of workflow engines by using workflows. Additionally supported is the use of several heterogeneous quantum and conventional cloud providers with varying features. However, more knowledge is needed to describe orchestrations in order to implement them on specialized middleware, which might result in overhead for straightforward use cases like circuit design and testing.

Known Uses:

Business Process Model and Notation (BPMN) and Business Process Execution Language (BPEL) are two instances of standardized workflow languages. Various workflow engines, such as the Camunda BPMN engine, are available for the execution of various workflow models.

To make the modeling of processes in the field of quantum computing easier, there is also a modeling extension tailored specifically for quantum computing. Two examples of quantum-specific orchestration tools are Agnostiq's Covalent platform and Zapata's Orquestra, which employ a bespoke YAML-based language and need control flow to be specified using a Python-based domain-specific language.

Similar Patterns:

If the workflow has to execute many quantum circuits, waiting times can be decreased by using the PRIORITIZED EXECUTION pattern. This design may also be used to combine many different quantum applications that are made accessible using the PRE-DEPLOYED EXECUTION method.

8.3 Quantum Encoding Patterns

This section explains the pattern format and the process for gathering patterns. The display of patterns that follows, of which the figure below provides an overview, comes next. Angle encoding, qram encoding, and schmidt decomposition are three patterns for data encoding and state preparation that are also described. A measurement pattern called post-selective measurement follows the introduction of two patterns for unitary transformations: matrix encoding and quantum phase estimation.

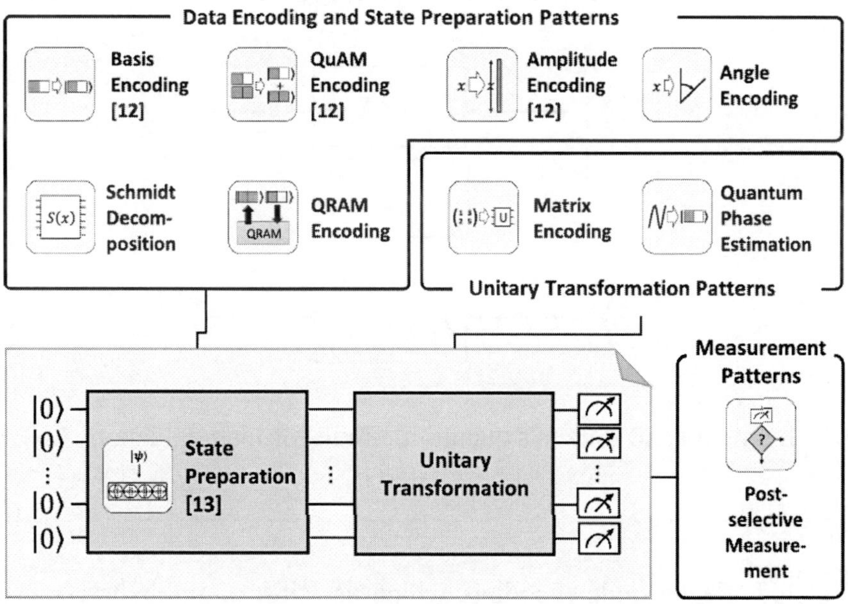

Fig.8.12 Overview of patterns.

8.3.1 Angle Encoding

Alias: Qubit Encoding, (Tensor) Product Encoding.

Context: After the data has been loaded, an algorithm needs an effective encoding scheme in order to execute as many operations as possible within the decoherence time.

Solution:

The first step is to normalize all data points that need to be encoded to the $\left[0, \frac{\pi}{2}\right]$ interval. Then, as shown in below figure, each value xi is represented by a single qubit by applying a rotation around the Bloch Sphere's y-axis. As a result, the data value determines the rotational angle.

Result: This encoding produces a separable quantum state, meaning that the qubits are not entangled:

$$|\psi\rangle = \begin{pmatrix} \cos x_0 \\ \sin x_0 \end{pmatrix} \otimes \begin{pmatrix} \cos x_1 \\ \sin x_1 \end{pmatrix} \otimes \ldots \otimes \begin{pmatrix} \cos x_n \\ \sin x_n \end{pmatrix}$$

This encoding's primary benefit is its exceptional operational efficiency: No matter how many data values need to be encoded, a certain amount of parallel processes are required. However, the number of qubits required depends on the number of data values: To encode a single component of the input vector, one qubit is needed. Therefore, the state preparation is efficient because only one qubit rotation is needed, but the number of qubits for this encoding is not ideal.

Connected Patterns: This pattern enhances STATE PREPARATION much more.

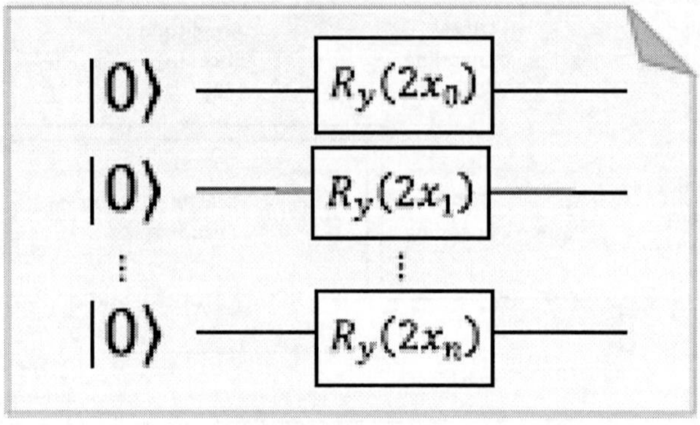

Fig.8.13 Leymann and Barzen's quantum circuit for loading data in ANGLE ENCODING.

Variants:

Alternatives include dense angle encoding, which uses just n2 qubits to represent n data points by taking advantage of a further qubit characteristic called relative phase.

Known Applications:

Using the encoding in quantum image processing One qubit represents a pixel's color information in the so-called flexible representation of a quantum image, while another register encodes the pixel's position. Quantum neuron (quron) is the term used to describe a qubit that uses this encoding in quantum neural networks. An angle encoding state preparation approach that allows the rotational axis (x, y, or z) to be specified. It is simple to prepare this encoding using normal qubit rotations if no loading routine is supplied.

8.3.2 Quantum Random Access Memory (QRAM) Encoding

Context: An algorithm needs random access to the input data values.

Solution: The data stored at a location with a memory index is loaded into an output register using a traditional RAM. Although the address and output registers are quantum registers, quantum random access memory offers the same functionality. Consequently, the output register and the address may both have numerous values superposed on each other.

The fundamental operation of a QRAM is depicted in the picture below. It loads the matching data values into an empty output register after receiving a superposition of the first two addresses

$\left(\frac{1}{\sqrt{2}}|00\rangle + \frac{1}{\sqrt{2}}|01\rangle\right)$ as input. As a result, the total quantum system is in the following state:

$$|\psi\rangle = \frac{1}{\sqrt{2}}|00\rangle|000\rangle + \frac{1}{\sqrt{2}}|01\rangle|110\rangle$$

Thus, loading m of n data values into a QRAM can often be explained as the following process.

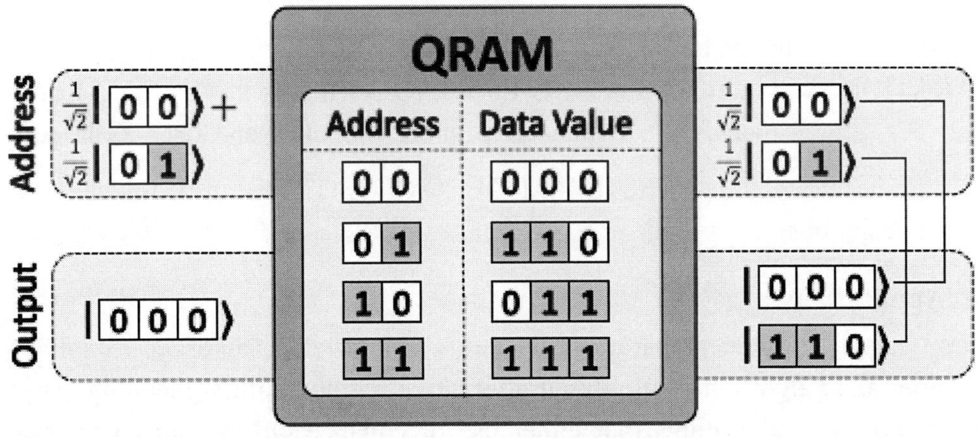

Fig.8.14 The fundamental operation of a quantum random access memory.

QRAM generates a superposition of addresses and their data values $\frac{1}{\sqrt{2}}|00\rangle|000\rangle + \frac{1}{\sqrt{2}}|01\rangle|110\rangle$ given an address register that is in a superposition of addresses ($|00\rangle$ and $|01\rangle$):

$$\frac{1}{\sqrt{m}}\sum_{i=0}^{m-1}|a\rangle_i|0\rangle \xrightarrow{QRAM} \frac{1}{\sqrt{m}}\sum_{i=0}^{m-1}|a\rangle_i|x_a\rangle$$

where the output register is the second register and the address register, which is the first register, is a superposition of all m addresses to be loaded. Additionally, xa is the data value linked to the address |a⟩i, which indicates the address of the ith data value to be loaded. Each data value |xa⟩ is loaded into the output register by the QRAM so that |a⟩i|xa⟩ is present in the combined state of both registers. This state could be entangled based on the data values.

Result: To encode the data values using BASIS ENCODING, l qubits are required for this encoding. For a maximum of n addresses, ⌈log(n)⌉ more qubits are needed by the address register. The computational characteristics are comparable to those of QUAM ENCODING and BASIS: When a superposition of the encoded data values is ready, arithmetic operations like addition and multiplication can be performed and data can be processed in parallel (quantum parallelism).

An algorithm that makes use of QRAM makes the assumption that there is an effective method for preparing states in logarithmic runtime. A state preparation technique that mimics a QRAM's loading procedure must be employed as long as there are no hardware implementations of QRAM. The primary disadvantage of QRAM encoding is that, generally speaking, there isn't a state preparation technique as effective as a QRAM for arbitrary input data. An algorithm that uses QRAM can only achieve the promised speedup if data can be efficiently encoded using a proven state preparation technique.

Related Patterns: This pattern makes use of BASIS ENCODING and improves STATE PREPARATION even more. CREATING ENTANGLEMENT: For instance, loading the first and last address yields the entangled 5-qubit Greenberger-Horne-Zeilinger state, $\left(\frac{1}{\sqrt{2}}|00\rangle|000\rangle + \frac{1}{\sqrt{2}}|11\rangle|111\rangle\right)$. SCHMIDT DECOMPOSITION can be utilized as a state preparation technique.

Known Applications:

By circuit family, a state preparation algorithm is provided. In order to solve semi-definite programs, algorithms employ an alternative method called encoding. There are numerous additional algorithms that either use or enhance QRAM. In an intermediate phase of the Harrow-Hassidim-Lloyd (HHL) algorithm for solving linear equations, eigenvalues are represented via QRAM ENCODING.

8.3.3 Schmidt Decomposition

Context:

An empty n-qubit register must be used to prepare a state |s⟩. An arbitrary state can be created in its place if there isn't a state preparation technique that effectively uses the structure of this state.

Forces:

The following forces are present while building a circuit for an arbitrary state:

1. The designed state preparation circuit should ideally have a shallow depth.
2. The possible advantage of utilizing a quantum computer should not be outweighed by the runtime required to build the state preparation circuit on a classical computer.

Solution:

In order to create a circuit for |s⟩, it must first be described in terms of two subspaces that span $H\otimes^n$, V and W. First, a linear combination of the orthogonal basis vectors {f1, ..., fk} ∈ V and {g1, ..., gk} ∈ W is used to represent |s⟩:

$$|s\rangle = \sum_{i,j} b_{ij} \cdot f_i \otimes g_j$$

Next is the computation of the matrix M = {bij}'s singular value decomposition (SVD):

$$M = (\,U_1 U_2\,)\begin{pmatrix} A \\ 0 \end{pmatrix} V^*$$

where U1 and U2 rewrite the matrix U that the SVD produced. The Schmidt decomposition of |s⟩ is defined as the set {α1, ...αm}, which is constructed from the entries of the diagonal matrix A:

$$|s\rangle = \sum_{i=1}^{m} \alpha_i \cdot u_i \otimes v_i,\, \alpha_i \in \mathbb{R} \geq 0, \text{where} \sum_{i=1}^{m} \alpha_i = 1$$

where the Schmidt coefficients for the Schmidt bases {ui}, {vi} are α1, ..., αm. To prepare |s⟩ on an empty register, use the circuit shown in the diagram below. First, B converts the first register's amplitude to the Schmidt coefficients. This state is then copied to the second register using a sequence of CNOT operations. Lastly, the Schmidt basis states are created by U1 and V from the computational basis states {ei}:

$$(U_1 \otimes V) \sum_{i=1}^{m} \alpha_i \cdot e_i \otimes e_i = \sum_{i=1}^{m} \alpha_i \cdot u_i \otimes v_i$$

The unitary matrices need to be further broken down into one and two qubit gates in order to be executed on a quantum computer.

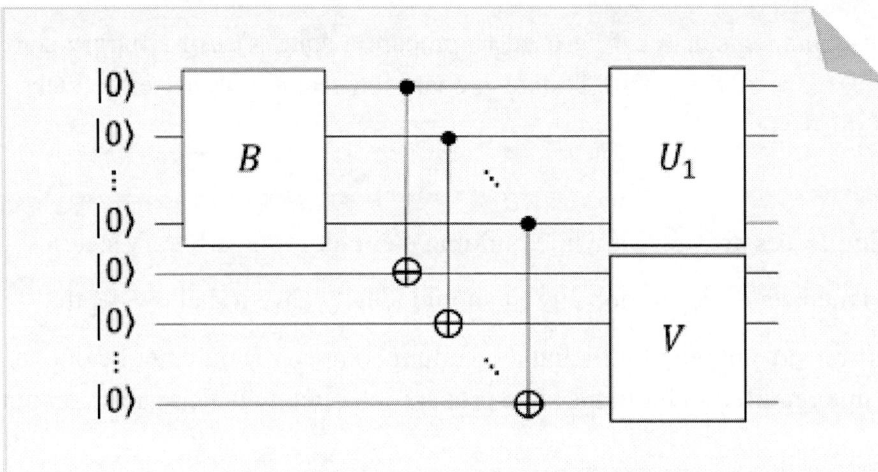

Fig.8.15 State preparation circuit for |s⟩.

Result: The register creates the state |s⟩. The Schmidt coefficients αi, which can be used to measure entanglement, are known for this state. If and only if precisely one of the Schmidt coefficients is non-zero, the state |s⟩ is separable. The circuit's depth is exponential in the worst scenario, or more specifically, $\frac{23}{48}2^n)$. It should be noted that arbitrary state preparation was demonstrated to have exponential complexity, meaning that in the worst scenario, an exponentially deep circuit will always be required.

Related Patterns: This pattern improves STATE PREPARATION and can be used to QRAM or AMPLITUDE state preparation.

Known Applications: Random states with a regulated degree of entanglement can be produced using this pattern.

8.4 Data Encoding Patterns

At the start of a quantum algorithm, each pattern explains how incoming data is loaded in a particular encoding. Since the INITIALIZATION process involves loading data, each encoding pattern improves on the previous one. Thus, begin with providing a brief synopsis of INITIALIZATION, followed by a thorough explanation of the pressures to expand the initial pattern. We leave this portion out of the encoding patterns as these are also the driving forces behind the new ones.

Here, QUAM (QUANTUM ASSOCIATIVE MEMORY) and AMPLITUDE ENCODING are introduced after the most basic encoding, BASIS ENCODING. Since the primary focus of quantum computing in the past has been on solving quantum physical problems, input data for quantum algorithms is frequently numerical. As a result, each pattern's context assumes that the input data, X, is numerical.

Initialization

An algorithm's initial state is prepared at the start: First, the |0…0> state is used to initialize the registers. If the method uses input data, the data is encoded using a particular encoding using a suitable state preparation procedure.

Forces

Data encoding in qubits is a challenging task. Only a small number of qubits that are stable for a brief period of time are present in current devices. The representation must be small and require only a few qubits and quantum gates in order to utilize existing equipment. The number of actions required to prepare the quantum state must be minimal since qubits decay quickly and quantum gates are prone to errors. A logarithmic or linear runtime—that is, a state preparation procedure with a logarithmic or linear number of concurrent operations—is optimal for efficiently encoding even a high number of data values.

In essence, any encoding involves a trade-off between two main factors: (i) the quantity of qubits needed and (ii) the loading process's runtime complexity. In addition, another force mandates that data be formatted appropriately for subsequent processes. It is frequently necessary to express the precise values of the data for arithmetic operations like addition and multiplication. For other operations, it could be enough to just express their relative values (for example, using AMPLITUDE ENCODING to express a quantum state's comparatively small or high amplitude).

Basis Encoding

Context.

Quantum algorithms need numerical input data (X) in order to perform additional computations.

Solution.

Using the computational base $\{|0...00\rangle, |0...01\rangle, \ldots, |1...11\rangle\}$ to encode the input data is the primary concept behind this encoding: An input integer x is converted into the associated basis vector $|x\rangle := |b_{n-1} \ldots b_1 b_0\rangle$ after being approximated using the binary format $x := b_{n-1} \ldots b_1 b_0$. For instance, "2" is represented as 10, which is subsequently encoded by $|10\rangle$. For instance, the number "2" is encoded by $|10\rangle$ and rendered as 10. This generally results in the encoding that follows. $X \approx \sum_{i=-k}^{m} b_i 2^i \mapsto |b_m \ldots b_{-k}\rangle$. where X is represented by a basis vector after being roughly estimated with a precision of k+m significant digits.

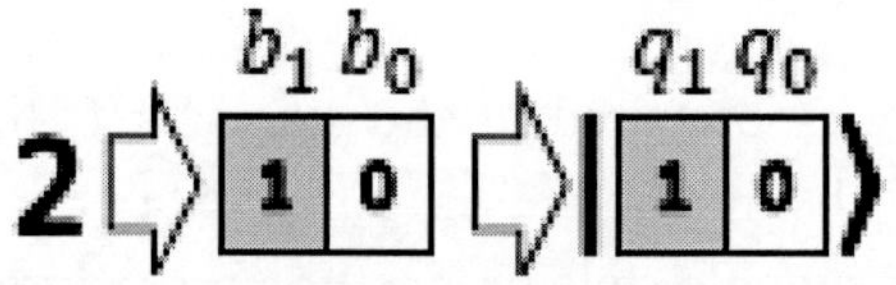

Fig.8.16 Encoding of bases. The first phase involves approximating a number using a binary bit string, and the second step involves encoding it using a computational basis state.

Result.

Since this encoding is appropriate for arithmetic computations, it can be classified as digital encoding. To represent input numbers that are roughly represented by l digits, l qubits are required. The initial $|0\rangle$ state of qubits representing a "1" digit must be changed into $|1\rangle$ in order to implement this encoding. This can be accomplished in a single operation for a single qubit, allowing for the preparation of this encoding in linear time.

Associated Pattern.

INITIALIZATION is improved upon by this pattern. If several numbers are needed as input for an algorithm, they can all be encoded using BASIS ENCODING and processed by the QUAM pattern.

Known Applications.

Algorithms used in BASIS ENCODING that carry out arithmetic operations on integers. This state preparation procedure can be easily implemented because just one quantum gate is required to obtain this encoding.

QUAM (QUANTUM ASSOCIATIVE MEMORY)

Context.

Several numerical numbers X must be entered into a quantum algorithm in order to do additional computations.

Solution.

In the same qubit register, create a superposition of basis-encoded values using a quantum associative memory (QuAM). This is shown in binary format for the three numbers x1, x2, and x3 in the picture below. Keep in mind that the final encoding is a superposition of the base encoded values that is equally weighted; that is, all of the amplitudes have the same magnitude.

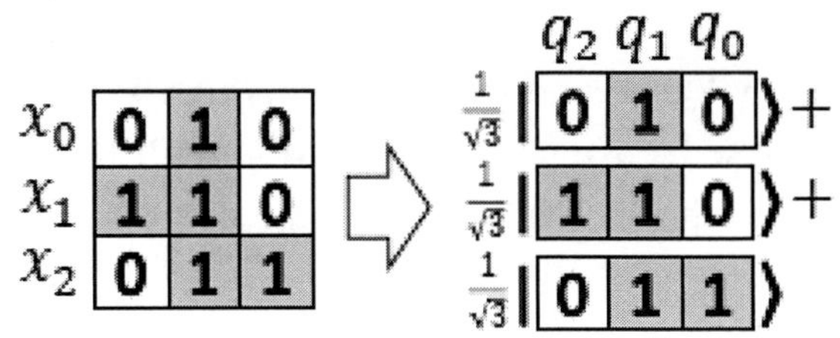

Fig.8.17 Resulting Encoding. Every row on the left represents a data value that has an amplitude of $\frac{1}{\sqrt{n}}$. and is encoded using BASIS ENCODING.

The quantum associative memory's register loads data by superposing two states: a processing state and a memory branch (see below figure). Each branch has a storage section and a load section. Step 1 involves first preparing an extra component for the load portion of both branches. The processing branch is then divided so that the newly added element receives the appropriate amplitude (step 2) and may be stored by superposing it with the previously added elements (step 3). Both branches are then cleaned by a UNCOMPUTE so they are prepared for the following iteration.

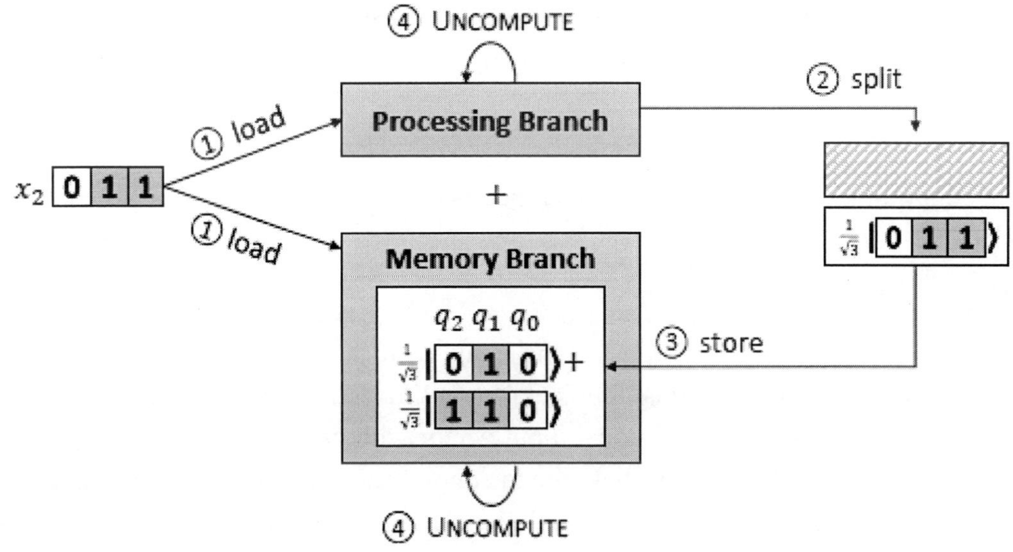

Fig.8.18 State preparation routine illustration of Ventura and Martinez. Every iteration loads a new element and places it in superposition with the previously stored elements.

Outcome.

Since the resulting encoding is digital, it can be used for mathematical calculations. This format requires l qubits for input n numbers that are roughly represented by l digits. A basis vector with an amplitude of $\frac{1}{\sqrt{n}}$. represents each of the n encoded input values. The register's other two amplitudes $2^l - n$ are all 0. In this case $|000\rangle$, $|001\rangle$, $|100\rangle$, $|101\rangle$, and $|111\rangle$;i. For this encoding, the amplitude vector is frequently sparse.

Associated Pattern.

This pattern utilizes UNCOMPUTE and improves INITIALIZATION. All computational basis states are superposed using UNIFORM SUPERPOSITION. In BASIS ENCODING, a value is also represented by each of the computational basis states.

Known Applications.

Anytime numerous data values need to be represented in BASIS ENCODING, the Ventura and Martinez-based state preparation procedure can be utilized. This encoding is essential to Grover's method for unstructured search, Shor's algorithm for factorization of prime numbers, and a quantum version of the Fourier transform. This encoding is also used by other algorithms that extend or utilize Grover's technique.

Amplitude Encoding

Alias

LaRose and Coyle have also called this encoding as Wavefunction Encoding. The wavefunction of each quantum system describes it and establishes the measurement probability. Given that data is encoded via the wavefunction ψ, it follows that amplitudes of the quantum are employed to depict data values.

Context

For an algorithm to work, a numerical input data vector $(x_0, \ldots, x_{n-1})^T$ needs to be encoded.

Solution

The data is encoded using amplitudes. The input vector must be normalized to length 1 since the squared moduli of a quantum state's amplitudes must add up to 1. The image below shows this for a two-dimensional input vector with two data points in it. Since the vector space of a n qubit register has dimension 2^n, the dimension of the input vector must be a power of two in order to correlate each amplitude with a component of the vector. If this isn't the case, you can expand the input vector's dimension by padding it with more zeros. The following is how the input vector is encoded in the quantum state's amplitudes using an appropriate state preparation procedure (see Known Uses): $|\psi\rangle = \sum_{i=0}^{n-1} x_i |i\rangle$

The process of encoding the data—but not the encoding itself—is frequently referred to as arbitrary state preparation as the amplitudes are dependent on the data.

Outcome.

$\lceil log_2(l) \rceil$ qubits can represent a data input vector of length l; this is a fairly compact representation, in fact. It is known that at least one $\frac{1}{n}2^n$ parallel operation is required for an arbitrary state represented by n qubits, which corresponds to 2^n data. Compared to 2^n operations, current state preparation procedures perform somewhat better. However, an encoding in a logarithmic runtime might still be achievable, depending on the data.

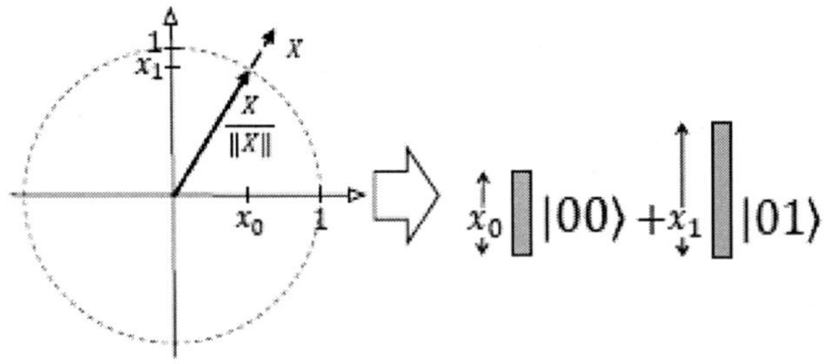

Fig.8.19 Three data points with amplitude encoding. The amplitudes in the final encoding represent the normalized input vector (left).

Applying a Hadamard gate to each of the n qubits, for instance, can produce a UNIFORM SUPERPOSITION. This can be done in simultaneously, and so in a single step. All of the data items in this 2^n-dimensional vector are $\frac{1}{\sqrt{n}}$. Likewise, it is possible to prepare sparse data vectors more effectively. It should be mentioned that in order to get a reliable estimate of the output result, several measurements must be made if the output is also encoded in the amplitude. Since n qubits have 2^n amplitudes, the number of measurements increases as the number of amplitudes does.

Similar patterns.

INITIALIZATION is refined by this pattern. Compared to BASIS, ANGLE, or QRAM ENCODING, the encoding is more compact (in terms of qubits).

Known Applications.

Many algorithms for quantum machine learning require AMPLITUDE ENCODING. Another illustration is the Harrow, Hassidim, and Lloyd algorithm (often known as the HHL algorithm), which is used to solve linear equations. A common premise in machine learning, such as in support vector machines, is that the data values can be normalized. For this encoding, a state preparation method can be built in a variety of ways. PennyLane, for instance, provides a loading procedure for amplified encoding. Additionally, the library has a method for preparing arbitrary states using the Möttönen and Vartiainen algorithm. To encode 2^n data values, Möttönen and Vartiainen's state preparation procedure necessitates an exponential number of processes. The pattern classification algorithm using k-nearest neighborhoods to the intended amplitude encoding is provided by Q#.

The Pattern Classification Algorithm Using K-Nearest Neighbors

The goal of a pattern classification challenge is to use a rule that was learned from a collection of example classifications to assign a pattern to one of several classes. Therefore, there is an issue with supervised learning, or learning from training information. A remarkable variety of significant real-world decision-making issues are included in this abstract formulation. Examples include a doctor making a diagnosis based on a variety of symptoms and his experience with other instances, an email being automatically classified as "important" or "spam" based on past correspondence, or a scanning gadget identifying a handwritten number on a postal envelope.

Furthermore, choice issues can be used to characterize how humans think. For instance, we use sensory stimuli to determine if a situation is harmful or not, or we use them to "recognize" (= classify) persons, objects, and odors around us. Pattern recognition, which is a more generalized term that examines the issue of recognizing patterns without classifying them, template matching, or associative memory—in which a close example from learned data is retrieved upon an input—is used by some authors in place of the term pattern classification.

The 'training set' for the problem is a collection of n-dimensional data vectors $\vec{v}^k$ and their class assignments c^p, $\mathcal{T} = \{(\vec{v}^p, c^p)\}_{p=1,\ldots,N}$. This provides a more detailed description of the pattern classification problem. *n* characteristics v_i^p are encoded by each vector. These characteristics could indicate the frequency of a certain phrase in a text sample, the grey shade of a particular pixel, or whether a patient has a family history of cancer. Binary, integer, or real-valued values are used to represent the features, and a finite number *d* of positive integers $c \in \{1,\ldots,d\}$ is frequently used to encode the class c^p of a feature vector.

Additionally provided is an unclassified input vector $\vec{x}$ that encodes *n* characteristics and comes from the same vector space as the training vectors. Matching the new vector $\vec{x}$ to a class using knowledge from the training data is the task of pattern classification. Usually, to accomplish this, a distance measure is defined, and the class whose members are most "similar" in terms of this distance is given the new input vector. The Euclidean metric, or the Hamming distance in the case of binary characteristics, is a widely used distance measure.

Several algorithms were created by the machine learning field to address the pattern classification issue. The most well-known is the k-nearest neighbor (kNN) approach. The *k* training vectors that are closest to the input vector, given a training set *T* that is kept in memory, are chosen. The input vector then receives the class that the majority of these neighbors belong to. This straightforward approach has numerous variations. Closer neighbors have a greater influence on which class is chosen in the distance-weighted kNN, for instance, because the neighbors are weighted according to their distance from the input vector. Preprocessing the training data and calculating the centroid $\vec{v}_c = |\vec{x} - \frac{1}{L}\sum_{l\in c} \vec{v}^l|$ is an additional variant of every class $c \in \{1, ..., d\}$ $(l = 1, ..., L_c$ is the index for students in class c). The nearest centroid vector then joins the input vector as a member of the class.

The simplicity of the kNN method and its variants is not the sole benefit. Since they don't require prior knowledge of the vector distribution, they are *nonparametric* instances of supervised learning.

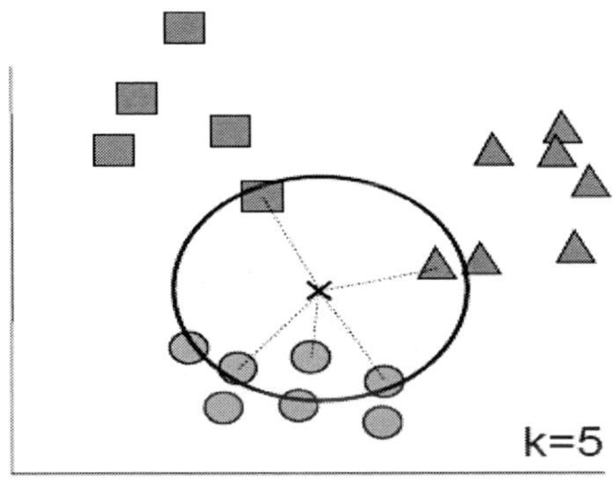

Fig.8.20 An example of the kNN pattern classification method in action. The new vector (cross) is allocated to the class that most of its k nearest neighbors belong to, which in this instance would be the circle. The value of k in this instance is 5.

The sole presumption regarding the data utilized is that comparable inputs yield comparable results; in this instance, identical input vectors ought to be members of the same class. The original kNN technique requires finding a compromise between noise reduction and preserving locality information, which is a crucial challenge. For instance, if k! all is used, the class assignment will always go to the class with the most members. Because the weights implicitly conceal the number of nearest neighbors, the distance-weighted kNN version has the advantage of being independent of the choice of k. Assuming that "close" feature vectors carry the class that should be assigned to the new vector, the quantum technique presented below is founded on the same idea as kNN.

Characterization of quantum patterns

The pattern classification problem can be translated into quantum physics as follows. Used here the quantum states to represent the feature data set. The class of feature vector $\vec{v}^p$ is stored in the qubit $|c^p\rangle$, and $\{|v_1^p ... v_n^p, c^p\rangle\} \in \mathcal{H}_2^{\otimes n} \otimes \mathcal{H}_d$, where p = 1,….N loops over the training states. The feature space is thus represented by the product state of n 2-dimensional Hilbert spaces, but the d potential classifications are encoded by the additional qudit in $\mathcal{H}_d$. A quantum state $|x_1, ..., x_n\rangle$ from the feature Hilbert space $\mathcal{H}_2^{\otimes n}$ serves as the input vector. Since it is now working with quantum information, it is necessary to either convert classical data into quantum states or extract it from a quantum random access memory (particularly if the machine learning method is a subroutine to a bigger calculation on a future quantum computer).

Classification algorithm for quantum patterns

The distance-based classification method used by the quantum pattern classification (QPC) algorithm is the same as that of kNN; however, the distance of the complete training vector set is taken into account rather than just the nearest neighbors (see image below). The algorithm it uses is one that was introduced in relation to quantum associative memory. Creating a superposition of the training data set and "writing" the input state's Hamming distance into each vector's amplitude is the process. The requested class is then retrieved with the highest probability once class-qudit has been measured. Furthermore, if the procedure is run frequently enough to reach statistical significance, it produces a probability distribution that shows how near each class member is to the input vector.

Please take note that comprehension of the quantum computing circuit model is necessary for the following. Building a "training set superposition" is the algorithm's first stage.

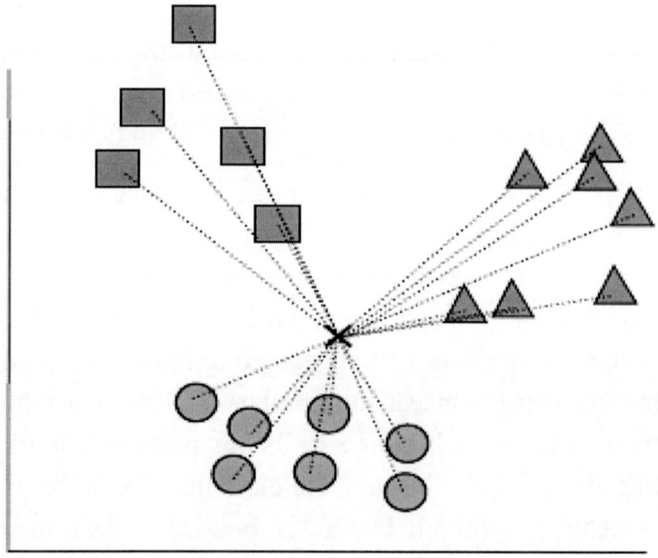

Fig.8.21 A representation of the fundamental idea behind the classification of quantum patterns. The nearest members of the class are given the new vector, which is a black cross.

Comprising the training data,

$$|T\rangle = \frac{1}{\sqrt{N}} \sum_{p} |v_1^p \ldots v_n^p, c^p\rangle$$

Although this "training phase" is insignificant in the classical scenario, there are still unanswered problems regarding quantum memory devices and the effective setup of a quantum system in an arbitrary initial state. However, just as accessing every bit from a classical memory would have linear complexity, procedures to create the beginning state from a ground state can be found. This construct yields the initial state.

$$|\psi_0\rangle = \frac{1}{\sqrt{N}} \sum_p |x_1 \ldots x_n; v_1^p \ldots v_n^p, c^p; 0\rangle$$

It is composed of three registers: the input state is stored in the first, the superposition $|T\rangle$ is stored in the second, and an ancilla qubit set to zero is stored in the third. The first stage involves using a Hamadard gate to superimpose the ancilla, which results :

$$|\psi_1\rangle = \frac{1}{\sqrt{N}} \sum_i |x_1 \ldots x_n; v_1^p \ldots v_n^p, c^p\rangle \otimes \frac{1}{\sqrt{2}}(|0\rangle + |1\rangle)$$

For the time being, excluded the ancilla state for readability purposes. In a further step, the Hamming distance between each qubit in the first and second register,

$$d_k^i = \begin{cases} 1, & \text{if } |v_k^p\rangle = |x_k\rangle \\ 0, & \text{else,} \end{cases}$$

swaps out the second register's qubits. This is accomplished by using a cNOT(a,b)-gate, which replaces entry b with 0. Sincc it ultimately needs a strong "signal" for small Hamming distances, reverse the states in the second register using the X gate if a = b and else with 1.

Keep in mind that the class and ancilla states are unaffected by the gates. Consequently, the second step reads

$$|\psi_2\rangle = \prod_k \mathrm{X}(x_k)\ \mathrm{cNOT}(x_k, v_k^p)\ |\psi_1\rangle$$

$$= \frac{1}{\sqrt{N}} \sum_p |x_1 \ldots x_n; d_1^p \ldots d_n^p, c^p\rangle \otimes \frac{1}{\sqrt{2}}(|0\rangle + |1\rangle)$$

Next, the unitary operator is employed.

$$U = e^{-i\frac{\pi}{2n}H} \qquad H = 1 \otimes \sum_k \left(\frac{\sigma_z + 1}{2}\right)_{d_k} \otimes 1 \otimes (\sigma_z)_c$$

to add up each training vector $|v_1^p \ldots v_n^p\rangle$ reverse single-qubit Hamming distances d_k^p To write the entire reverse Hamming distance, $\bar{d}_H(\vec{x},\vec{v}^p)$, between the input vector and the pth training vector into the phase of the *i*th state of the superposition, use vpn i. If the ancilla qubit is $|1\rangle$, this value will also have a negative sign. Following the third stage, the state is subsequently provided by

$$|\psi_3\rangle = U\,|\psi_2\rangle = \frac{1}{\sqrt{2N}}\sum_p e^{i\frac{\pi}{2n}\bar{d}_H(\vec{x},\vec{v}^p)}\,|x_1 \ldots x_n; d_1^p \ldots d_n^p, c^p; 0\rangle|$$

$$+\, e^{-i\frac{\pi}{2n}\bar{d}_H(\vec{x},\vec{v}^p)}\,|x_1 \ldots x_n; d_1^p \ldots d_n^p, c^p; 1\rangle$$

The phase information is written into the amplitudes via another Hadamard transformation on the ancilla state, $H = 1 \otimes 1 \otimes 1 \otimes H_a$.

$$|\psi_4\rangle = H\,|\psi_3\rangle = \frac{1}{\sqrt{N}}\sum_p \cos\left[\frac{\pi}{2n}\bar{d}_H(\vec{x},\vec{v}^p)\right]|x_1 \ldots x_n; d_1^p \ldots d_n^p, c^p; 0\rangle$$

$$+ \sin\left[\frac{\pi}{2n}\bar{d}_H(\vec{x},\vec{v}^p)\right]|x_1 \ldots x_n; d_1^p \ldots d_n^p, c^p; 1\rangle$$

In addition to enabling this technique, the ancilla provides us with the ability to determine whether the input $|x\rangle$, which would want to classify, and the states $|v^p\rangle,\ p = 1,\ldots,P$ have an average big or small Hamming distance. The likelihood of measuring the ancilla in state $|1\rangle$ is significantly higher if the new input is far from the majority of training patterns; if the input is near numerous patterns, we end up in state $|0\rangle$. Trugenberger claims that an associative memory can only be dependable in this situation, which is why his quantum associative memory only accepts inputs with a sufficiently high probability of an ancilla state in $|0\rangle$. In order to retrieve the cosine half of the sum in the subsequent retrieval phase, we must measure the ancilla until we obtain a $|0\rangle$, even though our QPC algorithm shouldn't rely on the average distance between the input and the training vectors.. Naturally, the likelihood of success increases with the input's proximity to the training set. The simulations indicate that the likelihood of this measurement,

$$P(0_a) = \frac{1}{N}\sum_p \cos^2\left[\frac{\pi}{2n}\bar{d}_H(\vec{x},\vec{v}^p)\right]$$

is greater than 2/3 for typical examples, such as the MNIST handwritten digit database. In one version, the class of vectors that are on average closer to the input is assigned using the "$k \rightarrow$ all" method. In the other version, the pattern register is measured, neighbors are retrieved using a probability weighed by their distance, and the class most represented by this pool is selected. A measurement of the class-qudit along the standard basis is the final step after the first version. To choose the most likely (i.e., close) candidate, step two is reversed in order to measure along the basis of the training vectors. The distance between each class's members and the input to be classified determines how weighted the various classes look in superposition $|\psi_4\rangle$. If we rewrite state $|\psi_4\rangle$ as follows, it becomes clear:

$$|\psi_4\rangle = \frac{1}{\sqrt{N}}\sum_{c=1}^{d}|c\rangle \otimes \sum_{l\in c}\cos\left[\frac{\pi}{2n}\bar{d}_H(\vec{x},\vec{v}^l)\right]|x_1...x_n; d_1^l...d_n^l; 0\rangle$$
$$+\sin\left[\frac{\pi}{2n}\bar{d}_H(\vec{x},\vec{v}^l)\right]|x_1...x_n; d_1^l...d_n^l; 1\rangle$$

where all training vectors classified with the label *c* are processed through by *l*. Given already the measured ancilla in 0, the probability of measuring a specific class $c \in \{1, ..., d\}$ is given by

$$\mathrm{P}(c) = \frac{1}{NP(0)}\sum_{l\in c}\cos^2\left[\frac{\pi}{2n}\bar{d}_H(\vec{x},\vec{v}^l)\right]$$

The average Hamming distance between the input and every training vector in this class determines the value. The best class label for $|x_1 ... x_n\rangle$ can be obtained by measuring the class qudit of a sufficient number of copies of superposition $|\psi_4\rangle$. This can be transformed into a new training vector or further processed as classical information $|v_1^{P+1}, ..., v_n^{P+1}, \bar{c}^{P+1}\rangle = |x_1...x_n, c_x\rangle$. The qubits $d_1 ... d_n$ in the second register are discarded.

Fig.8.22 Sample of an unclear input image for the handwritten digit recognition test. The image, which comes from the MNIST database's training set, displays both the original (left) and binarized (right) examples of a handwritten "9" that is plainly distinguishable as either a 0 or a 9.

8.6 Patterns of Unitary Transformation and Measurement

Best practices for operations following the creation of an initial state are described by unitary transformation patterns. Initially, MATRIX ENCODING explains how an operation can be represented as a matrix. The QUANTUM PHASE ESTIMATION routine, which employs two of the previously described data encoding patterns to estimate the eigenvalues of an operation, is then briefed. Lastly, a measuring pattern known as POST-SELECTIVE measuring was described.

8.6.1 Matrix Encoding

Alias: Dynamic Encoding.

Context: On a quantum computer, a matrix A must be represented as an operation U. Because a data encoding pattern does not describe an operation, it is insufficient to represent the matrix's entries.

Forces: An operation's representation strikes a balance between the following forces:

1. It is ideal for the circuit representing the operation to have a shallow depth.
2. A's eigenvalues and eigenvectors ought to match those of the quantum operation.

Solution: Encode if A is not Hermitian.

$$H = \begin{pmatrix} 0 & A \\ A^{\dagger} & 0 \end{pmatrix}$$

rather than A. $U = e^{-iHt}$ is unitary and can be used to encode H since H is Hermitian. The period for which the operation is applied is denoted by t, which is often set to be modest.

Result: Each state vector $|\psi\rangle$ may be expressed as a linear combination of the eigenvectors $\{|vi\rangle\}$ of the n * n matrix H since they form a basis:

$$|\psi\rangle = \gamma_1|v_1\rangle + \cdots + \gamma_n|v_n\rangle$$

The following state is produced when U is applied to this state.

$$e^{-iHt}|\psi\rangle = e^{-i\lambda_1 t}\gamma_1|v_1\rangle + \cdots + e^{-i\lambda_n t}\gamma_n|v_n\rangle$$

If just one $\gamma i \neq 0$ and $|\psi\rangle$ is an eigenvector of H, the state gains a global phase shift: $U\gamma_i|v_i\rangle = e^{-i\lambda_i t}\gamma_i|v_i\rangle$. This effectively illustrates how a scaling factor results from applying matrix A to an eigenstate. The primary disadvantage of this encoding is that the circuit depth that implements U may increase exponentially.

Related Patterns: A unitary operation can be defined using this pattern as an input for a quantum phase estimation.

Known Applications: This encoding is frequently used to simulate quantum systems. One approach that combines MATRIX ENCODING and QUANTUM PHASE ESTIMATION is the HHL algorithm for solving linear equations.

8.6.2 Quantum Phase Estimation

Alias: Phase estimation algorithm (PEA).

Context: The matching eigenvalue needs to be found given a unitary matrix U and one of its eigenstates. In BASIS ENCODING, the eigenstate $|v\rangle$ is provided on a register. A global phase is produced when U is applied to the eigenstate $|v\rangle$:

$$U|v\rangle = e^{2\pi i\varphi}|v\rangle$$

where $\varphi \in [0, 1]$ is the only factor that can determine the eigenvalue $\lambda = e^{2\pi i\varphi}$. For this reason, φ can be estimated.

Forces: The following forces are balanced by this pattern:

1. A global phase cannot be quantified.
2. It is important to estimate φ as precisely as possible.
3. The implemented quantum circuits must have a low depth and width in order to operate on the NISQ computers of today.
4. The quantum computer should ideally only require a small number of executions.

Solution: To approximate θ, use the circuit depicted in the diagram below. Initially, a UNIFORM SUPERPOSITION is created from a register of m ancillae. Then, using the approach shown in the provided figure, controlled versions of U's powers are applied to the eigenstate's register. Every time a controlled-U operation is applied, the control qubit experiences a phase kickback, meaning it gains a relative phase of φ.

As a result, the general state is:

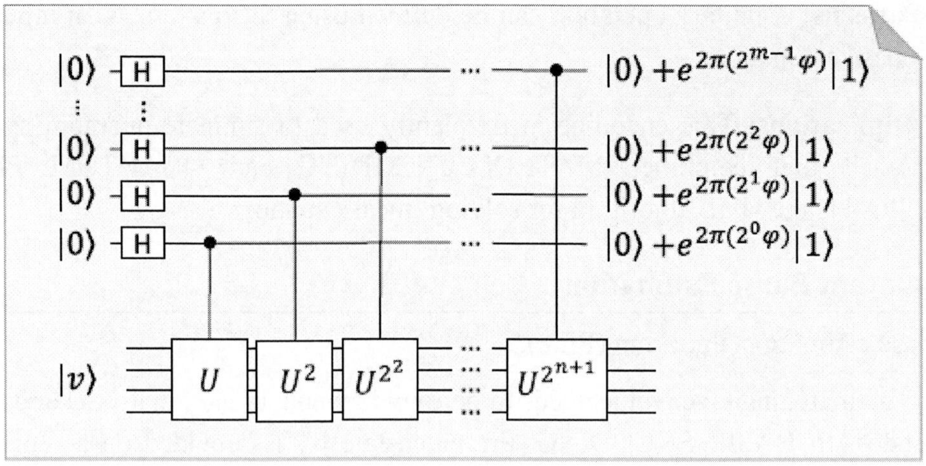

Fig.8.23 Routine of Quantum phase estimation.

$$|\psi\rangle = \sum_{y=0}^{2^m-1} e^{2\pi\varphi y}|y\rangle$$

where the relative phase encodes φ. The ancillae register is subjected to the inverse of the quantum Fourier transformation in order to obtain this data.

Result: The eigenvalue in BASIS ENCODING is contained in the ancillae register if φ is a rational number (assuming a proper number of ancillae). Otherwise, there is a probability of at least 4π that an approximation will be generated. Adding more ancillae to boost the approximation's precision is expensive because it necessitates more controlled-U operations. The algorithm is frequently considered unsuitable for NISQ devices due to its high hardware requirements.

Variants: An arbitrary quantum state, which is always a linear combination of eigenvectors, can also be used to initialize the second register. In this instance, the algorithm uses the output register to approximate a superposition of eigenvalues for these eigenvectors. Other variations of this approach require fewer measurements or further enhance the circuit's depth.

Related Patterns: This pattern generates an output in BASIS ENCODING using AMPLITUDE ENCODING and MATRIX ENCODING as inputs.

Known Applications: The foundation of many algorithms is quantum phase estimation. The HHL algorithm, which solves a set of linear equations, is a well-known example. Similar principles are used by other quantum machine learning techniques, such as quantum principal component analysis and quantum support vector machines (QSVM).

Examine the following issue as a preliminary use of the quantum Fourier transform: The eigenvector $|u\rangle$ of a unitary operator U has an eigenvalue of $e^{i\phi}$ $(0 \leq \phi < 2\pi)$. Assume that the state u can be prepared and that a black box routine, with j being a non-negative integer, can carry out the actions controlled -U^{2^j}. The best n-bit estimate of ϕ is what we want.

Below Fig. depicts the quantum circuit that resolves this issue. Depending on the level of accuracy needed for ϕ, the first register has n qubits. The m qubits required to store $|u\rangle$ are in the second register. On a state $\frac{1}{\sqrt{2}}(|0\rangle+|1\rangle)|u\rangle$ the gate $C-U^{2^j}$ action is provided by

$$\begin{aligned} C-U^{2^j}\frac{1}{\sqrt{2}}(|0\rangle+|1\rangle)|u\rangle &= \frac{1}{\sqrt{2}}(|0\rangle|u\rangle+|1\rangle U^{2^j}|u\rangle) \\ &= \frac{1}{\sqrt{2}}(|0\rangle|u\rangle+|1\rangle e^{i2^j\phi}|u\rangle) \\ &= \frac{1}{\sqrt{2}}(|0\rangle+e^{i2^j\phi}|1\rangle)|u\rangle\,. \end{aligned} \tag{1}$$

Considering this outcome, it is simple to verify that the circuit's output (figure) is provided by

$$\begin{aligned} &\frac{1}{\sqrt{2^n}}(|0\rangle+e^{i2^{n-1}\phi}|1\rangle)\cdots(|0\rangle+e^{i2\phi}|1\rangle)(|0\rangle+e^{i\phi}|1\rangle)|u\rangle \\ &\qquad = \frac{1}{\sqrt{2^n}}\sum_{y=0}^{2^n-1}e^{i\phi y}|y\rangle|u\rangle\,. \end{aligned} \tag{2}$$

The crucial element in both Deutsch's and Grover's algorithms is that the quantum register used to store $|u\rangle$ is set up in an eigenstate of the operators U, U^2, U^4,.. Consequently, the phase factors $e^{i\phi}, e^{2i\phi}, e^{4i\phi}, \cdots$ are transmitted backwards in the control register and the value of this register remains constant.

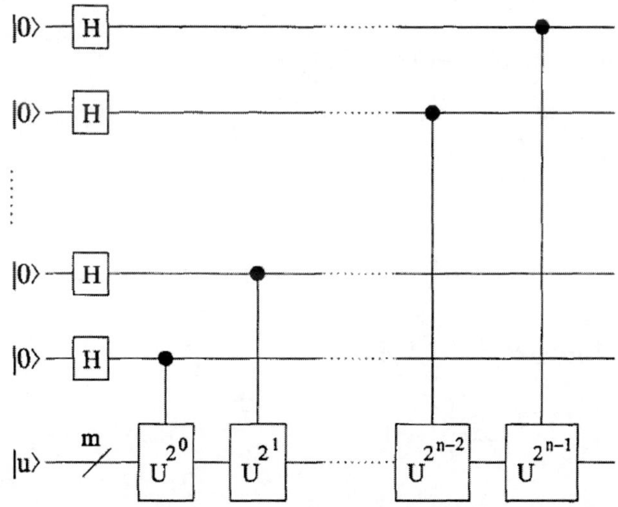

Fig.8.24 In the phase estimation issue, the state (2) is obtained using a quantum circuit. A set of m qubits is represented by the dashed wire.

We now solely look at the control register and demonstrate that the best n-bit estimate of ϕ with high probability may be obtained from its quantum Fourier transform. It is convenient to write

$$\phi = 2\pi\left(\frac{a}{2^n} + \delta\right) \tag{3}$$

Since $2\pi a/2^n$ is the best n-bit approximation of ϕ, where $a = a_{n-1}a_{n-2}\cdots a_1a_0$ (in binary notation), $0 \leq |\delta| \leq 1/2^{n+1}$. It is possible to verify that, when applied to the state (2), the inverse quantum Fourier transform of the first register yields

$$\frac{1}{2^n}\sum_{x=0}^{2^n-1}\sum_{y=0}^{2^n-1} e^{2\pi i(a-x)y/2^n} e^{2\pi i\delta y}|x\rangle \tag{4}$$

The first $(|x\rangle)$ register is now subjected to a standard measurement. The wave vector (4) decreases to $|a\rangle$ if $\delta = 0$. Thus, in this instance, the phase ϕ is precisely calculated and a standard measurement of the first register yields a result with certainty. The best n-bit estimate of ϕ in the general situation $\delta \neq 0$ is provided by a, which is derived from a standard measurement of the first register with probability $p_a = |c_a|^2$. Here, ca stands for the wave function (4)'s projection onto state $|a\rangle$, which is provided by

$$c_a = \frac{1}{2^n}\sum_{y=0}^{2^n-1}\left(e^{2\pi i\delta}\right)^y = \frac{1}{2^n}\sum_{y=0}^{2^n-1}\alpha^y \qquad (\alpha \equiv e^{2\pi i\delta}) \tag{5}$$

You can add this finite geometric series to get

$$c_a = \frac{1}{2^n}\left[\frac{1-\alpha^{2^n}}{1-\alpha}\right] \tag{6}$$

Given that $2z \leq \sin(\pi z) \leq \pi z$ for each $z \in [0, \frac{1}{2}]$, we get

$$\begin{aligned} \left|1 - e^{2\pi i\delta 2^n}\right| &= 2\left|\sin(\pi\delta 2^n)\right| \geq 4|\delta|\,2^n, \\ \left|1 - e^{2\pi i\delta}\right| &= 2\left|\sin(\pi\delta)\right| \leq 2\pi|\delta|. \end{aligned} \tag{7}$$

By adding these two inequalities to (6), we can get

$$|c_a|^2 \geq \frac{4}{\pi^2} \approx 0.405 \tag{8}$$

Consequently, it is high likely that the $|c_a|^2$ n-bit estimate of ϕ will be found.

For a sufficiently high number of qubits (n), we note that the optimal l-bit approximation of the phase ϕ can be obtained with probability arbitrarily near to 1. Specifically, if the circuit of above Fig. has $n = l + O(\log(1/\epsilon))$ qubits in the first register, the best l-bit approximation of ϕ is found with probability $> 1 - \epsilon$. As a result, increasing n increases both the likelihood that our algorithm will succeed and the precision of phase estimate.

To summarize, the inverse quantum Fourier transform is utilized by the quantum-phase estimation technique to convert the state (2) to the state (4). As demonstrated above, this later state provides a highly probable accurate estimate of the phase ϕ. when measured. Assuming that the unitary operator U can be efficiently decomposed into elementary gates on a quantum computer (i.e., U\u) can be computed in a number of elementary quantum gates polynomial in the number m of qubits required to store $|u\rangle$), It is emphasized that this algorithm is exponentially efficient in comparison to any known classical algorithm solving the phase estimation problem.

8.6.3 Post Selective Measurement

Context: Quantum operations carry out linear changes since they are unitary. Nonetheless, there are instances where a non-linear transformation is preferable. As an illustration, if a computation's output is kept in one branch of the superposition, the remaining superposition should be discarded in favor of moving forward with |1⟩|f(x)⟩.

$$|\psi\rangle = \frac{1}{\sqrt{2}}|1\rangle|f(x)\rangle + \frac{1}{\sqrt{2}}|0\rangle|g(x)\rangle$$

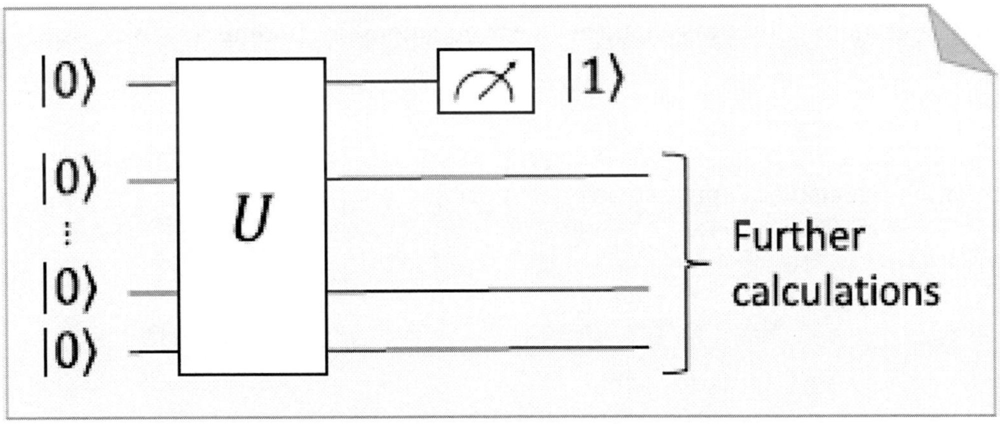

Fig.8.25 An illustration of a post-selective measurement circuit.

Solution:

To make the quantum state collapse into one of the two branches, use measurement. In the aforementioned example, measuring the computational basis's initial qubit yields either |0⟩ or |1⟩. Further computations (shown in the above image) can be carried out if the measurement shows that the preferred branch was chosen (in our example, |1⟩). If not, the current calculation is discarded and begun over, which entails first setting each qubit to |0⟩ and then the remaining circuit actions.

Result: Because the resulting method is probabilistic, the amplitude of the chosen branch determines the average number of repetitions required. The algorithm runs with a 50% chance in the aforementioned situation.

Related Patterns: It is possible to utilize AMPLITUDE AMPLIFICATION to raise the likelihood of choosing a specific branch.

Known Applications: When creating quantum neural networks, a non-linear transformation may be advantageous. This method is employed by the HHL algorithm as well as several other algorithms that build upon it, such as the QSVM. Post selective measurements are also employed in repeat-until-success circuits, which, rather than starting the computation from scratch, use a recovery operation to return to the state before to the measurement. The ability to formally model such a strategy using measurements inside a while loop is introduced by OpenQASM 3.0.

8.6.4 Use Case: HHL Algorithm

A use case illustrating the application of data encoding patterns in a quantum algorithm is briefed in this section. As a result, rephrase the well-known HHL algorithm, emphasizing the data conversions and encoding patterns that are employed throughout. For the sake of simplicity, we shall disregard potential future algorithmic advances, assume a sufficient number of ancillae, and ignore normalization constants in the following.

The HHL algorithm solves a system of linear equations by finding $A \in \mathbb{C}^{n \times n}$.such that A|x⟩ = |b⟩ given a matrix $|x\rangle \in \mathbb{C}^{n}$ that satisfies specific requirements4 and a vector $|b\rangle \in \mathbb{C}^{n}$.

This equation can also be expressed as |x⟩ = A−1|b⟩.

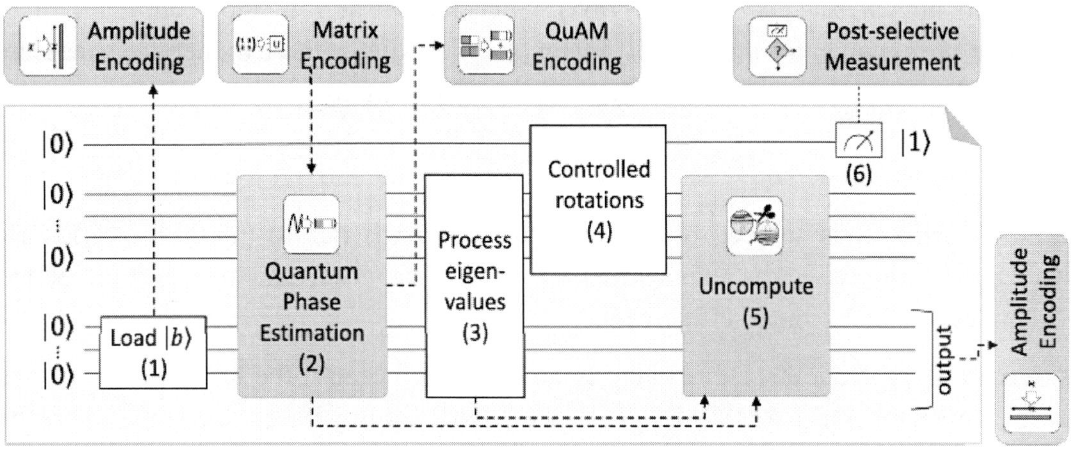

Fig.8.26 The HHL Algorithm's circuit and used patterns.

The spectral theorem allows |b⟩ to be expressed in terms of A's eigenvectors {ui}, which means $|b\rangle = \sum_{j=0}^{n-1} \beta_j |u_j\rangle$. Consequently, the equation can be rewritten as follows:

$$|x\rangle = \sum_{j=0}^{n-1} \lambda_j^{-1} b_j |u_j\rangle$$

which is, in fact, the HHL algorithm's output.

Using the circuit shown in the preceding image, the state of Equation is created. The vector |b⟩ is first loaded into the first register (step 1) as AMPLITUDE ENCODING.

$$|b\rangle = \sum_{i=0}^{n-1} b_i |i\rangle$$

Next, a QUAM ENCODING of the estimated eigenvalues in the second register that is entangled with |b⟩ is produced by the QUANTUM PHASE ESTIMATION (using a MATRIX ENCODING of A as an input in the steps):

$$\sum_{j=0}^{n-1} \beta_j |\lambda_j\rangle |u_j\rangle$$

The procedure reverses the eigenvalues and changes them from QUAM ENCODING, a digital encoding, to an equivalent AMPLITUDE ENCODING in the subsequent phases. An UNCOMPUTE operation is used to untangle the registers. Due to the fact that the inversion of the eigenvalues is a probabilistic operation, a POST-SELECTIVE MEASUREMENT indicates if the method as a whole was successful (i.e., collapsed into the desired state of Equation) or if it needs to be repeated. Additionally, the encodings employed throughout the method highlight the primary algorithmic flaws that were noted in.

Loading |b⟩ in AMPLITUDE ENCODING, often known as the "input problem," may necessitate an exponential amount of operations, destroying the exponential speed-up. Although the HHL method can theoretically be applied to the output of an earlier algorithm, its hardware requirements are higher than those of NISQ devices at the moment.

The input matrix A is subject to a number of restrictions due to the QPE's MATRIX ENCODING; otherwise, the exponential speed-up disappears and this portion of the algorithm cannot be executed effectively.

A straightforward readout of this value is not possible because the technique generates the solution vector |x⟩ in AMPLITUDE ENCODING. Multiple algorithm repeats can be used to estimate the amplitudes; however, this also eliminates speedup and has been dubbed the "output problem."

8.7 Circuit Optimization and Quantum Gate Pattern Recognition for Scientific Uses

Encoding a quantum algorithm into a quantum circuit is not a special process. To make the most of quantum devices produced over the next ten years, circuit optimization is crucial due to their limited qubit counts, connectivity, and coherence times. There is a multi-tiered quantum circuit optimization protocol called AQCEL and combine the two distinct concepts for circuit optimization. Future hardware optimization is made possible by the first ingredient, which is a technique to identify the recurring patterns of quantum gates. The second ingredient identifies zero-or low-amplitude computational bases and redundant gates in order to reduce circuit complexity. AQCEL is used as an example on an iterative and effective quantum algorithm intended to model final state radiation in high energy physics. Our optimization strategy for this algorithm results in a notable decrease in the number of gates without sacrificing accuracy when compared to the original circuit. This method is generic and applicable to a broad range of quantum algorithms.

Circuit optimization, sometimes referred to as circuit compilation, is one of the commonly used methods for enhancing the performance of NISQ computers. There is a unique method for encoding a quantum algorithm in a collection of gates, and some algorithmic realizations may be more appropriate for a quantum device that is already in operation. A popular toolkit that includes both architecture-specific and architecture-agnostic procedures. For instance, Clifford identities like CNOT2=Identity are automatically identified, whereas CNOT is a Pauli-Xgate-controlled entity. Other toolkits for circuit optimization exist as well, such as hardware-specific packages for quantum circuits. It will serve as baseline because it is a generic framework that includes numerous algorithms that have already been benchmarked against other procedures.

Introduction of two strategies that complement current approaches and can be utilized to optimize circuits. Finding recurrent sets of quantum gates in a circuit is the main goal of the first. Finding these recurring sets of gates (RSGs) can be crucial because optimizing these RSGs has a greater impact on the circuit as a whole. Finding recurrent gate sets can also be helpful for future hardware optimizations where the cost of other, less common operations can be reduced while maintaining the fidelity of some common operations.

The second technique optimizes a generic circuit by eliminating unnecessary gates or unused qubits so that the circuit depth becomes as short as possible. An example of how such optimization can result in simplification is when a quantum circuit is designed with complete generality in mind. In this scenario, the circuit only reaches a select set of intermediate states for a certain initial state, making some operations simple and even possible to eliminate. Controlled procedures such as a ToffolioraCNOTgate (a controlled-controlled Pauli-Xgate) are the main focus of the removal of superfluous gate operations that were presented here. The discovery of zero- or low-amplitude computational basis states, which allow us to ascertain if the entire gate or (part of) qubit controls can be altered, is the fundamental component of the elimination technique. The optimization protocol known as Aqcel, or Advancing Quantum Circuit by ic Epp and Lbnl, combines both of these methods.

The linear final state radiation from energetic charged (underanyforce) particles is the particular algorithm that is examined. Due to its exponential speedup over the most effective known classical algorithm and its precision-tunable circuit depth, this approach considered as a valuable benchmark. The protocol has broad relevance for quantum computing applications in both research and industry.

8.7.1 Aqcel optimization protocol

The two components of the Aqcel optimization protocol are locating recurrent quantum gates and removing superfluous gates and qubits. Instead of focusing on a particular implementation employing derivative gates for a particular quantum device, this approach focuses on circuit optimization at the algorithmic level. Below is an explanation of each optimization phase.

8.7.2 Pattern recognition of gatesets

The Aqcel first looks for gateset patterns in a random quantum circuit in order to extract RSGs from it.

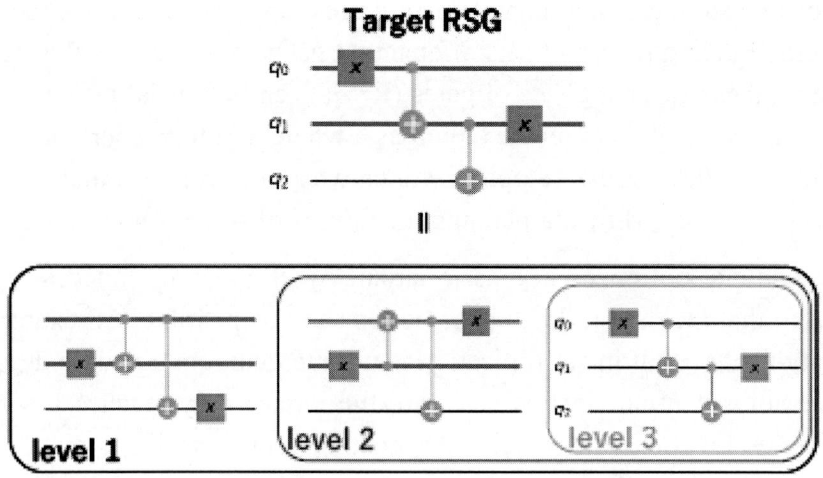

Fig.8.27 The goal RSG is consistent with possible RSG patterns for the three matching criteria levels.

8.7.2.1Directional depiction of acyclic graphs

A structure like this can be described by a directed acyclic graph (DAG). Verifying qubit dependencies and extracting a subset of the circuit that works for particular tasks are made simple by the DAG. Since gate operations in a quantum circuit alter individual qubits one at a time, subsequent gate operations shouldn't have an impact on the quantum state represented at a particular point in the circuit. The initial step in transforming a quantum circuit into the DAG format is to use the DAG circuit class in Qiskit TerraAPI, where an edge connecting the two nodes represents a qubit and anodere denotes an operation by a quantum gate. Three incoming edges (qubits prior to the gate operation) and three outgoing edges (qubits subsequent to the gate operation) are present in the node that corresponds to a Toffoligate. The gateset pattern recognition problem can then be resolved using the DAG format. Verifying the identity of the DAGs of two circuits as a graph isomorphism issue will guarantee the identity of the RSG functionality.

According to the Network X library, the gateset pattern recognition technique is composed of two steps: (1) utilizing depth-first search with heuristic pruning to locate RSG candidates with DAG representation, and (2) using graph hashing using WeisfeilerLehman graph hash to confirm the DAG isomorphism.

8.7.2.2 Recurring gateset extraction in tiers

Three tiers of matching criteria are used to determine the gate recurrence in order to take into consideration various patterns:

Level 1: Ingate types alone must match;

Level 2: Ingate types and the roles of qubits the gates acton must match; and

Level 3: Ingate types must match both the roles and indices of qubits the gates acton.

The precise encoding of the quantum method may affect how RSGs appear in a circuit.

Regardless of the qubits they act on, Level 1's least stringent matching criterion merely identifies the same sets of quantum gates that show up in the circuit. Level 2 is stricter and ensures that the qubits in the RSGs play the identical roles. To put it another way, the qubit connections between the gates within a single RSG are preserved even when the qubit indices may vary between RSGs. Level 3 applies the strictest requirement, requiring that the RSGs appear on the same set of qubits in the circuit and that the qubits they act on have the same qubit indices and responsibilities. The RSGs' appearance pattern for the three matching criteria is displayed in above given figure.

A predetermined number of the circuit's top-ranked RSGs are removed in this step. The number of gates that comprise the discovered RSGs and the frequency of their occurrence in the circuit are multiplied to determine their ranking.

8.7.3 Heuristic circuit optimization

After trying to find RSGs in the circuit, a heuristic optimization procedure is employed to eliminate unnecessary qubits or redundant gates in order to minimize the circuit depth. There are two optimization levels in this step:

Level 1: Optimize the circuit as a whole, including the RSGs;

Level 2: Optimize the circuit as a whole, but only eliminate the nearby gate pairs (see below) for the RSGs.

While Level 2 would typically produce a deeper circuit than Level 1 and offer more opportunity for development in subsequent compilation stages if the RSGs have specialized low-level implementations, Level 1 would offer a shorter, more effective circuit.

8.7.3.1 Fundamental concept of eliminating unnecessary controlled processes

Depending on the quantum state of the system at the moment the gate is applied, a controlled operation, such as a CNOT or a Toffoli gate, executes a different operation. Assuming that this $|\psi\rangle$operation's control qubit count is

$$|\psi\rangle = \sum_{j,k} c_{j,k} \, |j\rangle_{\text{ctl}} \otimes |k\rangle$$

Where $|\cdot\rangle_{\text{ctl}}$ indicates the state of the control qubits, while the unsubscripted ket indicates the other state of the system. The states are expressed as integers with $0 < j < 2^m - 1$ and $0 < k < 2^{n-m} - 1$. We suppose that the controlled operation for the gate is applied when all of the control qubits are in the $|1\}$state, which is the state

$|j\rangle_{\text{ctl}} = |11\ldots1\rangle = |2^m - 1\rangle_{\text{ctl}}$. This enables one to use the amplitudes to categorize the system's state into three general classes $c_{j,k}$.

Cause: $c_{j,k} \neq 0$ iff $j = 2^m - 1$

All computational bases in the superposition use the gate's controlled operation.

Non-Triggering: $c_{2^m-1,k} = 0$ for all k. The controlled operation is never used.

Unknown: The state is either non-triggering or triggering.

The current technique cannot simplify an uncertain single-qubit controlled gate, but it can simplify an indeterminate multi-qubit controlled gate by removing control on some of the qubits, as long as the system state meets a specific requirement. One way to simplify a circuit with triggering or non-triggering controlled gates is to remove all controls (triggering case) or the gate entirely (non-triggering case).

As an illustration of this idea, look at the simple circuit below: Since the |0> is the CNOT's henon-triggering state, the first CNOT gate has no effect and can be removed from the circuit if the second qubit is in the initial state |0>. The triggering state |1> contains the second qubit prior to the second CNOTgate. Thus, it is possible to remove the qubit control from the second CNOT gate.

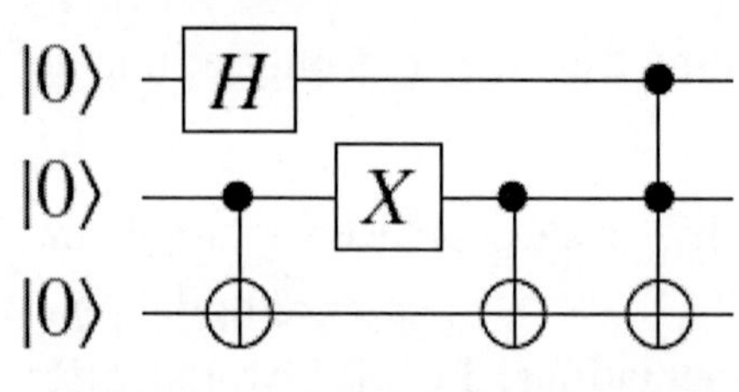

Fig.8.28 The Henon-triggering state.

Before the Toffoligate, the first two qubits are in the superposition of |01> and |11>, which is an unknown state for the Toffoligate. This second qubit control can be removed from the Toffoligate and replaced with a CNOTgate controlled only on the first qubit because the Toffoligate has a triggering bitstring{11} and the second qubit is always in the|1> state.

Consequently, the heuristic circuit optimization for each controlled gate necessitates determining the possible states that the control qubits can adopt as well as eliminating extraneous components from the controlled processes. The following goes into further depth about these two steps.

An arbitrary multi-qubit controlled-U gate with m control qubits can be converted into an O(m)Toffoli and controlled-U gate. All controlled gates are thus reduced to singly-controlled unitary operations (C[U]) and Toffoli gates (C^2[X]). Therefore, {1} or {11} are the only triggering bitstrings that need to be considered. This decomposition results in at most˜ N=nN controlled gates for a qubit circuit composed of N multi-qubit controlled gates, each of which has a maximum of n control qubits.

8.7.3.2 States of the computational base establishment

A circuit consisting of n qubits generally generates a quantum state described by a superposition of the fall of the 2n computational base states, giving birth to the three classes of the system's states. However, it is very typical for a given circuit to generate a quantum state in which the amplitudes of only a subset of the computational basis states are nonzero. Furthermore, the beginning state determines the number of finite-amplitude basis states.

Either a complete calculation of the amplitudes or repeated measurements of the control qubits can be used to determine the state classification of each controlled gate. A traditional simulation involves running the circuit directly in front of the controlled gate and repeatedly measuring the control qubits at the truncation point. Although it falls within the statistical uncertainty of the observations, the distribution of the produced bitstrings can be used to deduce the finiteness of the relevant amplitudes. Because it requires less computing power, Aqcel employs the latter approach.

It is important to take into account a few observations regarding the computing costs of the two approaches. A circuit with N controlled gates and n qubits. As was previously said, O(N) single or double controlled gates are produced by reducing this to either $C^2[X]$ or C[U]. The number of qubits in a classical simulation of the state vector prior to a controlled gate scales exponentially, requiring $O(2^n)$ calculations. However, O(M) operations are needed to measure them=1 or 2 control qubits Mtimes, which yields Mbit strings of length m. It takes $O(\tilde{}N2^n)$ for the classical simulation and $O(N^2M)$ for the quantum measurements to repeat this for all N gates.

8.7.3.3 Elimination of superfluous controlled procedures

Once zero-amplitude computational basis states have been identified, each controlled gate—or its controls, if feasible—is shifted. The entire circuit for eliminating unnecessary controlled processes is analyzed before the control elimination step in classical simulation. When quantum measurements are used instead, circuit execution, measurements, and circuit optimization are performed individually at each controlled gate.

The control elimination process for each controlled gate looks like this: Determine the likelihood of observing|01> of the control qubit for a C[U] gate. Remove the control and retain only the single unitary gate U if the probability is 1. Take the controlled gate out of the circuit if the probability is zero. If not, leave the restricted gate in place. For a $C^2[X]$ (Toffoli)gate, determine the probabilities of the four possible states: Determine the probability of each of the following four states: |00>, |01>, |10>, and |11>.

If the probability of |11{ is 1, remove the two controls and leave the Xgate in place; if the probability of |11> is 0, remove the entire Toffoligate; if either of those two conditions is true (the unidentified class), one of the two controls can still be eliminated; this is the case if the probability of the state|01>(|10>)is zero, in which case the first (second)control can be eliminated.

Setting thresholds is necessary to decide whether to call a state triggering, non-triggering, or undecided. After setting a threshold, the number of measurements required must be high enough to ensure that the statistical uncertainty is below the threshold. Note that the measurements of the states will be imprecise for noisy quantum circuits, and one should anticipate inaccuracies in the probabilities to witness specific bit strings.

It is possible to calculate the probabilities for every potential bit-string given the measured bit strings, which may be found using O (˜N^2M) operations. This allows one to decide whether to use O(˜N) operations to simplify a controlled process. Because of this, determining the computational cost of removing control from the entire controlled operation is made simple.

It should be mentioned that the so-called ZXcalculus can also be used to identify and remove unnecessary controlled operations. Since the ZXcalculus is comprehensive in the sense of formal logic, it is always possible to demonstrate that an unneeded gate can be shifted with its help. But generally speaking, this has no scalability advantage over just computing the state vectors because it consumes exponential resources. Undoubtedly, the ZXcalculus remains immensely potent and serves as the foundation for numerous quantum compiler optimization methods, such as the one we compare later.

8.7.3.4 Removing neighboring gate pairs

It is possible to exclude the gates that implement unitary operators A and their Hermitian conjugate A from the circuit if they act on the same set of qubits next to one another and produce an identity operation. A circuit with such canceling gate pairs can be achieved by moving gates through the optimization processes described above, albeit this is obviously oversimplifying the situation. Because of this, the gate reduction step is used both before and after eliminating redundant controlled activities.

8.7.3.5 Removal of unnecessary qubits:

Following the previously outlined procedures, the circuit is inspected for qubits in which no gate is applied, and those qubits are subsequently eliminated. For instance, this happens when a quantum circuit that is designed to function generically with various initial states is run with a particular initial state. These exponential algorithms that we examine below are an example of such a circuit.

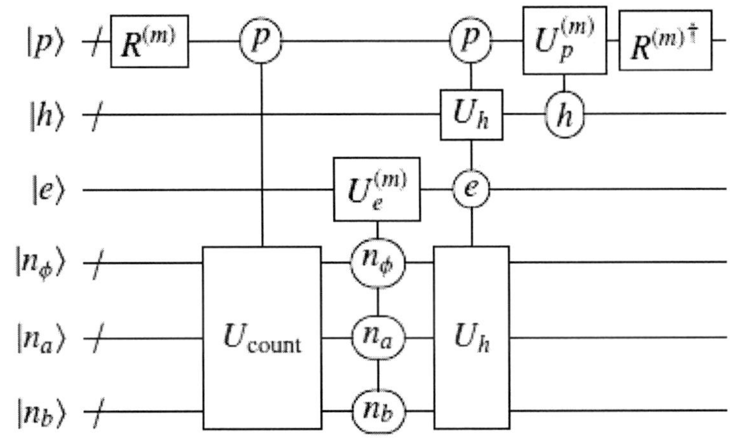

Fig.8.29 The algorithm's m[th] stage in the quantum circuit.

The particles at this step are contained in the physical register |p>; the Branchinghi tale is represented by |h>; and the binary variable |e> indicates whether or not an emission is present at this step. The exact form of the rotation matrices R(m) and the unitary operations U_{count},U_e $^{(m)}$,U_h, and $U_p$$^{(m)}$ are uncomputed before the circuit ends. The three lower registers count the number of particles of type, $|\phi$: a, and b.

8.8 Use of Quantum Algorithms

The circuit optimization protocol has been applied to a quantum algorithm developed for HEP, and the heuristic optimization is carried out at Level 1 for the optimization on current quantum hardware.

8.8.1 The Quantum Partonshower technique

An aquan-tum computer with polynomial resources has been shown to be capable of efficiently simulating the agenerics scattering process. However, in the context of near-term devices, such circuits demand prohibitive resources. One of quantum computing's most prominent scientific uses is quantum parton-shower algorithms.

When the charge of all particles capable of radiating is different, the quantum partonshower (QPS) technique provides an exponential speedup over existing algorithms. Specifically, an approach to model the collinear radiation from particles with a fundamental charge that is not zero. Since this radiation is similar to the remaining scattering amplitude, it can be handled separately. Partonshower Monte Carlo generators in HEP are based on this factorization.

The particles start with either type f1 or f2 n fermions. These fermions can radiate a scalar particle $|\phi$:, which in turn can split into fermion-anti-fermion pairs (of the same or different type). The three couplings g1, g2, and g12 between f1and $|\phi$:, f2 and $|\phi$:, and

$f_1\bar{f}_2$ $(\bar{f}_1 f_2)$ and ϕ, respectively, are the pertinent parameters. A particle may radiate, split, or do nothing at each of the Novel steps that make up the shower development. When N_{evol} is high, the result is more accurate.

The quantum circuit block for the mth step of the circuit is shown in the above picture. Rotating the fermions into a new basis, f_a and f_b, where the effective mixing g_{ab} between $f_a\bar{f}_b$ $(\bar{f}_a f_b)$ and ϕ is zero, is the first stage. The registers n_a, n_b, and n_ϕ are then used to hold the number of particles of each type. The existence or absence of an emission is then determined by computing a Sudakov factor. The total number of particles of each type is the only factor that affects this process. Due to the coupling constants being run with energy scale, some of the stages in this method are universal (i.e., independent of m), while others are m-dependent. Following the emission stage, the fermions are rotated back into the f1 and f2 bases and the particle and history registers are suitably updated.

8.9 Integrated Patterns of Quantum Computing for Real-Time Cryptography in Various Domains

Quantum bits, or qubits, are essential to quantum computers, which manipulate knowledge through quantum-mechanical events. Superconductivity is one of the methods for generating a quantum state, although there are other ways to make a qubit. They need to be kept extremely cold in order to work on these superconductive qubits for extended periods of time. All computer systems have the ability to store and manipulate information. Traditional computers today process single bits that are stored in binary states of 0 and 1. Quantum computers are superior to the vacuum of space at temperatures close to absolute null because every temperature factor within the device may be changed.

Think about how a quantum computer with more than 2000 parts creates a cold environment for the qubits within its dilution refrigerator. Today, researchers from all across the world are testing algorithms for various fields of operation using real quantum processors. However, a few decades ago, quantum processing was purely theoretical. Using the concepts of quantum mechanics, quantum cryptography—also referred to as quantum encoding—encrypts messages so that no one else can decipher them. Together with its "theory of no transition," which stipulates that it cannot be unintentionally broken, it supports quantum states. Calculations using quantum-improved AI are particularly relevant in this field. In order to ensure safe and integrity-aware communication generally, this section provides a brief overview of the patterns of quantum computing implementation in real-time cryptography.

Ions or photons, the crucial component of quantum mechanics, are used as qubits in commonplace quantum computers. Generating, managing, or modifying qubits for high-performance and multidimensional techniques is an essential component of creative problem solving. Many businesses, including IBM, Google, and Rigetti, have found that superconductive circuits can function at temperatures as low as those seen in space. IonQ researchers capture individual atoms in electromagnetic fields using ultra-high vacuum chambers. It is intended to be isolated in a different way for each scenario, though. Computers nowadays run on "pulses," which are an electrical or optical stream of ones and zeros, according to current technology.

A more thorough summary of the core ideas of quantum computing can be found in The Fundamentals of Quantum Computing. This will include an explanation of quantum bits (qubits), their special characteristics, and the entanglement and superposition concepts that set quantum computing apart from traditional computing. By exploring the world of quantum mechanics and providing previously unheard-of processing power and efficiency, the advent of quantum computing completely transforms our understanding of computation. Quantum computers use quantum bits, or qubits, which can exist in several states concurrently due to concepts like superposition and entanglement, in contrast to classical computers, which are based on bits in binary values of 0 and 1. These special characteristics make quantum computers very interesting for a variety of applications since they allow them to tackle complicated problems tenfold faster than classical computers.

From gate-model quantum computers that use quantum circuits and logic gates to adiabatic quantum computers and quantum annealers that address certain problem classes, quantum computing architectures come in a variety of styles. Recent developments in quantum computing, including proofs of quantum supremacy, enhancements to quantum error correction methods, and the scalability of qubit systems, demonstrate the field's quick development. Practical uses of quantum computing in a variety of fields are demonstrated by real-world applications such as quantum-enhanced optimization algorithms, material science simulations, and cryptography advances made possible by algorithms like Shore's for integer factorization.

But these developments also bring with them some serious difficulties. Maintaining quantum coherence and performing calculations without errors are still severely hampered by qubit decoherence, which results from interactions with the environment. Developments in scalable quantum hardware and fault-tolerant quantum computing are needed to meet these hurdles, opening the door for real-world use across a range of industries.

Unlocking the full potential of quantum computing, creating fault-tolerant quantum computers, investigating novel quantum algorithms for machine learning and optimization, and transforming sectors like healthcare and finance are the goals of current research projects. Real-time cryptography combined with quantum computing creates new possibilities for safe data processing and communication, with ramifications for smart cities, the Internet of Things, and other areas.

The main developments in quantum computing are included in the fundamental principles section of the article. This could include new algorithms, significant advancements in the real-world application of quantum processors, and current developments in quantum hardware. Additionally, the usefulness of quantum computing in actual applications.

Supersonic medication plans, in silico clinical preliminary procedures with virtual people replicated "live," maximum control over all genetic sequencing and examination, cloud-based emergency clinic development, prescient health, or clinical information security using quantum vulnerability and high-performance quantum computers are all possible with quantum registering. Because qubits have some peculiar quantum characteristics, a collection of them can provide significantly more computing power through interlocking, where high integrity is needed for the essential dimensions. The fundamental building blocks of quantum computing are qubits, which are employed in many different applications, such as security, privacy, integrity, optimization factors, and many more.

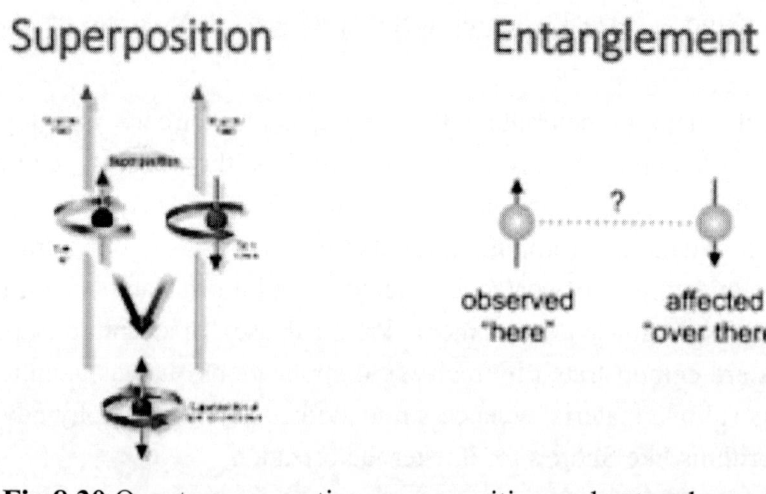

Fig.8.30 Quantum computing: superposition and entanglement.

Quantum bits, or qubits, are used in quantum computing. Due to the rules of superposition and entanglement, qubits can exist in several states simultaneously. Only 0 or 1 can be utilized as traditional bits in classical computing. The application of cryptographic techniques to guarantee data security even during rapid data transmission is known as real-time cryptography.

These methods need to be fast enough to encrypt and decode data in order to satisfy demands for processing or real-time communication. Integrated Patterns are tried-and-true frameworks or techniques for implementing quantum computing ideas in a range of sectors, such as finance, healthcare, and telecommunications, to improve processes or address difficult problems in a number of different domains.

Superposition And Overlays

Many combinations of 1 and 0 can be used as qubits at the same time. We refer to this ability to exist simultaneously in multiple states as superposition. Researchers control qubits by using precision lasers or microwave beams. This method attains a greater level of precision with respect to the patterns of implementation.

Concurrent "existence" of several states. [Prior to Measurement]

Interaction between two distinct systems

Table 8.1 Computing: classical versus quantum

Parameters of comparison	**Classical Computing**	**Quantum Computing**
Information processing	Using Logic gates like AND, OR	Using quantum logic
Error rates	Classical computing has a less error rate	Quantum computing has a high error rate
States and Phases	Discrete	Continuous
Suitability	Classical computing is best suitable for the daily processing	Quantum computing is best appropriate for data analysis
Operations	Linear algebra	Boolean algebra

The key advantage of quantum computers is that, in a conventional device, doubling the computational power doubles the number of bits. However, a quantum computer's numerical reduction capacity increases exponentially with the number of qubits added.

In quantum computing, superposition and entanglement are depicted in previous Figure. Quantum computers operate by means of a quantum daisy chain made up of entangled qubits. This is the cause of the excitement surrounding their potential to use certain quantum methods to speed up computations. It serves as the crucial foundation for quantum systems with extreme precision and low error rates.

Quantum Decomposition and Decoherence

Coherence and decoherence are combined in quantum computing, which is known as the breakdown between qubits and their environment. The characteristics of two or more quantum particles may be unpredictable or random when they are extremely near to one another. They may overlap until their duty is completed correctly due to the slight temperature or vibration variations, which are referred to as quantum-speak "noise." For this reason, scientists are working hard to keep qubits in vacuum rooms and super cooled refrigerators isolated from the outer world. For performance in quantum system implementation scenarios, this cooling factor and the regulated temperature are combined.

Nevertheless, noise also causes a number of errors to creep into equations in spite of their best efforts. Intelligent quantum algorithms that can assist in adding extra qubits can compensate for any of them. However, hundreds of stable qubits will probably be needed to create a single, incredibly stable "logical" qubit. This envisions the computational power of a quantum computer for various implementation phases and levels. In order to solve a mathematical equation, the quantity of bits must be managed with extreme precision and throughput, which is obviously beyond the capabilities of even the most potent supercomputer. Because researchers are always finding new techniques to increase the efficiency of traditional machines and supercomputer software is getting better, it is still unclear how many qubits are needed to do this.

Within the scientific community, there is a lot of debate regarding the significance of reaching this milestone. Rather than waiting for the dominance to be announced and for corporate giants to implement quantum computing at massive levels for social and corporate segments, companies are now starting to test quantum computers from companies like IBM, Rigetti, and D-Wave, a Canadian company.

Comparing Quantum and Classical Cryptography Algorithms

Explored here how quantum and conventional algorithms differ fundamentally in the field of cryptography, clarifying how their unique characteristics affect how they operate.

Fundamentals of Quantum Algorithms

1. **Quantum Bits (Qubits):** The way information is represented is one of the fundamental differences. Quantum algorithms use quantum bits, or qubits, whereas classical algorithms use classical bits, which can be in the states of 0 or 1. Because qubits can exist in numerous states at once due to the principles of superposition and entanglement, quantum algorithms are able to execute parallel calculations in a manner that is not possible with classical algorithms.

2. **Quantum Parallelism:** To process numerous possibilities at once, quantum algorithms take advantage of quantum parallelism. In contrast, classical algorithms handle every alternative one after the other. Quantum algorithms may have an edge in some computational tasks due to their intrinsic parallelism.

3. **Algorithms for Quantum Cryptography:**

    - Shor's Integer Factorization Algorithm: Shor's algorithm is a well-known illustration of the quantum advantage in encryption. Compared to the most well-known classical algorithms, this quantum algorithm calculates huge integers exponentially more quickly. The difficulty of factoring big numbers is what makes popular cryptographic systems like RSA secure. The classical security presumptions that underlie such techniques are threatened by the quantum speedup introduced by Shor's algorithm.

- Grover's search technique, which offers a quadratic speedup in unstructured search problems, exemplifies yet another aspect of quantum superiority. This algorithm can be used in cryptography to search a database or an unsorted list, greatly cutting down on search time when compared to traditional search algorithms.

1. QKD, or Quantum Key Distribution

Quantum Key Distribution (QKD) is a cryptographic algorithm that uses quantum mechanics to protect communication channels. One of its features is quantum entanglement. By using quantum entanglement, QKD creates a shared secret key between two parties, in contrast to traditional key distribution techniques. Quantum mechanical principles ensure the key's security, making it impervious to eavesdropping efforts.

No-Cloning Theorem: According to this essential tenet of quantum physics, an arbitrary unknown quantum state cannot be accurately replicated. In quantum cryptography, this theory is used to identify any effort to copy or intercept quantum keys. This intrinsic quantum protection is not advantageous for classical key distribution systems.

2. Post-Quantum Encryption

Classical cryptography faces new threats from quantum computing: classical cryptography systems now face additional difficulties.

Shor's algorithm is one that has the potential to crack popular public-key cryptosystems. To guarantee the ongoing security of communication in a post-quantum age, the discipline of post-quantum cryptography is actively investigating cryptographic algorithms that withstand quantum attacks.

3. Protocols for Quantum Cryptography

Quantum Coin Protocols: Examples of quantum cryptography protocols that highlight the special benefits and difficulties of quantum communication are quantum coin disputes. These protocols create safe, tamper-evident channels of communication between untrusted parties by utilizing the characteristics of quantum physics.

4. Opportunities and Challenges

Due to the fragile nature of quantum states, quantum algorithms are susceptible to issues like mistakes and noise. It becomes essential to use error-correction algorithms in order to preserve the integrity of quantum cryptography systems. This similar problem is not faced by classical algorithms since they are not susceptible to quantum noise.

The principles of quantum mechanics are used by quantum algorithms in cryptography to carry out operations and create secure communication channels in ways that are not possible with classical algorithms. The unique features of quantum cryptography, the parallelism qubits offer, and the efficiency with which they address certain problems demonstrate the revolutionary potential of quantum technologies in the information security space.

8.9.1 Quantum Computing: Use Cases

The ability to use quantum mechanical features to perform encryption operations is known as quantum encryption. A quantum key distribution that offers an informatively safe solution to the crucial exchange problem is best exemplified by quantum encryption. The advantage of quantum cryptography is that it is possible to prove or infer that it is implausible that various cryptographic operations could be completed with traditional (nonquantum) communication alone. For example, it is impossible to duplicate data that is encoded in a quantum state. By collapsing the wave function (no-cloning theorem), you attempt to decode the coded data, changing the quantum situation. This can monitor the quantity of major deliveries that are being overheard.

The most powerful link in the data-protection chain is cryptography. However, stakeholders don't think encryption keys are always stable. Quantum cryptography includes a variety of cryptographic techniques and protocols. Some of the more important protocols and applications are covered in the following. The most popular method for circumstances when a third party cannot decipher the key despite information transmission between Persons 1 and 2 is quantum key distribution, or QKD. Persons 1 and 2 would be inconsistent if a third party wanted to consider the key that needs to be located. After then, the key is typically used for secure communications via conventional means. For instance, symmetric cryptography can make advantage of the shared key.

Quantum Key Distribution (QKD), in contrast to traditional key distribution, was mathematically demonstrated to not impede an adversary's ability to eavesdrop. Known as "unconditional security and protection aspects," it requires certain rules of quantum physics, such as Person-1's ability to authenticate him and Person-2's inability to impersonate him.

Despite QKD's attractive appearance, its practical implementation is unlikely. The inadequate separation between primary and secondary power plants is the cause of this. The outcomes of recent and ongoing research have only expanded the parameters. Though it actually exceeded it at 200 km before encountering the loss-scaling of its non-repeating primary capability, the two-field QKD (TF-QD) approach could theoretically solve the scaling out of a failure channel in the twinning flow method and show that its covert function, known as the PLOB, was no longer present at 340 km of optical fiber. They could not follow up. "550-kilometer standard fiber," which is still the benchmark for contemporary communications, can achieve ideal performance, according to the investigation. Despite the tendency for TF-QD to expand local network bandwidth, the Sending-Not-Sending (SNS) Version achieves remarkable overall performance over extended distances.

8.9.2 Aspects of Quantum Encryption and Security

In distrustful cryptography, the participants lack mutual trust. Persons 1 and 2, for instance, combine private entries to perform the computation. They collaborate. However, Person-2 has no faith in Alice, and Person-1 has no faith in Person-2. Therefore, after the computation is finished, a stable cryptography job requires that Person-1 be able to guarantee that Person-2 has not cheated, and that Person-2 is thus certain that Person-1 has not deceived.

In mistrusted cryptography, for instance, promises and steady computations—including additional instances of coin flipping and forgetful transfers—work. The distribution of keys does not fall under the category of unreliable encryption. Utilizing quantum systems, cautious quantum cryptography investigates the field of manipulating cryptography and can be combined to monitor communication and sniffing attempts.

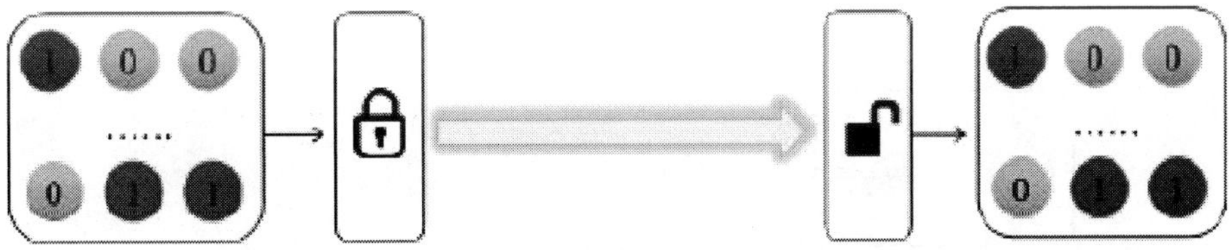

Fig.8.31 Secure communication based on quantum technology.

In addition to using quantum mechanics, protocols that make use of special relativity may offer complete security. Mayers both offered examples of unconditionally secure quantum bit participation that may be referred to as "confirmed proof."

Here's the procedure: There was no way for Lo and Chau to deliver more bricks to the assignment once they had achieved the ideal quantity gold. One out of every two naive transfers would still be dangerous, as demonstrated by Lo. As I go through the list, I'm writing the following sentences: These "primitive" and "relativistic" protocols, however, have been demonstrated by Kent to be fairly conservative.

A. Quantum computation and real-time cryptography

In contrast, quantum coins are a protocol between two parties who do not trust one another, unlike the distribution of quantum keys. Qubits allow users to communicate and exchange information. Everyone wants the other to lie because Persons 1 and 2 are insecure about one another over a quantum channel. Therefore, more effort must be made to guarantee that neither Person-1 nor Person-2 will significantly outperform the others in order to produce the intended outcome. Bias is the ability to influence a specific result, and procedures are created to lessen the bias of dishonest players. Other names for stealing are depicted in the above figure.

Although there are clear safety advantages to quantum communication protocols, such as the quantum coin reversion, over conventional communication, they are challenging to implement in real-world scenarios.

A player engages in manipulation and tampering when they attempt to change a particular result or raise its probability. Person-1 might cheat, for instance, by claiming that Person-2 miscalculated her starting foundation when he estimated it properly. However, Person-1 would still need to construct a new string of qubits that precisely corresponds to Person-2's calculation on the opposite side of the table? If Person-2 detects a misunderstanding, he will be aware that she lied, and her chances of generating a similar qubit will decrease dramatically.

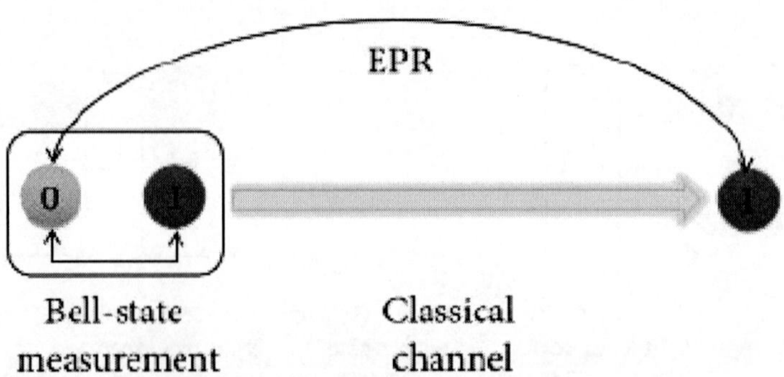

Fig.8.32 Quantum-based channel.

Person-2 may see that Person-1's chain somewhat (but not completely) coincides with the two sides of the table and realizes that she is being deceived. Person-1 can also construct a chain of photons using a combination of states. Existing quantum devices still have an inherent flaw. Gaps in Bob's measurement table and an effect on Person-2's measures can result from errors and lost qubits. The ability of Person-2 to validate the qubit sequence of Person-1 would be hampered by significant calculation losses. The Einstein-Podolsky-Rosen (EPR) conundrum is definitely conceivable. Two polarized photons in an anisotropic state are in an EPR pair as long as they are measured in the same manner.

A person could accomplish this. Person-1 could send Person-2 a single photon while preserving Person-2's bits. Person-2 will be on the opposite side of the room, figuring out her EPR photon pairs and setting up a perfect relationship with the other table in the meantime.

For as long as that worked, she was unaware that she was breaching the rules. It will require a quantum-based technology that does not yet exist, which is actually not feasible. Person-1 must be able to efficiently store and count almost all of the photons, as seen in the figure above, in order to be effective. This might be the case since every missed photon in the sequence counts as a null. All communications made using this method are closely watched and traceable.

Disputes involving quantum coins usually occur when there is mistrust. You must measure a benefit that Person-1 cannot change in order to create a reward scheme, and beneficiaries won't be aware of it until Person-1 has had an opportunity to provide feedback. It is unchangeable. In cryptography, such tactics are frequently employed. The ability to build an absolute-safety procedure out of a quantum tube and a commitment has been included. Kilian, on the other hand, created a subtle touch at the same time. This technique, known as "secure multiparty computation," allowed for the safe transportation of nearly any computing equipment. To clarify, we are uncertain about the exact phrase because we only understand the general idea of the concept.) Multiparty computation is possible with commitment and a quantum channel (which need not be physical). You risk losing the ability to defend the study's findings because researchers are not allowed to make any assertions on "possibility."

It has been demonstrated that protocols for the initial phases of quantum engagement are ineffective as a result. Mayers demonstrated that there can be no quantum protocol that is absolutely stable; instead, an attacker with limited computing power could only start an ongoing botnet attack. Even although Mayers can be effectively used in scenarios that are far less powerful than what is needed for multi-card computation, quantum protocols (and, consequently, multiparty protocols) are still possible. Here is an example of how engagement protocols can be developed using quantum communication. The November 2013 movement brought "conditional encryption," which was initially seen globally. The present situations are gaining knowledge about a novel strategy known as "perfectly unconditional hiding."

The purpose of BQSM processes was never to assist aspiring engineers in preserving quantitative data for everybody. At the very least, these duties can be completed with the help of today's cutting-edge technological protocol implementations. Since the adversary only knows one thing—everything that has ever been written—the correspondence of creativity is only more important than the adversary's restriction set. By presuming that the competitors' quantum memory is weak, it gives the BCNOS algorithm an edge. Nowadays, single-qubit storage is difficult to implement. The precise protocol will determine this.)

More time can be spent in the quantum storage cycle by postponing the protocol. An opponent can utilize accessible quantum devices of different sizes in an imperfect manner rather than restricting the physical scale of memory. Sound canals are unavoidable because of the ongoing quantum-level uncertainty. Primitives, a model regarding noisy storage models, are returned with noise levels that are as high as those in the BQSM.

B. Position-Depending Quantum Encryption

The goal of quantifying quantitative placement is to use a player's location as its (sole) credential. To make sure a message can only be read by a player in a specific position, for example, you want to deliver it to that player. In the straightforward task of confirming that she is in a specific location, Alice, the player, must convince the (honest) verifiers. Checking postures against collusive opponents utilizing traditional protocols (those who control all processes other than the prover's purported location).

C. Unified Model For Real-Time Cryptography and Quantum Computing

This section is to provide a thorough knowledge of the mutually beneficial relationship between real-time cryptography and quantum computing.

1. Protocols for Untrusted Participants in Quantum Coin

The dynamics between Person-1 and Person-2 must be examined in order to introduce quantum currencies as a protocol between untrusted players. Using qubits and a quantum channel, both people negotiate a situation in which mistrust between them predominates. The purpose of protocols is to reduce biases and keep any person from having a major advantage. The procedures used in quantum coin disputes, which frequently occur in untrustworthy circumstances, assess advantages that are difficult for Person-1 to modify and are consistent with cryptography principles.

2. Modifications To Quantum Communication Protocols

Although quantum communication protocols—including those involving quantum coins—show notable safety advantages over conventional communication, there are still real-world obstacles to overcome.

Threats include manipulation and tampering, in which a player tries to change results or make them more likely. This explores situations in which exponential probability drops, photon chain correlations, and inherent flaws in current quantum devices make it difficult for Person-1 to attempt deception.

3. Cryptographic Methods And Quantum Coin Disputes

Disputes over quantum coins are especially pertinent when there is mistrust. The use of cryptographic techniques to create a reward system with advantages that are impervious to manipulation is highlighted in this section. Pledges and quantum channels are used to integrate absolute-safety protocols, highlighting the possibility of secure multiparty computation.

4. Quantum protocols: opportunities and challenges

It highlights the limitations of Mayers' work on unconditionally stable quantum protocols under computationally constrained attacks. Conditional encryption and the investigation of "perfectly unconditional hiding" offer contemporary developments and situations, taking into account quantum memory limitations and possible unethical behavior.

5. Noise Levels And Quantum Memory Considerations

A briefing is given on the BCNOS algorithm and its advantages over opponents with weak quantum memory. The inevitable existence of sound canals and their effect on quantum storage are highlighted by considerations of noise levels in storage models like the BQSM.

6. Real-Time Model Implications

The ramifications of real-time models are then determined by synthesizing the collective insights from real-time cryptography and quantum computing. Described in detail how cryptographic techniques and quantum protocols work together to improve the security and effectiveness of real-time communication.

8.9.3 Advances for Applications in the Real World

A. Applicable Implementation Methods

This component aims to close the gap between theoretical ideas and real-world applications of encryption and quantum computing. It entails dealing with difficulties relating to scalability, hardware constraints, and making sure that the system is compatible and interoperable with current ones. The technical elements of incorporating quantum technologies into actual situations are to be examined via practical implementation strategies, which take into account variables like system stability, performance optimization, and resource limitations.

B. QKD (Quantum Key Distribution) Advances

Quantum Key Distribution (QKD) is an essential part of quantum-safe cryptography, and new developments in this area have made cryptographic communication much more secure. With this innovation, the focus is on investigating state-of-the-art QKD algorithms that enhance the production and dissemination of cryptographic keys in real-time situations. By integrating these developments, research stays at the forefront of guaranteeing safe routes of communication in situations involving quantum computing.

C. Standards for Quantum-Safe Cryptography

The development of quantum-safe cryptography standards and protocols is urgently needed since quantum computing could endanger established cryptographic systems. Examining the most recent advancements in cryptographic methods that are resistant to quantum assaults is part of this innovation.

D. Integration of Quantum Cloud Computing

Modern IT infrastructures now cannot function without cloud computing, and integrating quantum computing with cloud platforms offers both possibilities and difficulties. This invention investigates the deployment and management of quantum algorithms in cloud environments to take use of distributed computing capabilities and scalable resources. It is essential to comprehend the advantages and difficulties of quantum cloud computing in order to successfully implement quantum applications in practical settings.

E. Applications spanning multiple disciplines

Beyond traditional IT and cybersecurity, quantum computing and cryptography have the potential to revolutionize a number of fields. This invention demonstrates the many ways that quantum technologies are being used in industries like healthcare, banking, logistics, and more. This illustrates the wide range of real-world situations where quantum solutions can provide notable breakthroughs and enhancements by presenting cross-disciplinary applications.

F. Aspects of Quantum Error Correction

Because of quantum decoherence and external influences, quantum systems are prone to errors by nature. Techniques for quantum error correction are essential for reducing these flaws and enhancing the dependability of quantum calculations. This invention focuses on talking about the most recent cutting-edge error correcting techniques and how well they work in actual quantum computing situations. The practical feasibility of quantum computing technology depends on resolving error correcting issues.

G. Advances In The Adoption Of Quantum Cryptography

Quantum-safe cryptography adoption entails more than just technical considerations. In this innovation, practical factors including user acceptability, regulatory compliance, integration with current communication infrastructure, and general viability are examined. Successful implementation and deployment of quantum cryptography in actual communication systems depend on an understanding of the prospects and difficulties related to its adoption.

Chapter - 9
Quantum as a Service

Although quantum computer technology has only begun to leave the lab, full-scale commercialization is probably still a few years away. According to a recent GlobalData research, the market for quantum computing is expected to grow from $500 million to $1 billion in 2022 to $10 billion sometime between 2026 and 2030. Businesses that wait for this enormous expansion to happen, however, run the danger of slipping behind their rivals. They must begin developing their quantum plans right now.

How can businesses of today be ready for the quantum future?

Businesses must first decide which use cases are a suitable fit for quantum. Despite popular belief, quantum computers will not completely replace traditional computers. Existing high-performance computing (HPC) systems will be enhanced by quantum computers, each of which will be utilized to serve specific use cases. Making the most of both technologies and integrating them so they work effectively together as part of an overall IT architecture will be the problem facing businesses in the future.

In particular, highly demanding use cases like building machine learning models, running extensive simulations, or resolving complex optimization issues are the ideal fits for quantum computers. Although these use cases will appear across a variety of industries, the automotive, healthcare, and financial services sectors will see the highest concentration of them.

Given that quantum algorithms have the potential to accelerate established solutions to a number of challenging computer science issues, software research. In recent years, there has been a rise in the development of quantum computing. Quantum algorithms take advantage of unique quantum-specific characteristics like superposition or entanglement to outperform classical algorithms in terms of speed. The quantum software stack facilitates the use of quantum algorithms. Some of the available tools for creating quantum softwares are briefed in this section. We also go over various service models, deployment etc.,

Noisy Intermediate-Scale Quantum (NISQ)

The NISQ Era: With exponential improvements over conventional systems, quantum computing has the potential to completely transform processing capability. Quantum computers can compete with today's supercomputers by using well-designed algorithms, and future predictions indicate an order of magnitude improvement. Qubits, the fundamental building blocks of quantum information, are essential to the effectiveness of quantum computing; their quantity and caliber dictate computational efficiency. Coherence, or the length of time that quantum information is preserved, and gate fidelity, or the precision of quantum gate operations, are important metrics since qubits can be disrupted. Despite advancements, problems like error rates and coherence durations still plague modern quantum computers, which are part of the Noisy Intermediate-Scale Quantum (NISQ) era.

Today, we live in the age of hundreds of noisy qubits, or Noisy Intermediate-Scale Quantum (NISQ) computing. Technologies like as trapped ions and superconducting Josephson junctions are used to create physical qubits. Even if there are still obstacles to overcome, quantum computing is quickly becoming more widely used.

Tech behemoths like Google and IBM, as well as up-and-coming nations like China, are driving the race toward scalable quantum computing. Significant events like IBM's release of Eagle, a 127-qubit processor, and Google's assertion of quantum supremacy with Sycamore highlight the field's quick development. Within ten years, quantum computing is expected to become widely used, marking the beginning of a new age. Quantum computing has the potential to revolutionize a number of fields, including materials research, medicine development, and encryption. The commercialization of quantum computing, despite its futuristic appeal, is no longer limited to large organizations and research institutions; startups and QaaS providers are well-positioned to democratize access to this ground-breaking technology, spurring creativity across sectors.

Why QCaaS?

For a number of reasons, businesses can profit from a Quantum Computing as a Service (QCaaS) business model. The first is the obvious: anyone other than the biggest corporations with the most money cannot afford to purchase a quantum computer since they are still very costly and fast become outdated.

Traditionally, quantum computing required hefty investments in infrastructure, expertise, and specialized hardware. However, with the advent of QCaaS, businesses can now access quantum computing resources via the cloud on a pay-per-use basis, similar to other cloud services.

QCaaS democratizes access to quantum computing resources, akin to Software as a Service (SaaS) models. By providing on-demand access to quantum computers via the cloud, QCaaS enables businesses to accelerate innovation and problem-solving.

Additionally, not all quantum computers are made similarly, so businesses should avoid using a one-size-fits-all strategy. Nowadays, there are several different quantum modalities accessible, and certain quantum computers are more suitable than others to tackle specific tasks more quickly and with fewer errors. An organization would still be restricted to using only one kind of quantum computer even if it were able to get beyond the expense and difficulty of purchasing, setting up, and maintaining its own. On the other hand, a business that use QCaaS might be as flexible as possible, possibly utilizing the greatest computer for every task.

Key Players

The creation of quantum cloud platforms has been led by major computer companies including IBM, Google, Microsoft, and Amazon. These platforms give customers access to state-of-the-art quantum processors, sophisticated simulators, and extensive development tools. Leading cloud service providers, such as Microsoft Azure and Amazon Web Services (AWS), have introduced Quantum Computing as a Service (QCaaS) platforms, enabling a wide range of users, including developers, researchers, and businesses, to explore the world of quantum algorithms and applications.

Nonetheless, a few major companies are making noteworthy advancements in creating and providing QaaS solutions:

IBM:

A pioneer in quantum computing, IBM provides IBM Quantum Experience, a sophisticated QaaS platform. In addition to tools and tutorials to get users started, this platform offers cloud-based access to a fleet of genuine quantum computers.

Amazon Braket:

With its Amazon Braket platform, Amazon is also venturing into the QaaS space. In addition to its own quantum simulation tools, Braket provides access to quantum computers from many vendors, such as IonQ and Rigetti Computing.

Microsoft Azure Quantum:

With its Azure Quantum platform, Microsoft is another significant contender. A range of quantum computing resources, such as hardware and simulators from various suppliers, are accessible through Azure Quantum. Additionally, it offers libraries and tools for creating quantum algorithms.

Google Quantum AI:

As a pioneer in quantum research, Google provides access to their quantum hardware. Google is aggressively creating cloud-based access solutions, even if they aren't quite a QaaS platform yet.

Rigetti Computing:

As part of its Quantum Cloud Services, the hardware manufacturer Rigetti Computing makes its own range of quantum computers available online.

IonQ: Through its IonQ Cloud platform, IonQ, another hardware supplier, offers cloud access to its trapped-ion quantum computers.

How to access QcaaS

Enterprise clients still have certain unmet needs with even some of the QCaaS solutions that are currently on the market. Academic and research institutes have been the main early users of QCaaS. These clients usually use their own on-site facilities, which are usually university labs, to access the services. These settings make it difficult to connect with commercial ecosystem partners; although this might not be a major problem for academic institutions, it is a significant barrier for businesses.

Businesses nowadays can also use public cloud platforms to directly use QCaaS. A cloud-only strategy does have certain disadvantages, though, such as the potential for vendor lock-in, which reduces flexibility. When it comes time to move data out of the public cloud, moving it there might result in extremely hefty data egress fees.

To get ready for quantum's future, have a peek at

What is the best course of action for businesses wishing to plan their quantum strategy if both public cloud QCaaS and on-premises quantum computers have serious disadvantages?

Generally speaking, quantum innovation to be essentially forward-looking. However, it could be useful to put some of the knowledge we have gained about digital infrastructure to use in order to go from idea to commercialization. Many businesses have realized in recent years how much commercial value they may create by deploying in dispersed, networked data centers.

They have been able to optimize the value of their company data and guarantee infrastructure agility wherever they require it by placing themselves in close proximity to ecosystem partners and potential clients. In order to capitalize on all the advantages that data centers provide, digital leaders have made them the focus of their operations. It won't be shocking if QCaaS experiences the same issue in the future.

Quantum service providers will gain the network connectivity necessary to transfer massive data sets rapidly by establishing in or close to key data center sites, which will benefit both their business clients and themselves. Additionally, QCaaS providers may increase their workloads while maintaining minimal administrative costs by being close to dense ecosystems of potential consumers.

9.1 Equipment

In recent years, a number of systems that use the recently announced quantum computing stack have been made available (LaRose, 2019). This include platforms from third-party suppliers like ProjectQ, as well as platforms from quantum computer providers like IBM's Qiskit (Qiskit, 2020) or Rigetti's Forest (PyQuil, 2020).

So-called quantum circuits, which are organized sets of quantum gates, are used to define quantum algorithms. These gates are unitary transformations on the quantum register. Any quantum algorithm may be implemented using the universal set of gates that each platform offers. A basic illustration of one of these circuits is shown in the below Figure. It makes use of two qubits, each of which is initialized to $|0\rangle$ and is represented by a horizontal line. The measurement data are shown as a single line in a traditional two-bit register c. The qubit at quantum register position 0 is subjected to the Hammard gate (H), which produces an equal superposition of the two base states $|0\rangle$ and $|1\rangle$.

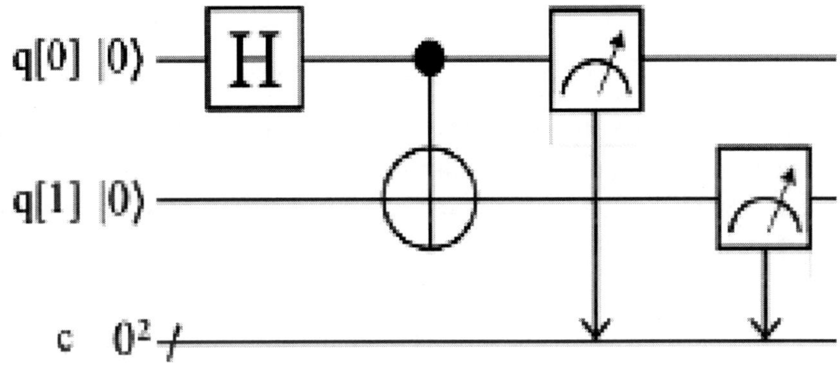

Fig.9.1 A quantum circuit example.

The qubits at quantum register locations 0 and 1 are then subjected to the Controlled Not gate (CNOT), where the former serves as the control-bit and, if the control qubit is $|1\rangle$. a NOT operation is done to the second qubit. Both qubits are then given measurement gates, which indicate that they will be measured and that the results will be saved in the classical bit register.

Different quantum programming languages that are embedded in traditional host languages are supported by the various platforms. For example, PyQuil from Forest is embedded in Python, while Qiskit is embedded in Python, JavaScript, and Swift. The platforms offer libraries that contain techniques for putting a quantum circuit into practice. A code snippet example of the design and operation of the circuit from Figure is displayed in Listing 1.

```
1  from SDK import lib
2  # create circuit and add gates
3  circuit = lib.Circuit()
4  circuit.H(0)
5  circuit.CNOT(0, 1)
6  ...
7  # many more
8  ...
9  circuit.measure()
10 # choose QPU
11 backend = lib.getBackend('...')
12 # compile circuit and send to QPU
13 result = lib.execute(circuit,
```

Listing 1: An example of a line of code that creates and runs a quantum circuit.

The library is imported in the first line. The gates are then accumulated in consecutive order using a circuit object that has been built. In line 4, Gate H is added to the circuit, and in line 5, the CNOT gate is added. Lastly, line 9 adds measurement to the circuit. Following circuit construction, line 11 selects a concrete backend, which may be a QPU, a local simulator, or a cloud simulator. Line 13 is where the circuit's execution begins. The circuit, the selected backend, and the quantity of shots are required inputs for this execute method.

A quantum algorithm often runs several times, and the shots parameter allows you to specify how many times it runs. The platform's compiler then transforms the circuit into quantum assembler language. The corresponding platform's compiler subsequently transforms the circuit into quantum assembler language.

Despite the fact that vendor-specific libraries are included into high-level programming languages, a thorough understanding of quantum computing is necessary to develop quantum algorithms utilizing universal sets of gates. Thus, in relation to their offered subroutines, libraries occasionally already offer subroutines for popular quantum algorithms, such the Quantum Approximate Optimization Algorithm or the Variational Quantum Eigensolver. Nevertheless, it is frequently impossible to invoke these subroutines without assuming the QPU being used and how they are actually implemented.

At the moment, the majority of platforms are vendor-specific and offered by the quantum computer suppliers. But there are other vendor-agnostic methods, such ProjectQ or XACC, which are both software platforms that are expandable and enable the creation of vendor-agnostic source code that may be executed on many QPUs.

9.2 Quantum Application as a Service and Deployment

A number of suppliers provide cloud-based access to their quantum computers. Quantum Computing as a Service (QCaaS) is another name for this cloud service concept. Additionally, cloud service providers like Amazon and 1Qbit have added QCaaS products to their portfolio. For quantum applications to be realized, traditional and quantum computer infrastructure must be combined.

Usually, a quantum computer is used in conjunction with a conventional computer; the latter are still required for data storage, pre- and post-processing, user interface, and other tasks.

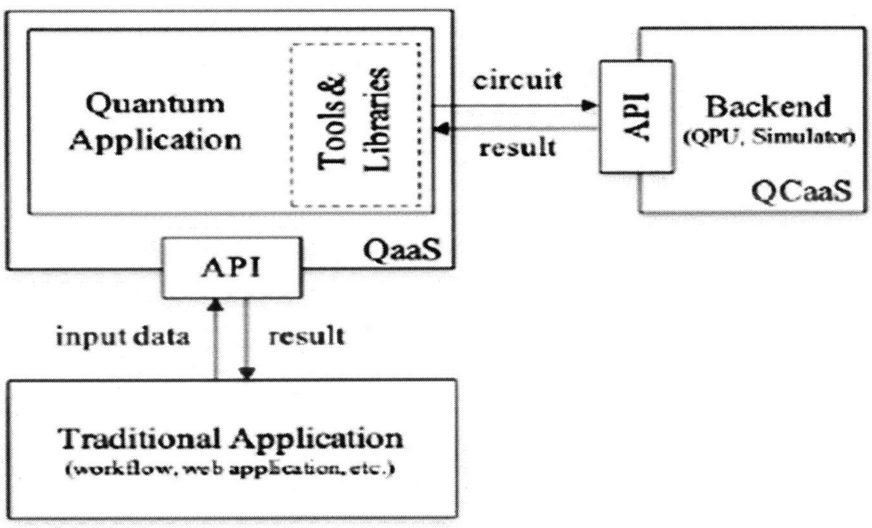

Fig.9.2 Quantum Computing as a Service (QCaaS) and Quantum Algorithm as a Service (QaaS).

Consequently, a hybrid architecture comprising both quantum and conventional components is the end result of a quantum application. As can be seen in Listing 1, the source code currently contains the deployment logic for the quantum portion. Installing the appropriate platform on a classical computer is the first step in executing a quantum application. Next, the circuit must be constructed, the backend must be chosen, and finally, the circuit must be operated. As a result, there is an alternative service model, which is shown in below figure and refer to as Quantum Application as a Service (QaaS). All of a quantum application's application and deployment logic, including the quantum circuit and data pre- and post processing, are wrapped in the QaaS offering. It also offers APIs that may be used to integrate with more conventional applications, such as web apps or workflows.

The API receives input data from the conventional application. To initialize the quantum register for the subsequent calculation, this input data must be correctly encoded. The service takes care of this data encoding, building a suitable quantum circuit, compiling it, and deploying it. A QCaaS solution may be utilized for the circuit's actual execution. The dynamical selection of various QCaaS would also be made possible by hardware-agnostic processing of quantum algorithms. The quantum application interprets the execution's outcome before returning it to the conventional application.

This concept would make it possible to distinguish between quantum and conventional applications, especially in terms of deployment. Furthermore, because QaaS makes it possible to employ popular technologies of service-based architectures, integrating characteristics of quantum computing may be made easier.

9.3 QaaS Design Patterns

The Quantum as a Service (QaaS) design pattern refers to a set of architectural patterns that enable the integration, deployment, and management of quantum computing resources in cloud-based or hybrid environments.

9.3.1 Key QaaS Design Patterns

1. **Quantum Resource Pool Pattern**: Centralizes management and scheduling of quantum resources, optimizing allocation and performance while maintaining availability and scalability.

Core Implementation

The resource pool contains multiple quantum devices (hardware and simulators) managed collectively to handle demand from many users and tasks.

Access, scheduling, and health monitoring are automated by orchestration software, which assigns quantum jobs to the available resources in the pool for optimal utilization and fairness.

Key Mechanisms

Centralized Resource Management: A dedicated control layer tracks the availability, workload, and health of each quantum device. Jobs are routed to the next available, best-fit resource.

Intelligent Scheduling: An orchestrator (or scheduler) uses rules or algorithms to prioritize quantum tasks, balance loads across the pool, and ensure high availability.

Automated Optimization: The pool continually evaluates its resource performance and adapts to changing demand, integrating new quantum devices and updating allocation strategies autonomously

Benefits

Efficient Resource Utilization: Scarce and expensive quantum computers are shared among many users, preventing idle periods and reducing costs.

Scalability: As more quantum devices become available, the architecture can easily expand the pool and manage increased demands.

Resilience and Reliability: Health and error monitoring boost overall reliability, enabling automatic failover or rerouting of jobs if a resource encounters issues.

2. **Hybrid Microservices Pattern**: Adapts traditional microservices to quantum computing, integrating quantum and classical components via standardized APIs and orchestration frameworks.

The Hybrid Microservices Pattern is an architectural approach that enables the integration of quantum and classical services, allowing complex problems to be solved by orchestrating both types of computing resources within a distributed microservices ecosystem.

Pattern Characteristics

Service Wrapping: Quantum algorithms are encapsulated as micro services that expose well-defined APIs, allowing them to be invoked remotely like any classical service.

Classical–Quantum Coexistence: Hybrid micro services architectures treat quantum and classical services as independent, distributed units that interact seamlessly using messaging protocols or RESTful interfaces.

Elastic Deployment: These micro services are typically deployed on cloud infrastructure, benefiting from the scalability and resilience of containerized orchestration (e.g., Kubernetes).

Orchestration Challenges: Current quantum services tend to be tightly coupled to specific hardware and lack the composability and flexibility of classical micro services, presenting challenges for maintainability, scalability, and service abstraction.

Implementation Steps

Wrap quantum algorithms using classical services that manage access to quantum hardware and interpret results.

Integrate quantum micro services into existing classical micro service architectures, supporting workflows where the quantum service is invoked as needed for specialized tasks.

Address coupling issues by designing middleware or APIs capable of managing diverse quantum platforms, error scenarios, and data formats.

Leverage cloud QaaS platforms (like AWS Braket, IBM Quantum) to execute actual quantum jobs as part of the micro service flow.

Benefits

Modularity: Quantum and classical services can be substituted, upgraded, or scaled independently, facilitating agile development and deployment.

Task Specialization: Quantum micro services handle compute-intensive or specialized quantum workloads, while classical micro services handle supporting logic, orchestration, and data management.

Limitations

Despite its promise, the Hybrid Micro services Pattern faces hurdles like platform coupling, error propagation, and limited orchestration flexibility owing to the evolving nature of quantum software engineering.

Hybrid Micro services are essential for modern quantum applications, providing the structure for integrating quantum computing into enterprise software and distributed cloud systems

3. **Asynchronous Pipeline Pattern**: Manages data flow and parallel execution between classical and quantum processes, facilitating complex hybrid algorithms such as variational quantum methods.

The Asynchronous Pipeline Pattern is an architecture used in quantum computing and software systems to coordinate sequential processing stages where operations, including quantum-classical tasks, are executed independently and asynchronously, facilitating scalability, continuous workflow, and efficient resource utilization.

Workflow

Work tasks (e.g., data, commands, or jobs) move through a series of asynchronous processing stages (the pipeline). Each stage can perform operations, including calls to quantum or classical services, and pass output to the next stage.

In quantum-classical scenarios, asynchronous pipelines often coordinate classical pre-processing, quantum execution, post-processing, and results integration, with each phase able to proceed as soon as its dependencies are available—no global synchronization is required.

Asynchronous execution enables overlap and concurrency between stages, boosting utilization and throughput by keeping resources busy even if some stages are temporarily delayed.

Quantum Example

A quantum pipeline may include stages for data preparation, quantum circuit creation, and quantum execution on a QaaS platform, result post-processing, and integration into a larger classical workflow.

Each stage can asynchronously send requests and receive replies (the "request-reply" pattern), managing delays and resource bottlenecks dynamically, especially valuable with cloud-based quantum resources.

Advantages

Scalability: Asynchronous pipelines allow work to scale horizontally, handling increased task loads efficiently by distributing them across multiple workers and quantum devices.

Resilience: Failures or delays in one stage do not halt the entire workflow, aiding reliability and fault tolerance.

Decoupling: Each stage can be modified, replaced, or scaled independently, supporting rapid development and testing in complex hybrid environments.

The Asynchronous Pipeline Pattern is increasingly adopted for hybrid quantum-classical workflow orchestration, real-time data processing, and scalable cloud-based quantum computing in QaaS architectures.

4. **Quantum Auto-Tuning Framework**: Automates optimization of quantum system parameters, algorithm performance, and resource usage to simplify management in dynamic environments.

The Quantum Auto-Tuning Framework is an automated software architecture that optimizes quantum algorithms, quantum circuit design, and quantum machine learning pipelines, often using advanced search strategies and probabilistic models to minimize manual intervention and maximize performance.

Core Concepts

Automated Circuit Design: Auto-tuning frameworks iteratively search for optimal quantum circuit topologies and gate configurations using algorithms like topology-driven search and neural architecture search (QuantumSupernet).

Hyperparameter Optimization: Techniques such as Bayesian optimization, genetic sampling, and shared-parameter training automate the configuration and tuning of quantum models, encoding circuits, and preprocessors for tasks like quantum machine learning (QML).

End-to-End Pipelines: Frameworks like AutoQML build and optimize complete QML pipelines—from classical data preprocessing, through quantum feature encoding and circuit execution, to post-processing—in a unified, modular workflow.

User-Friendliness: Many frameworks provide interfaces close to classical optimization tools, enabling users to specify the problem, constraints, and criteria, with the system managing algorithm and hardware selection and transformation automatically.

Implementation Workflow

Define the search space for quantum circuit topologies and gate types.

Use probabilistic or AI-driven algorithms to explore the space and evaluate candidate circuits for performance (e.g., accuracy, loss).

Share parameters across circuit candidates for efficient optimization and reuse, often using parameter-sharing supernets.

Automatically select, train, and fine-tune the best-performing quantum circuits, hyperparameters, and pipeline configurations.

Output optimized pipelines for deployment on actual quantum hardware or simulators, abstracting hardware-specific details for portability.

Advantages

Efficiency: Reduces computational cost, training time, and manual tuning efforts, enabling rapid, scalable quantum software development.

Accessibility: Makes quantum solutions manageable for non-experts, democratizing access to advanced quantum capabilities.

Adaptability: Easily adapts to new quantum computers, algorithms, or workloads as technology evolves.

Quantum auto-tuning frameworks form a central pillar of advanced QaaS and quantum software engineering, supporting robust, automated development and deployment in real-world use cases for optimization, machine learning, and simulation.

9.3.2 Quantum-Classical Split Patterns

1. **Quantum Monolith**: Implements a single, unified quantum component within the system, usually for specialized workloads. It is an architectural pattern in quantum-classical software systems where the core computational task—especially inference for AI or data processing—is handled entirely by a single, unified quantum component, with minimal or no classical post-processing beyond initial data preparation and final output interpretation.

Pattern Overview

Description: Input data is encoded directly as quantum states and processed exclusively by the quantum computer. The whole inference or processing task is delegated to this quantum "monolith"; classical computation is limited to basic pre- and post-processing.

Purpose: This pattern aims to maximize quantum advantage by leveraging quantum computation for the entire critical workload, rather than splitting tasks between quantum and classical components.

Context: Often adopted in proof-of-concept applications or for research, especially where quantum circuits can address the problem size and hardware limitations (NISQ-era devices).

Key Features

Simplicity: System design and data flow are straightforward, as quantum computation is isolated and centralized.

Full Quantum Delegation: All inference or problem-solving logic is performed by the quantum component, making this suitable when the whole workflow fits within quantum device constraints.

Known Limitations: While potentially efficient, scalability is restricted by current quantum hardware capabilities (qubit count, noise, decoherence). There is little flexibility for incremental adoption in larger, hybrid systems.

Use Cases

Prototyping quantum AI and machine learning algorithms where end-to-end quantum processing is feasible.

Benchmarking quantum algorithms against classical baselines in tasks like classification, search, or optimization using purely quantum models.

Exploring quantum "proofs of concept" to evaluate future quantum advantage as hardware matures.

The Quantum Monolith pattern, while foundational in early quantum AI, is likely to evolve toward hybrid patterns as systems scale and classical–quantum integration becomes crucial for real-world applications.

2. **Multi-Layer Architecture**: Positions quantum computation at multiple architectural layers, enabling flexible integration for feature engineering, inference ("quantum head"), or acceleration tasks. The Multi-Layer Architecture in Quantum-Classical Split Patterns is an architectural approach that distributes quantum and classical computations across multiple integrated layers to optimize performance, flexibility, and scalability in hybrid quantum-classical systems.

Architecture Overview

Layered Structure: Quantum computing tasks are segmented across distinct architectural layers, where each layer is responsible for specific roles such as quantum feature extraction, intermediate quantum processing, or classical computation management.

Flexible Integration: This pattern allows quantum operations to be embedded strategically at different points in the classical processing stack—e.g., data preprocessing, model inference, or acceleration layers—enabling hybrid workflows that leverage the strengths of both quantum and classical systems.

Modularity: Each layer can be independently developed, deployed, and optimized, facilitating system evolution as quantum hardware and software mature.

Key Characteristics

Quantum Layers: May include quantum feature encoders, quantum neural network layers, or quantum accelerators embedded between classical layers.

Classical Layers: Responsible for complex orchestration, interfacing with traditional databases, user interfaces, or further classical machine learning components.

Communication Bridges: Well-defined interfaces and protocols connect layers, ensuring smooth data exchange and synchronization while enabling asynchronous or parallel execution.

Benefits

Performance Optimization: Balances quantum resource usage with classical computing power, maximizing overall efficiency and enabling difficult tasks beyond current quantum hardware limits.

Scalability and Maintainability: Supports incremental adoption of quantum technologies without overhauling entire systems, easing integration in existing IT architectures.

Enhanced Flexibility: Adapts to various problem domains by tailoring the placement and depth of quantum layers according to workload complexity and hardware capabilities.

Use Cases

Hybrid AI/ML pipelines where quantum layers perform certain feature extraction or inference tasks, while classical layers handle data management and user interfacing.

Scientific simulations or optimization problems where quantum layers accelerate core computations embedded within broader classical workflows.

The Multi-Layer Architecture pattern is central to realizing practical hybrid quantum-classical systems, offering a structured yet flexible framework for leveraging quantum computing's potential alongside classical infrastructure.

3. **Intermediate Quantum Layer**: Embeds quantum computation between classical layers for optimized workflows in AI or data processing pipelines. It is a hybrid architectural pattern where a quantum inference engine is embedded between classical inference engines in a processing pipeline.

Pattern Description

In this approach, classical components handle the initial stages of feature extraction and preprocessing of input data and also finalize the output by interpreting measurement results from the quantum component.

The quantum component occupies the intermediate layer, substituting several classical layers with quantum circuits to leverage quantum advantages without overwhelming hardware constraints like limited qubit counts and circuit depths (typical of NISQ-era devices).

The pattern combines concepts from the Quantum Head and Quantum Feature Engineering patterns, where classical and quantum components collaborate closely in the pipeline.

Benefits

Scalability for NISQ Hardware: Classical layers ensure manageable input/output dimensionality by adapting data to available quantum resources.

Parameter and Complexity Reduction: Replacing multiple classical layers with the quantum intermediate layer reduces model parameters while maintaining or enhancing expressiveness.

Versatility: Suitable for classification tasks, variational autoencoders, anomaly detection, and other hybrid quantum-classical applications.

Challenges

High-speed Communication Required: The pattern requires fast, low-latency communication channels between classical and quantum components, which is technically demanding.

Resource Intensive: Significant computational resources on the classical side are needed to support data transformations and interaction with quantum hardware.

Use Cases

Financial forecasting improvements using hybrid pipelines.

Multi-class classification of remote sensing imagery and medical imaging.

Quantum variational autoencoder architectures for anomaly detection.

The Intermediate Quantum Layer pattern strategically balances classical and quantum computing strengths, enabling practical hybrid systems that navigate current hardware limitations while enhancing computational capabilities.

9.3.3 Quantum Middleware Patterns

1. **Service or Micro services Wrapper**: Encapsulates quantum hardware or algorithms in micro services, allowing for standardized deployment and easy access within complex software ecosystems. It refers to encapsulating quantum computing resources, algorithms, or hardware access within classical services or micro services to enable seamless communication, integration, and deployment in hybrid quantum-classical systems.

Overview

This pattern wraps quantum components into small, loosely coupled, and independently deployable services or micro services.

These wrappers provide standardized APIs that abstract the complexity of quantum resources, enabling easy invocation and data exchange from classical applications or other quantum services.

The micro services encapsulate vendor-specific quantum hardware or simulators, mitigating technology and vendor lock-in issues and facilitating portability and flexibility.

Problem Addressed

Quantum hardware access is mostly cloud-based via APIs from providers like AWS Braket, IBM Quantum, Microsoft Azure Quantum, and others, often with differing interfaces.

Direct interaction with these quantum resources is complex, non-portable, and challenging for maintainability and resilience.

The wrapper pattern simplifies this by abstracting the hardware specifics and providing uniform service interfaces.

Key Benefits

Interoperability: Classical systems interact seamlessly with quantum functionality through well-defined micro service APIs.

Modularity: Quantum capabilities evolve independently within services, allowing upgrades or replacements without disrupting the whole system.

Scalability & Deployment: Micro services can be independently deployed, scaled, and managed in cloud or hybrid environments, supporting flexible quantum workload distribution.

Maintainability: Encapsulation limits the impact of quantum technology changes on classical clients.

Usage

Wrapping quantum machine learning modules, optimization routines, or simulators as micro services accessed by classical orchestration engines.

Enabling hybrid workflows where classical preprocessing or post-processing is split from quantum execution by interacting services.

Facilitating multi-cloud or multi-vendor quantum strategies by routing requests transparently across wrapped quantum service endpoints.

The Service or Micro services Wrapper pattern is foundational in modern QaaS architecture, enabling efficient and flexible quantum-classical integration while abstracting hardware complexity and fostering the growth of quantum-enabled applications.

2. **Quantum API Gateway**: Routes requests and manages communication between quantum and classical systems, enabling interoperability and resource efficiency. It acts as the single entry point for clients accessing various quantum services, managing and routing API requests between quantum and classical components efficiently.

Pattern Description

The Quantum API Gateway routes client requests to the most suitable quantum micro services based on real-time information about available quantum computers, including their topology, error rates, fidelity, cost, and expected response times.

It abstracts hardware specifics, enabling the quantum applications to remain hardware-agnostic and facilitating composability by splitting a single client request into multiple backend service calls as needed.

The gateway may also aggregate results from multiple quantum services and create client-specific API interfaces tailored to different types of consumers.

This pattern is an adaptation of the traditional API Gateway pattern from classical micro services, customized to meet the particular needs of quantum service deployment and orchestration.

Benefits

Optimized Deployment: Dynamically selects the best quantum resource at runtime, improving efficiency and reducing latency in quantum service invocation.

Hardware Decoupling: Hides the complexity and differences across multiple quantum hardware platforms from clients, making applications more portable and maintainable.

Service Composability: Enables using heterogeneous quantum services together by routing and managing requests seamlessly.

Challenges

The API Gateway may introduce a performance bottleneck or a single point of failure if not properly scaled and managed.

Known Uses

Implemented as a proof of concept for platforms like Amazon Braket.

Considered a core component in quantum service-oriented architectures for simplifying quantum resource access and facilitating multi-cloud quantum strategies.

The Quantum API Gateway pattern is fundamental for building scalable, flexible, and user-friendly quantum middleware systems that streamline access to diverse quantum computing resources and services in cloud or hybrid environments.

3. **Quantum Workflow Orchestration**: Automates deployment, scheduling, and execution of quantum workflows, supporting both continuous and event-based quantum programming models. It is designed to automate the deployment, scheduling, and execution of quantum components within hybrid quantum-classical workflows, managing complex interdependencies and interactions across quantum AI systems.

Pattern Overview

The orchestrator middleware parses high-level quantum programming code, identifies quantum components, and automatically decomposes workflows into sequences of classical and quantum tasks.

It supports continuous, event-based, or time-based executions by scheduling quantum programs on the most appropriate quantum hardware providers, considering constraints like availability and performance.

The workflow is often modeled as a directed graph where nodes represent tasks and edges represent execution order and data flow, enabling flexible and dynamic control over the execution sequence.

Components

Orchestrator Engine: Manages task dependencies and overall workflow execution logic.

Language Translator/Generator: Converts high-level code into executable API calls for classical and quantum services.

Scheduler: Allocates resources, queues jobs, and directs tasks to quantum or classical backends based on runtime information.

Benefits

Autonomy: Minimizes human intervention by automating quantum program scheduling and deployment.

Hardware Decoupling: Abstracts quantum software from specific hardware constraints, promoting portability.

Availability: Ensures quantum components are available and invoked when needed within larger applications.

Challenges

Reliability: Middleware constitutes a critical single point of failure, with disruptions potentially impacting the entire system.

Response Time and Performance: Additional orchestration layers introduce latency and system complexity, possibly slowing down response and throughput as workflow and data volumes increase.

Use Cases and Implementations

Used in hybrid quantum-HPC integration to manage concurrent quantum and classical tasks.

Implementations like Qiskit Serverless and Covalent orchestrate workflows across distributed CPU, GPU, and QPU resources.

Workflow systems integrate with high-level quantum programming libraries such as Qiskit, PennyLane, and CUDA Quantum to implement automated execution of complex quantum-classical pipelines.

Quantum Workflow Orchestration is pivotal for orchestrating the growing complexity of quantum ecosystems, enabling scalable, efficient, and reliable execution of hybrid applications in emerging QaaS environments.

9.4 Benefits of QCaaS

Quantum computing-as-a-service (QCaaS) promises companies never-before-seen capacity to address difficult issues. It marks a dramatic change in computational access. Similar to Software-as-a-Service (SaaS), QCaaS provides cloud-based quantum computing capabilities, giving companies online access to quantum processing capacity whenever they need it. Through the use of remote hardware and hybrid computing engines, QCaaS helps businesses use quantum computing solutions to solve a variety of business problems, greatly speeding up decision-making and streamlining operations.

Cloud-based quantum computing facilitates the creation of quantum algorithms and makes current quantum hardware accessible. The cloud increases the financial viability of quantum computing by emulating quantum behavior and providing access to a limited number of quantum computers, democratizing access for numerous users and encouraging creativity across sectors.

Making the switch to QCaaS provides companies with a number of strong advantages:

Accessibility: Without requiring large upfront expenditures, QCaaS systems offer easy access to quantum computing resources. Startups, SMEs, and large corporations may all investigate quantum algorithms and applications because to this accessibility, which democratizes quantum computing.

Scalability: Businesses may modify computational resources according to their requirements thanks to the scalable solutions provided by cloud-based quantum computing systems. Whether running small-scale simulations or tackling complex optimization problems, users can dynamically scale their quantum computing resources as required.

Cost-Effectiveness: QCaaS spares businesses from having to buy and manage specialized infrastructure for quantum technology. Alternatively, companies may use pay-as-you-go cloud-based solutions to optimize expenses and save capital expenditures.

Cooperation and creativity: QCaaS promotes cooperation and creativity in the corporate and scientific sectors by democratizing access to quantum computing resources. The discovery of new quantum algorithms and applications can be accelerated by the smooth collaboration of researchers, developers, and subject matter experts.

9.5 Applications of QCaaS

Across a wide range of businesses, QCaaS systems provide countless opportunities:

Optimization: Supply chain management, portfolio optimization, and route optimization are just a few of the optimization issues that quantum algorithms are excellent at resolving. Companies may increase operational efficiency, save expenses, and improve resource allocation by utilizing QCaaS.

Drug Discovery: Molecular modeling and drug discovery might be accelerated by quantum computing. Scientists can find novel drug candidates and expedite the drug development process by modeling molecular interactions and structures.

Financial Modeling: By carrying out intricate simulations and scenario analysis, quantum algorithms can improve financial modeling and risk assessment. QCaaS may be used by banks, financial businesses, and insurance organizations to better understand market dynamics and make well-informed judgments.

Cryptography and Security: Cryptography and cybersecurity are also affected by quantum computing. QCaaS platforms can assist researchers in creating quantum-resistant encryption algorithms and security protocols, even if quantum computers threaten current cryptographic techniques.

Quantum computing commercialization

An important turning point in the commercialization of quantum computing has been reached with the introduction of QCaaS. Quantum technology moves from abstract ideas to real-world uses as more companies adopt it via cloud platforms. Quantum algorithms are being studied by a variety of industries, including materials science, logistics, healthcare, and finance, in an effort to solve challenging issues, improve workflows, and get a competitive advantage. The demand for quantum-as-a-service (QaaS) providers is anticipated to increase due to the significant expenses and resource allocation required for the development of quantum labs.

The commercialization of quantum computing is being led by major companies like Google, IBM, and Intel. IBM's Eagle and Google's Sycamore are noteworthy examples of quantum supremacy and scalability. With developments in both superconducting and photonic qubits, China's advances in quantum computing further highlight its influence on the world stage.

These companies facilitate test beds for device characterization, give remote cloud access to quantum computers, and even supply manufacturing services through foundries. In order to attract entrepreneurs to enter the rapidly expanding quantum environment, these services are essential. In the long run, QaaS suppliers will be essential to standardizing the manufacture, characterization, and operation of devices. In turn, this standardization will make it easier to benchmark quantum computers and other supporting technologies, which will promote innovation and progress in the area.

A fundamental change in computing, Quantum Computing as a Service gives companies previously unheard-of access to quantum computing capacity via cloud platforms. As QCaaS platforms develop further, they will enable businesses to explore new avenues, spur innovation, and address some of the most important issues facing the globe. The future appears bright for companies adopting this game-changing technology as quantum computing enters the commercialization stage.

9.6 Obstacles and Prospects for the Future

Even with its enormous potential, QCaaS still has to overcome a number of obstacles, such as algorithm optimization, hardware scalability, and quantum error correction. Nevertheless, these issues are being addressed by current research and developments in quantum technology, opening the door for future widespread use of QCaaS. We may anticipate that QCaaS will be essential in fostering creativity, resolving challenging issues, and influencing the direction of technology as quantum computing develops further.

While cloud-based quantum computing faces technical hurdles and a steep learning curve, its potential to revolutionize industries mirrors the transformative impact of AI and machine learning. As cloud providers invest in specialized infrastructure and software stacks, quantum computing is poised to integrate seamlessly with existing computing resources, paving the way for a future where quantum capabilities augment classical computing and AI services.

Chapter - 10
Quantum Robotics

Quantum robotics applies the principles of quantum computing—including superposition, entanglement, and quantum algorithms—to overcome some of the most pressing challenges in robotics. These challenges include the ability to process vast sensory data streams in real time, to enable adaptive decision-making under uncertainty, and to support cognitive and even emotional functions that approximate human intelligence.

Unlike traditional robots, which rely on the deterministic limits of binary computation, quantum robots—or "qubots"—leverage the probabilistic nature of quantum mechanics. This allows them to explore multiple possibilities simultaneously, coordinate across distributed systems with unprecedented efficiency, and optimize complex tasks in ways that classical architectures cannot.

Although quantum robotics remains largely theoretical and experimental, it holds the potential to transform areas such as autonomous navigation, swarm robotics, human–robot collaboration, and robotic cognition. By expanding the computational and functional horizons of robotics, quantum technologies may ultimately redefine what it means for machines to act, learn, and interact in human-centered environments.

Quantum computing offers significant advantages for addressing optimization problems, advancing machine learning, improving classical artificial intelligence algorithms, and enhancing data mining and analysis in robotics. Quantum algorithms such as Grover's search, the Harrow–Hassidim–Lloyd (HHL) algorithm, and qBLAS have demonstrated superiority over classical approaches in various scenarios. Even with a limited number of qubits, quantum computing can effectively manage complex problems involving large-scale data.

Quantum methods show strong potential for accelerating supervised learning processes, improving image processing, and optimizing control systems. To fully exploit both local quantum processing units (QPUs) and high-performance cloud services, the integration of quantum computing into robotics requires application-centric, hardware-agnostic, and scalable protocols. By doing so, quantum computing could fundamentally transform robotic capabilities and efficiency across multiple domains.

Future research directions may include the design of highly specialized quantum algorithms for robotic tasks, exploration of quantum reinforcement learning techniques, and advancement of quantum image processing methods. Additionally, efforts could focus on demonstrating impactful applications of quantum image processing and developing the supporting hardware and software toolkits. Ultimately, scalable protocols and intelligent scheduling algorithms will be critical for the effective adoption of quantum computing in robotics.

Free-Space Quantum Communication on Mobile Platforms

The concept of free-space quantum communication between mobile platforms was first proposed in 2017 for reconfigurable Quantum Key Distribution (QKD) applications using drones. Since then, this approach has evolved rapidly, demonstrating the feasibility of secure quantum communication in dynamic and mobile environments.

Building on the initial drone-based QKD experiments, researchers have extended the technology to a variety of mobile configurations, including drone-to-drone, drone-to-moving vehicle, and vehicle-to-vehicle systems. These advancements highlight the adaptability of quantum communication systems for diverse real-world applications, such as secure battlefield communications, disaster recovery, and mobile network security.

A key milestone in this progression was the demonstration of BB84 quantum key distribution protocols in airborne optical downlinks. This involved both the development of quantum communication system technology for aircraft and the successful demonstration of an airborne QKD receiver payload. These results confirm that quantum-secure communication is not only viable in static ground-based systems but can also be extended to high-mobility platforms operating in challenging atmospheric conditions.

Together, these achievements mark significant steps toward the integration of mobile QKD systems into future communication infrastructures, paving the way for a quantum-secure Internet of Things (IoT) and resilient global networks.

Free-Space Quantum Communication in Robotics and Mechatronics

Subsequent research extended free-space quantum communication to address practical constraints of mobile platforms. For example, efforts have focused on the development of low size, weight, and power (SWaP) QKD systems for integration into small-form unmanned aerial vehicles (UAVs). Additional contributions include the characterization of polarization-based receivers for mobile free-space optical QKD and demonstrations of optical-relayed entanglement distribution using drones as mobile quantum nodes.

Originally conceived to enable free-space QKD and entanglement distribution across mobile nodes, this field has since expanded into the robotics domain as an emerging interdisciplinary area now referred to as quantum robotics or quantum mechatronics. This integration explores the interface between quantum technologies and robotic systems, particularly in multiagent and cooperative autonomous systems where secure communication is critical. The central advantage of such integration is the guaranteed security of inter-agent communication, a feature that classical methods cannot fully ensure.

Although still in its infancy, this emerging field holds promise for broader benefits in future research. By leveraging the forthcoming quantum advantage, robotic systems could gain not only secure communication channels but also enhanced capabilities in decision-making, distributed sensing, and swarm intelligence. However, this progress depends on laying a foundational framework for quantum robotics and quantum mechatronics.

Beyond its immediate technical implications, this integration also provides an opportunity to modernize the mechatronics discipline with quantum engineering. Embedding quantum principles into educational curricula ensures that the future engineering workforce is equipped to meet the demands of a rapidly evolving industry. Key quantum concepts — including quantum entanglement, cryptography, teleportation, and the Bell test — are central to this training, bridging the gap between classical engineering methods and the quantum era.

Alice Robot, Bob Robot, and Eve Robot in Quantum Robotic Communication

In classical quantum communication protocols, the characters Alice (sender), Bob (receiver), and Eve (eavesdropper) are widely used to explain information transfer and security challenges. Extending this metaphor into the domain of quantum robotics and mechatronics provides a powerful framework for conceptualizing secure communication between mobile robotic platforms.

Alice Robot: Functions as the transmitter platform, such as a drone or autonomous vehicle, responsible for preparing and sending quantum states (e.g., entangled photons or qubits).

Bob Robot: Acts as the receiver platform, equipped with specialized detectors to measure the transmitted states and reconstruct the information. Bob Robot represents the trusted recipient in a cooperative multi-agent system.

Eve Robot: Represents the adversarial platform, attempting to intercept, measure, or manipulate the quantum states transmitted between Alice Robot and Bob Robot. In practice, Eve Robot could be another drone or autonomous system trying to compromise the network.

Just as in traditional Quantum Key Distribution (QKD) protocols, the presence of Eve Robot introduces the possibility of eavesdropping. However, the laws of quantum mechanics (e.g., the no-cloning theorem and measurement disturbance) ensure that any interception attempt by Eve Robot introduces detectable anomalies in the communication channel. This property guarantees that Alice Robot and Bob Robot can detect and counter intrusions, providing information-theoretic security for robotic networks.

By extending the Alice–Bob–Eve analogy into quantum robotics, researchers can not only illustrate the inherent security advantages of quantum communication but also contextualize the challenges of deploying these technologies in real-world robotic swarms, autonomous vehicles, and drone networks. This metaphor thus bridges abstract quantum protocols with practical multi-agent mechatronic systems, emphasizing the need for both robust engineering and quantum-aware cybersecurity strategies.

Security is a critical concern, since quantum robots integrated into industrial Internet of Things (IIoT) systems and other connected networks become susceptible to cyberattacks. Although quantum communication offers inherently stronger security guarantees, adapting these protocols to hybrid quantum–digital infrastructures will demand substantial innovation.

Major hurdles for quantum robotics include the immaturity of both hardware and software, as well as the persistent difficulty of interfacing fragile quantum systems with robust classical architectures. The extreme sensitivity of quantum states remains a key bottleneck for practical deployment. Equally pressing is the challenge of quantum–digital conversion, which is essential for enabling seamless hybrid operations.

Because the field is deeply interdisciplinary—spanning quantum mechanics, computer science, control theory, and electrical engineering—rapid progress will require close collaboration across domains. Future research is likely to investigate how quantum-inspired algorithms, such as quantum particle swarm optimization, can enhance robotic navigation, multi-agent cooperation, and autonomous decision-making.

A portable physical device that senses its environment and internal condition by using the quantum features of a quantum system is called a quantum robot. It is also capable of certain functions and the manipulation of quantum information. Three interactive parts make up the quantum robot system (see Fig. below): data acquisition units, a quantum actuator and controller, and a multi-quantum computing unit (MQCU). Initially, however, cloud services for quantum computing will be accessible, as well as the potential for quantum processing units (QPUs) to work in tandem with traditional computers.

Superposition and entanglement are two unique characteristics of quantum computing that, when compared to conventional computing methods, may significantly increase processing capability and successfully handle complex problems. By employing quantum algorithms like Grover's method, Harrow-Hassidim-Lloyd (HHL), and qBLAS, researchers can address optimization problems, machine learning tasks, image processing, artificial intelligence, and data mining in robotics. Pathway planning, robot vision, task allocation, kinematics, perception, localization, control systems, and data processing could all advance as a result of combining quantum computing and robotics.

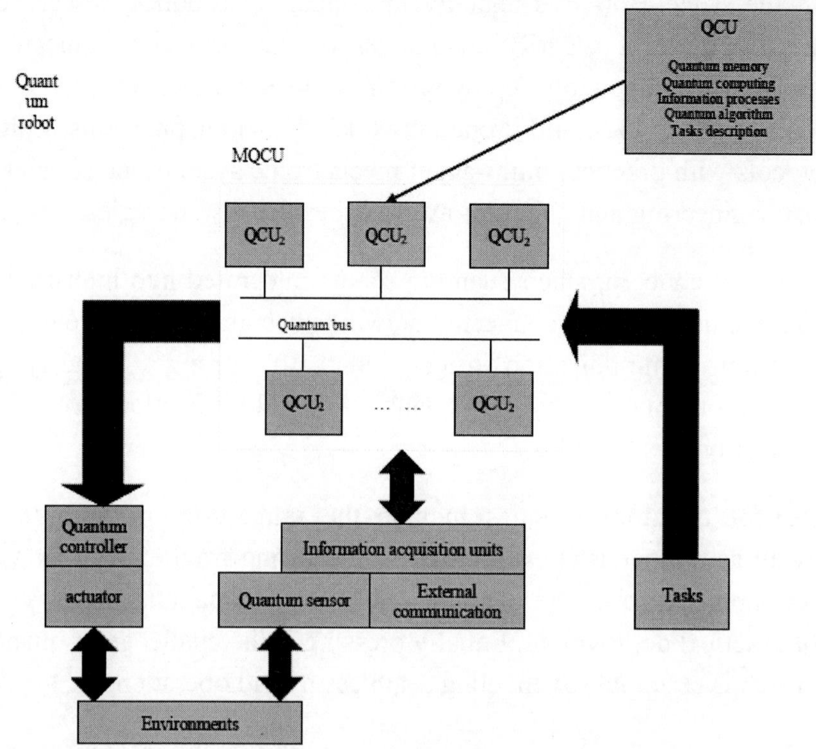

Fig.10.1 The structure of a quantum robot system.

10.1 Core Quantum Robotics Architecture

A quantum robot system typically includes three fundamental components:

1. **Multi Quantum Computing Units (MQCU):** Serve as the main computational core, utilizing quantum algorithms for tasks like fast searching and reinforcement learning.

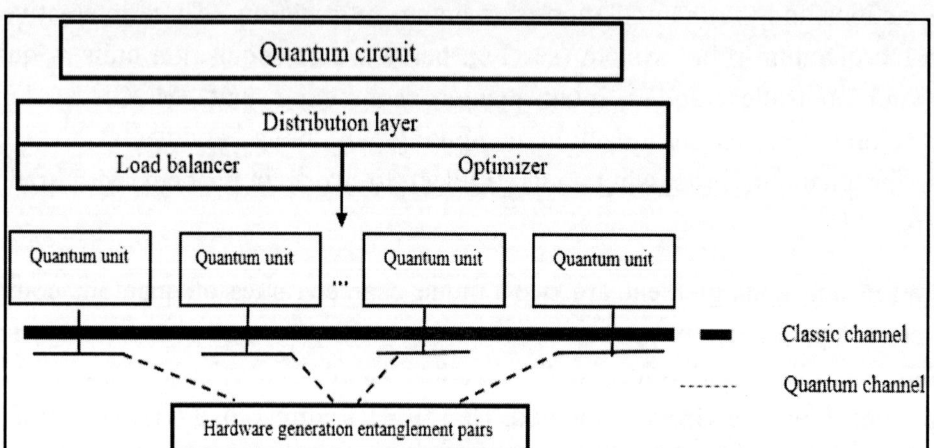

Fig.10.2 Multi Quantum Computing Units.

Multi Quantum Computing Units (MQCU) refer to a structural approach in quantum computer architecture where multiple quantum processors (or QPUs) are interconnected and work together to solve problems that surpass the limitations of a single quantum chip. This setup is critical as modern quantum algorithms and error correction demand both scalability and high qubit fidelity.

MQCU Overview

MQCU leverages modular architectures, combining several quantum processing units—each with its own set of physical qubits, control electronics, and error correction layers.

These units may be connected via quantum buses, optical links, or other quantum networking techniques, forming a unified computational platform.

Architectural Layers in MQCU

The architectural stack for MQCU generally features:

Physical Layer: Multiple qubit chips, cooling infrastructure, and quantum interconnects.

Logical Layer: Quantum error-correcting codes spanning different chips, logical qubits encoded using distributed physical qubits.

Control Layer: Coordinated pulse and gate generation, synchronization of quantum operations across several QPUs.

Software & Compiler Layer: Tools to split, allocate, and optimize quantum circuits for execution across the MQCU system.

Application **Layer:** End-user task orchestration like distributed simulation, optimization, cryptography, and machine learning.

Key Features and Benefits

Enables scaling to larger numbers of qubits, which is essential for complex quantum algorithms.

Improves error correction by distributing logical qubits over many redundant physical qubits.

Facilitates advanced quantum networking and distributed quantum computing, supporting secure communications and global collaboration.

Drives versatility in algorithm implementation—for instance, modular quantum FPGAs integrate different quantum computing models for efficient logic construction.

MQCU is a foundational concept in scaling quantum computing, and its architecture mirrors clustered CPUs in classical systems but with unique quantum mechanical connectivity and operational challenges.

1. **Quantum Controller and Actuator:** Governs the robot's interactions and movement, utilizing quantum control techniques to improve motion accuracy and stability.

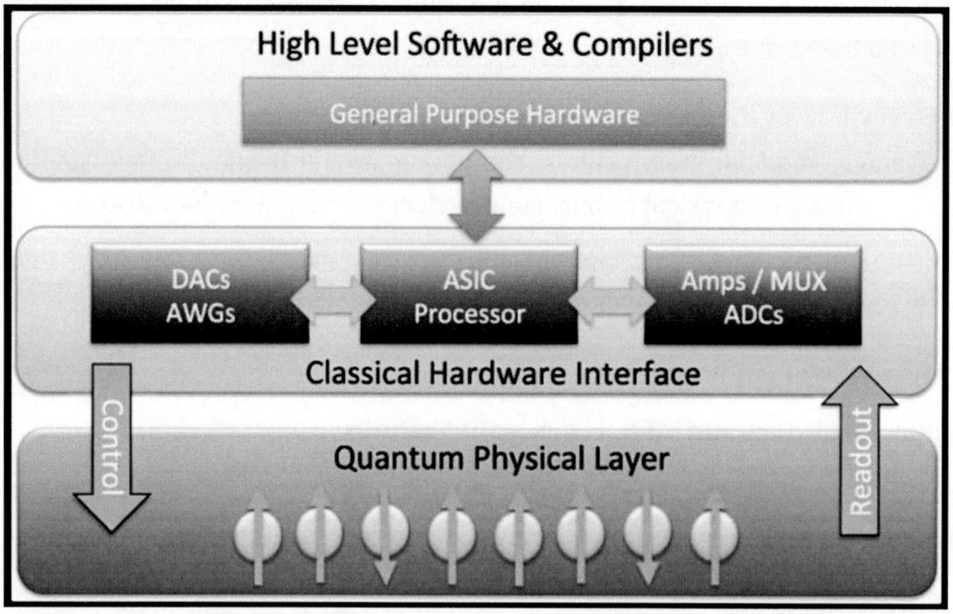

Fig.10.3 Quantum controller and actuator layers.

A Quantum Controller and Actuator are key components within quantum robotic or quantum system frameworks that enable control and actuation based on quantum information processing.

The Quantum Controller acts as the processing and control unit that receives task instructions from a quantum computing core (like MQCU - Multi Quantum Computing Units). It processes these instructions and sends signals to the actuator on what operations to perform. The controller can itself be a quantum system or a classical-quantum hybrid implementing quantum control algorithms to manipulate quantum states or qubits.

The Quantum Actuator is the execution apparatus responding to signals from the quantum controller. It carries out physical or logical operations on the quantum system or its environment. The actuator can be a pure quantum system or a semi classical device capable of handling quantum information. It serves as the interface that converts control signals into actual state changes or interactions—effectively the "motion" or "action" part of the system.

Together, they form the execution and control elements that enable a quantum system or quantum robot to perform tasks by processing quantum information, making decisions through the controller, and physically or logically acting via the actuator. This setup allows quantum robots and systems to sense, compute, decide, and act in a manner leveraging quantum effects such as superposition and entanglement.

This concept is notably described in the structure of a quantum robot, consisting of MQCU (quantum computing core), quantum controller and actuator (execution/control interface), and information acquisition units (sensors). The quantum controller and actuator are essential for translating quantum computations and algorithms into actual operational changes in the system or environment.

An actuator, in general (including quantum or classical contexts), is a device that transforms control signals into mechanical motion or other forms of physical action using energy sources and mechanical elements. In quantum systems, this actuator operates with quantum information signals to affect quantum states or surroundings.

Hence, a Quantum Controller orchestrates what needs to be done, and the Quantum Actuator carries out those instructions in the quantum domain.

2. **Information Acquisition Units:** Sensors and interfaces, potentially quantum-enhanced, for environment perception and state feedback.

In a quantum robot system, Information Acquisition Units are critical components responsible for perceiving and gathering information from the robot's environment. Similar to sensors in traditional robots, these units can include quantum sensors specially designed to detect and acquire both classical and quantum information from surroundings.

Quantum sensors leverage quantum effects to achieve extremely high sensitivity and precision. Examples include superconducting quantum interference devices (SQUIDs), which can detect minute magnetic fields, and quantum well Hall sensors, which measure faint electromagnetic signals with high temperature stability. These sensors enable the quantum robot to sense faint signals and complex quantum information that traditional sensors might not detect adequately.

Besides sensing, information acquisition units also include communication interfaces that allow the robot to receive information from distant mainframes or other quantum robots through quantum communication, enabling secure and efficient data exchange.

A significant challenge in information acquisition in quantum systems is the nature of quantum measurement, which often disturbs the quantum state being measured. Quantum nondemolition (QND) measurement techniques are thus important for acquiring quantum information without destroying it.

Overall, information acquisition units allow a quantum robot to perceive its environment accurately, feeding sensing data into its quantum computing unit (MQCU) for processing and decision-making, which then directs the quantum controller and actuator for appropriate actions.

These units typically consist of quantum sensors designed with quantum physical effects to detect various signals and are vital to the robot's ability to interact intelligently with its environment.

10.1.1 Hybrid Quantum–Classical System Design

The most practical architectures today are hybrid, with a layered approach:

Hardware Layer: Combines quantum processors (for intensive tasks like optimization) with classical systems for control, memory, and resource management.

Middleware Layer: Orchestrates task allocation, handles error correction, and enables scalable, fault-tolerant system expansion—often through modular designs that allow easy component replacement and scaling.

Software Layer: Connects robot cognition (perception, reasoning, action planning) to quantum and classical backends, typically using frameworks like Qiskit and OpenQASM for programming algorithms.

Hybrid Algorithm Workflow

The workflow typically operates in a feedback loop:

The quantum processor tackles specialized subroutines such as optimization or simulation.

Classical systems manage preprocessing, error correction, iterative optimization, and decision logic.

The two exchange results iteratively, dynamically partitioning tasks either statically (predefined distribution) or dynamically (real-time based on system state and workload).

Key Architectural Design Principles

Modularity: Quantum hardware is increasingly built with modular interconnects (like Lego-like quantum chips), making robotics systems adaptable and upgradable.

Scalability: Hybrid architectures enable gradual expansion and integration of quantum devices as technology matures.

Task Partitioning: Certain robotic operations (like motion planning, path optimization, or high-dimensional state navigation) are processed by quantum subsystems, while routine and deterministic tasks remain classical.

Application Examples

Motion Planning: Quantum algorithms such as Grover's search or QAOA can optimize robotic paths in complex environments, leveraging quantum parallelism for efficiency.

Dexterous Manipulation: Quantum optimization helps solve intricate grasping and manipulation challenges, leading to improved precision in tasks such as surgical robotics and manufacturing automation.

Cognitive Architectures: Quantum-inspired models are being developed for perception, reasoning, and decision-making in robots, pushing forward capabilities in autonomy and intelligent behavior.

Integration Challenges

Challenges include:

Error Propagation: Quantum errors impact hybrid workflows, making correction and mitigation crucial.

Latency: Synchronization between quantum and classical cycles is essential to minimizing delays.

Resource Heterogeneity: Middleware must efficiently manage diverse resources and workloads at scale.

Hybrid quantum–classical system design is paving the way for wider quantum adoption, with ongoing research focused on improving orchestration, error mitigation, and seamless integration between quantum and classical computing resources.

10.2 Robotics: Possible Applications

To anticipate how quantum computing may reshape robotics, we organize potential applications according to the conventional sense–think–act cycle, complemented by an overarching observe stage that addresses system-level monitoring and diagnostics.

1. Sense (Perception and Data Acquisition)

Quantum-enhanced sensing: Leveraging quantum sensors (e.g., quantum magnetometers, gravimeters, and LIDAR) to achieve higher precision in navigation, mapping, and environmental monitoring.

Quantum imaging and vision: Exploiting entangled photons or quantum illumination to enhance object detection in low-light or noisy environments.

Multi-modal fusion: Quantum algorithms for combining heterogeneous sensor inputs (vision, haptics, acoustics) more efficiently than classical approaches.

2. Think (Computation, Planning, and Learning)

Quantum machine learning: Accelerating training and inference for robotic perception, classification, and decision-making tasks.

Quantum optimization: Applying algorithms such as quantum annealing or variational quantum eigensolvers for motion planning, task allocation, and multi-robot coordination.

Quantum-enhanced control: Using quantum linear algebra solvers to improve real-time trajectory optimization and adaptive control in dynamic environments.

3. Act (Execution and Manipulation)

Quantum-optimized motion control: Refining actuator control strategies through quantum-inspired algorithms (e.g., quantum particle swarm optimization).

Precision manipulation: Enabling nanoscale or microscale robotic systems to operate with higher accuracy, relevant in fields like medical robotics and Nano manufacturing.

Swarm robotics: Leveraging quantum entanglement analogies or quantum-inspired algorithms for emergent, collective behaviors in large robotic teams.

4. Observe (System Diagnostics and Meta-Control)

Quantum monitoring of system states: Using quantum-enhanced diagnostic tools to detect hardware faults, energy inefficiencies, or performance drift.

Quantum communication security: Ensuring system resilience against cyberattacks by integrating quantum key distribution (QKD) into robotic networks.

Digital–quantum health checks: Continuous validation of hybrid operations, ensuring coherence and consistency between quantum and classical subsystems.

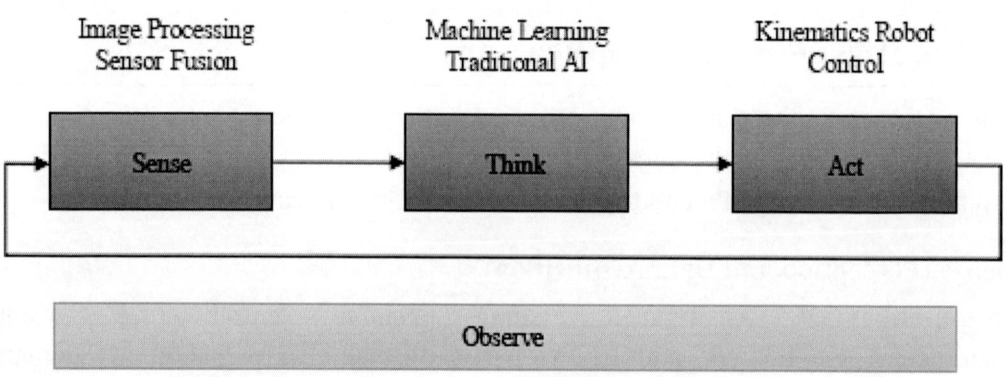

Fig.10.4 The Application of New Technologies to the Perception, Evaluation, and Reaction to Inputs.

Sense: Sensor Data Processing, Vision, and Perception

Autonomous robots rely heavily on rapid visual processing to perceive and interpret their environments. Contemporary computer vision and image processing techniques are computationally intensive, especially given the need to analyze high-resolution data across millions of pixels in real time.

Quantum computing offers a promising pathway to overcome these challenges by leveraging entanglement, superposition, and parallelism to accelerate visual data processing. A growing area of research, known as Quantum Image Processing (QIP), explores how visual information can be encoded and manipulated on quantum systems. The central concept is to represent image features—such as pixel positions and color intensities—as qubit lattices, allowing operations on entire images to be performed in parallel rather than sequentially.

This paradigm has been extended beyond static images to video and dynamic scene analysis, opening possibilities for real-time robotic perception in complex environments. The rise of quantum computing has therefore sparked a surge of interest in QIP, with researchers investigating quantum-based methods for tasks such as object recognition, pattern detection, image enhancement, and even video compression.

For robotics, the implications are significant: quantum-enhanced perception could enable robots to navigate more efficiently, recognize objects under adverse conditions (e.g., low light, occlusion, or noise), and fuse multi-sensor inputs into a more coherent understanding of their surroundings. This makes QIP a foundational step in equipping future quantum robots with superior sensing and perception capabilities.

The study of Quantum Image Processing (QIP) is generally divided into two complementary domains: quantum image representation methods and quantum image processing techniques. Among these, representation is particularly fundamental, since it defines how visual data is encoded within a quantum computer and thus determines the efficiency and scope of subsequent processing tasks.

The paradigm of image representation is crucial because it governs how portions of an image—such as pixel locations, intensities, or colors—are mapped into quantum states. A well-designed representation provides the foundation for scalable and efficient quantum operations on images.

Over the past decade, several models for quantum image representation have been proposed. One of the most prominent is the Qubit Lattice model, which encodes image features into structured arrays of qubits, allowing parallel manipulation and efficient retrieval of visual information. Such representations form the basis for advanced QIP applications, including image compression, encryption, pattern recognition, and video processing.

Quantum Image Representation Models

A central challenge in Quantum Image Processing (QIP) is how to represent classical images within a quantum computer in a way that supports efficient encoding, storage, and manipulation. Over the years, a variety of Quantum Image Representation (QIR) models have been proposed, each introducing distinct encoding strategies for pixel position, color, and intensity. These representations differ in terms of complexity, scalability, and suitability for specific applications, such as object recognition, compression, or encryption.

Some of the most prominent QIR models include:

- **Foundational Representations**
  - **Flexible Representation of Quantum Images (FRQI)** – One of the earliest and most widely studied models, encoding pixel colors as amplitudes and positions as qubit indices.
  - **Novel Enhanced Quantum Representation (NEQR)** – Uses binary encoding of pixel values, allowing direct manipulation of grayscale images.
  - **Generalized NEQR (GNEQR)** – Extends NEQR to support broader image formats.
  - **Improved NEQR (INEQR)** – Optimizes memory efficiency and processing speed.
- **Color and Multi-Channel Models**
  - Quantum Representation of Color Digital Images (QRCI, NCQI, OCQR) – Extensions of FRQI/NEQR designed for colour images.
  - Multi-Channel Quantum Image Representations (MCRQI, MCQI, QMCR – Encode RGB or hyperspectral data across multiple qubit registers.
  - Quantum Representation of Multi-Wavelength Images (QRMW) – Supports spectral imaging beyond the visible range, relevant for remote sensing and medical robotics.
  - Double Quantum Color Images Representation (DRQCI) – Encodes dual-channel image data for higher information density.
- **Specialized Representations**
  - **Bitplane Representation of Quantum Images (BRQI)** – Encodes images as layers of bitplanes, facilitating compression and error correction.
  - **Quantum Block Image Representation (QBIR)** – Divides images into blocks for more efficient large-scale image encoding.
  - **Order-Encoded Quantum Image Model (OQIM)** – Employs ordered encoding to reduce computational complexity.
  - **Simple Quantum Representation of Infrared Images (SQR)** – Designed for infrared imaging, useful in surveillance and autonomous navigation.
  - **Quantum Log-Polar Images (QUALPI)** – Represents images in log-polar coordinates, beneficial for rotation- and scale-invariant recognition tasks.

- **Quantum Representation Model for Multiple Images (QRMMI)** – Encodes several images simultaneously, useful for robotics applications requiring dataset-level analysis.

- **Novel and Hybrid Approaches**
  - **Entangled Image Representation** – Leverages entanglement for image correlation and joint analysis.
  - **Caraiman's Quantum Image Representation (CQIR)** – Introduces optimized qubit structures for improved fidelity.

Each of these models encodes **pixel position and intensity** differently, resulting in trade-offs in terms of **storage efficiency, processing complexity, and resilience to noise**. For robotics, the choice of representation model will directly influence the efficiency of tasks such as **real-time perception, object recognition, sensor fusion, and navigation under uncertain conditions**.

However, most of the aforementioned representation methods are restricted to two-dimensional images, which is insufficient for advanced robotic perception. In practice, robots often rely on multiple sensor modalities—such as stereo cameras, LiDAR, and depth sensors—to construct a three-dimensional point cloud of their environment. This richer representation enables not only object detection but also precise localization and mapping, both of which are essential for navigation and interaction with complex surroundings.

At present, only a limited number of quantum representations for 3D data have been explored, such as quantum point cloud models. These methods aim to extend QIP principles to higher-dimensional datasets, but the field is still in its infancy. Given the exponential parallelism of quantum systems, it is widely anticipated that Quantum Image and Point-cloud Processing (QIMP) will eventually surpass classical approaches in both speed and efficiency, particularly for large-scale perception tasks in robotics.

To convincingly demonstrate the superiority of QIMP over traditional methods, the research community must focus on:

1. **High-impact applications** – Examples include real-time 3D object recognition for autonomous vehicles, quantum-enhanced SLAM (Simultaneous Localization and Mapping), or multi-robot collaborative perception.
2. **Toolkits and frameworks** – Practical quantum software libraries, simulators, and hybrid algorithms that allow robotics researchers to experiment with QIMP without requiring direct access to large-scale quantum hardware.
3. **Hardware integration** – Specialized quantum devices, possibly coupled with classical GPUs/TPUs, that can efficiently encode and process 3D visual information.

Although several early techniques have demonstrated potential advantages of quantum-based image and point cloud processing, further evidence, benchmarking, and experimental validation are urgently needed. Establishing these foundations will be critical before QIMP can be deployed in real-world robotic platforms.

10.2.1 Think: Traditional AI in Robotics

Traditional Artificial Intelligence (AI), often referred to as **Weak AI** or **Narrow AI**, is designed to perform specific cognitive tasks with efficiency and precision. Such systems are not capable of general intelligence or creativity but are instead built to respond to well-defined inputs and produce context-specific outputs. They acquire knowledge from data, apply pre-established rules, and make decisions or predictions accordingly.

A simple analogy is that of a **computer chess program**: the system knows the rules of the game, can anticipate the player's moves, and chooses responses based on a combination of heuristics and predefined strategies. Importantly, it does not invent new styles of play but rather selects from the strategies encoded within its framework. In this sense, traditional AI functions like a skilled strategist—capable of making informed decisions within a fixed domain but without the ability to extend beyond it.

Examples of such systems are commonplace in everyday technology. Voice-based assistants such as **Siri** or **Alexa**, personalized recommendation systems on **Netflix** or **Amazon**, and **Google's search algorithms** all embody traditional AI principles. They operate effectively within their assigned domains but lack the ability to generate novel content or transfer knowledge across domains.

In robotics, traditional AI has been widely applied in tasks such as:

- **Knowledge inference** – deriving new information from a set of facts and rules.
- **Route planning and navigation** – computing efficient paths through structured or unstructured environments.
- **Reasoning and decision-making** – selecting appropriate actions based on predefined goals and constraints.
- **Multi-agent coordination** – managing cooperation and task distribution among several robots.
- **System diagnosis** – identifying faults or inefficiencies within a robotic system.
- **Goal-oriented action planning** – sequencing actions to achieve specified objectives.

Many of these applications rely on **search algorithms**, which explore possible states in a graph or tree-like structure. Each node represents a potential state, while edges denote transitions to subsequent states. Traditional AI methods employ both **uninformed (blind)**

search algorithms, which systematically explore without prior knowledge, and **informed (heuristic) search** algorithms, which incorporate domain-specific knowledge to guide the exploration process more efficiently.

Although these approaches have proven effective in robotics, their reliance on formal knowledge representations and fixed rules means they are inherently limited compared to contemporary **machine learning** methods. Nonetheless, they provide the foundational reasoning frameworks upon which more advanced hybrid and quantum-enhanced robotic intelligence can be built.

Quantum Approaches to Search and Stochastic Algorithms in Robotics

Robotics research has long relied on search algorithms for tasks such as trajectory planning and multi-robot coordination. Traditional combinatorial and graph-based search methods, while effective, often suffer from exponential complexity as the problem size grows. This is where quantum computing offers a promising advantage.

Quantum-enhanced combinatorial search: Classical combinatorial search algorithms can be reformulated as quantum problems by leveraging Grover's algorithm, which provides a quadratic speedup in searching unsorted solution spaces. For robotics, this translates to faster exploration of feasible paths in trajectory planning or optimal role allocation in multi-robot coordination.

Quantum graph search via random walks: Graph search algorithms are central to route planning and task scheduling. Quantum versions of these methods utilize quantum random walks, which exhibit markedly different spreading behaviour compared to classical random walks. This difference can yield faster convergence when identifying optimal paths through a state space, enabling more efficient robotic navigation.

Stochastic decision-making: Many robotics problems involve uncertainty, where outcomes cannot be determined with certainty. Classical AI often models such processes with Markov chains or Bayesian networks, which represent probabilistic transitions between states. Quantum analogs—such as quantum Markov processes and quantum Bayesian networks—extend these models by replacing classical probability distributions with quantum amplitudes. This can lead to richer representations of uncertainty and potentially faster inference.

Quantum stochastic optimization: Algorithms such as Monte Carlo simulation, evolutionary algorithms, and simulated annealing are widely used for trajectory optimization and adaptive control. When reformulated for quantum systems, these methods typically achieve polynomial or quadratic speedups. For example:

Quantum simulated annealing may accelerate convergence to near-optimal trajectories in high-dimensional search spaces.

Quantum-inspired genetic algorithms can enhance adaptability in multi-robot cooperation problems.

Quantum Monte Carlo techniques may improve sampling efficiency in probabilistic path planning.

Collectively, these quantum formulations promise to reduce computational overhead while maintaining or even improving solution quality. In particular, the distinct properties of quantum random walks—including faster state space exploration and interference-based biasing—could play a transformative role in real-time path planning and distributed robotic coordination, two of the most computationally intensive tasks in robotics.

Kinematics and Dynamic

For a long time, attempts have been made to use artificial intelligence techniques as a practical solution for traditional robotic jobs. Thus, it should come as no surprise that comparable studies are being conducted to use quantum neural networks to solve kinematic challenges. Examples include utilizing a quantum evolutionary algorithm for trajectory planning and resolving the inverse kinematics problem. The classification of basic optimization options that might be applied to the creation of a manipulator and its kinematic control is shown in the figure below. Opportunities could be viewed as a planner partial specification, where the path between select and place poses is not stated.

Additionally, each of these options leads to a discrete or continuous optimization problem that grows exponentially with the number of extra actuators. The traveling salesman problem, which belongs to the NP-complete complexity class, is a challenging problem that can be used to illustrate the order of sub jobs in an issue. There is a chance that a quantum computer could be used to solve this issue successfully.

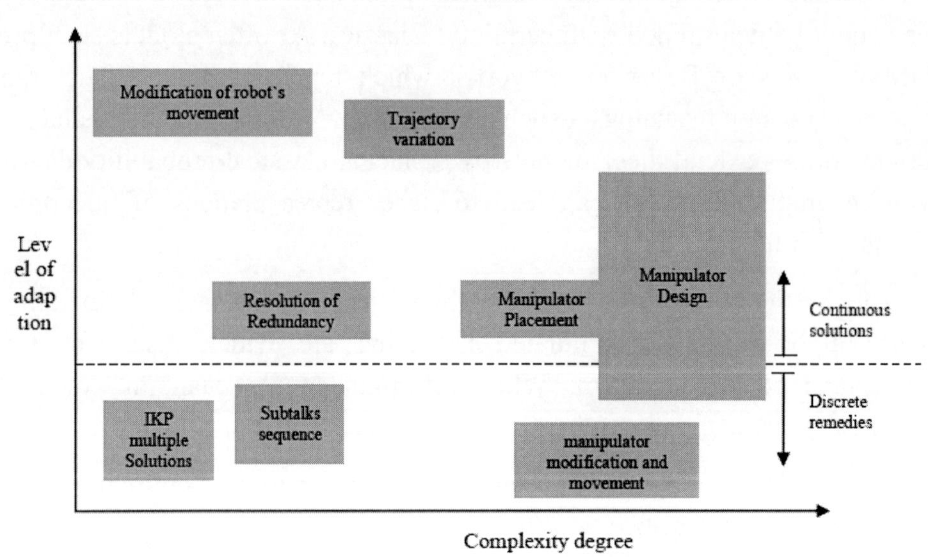

Fig.10.5 Taxonomy of Robotic Manipulator Optimization Techniques.

A nonlinear optimization problem is the process of eliminating redundancy in a robot's over-determined system. Global solutions can only be computed for basic kinematic chains. Consequently, the most popular method for obtaining a local solution is to evaluate the Jacobian matrix. The question of whether globally optimum solutions for generic redundant manipulators can be found is not conclusively answered by current knowledge. A cost function between the starting and ending points is either minimized or maximized as a result of the trajectory change, which instantly modifies the end-effector posture function. When considering dynamic models instead of only kinematics, the computing complexity of figuring out the optimal motion execution increases significantly.

Additionally, the two levels of robotics regulation—exact movement-planning and abstract task-planning—which are currently frequently handled separately due to their combined complexity have been expected to be resolved more cohesively through the application of quantum computing. Quantum optimization holds promise for control systems that employ online optimization, such as model-predictive control or the more conventional dynamic programming methods to control issues. Because the search region is so large, it is especially challenging to place the manipulator and optimize its design. Furthermore, the overarching problem takes into account all potential optimization options at once, making standard methodologies completely insufficient in determining the most optimal solution. In a similar vein, we would incorporate elements like joint friction and the inertia moments of the manipulator components if we increased the quality of mathematical modelling to encompass dynamic scenarios. Some robotics experts think that using quantum reinforcement learning—which uses models that can improve themselves—is the only way to solve this problem.

Hybrid quantum-classical algorithms offer an additional efficient method for addressing these combinatorial problems. Furthermore, using quantum computers in a multi-state operation appears to be beneficial for figuring out the overall answer to complex optimization problems. Two quantum computing resources are used to accomplish this goal: one is used to generate initial solutions, and the other is used to identify optimal solutions.

Data-Centric Robotics and the Role of Data Mining

At a macroscopic level, **robotics fundamentally revolves around data**. Every robot agent, whether an industrial manipulator, an autonomous drone, or a service robot, depends on the **acquisition, processing, and interpretation of data** to carry out its assigned tasks. This data may originate from external sensors (e.g., cameras, LiDAR, radar, tactile sensors), internal states (e.g., joint encoders, battery health, thermal conditions), or higher-level interactions with other agents and networks.

Given the wide spectrum of robotic applications — from manufacturing and healthcare to autonomous mobility and space exploration — the **challenge of effectively collecting,**

organizing, and utilizing this data becomes a central issue. Data is not only a raw input but also an **asset of knowledge and insight** that defines the robot's capacity for **adaptability, intelligence, and resilience**.

This is where **data mining** plays a pivotal role. Traditionally associated with uncovering hidden structures and patterns within large datasets, data mining has been widely applied in domains such as finance, healthcare, and social sciences. Its integration into robotics, however, has emerged more recently as a transformative methodology for:

1. **Behavioural Modelling** – Discovering correlations in sensorimotor patterns that allow robots to anticipate, adapt, and learn from experience.
2. **Fault Detection and Predictive Maintenance** – Mining internal system data to identify early signs of wear, malfunction, or anomalous operation.
3. **Human–Robot Interaction (HRI)** – Analyzing communication and interaction logs to personalize and improve robot responses.
4. **Swarm and Multi-Agent Systems** – Identifying coordination patterns and emergent behaviours across distributed robotic networks.
5. **Autonomous Decision-Making** – Enhancing path planning, task allocation, and resource optimization by uncovering latent relationships in high-dimensional data.

Despite these advances, **research remains fragmented** across sub-disciplines, with limited unifying frameworks. Some **overlooked prospective areas** include:

- **Ethics-aware data mining for robotics:** ensuring that mined insights respect privacy, fairness, and bias constraints in human-centered environments.
- **Quantum-enhanced data mining:** leveraging quantum computing to accelerate complex data mining tasks in real-time robotic applications.
- **Cross-domain knowledge transfer:** mining data from heterogeneous robotic platforms to enable shared learning across different environments or tasks.
- **Security-driven data mining:** detecting adversarial attacks or eavesdropping attempts (e.g., Eve Robot scenarios) in robotic communication systems.
- **Sustainability-oriented mining:** analyzing robotic operation data to optimize energy consumption and extend system lifetime, aligning with SDG goals.

Fault Diagnosis in Robotics through Data Mining and Quantum Approaches

In contemporary robotics, empirical evidence demonstrates that even meticulously designed and manufactured robots are prone to **malfunctions and performance degradation**. Causes include the **gradual deterioration of mechanical or electronic components**, environmental uncertainties, and incomplete knowledge of operating conditions. As robotic systems are deployed in increasingly complex and safety-critical domains — such as autonomous driving, medical assistance, and industrial automation — the need for **reliable fault diagnosis** becomes paramount.

Fault diagnosis may be defined as the task of identifying the components or subsystems that best explain the discrepancy between the robot's **actual behaviour** and its **expected behaviour**. Over the years, a wide spectrum of diagnostic methods has been developed, typically categorized into three broad families:

1. **Systems theory approaches**, leveraging analytical redundancy and mathematical modelling of system dynamics.
2. **AI-based methodologies**, employing rule-based reasoning, expert systems, and machine learning models for pattern recognition.
3. **Hybrid approaches**, which combine model-driven and data-driven methods to exploit their complementary strengths.

A prominent example is the **consistency-based approach**, where diagnosis is inferred by identifying minimal sets of components whose malfunction explains the observed inconsistency. This method is formally expressed as a **minimum hitting-set problem**, a classical optimization challenge widely studied in AI. Interestingly, this problem can also be reformulated as a **vertex cover problem**, for which quantum computing methods — including **quantum annealing** and **variational quantum algorithms** — have been investigated as potential accelerators.

Parallel to these approaches, **data mining** emerges as a powerful tool for diagnosing robotic systems. By systematically extracting patterns and insights from large-scale robot data logs, data mining enables the identification of recurring failure modes, correlations between sensor anomalies and system faults, and predictive indicators of degradation. For example, log files can reveal subtle trends in actuator performance, battery decay, or environmental interactions that precede failures.

- The process of data analysis and mining typically draws on techniques from:
- **Database systems** (e.g., index searches and query optimization for handling large robot logs),
- **Statistical methods** (e.g., anomaly detection, regression models), and
- **Machine learning algorithms** (e.g., clustering, classification, neural networks).

These methods are computationally intensive, particularly when scaled to the **high-dimensional, multimodal datasets** generated by modern robots. Here, **quantum algorithmic approaches** provide promising opportunities:

- **Quantum search algorithms** (e.g., Grover's algorithm) for accelerating database-style searches over large diagnostic datasets.

- **Quantum machine learning** for clustering and classification of anomalous patterns in robotic sensor data.
- **Quantum optimization methods** for efficiently solving hitting-set and vertex cover formulations of diagnostic tasks.

Together, these advances suggest that the **fusion of data mining with quantum-enhanced algorithms** could lay the foundation for **next-generation robotic fault diagnosis systems** — systems capable of **real-time, scalable, and predictive diagnosis** in highly complex environments.

10.3 Architectures for Quantum Computing Integration with Robotic Systems

The integration of quantum computing into robotics is not envisioned as a wholesale replacement of classical computing frameworks, but rather as a **layered and hybrid architecture** where quantum processors complement existing classical systems. This progression is expected to unfold in distinct stages:

1. **Cloud-based Quantum Computing Access**
    - In the near term, the primary method for robotic systems to leverage quantum computation will be through **cloud-hosted quantum services**.
    - Analogous to today's cloud GPU processing for machine learning, such services will support computationally demanding but non-real-time robotic tasks (e.g., offline optimization, path planning in complex environments, or post-mission data analysis).
    - Latency and bandwidth constraints mean this model is best suited for deferred, high-value computations rather than immediate control loops.
2. **Hybrid Quantum-Classical Architectures (Co-processors as Accelerators)**
    - As hardware matures, **quantum processing units (QPUs)** are expected to function as **co-processors** alongside classical CPUs and GPUs in **High Performance Computing (HPC) systems.**
    - These QPUs will be selectively employed to accelerate **specialized computational tasks** within robotics, such as:
        - Solving combinatorial optimization problems in task scheduling,
        - Quantum-enhanced machine learning for real-time sensor fusion,
        - Quantum simulations of environments for adaptive planning.

- The efficacy of this model will be determined by benchmarking **hybrid workflows** (classical + quantum) against purely classical baselines.

3. **Embedded and On-board Quantum Processors**
   - With continued miniaturization, future architectures will integrate compact QPUs directly into robotic platforms.
   - This would enable **real-time quantum-enhanced computation** for autonomous agents, particularly in domains requiring high-speed decision-making under uncertainty (e.g., swarm robotics, defence applications, or space exploration).
     - Achieving this stage requires breakthroughs in **hardware stability, error correction, and energy efficiency** for portable QPUs.

10.3.1 Quantum Characterization, Verification, and Validation (QCVV) Criteria

To ensure that quantum processors — whether cloud-based, hybrid, or embedded — can reliably support robotic applications**, QCVV methods** must meet the following criteria:

1. **Scalability**
   - The QCVV framework must be capable of handling increasing numbers of qubits and circuit depth as hardware evolves.
   - Scalable metrics are essential for comparing performance across devices and tracking improvements over time.

2. **Task-specific Reliability**
   - Beyond raw qubit fidelity, QCVV must assess whether quantum hardware can **reliably solve domain-specific robotic tasks**, such as optimization or classification.
   - Metrics should therefore incorporate **application-level benchmarks** that reflect practical robotic workloads.

3. **Hybrid Integration Assessment**
   - Since robotic systems will use **hybrid quantum-classical workflows**, QCVV must evaluate **end-to-end system performance**, not just isolated quantum hardware.
   - This includes measuring how quantum acceleration impacts latency, accuracy, and energy consumption in realistic robotic pipelines.

Table 10.1 An Evaluation Based on High-Performance Computing.

Application-centric	A single integer (or short number) that distinctly illustrates a particular QPU's capacity to handle a real-world HPC application should be provided via the protocol. The processor's entire performance, including its performance in other applications, should ideally be indicated by the QPU's score for this particular application.
Hardware-agnostic	All upcoming and existing hardware advances should be treated fairly by the protocol. In particular, it should avoid displaying an overt preference for one technology over another. The benchmark ensures that hardware makers are driven to make significant improvements across the board by giving priority to applications, as opposed to making particular changes meant to trick the benchmark, which is more likely to happen at the gate or circuit level.
Scalable	For a significant number of qubits to be supported, the protocol must be scalable. In particular, the computational complexity required to generate the metric and handle the quantum output should be suitably low. Because of this restriction, protocols that require classical calculations that have an exponential cost in respect to the number of qubits are eliminated.

Naturally, local QPUs will not match the computational capacity (in terms of available qubits) of their cloud-based counterparts. Therefore, intelligent task distribution becomes a key determinant in realizing the benefits of quantum computing. To effectively leverage both local QPUs and high-performance cloud services, it is essential to employ intelligent scheduling between the QPU and CPU across different scenarios.

Strategies developed for CPU–GPU scheduling can serve as starting points, whether through domain-specific languages (DSLs) or program profiling. However, several unique factors must be considered, such as robot mobility and the significant latency associated with cloud access. GPU scheduling typically assumes fixed program flows to maximize optimization, including profiling-based methods. In contrast, robotic tasks exhibit strong interdependence with their environment, making program flows inherently unpredictable. The scale and nature of algorithmic challenges shift dynamically with environmental changes.

As a result, scheduling techniques must be context-sensitive and adaptive. Two conditions are fundamental for this: (1) robot programs must be executable on both CPU and QPU, and (2) a real-time, competent decision engine must be available to operate under incomplete information. These variables substantially increase the complexity of

CPU–QPU scheduling. An intriguing possibility is that quantum computing itself could be used to enhance the scheduling method.

10.4 Quantum Robot: Architecture, Algorithms, and Applications

A quantum robot can be regarded as a complex quantum system, typically composed of three fundamental components: **multi quantum computing units (MQCU),** a **quantum controller/actuator**, and **information acquisition units**. Based on this system architecture, several learning control algorithms—such as quantum search algorithms and quantum reinforcement learning—have been proposed for quantum robots.

Theoretical analyses indicate that a quantum robot can reduce the computational complexity of traditional robotic approaches from $O(N^2)$ to $O(N\sqrt{N})$ by employing quantum search algorithms. Furthermore, simulation results demonstrate that quantum robots achieve more efficient learning compared to classical robots when equipped with novel quantum reinforcement learning methods.

The emergence of robots and the establishment of robotics represent one of the most significant achievements in science and technology during the 20th century. With continuous technological advancement, robots now serve society in diverse domains such as industrial production, military operations, national defence, healthcare and sanitation, navigation and space exploration, and public security. Furthermore, novel forms of robots—such as Nano robots, bio robots, and medical robots—have emerged through the integration of nanotechnology, biology, and biomedical engineering into robotics.

From the perspective of developmental trends, **intelligentization** and **miniaturization** are two critical directions in robotics. The essence of intelligentization lies in improving sensor performance, accelerating learning processes, and enhancing decision-making capabilities. Meanwhile, continuous progress in miniaturization inevitably gives rise to quantum effects, which pose both challenges and opportunities that require novel approaches.

In parallel, quantum theory—another landmark achievement of the 20th century—has seen rapid development. In particular, advances in quantum information science have demonstrated that quantum computers can significantly improve efficiency in solving important classical problems and even address computationally intractable tasks beyond the reach of classical systems. Similarly, quantum communication enables ultra-secure information transfer and enhances channel capacity. Consequently, the manipulation of quantum systems and the exploitation of quantum effects have become a central focus of contemporary scientific research.

The fusion of quantum theory and robotics gives rise to a novel paradigm: the **quantum robot**, a new class of robots constructed on the basis of quantum systems. The concept of the quantum robot was first introduced from a physics perspective by Benioff in 1998, where he emphasized the central role of the quantum computer. In this original conception, the quantum robot neither perceived its environment, nor made decisions, nor conducted experiments or measurements.

From an engineering standpoint, however, the structure of a quantum robot can be expanded to include mechanisms for **information exchange** and **learning control**. By exploiting quantum effects, quantum robots are capable of addressing challenges that arise from extreme miniaturization. Furthermore, their capabilities can be significantly enhanced by incorporating quantum sensors, which improve sensing performance, and by leveraging the power of quantum algorithms. Quantum computation provides massive parallelism, rapid search capabilities, and efficient learning mechanisms, thereby accelerating both the learning process and behavioral decision-making of robots.

10.4.1 System Structure of Quantum Robot

The concept of the quantum robot was first introduced by Benioff in 1998, where it was described as a **mobile quantum system** equipped with an on-board quantum computer and the necessary ancillary subsystems. In this initial definition, the emphasis was placed on the role of the quantum computer, while the robot itself lacked environmental awareness, decision-making capabilities, and measurement functions.

Here, we adopt an alternative definition that extends beyond computation to include **sensing and information processing**. A **quantum robot** can be defined as a mobile physical apparatus designed by leveraging quantum effects, capable of perceiving both its external environment and internal states, processing quantum information, and executing tasks.

The system structure of a quantum robot consists of three interdependent components (Below Fig.):

1. **MQCU (Multi Quantum Computing Units)** – the computational core responsible for quantum information processing, algorithm execution, and decision-making.

2. **Quantum Controller and Actuator** – the module that translates computational outcomes into physical actions, enabling interaction with the environment.

3. **Information Acquisition Units** – the sensing subsystem, which includes quantum sensors and measurement devices to capture environmental and state-related data.

These three components form an integrated architecture that enables the quantum robot to sense, process, and act within its operating environment.

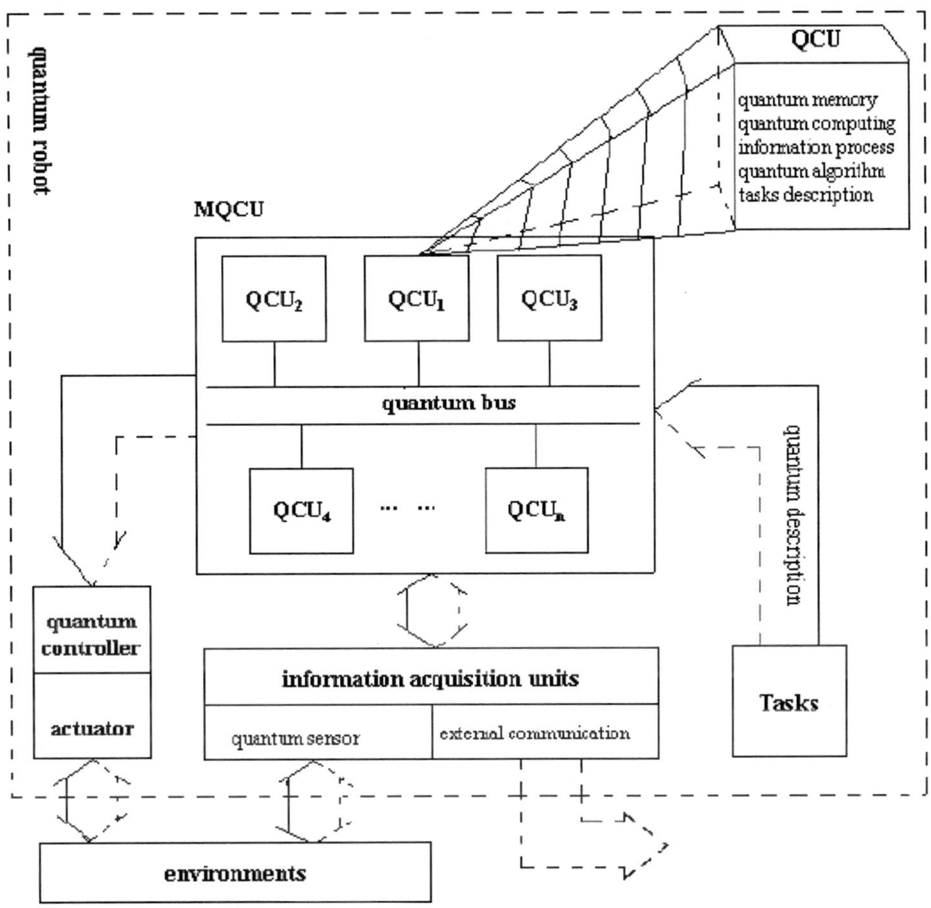

Fig.10.6 Quantum robot system structure. The MQCU, quantum controller and actuator, and information acquisition units are the three essential components of a quantum robot.

MQCU (Multi Quantum Computing Units)

The **MQCU** serves as the information-processing centre of the quantum robot, functioning analogously to its *cerebrum*. It receives tasks described in quantum language and exchanges information with the environment through quantum sensors or external communication channels. By storing, analyzing, computing, and processing diverse forms of information—including task-related, environmental, and sensory data—the MQCU constructs appropriate quantum control algorithms. It then generates output signals that are transmitted to the quantum controller, guiding the actuator in executing the required operations.

Typically, the MQCU is composed of multiple **Quantum Computing Units (QCUs),** with each QCU dedicated to specific functions. These units communicate through a **quantum bus,** which may consist of a refreshable entanglement resource or other quantum circuits. In addition to the conventional roles of classical buses (e.g., CAN bus, PCI bus, PC104 bus), the quantum bus must also support the exchange and pre-processing of quantum information. According to quantum information theory, QCUs can exchange data with greater speed and security than the MCUs of classical robots.

Each **QCU** acts as a quantum information processor, capable of tasks such as quantum computing, quantum memory management, and task description. In practical implementations, a **quantum computer** can serve as the core of a QCU. A quantum computer is a physical apparatus designed to manipulate quantum states in a controlled manner, thereby enabling quantum information processing and massively parallel computation. Its fundamental unit of information—the **quantum bit (qubit)**—can exist in a coherent superposition of the logical states 0 and 1. This property allows a quantum computer to simultaneously represent multiple states, significantly accelerating the solution of certain classical problems and even enabling the resolution of problems intractable for classical computers.

The essential characteristics underpinning quantum computation are **quantum superposition** and **quantum coherence**. With the rapid progress of quantum technologies, various quantum computer models have been realized using nuclear magnetic resonance (NMR), ion traps, and photonic systems. Within a quantum robot system, such quantum computers can act as QCUs, carrying out dedicated tasks such as storing, analyzing, computing, and processing information, ultimately enabling the MQCU to formulate effective quantum control algorithms.

Quantum Controller and Actuator

The **quantum controller** and **actuator** together form the execution and control apparatus of the quantum robot. The quantum controller receives and processes indication signals from the MQCU and transmits corresponding instructions to the actuator, thereby functioning as the link between the *cerebrum* (MQCU) and the *limbs* (actuator) of the robot.

The quantum controller is typically realized as a quantum system, such as a **quantum CNOT gate**, and may be further designed and optimized based on the principles of the rapidly developing field of **quantum control theory**. Its primary function is to transform the computational outputs of the MQCU into actionable commands for the actuator.

The **actuator** executes the actions determined by the controller. It may be implemented either as a pure quantum system or as a semi classical apparatus capable of processing both quantum and classical information. In general, the actuator maintains bidirectional information exchange with the controller, handling both quantum and classical signals. In certain configurations, the actuator and controller can be regarded as a unified apparatus, directly receiving commands from the MQCU and interacting with the external environment.

Alongside the quantum sensor, the actuator constitutes a critical interaction channel between the quantum robot and its surroundings, enabling the system not only to perceive but also to act upon the environment in a quantum-enhanced manner.

Information Acquisition Units

As with traditional robots, a quantum robot must be able to perceive its environment and gather information through dedicated **information acquisition units**. In such systems, data may be obtained from two primary sources: (1) the **quantum sensor**, which directly measures environmental conditions, and (2) an **external communication unit**, which enables information exchange with remote mainframes or other quantum robots. The information acquired can include both **quantum information** and **classical information**.

However, unlike classical sensing, the acquisition of quantum information presents significant challenges. According to quantum theory, measurement typically disturbs or even destroys the quantum state of a system. To address this issue, **quantum nondemolition (QND) measurement** plays a crucial role in enabling information acquisition without collapsing the quantum state.

Within the quantum robot system, the **quantum sensor** is the core device for environmental perception. These sensors are microstructure devices designed by exploiting quantum effects, offering extreme sensitivity to weak signals. Two well-developed types of quantum sensors that can be integrated into quantum robots are:

- **Superconducting Quantum Interference Device (SQUID) sensors** – extremely sensitive magnetic sensors based on the principles of superconductivity, including the Meissner effect, flux quantization, and the Josephson effect. By exploiting the Josephson effect, SQUID sensors convert minute variations in current or magnetic fields into measurable voltages, enabling detection of magnetic fields as small as 10−1010^{-10}10−10 Tesla.
- **Quantum Well Hall sensors** – high-performance micro Hall sensors that utilize two-dimensional electron gases to balance high mobility and high carrier concentration while maintaining high sheet resistance. For example, a quantum well Hall sensor can be fabricated by sandwiching thin InAs layers between AlGaSb layers, producing high magnetic sensitivity and excellent temperature stability due to strong confinement of the two-dimensional electron gas. Such sensors are effective for detecting faint electromagnetic fields under a variety of conditions.

By leveraging their high sensitivity and thermal stability, quantum sensors enable quantum robots to measure extremely weak electromagnetic fields. Ongoing research into new types of quantum sensors aims to extend this capability to direct acquisition of quantum information. Once realized, such sensors could allow quantum robots to detect and process diverse quantum signals and feed them into the MQCU for further computation.

In addition to sensing, the **external communication interface** allows the quantum robot to exchange information with remote systems or other quantum robots, enabling the construction of a **multi-quantum robot system** (Fig.). Through quantum communication, advantages such as ultra-high channel capacity, perfect security, and **quantum teleportation** can be fully utilized, further enhancing the performance and scalability of quantum robotic networks.

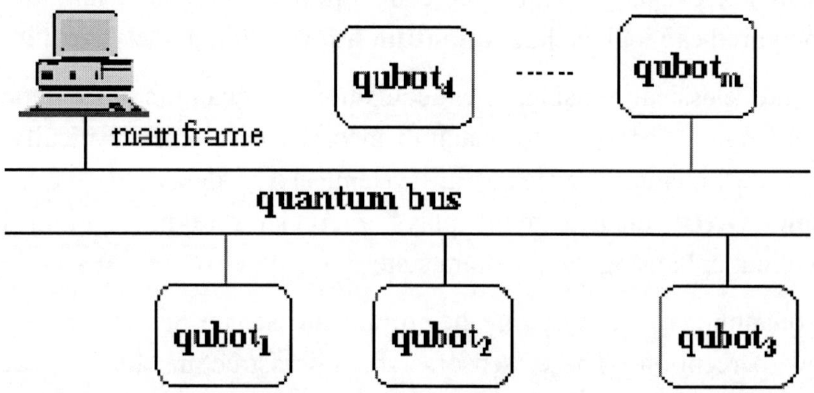

Fig.10.7 A system of several quantum robots (where qubot, or quantum robot, is used).

Based on the above structure, a quantum robot can be regarded as a specialized robotic system capable of accomplishing tasks by **perceiving its environment through sensors** and **acting upon that environment through actuators**. Its distinguishing characteristics arise from its physical implementation and unique processes of information acquisition, processing, and control.

For example, consider a quantum robot designed to assist doctors in biomedical applications. In such a scenario, the task decomposition, expressed in quantum language, is transmitted to the MQCU. Simultaneously, the MQCU receives sensing information from the external environment. Each QCU within the MQCU may be responsible for specific functions such as tracking, navigation, estimation, or diagnosis. Based on the processing results, the MQCU formulates control strategies and generates indication signals. These are sent to the quantum controller, which then directs the actuator to perform the corresponding actions on the environment.

The operational cycle of a quantum robot involves continuous interaction between its core subsystems. The **information acquisition units** repeatedly perceive the environment and transmit sensing data to the MQCU. The MQCU then processes this information and generates new signals or learning control algorithms, which are subsequently communicated to the quantum controller and actuator. This iterative process continues until the assigned task is successfully accomplished.

Within this cycle, the design of **learning control algorithms** plays a central role. Considering the unique characteristics of quantum robots, two representative algorithms are particularly noteworthy: the **quantum Grover algorithm,** applied to robotic searching tasks, and the **quantum reinforcement learning algorithm**, designed to enhance the learning capabilities of quantum robots.

10.4.2 Quantum Robot Control Algorithms

As with traditional robots, a key challenge for quantum robots lies in the design of high-efficiency learning control algorithms. For classical robots, executing algorithms with high computational complexity is difficult, particularly when real-time processing is required. This limitation arises from the restricted speed of CPUs and the constraints of chip integration.

In contrast, a quantum robot is inherently composed of multiple quantum systems, with the MQCU occupying the central position in its architecture. By harnessing the capability of quantum parallel processing, it becomes possible to design specialized learning control algorithms that can significantly reduce computational complexity and accelerate information processing. This advantage enables quantum robots to meet real-time requirements more effectively and to handle tasks that are computationally prohibitive for traditional robots.

Parallel Processing of Quantum Robot

A quantum robot is essentially a complex quantum system, and its overall configuration can be described by a **quantum state**. To facilitate efficient information processing, all forms of data—task-related, sensory, or environmental—can be encoded into **qubits**.

In quantum information theory, the state of an arbitrary qubit can be expressed as a **superposition state**:

$$|\psi\rangle = \alpha|0\rangle + \beta|1\rangle \qquad (1)$$

where α and β are complex probability amplitudes that satisfy the normalization condition $|\alpha|^2 + |\beta|^2 = 1$. This superposition property enables a qubit to simultaneously represent both logical states 0 and 1, providing the foundation for **quantum parallelism**. By extending this representation to multiple qubits, a quantum robot's MQCU can encode and process an exponentially large amount of information in parallel, thereby accelerating learning control algorithms, optimization, and decision-making tasks.

Two orthogonal states that correspond to logic states 0 and 1 are $|0\rangle$ and $|1\rangle$. These states are also known as eigenstates of quantum state $|\psi\rangle$. When this qubit is measured, the occurrence probability of $|0\rangle$ is represented by $|\alpha|^2$, and the probability of getting result $|1\rangle$ is represented by $|\beta|^2$. Unlike a classical bit, which can take only a Boolean value of either 0 or 1, a qubit can be prepared in a coherent superposition of both states. In other words, a qubit can simultaneously encode 0 and 1. This fundamental property of quantum information is one of the key distinctions between a traditional robot and a quantum robot, as it allows the latter to exploit quantum parallelism for faster computation, learning, and decision-making.

In **quantum information theory**, any quantum computation can be described as a **unitary transformation** UUU that maps an **input quantum state** to an **output quantum state**. Since UUU is linear, its action on a superposition follows the principle of linearity: if the input state is a superposition of basis states, the transformation applies to each basis state individually, and the results are then recombined into a new superposition.

For a **quantum robot**, which is essentially a complex quantum system with a **multi-qubit control unit (MQCU)** at its core, certain processes can also be represented as such transformations. When the robot applies **U** to a superposition state, the operation is performed **simultaneously on all components of the superposition**.

For example, if the robot processes a function f(x) through quantum computation, then instead of evaluating f(x) for a single classical input, the quantum robot can encode multiple inputs into a superposition and apply **U**. The output will then be a superposition of all corresponding results f(x).

This property—**quantum parallelism**—is directly analogous to **parallel processing** in classical systems but is exponentially more powerful. Whereas a classical robot must evaluate inputs one at a time (or in limited parallelism constrained by hardware), a quantum robot can exploit superposition to explore **many possibilities in one computational step**.

Thus, the **strong parallel processing ability** is a fundamental advantage of a quantum robot over a traditional robot, enabling it to handle complex tasks such as search, optimization, and learning in ways that are computationally infeasible for classical robots.

Take the following superposition state for an n-qubit cluster:

$$|\psi\rangle = \sum_{x=00\cdots0}^{11\cdots1} C_x |x\rangle, \quad \sum_{x=00\cdots0}^{11\cdots1} |C_x|^2 = 1 \qquad (2)$$

where C_x stands for complex coefficients, x is of length n, and $|C_x|^2$ is the occurrence probability of $|\, x\rangle$ measuring state $|\psi\,\rangle$. Since $|\, x\rangle$ has 2^n values, the superposition state can be thought of as the superposition state of every integer between 1 and 2^n. The processing function f (x) can be used because **U** is linear.

$$U \sum_{x=00\cdots0}^{11\cdots1} C_x \,|\, x,0\rangle = \sum_{x=00\cdots0}^{11\cdots1} C_x U \,|\, x,0\rangle = \sum_{x=00\cdots0}^{11\cdots1} C_x \,|\, x, f(x)\rangle \qquad (3)$$

where the input joint state is denoted by $|\, x,0\rangle$ and the output joint state by $|\, x, f(x)\rangle$. It is clear from the analysis above that an n-qubit cluster may handle 2n states at once. However, quantum parallel processing does not always require a trade-off between processing time and required physical space, which sets it apart from classical parallel processing. Actually, it gives the n-qubit linear physical space an exponential-scale processing space. Therefore, quantum robots can efficiently speed up information processing and solve specific issues like decision-making and navigation more quickly.

10.4.4 Quantum Robot's Search Algorithm

Similar to conventional robots, the majority of quantum robot planning and control issues can be reduced to searching issues. As an example, we will use the quantum Grover algorithm to solve an abstract robot planning problem.

Let's start by looking at a robot planning system whose state changes based on specific transition probabilities that are dependent on a control **u**. A robot in state ***i*** will go to state ***i*** with probability $\mathbf{p}_{ij}\,\mathbf{(u)}$ and cost ***g(i,u,j)*** if it selects control ***u*** in accordance with policy $\boldsymbol{\pi}$. Assume for a moment that a state's value, or V, is the definition of its worth. The robot planning system's job is to determine the ideal **V(state)** sequence that fulfils certain Bellman's equation applications.

Bellman's equation

$$V^*(i) = \min_u E[g(i,u,j) + V^*(j) \,|\, i,u] \qquad \text{(for all } i\,,j\,) \qquad (4)$$

In this case, the expected value is **E[· | i,u]**. So at a certain state ***i***, the robot planning problem is simply an unstructured searching problem to find the action a_i (or the next state ***j***) which is the optimal.

The algorithm complexity for unstructured searching issues with a searching space of N is **O(N)** in classical computation. Searching action space for the right action depending on the robot's present condition is a crucial task in robotics. A quantum robot can use the

Grover searching algorithm to reduce the complexity to $O(N\sqrt{N})$ if the state (or action) space complexity is **O(N).** In contrast, a regular robot's problem complexity is **O(N ^{2}).**

If there are N actions ($2^n \geq N \geq 2^{n-1}$), express them with n qubits:

$$|\psi_0\rangle = \sum_{l=00\cdots0}^{11\cdots1} a_l\,|l\rangle \tag{5}$$

where the length of l is n. For convenience, formula (5) can also be expressed as

$$|\psi_0\rangle = \sum_{i=1}^{2^n} a_i\,|i\rangle \tag{6}$$

Now that we know the cell to be located corresponds to | k⟩, we may finish the search using the quantum Grover algorithm.

First, a quantum state is prepared.

$$|s\rangle = \frac{1}{\sqrt{2^n}}\sum_{i=1}^{2^n}|i\rangle \tag{7}$$

It is a superposition state of equal weight. Applying the Hadamard transformation to every qubit in the n-qubit state 00L00 will achieve this $|00\cdots00\rangle$. Next, we build a reflection transform.

$$U_s = 2|s\rangle\langle s| - I \tag{8}$$

When U_s acts on an arbitrary vector, it flips the component in the hyperplane orthogonal to |s⟩ and maintains the component along |s⟩. Therefore, if we apply U_s to ⟩ | ψ_0 , we obtain

$$U_s|\psi_0\rangle = 2|s\rangle\langle s|\psi_0\rangle - |\psi_0\rangle = 2|s\rangle\sqrt{2^n}\langle a\rangle - |\psi_0\rangle$$
$$= 2\frac{1}{\sqrt{2^n}}\sum_{i=1}^{2^n}|i\rangle\sqrt{2^n}\langle a\rangle - \sum_{i=1}^{2^n}a_i|i\rangle = \sum_{i=1}^{2^n}(2\langle a\rangle - a_i)|i\rangle \tag{9}$$

where

$$\langle a\rangle = \frac{1}{2^n}\sum_{i=1}^{2^n}a_i \tag{10}$$

Now we give another reflection transform

$$U_k = -2|k\rangle\langle k| + I \tag{11}$$

where $|k\rangle$ is the *k*-th eigenstate and by applying it to state $|\psi_0\rangle$, we obtain

$$U_k|\psi_0\rangle = -2|k\rangle\langle k|\psi_0\rangle + |\psi_0\rangle = -2|k\rangle a_k + |\psi_0\rangle = \sum_{i=1, i\neq k}^{2^n} a_i|i\rangle - a_k|k\rangle \tag{12}$$

It is easy to see that U_k only changes the amplitude's sign of $|k\rangle$ in the superposition state. Thus we can form a unitary transformation (Grover iteration)

$$U_G = U_s U_k \tag{13}$$

The probability amplitude of k⟩ can be increased while the amplitude of all other states ***i*** ≠ k is suppressed by repeatedly applying the transformation U_G on ψ_0. With a probability of nearly one, we can measure the system to make the state ψ_0 ⟩ collapse into k⟩ after repeating the transformation enough times.

Define angle θ satisfying $\sin^2\theta = 1/2^n$. After applying the U_G *j* times to $|\psi_0\rangle$, the amplitude of $|k\rangle$ will become

$$a_k^j = \sin((2j+1)\theta) \tag{14}$$

If $j = (\pi - 2\theta)/4\theta$, then $(2j+1)\theta = \pi/2$ and $a_k^j = 1$. We are required to carry out an integer number of iterations, though. By doing the Grover iteration int(π / 4θ) times (here, the function int(x) returns the integer component of x), Boyer has demonstrated that the likelihood of failure is no greater than $1/2^N$. The Grover algorithm states that a quantum robot may determine the action corresponding to $|k\rangle$ with a high probability of [1-O(1/N)] when N is large.

Given that the Grover algorithm can get the required result in N steps with about a one percent chance, a quantum robot can select the appropriate action from action space based on the robot's current state, reducing complexity. Below table compares the issue complexity of traditional and quantum robots when the number of states is 10^4 and varied numbers of actions are taken into account. The table shows that as the number of actions increases, the benefit of the quantum robot becomes more noticeable.

Table 10.2 Traditional and quantum robots' issue difficulties are compared.

Number of actions	10^2	10^3	10^4	10^5	10^6	10^7	10^8
Complexity in traditional robot	10^6	10^7	10^8	10^9	10^{10}	10^{11}	10^{12}
Complexity in quantum robot	10^5	3.2×10^5	10^6	3.2×10^6	10^7	3.2×10^7	10^8

10.4.5 Robot Learning and Its Paradigms

The essence of robot learning lies in modelling and optimizing the **state–action relationship**, typically represented as pairs {State(t),Action(t)}. Learning methods are usually classified into three broad categories: **supervised learning, unsupervised learning, and reinforcement learning (RL).**

- **Supervised learning** requires explicitly labelled input–output pairs, from which it infers a mapping function. This is suitable when accurate demonstrations or annotated datasets are available.
- **Unsupervised learning** operates only on input data without labels, aiming to uncover hidden patterns, clusters, or representations.
- **Reinforcement learning (RL)** is fundamentally different: it evaluates state–action pairs using a scalar feedback signal called a **reward**. Through repeated interaction with its environment and a trial-and-error mechanism, RL agents learn policies that maximize cumulative reward.

Since the 1980s, reinforcement learning has emerged as one of the most significant approaches to machine intelligence. Its strength lies in the ability to **adapt online**, cope with **uncertainty and dynamism**, and learn effective control strategies for **complex nonlinear systems**. Consequently, RL has found wide application in artificial intelligence and robotics, particularly in tasks requiring **autonomous adaptation, sequential decision-making, and long-term planning**.

To adapt learning algorithms to the framework of quantum robots, a novel method termed Quantum Reinforcement Learning (QRL), which is inspired by the principles of quantum superposition and quantum parallelism.

In QRL, the agent's state–action space is encoded into quantum states, enabling the learning process to exploit the parallel evaluation of multiple state–action pairs simultaneously. Unlike classical reinforcement learning, where the agent explores one trajectory at a time, QRL allows the quantum robot to explore a superposition of possible trajectories in a single computational step. The transformation of these quantum states through appropriate unitary operators enables the agent to update its policy by amplifying favourable actions (those associated with higher rewards) and suppressing unfavourable ones.

This mechanism combines the trial-and-error adaptation of RL with the computational advantage of quantum parallelism, potentially leading to faster convergence and more efficient policy learning. For quantum robots operating in complex, uncertain, and dynamic environments, QRL offers a promising pathway to achieve real-time adaptation, robustness, and scalability beyond the limits of classical methods.

Assuming that N_s and N_a represent the number of states and actions, select m and n, which are defined by the subsequent equations:

$$N_s \le 2^m \le 2N_s, N_a \le 2^n \le 2N_a \tag{15}$$

State set S={s} and action set A={a} can be represented by m and n qubits, respectively:

$$s: \begin{bmatrix} a_1 \middle| a_2 \middle| \cdots \middle| a_m \\ b_1 \middle| b_2 \middle| \cdots \middle| b_m \end{bmatrix}, \text{ where } |a_i|^2 + |b_i|^2 = 1,\ i = 1,2,\ldots m$$

$$a: \begin{bmatrix} \alpha_1 \middle| \alpha_2 \middle| \cdots \middle| \alpha_n \\ \beta_1 \middle| \beta_2 \middle| \cdots \middle| \beta_n \end{bmatrix}, \text{ where } |\alpha_i|^2 + |\beta_i|^2 = 1,\ i = 1,2,\ldots n$$

They might therefore be in a superposition state:

$$|s^{(m)}\rangle = \sum_{s=00\cdots0}^{11\cdots1} C_s |s\rangle,\ |a^{(n)}\rangle = \sum_{a=00\cdots0}^{11\cdots1} C_a |a\rangle \tag{16}$$

where $C_s = x_s + iy_s$ and $C_a = u_a + iv_a$ are complex numbers. The mapping from states to actions is $f(s) = \pi : S \to A$ and we will get:

$$f(s) = |a_s^n\rangle = \sum_{a=00\cdots0}^{11\cdots1} C_a |a\rangle \tag{17}$$

$|C_a|^2$ denotes the probability of $|a\rangle$ when $|a_s^n\rangle$ is measured. Based on the above express, the procedural form of QRL can be described as follows.

The QRL process

Initialize $|s^{(m)}\rangle = \sum_{s=00\cdots0}^{11\cdots1} C_s |s\rangle$, $f(s) = |a_s^n\rangle = \sum_{a=00\cdots0}^{11\cdots1} C_a |a\rangle$ and $V(s)$ arbitrarily

Repeat (for each episode)

For all states $|s^{(m)}\rangle = \sum_{s=00\cdots0}^{11\cdots1} C_s |s\rangle$:

(1) Observe $f(s)$ and get $|a\rangle$;

(2) Take action $|a\rangle$, observe next state $|s'^{(m)}\rangle$, reward r

Then update: $V(s) \leftarrow V(s) + \alpha(r + \gamma V(s') - V(s))$

$$C_a \leftarrow e^{\lambda(r+V(s'))} C_a$$

Until for all states $|\Delta V(s)| \leq \varepsilon$.

QRL is inspired by two fundamental ideas from quantum mechanics: the **superposition principle of quantum states** and **quantum parallel computation**. In this framework, the **state value** is encoded as a quantum state. By performing a measurement on this simulated quantum state, the system collapses to a specific outcome in accordance with the **quantum measurement postulate**. The probability of observing a particular eigenvalue corresponds to its **probability amplitude**, which evolves dynamically as the learning process updates according to received rewards.

In effect, the entire **state–action space** of the quantum robot is represented as a **superposition of quantum states**. This representation naturally balances **exploration and exploitation**:

- *Exploration* arises from the probabilistic sampling inherent in quantum measurement.
- *Exploitation* is reinforced as probability amplitudes are adjusted to favour actions associated with higher rewards.

Moreover, this representation is fully consistent with the principles of quantum parallelism, allowing the robot to evaluate multiple state–action pairs simultaneously. As a result, QRL has the potential to significantly accelerate the learning process compared to its classical counterpart, especially in high-dimensional or complex environments.

Verification of stochastic iterative algorithms shows that, when the following holds true (where k αk is step size), they converge at the optimal state value function V (s)* with probability 1 under specific exploration policies:

$$\lim_{T\to\infty}\sum_{k=1}^{T}\alpha_k = \infty, \qquad \lim_{T\to\infty}\sum_{k=1}^{T}\alpha_k^2 < \infty \tag{18}$$

Additionally, QRL is identical to classical RL; the only distinctions are that (1) its exploration policy is predicated on the collapse theory of quantum measurement while being observed, and (2) it computes in parallel. Thus, QRL algorithms converge and the characteristic of convergence is unaffected by changes to RL.

Consider the grid world setting of four rooms and surrounding corridors, as seen in below figure, as an example of typical rooms with corridors to assess the QRL algorithm in practice. Every grid cell represents a distinct environmental condition. The robot (or agent) can move in one of four main directions from any state: up, down, left, or right. Actions that would enter a blocked cell are not carried out. The algorithms' job is to determine the best course of action that will enable the robot to travel from point S to point G while minimizing costs and maximizing benefits.

The collapse theory of quantum measurement serves as the inspiration for QRL's action selection policy, which is clearly distinct from that of conventional RL algorithms. Additionally, probability amplitudes | Ca|^2 are used to indicate the likelihood of an action that is specified as

$$f(s) = |a_s^n\rangle = \sum_{a=00\cdots0}^{11\cdots1} C_a |a\rangle$$

Every one of the four cell-to-cell operations | Ca|^2 has a uniformly initialized. This 13x13(0~12) grid globe has cell(4,4) as the starting point and cell(8,8) as the end goal.

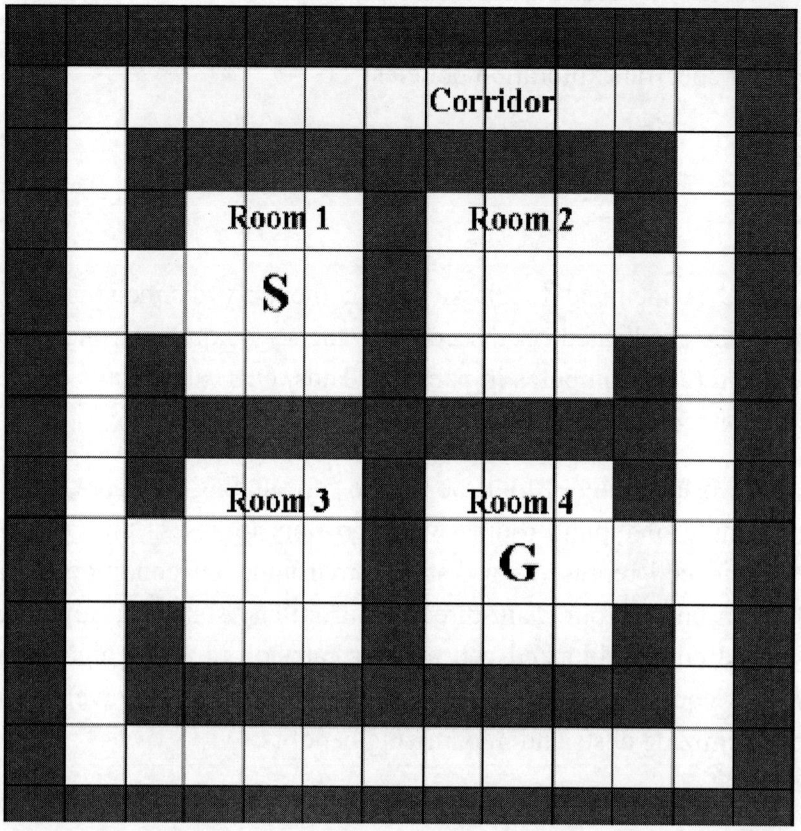

Fig.10.8 A gridworld setting with cell-to-cell movements (up, down, left, and right) serves as an example of a chamber with a corridor. The initial condition is indicated by the labels S and G.

10.5 Swarm Robotics

Swarm robotics is the study and design of **large groups of simple robots** that can cooperate to perform complex tasks. They are inspired by **natural swarms** (ants, bees, birds, fish schools) where simple local rules produce intelligent collective behaviour. When **quantum computing, communication, and sensing** are integrated, swarms can become **more efficient, secure, and intelligent.**

Robotic swarms use a number of simple robots, each of which completes a basic duty, to accomplish complicated goals. Autonomy, collaboration, scalability, cost-effectiveness, and flexibility are some of the benefits of swarm robotics. Because each robot in a swarm makes local decisions based on how they perceive their surroundings and the signals they exchange with their peers, the robots are autonomous. Swarms of robots work together to accomplish a challenging task, such as shape development or search and rescue. Because of the scalability, the behaviour of the whole is unaffected even if one unit is lost. As a result, they offer a financial edge over individual, less costly, less sophisticated robots, particularly in hazardous scenarios, making the entire system more cost-effective. Another way to test theories about the development and behaviour of natural swarms is by using a robotic swarm as a model. In a different use, tiny robots enter the human body to precisely and locally administer medication.

Both simulators and actual hardware can be used to study quantum computing. The same is true with robotics: there are real and virtual equipment. Working in a simulation environment enables one to build new robots, assess their viability, conduct tests that take into account the system's physics without causing any damage to costly equipment, and evaluate how well a prototype or algorithm performs a task.

1. **Quantum Communication in Swarms**

- **Entanglement-based Coordination:**

Swarm members can share information via quantum entanglement, allowing instant synchronization of states across the swarm.

- **Quantum Key Distribution (QKD):**

Communication between swarm robots becomes **unhackable**, crucial in defence or financial applications.

- **Reduced Latency in Coordination:**

Secure quantum channels eliminate delays in multi-robot decision-making, enabling faster collective action.

2. **Quantum Sensing for Collective Awareness**

- **Enhanced Environmental Mapping:**

Each robot equipped with quantum sensors (magnetometers, gravimeters, quantum lidar) contributes ultra-precise local measurements to a **global swarm map**.

- **Subterranean & Underwater Exploration:**

Swarm drones could map underground tunnels or deep oceans without GPS, using quantum accelerometers and gyroscopes.

- **Disaster Response:**

Swarms of quantum-sensor-equipped robots can detect survivors under rubble, measure gas leaks, or sense weak magnetic anomalies.

3. **Quantum Computing for Swarm Intelligence**

- **Optimization of Swarm Behaviour:**

Quantum algorithms (like Grover's search or QAOA) allow efficient task allocation, path planning, and coverage optimization across thousands of robots.

- **Quantum Reinforcement Learning (QRL):**

Each robot can "learn" policies faster via quantum-enhanced decision-making, enabling adaptive behaviours in uncertain environments.

- **Emergent Collective Intelligence:**

With quantum parallelism, swarms can evaluate many strategies simultaneously, converging on optimal solutions much quicker than classical methods.

4. **Applications of Quantum Swarm Robotics**

- **Defence & Security:**
  - Swarms of drones for surveillance that are resistant to electronic jamming.
  - Quantum stealth detection by monitoring magnetic/gravitational anomalies.
- **Space Exploration:**
  - Swarm rovers on Mars/Moon collaboratively explore, map, and communicate securely with Earth.
  - Self-healing swarm networks that adapt if some robots fail.
- **Environmental Monitoring:**
  - Oceanographic swarm robots mapping currents, salinity, and pollution with quantum precision.
  - Large-scale climate and ecosystem tracking.

10.6 Quantum and Swarm Robotics

Mixing quantum algorithms with swarm robotics involves enhancing classical robotic controllers using quantum paradigms, especially for decision-making and optimization tasks. While robots operate in a classical physics domain—where direct quantum effects like Heisenberg indeterminacy do not apply—quantum-inspired methods provide speed-ups via mathematical analogies and probabilistic modelling.

Quantum Algorithms in Robotic Controllers

Quantum algorithms, such as Grover's search and Quantum Approximate Optimization Algorithm (QAOA), allow robots to explore multiple possible paths or states simultaneously via superposition, dramatically reducing the computation time for tasks like path planning, localization, and global coordination compared to classical methods. These algorithms typically replace or augment portions of classical control, such as neural network layers in reinforcement learning systems, leading to better performance with fewer learnable parameters.

Mathematical Quantization and Probability

Since direct quantum physical effects are unavailable, the integration is mathematical. Decision spaces, for instance, can be modelled using probability amplitudes and superposition, allowing controllers to represent and compute on multiple robot states (like positions or rewards) analogously to quantum states in quantum mechanics. This maintains a classical substrate but benefits from quantum logic's ability to encode and efficiently resolve complex decision scenarios.

Applications and Advantages

Swarm Coordination: Embedding quantum circuits or algorithms in swarm control allows each robot to process interactions with probabilistic logic, leading to faster and more robust emergent global behaviours.

Reinforcement Learning: Quantum-enhanced RL can speed up learning and exploration strategies, leading to improved autonomy for complex tasks such as robotic arm manipulation or search-and-rescue operations.

Complexity Reduction: Quantum algorithms can reduce computational complexity in optimization and search tasks, which is crucial for large robotic swarms and real-time control.

Conceptual Integration

In practice, this integration occurs mainly at the algorithmic level:

Robotics controllers mimic quantum behaviours by quantizing variables, using reversible gates, and modelling decision states as superpositions. These enhancements do not violate classical robotic operation but provide efficiencies and new perspectives for controller design and swarm behaviour analysis. Mixing quantum algorithms with swarm robotics mathematically augments classical controllers, leveraging quantum-inspired approaches to optimize decision processes, model probabilistic phenomena, and achieve computational speed-ups—without requiring actual quantum physical effects in the robots' embodiment.

10.7 Why Quantum and Swarm Robotics

Combining swarms of robots with quantum computing provides a significant computational speed-up, leading to increased efficiency and scalability in multi-robot missions. This integration enables tasks to be solved faster and with fewer resources, translating to savings in both computational time and operational costs such as the number of robots required.

Efficiency and Scalability Advantages

Computational Efficiency: Quantum algorithms drastically reduce the time required for decision-making, optimization, and task allocation within swarms. Classical algorithms have higher complexity (e.g., O(n)O(n)), while quantum solutions can scale down search and allocation complexities (e.g.,

O(n)O($\sqrt{n}$)), enabling swarms to solve problems faster and more efficiently.

Operational Cost Savings: Enhanced algorithms mean that a given mission may require fewer robots or allow existing robots to handle larger tasks effectively, saving money on hardware and maintenance.

Resource Optimization: Swarm behaviour powered by quantum computing leads to more coordinated collective actions, minimizing duplicated effort and improving robustness—even with simple, inexpensive robots.

Time and Money" Implications

Time: Quantum-enhanced swarm controllers optimize path planning, task assignment, and adaptation in dynamic environments, outperforming classical algorithms in speed.

Money: Missions can deploy lower-cost robots or use smaller fleets, leveraging advanced coordination and quickly adapting to failures or environmental changes—ultimately reducing setup, operational, and development costs.

Quantum computing thus amplifies the benefits of swarm robotics by providing faster and more scalable solutions, achieving ideal savings in both computational time and financial investment in real-world deployments.

The application of 'quantum translation'—recasting classical algorithms in quantum terms—indeed extends to swarm robotic controllers, enabling both theoretical exploration and computational tests. This translation involves implementing reversible logic gates, measurements, and superposition as constitutive elements of quantum circuits, which can be embedded within classical algorithms to model interactions, decision-making, and emergent behaviours in robot swarms.

Quantum Translation and Swarm Robotics

Reversible Logic Gates: These gates form the basis of quantum circuits, enabling the representation and processing of information in a way that preserves computational reversibility—a key property for optimization and resource efficiency in large distributed systems such as swarms.

Superposition and Probability Amplitudes: By modelling robot positions, rewards, and states as probability amplitudes and eigenstate superpositions, robots can encode a spectrum of possibilities rather than binary outcomes, mirroring quantum mechanics' approach to complex system modelling.

Entanglement for Communication: Quantum entanglement supports stronger, more cohesive communications in swarms, allowing information from one robot to influence others as if the robots were "particles of the same system." This could lead to adaptive, resilient, and highly coordinated swarm behaviours.

Deepening Knowledge of Complex Systems

Quantum modelling of swarm behaviours extends beyond technical optimization: Robots can be metaphorically treated like particles, enabling researchers to study emergent phenomena and collective dynamics by observing how simple, locally defined quantum rules lead to complex global behaviours.

This framework aids in understanding natural swarms, distributed control, and collective intelligence—not just improving optimization but inspiring new paradigms in AI and robotics.

Applicability Limits and Potentialities

While quantum algorithms can be embedded in classical robot controllers or external quantum centers, direct implementation in small robots faces technological barriers (e.g., miniaturization, robustness).

Most research is currently theoretical or simulation-based, utilizing quantum-inspired frameworks to test how superposition, entanglement, and quantum gates shape swarm coordination, adaptability, and emergent outcomes.

Future advancements may allow broader application not only for optimization but also for discovery in natural sciences, engineering, and group intelligence.

Example: Quantum Circuit for Swarm Exploration

In simulated search-and-rescue missions, quantum circuits help select exploration directions based on the most successful robot's position and reward. The entire swarm then adapts its configuration by communicating and updating strategies through quantum gate-based algorithms, supporting distributed control and rapid convergence on tasks.

Quantum translation empowers swarm robotics with powerful modelling tools, deeper insights into complex adaptive systems, and the promise of collective intelligence shaped by quantum phenomena such as superposition and entanglement.

10.8 How Quantum and Swarm Robotics works

Pioneering research in quantum robotics is beginning to address the practical and theoretical integration of quantum computing with swarm robotic applications, though only a limited number directly focus on swarms. The quantum paradigm can enhance both single-robot decision-making and the interactions within a robotic swarm, leading to efficiency in tasks such as path planning and more sophisticated emergent collective behaviours.

Quantum-enhanced Single Robot Decision-Making

Path Planning: Quantum algorithms like Grover's search are being adapted for robot path planning. They allow a robot to evaluate possible paths in superposition, providing faster and more resource-efficient solutions than classical techniques.

Task Allocation and Optimization: Quantum-inspired algorithms (e.g., quantum annealing, quantum walks) have demonstrated superior results in assigning tasks and planning routes for individual robots, outperforming classical approaches in simulation.

Quantum Influence on Swarm Interactions

Pairwise Quantum Gates: Studies have deployed quantum circuits to model the interaction between robots in a swarm. Each pairwise exchange of data—such as positional or reward information—is processed using quantum logic gates, fundamentally shaping both individual decisions and the global emergent behaviour.

State Superposition: Positions and success metrics for individual robots are treated as quantum states, enabling richer state representations and probabilistic behaviours that naturally generate swarm-level coordination and adaptability.

Research Highlights and Applications

Early efforts have successfully demonstrated quantum-inspired collective movement and target search in simulated environments, such as search-and-rescue missions and foraging-like behaviours, showing rapid convergence and improved coordination compared to traditional models.

Quantum algorithms and circuit models also provide new perspectives for simulating complex systems and modelling natural phenomena—from collective intelligence to self-organization of agents—moving beyond mere optimization into deeper understanding and control of emergent behaviours.

While quantum robotics is an emerging field, its potential to shape single-robot decision systems and influence swarm interactions is increasingly evident, promising advances in efficiency and emergent coordination for real-world applications.

Quantum algorithms for swarm robotics focus on optimization, decision-making, path planning, and collaborative intelligence, leveraging quantum computational models to enhance classic swarm behaviours. The leading approaches embed quantum circuits inside classical algorithms, enabling local interactions between robots that lead to more intelligent global swarm behaviours.

Quantum Path Planning Algorithms

Grover's Search Algorithm: Used for fast target-search and path planning by reducing classical search complexity. Robots encode their positional and reward information (proximity to a target, success rates) into a quantum circuit, and Grover's search identifies optimal candidates or directions for exploration. Outperforms classic ant-foraging simulations, reducing the time and steps needed to reach targets in cluttered arenas.

Quantum Pairwise Interaction Models

Local-to-global swarm behaviours emerge from rules encoded as quantum logic gates. Pairwise interactions are modelled through quantum gates (such as Hadamard or CNOT gates) applied to qubit representations of robot states, allowing probabilistic and entangled decision-making for tasks like search-and-rescue. These quantum circuits can direct robots to follow high-reward peers or scatter depending on current mission needs, and can be adapted for obstacle avoidance.

Quantum Optimization and Task Allocation

Quantum-inspired or quantum-annealing algorithms solve complex combinatorial problems, such as multi-robot task allocation, more efficiently than classical methods. Quantum walks (random walks of quantum particles) can guide robots in finding optimal paths or resource allocation for distributed tasks, outperforming classical path-planning.

Quantum-Enhanced Swarm Learning

Quantum clustering and quantum-enhanced deep learning algorithms have been applied to increase the efficiency of swarm intelligence, adaptive learning, and emergency vehicle dispatch forecasting.

These algorithms allow swarms to learn collectively in real time, adapting behaviours based on shared sensory information via quantum communication networks.

Implementation Scenarios and Challenges

Robots typically send positional and reward information to an external quantum computer, which processes decision cycles and relays instructions for swarm movement.

Real-time simulation environments combine robotics toolkits (e.g. Webots) with quantum simulators (IBM Q Experience) to visualize quantum-driven swarm behaviours.

Quantum hardware limitations, programming paradigms, and interoperability with robot software currently restrict large-scale real-world deployment.

Example Procedure: Quantum-Driven Search-and-Rescue Mission

- Robots randomly explore the arena, reporting their positions and rewards (target proximity) to a quantum processor.

- The quantum circuit compares rewards and identifies the region for further exploration.
- Swarm robots move into identified regions, avoiding overlap via randomized quantum instructions.
- Steps repeat until the target is found, often in fewer cycles and travel distances than with a classical algorithm.

Quantum algorithms bring powerful speed-ups and richer behaviours to swarm robotics, offering new directions for multi-agent intelligence and real-world deployment as hardware and frameworks mature.

10.9 Architecture

The architecture for quantum and swarm robotics blends quantum computation with classic swarm control frameworks, enabling robust, efficient, and scalable decision-making across robotic collectives. This hybrid architecture uses quantum circuits for critical local interactions or global planning stages, while classical algorithms handle real-world sensing and basic movement.

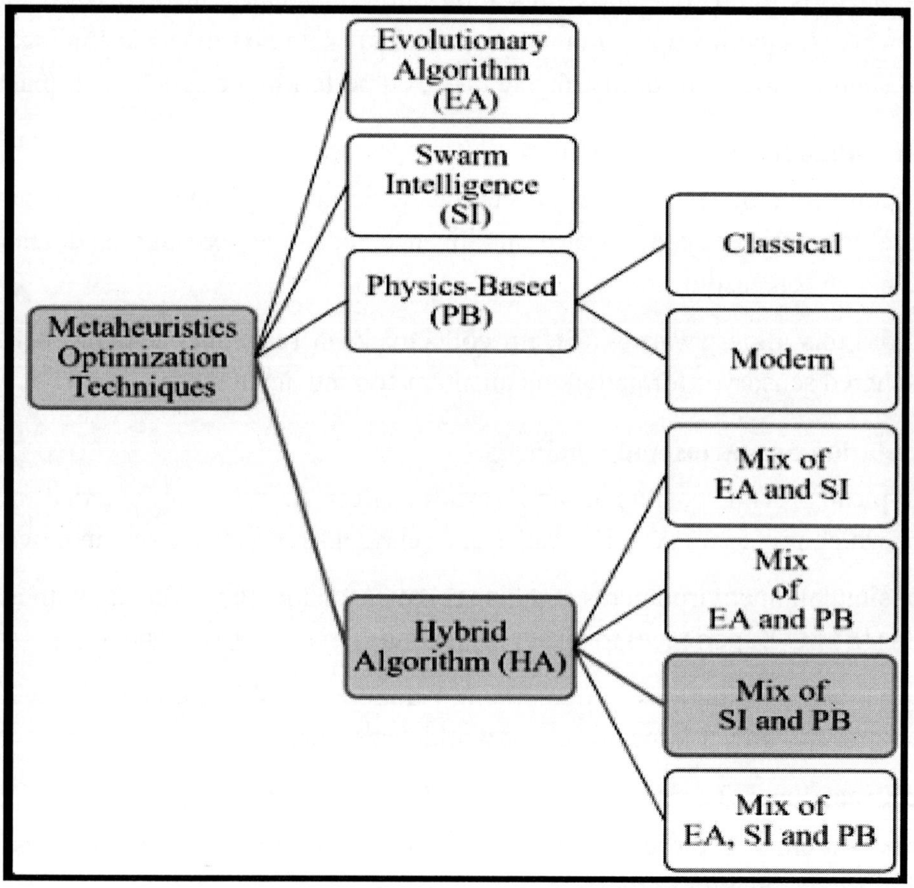

Fig.10.9 Quantum and swarm robotics architecture.

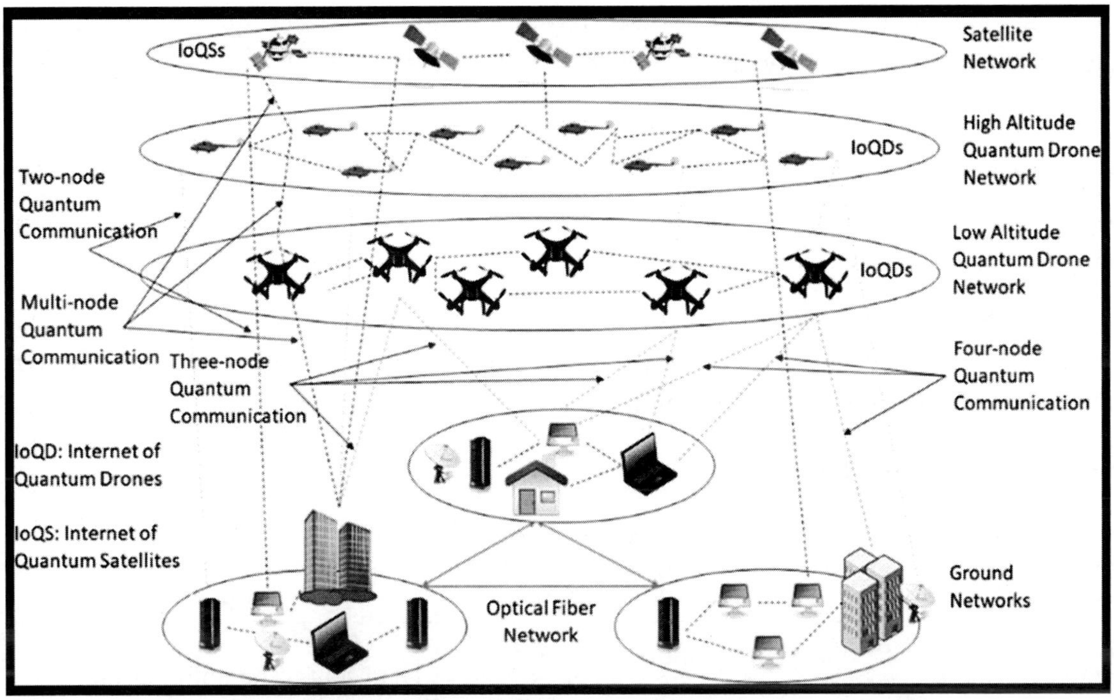

Fig.10.10 Futuristic disruptive technologies using drones.

Key Components of Quantum Swarm Architecture

1. Quantum-Classical Hybrid Control

Quantum circuits are embedded inside classical algorithms, acting as modules for decision-making and coordination (e.g., during search and rescue tasks).

Local rules (decisions, movement) are processed with reversible logic gates and quantum measurements, enabling superposition and probabilistic decisions among possible paths or actions.

2. Distributed vs. Centralized Models

In practice, robots usually lack on board quantum computers due to physical constraints. Instead, robots rely on an external quantum server that receives data (positions, rewards) from the swarm, executes quantum circuits, and sends back decisions or path suggestions.

Some architectures use nested matrices: diagonal blocks represent the internal state of individual robots; off-diagonal blocks represent pairwise interactions modelled via quantum gates.

3. Pairwise Quantum Interactions

Global behaviour emerges from quantum-modelled pairwise exchanges: the success (reward, proximity to goal) and current position of each robot inform collective movements via quantum logic.

When a robot achieves a higher reward, its information enters the quantum circuit to suggest exploration areas for the rest of the swarm, promoting efficient convergence to targets.

4. Information Exchange and Simulation Loop

Robots simulate sensor-based perception and message passing, exchanging information about their positions and observations.

Data cycles between robot simulators (e.g., Webots) and quantum computation platforms (e.g., Qiskit-Jupyter), updating robot positions after quantum-guided measurements and iteratively refining the swarm configuration until the target is found.

Architectural Workflow

Table 10.3 Architecture workflow of classical and quantum components.

Step	Classical Component	Quantum Component
Data Collection	Robots sense positions, rewards, states	Data sent to quantum circuit
Local Interaction	Decides movement, avoids obstacles	Pairwise logic gates analyze info
Decision Making	Compares rewards, sets exploration	Grover's or other quantum algorithm
Global Coordination	Updates swarm configuration	Calculates emergent best areas
Feedback Loop	Applies new position, updates sensors	Next round of quantum measurements

Quantum and swarm robotics architectures are evolving hybrids, usually relying on centralized quantum computation to augment classic local robotics algorithms. Quantum circuits inform the most critical steps of swarm coordination, especially in complex missions like search-and-rescue, leading to faster convergence and enhanced adaptability compared to purely classical approaches.

10.10 Cloud with Quantum robotics

Cloud-enabled quantum robotics refers to the integration of cloud computing, quantum computing, and robotic systems (including swarm robotics), offering scalable computational resources and advanced algorithms for decision making, path planning, and collaborative tasks in robotics. Leveraging the cloud enables remote access to quantum processors for enhanced swarm intelligence, optimization, and simulation, overcoming hardware and programming limitations in individual robotic agents.

Architecture Overview

Quantum Cloud Platforms provide layered architectures:

The Quantum Processing Unit (QPU) layer executes quantum computations via cloud interfaces.

The Quantum Control and Calibration (QCC) layer manages quantum hardware operations.

The Quantum Application and Interface (QAI) layer connects users and classical systems to quantum services, often through programming frameworks like Qiskit and Cirq.

Robotic simulators such as Webots can integrate with quantum simulators (e.g., IBM Quantum Experience) for real-time interactions, influencing swarm behaviour and decision cycles.

How Quantum and Cloud Robotics Work

Architecture: Robotic systems connect to quantum processors via cloud interfaces, enabling real-time access to quantum computing power without requiring specialized on-site hardware. Quantum cloud platforms offer APIs for running quantum algorithms such as Grover's search, HHL, and quantum machine learning directly on computational tasks like path planning, vision, and task allocation.

Resource Allocation: Workloads may be distributed between local Quantum Processing Units (QPUs) embedded in robots, and remote quantum services in the cloud, balancing speed, mobility, and operational delays.

Hybrid Systems: Most practical approaches use hybrid quantum-classical architectures, combining conventional CPUs and quantum resources via cloud frameworks, to solve problems that surpass traditional computation

Quantum and cloud robotics architecture typically involves a hybrid system combining classical cloud infrastructure, quantum processing units (QPUs), and robotic control components, enabling efficient, scalable, and secure quantum-augmented robotic applications. This architecture supports the remote execution of quantum algorithms via the cloud, alongside classical control and pre/post-processing in robotics.

Core Architecture Components

Quantum Processing Unit (QPU): The heart of quantum computation, QPUs perform quantum operations on qubits using gates such as Hadamard, CNOT, and Pauli gates. QPUs are accessed remotely in the cloud and provide quantum speedup for tasks like optimization, learning, and path planning.

Classical Processing Unit (CPU): Handles classical data processing, preparation of quantum circuit instructions, and interpretation of quantum results. CPUs often run on local robots or cloud servers, coordinating with QPUs in hybrid quantum-classical workflows.

Quantum Control Plane: Manages communication, scheduling, error correction, and calibration between classical and quantum components. It ensures efficient execution of quantum tasks and data flow, optimizing hybrid operations for robotics use cases.

Cloud Infrastructure: Provides scalable, on-demand quantum compute resources and storage, accessible over standard APIs and interfaces. Cloud platforms (such as IBM Quantum Experience, Microsoft Azure Quantum) host QPUs and offer quantum software development kits (Q-SDKs) and quantum cloud services for robotics integration.

Robotic Interface Layer: Connects physical robots or simulators to the cloud quantum services, managing sensor data, actuator commands, and quantum-enhanced decision support. This may include APIs for task offloading or client applications for hybrid quantum-classical control.

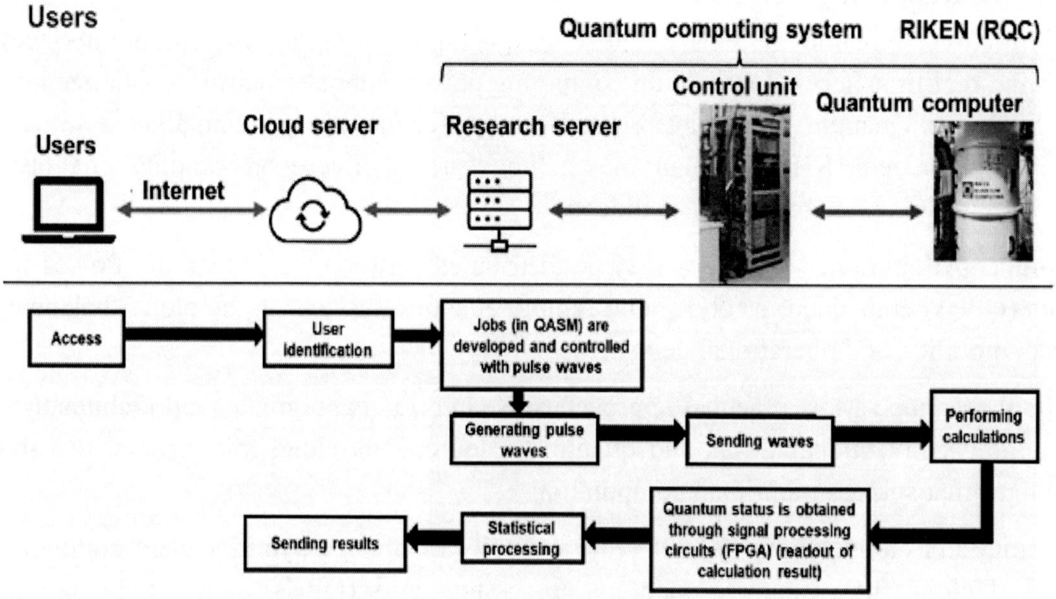

Fig.10.11 Cloud Quantum Architecture.

Architecture Layers

Physical Layer: Quantum chips, error correction, cryogenics, and classical hardware.

Control and Middleware Layer: Orchestrates quantum operations, error correction, data exchange, and scheduling.

Hybrid Computing Layer: Integrates quantum and classical computational tasks, enabling quantum-classical algorithms suited for robotics.

Application Layer: Quantum algorithms for robot path planning, swarm optimization, AI-enhanced sensing, and control, accessible via cloud APIs.

User Interface Layer: Developer tools, management consoles, and APIs facilitating quantum service deployment and monitoring.

Hybrid Quantum-Classical Workflow

Quantum cloud robotics leverages hybrid models where quantum circuits are prepared and results processed classically. These workflows optimize resource use and overcome current quantum hardware limitations by offloading parts of algorithms to classical processors while harnessing quantum acceleration where most beneficial.

This layered, hybrid architecture enables flexible deployment of quantum-enhanced robotic applications, facilitating innovation in swarm robotics, autonomous vehicles, optimization, and AI-driven robotics through a cloud-connected quantum computing paradigm.

10.11 Quantum Robot Applications

Before exploring the potential applications of quantum robots, it is essential to highlight the distinctions between them and conventional robots. Traditional robots are primarily limited to processing **classical information**, which constrains their computational efficiency and adaptability. In contrast, **quantum robots** integrate principles of quantum mechanics—such as superposition, entanglement, and quantum parallelism—into their architecture. This enables them to:

- **Process quantum information** directly, allowing faster and more complex computations than classical processors.
- **Exploit quantum effects** to enhance decision-making, learning, and sensing capabilities in uncertain or dynamic environments.
- **Leverage quantum communication** for secure data exchange and coordination in multi-robot systems.

These unique properties extend the potential application areas of quantum robots far beyond the scope of conventional robots, making them suitable for tasks in fields such as **space exploration, cryptography, advanced manufacturing, biomedical engineering, and intelligent autonomous systems**.

Table 10.4 Quantum robot and conventional robot comparisons.

Comparable Items	Quantum robot	Conventional robot
Attribute of the system	Quantum system	Mechanical system
Internal Sensors	Quantum sensors, including quantum well Hall and SQUID sensors	CCD cameras, infrared sensors, ultrasonic sensors, and more.
Law to abide	The law of quantum mechanics	The law of classical mechanics
Information processing	MQCU stands for multiple quantum computing units.	Classical computers and other processors
Information	Both conventional and quantum information	Traditional data
Intricacy	Superior	Significantly reduced
Space size	Microcosmic	Primarily macro
Technical issues	More challenging	Simpler
Mode of communication	Classical communication and quantum communication	Traditional modes of communication
Parallel Process Execution	Influential	Feeble

Thus, it can be seen that the quantum robot, as a novel class of robotic systems, has the potential to overcome many challenges associated with miniaturization and precision. By integrating quantum sensors, it is capable of acquiring both quantum and classical information from its environment with exceptional sensitivity. This extremely high resolution and delicacy effectively transcend the limitations of conventional sensor performance. Moreover, quantum robots can directly harness the advantages of quantum information processing, significantly accelerating their control, learning, and decision-making processes. Consequently, quantum robots hold promising application prospects across a wide spectrum of domains, including military and national defence, aerospace exploration, biomedicine, scientific research, safety engineering, and even daily life.

10.11.1 National Defence and Security

- **Quantum Sensing for Surveillance:**

Quantum magnetometers and gravimeters allow robots to detect faint disturbances in magnetic or gravitational fields. For example, if submarines, nuclear materials, or stealth vehicles approach a restricted zone, quantum robots could detect them even when cloaked or shielded.

- **Navigation without GPS:**

Quantum gyroscopes and accelerometers enable precise navigation in environments where GPS is jammed or unavailable (underwater, underground, deep space).

- **Robotic Patrol Warriors:**

Autonomous quantum robots equipped with quantum sensors could monitor ports, air bases, or borders. They would "forewarn" commanders by detecting anomalies invisible to classical sensors.

10.11.2 Space Exploration

- **Planetary Rovers with Quantum Navigation:**

Quantum-enhanced navigation allows rovers on Mars or the Moon to operate without reliance on Earth-based GPS or frequent communication.

- **Resource Detection:**

Quantum gravimeters could detect underground water, mineral deposits, or lava tubes beneath planetary surfaces.

- **Quantum Communication with Earth:**

Entanglement-based communication allows secure, high-speed, and long-distance communication between Earth and space robots.

10.11.3 Medical and Healthcare Robotics

- **Quantum Imaging for Surgery:**

Robots equipped with quantum-enhanced MRI or quantum optical imaging could perform minimally invasive surgery with unprecedented precision.

- **Drug Discovery and Delivery:**

Quantum computation speeds up molecular simulation; robotic systems then use this knowledge for targeted drug delivery or nanoparticle-based treatments.

- **Neuroprosthetics:**

Quantum sensors can detect extremely faint neural signals, helping robots interface directly with the brain to control prosthetics or rehabilitation devices.

10.11.4 Industrial and Energy Sectors

- **Oil, Gas, and Mining Robots:**

Quantum gravimeters and magnetometers let robots map underground resources more accurately and safely than seismic methods.

- **Nuclear Facility Monitoring:**

Quantum radiation detectors and robotic systems inspect reactors, pipelines, or waste storage sites with ultra-high sensitivity to prevent leaks or accidents.

- **Quantum Manufacturing Robots:**

Integration of quantum algorithms for optimization in scheduling, resource allocation, and defect detection enhances smart factories.

10.11.5 Environmental Monitoring

- **Climate and Ecosystem Robotics:**

Quantum lidar and gravimetry allow robots to detect subtle changes in ice sheets, groundwater, and forest biomass.

- **Oceanography:**

Quantum robots can measure salinity, magnetic signatures, and ocean currents in deep sea environments. They can also detect hidden pollutants or undersea volcanic activity.

- **Disaster Response:**

Quantum-enhanced imaging robots can see through rubble (using quantum ghost imaging) to locate survivors during earthquakes or collapsed buildings.

10.11.6 Transportation and Autonomous Vehicles

- **Quantum Navigation Cars & Drones:**

Self-driving cars and aerial drones can navigate even without GPS, relying on quantum gyroscopes.

- **Traffic Optimization:**

Quantum algorithms applied in robotic traffic management systems optimize routing and reduce congestion in smart cities.

- **Maritime Robotics:**

Quantum compasses allow unmanned submarines to navigate stealthily in contested waters.

10.11.7 Artificial Intelligence & Quantum Machine Learning in Robotics

- **Quantum Reinforcement Learning (QRL):**

Robots can use quantum parallelism to learn policies and optimal strategies faster than classical reinforcement learning.

- **Pattern Recognition:**

Quantum-enhanced AI improves a robot's ability to recognize complex objects, signals, or threats.

- **Swarm Robotics:**

Quantum communication protocols synchronize multiple robots securely and efficiently, enabling collective tasks such as search-and-rescue or planetary exploration.

10.11.8 Cybersecurity and Quantum Communication in Robotics

- **Unhackable Robot Communication:**

Robots in defence or finance use quantum key distribution (QKD) to prevent interception of command-and-control signals.

- **Secure Multi-Robot Coordination:**

Swarms of drones or industrial robots share encrypted entanglement-based data to coordinate actions without external eavesdropping.

Quantum robots combine **quantum sensing** (ultra-precise measurement), **quantum computing** (optimization, AI, simulation), and **quantum communication** (secure data exchange) with classical robotic platforms. This makes them applicable to **defence, space exploration, medicine, industry, environment, transport, and AI-driven autonomy**—tasks where classical robots are limited by noise, uncertainty, or security vulnerabilities.

Chapter - 11
Secure Cloud Computing Using Quantum Cryptography

Cloud computing is in high demand both now and in the future, as evidenced by the fact that 65% of the world's largest businesses utilize it. Amazon, Twitter, and Google are all heavily focused on the cloud.

The most recent security breach occurred in 2014 when several account security passwords to Drop box records were exposed. Online hackers were able to launch numerous more consideration information launches in return for Bitcoin. 400 carefully considered security passwords and usernames were disclosed on the website Paste bin by hackers, who were evidently able to get weak logins and security passwords through a third-party service.

The article said that 6.9 thousand more material, including pictures and videos, had been obtained for Drop box consideration. Another report warns of fear as over 54,000 Twitter accounts are hacked by the Islamic Region's "cyber caliphate." Twitter and Drop Box are two services that are housed in cloud computing, where security issues are still being worked out. 4,5 does not include any additional standards for protecting and decrypting data. Instead, it's a method of quantum cryptography that creates a cryptographic key using photons and sends it to a receiver via the proper interaction channel. The most important tool in cryptography is a cryptographic key, which is used to safeguard and decode data.

Quantum cryptography and the cloud are the ideal combinations to create a secure cloud environment, whereas quantum mechanics relies on photons and physics to generate cryptographic keys.

11.1 Current Cloud Cryptography Technology

Traditional cryptography algorithms are used by current cloud technologies to encrypt data securely. Various algorithm types are employed based on various service providers. The algorithms that are most frequently utilized are

11.1.1 RSA

A cryptography standard with a community security key that differs from a secret decryption key ii) Conventional Information Encryption (DES) and Facilitates Conventional Information Encryption (S-DES), in which DES employed a symmetrical key for both security and decryption

11.1.2 128 Bit Secure Outlet Layer (SSL) Protection

It is a widely used technique that leverages community to manage the security of a communication transmitted over the Internet and a security mechanism with private keys. Nonetheless, there is a weakness in the conventional encryption scheme as hackers may duplicate both the public and private keys.

11.2 Quantum Cryptography

Encryption's Evolution

What if we could use a secret code to lock our diary? It works roughly like how our digital data is protected by encryption. Simple techniques like rearranging words or altering letters in a message were used in the past to keep secrets. Information encoding has grown more complex as technology has progressed. We therefore created various methods of encoding our data using intricate mathematics, making it more challenging to decipher the code. Consider a password that we use, for instance, to prevent unwanted access to the data on our computers or phones. It's also an encryption method! To put it simply, encryption is the act of transforming plain text, or our data, into cipher text, or a secret code, in order to protect it from unwanted access.

Synopsis of the encryption method

Encryption techniques were less complex in the past than they are now. Individuals used substitution ciphers, in which different symbols were used in place of letters. Julius Caesar invented the Caesar Cipher, which is an example of a message that is encoded by moving each letter in the message by a predetermined number of alphabetic positions. In terms of encryption technology, the Germans' Enigma machine during World War II established a new standard. Deciphering it was challenging because it changed the letter substitutes every day. Nevertheless, cryptography continued to advance and employ techniques such as frequency analysis. By examining the frequency of letters in the encrypted message, experts were able to decode substitution ciphers. Patterns could be discovered and the original message could be deduced through methodical analysis. This aids in the substitution cipher's decryption. The sophistication of encryption systems increased along with the advancement of computers. Symmetric and asymmetric encryption are the two types of encryption used by modern computers.

There is nothing new about quantum cryptography as a means of securing and decrypting data. Instead of employing a statistical method, this technique uses photons to generate a cryptographic key, then give it back to the receiver choosing a suitable relationship-building route. An encryption Key functions to a larger extent in cryptography; they are employed in information that is encrypted or guarded. Two categories of cryptography exist.

1. Symmetric and
2. Asymmetric Cryptography

11.2.1 Symmetric Cryptography

Cryptography that protects plaintext using symmetric-key methods and decrypts cipher text using the same cryptographic key components. The two essential components could be the same or they might require a small modification to transition between them. In work out, the key elements stand in for a key that is assigned between two or more activities and may be utilized to create a unique information weblink. Compared to public-key protection, the main disadvantage of shaped key protection is the requirement that all parties have access to the key.

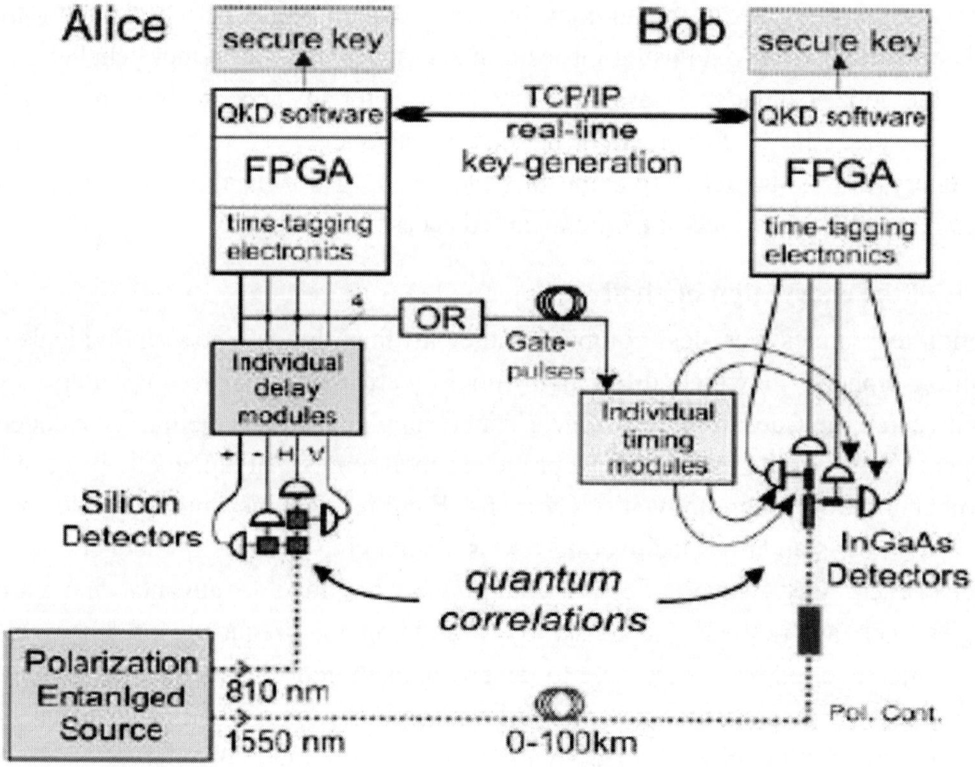

Fig.11.1 Quantum mechanics in communication cryptography.

Symmetric-key protection can circumvent ciphers or employ circulation ciphers. i) Flow ciphers safeguarded an idea's figures one at a time, usually in the form of bytes. ii) Avoid using ciphers take a variety of objects and safeguard them individually, ensuring that the plaintext is supported to prevent multiple sizing issues. 64-item stops have often been utilized. 128-bit prevents are used in the Impressive Security Traditional (AES) standards, which were authorized by NIST in December 2001.

11.2.2 Asymmetric Cryptography

Asymmetric cryptography, often known as public-key cryptography, is a type of encryption where an email is secured and decrypted using several key parts to ensure its security. A system client first receives a group and key several from accreditation power. From a group record, any other client that wishes to contribute a securely developed idea can obtain the developed recipient's group key.

They give the recipient this key, which they employ to safeguard the concept. Once the recipient understands, they decode it using a unique key that they shouldn't share with anybody else.

11.2.3 Mechanism of Quantum Cryptography

In quantum cryptography, any future information that has to be conveyed may be decrypted using a key that the source gives to the recipient. After the key has been successfully provided and received, the recipient must be given appropriately protected information, which it must then decode and process. The primary component of cryptography is the key, which needs to be sent in a very safe manner. The method used by huge cryptography 1,2,3 to give the recipient the key is distinct. Photons are used to offer a key in it.

11.2.3.1 How does Proton being utilized?

The smallest known particle of light is a photon. There are three different kinds of spins on it: horizontal, vertical, and diagonal (left and right).

A photon may simultaneously rotate in all three directions. A photon can be polarized (passed through a filter) to give it a certain movement, such as tilting, side to side movement, or direct movement. Polarization purification is the process used to polarize a photon.

Heisenberg's Doubt Concept claims that a substance's situation will change when assessed and that it does not appear to be feasible to assess a substance's velocity and location together with the utmost possible perfection. In other words, if an eavesdropper catches downfall photons and passes them through its polarizer, the receiver will get a different photon if the protocol is incorrect. Thus, the connections that are being intercepted will be recognized.

11.2.3.2 How to use photons to communicate information

An essential issue prior to utilizing big cryptography is the method of online detail retrieval using photons. It is simple to settle this issue by allowing each photon to travel as either 0 or 13. The paragraph that follows will describe how to use photons to communicate details:

Spin	Horizontal Spin (–)	Vertical Spin (|)	Left Diagonal Spin (\)	Right Diagonal Spin(/)

Therefore, data that is appropriately encrypted may be sent and decrypted upon receipt.

Value	0	1	0	1

Consider Alice applies polarizations to photons, observes their rotation, and records it. There is a value attached to each rotation.

Polarization	x	x	+	+	x	+	+	+	+	+	x	+	+	x	x	x
Spin	\	/	-	|	/	-	-	|	|	-	/	-	|	\	/	/
Value	0	1	0	1	1	0	0	1	1	0	1	0	1	0	1	1

Alice uses four different types of sensors—horizontal, straight, right-tilted, and diagonal—to detect the movement of photons following polarization.

The secret to binary structure now is: 0101100110101011

Depending on which consumers are chosen to participate in the conversation, this binary data can take on additional forms such as sequence and integer. Since Alice is likely interested in an integer structure, the key will be:

Binary Data	0101100110101011
Integer Data	22955

11.3 Predicated on the Uncertainty Principle of Heisenberg

BB84 and its variations: A polarizer is used to pass a single photon pulse through. Alice is able to polarize a single-photon pulse using a certain polarizer and encode binary value bits to the result of a specific polarizer type (vertical, horizontal, circular, etc.). Bob would predict the polarizer upon receiving the photon beam. By matching the examples with Alice, Bob is able to determine whether or not his guesses were accurate. If Eve had been attempting to decipher, her polarizer would have created differences in Bob and Alice's match instances, letting them know that they were being eavesdropped on. Therefore, with such a setup, Alice and Bob will be alerted if Eve tries to listen in.

- Unlike the four polarization states in the original BB84, the B92 protocol has just two.
- A comparable technique, SSP, is used by BB84, which encodes its bits using six states.
- Another technique that makes use of attenuated lasers is SARG04, which outperforms BB84 in multiple photon systems.

11.4 Stemming from Quantum Entanglement

E91 and Variants: Two entangled photons are emitted by a single source, and each particle is received by Alice and Bob. For every photon sent, Alice and Bob would trade encoded bits and match cases, much like in the BB84 system. However, because of the Entanglement principle, the results of Alice and Bob's match instances will in this case be the reverse. The complement bits in bit strings will be interpreted for any of them. After that, one of them can flip pieces to decide on a key.

This test can validate the lack of eavesdroppers since entangled particles should not satisfy Bell's inequality. This system is completely safe since it is nearly impossible to have a third photon in entanglement with energy levels high enough to be undetectable.

Entangled particles theory may be extended to SARG04 and SSP protocol models.

11.5 Potential Points of Attack for Quantum Cryptography

Photon Number Splitting (PNS) Attack: A pulse is delivered instead of a single photon since it is not possible to send a single photon. Eve has the ability to catch some of the photons from a pulse. Once Alice and Bob have matched the bits, Eve may utilize Bob's polarizer to obtain the key covertly.

Faked-State Attack: Eve uses a copy of Bob's photon detector to intercept and pass on the photons that were meant for Bob. Bob believes he got the encoded bit from Alice, even though Eve is aware of it.

11.6 How Operates in Quantum Cryptography?

The fundamental idea behind quantum cryptography is the phenomenon known as quantum entanglement, in which two particles are coupled enough that their states are affected by one another even when they are separated by a great distance. In quantum cryptography, a secure communication channel is established between Alice and Bob using a pair of entangled particles.

The following steps are involved in the process:

- Bob receives a stream of photons, or light particles, from Alice.
- Bob takes a random sample of photons and measures the direction of oscillation, or polarization.
- Bob uses a traditional communication connection to send Alice the results of his measurements.
- Bob and Alice compare a portion of their measures in order to identify any listening in.
- They encrypt their message using the remaining photons if they detect no eavesdropping.
- Next, the message is encoded and transmitted using a traditional communication channel.

11.7 Interception of Connections

The client must arbitrary add polarization to the photons supplied when he is intercepting the connections between the emailer and the recipient. The client will forward it to the first emailer after polarization. It's challenging for the eavesdropper to efficiently consider all polarizations, though.

Thus, connection interception will be detected when Bob and Alice confirm the polarizations and Bob is unable to decipher the specifics.

11.8 Combining Quantum Cryptography with the Cloud

Users embrace cloud computing because it offers cost-effectiveness, availability, and development flexibility. Because it may be accessed from anywhere, security is a major concern, and most current methods fall short of providing adequate precautions.

Table 11.1 Output spin for polarization in execution.

Polarization	Output Spin	
Rectilinear Polarization (+)	Horizontal Spin (–)	Vertical Spin (|)
Diagonal	Left Diagonal Spin (\)	Right Diagonal Spin (/)

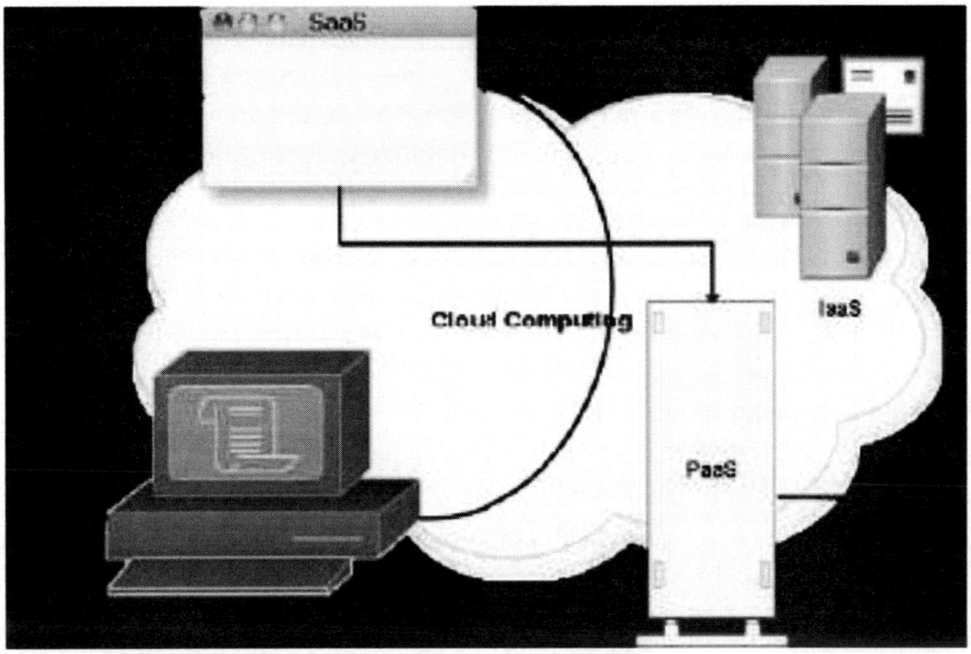

Fig.11.2 Cloud Computing: Cryptography as a Service (CaaS).

Protons are used in quantum cryptography to create encryption keys that are nearly hard for hackers to crack. This would support the buyers' belief that technological advancement will take millions of years to manifest. Furthermore, the quantum thinking pair security would provide exceptional management capabilities with you of many things. This implies that consumers will be able to use the internet to use the incredibly quick and secure technology of thought management from any location.

Such technology would pave the way for subsequent advancements in management that would provide easier, more secure management and maybe spark a revolution in the mobile phone industry.

11.9 Applications of Quantum Cryptography

Quantum cryptography offers a safe communication route that is impervious to cyberattacks, which has the potential to completely transform the way humans communicate.

The following are a few uses for quantum cryptography:

Financial transactions: By offering a secure communication channel, quantum cryptography helps prevent thieves from intercepting and stealing confidential financial data. Forecasting the market to increase profits is a key component of finance! Currently, there are several algorithms that predict future market patterns using a variety of probabilities and assumptions. In this case, quantum computers can be of great assistance as they can remove blind spots and data mistakes that result in inaccurate financial projections and, consequently, financial loss!

Government and military communication: Sensitive information may be safely sent using quantum cryptography by government and military organizations without having to worry about it being intercepted.

Healthcare: Patient data and medical research may be secured with the use of quantum cryptography.

Do you want a medication customized for your particular genome and DNA structure?

Quantum computing may be able to help with this. It is quite challenging to study an organism's whole DNA with classical computing since it takes a lot of processing power and storage capacity. Quantum computing, on the other hand, would greatly simplify this procedure and enable us to both heal numerous genetic illnesses and get a greater understanding of individual DNA.

Internet of Things (IoT): Because IoT devices have minimal processing power and are therefore susceptible to cyberattacks, quantum cryptography can be employed to safeguard their communication channels.

Cyber Security: Are you aware that the cryptographic protocols protecting our private messages and sensitive data might be cracked by using the incredibly fast speed of quantum computers? However, employing quantum encryption, quantum computers might also be used to safeguard data from hackers. In order to safeguard the data, photons are sent across great distances while utilizing the Entanglement Principle.

Agriculture: The use of fertilizers is crucial to agricultural success! And ammonia is the main ingredient in them. However, did you know that we still produce ammonia using a method that dates back to the early 1900s and calls for high heat and pressure? Furthermore, there are millions of different catalyst combinations to explore; no new method for producing ammonia has been found. On a quantum computer, this issue can be solved quickly and simply, but it can take a long time on a classical computer.

Artificial Intelligence: Quantum computing has the potential to make artificial intelligence—which is already fascinating—virtually infinitely varied. Quantum computers may be able to develop sophisticated algorithms that map out the billions of neurons in the human brain, making significant contributions to the study of neural networks. Additionally, quantum computing and machine learning might be used to build highly networked Internet of Things devices with incredibly complex cybersecurity rules.

11.10 Difficulties with Quantum Cryptography

Despite being a promising technology, quantum cryptography is not without its difficulties. Among the difficulties are:

Cost: Large-scale implementation of quantum cryptography is challenging due to its high cost and need for specialized infrastructure and equipment.

Limitations on distance: The attenuation of photons during transmission, which may have an impact on the communication channel's quality, sets a limit on the distance between the two parties.

Real-world use: Quantum cryptography is still in its infancy as a practical application, and further study and development are required to make it more scalable and useful.

11.11 Classical and Quantum Cryptography Distinctions

Classical Cryptography: This mathematically based method depends on the computational challenge of factorizing big numbers. The enormous mathematical difficulty of the instance factorization of huge numbers is the foundation for the security of traditional cryptography.

Quantum Cryptography: The principles of quantum mechanics are the foundation of quantum cryptography, which is a branch of science. A new technology is emerging that highlights the phenomenon of quantum physics, which allows for safe communication between two parties thanks to the invariance of quantum mechanical principles.

Table 11.2 Distinctions between Classical and Quantum Cryptography.

Classical Cryptography	Quantum Cryptography
Its foundation is mathematical calculation.	Quantum mechanics serves as its foundation.
Many people utilize it.	It's advanced.
Presence of Digital Signature	Digital signature is absent
Bit rate is influenced by processing power.	1 MBPS is the average bit rate.
2n n-bit strings for bit storage.	One n-bit string is stored in a bit.
The range of communication is millions of miles.	The maximum communication range is ten miles.
Tested and deployed.	Not thoroughly tested in the early phases.
Upgrades are necessary when processing power rises.	The rules of physics form its foundation.
Irrespective of the communication channel.	Depending on the communication channel.
Less Expenditure	More Expenditure

Post-quantum Cryptography

Classical cryptography has evolved into PQC. PQC is built on mathematical problems, just as traditional cryptography. PQC, on the other hand, applies the intractability feature of conventional cryptography to quantum computers. PQC uses even more challenging mathematical problems—problems that are thought to be intractable even for quantum machines—to accomplish this.

One intriguing advantage of both classical and post-quantum systems' reliance on mathematical problems is that PQC answers are simple to create in code and distribute to any device through software updates.

Although symmetric systems are also being developed, post-quantum cryptography technologies are mostly asymmetric (public-key). Since symmetric cryptography is thought to be impervious to quantum computers, at least for the foreseeable future, PQC systems often have an asymmetric design.

The private key and the public key in asymmetric cryptography are mathematically connected. This implies that hackers might extract the private key from the public key—which is accessible to everyone—if they had sufficient processing power. Classical computers cannot accomplish this, but quantum machines will make it extremely simple.

Your public key could be used by hackers to gain access to your company network. Since symmetric methods assume that the encryption/decryption key is never made public, they are immune to this flaw. Because of this, the majority of PQC algorithms are now asymmetric or public-key.

11.12 Benefits

Unconditional security: An eavesdropper cannot intercept or duplicate data being transmitted without being discovered thanks to quantum cryptography, which offers unconditional security.

Key distribution: A safe method of key distribution is possible with quantum cryptography and is a fundamental element of many encryption techniques.

Speed: Secure communication at very high rates can be achieved with quantum cryptography, which is crucial for applications that need to transport data in real time.

Long-term security: Data encrypted with quantum cryptography will continue to be safe since it is impervious to assaults by upcoming quantum computers.

Security verification: Quantum cryptography detects any effort to intercept or alter data, giving a means of confirming the communication's security.

11.13 Drawbacks

Cost: Because quantum cryptography requires specialized hardware and software, implementation can be costly.

Distance restrictions: Because of the nature of quantum entanglement, quantum cryptography is currently only applicable to short-range communication.

Complexity: The implementation and upkeep of quantum cryptography calls for certain knowledge and abilities due to its complexity.

Limitations on key distribution: One possible flaw in quantum cryptography is the requirement for a reliable third party to deliver the cryptographic keys.

Side-channel attack susceptibility: Quantum cryptography is susceptible to side-channel attacks, which include assaults on the system's implementation software or hardware.

Chapter - 12

Quantum Computing in Big Data Analytics

Data intrusion at all levels is celebrated in our society. We prefer data that is generated and absorbed. If we want to handle data efficiently, we also need order. Big data was therefore intended to manage and make data appear meaningful. The amount of data generated is substantial. Without creating placeholders, we wouldn't be able to manage this volume of data. Improved data encoding is necessary for placeholders to function. Level-adept handlers are necessary for encoders to proceed. This is where quantum computing comes in. It provides massive data managers and simplifies big data. We can achieve data sufficiency in our environment when quantum coding is used appropriately.

Data is created more quickly in the modern world. Every day, producing exabytes of data. It indicates that producing data based on the 90-minute movie running time. New theories are required to deal with this enormous volume of data. Big data presents many difficulties. It is so enormous that neither classical physics nor conventional computers can adequately describe it. To get the correct result, we need a new solution. The quantum computer then enters the picture. According to Moor's law, the speed of a microprocessor should double every 18 years. Quantum computing is the answer to justify the volume of data being generated and to provide Moore's law an advantage.

Larger-scale problem solving requires speed. The amount and complexity of datasets are growing as a result of our need for answers to every challenge at a much faster rate. Quantum computing is required in order to handle massive data sets. The way we view data has been altered by big data. The same is being done via quantum computing. The simplest method to view the data is to arrange it so that the outcome is obtained in a split second. Every day, millions of data are generated as a result of consumers interacting with computers. Therefore, that data needs to be well organized. Transistors were the only means of producing data in the past, but quantum manufacturing has changed how data appears today. We mean paradox by entanglement.

There is a dilemma associated with every feature of a quantum particle. There will also be a correlated reverse feature if one particle has a spin. Another crucial factor is the wave particle's dual use. The Heisenberg theory of nature's duality also enters the scene. Both can coexist at the quantum level. The existence of n-bit variables is hinted at by the qubit, the fundamental data particle. These days, Toshiba and ID Quntique use quantum computing. This is the next level of data sophistication following transistor miniaturization. Heisenberg's theory is explained by a bridge that connects quantum computing and classical theory by producing electron spin.

The battle for data dominance rages on. Organizations strive to enhance their data management capabilities continuously. Beyond just managing data, we must also invest in modern technologies to achieve our strategic objectives. While the notion of data as a valuable resource is appealing, in reality, we perceive data pools as resources, assets, or indicators of impending change. We must leverage skilled data handlers as a symbol of technological advancement. Improved data handlers are required, both at the quantum level and the macro level.

12.1 Overview of Big Data

Our world is fed by data. The industry generates thousands of data points for analysis. Data becomes outdated if we don't analyze it. It turns into dark data. There is no use for dark data. Data is what needs to be processed. Proper analysis of data depends on the needs and trends of the future. Big data is a new area of computing that involves analyzing vast amounts of data in order to make money. Data processing is how we get analysis done. We think of petabytes and terabytes when we discuss huge data. Data analysis is an extremely difficult undertaking due to the vast amount of data. Since every piece of data informs us something about its successor, we are powerless to stop data waste.

Additionally, all data points to consumer behaviour. Without analyzing consumer behaviour, we will be unable to take advantage of opportunities. Therefore, it becomes essential for the business to analyze big data in order to have a competitive edge over rivals. There are three sources of big data. The first is the data that the user has created. He creates what is known as user-related data when he logs on to the system. Second, data is also generated when he uses internet of things devices, such as mobile phones and utility devices. Data generated by web interaction is referred to as "internet of things data." The data that has been aggregated by outside resources comes in third. Because it reflects consumers' thinking, such data is also very important.

We consider data to be a tool for forecasting client net usage when discussing positioning competitive advantage. Value velocity, truthfulness, diversity, and volume are some of the parameters that make up data. All of these indicate data tampering. While value refers to data as money, velocity is a concept used to assess the rate of data growth. Data distinction can be inferred from veracity. Volume helps us comprehend the overwhelming amount of data. It is impossible to interpret data by itself. Data needs to stored and should be manipulated by algorithms for data to be useful for public. We also need four factors for that to occur. They are segmentation, accuracy, reliability, and authenticity. By segmenting the data into classes and employing a single variable, a regressive value may be obtained. Regression is the process of identifying complex class behavior by focusing on a single variable. Next, we must verify the class validity or dependencies.

Data must be authentic if it is arranged in a class. Authenticity and dependability provide a competitive advantage. We also employ algorithms to manipulate data. We employ fundamental techniques such as cluster approaches and regression. Large businesses use rather sophisticated data mining tools. One of the big businesses that began utilizing data mining was Walmart. The American purchasing trend was halted when the hurricane hit the country. They discovered that one product was preferred above others. Walmart then began selling those products, and when the next hurricane hit, it made a huge profit. Data mining and manipulation are carried out in this manner, which eventually becomes beneficial. The field of quantum computing is extremely competitive. The fact that it can handle petabytes of data in a matter of seconds suggests its value as a computing device. As we progress, we will eventually live in a society that depends on data to make decisions.

We must realize that without competent analysis, data cannot make much of a difference. The reality of today is complex computing outcomes. Massive amounts of data are produced when we report on the weather, deal with stocks, or discuss the electrical system. Big data is that. This is where quantum computing comes in handy. Conventional computers cannot provide a comprehensive understanding of the true meaning of diverse data. Quantum computing is essential to modern computing. It must use algorithms designed for discrete computing to make data monetized. Discrete mathematics is essential to quantum computing. Qubits are the fundamental building block of data storage in quantum computing.

The n-bit qubit variable is obtained by superimposing the states, which results in a compounded state set. Since quantum computing derives its state from the curvature of photons, it is a rapidly expanding subset of current computing. Big data issues can be resolved by quantum computing. In nanoseconds, we can achieve faster outcomes, and quantum computing excels in situations where time is a variable. In the commercial world, every bit of information matters. Quantum computing provides a comprehensive understanding of the capabilities of data. Qisbit is one open source program that can handle quantum computing. Since the field is expanding, many researchers are encouraged to obtain a reliable data report.

12.2 Characteristics of Big Data

In recent years, large amounts of big data have been accumulated across various domains, including healthcare, public administration, retail, biochemistry, and other interdisciplinary scientific research fields.

According to the Gartner definition, the key characteristics of big data are its high volume, high velocity, and high variety, which require new handling approaches to enable better decision-making, knowledge discovery, and process optimization. These "three Vs" - volume, velocity, and variety - are considered the fundamental traits of big data. However, various organizations and institutes have proposed alternative definitions.

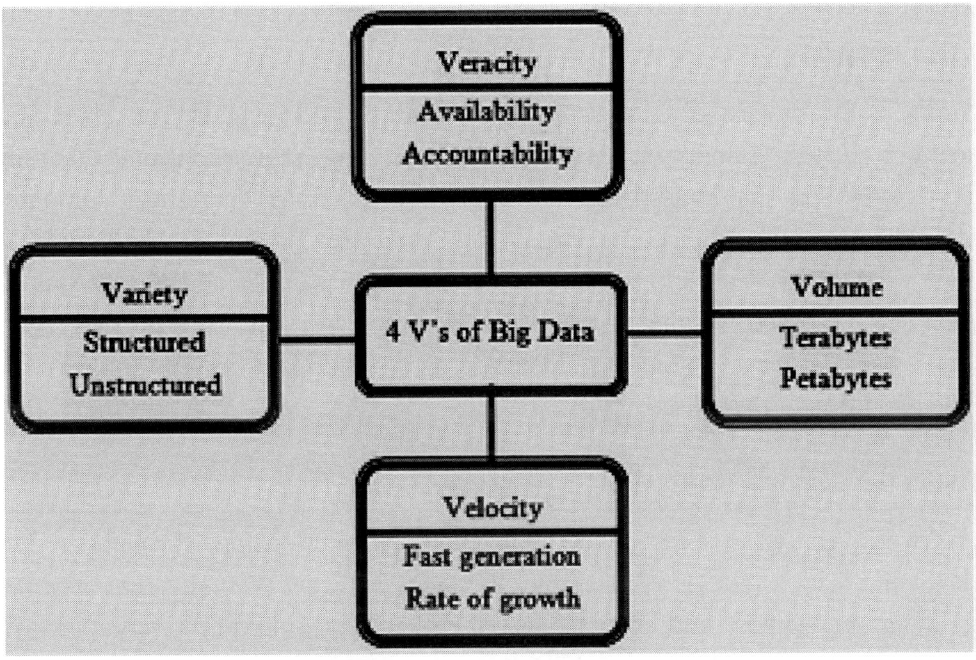

Fig.12.1 4 V's of Big Data.

12.3 Supporting Techniques and Tools

Big Data Analytics encompasses a wide range of techniques, including data mining, statistics, neural networks, machine learning, social network analysis, pattern recognition, signal processing, optimization methods, and visualization approaches. This summary provides an overview of these key analytical methods.

12.3.1 Statistics

Techniques are used to collect, organize, and interpret data. An efficient approximate algorithm has been proposed for large-scale multivariate monotonic regression, which exploits the causal relationships and correlations among distinct objectives. This approach estimates functions that are monotonic with respect to input variables. Another trend in data-driven statistical analysis focuses on scaling and parallel implementation of statistical algorithms. Statistics generates numerical descriptions of data. Statistical learning and statistical computing are two active research subfields.

12.3.2 Optimization Techniques

Optimization methods are commonly applied to solve quantitative problems. Much research focuses on scaling up large-scale optimization through co-evolutionary algorithms. Additionally, real-time optimization is crucial for various big data applications.

12.3.3 Data Mining

Data mining is the process of extracting useful patterns and insights from data, such as classification, clustering analysis, association rule mining, regression, and discriminant analysis. It involves methods from statistics and machine learning. Compared to conventional data mining algorithms, Big Data mining presents unique challenges. Many extensions of traditional algorithms rely on analyzing a sample of the Big Data, then using the sample-based results to derive a partition for the overall data. Genetic algorithms have also been applied to clustering as an optimization criterion, in order to reflect the goodness of the clustering results.

12.3.4 Social Network Analysis

Social Network Analysis (SNA) conceptualizes social relationships through the lens of network theory, which models connections as nodes and ties. Visualization approaches, such as diagrams, tables, and images, are then employed to intuitively display and facilitate understanding of the data.

12.3.5 Artificial Neural Networks

Artificial Neural Networks (ANNs) are a mature and versatile technique, with successful applications spanning pattern recognition, image analysis, adaptive control, and various other domains. The majority of contemporary ANNs employed in artificial intelligence leverage statistical estimation, classification optimization, and control theory principles.

12.3 6 Deep Learning

Powered by neural networking, Deep Learning shows immense potential for solving complex business problems. It can efficiently recognize relevant insights from massive amounts of unstructured and binary data, and deduce meaningful relationships without relying on predefined models or programming instructions.

12.3.7 Visualization

Visualization approaches employ tables, images, diagrams, and other intuitive displays to help understand data. For large-scale data visualization, many researchers first use feature extraction and geometric modeling techniques to significantly reduce the data size before rendering the visualizations.

12.3.8 Column-Oriented Databases

To handle the unstructured nature of big data, column-oriented databases have been introduced. These databases enable significant data compression and very fast query times. However, the trade-off is that they typically only support batch updates, resulting in much slower update speeds compared to traditional database models.

12.3.9 Schema-Less Databases or NoSQL Databases

NoSQL database systems offer key-value storage, with a focus on highly scalable and high-performance data storage. They provide low-level access mechanisms, making them highly flexible for data modeling. Additionally, NoSQL databases enable easy updates to application development and deployment.

12.3. 10 Tools

The major categories of Big Data tools can be classified as

1. Batch processing tools,
2. Stream processing tools, and
3. Interactive analysis tools.

Several batch processing tools are available, including Apache Hadoop, MapReduce, Dryad, Karmasphere Studio and Analyst, Jaspersoft BI, Skytree Server, Pentaho Business Analytics, Apache Mahout, Tableau, and Talend Open Studio. Prominent stream processing platforms include Storm, S4, SQLstream, Splunk, Apache Kafka, and SAP Hana. Interactive analysis tools, such as Google's Dremel, Hive, PIG, Wibidata, and PLATFORA, are also available through open-source channels.

The table below outlines the specific uses and advantages of various tools.

Table 12.1 Batch Processing.

Tool Name	*Specified Use*	*Advantage*
Apache Hadoop	Infrastructure and platform	High scalability, reliability, completeness
Drad	Infrastructure and platform	High performance distributed execution engine, good programmability
Apache Mahout	Machine learning algorithms in business	Good maturity
Jaspersoft BI Suite	Business intelligence software	Cost-effective, self-service BI at scale
Pentaho Business Analytics	Business analytics platform	Roboustness, scalability, flexibility in knowledge discovery
Skytree Server	Machine learning and advanced analytics	Process massive datasets accurately at high speed
Tableau	Data Visualization, Business analytics	Faster, smart, fit, beautiful and ease of use dashboards
Karmasphere studio and analyst	Big data workspace	Collaborative and standards-based unconstrained analytics and self service
Talend open studio	Data management and application integration	Easy –to-use,edipse-based graphical environment

Table 12.2 Streaming data processing tools leverage real-time analytics to provide immediate insights.

Tool Name	*Specified Use*	*Advantage*
Storm	Realtime computation system	Scalable, fault-tolerant, and is easy to set up and operate
S4	Processing continuous unbounded streams of Data	Proven, distributed, scalable, fault-tolerant, pluggable platform
SQLstream s-Server	Sensor, M2M, and telematics applications	SQL-based, real-time streaming Big Data platform
Splunk	Collect and harness machine data	Fast and easy to use, dynamic environments, scales from laptop to Data center
Apache Kafka	Distributed publish-subscribe messaging system	High-throughput stream of immutable activity data
SAP Hana	Platform for real-time business	Fast in-memory computing and real time analytic

12.4 Algorithms

Data is processed using algorithms. To make the data appear familiar to us, we employ a random method. We employ algorithms to make work that is derived from data appear believable. Massive data levels are related to big data. Big data generates so much data that it takes the best possible use of algorithms to extract any useful information from it. In order to make sense of diverse data, regression is used. Finding a relationship between two sets of independent and dependent variables is what we usually mean when we talk about regression. The problem set determines whether the two data sets are finite or infinite.

The mathematical function that establishes a relationship between the two is what decides how the two data variables can vary or how a change in one set of variables will affect the other. The regression technique is best suited for prediction and forecasting. When we discuss regression, we often imply a parameterized function and the observational data that goes along with it. The relationship between casualty and effect is discussed more frequently.

Regression points are displayed in the model

There are two categories of regression procedures. There are two types of regression: logistic regression and linear regression. Both are different in two ways. The observational data set and the way a function reacts to a change in variable are used to establish the difference. Whereas logistic data requires limited sets of data, linear regression works with infinite data. While logistic regression is commonly employed in big data analytics, linear regression is used in business models rather regularly. The variables used in linear regression are a set of scalar variables.

As the name implies, while creating a relationship or examining the linear cause and effect between two sets of data, we must deal with a linear model. Linear regression provides a scalar point of view, while logistic regression provides regression analysis that is more of continuous variability. When an error reduction is necessary, linear regression is also employed. Linear regression is used when we continuously rectify and obtain a pattern, which is a fairly basic perspective of data relations. In a similar vein, logistic regression must address a higher level. In this model, we use either a binomial or multinomial relationship. David Cox was the one who created it.

A typical linear regression function is displayed in the function above. The sigma provides the total of mistakes while representing regressive coefficients. x1 and x2 provide the coefficients, as do additional independent variables. A clear picture is provided by the graphical examination of both regression models. Logistic regression creates a sigmoid graph, whereas linear regression yields a straight line on the y variable. In more models, the graph quality varies.

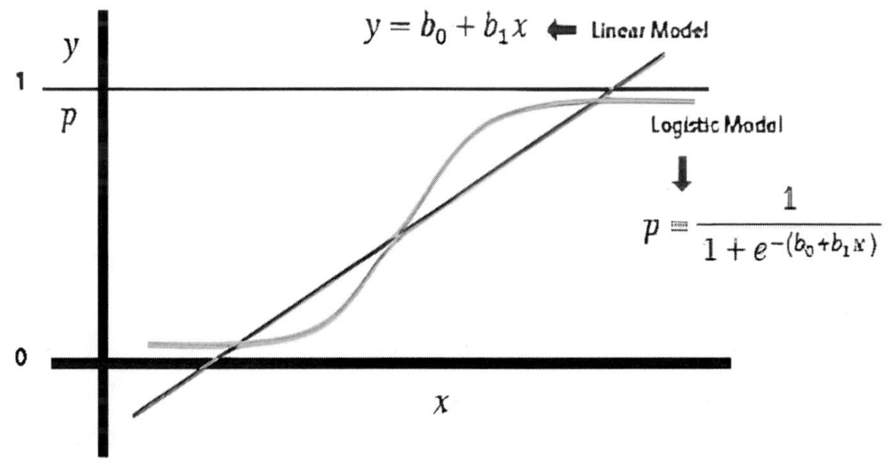

Fig.12.2 Big data analytics algorithms include the following: K-means techniques for clustering.

As the name implies, clustering algorithms use data clustering. In order to create veronoi cells, the data clusters are arranged so that each cluster displays a single variable that must be mapped to another variable and its closest mean distance determined. The creation of cells that function on a distance basis from the mean principle is referred to as veronoi cells. Weather forecasting and machine learning both make use of it. Vector quantization is one of the most intriguing features. Segmentation should be taken into consideration while utilizing the K clustering algorithm. As stated, we have distinct segments according to variable k.

The variable k determines the closer samples in which we generate the colour palette. Other useful applications, like as computer graphics and image segmentation, further support the idea that the k clustering algorithm is a reliable method of separating data into clusters. Clustering relies on the difficult-to-find variable k. Additionally, this approach is employed in both supervised and unsupervised learning, where learning requires revisiting each data cluster. The cluster algorithm is defined by the variable k and Euclidean distance. In Euclidean space, the Euclidian distance is a type of straight distance between two locations. It is one of the metrics for segregation using k clustering.

Algorithm for association rule mining

An effective method for evaluating qualities based on relationships with data similarity in a data structure is the association rule mining algorithm. Data is mapped in a way that yields insights and meaning that support industry. The association rule mining algorithm is used to gain a deep knowledge of data, particularly in business contexts. We create a rule between two sets of data groups in this algorithm. In professional settings, this works. When discussing relationships, we look for intriguing interpretations of the provided data. It helps in forecasting and it also helps in bioinformatics and data mining. It can also be used in other sectors. Here, we search for relationships, and if one is found, a certain level of confidence is produced. Let's go to the degree of conviction if this confidence is higher. Finding a relationship is support, and obtaining a good probability is conviction. Thus, the four ideas of lift rules, confidence, conviction, and support. A degree of confidence is given by the minimal support between datasets. For example, we may use a probability function to imply that a man is likely to buy cheese and hamburgers if we state he is certain to buy potatoes and tomatoes from the store. Here, supporting the argument with a probability function.

Vector machine support

A unique method of data segregation based on hyperplane is the support vector machine. The data is separated into its distance measured from the mean by a superficial hyperplane. There is a superficial hyperplane that separates two data sets. The data will be separated by the hyperplane. For supervised learning, support vector machines are used. It is a frequently used algorithm in machine learning. Continuous data categorization is necessary for machine learning. We can determine how a piece of data must be used by deriving a (p-1) set of hyperplanes from a set of points.

The segregation of a pair of data sets is determined by the kernel function. This support vector approach is frequently used in handwriting analysis and character imaging. Its potential is being used to identify images. We have the idea of a soft margin classifier because it is nearly impossible to separate large amounts of data virtually. This is a straightforward method of grouping data according to how far away they are from the kernel function's k variable. The line that assesses the effectiveness of data separation is known as the maximum margin classifier.

12.5 Quantum computing's emergence in big data analytics.

A revolutionary age in data processing and analysis has begun with the introduction of quantum computing to the field of big data analytics. This integration promises previously unheard-of computational power and efficiency, and it is not just a small step forward but a paradigm change. The increasing complexity and volume of data in this field is driving the emergence of quantum computing, which calls for more potent and advanced analytical tools.

Characterized by concepts like entanglement and superposition, quantum computing presents a fresh method of data processing that is essentially distinct from classical computing. In contrast to conventional binary computing, quantum computing makes use of qubits, which have the ability to exist in several states at once and provide exponential processing power development. Big data, which includes enormous and varied datasets that are frequently outside the purview of traditional computing techniques, benefits greatly from this quantum advantage.

Quantum computing's incorporation into big data analytics is not merely a theoretical idea; it is becoming more and more real in real-world applications. For example, complicated data analysis tasks that were previously thought to be unfeasible are now being addressed by quantum algorithms. These include tasks involving machine learning, pattern recognition, and optimization where quantum computing may be able to provide answers more quickly and effectively than traditional techniques.

A major advancement that ushers in a new age in data processing and analysis is the introduction of quantum computing into big data analytics. In the era of big data, its capacity to effectively manage intricate and huge datasets makes it a priceless instrument. As quantum computing develops further, it has the potential to completely transform big data analytics by providing fresh opportunities and answers to challenging analytical problems.

A revolutionary new frontier in data processing and analysis is represented by quantum-accelerated big data analytics on cloud platforms. We can overcome the drawbacks of classical computing and open up new avenues for deriving insightful information from enormous and intricate datasets by utilizing the special powers of quantum computing, such as parallel computation, quantum algorithms, and quantum phenomena like superposition and entanglement. Despite the fact that quantum computing is still in its early stages, the quick development of quantum hardware and software, as well as the growing accessibility of quantum computing resources on cloud platforms, open the door to the possibility of quantum-accelerated big data analytics in the future. However, scalability, algorithm development, data encoding, interaction with current frameworks, and security and privacy issues are just a few of the major obstacles that must be overcome in order to fully realize the potential of quantum-accelerated big data analytics.

To further this discipline, scholars, data scientists, industry professionals, and cloud service providers must collaborate and conduct ongoing study. We can speed the development and use of quantum-accelerated big data analytics by promoting interdisciplinary collaborations and utilizing cloud computing's capabilities. This will open up new avenues for scientific discoveries, technical improvements, and data-driven decision-making.

12.6 The Effect of Quantum Computing on Data Analysis

A major change in data analysis capabilities is signalled by the incorporation of quantum computing into big data analytics, which has substantial ramifications for numerous industries. Large dataset handling, analysis, and interpretation are about to undergo a radical change thanks to quantum computing's special processing capabilities. The ability of quantum computing to process and analyze data at scales and rates that are not possible with traditional computing techniques is the main factor influencing big data analytics. By using quantum algorithms that can evaluate many data sets at once, quantum computing makes it possible to quickly collect and analyze enormous volumes of data. This skill is especially important in a time when the volume and complexity of data are increasing at an exponential rate, surpassing the capacity of conventional computing technology.

Quantum computing has more possibilities than just speed and economy. Big data analytics in many different industrial areas could be completely transformed by quantum computing, whose sophisticated algorithms and tools can offer fresh perspectives and answers to challenging issues that were previously unsolvable. This revolutionary influence extends beyond particular sectors and encompasses a wide range of fields, including healthcare and finance, providing a universal set of tools for innovation and data-driven decision-making.

For example, the impact of quantum computing is especially noticeable in the healthcare industry. Quantum computing's use in predictive modeling and spine care shows how it can handle the challenges of big data and artificial intelligence in this area. Quantum computing allows for more accurate and effective analysis by reducing the space and time dimensions in computational processes, opening the door to better patient care and results. The potential of quantum computing to improve data security is another factor that makes it significant for big data analytics. Incorporating quantum algorithms into data security procedures can offer stronger defense against online attacks, which is becoming a more crucial factor in the digital world. This is a crucial component of quantum computing.

Additionally, new study avenues are made possible by the investigation of quantum computing in big data analytics. The limits of data analysis will continue to be pushed by the continuous advancement of quantum computing equipment, software, and algorithms.

Realizing the full potential of quantum computing in big data analytics depends on this continuing research, which also makes sure that the technology advances to satisfy the ever rising needs of data-driven enterprises.

The impact of quantum computing on data processing is extensive and has many different facets. Its disruptive potential is highlighted by its capacity to handle enormous datasets quickly, offer fresh perspectives on challenging issues, improve data security, and spur innovation in a variety of industries. The field of data analysis and decision-making is about to undergo a transformation as quantum computing advances and becomes an essential tool in the big data analytics toolbox.

12.7 Historical Development: Quantum Paradigms to Classical Data Processing.

A major advancement in big data analytics may be seen in the historical progression of data processing from classical computing paradigms to quantum computing. This change represents a departure from conventional approaches, which frequently find it difficult to handle the enormous volume and complexity of big data, to more sophisticated quantum computing strategies that offer exponential gains in processing efficiency and speed.

The constraints of conventional machine learning (ML) models, which are usually taught using historical data, are the reason behind the transition from classical to quantum computing in data processing. The transition to quantum computing is further demonstrated by the creation of big data classification models and algorithms. Data-parallel optimized computing has an effective solution that makes use of quantum computing methods. By combining clever algorithms with the ideas of quantum computing, this method overcomes the shortcomings of conventional large data categorization models, such as lengthy processing times. The outcome is a more effective and efficient way to handle big data categorization and multivariable system identification.

A change in the focus of computing technologies is another indicator of the transition from classical data processing to quantum paradigms. Although many computation-intensive fields have made extensive use of classical computing, the emergence of large data has made the development of more potent computing methods necessary. This need is met by quantum computing, which provides a more effective method of processing and analyzing big datasets due to its low energy consumption and increased speed over conventional computers.

One important advancement in the field of big data analytics is the historical transition from conventional data processing to quantum paradigms. The use of quantum computing techniques, which provide exponential advances in processing speed, efficiency, and accuracy, is the result of this shift, which was prompted by the constraints of classical computing methods in managing massive data. Quantum computing is poised to revolutionize data processing and analysis as it develops further, making it a vital instrument in the big data era.

12.7.1 Important developments and technologies in quantum data processing.

Numerous important technologies and developments are influencing the development and implementation of quantum data processing, a continuously changing subject. In addition to expanding the potential of quantum computing, these developments are fusing it with other fields to produce game-changing results.

The creation of 3D integration technologies is one of the most important technical developments in quantum computing. The practical implementation of quantum computing requires the modular and flexible building of integrated circuits, which is made possible by 3D integration. This method is especially applicable to many quantum bit (qubit) candidates that are compatible with sophisticated CMOS fabrication techniques, such as trapped ions, superconducting circuits, silicon spin, and photons.

Cybersecurity is another important area where quantum data processing is being innovated. One of the fundamental components of quantum cryptography is the quantum key distribution (QKD) mechanism. By utilizing the concepts of quantum mechanics, QKD provides a more secure approach to data encryption. It simulates actual situations on the future Internet by evaluating the QKD protocol in both noisy and noise-free channels. In the age of quantum computing, this is essential because conventional cryptography techniques could be subject to quantum assaults. When it comes to ordinary communications infrastructure utilized in cyber-physical systems, quantum cryptography offers an impenetrable security layer.

Additionally, new research and application opportunities are being created by the integration of quantum computing with other Information, Communication, and Computing Technologies (ICCT). The enormous potential that results from combining fundamental technologies like data analytics, cryptography, artificial intelligence, and communication networks with quantum computing. The goal of this multidisciplinary investigation is to unleash hitherto unheard-of computational power and efficiency, which will transform a number of scientific fields and enterprises One study develops postulates that illustrate the revolutionary gains in computational power, security, and efficiency across a range of applications by using an ABCD analytical methodology to assess the advantages, benefits, limits, and drawbacks of this integration.

The sector is moving toward new horizons of efficiency, security, and application thanks to the major technologies and advancements in quantum data processing. The dynamic and transformational aspect of this subject is highlighted by the development of 3D integration technologies, quantum cryptography breakthroughs, and the integration of quantum computing with other ICCT. The integration of quantum computing with other technologies will open up new avenues for innovation and the creation of increasingly complex and potent information and communication systems as the technology develops.

12.8 Landscape and Developmental Patterns in Big Data Quantum Computing.

The discipline of computer science and engineering is changing rapidly due to notable breakthroughs and new trends in the field of quantum computing, particularly in the area of big data analytics. A transition from theoretical research to real-world applications characterizes this progression, with quantum computing emerging as a crucial component in managing the intricacies and enormous volumes of big data.

Recent studies explore the most recent developments in quantum computing and emphasize how it is revolutionizing a number of technological fields. Quantum computing is at the forefront of these developments due to its capacity to process data at previously unheard-of rates and scales. The study emphasizes how crucial quantum computing is for handling the ever-increasing complexity of large data by providing answers that were previously impossible to obtain using traditional computer techniques.

A crucial part of this progression is the shift of quantum information from theoretical study to real-world use in the information and communications technology (ICT) industry. Quantum computing is known for being faster and more secure than traditional digital computers. In the big data era, where data volumes are predicted to increase exponentially and need for increasingly sophisticated computer solutions, this shift is especially pertinent.

Moreover, quantum computing is being used in fields other than classical computing. It investigates its use in relation to digital landscape design and smart city. It illustrates the potential of quantum computing in urban planning and development by optimizing landscape and environmental design through the use of big data analysis. It highlights how quantum computing might improve the efficacy and efficiency of data processing in intricate urban planning and environmental contexts.

A dynamic interaction between notable developments and a move toward real-world applications characterizes the state of quantum computing in the big data setting today. In addition to improving computer science and engineering, quantum computing is revolutionizing urban planning and solving difficult data processing problems. The field's unique ability to handle huge and complicated data sets positions it to provide creative solutions across a range of areas as it continues to develop.

12.9 Methods of Quantum Computing for Big Data Analysis

There are already a number of quantum computing techniques available, each with unique advantages and applications for various big data analytics workloads. The most well-known methods and their possible uses in the big data analytics space are examined in this section.

1. Quantum computers based on gates:

The most versatile and general type of quantum computing are gate-based quantum computers, sometimes referred to as universal quantum computers. To control qubit states and carry out calculations, they use a number of quantum gates and circuits. Because these computers can run any quantum algorithm, they can be used for a variety of large data analytics activities, such as simulations, machine learning, and optimization issues. For some computational tasks, gate-based quantum computers use quantum phenomena like superposition and entanglement to achieve exponential speedups.

They do very well on jobs involving the factoring of huge numbers, finding large solution spaces, and resolving challenging linear algebraic problems. Scalability issues, quantum error correction, and the requirement for extremely controlled settings to preserve quantum coherence are problems for gate-based quantum computers. Considerable research is being done to overcome these obstacles and create large-scale, fault-tolerant quantum computers.

2. Quantum Annealing:

This method of quantum computing finds the global minimum of an objective function by using quantum fluctuations. It works especially effectively for resolving optimization issues, like those that arise in scheduling, logistics, and resource allocation assignments. Systems for quantum annealing, such as those made by D-Wave Systems, employ specialized hardware made to take advantage of quantum effects in order to investigate the energy landscape of an issue and identify the lowest energy state, which is the ideal solution.

Quantum annealing systems provide benefits in terms of stability and scalability, but their applications are more constrained than those of gate-based quantum computers. These systems may be able to function at higher temperatures and manage larger issue sizes, which would lessen the requirement for strict environmental controls. Quantum annealing is a useful technique for big data analytics jobs requiring resource allocation, scheduling, and route optimization since it has demonstrated encouraging results in handling a variety of combinatorial optimization issues.

3. Quantum Simulators:

These software-based instruments mimic how quantum systems behave on traditional computers. They offer a way to investigate and evaluate quantum protocols and algorithms without requiring real quantum gear. In the early phases of developing quantum algorithms and for teaching, quantum simulators are especially helpful. They give scientists and engineers the chance to test novel quantum algorithms, play with the ideas of quantum computing, and learn more about how quantum systems behave.

Quantum simulators are useful tools for testing, benchmarking, and comprehending the limitations and potential of quantum algorithms for big data analytics workloads, even though they do not provide the exponential speedups that physical quantum computers promise. The performance of quantum machine learning algorithms, quantum optimization procedures, and the possible uses of quantum computing in fields like data encryption and cryptography can all be investigated with the help of quantum simulators.

12.10 Use Cases for Quantum-Accelerated Big Data Analytics

Numerous potential use cases and applications in a variety of disciplines are made possible by the incorporation of quantum computing with big data analytics on cloud platforms. The potential advantages of quantum-accelerated big data analytics are highlighted in this section along with some of the intriguing use cases.

1. Risk Analysis and Financial Services:

Big data analytics is essential to fraud detection, portfolio optimization, and risk assessment in the financial industry. By facilitating faster optimization techniques, improved machine learning models, and more effective simulations, quantum computing can greatly speed up these procedures. To enhance fraud detection skills, for instance, large financial data sets can be searched for patterns and anomalies using quantum algorithms like Grover's algorithm. The best asset allocation strategies can be found more quickly with quantum annealing algorithms than using traditional techniques when applied to portfolio optimization challenges.

2. Medical Imaging and Biomedical Research:

The healthcare sector produces enormous volumes of data from a variety of sources, including genomic information, electronic health records, and medical imaging. More precise disease modeling, drug discovery, and personalized therapy are made possible by quantum-accelerated big data analytics, which has the potential to completely transform biomedical research. It may be challenging to find patterns and connections in complex biomedical data using traditional techniques, but quantum machine learning algorithms can help. Protein folding simulations and molecular dynamics simulations, two computational biology activities that are crucial for comprehending biological processes and creating novel therapeutic approaches, can be accelerated by quantum computing.

3. Logistics and Supply Chain Optimization:

For companies that operate internationally, effective supply chain management and logistics are essential. Big data analytics is essential for resource allocation, inventory control, and transportation route optimization. When it comes to resolving these intricate optimization issues, quantum computing can offer substantial benefits. Algorithms for quantum annealing can be used to optimize scheduling and routing issues, reducing transportation expenses and speeding up delivery. More efficient resource allocation and inventory management are made possible by the application of quantum machine learning algorithms to supply chain data analysis and demand pattern prediction.

4. Climate and Environmental Modeling:

This type of modeling entails processing and examining enormous volumes of data from numerous sources, including weather stations, sensor networks, and satellite imagery. More precise and thorough simulations and forecasts are made possible by the speed at which quantum computing can complete these computationally demanding tasks. Environmental and climatic data can be processed and analyzed efficiently using quantum algorithms such as the Quantum Fourier Transform. We can better comprehend climate change and its effects by using quantum machine learning techniques to find patterns and connections in complicated environmental information.

5. Data encryption and cybersecurity:

Although quantum computing presents difficulties for traditional encryption approaches, it also offers chances to create new secure data processing methods and quantum-resistant cryptographic protocols. To guarantee the confidentiality and privacy of sensitive data, big data analytics frameworks can use quantum cryptography techniques. Big data analytics applications can create secure communication channels and safeguard data transmission by utilizing quantum secure direct communication protocols and quantum key distribution. It is possible to create encryption algorithms that are resistant to quantum cryptanalytic attacks in order to protect data processing and storage.

12.11 Challenges in the integration of quantum computing into big data analytics on cloud platforms

It is important to carefully evaluate and handle the benefits and problems that come with integrating quantum computing with big data analytics on cloud platforms.

1. Scalability and Computational Power:

The number of qubits and the fidelity of quantum operations limit the computational power and scalability of quantum computers, notwithstanding the possibility of exponential speedups in specific computing workloads. It is still very difficult to create large-scale quantum processors that can process enormous datasets.

2. Development of Quantum Algorithms:

It is a challenging undertaking to create effective and efficient quantum algorithms for particular big data analytics workloads. It necessitates proficiency in data analysis and problem-solving methodologies in addition to a thorough comprehension of quantum computing principles [8]. Research is currently underway to create new quantum algorithms specifically suited for big data analytics.

3. Data Encoding and Quantum Input/Output:

One of the most important challenges is providing and encoding classical data in a quantum format that can be processed by quantum computers. Leveraging the full potential of quantum computing in big data analytics requires effective input/output systems and data encoding.

4. Integration with Current Data Processing Frameworks:

One of the biggest challenges is incorporating quantum computing capabilities into big data analytics tools and current data processing frameworks. It is necessary to deal with compatibility problems, data format transformations, and the synchronization of resources for both classical and quantum computing.

5. Security and Privacy Considerations:

With the growing popularity of quantum computing, it is critical to address any possible security and privacy issues related to big data analytics that are accelerated by quantum technology. Certain classical encryption algorithms may become vulnerable to quantum cryptanalysis techniques, which calls for the creation of safe data transport systems and quantum-resistant cryptographic protocols.

12.12 Opportunities in the integration of quantum computing into big data analytics on cloud platforms

1. Exponential Speedups and Increased computing Power:

For some computing jobs, such factoring big numbers, scanning unstructured databases, and resolving optimization issues, quantum computers may offer exponential speedups. These features have the potential to greatly speed up big data analytics procedures, allowing for more effective data processing and analysis.

2. Better Machine Learning and Pattern Recognition:

Quantum computing presents special chances to improve algorithms for machine learning and pattern recognition. Better decision-making and insights from complicated datasets may be possible with the use of quantum-accelerated machine learning techniques, which may provide more accurate and effective models.

3. Optimization and Combinatorial Problem-Solving:

A lot of big data analytics work entails resolving intricate optimization and combinatorial issues, like scheduling, routing, and resource allocation. With its capacity to effectively explore large solution areas, quantum computing can offer substantial benefits in addressing these issues.

4. Secure Data Processing and Encryption:

Although quantum computing makes traditional encryption techniques more difficult to use, it also offers chances to create new secure data processing methods and quantum-resistant cryptographic protocols [10]. Big data analytics privacy and data protection can be improved by utilizing quantum features like entanglement and superposition to facilitate safe data transfer and storage.

5. Cloud-Based Quantum Computing Services:

By incorporating quantum computing capabilities into cloud platforms, specialist hardware and infrastructure are not as necessary, allowing on-demand access to quantum computing resources. This adaptable and scalable method can hasten the adoption of big data analytics powered by quantum technology, encouraging creativity and cooperation in a variety of fields.

12.13 Quantum computing applications in data analytics

Despite being a relatively new technology, data analytics is already utilizing quantum computing. Here are some examples of how big data analysis is being aided by quantum computing:

- Quantum computing provides high-speed detection, analysis, integration, and diagnosis capabilities when working with huge, dispersed data sets.
- By concurrently seeing every item in a massive database, quantum computers are able to swiftly identify patterns in big, unsorted data sets.
- Quantum computers may do incredibly complex computations in a matter of seconds, but non-quantum computers may take hundreds of years to complete.
- These days, artificial intelligence systems are frequently used to manage large data sets and assist in the analysis of datasets in order to identify patterns. Despite the technology's quick development, traditional computers can only process a finite amount of data. This constraint, however, does not apply to quantum computers. The speed and capabilities of quantum computing are advantageous in three areas of artificial intelligence:

Natural Language Processing: The first natural language processing operation driven by quantum technology was completed in 2020. Grammatical statements have been successfully converted into quantum circuits by scientists. These algorithms were able to answer questions after they were executed on a quantum computer, which has significant ramifications for big data.

Machine Learning: Quantum machine learning uses a quantum computer to carry out machine learning algorithms. By using more computational power than a conventional computer could, this innovative technique can significantly speed up processing.

Predictive analytics: AI can be used to mine databases for current information and important historical facts. More data is processed when paired with quantum computing, producing pertinent data that can then be utilized for forecasting. However, because a predictive model must take into consideration a large number of decisions, elements, and variables, the vast amount of data accessible can occasionally be too much. Without slowing down the process, quantum computing helps create predictive models that are more scalable.

Environmental factors like temperature changes or vibrations can lead most quantum computers to suffer a condition of decoherence that renders them essentially worthless, preventing them from reaching their full potential. Because of this, it might still be years before most businesses use quantum computing or it becomes a commonplace data analytics tool.

Quantum computing is still an emerging technology in 2021. At the moment, machine learning algorithms are still getting better thanks to developments in quantum computing technology. There is still much to discover about the potential of quantum computing and its implications.

Chapter - 13
Quantum Computing Applications

13.1 Healthcare

The chapter discusses the benefits and drawbacks of applying quantum computing to the medical field. It covers topics including the computer's power, how algorithms are created, and information security. This chapter demonstrates how Quantum computing has the potential to improve healthcare and introduce novel concepts to the field of medicine.

Quantum computers can make predictions more accurately and more quickly. Predicting and acting promptly are crucial when it comes to a patient's health. Quantum computing and healthcare are related in a way that is similar to a completely new, extremely sophisticated technology. It might significantly alter the way we practice medicine. Utilizing unique scientific principles, quantum computing has the potential to transform healthcare in ways that were previously unthinkable. Finding new medications, comprehending genes, and improving healthcare are just a few of the difficult issues that this new technology can help us with. Investigating the potential benefits of quantum computing in healthcare reveals that it has the potential to significantly alter healthcare practices, speed up research, and provide new insights.

The fundamentals of quantum computing, its advantages over conventional computing, and how it can transform healthcare to make it more precise, quicker, and patient-specific will all be covered in this investigation.

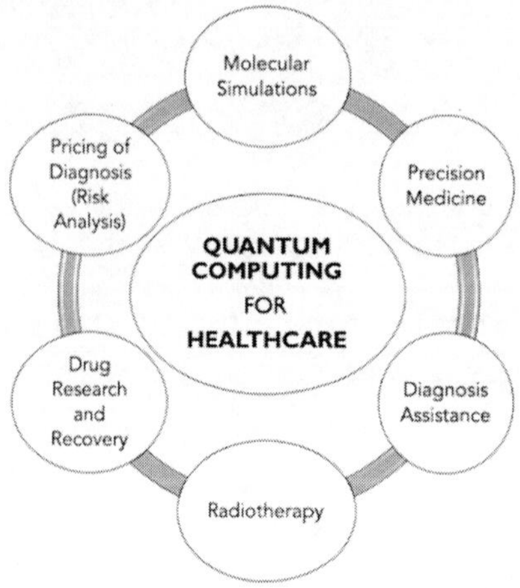

Fig.13.1 Quantum Computing for Healthcare.

Applications of Quantum Computing in Healthcare In the Internet of Things (IoT) era of digital healthcare, computing is particularly useful for demanding healthcare activities. It's similar to having incredibly powerful computers that are capable of incredible feats. It can assist, for instance, with cloud-based or Internet-connected medical devices. Significant advancements in healthcare could result from this supercomputer capability. Research in healthcare can greatly benefit from the switch from conventional to quantum computers. It's similar like going from a sluggish car to one that is extremely quick. It can greatly speed up processes like researching proteins, determining how medications and chemicals work together, and even testing novel medications. One intriguing development is the lightning-fast DNA sequencing capabilities of quantum computers, which may pave the way for personalized medicine.

Complex healthcare operations are well suited for quantum computers, particularly when it comes to networked medical devices like sensors that are connected to the cloud or the Internet. Significant advances in healthcare research can also be made with the aid of these potent computers. They can expedite processes such as determining how chemicals, such as medications, fit together, measuring the strength of molecular bonds, and researching how proteins fold. Here are some instances of the potential applications of quantum computers in healthcare, such as the ability to swiftly read DNA to customize medication.

Supersonic drug design:

Comparing molecules is the most crucial stage in creating novel medications. Many of them can be compared by standard computers, but very large molecules are beyond their capabilities. Larger molecules can be compared using quantum computing. This implies that we can advance the creation of medications and the discovery of treatments for various illnesses. Healthcare professionals can model intricate molecular interactions at a very small scale thanks to quantum computing. For medical research and the development of new medications, this is significant. Experts will soon be able to model and comprehend the functions of all 20,000 proteins found in the human genome.

Additionally, they will be able to model the interactions between these proteins and both novel and old medications. The traditional method of producing medications through drawn-out and costly clinical trials is no longer the sole choice. To expedite the process and lower the cost of drug discovery and development, scientists and pharmaceutical corporations are increasingly experimenting with various techniques like artificial intelligence, human organs-on-chips, and in silico trials. For example, it uses supercomputers to look through a huge database of molecular structures for possible treatments. AtomNet, one of its potent technologies, analyzes more than 100 million molecules.

In 2015, Atomwise looked for safe medications that were already on the market that could be modified to treat Ebola. Surprisingly, they found two possible medications in less than a day, although normally it takes months. In a different instance, InSilico Medicine made headlines when they disclosed that they were able to create a new medication candidate in just 46 days because to their clever algorithm.

Advancing to the stage of clinical trials conducted in silico. This entails testing medications or treatments using computer models rather than humans, animals, or cells. These simulations can be substantially enhanced by quantum computing, which enables intricate models like HumMod, which replicates different bodily activities, and detailed "virtual humans." Customized 'live' studies with virtual patients might result from this, which would speed up, improve, and complete the trials. New medications may be released onto the market a few weeks after they are discovered.

Full-speed DNA sequencing and analysis:

Genetics and genomics have changed significantly over the last 20 years. During the Human Genome Project, which started in 1990 and released its final findings in 2006, decoding the human DNA once required more than 15 years and billions of dollars. However, direct-to-consumer genetic testing companies now offer over 2,000 genetic tests for a variety of human problems, and you can even obtain them online. These tests help medical professionals diagnose conditions and let people learn about their hereditary disease risks.

The time, cost, and technical requirements for genome sequencing have all improved by a factor of ten in less than a decade. Nonetheless, we believe that a major revolution in this subject is still possible. This revolution could be advanced by quantum computing. It might make it possible to sequence the genome more quickly and analyze the complete genome more thoroughly. By taking into account even more data than conventional computers, quantum computers may also be able to incorporate all genomic data into medical records and produce forecasts that are more accurate. Everyone's health could improve if genetic and genomic ambiguities are eliminated via quantum computing.

Making the patient at the center of care:

Even while we can currently measure a vast amount of personal health data, we are aware that it is still not very common. In the future, zettabytes of patient data may be sent to the cloud via wearable technology, health sensors, and small medical devices. For example, the digital universe, or the information we create and copy every year, is expected to grow to 175 zettabytes, or 175 trillion gigabytes, by 2025, compared to 4.4 zettabytes in 2013. These massive volumes of data, including tidbits of health information, will be understandable by quantum computers.

Furthermore, patient monitoring via interconnected sensory systems may eliminate the need for physical hospitals and genuinely put the patient at the center of care. These technologies could operate seamlessly on the "home front" thanks to quantum computing.

Developing the ideal system for decision support:

The days when a single professor's mind could contain all of the medical experts' collective knowledge are long gone. It's simply too a lot. There are 34 million papers on Pubmed. It would take a lifetime for a single doctor to study three to four papers in their field of expertise, and millions more would be published in the interim. That has long been an issue, so IBM developed IBM Watson, a supercomputer and algorithm that can quickly scan through millions of research. However, it is unclear what will happen to these efforts once Watson is sold.

That would be enhanced with unique abilities and taken to a whole new level by quantum computing. What if these machines were able to provide doctors with flawless decision support? They might quickly go through all of the research at once, discover connections and causes that the human eye would never notice, and perhaps discover diagnoses or courses of therapy that a human physician could never have discovered on their own. At the absolute end of this evolution, quantum computers may provide a better version of PubMed, where data would be stored in qubits rather than the conventional written format because only the computer would be able to "read" the research.

Using quantum uncertainty for encryption is one of the most likely uses of quantum computing to create the safest medical data systems ever. According to her, it could be used to generate private keys that would encrypt messages sent between locations, making it impossible for hackers to duplicate the key exactly because of quantum uncertainty. To hack such keys, they would need to violate the principles of quantum physics. Consider that degree of protection for private medical data, such as genetic and genomic information, electronic health records, or any other information the health system produces about our bodies. Some samples are already available. A team from China and Austria demonstrated in January 2018 that using quantum encryption to communicate across continents was feasible.

Combining quantum communication from the Micius satellite with Beijing's fiber optic network is the most recent innovation made by this team. It is the first concrete evidence that networks can currently employ the technology that enables quantum encryption. Theoretically, quantum computing does have incredible promise. This is more science fiction at the moment, though, as we still have a long way to go before any of this can be used in the actual world. Furthermore, a further issue with quantum computing is that not many people fully comprehend what it is and how it operates.

Radiotherapy:

One common cancer treatment is radiotherapy. Additionally, it employs radiation to either kill or stop the growth of malignant cells. To lessen the harm to healthy tissues and body components, a radiation plan must be developed. Additionally, it handles intricate optimization issues involving thousands of variables. As a result, it takes several simulations to arrive at the best radiation plan until an ideal one is found. Because of this, a wide range of possibilities are taken into account in each simulation when using quantum computing. Consequently, it enables medical practitioners to run multiple simulations at once and create the best possible plan.

Healthcare Data:

Patients desire to protect and preserve their health information. Therefore, it is essential to analyze and evaluate every hacking approach. For instance, ID Quantique is a company that secures data using elements of quantum mechanics. Consequently, one of the more useful applications is the use of quantum entanglement, and the data is protected by quantum cryptography.

Genomics

The study of an organism's entire genetic makeup is known as genomics. In other words, it integrates bioinformatics, DNA sequencing techniques, and recombinant DNA. Additionally, it necessitates the sequencing, assembly, and analysis of genomic structures and functions. Additionally, the most recent methods divide DNA into tiny pieces. It also covers looking for specific biomarkers and any mutations linked to the condition. This ultimately boils down to two significant effects that require attention. First of all, the procedure takes too long. Second, when just manual procedures are used, it becomes slower.

Traditional computers are therefore insufficiently active for the tasks. Because quantum computing offers greater processing and storage capacity, it is the best course of action. Additionally, the results will be more precise, assisting in the provision of accurate diagnoses and customized drugs. Additionally, it will allow experts to compile a database of genomes in order to find unidentified mutations and biomarkers. By taking into account many aspects like lifestyle and surroundings, it will also transform the treatment.

Enhancing Imaging Solutions:

Single molecules can be seen thanks to the creation of incredibly accurate images made possible by quantum imaging technologies. Additionally, experts and physicians can better analyze the results with the aid of machine learning and quantum computing. Additionally, quantum computing offers the interpretation of the findings and their remedies, while machine learning aids in the detection of anomalies in the body. However, the radiologist must assess the areas of light and dark that are detected by conventional MRIs. Therefore, in order to facilitate more accurate imaging, quantum imaging technologies aid in tissue type differentiation.

Healthcare Using Quantum Algorithms for Cognitive Function:

The amount of data in the healthcare sector is growing at the same time that healthcare costs are increasing. Big data, sophisticated machine learning, supercomputers, and cloud services are all used in cognitive computing in healthcare to assist physicians identify illnesses early, enhance treatment results, and eventually lower healthcare costs. Siemens Healthineers and UCL are examining how quantum machine learning algorithms can enhance cognitive computing in the medical field. Problems that are computationally unsolvable with traditional computers may be resolved by algorithms that execute incredibly quickly on quantum processors. When it comes to deriving valuable, decision-level information from medical images, this holds great promise.

Classifying Images Using Auto-encoders and Quantum Pre-training:

Applications for computer vision are numerous and include robots and medical image analysis. Machine learning has revolutionized the area in recent years, and it could gain from future developments in quantum computing. The primary obstacle to image processing on existing and upcoming quantum devices is the volume of data that these devices can handle. Large, multi-dimensional, and multi-channel images are possible. In order to fit the images onto the device, current machine learning techniques for computer vision that take advantage of quantum resources necessitate a large amount of human pre-processing.

The challenge of processing massive amounts of data on tiny quantum devices has a solution. It operates on huge grayscale and RGB images and doesn't require any information or processing particular to datasets. Additionally, when larger quantum hardware architectures become available, it can scale to accommodate them. This method compresses the image data to a size that can be put into a quantum device by training a classical autoencoder. The compressed data is then utilized to train a Restricted Boltzmann Machine (RBM) on the D-Wave device. A neural network for picture classification is then initialized using the weights from the RBM.

Training and Meta-Training Binary Neural Networks with Quantum Computing:

For a variety of applications, quantum computers offer notable benefits over classical computers. We demonstrate that the quantum state output of a quantum computer may be used to describe the whole loss function landscape of a neural network. Using a well-known mechanism called quantum amplitude amplification, It clearly illustrates that for a binary neural network and further demonstrate how a quantum computer may train the network by modifying this state.

Bits, or 0s and 1s, which stand for electrical impulses that indicate on and off, are processed in classical computing. A completely different method of information processing is used in quantum computing. It extends processing capabilities to previously unheard-of heights by utilizing qubits, which can simultaneously exist as a 1 and a 0, as well as the interplay, entanglement, and superposition of subatomic particles in quantum physics. The effectiveness of quantum computing for significant verticals like healthcare, where it can facilitate significant advancements in the creation of life-saving medications, speedy DNA sequencing, early disease detection, and other computationally demanding healthcare-related tasks. Traditional computational systems have been completely transformed by quantum computing, which offers previously unthinkable speed, efficiency, and dependability.

13.2 Material Science

Quantum computing has the potential to revolutionize fields like materials science and drug discovery by simulating the behaviour of molecules and materials with greater accuracy than classical computers. Major tech giants such as Google, IBM, Microsoft, and Intel have dedicated teams working on advancing quantum computing to tackle complex problems. However, the applications of quantum computing extend beyond just large enterprises, as smaller companies and start-ups are also exploring its potential. While regular computers often struggle with modelling intricate molecular interactions, quantum computers excel at handling such complexity. This capability can enable chemical and petroleum companies to accelerate the development of new products.

IBM's publicly accessible quantum computers were leveraged to study lithium hydride and beryllium hydride - chemicals critical to the chemical and petroleum industries. This research could lead to the development of improved catalysts and surfactants.

Leveraging the power of quantum computing, ExxonMobil is developing innovative energy and manufacturing technologies. The company foresees breakthroughs in optimizing power grids, creating more accurate environmental simulations, and discovering novel carbon capture materials to boost efficiency.

13.3 Finance

Quantum computing holds significant promise for transforming financial planning and risk management. In January 2023, quantum computing companies and France's Credit Agricole bank announced the completion of a 1.5-year study exploring how quantum-inspired techniques could enhance the valuation of financial assets and the assessment of loan risk.

The study found that applying these quantum-like approaches can dramatically improve computational speed and efficiency, even with relatively modest 50-qubit quantum processors. The researchers believe this technology will become even more powerful as qubit counts increase to 300 by 2024. Notably, the team developed the first computer program that combines quantum and classical techniques to predict changes in credit ratings.

Overall, the results suggest quantum computing could revolutionize key financial planning and risk management tasks, allowing for more accurate forecasting of market movements and better control over portfolio risks. As the technology continues to advance, financial institutions are poised to reap substantial benefits from this quantum leap forward.

13.4 Machine Language

Quantum computing has the potential to significantly enhance machine learning algorithms, allowing them to make faster and more accurate predictions. Quantum Machine Learning (QML) combines quantum computing with quantum sensing, a lesser-known area. While there are still significant challenges to overcome, such as the need for more qubits and better error correction, some experiments have already shown the advantages of QML. Even with a limited number of examples, quantum computers can outperform traditional computers, even those with unlimited resources. However, to fully realize the benefits of QML, we need to improve current quantum sensor technology and find ways to accurately transfer quantum states to quantum computers. The fact that today's quantum computers can already process this data and gain a learning advantage is an encouraging sign for the future of quantum machine learning.

13.5 Natural Language Processing (NLP)

Quantum computing holds immense potential for enhancing Natural Language Processing (NLP) and speech recognition, thereby making communication more accurate and efficient. In October 2021, Cambridge Quantum Computing (CQC) released the first quantum natural language processing (QNLP) toolkit and library, enabling the rapid development of QNLP applications such as automated dialogue, text mining, language translation, text-to-speech, language generation, and bioinformatics. Our latest research project in QNLP, conducted with researchers from [institution], has shown that even at this early stage, QNLP techniques can produce sentence classification results comparable to traditional methods. However, we recognize that the infrastructure for quantum computing must improve before these techniques can be commercialized. Importantly, the QNLP approach holds the promise of explainable AI, which could lead to more accurate and accountable intelligence - a crucial factor in fields like medicine. As this area is new and significant, the opportunity to gain practical experience in the experimental side of QNLP is invaluable for advancing NLP on actual quantum computers.

13.6 Quantum Computing applied to optimize tasks

Because it is thought to complete intricate optimization tasks far more quickly than conventional computers, quantum computing can be successful in industries like manufacturing and logistics. The Latin American business Quantum-South offers an illustration of how quantum computing aids in optimization. In June 2022, this Uruguayan business posted an article titled "Improving Cargo Loading Plans with Quantum Annealers" on its website. It describes how they improved cargo loading plans by optimizing goods in the lower compartments of passenger airplanes using a hybrid method that used quantum annealers via Amazon Braket. Based on the results of their early trials, the advanced use of this approach could more effectively arrange the mix of people, weight, and cargo on busy flights.

It will also enable greater process efficiency, which will cut down on the time needed for analysis and optimization. The solution has also been tried by International Airlines Group (IAG) subsidiary Quantum IAG Cargo. It might greatly increase the effectiveness of the workload. The method might optimize the entire network of freight carriers, whereas the existing optimization procedure only covers a subset of flights is constantly looking for new and creative ways to improve the efficiency of its operations," said Angel Cabeza, Head of Technology Change at IAG Cargo. He went on to say, "We're eager to proceed with further phases to confirm the positive outcomes we've observed."

"We started by closely studying the current IAG Cargo process at Adolfo Suárez Madrid–Barajas Airport in Spain," said Dr. Rafael Sotelo, co-founder and president of Quantum-South. He continued, "Our teams collaborated to integrate operational data into our algorithms and tailored two use cases to create a unique solution that fits IAG Cargo's specific needs." Put more simply, IAG Cargo is eager to enhance their procedures, and after closely collaborating with them to examine how things are now conducted at one of their airports, Quantum-South developed a unique solution. They are currently taking action to validate the favourable outcomes.

13.7 Security of Quantum Computing in Healthcare

Because healthcare applications deal with people's lives, security is essential. But the problem with healthcare is that its systems are frequently disjointed, making it difficult to exchange information and advance. According to Chuck Brooks, a cybersecurity specialist and the chair of the Quantum Security Alliance, in order to guarantee security, governments, industry, researchers, and academia must work together more effectively. Another crucial factor in quantum computing is security. It has the potential to greatly increase processing power, endangering existing cryptography techniques. Healthcare information security has historically been based on cryptography, but quantum computing offers robust security for healthcare communication by fusing classical encryption with quantum mechanics. Based on the principles of physics, quantum cryptography is a commercially available technology. There are number of security technologies that can enhance the security of healthcare data.

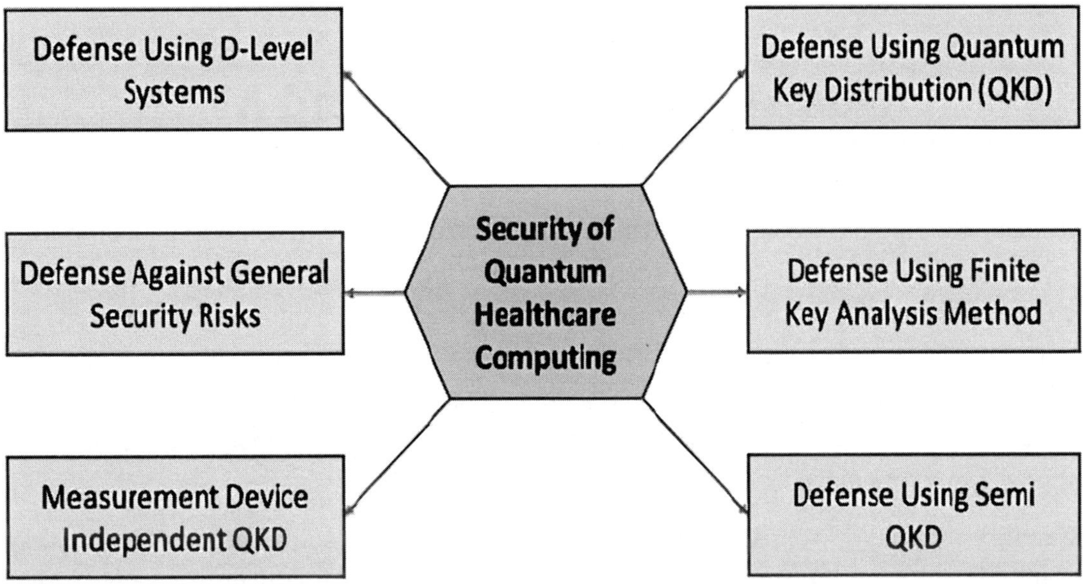

Fig.13.2 Categorization of key technologies for using quantum computing to securely process medical data.

Chapter - 14
Quantum Computing and AI

Artificial intelligence (AI) and quantum computing are two emerging computing revolutions with varying degrees of maturity and market impact. Despite having a strong scientific position in both fields, the European Union is still caught between the dominance of the United States and China's growing influence, especially in the field of artificial intelligence. The rise of DeepSeek in the major language models alone has demonstrated how creativity, scientific acumen, and open source models may drastically change the market balance.

The ability to develop robust, integrated software platforms, construct sizable, scalable, and effective computing infrastructure, and encourage the development of as general use cases as possible for end users ranging from the public and private sectors to the consumer markets are what give these domains their leadership. A key component of market success is the close coordination of industry R&D and academic research.

Although quantum computing is still in its infancy, there are already and will continue to be developing synergies between it and AI. The importance of mastering this dual discipline as an enabling technology is highlighted by the fact that many AI-driven techniques are already enabling significant advancements in quantum computing research and industry developments, from designing novel quantum algorithms to optimizing qubit control and quantum error mitigation (QEM) strategies in the early stage noisy intermediate-scale quantum (NISQ) regime.

However, even though the large-scale, fault-tolerant quantum computers (FTQC) required to achieve such an advantage are still a long-term goal, early evidence of quantum advantage in faster computing times, better results, or the need for less training data for solving specific machine learning problems shows how combining AI and quantum resources could bring value.

By expanding on the current research excellence in both areas and hastening the shift from lab to commercial applications, public investment in the convergence of AI and quantum computing might boost EU competitiveness. Developing AI-based solutions for healthcare, finance, materials research, and security is one of the strategic objectives of using quantum computing. Although it is a medium- to long-term goal, it will determine scientific and industrial leadership in both fields. The development of both open source and commercial integrated software engineering platforms should also be promoted by the EU's AI and quantum research environment.

Ensuring support for academic research and private-sector innovation at this intersection will not only secure the economic benefits associated with disruptive breakthroughs but also strengthen the EU's position as a major global player in emerging deep-tech ecosystems as international competition intensifies. A well-planned funding approach that includes basic research, talent development, and technology transfer incentives will guarantee a strong transition from innovative lab-scale studies to real, high-impact industry platforms and applications.

Today AI is seen in all sectors and is the most significant technological layer. The reach of AI, however, is limited to the capabilities of traditional computing, and these traditional consumers face constraints as well. Quite unreal to think that artificial intelligence has constraints as well isn't it? Yes, AI computational capability is low and it suffers from the same limitations as classical computers. With advances in quantum computing, AI and machine learning performance could be dramatically enhanced. The scale of quantum computation will be discussed in the future in terms of its applicability to artificial intelligence and its effects on many industries, enterprises, and the economy.

And if the statistics above from business insider are to be credible, and this is without a doubt the future of computing.

Quantum computers are millions of times faster than those nowadays.

By 2030 the quantum computing market is expected to reach a total revenue of $64.98 billion.

The race to build tools for quantum computers is gaining momentum with prominent companies such as Microsoft, Google, and Intel competing for the top spot.

The potential uses of quantum computing are becoming more and more popular in a variety of sectors. The prospective effects of this technology on artificial intelligence, however, have not received much attention. In addition to modeling large-scale systems and molecules, quantum computers can tackle decoding issues far more quickly than classical computers. Quantum computing will be essential to the advancement of artificial intelligence and other applications as it becomes more widely available. Additionally, they have the capacity to manage enormous volumes of data, which is necessary for artificial intelligence model training.

Artificial intelligence is becoming more widely used in many different areas, such as consumer electronics, smart cities, manufacturing, transportation and logistics, medical devices, retail, and utilities.

Quantum artificial intelligence (QAI) blends the human-like intellect of artificial intelligence (AI) with the strength and capabilities of quantum mechanisms like superposition and quantum gates to improve the speed, accuracy, and cloud environment's scalability. A number of reasons have contributed to the exponentially quicker development of quantum AI. First, the growing scalability requirements of cloud systems have led to the demand for quantum artificial intelligence. The growing demand for cloud services, which is mostly driven by the advantages and effectiveness of cloud environments for various personal and business uses, has made these scalability requirements worse.

Quantum AI's broad capabilities have also influenced its incorporation into cloud computing. By resolving issues like categorization and clustering, quantum AI technologies like quantum machine learning and quantum support vector machines (QSVM) simplify cloud computing. Furthermore, AI networks that are relevant to cloud computing and other diverse applications, such deep learning and neural networks, are vulnerable to dynamically rising computational demands and resources. These issues are successfully addressed by quantum methods, which use entanglement and superposition to solve optimization issues and model the massive data sets needed for deep learning.

Potential synergies abound at the nexus of artificial intelligence (AI) and quantum computing, which offers fresh methods for resolving challenging issues that are outside the scope of traditional computer paradigms. The creation of quantum machine learning algorithms, which take advantage of the processing capacity and intrinsic parallelism of quantum computing to improve on conventional machine learning methods, is one area of synergy. By using quantum principles to process and analyze data more quickly than their conventional equivalents, quantum machine learning algorithms show promise in tasks like classification, regression, and clustering. Significant speedups and increased accuracy are possible with quantum algorithms like quantum support vector machines and quantum neural networks, especially when working with huge datasets or complicated feature spaces.

Furthermore, quantum-inspired algorithms are showing promise as a solution for AI's optimization and pattern recognition problems. These algorithms create novel optimization techniques that surpass traditional methods by taking influence from the concepts of quantum computing. For example, quantum annealing and quantum-inspired optimization algorithms, such as the quantum approximate optimization algorithm (QAOA), provide effective solutions for combinatorial optimization problems, including graph partitioning and traveling salesman problems. AI systems can perform better on tasks including scheduling, logistics optimization, and resource allocation by utilizing quantum-inspired optimization approaches.

Quantum-enhanced data processing and analysis is another area where AI and quantum computing might work together. Superposition and entanglement, two special characteristics of quantum computing, allow for the effective manipulation of big datasets and intricate data structures. In high-dimensional data spaces, quantum techniques such as quantum principal component analysis (PCA) and quantum singular value decomposition (QSVD) provide methods for reducing dimensionality and obtaining valuable insights. Furthermore, jobs like anomaly detection, feature extraction, and data clustering, where conventional approaches might not be able to handle the computing needs or the complexity of the data, may benefit from the use of quantum-enhanced data analysis techniques. AI systems can open up new avenues for knowledge discovery and decision-making across a range of industries, including cybersecurity, healthcare, and finance, by utilizing quantum-enhanced data processing capabilities.

Attitudes toward Quantum Computing and AI

It's difficult (and odd) to be against quantum computing. Quantum computing is amazing on multiple levels. To those of us who have dedicated our lives to solving the wave equation of quantum mechanics and relating it to the very concrete world of chemistry, it is incredible to witness superposition and entanglement become operational reality and precise figures. We viewed such underlying quantum mechanical concepts as philosophical quandaries rather than the domain of human quantum mechanics like ourselves. And these concepts are put into practice today, rather than tomorrow. Designing the physical building pieces of a quantum computer, known as qubits, involves chemistry as well. Realizable qubits can be inorganic molecules or an addressable flaw in a crystal. Concerns concerning state fidelity and decoherence have led to the creation of a new bridge between chemistry and computation.

Artificial intelligence is now a reality, thanks to decades of computer use. Computing tasks, such as searching a library's holdings for a book title or plotting a wave function, are simple to express for humans using basic tools. The computer's method makes it straightforward to understand. The computer's quickness and the ease with which we may mislead it are always impressive. When it comes to machine translation from a foreign language, Google Translate and deepL use neural networks to achieve impressive results.

When it comes to facial recognition, the program's effectiveness can be overshadowed by the applications it may be used for.

Let's be specific: One of the study describes that used dating profile data to correlate sexual preferences with self-identification based on facial pictures and self-supplied profiles. Data scientists outperformed human evaluators in terms of correlation. Some institutions may utilize "identification" to evaluate job applicants, but it can also be used to mistreat some communities, such as Uighurs in western China, as part of "re-education". So the problem is human abuse, not the machine.

Two remarks on this

- Humans are fallible. Humans are prone to misusing technology, whether for personal gain, to injure others, or to create chaos. Legal structures that limit and govern computer conduct are the most effective way to address this issue. Of certainly, we should try. Human misuse, such as synthesizing addictive opioids or plagiarizing, often exceeds the reach of the norms and regulations in place. Hackers and trolls rely on mental energy, which is challenging to counter.

- To combat automated computer misuse, it may be necessary to implement computerized protection measures. Leaving the option to programs or robots does not resolve the ethical dilemma. Interestingly, this argument has been presented in another context:

Military specialists and roboticists contend that autonomous weapons systems are not only morally acceptable, but even ethically preferable to human warriors. According to roboticist Ronald C. Arkin, autonomous robots may act more "humanely" on the battlefield due to their lack of self-preservation instincts, potentially eliminating the need for a "shoot-first, ask questions later" approach. Autonomous weapons systems are immune to emotions like fear and frenzy, allowing them to process more sensory information without bias. The argument is weak, as robots may be designed to survive due to their high cost and potential use in non-judgmental tasks.

Algorithms cannot be responsible for taking lives or causing harm. Taking action entails great moral obligation. If we end up in a world where machines make life-or-death decisions, our society will have failed us.

The effects on artificial intelligence

Preliminary expert systems have been conceptualized and tried in recent works to perform reinforcement learning, infer interventions in quantum environments, and apply quantum computing applications outside of difficult multivariable optimization tasks. A quantum computing network that combines quantum processing, physical quantum memory, and a multi-layer neural network with deep learning capabilities and the fastest analytics speed possible was created and is presently being commercialized improved for use as an AI accelerator. Large-scale integration with top AI software stacks should be possible thanks to the co-designed programming interface, which will specifically enable previously unthinkable speedups of popular recurrent, generative adversarial, and cryptographic neural networks. The expectations and competitive comparisons related to quantum computing are also aiding the co-design's hardware advancements, which should lead to benchmarks, designs, and new features for quantum AI accelerators.

Such reactive approaches could quickly give way to more advanced technological stages, which would fundamentally alter deep learning applications. Indeed, novel AI models will appear and predicting accuracy should be significantly increased when entanglement or discord is generated between real and virtual quantum states. Given these predictions, the few in the conventional G8 or privileged races may not be the only ones who receive high-end digital computing leapfrogs in the so-called budding fourth industrial revolution during the last quarter of this decade. By offering renaissance chances through quantum computational advancements, quantum cloud computing could democratize transformational AI components with firsthand expertise in quantum technology and make local digital proliferation advantageous to more people worldwide.

1. Quantum Machine Learning

The energy used for training may be reduced by developments in quantum computing. The resource problem's compression may alleviate these energy limitations and facilitate quick debugging, enabling more learning iterations and speeding up the development of machine learning. A second area of research focuses on using quantum computing to create and execute algorithms that replicate or outperform logical operations that quantum systems are inherently capable of handling. Large-scale digital computation can benefit from quantum computing's specialization in eigenvalue problems, which adhere to the mathematical framework of quantum mechanics. It can expedite complicated tasks involving the interaction of many-body quantum coherence. Additionally, the dynamics of isolated quantum systems, which are represented by differential equations created in the mathematical formulation of quantum computing, are best simulated by quantum computing. Because a conventional computer finds it difficult to capture the dynamic evolution of quantum systems, quantum computing is crucial. Quantum material science, high-energy physics simulations of quantum field theories, and quantum chemistry simulations are only a few of the applications for quantum systems.

With a variety of issues in basic physics, associated sensory and data collecting, techniques to convert discoveries into workable algorithms, and hardware remaining unexplored, the development of quantum computing technologies and software applications is still in its infancy.

However, the mathematically complex problems associated with entanglement, high-dimensional control circuit manipulation, and scalable linear optical operations already demonstrate the toolkits of quantum computers. These problems offer the alluring promise of using quantum computing to transform artificial intelligence and machine learning, which first emerged as early experiments in its viability. The development of quantum computing technologies and software applications is still in its infancy due to a number of fundamental physics problems, related sensory and data collection methods, methods for turning discoveries into practical algorithms, and unexplored hardware.

Nevertheless, the toolkits of quantum computers are already evident in the theoretically challenging problems related to entanglement, high-dimensional control circuit manipulation, and scalable linear optical operations. These issues present the tantalizing prospect of transforming machine learning and artificial intelligence through the use of quantum computing, which initially surfaced as early trials in its feasibility.

2. Quantum Neurals Networks

The quantum community has been showing increasing interest in implementing quantum machine learning (QML), which includes quantum neural networks (QNNs) and quantum-enhanced support vector machines. Many quantum neural network architectures have been proposed since the first theoretical idea of a quantum Boltzmann machine using superconducting circuit quantum electrodynamics was presented in 2017. These architectures are based on ideas from deep learning algorithms, quantum state preparation, quantum algorithms, quantum algorithms, quantum approximate optimization algorithm, and tensor network state evolution to aid in training and classification.

Numerous QNNs have been taught using various quantum or hybrid quantum-classical learning techniques. Three broad categories can be used to classify current QNN proposals: 1) altering conventional quantum algorithms; 2) backpropagation from classical to quantum; and 3) acquiring classical neural network architectures. By improving the scalability, capacity, and enhanced efficiency of quantum algorithms for training classical machine learning models such support vector classifiers, the improvements to traditional quantum algorithms concentrate on upgrading from traditional quantum algorithms to QNNs. In order to train another large quantum data, the QNN training algorithm typically uses a small quantum device; therefore, it can be implemented using hybrid quantum-classical methods, where quantum processors improve the performance of the conventional stochastic gradient descent method for quantum machine learning.

There may be potential advantages to training QNNs via reinforcement learning using hybrid architectures, such as the policy gradient, deep Q-learning, and evolutionary strategy. In the center, quantum circuit learning makes use of a quantum device to identify unitary operations so that, as the input quantum state changes through the quantum circuit, the output is similar to those from the model to be trained. This is based on the assumption that the circuit ansatz structure of the taught model is present.

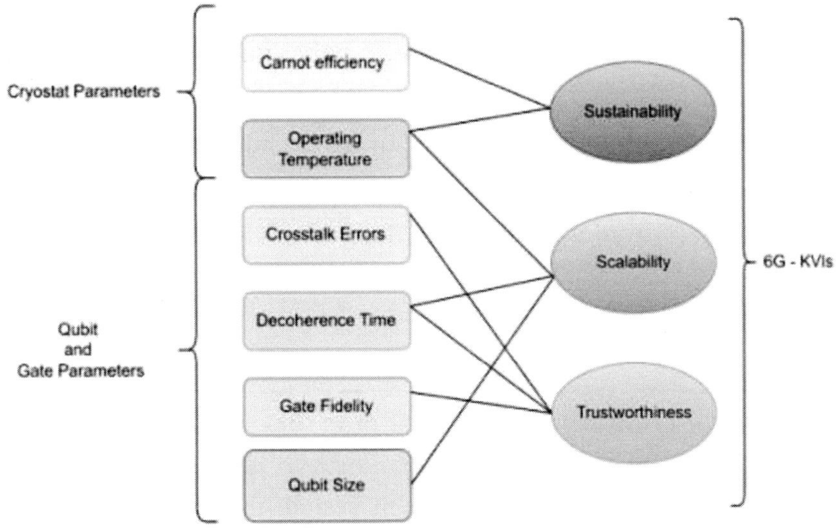

Fig.14.1 In-Network Quantum Computing.

The Positive Influence of Quantum Computing on Artificial Intelligence

Quantum computer's ability to process information outruns that of classical computers. In other words, there will be less time for AI systems to adapt and enhance. Algorithms might be able to leverage relationships between variables more efficiently if quantum entanglement is applied.

Quantum computers are able to optimize complex problems suitable for AI, which improves the performance of AI algorithms. This, in turn, could create artificial intelligence which is more advanced and sophisticated than the classical one as quantum computing principles are non-classical.

A number of AI tasks, including planning and scheduling, can be enhanced using quantum computing as it assists in the search for possible solutions to the tasks.

Quantum computing allows to engineer AI models more effectively and more at scale.

Some calculations can be done by quantum computers which classical computers cannot solve, and this enables new AI algorithms development. For example, a large number of integers can be factored using Shor's algorithm, and quantum computers are better than classical computers in simulating quantum systems.

Quantum Annealing helps to bring solutions to problems that couldn't be solved through classical means. Quantum Annealing can indeed help validate AI algorithms in terms of correctness and accuracy.

AI systems can advance through the development of high quality simulated environments condition in quantum computers so that performance in real life situations can be more optimal. For instance, quantum computers do not experience that type of memory loss that is often seen in old classical neural networks. As a result, any new things can be learned without forgetting all the old things which makes knowledge retention effective.

Sensitive information can be protected thanks to Quantum computers within AI systems. Furthermore, cybercrime could be combated through the use of parallel computing. Quantum computers can exist in multiple states at the same time, unlike classical computers, which operate from a single state. This allows for more effective algorithms to be discovered.

14.1 Quantum AI/ML

Machine learning and artificial intelligence, drug development and genomics, the chemical industry, molecular biology, cryptography, transportation and warehouse logistics, Internet communications, and quantum system modeling are just a few of the fields where quantum computing applications have already advanced. In example, quantum simulation may make it possible to quickly prototype materials and designs before components or assemblies are built using fast tooling, CNC machining, injection molding, or 3D printing.

The best quantum computers available today can only simulate a small number of particles and their interactions. However, intriguing hints are emerging that could help us comprehend the chemistry and manufacturing of eco-friendly carbon-neutral fertilizers and cements, model the intricacies of flight mechanics, aerodynamics, and fluid dynamics in the aerospace sector, and help us design next-generation EV batteries and solar panels. They may also help us understand the low-temperature behavior of exotic materials and superconductivity.

Here are a few of the more astounding advancements

The existence of the SIGINT programs "Penetrating Hard Targets" and "Owning the Net" to crack any type of robust encryption, obtain access to valuable secure digital communications networks, and create and target Quantum Key Distribution (QKD) protocols was verified by Edward Snowden's 2014 leak of National Security Agency documents. The agency intended to create a quantum "god machine" for these objectives, which would cost $80 million.

The study "Artificial Life in Quantum Technologies," presented by Unai Alvarez-Rodriguez of the University of the Basque Country in Spain in 2015, "paves the way for the realization of artificial life and embodied evolution with quantum technologies," according to him. Researchers from Ulm University in Germany found proof of quantum Darwinism in a room-temperature synthetic diamond test in 2019. A hypothesis known as quantum Darwinism describes how the whims of the quantum world give rise to our objective, classical physics. According to quantum Darwinism, the "quantum-classical transition" and evolutionary natural selection are comparable processes.

Since they are the "fittest" survivors, physical attributes chosen from a bouillabaisse of possibilities become concrete. This explains, for example, how different people can measure a quantum system and eventually agree on their results. In the past year alone, researchers have (a) revealed a proof of concept for a remote-sensing quantum radar, (b) built an impenetrable integrated quantum communication network that connects nodes over a 2,850-mile radius, and (c) devised a plan to use current telescope and receiver hardware to target and test possible quantum communications transmitted by extraterrestrials.

Information science and technology, economic activity and social paradigms, regulatory frameworks, and political and security structures will all undergo significant change as a result of the convergence of quantum computing and artificial intelligence, or quantum AL/ML [QAI]. Genetics, robotics, information, and nanotechnologies—the Fourth Industrial Revolution of GRI technologies—are expected to soon give rise to what the Dutch refer to as "Smart Humanity" and the Japanese refer to as "Society 5.0."

A post-scarcity golden age where quantum AI for good rules and advancements in quantum technologies enable the universal democratization of access to infinite computational possibilities could result from the next revolutionary change. It might also result in a post-apocalyptic hellscape. Maybe we should try to flee that technological dystopia since we are currently living in it. According to Johannes Otterbach of the quantum computer company Rigetti, machine learning and quantum computing are a good fit because they are both probabilistic by nature. Quantum computers have the potential to significantly accelerate machine learning training.

All three of the main subfields of machine learning—supervised learning, unsupervised learning, and reinforcement learning—will progress with quantum machine learning. In the fields of sampling, search, optimization, pattern recognition, predictive and risk analytics, and simulation, researchers are looking for quantum machine learning algorithms that show significant speedups over classical algorithms and that get past unsolvable exponential-time barriers to problem solving and decision-making.

Rapid developments in artificial intelligence in both scientific and industrial fields have highlighted the necessity of overcoming the computational constraints of traditional approaches and investigating alternate paradigms in order to develop scalable and effective AI solutions. The possibility that quantum-enhanced AI methods could surpass strictly classical approaches is suggested by recent developments in quantum computing, especially when it comes to solving computationally demanding tasks. One important avenue for this integration is the creation of hybrid quantum-classical systems, in which classical AI inference tasks are pre-processed by quantum computers. Long-term, early-stage fault-tolerant quantum computers with more than 50 logical qubits may allow for more complicated algorithms, whereas noisy intermediate-scale quantum devices with

100 to 200 physical qubits are anticipated to make this integration possible in the near to mid-term.

The main focus of quantum-enhanced AI is speeding up particular subroutines that are computationally costly for traditional approaches, like optimization, sampling, and high-dimensional data processing. In one example, high-performance computing (HPC) resources and quantum processors are combined to create hybrid systems that use quantum algorithms to address certain computational bottlenecks while maintaining the scalability and resilience of classical AI. Enhancing AI models using quantum-generated data is another exciting approach that may increase processing speed, computational complexity, modeling accuracy, and the quantity of data needed for training. Although these advancements demonstrate the revolutionary potential of quantum-assisted AI, sustained interdisciplinary efforts from the classical AI and quantum computing communities are necessary to achieve real-world impact.

The current status of quantum computing approaches and how they integrate with traditional processes are briefly described in this part, with a focus on machine learning methods. It also highlights the need for more study to enable widespread and efficient adoption by highlighting important AI subfields that are still understudied despite the enormous promise of quantum technologies, such as reasoning, optimization, and multi-agent systems.

14.1.1 Quantum-aided machine learning

14.1.1.1Supervised learning

Quantum supervised learning (QSL) is the process of solving supervised learning tasks using quantum algorithms. A model is trained on labeled data in supervised learning, a foundational area of machine learning, to discover the relationship between inputs (features) and related outputs (labels). To forecast the results for unknown inputs, the learnt connection must be generalized. Classification, in which the model allocates an input to a particular category, and regression, in which the model forecasts a continuous quantitative value, are typical instances of supervised learning tasks.

In many tasks, state-of-the-art techniques like neural networks have shown impressive performance, especially when huge datasets and specialized technology are available. These approaches, however, have a number of drawbacks, such as the requirement for large amounts of labeled data, lengthy training periods for intricate models, the inability to fully explain predictions, and the high computational expense of simulating high-dimensional, non-linear relationships. These drawbacks frequently make traditional techniques less scalable and useful in real-world situations.

Examples include the expenses associated with expert annotation in domains such as legal analysis and medical imaging, which restrict scalability, and the performance and generalization that are hampered by noisy labeling from crowd-sourcing or subjective tasks like sentiment analysis. By addressing issues that traditional approaches find challenging or unattainable, QSL seeks to overcome these obstacles. In general, there are several purposes for applying quantum algorithms to supervised learning problems: to streamline the training process in terms of training time and the number of optimization cycles needed; to enhance accuracy, or how well the models identify broad patterns in the data; and to increase efficiency by lowering the quantity of data required for training, with the goal of obtaining comparable or better results with less information.

According to the degree of quantum involvement and the kind of quantum hardware employed, this field includes a variety of methods that take into account incorporating quantum technologies into machine learning workflows. The differences between FTQC and NISQ technologies—where fault tolerance is not presumed to exist—have an impact on the theoretical potential and practical viability of QSL techniques and applications.

Effective quantum training of classical models

Enhancing the training phase of classical models is one important methodological application of quantum computing in supervised learning. By utilizing quantum algorithms to more effectively tackle the underlying parametric optimization issues, fault-tolerant quantum machine learning seeks to theoretically accelerate the optimization of well-defined classical techniques, including support vector machines, splines, and linear regression.

In order to speed up computationally costly linear algebra operations, these methods assume a specific functional form for the target function of interest, which is frequently expressed as a linear relationship with parameters to be estimated, as in least squares regression. This makes it possible to employ quantum techniques, such as variations of the Harrow-Hassidim-Lloyd (HHL) algorithm. These approaches rely on the availability of extended quantum circuits and error-corrected qubits, which allow for effective resolution of convex optimization problems with polynomial complexity. Since they emerge in the setting of quantum training pruned classical networks, strong guarantees for the performance of quantum training of classical models have been obtained, especially for models that are sparse and sufficiently dissipative.

Simultaneously, NISQ-based methods, like shadow models, seek to train classical surrogates of quantum neural networks that imitate quantum models by utilizing the current generation of quantum hardware, assuming that training them can be done more effectively.

Furthermore, classically inspired quantum approaches, such as quantum convolutional neural networks (QCNNs) or quantum perceptrons, modify well-established conventional architectures to take advantage of computing advantages during training in the neural network-based deep learning field. By limiting the use of quantum resources to the training stage, all of these methods allow for classical inference for scalability and wider end-user applicability. Ad hoc methods must be used in these situations, though, to guarantee that the quantum component is only utilized for training and that the algorithm remains completely classical for testing. Knowledge distillation is one such method in which a purely classical model is trained using guidance from a quantum-trained model.

A variational quantum circuit-based QNN is trained on a classification or regression problem to obtain softmax-like output probabilities, which is the first step in transferring knowledge from a QNN to a classical neural network. The soft labels that the QNN predicts are then used to train a traditional neural network rather than the ground truth. The objective is to produce a classical model that accurately captures the learnt representations of the QNN by simulating its decision boundary. When traditional models have trouble with optimization, generalization, or data efficiency, this method is especially helpful.

For example, in order to obtain effective convergence in image classification tasks, deep classical networks frequently need large labeled datasets and considerable hyper parameter tuning. Similar to this, long-range dependencies and high-dimensional correlations in time series forecasting present difficulties for classical models, requiring computationally costly training and considerable feature engineering. Classical models may have trouble using conventional feature representations to capture quantum mechanical features in molecular property prediction, which could result in less than ideal performance.

Learning with quantum models

In addition to training improvements, learning with quantum models integrates quantum computing into the training and inference stages with the goal of identifying data patterns that are unsolvable for classical systems. This involves leveraging complex quantum kernels and parameterized quantum circuits to represent data in ways classical models cannot. The variational paradigm, which relies on hybrid quantum-classical techniques in which a smaller variational quantum circuit is controlled by a classical algorithm, is particularly prominent in NISQ-based implementations, offering opportunities to explore novel hypothesis functions.

Initial findings suggest that quantum models may offer the ability to streamline the parameter space, decrease the amount of training data needed, and facilitate more effective training methods. However, these results are currently applicable only to particular cases involving quantum data. Exploring these benefits in data-heavy fields, such as genomics (for instance, DNA sequence analysis), financial modeling (like risk assessment in high-frequency trading), climate simulations (such as large-scale weather forecasts), and the industrial Internet of Things (for example, optimizing real-time sensor networks), might pave the way for quantum models to supersede traditional ones in both training and inference.

Nonetheless, considerable challenges remain, such as optimization plateaus and the absence of effective quantum versions of the classical back propagation training method. In certain cases, quantum models can be entirely dequantized, meaning that a viable classical algorithm for the same task can be identified, or classical alternatives can be developed. Additionally, it is crucial to ensure that the quantum circuit possesses enough expressiveness. Despite these hurdles, the incorporation of quantum computing into the supervised learning pipeline offers tremendous potential by tackling computational limitations and uncovering new insights into intricate data structures.

Diffusion models, particularly in the context of probability, can be regarded as a type of supervised learning. These models, especially those applied to generative tasks such as image creation, operate by incrementally introducing noise to the data in a forward diffusion phase, after which the model learns to reverse this noise process to retrieve the original data during the backward diffusion phase. Moreover, variations of HHL can offer quantum algorithms for diffusion models that demonstrate potential for a quantum advantage.

14.1.2 Reinforcement learning

Reinforcement learning (RL) is a subset of machine learning where an agent learns to make choices by engaging with an environment to maximize cumulative rewards, distinct from the categories of supervised and unsupervised learning. It finds applications in various domains such as robotics and large language models. In contrast to supervised learning, which depends on labeled datasets, RL emphasizes learning through trial and error, utilizing feedback from actions to enhance future outcomes. A significant difficulty in RL arises from its computational complexity, as numerous RL problems are represented through partially observable Markov decision processes (POMDPs), which require substantial computational resources.

The intricacy of this issue renders it computationally unfeasible to discover optimal solutions for large-scale challenges, which emphasizes the importance of effective algorithms and approximations. In practice, reinforcement learning depends on vast amounts of data and prolonged training durations, especially in advanced models that utilize deep neural networks. These challenges highlight the promise of quantum computing in overcoming the computational obstacles that are characteristic of reinforcement learning.

Efficient Quantum Training of Classical Models

One promising avenue in quantum machine learning involves leveraging quantum computing to enhance the training of classical reinforcement learning (RL) models through hybrid quantum-classical architectures. In many RL applications—such as robotic manipulation, autonomous navigation, and decision-making tasks—Actor-Critic frameworks are widely employed. These architectures decouple the decision-making (Actor) from the value estimation (Critic), where the Critic evaluates actions and provides feedback that stabilizes and guides policy updates for the Actor. The Critic's role is critical to the learning process: accurate value function approximation significantly impacts the stability and convergence speed of the overall model. Quantum-enhanced Critic modules, potentially implemented via variational quantum circuits (VQCs), offer an opportunity to perform more expressive and compact function approximations, potentially leading to improved sample efficiency and faster convergence in classical RL systems.

Despite their potential, achieving efficient training in complex reinforcement learning environments typically requires substantial computational resources and prolonged training periods. Hybrid quantum-classical architectures offer a promising solution by integrating quantum neural networks (QNNs) as the Critic, while retaining classical neural networks for the Actor. Employing QNNs in the Critic role allows for more effective capture of high-dimensional data patterns, improved trainability, enhanced stability, and stronger generalization capabilities during value estimation. Notably, after training is complete, the quantum component can be discarded—resulting in a fully classical system for deployment. This approach ensures that quantum resources are only used where they provide the greatest benefit: during training. As a result, the design maintains compatibility with existing classical infrastructure during inference, while still capitalizing on quantum advantages to optimize training efficiency and performance.

In Actor-Critic architectures, the Critic is exclusively involved during the training phase to evaluate actions and guide the Actor's policy updates. The Actor, typically a neural network that outputs actions based on observed states, is the sole component used during inference. Therefore, when incorporating a quantum neural network as the Critic, there is no need for model transfer or conversion after training. This is consistent with classical implementations, where the Critic is also discarded post-training. As a result, the quantum Critic serves only as a training accelerator, and the final deployed model remains entirely classical—ensuring compatibility with existing deployment environments while benefiting from potential quantum speedups during learning.

Learning with Quantum Models

Quantum machine learning (QML) leverages the principles of quantum computing to enhance the capabilities of traditional learning algorithms. In the context of reinforcement learning and neural networks, quantum models—such as variational quantum circuits

(VQCs) or quantum neural networks (QNNs)—offer potential advantages in expressivity, parallelism, and the ability to model complex high-dimensional data distributions.

These quantum models are particularly promising when integrated into hybrid learning frameworks. For instance, VQCs can serve as function approximators within reinforcement learning agents, particularly in the Critic component of Actor-Critic architectures. Their ability to represent non-classical correlations (entanglement) and perform high-dimensional transformations with relatively shallow circuits gives them a theoretical edge over certain classical counterparts, especially in settings with limited training data or highly non-linear value functions.

Training quantum models, however, presents unique challenges. Noisy intermediate-scale quantum (NISQ) devices are still limited in qubit count and fidelity, and quantum gradients can suffer from issues like vanishing gradients (barren plateaus). Nevertheless, various techniques—such as parameter initialization heuristics, quantum-aware optimizers, and hybrid training loops—have been proposed to improve the trainability and stability of quantum models.

Importantly, quantum models in current hybrid frameworks are typically restricted to the training phase. In applications like reinforcement learning, the quantum component (e.g., a QNN-based Critic) assists in optimizing the policy but is removed post-training. The deployed agent remains classical, relying solely on the Actor network, thereby avoiding the need for quantum inference infrastructure. This approach balances practicality with innovation—exploiting quantum advantages during training while maintaining compatibility with real-world deployment constraints.

14.1.3 Quantum Unsupervised Learning

Quantum unsupervised learning aims to harness the principles of quantum computing to address the inherent challenges of unsupervised learning tasks, including clustering, dimensionality reduction, and generative modeling. A key distinction in this emerging field lies in the nature of the algorithms being developed. Some quantum approaches are designed to accelerate existing classical methods, while others introduce fundamentally new, quantum-native paradigms that exploit properties such as superposition, entanglement, and quantum interference.

A prominent example is the q-means algorithm, a quantum variant of the classical k-means clustering technique. Q-means maintains conceptual alignment with its classical counterpart but is designed to offer significant computational advantages—potentially achieving exponential speedups under certain assumptions related to data access and encoding. By efficiently estimating distances and centroids in quantum Hilbert space, q-means exemplifies how quantum computing can enhance traditional unsupervised learning processes while preserving interpretability and usability.

Similarly, quantum algorithms have been used for spectral clustering, a widely used technique for detecting complex and non-convex cluster structures. These quantum variants offer theoretical polynomial speedups over their classical counterparts by exploiting efficient quantum linear algebra subroutines, such as quantum matrix exponentiation and eigenvalue estimation.

Despite these advancements, quantum unsupervised learning still faces substantial challenges. A major obstacle lies in the data encoding bottleneck—the process of embedding high-dimensional classical data into quantum states. Efficient amplitude encoding, which would enable such data to be loaded into quantum memory in logarithmic time, remains largely theoretical due to the current lack of scalable quantum random access memory (qRAM).

Moreover, while Parameterized Quantum Circuits (PQCs) and variational approaches have shown potential in various unsupervised learning tasks, their practical deployment is hindered by optimization difficulties such as barren plateaus, where gradients vanish and prevent effective training. These issues, coupled with hardware limitations and noise in near-term quantum devices, mean that current quantum unsupervised models are still far from outperforming classical methods on large-scale, real-world problems.

Classical Models of Effective Quantum Training

Quantum unsupervised learning leverages quantum algorithms to uncover patterns, structures, or groupings within unlabeled data. A central technique in this domain is clustering, which involves organizing data points into groups such that those within the same cluster exhibit higher similarity to each other than to those in other clusters. The objective is to partition the dataset in a way that captures the underlying structure without relying on predefined labels.

In classical clustering approaches, such as k-means, the algorithm operates by identifying a set of representative points—known as centroids—that define each cluster. During training, data points are iteratively assigned to the nearest centroid according to a distance metric, such as Euclidean distance for continuous data or Hamming distance for binary data. The centroids are then updated based on the current assignments, and this process repeats until convergence.

Quantum counterparts, such as the q-means algorithm, follow a similar high-level structure but utilize quantum subroutines to accelerate key computational steps. These may include distance estimation, centroid updates, and matrix operations—potentially offering significant speedups over classical methods under certain data access assumptions. By integrating these quantum methods into the training pipeline, researchers aim to improve the scalability and efficiency of clustering tasks, particularly in high-dimensional or large-scale datasets.

Once data points are assigned to clusters, centroids are recalculated to minimize the total distance between each point and its assigned centroid. This process repeats iteratively until convergence, which occurs when cluster assignments or centroid positions stabilize, or when an objective function—commonly the sum of squared distances—ceases to improve. Through this iterative optimization, the algorithm uncovers a stable and coherent partitioning of the data that reflects its underlying structure.

However, a major computational bottleneck in classical clustering arises from distance calculations, especially in large datasets with high-dimensional feature spaces. These calculations often require evaluating all pairwise distances, leading to substantial computational overhead as data volume increases.

Quantum clustering offers a potential solution to this scalability challenge by exploiting quantum computational primitives to accelerate key operations. A particularly important tool in this context is the quantum swap test, which allows efficient estimation of the similarity—or equivalently, the inner product—between quantum states. When classical data points are encoded as quantum states, the swap test enables rapid comparison of their similarity with significantly reduced computational complexity under ideal quantum conditions. This capability lies at the heart of several quantum clustering algorithms, where it can be used to efficiently assign data points to clusters or compute distances to centroids.

By leveraging such quantum operations, quantum clustering algorithms aim to dramatically reduce the time complexity associated with high-dimensional similarity evaluations, offering a promising path toward more scalable and efficient unsupervised learning.

A prominent example of quantum acceleration in unsupervised learning is found in quantum-enhanced variants of the k-means clustering algorithm. In classical k-means, each iteration involves assigning data points to the nearest centroid and updating centroid positions, both of which rely heavily on computing distances in high-dimensional space. These operations scale linearly with the number of data points and features, making them computationally intensive for large-scale datasets.

Quantum versions of k-means—particularly those targeting fault-tolerant quantum computing (FTQC) regimes—have the potential to exponentially reduce the time complexity of key steps such as distance evaluation. For example, distance computations that require

O

$($

N

d

)

O(Nd) time classically (where

N

N is the number of points and

d

d is the number of dimensions) can be performed in polylogarithmic time on a quantum computer, assuming efficient data encoding. Techniques such as the quantum swap test and amplitude encoding allow for rapid estimation of inner products between quantum-encoded vectors, significantly accelerating similarity calculations.

Moreover, quantum k-means algorithms can represent cluster assignments as quantum states, allowing for efficient quantum sampling and statistical inference without needing to explicitly process or output the full dataset. This approach enables analysis of global data properties while preserving compact quantum representations, offering new avenues for privacy-preserving or resource-constrained clustering.

Assuming that the overhead of encoding classical data into quantum states is negligible or can be mitigated by future advances such as quantum random access memory (qRAM), these quantum techniques could dramatically improve the scalability and efficiency of unsupervised learning. Such capabilities would be particularly valuable in real-world applications involving high-dimensional or large-volume data, where classical clustering methods struggle to maintain performance.

Importantly, while quantum algorithms can be employed to accelerate the computation of centroids during the training phase, it is also feasible to extract centroid information from the quantum system and subsequently perform the assignment of new, unseen data points using classical methods. This hybrid approach is particularly effective when the training dataset is sufficiently representative, and the number of new data points is relatively small. Under these conditions, the computational burden of classical distance evaluations for new assignments remains manageable, avoiding the need to re-engage quantum resources for inference.

By offloading the most computationally intensive operations—such as distance calculations during training—to quantum processors, and deferring inference to classical post-processing, this method strikes a balance between quantum acceleration and practical deployment. Such quantum-assisted clustering allows for substantial speedups during model training, particularly in high-dimensional or large-scale datasets, without requiring full quantum infrastructure during deployment. As a result, this paradigm enhances the scalability and accessibility of quantum clustering approaches, positioning them as powerful tools for addressing real-world unsupervised learning challenges.

Quantum Models learning

When quantum algorithms are employed during both the training and testing phases of clustering, they can be used to evaluate similarities, compute distances, and refine decision boundaries directly within high-dimensional quantum state spaces. This end-to-end quantum approach becomes particularly advantageous in scenarios where the training set is small, but the volume of unseen data is large, enabling the model to generalize more effectively without reverting to classical computation. However, the practical feasibility of this approach hinges on the scalability of quantum resources and the cost of transitioning between quantum and classical representations, which remains a significant bottleneck in current hardware architectures.

A more structured form of unsupervised learning is image segmentation, which aims to partition an image into semantically meaningful regions. Classical approaches to segmentation face substantial computational and practical challenges. While supervised segmentation methods—often based on convolutional neural networks—have achieved high accuracy, they rely heavily on large volumes of high-quality labeled data. Acquiring such annotations, especially in domains like medical imaging or remote sensing, is costly, labor-intensive, and subject to human bias, leading to inconsistent or unreliable labels.

Unsupervised segmentation techniques attempt to address this by eliminating the need for ground truth data. Traditional methods such as thresholding, clustering, region-growing, and edge detection operate directly on raw pixel values or low-level features. However, these approaches often suffer from poor scalability, limited robustness to noise, and difficulty in adapting to complex image structures or high-dimensional feature spaces.

More sophisticated graph-based segmentation methods model the image as a graph, where pixels or regions correspond to nodes, and edges represent similarity measures. Techniques such as minimum cut, normalized cut, and spectral clustering are then applied to partition the graph into coherent regions. While these methods offer better structure and flexibility, they are also computationally intensive, particularly when dealing with large images or 3D volumes, due to the combinatorial complexity of graph partitioning.

Quantum algorithms, especially those leveraging quantum linear algebra and eigenvalue estimation, have the potential to significantly accelerate key steps in graph-based segmentation, such as similarity computation and spectral decomposition. By reducing the time complexity of these operations, quantum-enhanced segmentation techniques may offer a scalable alternative to classical methods, particularly in high-dimensional or data-scarce environments.

Quantum computing presents a compelling alternative to classical graph-based segmentation methods by leveraging quantum annealing to efficiently solve the underlying combinatorial optimization problems. In this framework, the image segmentation task—particularly when modeled as a graph partitioning problem—can be reformulated as a Quadratic Unconstrained Binary Optimization (QUBO) problem. This transformation enables the use of quantum annealers, such as those developed by D-Wave, to approximate optimal segmentations by exploring the solution space in a highly parallel and probabilistic manner.

By encoding the graph's structure and segmentation objective into a QUBO formulation, quantum annealing seeks configurations of binary variables (e.g., node assignments) that minimize the total cut cost or maximize intra-segment similarity. This approach is especially attractive for large-scale segmentation problems, where classical combinatorial solvers become intractable due to the exponential growth of the search space. Although current quantum annealers are limited by noise, connectivity constraints, and precision, early research suggests that hybrid quantum-classical solvers—which combine classical preprocessing and post processing with quantum optimization cores—can outperform purely classical heuristics on specific instances.

Consequently, quantum annealing introduces a promising new tool for scalable, data-efficient image segmentation, particularly in applications where segmentation quality is critical but labeled data or computational resources are limited.

Quantum computing presents a compelling alternative to classical graph-based segmentation methods by leveraging quantum annealing to efficiently solve the underlying combinatorial optimization problems. In this framework, the image segmentation task—particularly when modeled as a graph partitioning problem—can be reformulated as a Quadratic Unconstrained Binary Optimization (QUBO) problem. This transformation enables the use of quantum annealers, such as those developed by D-Wave, to approximate optimal segmentations by exploring the solution space in a highly parallel and probabilistic manner.

By encoding the graph's structure and segmentation objective into a QUBO formulation, quantum annealing seeks configurations of binary variables (e.g., node assignments) that minimize the total cut cost or maximize intra-segment similarity. This approach is especially attractive for large-scale segmentation problems, where classical combinatorial solvers become intractable due to the exponential growth of the search space. Although current quantum annealers are limited by noise, connectivity constraints, and precision, early research suggests that hybrid quantum-classical solvers—which combine classical preprocessing and post processing with quantum optimization cores—can outperform purely classical heuristics on specific instances.

Consequently, quantum annealing introduces a promising new tool for scalable, data-efficient image segmentation, particularly in applications where segmentation quality is critical but labeled data or computational resources are limited.\

By encoding pixels as nodes in a graph and modeling similarities or dissimilarities as weighted edges, quantum annealing can be used to efficiently solve the segmentation task as a graph partitioning problem. This allows for the rapid identification of optimal or near-optimal partitions, and in some cases, quantum annealers have been shown to outperform classical solvers in runtime, particularly for large-scale or highly complex datasets where classical combinatorial methods become computationally prohibitive.

This approach is especially beneficial in domains characterized by limited, noisy, or unreliable labeled data, such as medical imaging or satellite remote sensing, where traditional supervised learning methods often struggle. By avoiding the reliance on labeled data and focusing on the inherent structure of the input, quantum segmentation methods offer a compelling alternative.

While current implementations primarily utilize quantum annealing, the same graph-based segmentation framework can be adapted for gate-based quantum computing. In such cases, variational quantum algorithms (VQAs), which are more qubit-efficient and compatible with near-term noisy devices, offer a promising path forward. These methods could enable flexible, hybrid quantum-classical segmentation pipelines, further expanding the range and scalability of quantum approaches.

Nevertheless, the widespread practical deployment of quantum segmentation methods depends on continued progress in quantum hardware development, including increased qubit counts, improved connectivity, noise reduction, and the design of efficient quantum-classical hybrid workflows. While empirical results demonstrate quantum advantage in specific scenarios, consistent, large-scale applicability will require overcoming current limitations in quantum system reliability and data encoding efficiency.

14.1.4 Quantum data pre-processing

Classical data processing methodologies encompass a range of well-established techniques used in conventional computing environments to prepare and refine data for analysis. These methods are foundational to modern data science and machine learning workflows, as they ensure that datasets are clean, consistent, and analytically meaningful.

One fundamental task is data cleaning, which involves identifying and correcting errors, inconsistencies, or missing values within a dataset. This step is essential for maintaining data integrity and preventing downstream analytical errors. Another critical component is feature selection, which seeks to identify the most relevant variables for the task at hand, thereby improving model interpretability, reducing overfitting, and decreasing computational complexity.

Normalization is also a core pre-processing technique, typically used to scale numerical features to a common range or distribution. This ensures that features contribute proportionately to distance-based algorithms and gradient-based optimization processes. In parallel, dimensionality reduction techniques, such as Principal Component Analysis

(PCA) and t-SNE, are employed to reduce the number of input features while preserving the essential structure and variability in the data. These techniques not only enhance computational efficiency but also help to mitigate the curse of dimensionality in high-dimensional datasets.

Collectively, these classical methods ensure that data is accurate, relevant, and suitably formatted for subsequent analysis. Their widespread adoption and proven effectiveness make them indispensable components of machine learning pipelines and data-driven decision-making processes.

Quantum data pre-processing builds upon classical methodologies by leveraging the unique computational capabilities of quantum systems to prepare data for quantum algorithms. This process involves two key components: the encoding of classical data into quantum states, and the manipulation of those states to facilitate efficient downstream processing.

A central goal of quantum pre-processing is to enable more compact storage and efficient transformation of large-scale and high-dimensional data, where classical techniques may become computationally expensive or intractable. Quantum algorithms offer potential speedups in these contexts due to their ability to operate in exponentially large Hilbert spaces and perform linear algebraic operations in parallel.

A fundamental step in quantum pre-processing is quantum state preparation, wherein classical data is mapped onto quantum states using a variety of encoding schemes. Common approaches include:

Amplitude encoding, which embeds data into the amplitudes of a normalized quantum state, allowing exponential compression but often requiring complex circuits or qRAM.

Basis encoding, where each data element is directly mapped to the computational basis states of qubits. Angle encoding (or parametric encoding), where data is encoded into the rotation angles of quantum gates applied to qubits.

These representations enable quantum parallelism, allowing the system to process multiple data components simultaneously and apply transformations across superpositions of states. As a result, quantum pre-processing can reduce the computational cost of tasks such as similarity estimation, kernel construction, and feature transformation, which are essential in many machine learning and signal processing applications.

Beyond encoding, quantum data pre-processing also includes the design of quantum subroutines capable of extracting meaningful information from quantum states—such as computing inner products, evaluating distances, or projecting data onto lower-dimensional quantum subspaces. When combined with variational quantum algorithms or hybrid quantum-classical frameworks, these techniques contribute to the scalability and practical utility of quantum machine learning systems.

While still in the early stages of development, quantum data pre-processing holds significant promise as a foundation for efficient quantum analytics, particularly as quantum hardware and memory access technologies (e.g., qRAM) continue to evolve.

Quantum algorithms have the potential to significantly accelerate key pre-processing steps in machine learning, such as dimensionality reduction and feature selection, by leveraging quantum linear algebra and optimization techniques. A prominent example is Quantum Principal Component Analysis (qPCA), which offers an exponential speedup over its classical counterpart under specific conditions. Unlike classical PCA, which scales polynomially with the number of dimensions and data points, quantum PCA utilizes quantum density matrix exponentiation to efficiently extract the principal components of a dataset encoded into a quantum system.

In this framework, the dataset is represented as a quantum density matrix, and multiple copies of this matrix are used to perform Hamiltonian simulation and extract the dominant eigenvectors—which correspond to the principal components—without requiring full reconstruction of the original matrix. This method is especially effective for low-rank matrices, where only a few components capture most of the data variance. However, the practical realization of qPCA depends on the availability of fault-tolerant quantum computers and efficient methods for preparing quantum states that represent the input data.

Similarly, quantum feature selection methods, particularly those built on variational quantum circuits (VQCs) and hybrid quantum-classical optimization, are being explored as a means to identify the most relevant input variables more efficiently than classical algorithms. By encoding data into quantum states and using parameterized quantum gates to transform these states, VQCs can exploit the quantum Hilbert space to model and evaluate complex feature interactions. Through quantum parallelism, these algorithms can potentially evaluate correlations and feature subsets simultaneously, accelerating the search for optimal feature combinations.

These quantum techniques aim not only to reduce computational overhead but also to improve the accuracy and interpretability of downstream learning models by focusing on the most informative features. As quantum hardware continues to evolve, such approaches may become integral components of scalable quantum machine learning pipelines, especially in domains characterized by high-dimensional, noisy, or incomplete data.

In addition to state preparation and encoding techniques, quantum distance metrics and quantum kernel methods play a pivotal role in the preprocessing stage of quantum machine learning by transforming classical data into a quantum-representable form optimized for further analysis.

Quantum distance metrics, such as the Quantum Hamming Distance and Quantum Euclidean Distance, enable the computation of similarities between data points by exploiting quantum parallelism. These methods can compare quantum-encoded vectors efficiently across exponentially large spaces, making it possible to uncover subtle correlations in high-dimensional datasets that may be computationally inaccessible through classical techniques.

Similarly, quantum kernel methods map data into higher-dimensional quantum Hilbert spaces, where complex, non-linear relationships become more easily separable through linear classification techniques. These methods are particularly useful for clustering, classification, and anomaly detection, and can provide quantum advantages over classical kernel approaches in both expressivity and computational efficiency. Quantum kernel estimation can be implemented using interferometric methods or variational circuits, and forms the basis for hybrid quantum-classical support vector machines and related models.

Furthermore, quantum generative models, such as Quantum Boltzmann Machines (QBMs) and Quantum Generative Adversarial Networks (QGANs), offer novel frameworks for data generation and augmentation. These models can be employed during pre-processing to synthetically expand training datasets, especially in scenarios with limited or imbalanced data. By learning quantum representations of the underlying data distribution, quantum generative models can potentially generate samples with higher diversity and fidelity than their classical counterparts, thereby improving model generalization.

Collectively, these quantum methods extend the scope of data pre-processing by enabling the efficient handling, transformation, and enrichment of complex datasets. When integrated into quantum machine learning pipelines, they offer the potential to significantly improve scalability, representation power, and model performance across various application domains—including bioinformatics, finance, cybersecurity, and quantum chemistry.

14.1.5 Optimizing Quantum

Optimization is a foundational challenge in artificial intelligence (AI) and broader computational domains, involving the identification of input configurations that minimize or maximize a given cost or objective function. Many AI-related problems are characterized by extremely large or high-dimensional search spaces, particularly in combinatorial settings where the number of possible solutions grows exponentially with the problem size. These problems are often NP-hard, exhibiting intractable worst-case complexity under classical computational paradigms.

In continuous domains, the challenge is further exacerbated by non-convex objective functions, which introduce multiple local minima and saddle points, significantly complicating the search for global optima. These features render classical optimization heuristics computationally intensive and frequently ineffective at scale.

Quantum computing offers several promising avenues to address these challenges

Quantum Speedup via Search and Acceleration

Quantum algorithms can explore classical solution spaces more efficiently by leveraging quantum parallelism and amplitude amplification. A prominent example is Grover's search algorithm, which offers a quadratic speedup for unstructured search problems. While this does not alter worst-case complexity classes, it provides practical improvements in large-scale search scenarios. Applied to dynamic programming, for instance in the Travelling Salesman Problem (TSP), quantum methods can reduce the runtime of classical approaches (e.g., Bellman–Held–Karp algorithm) via Grover-based acceleration. These applications typically yield polynomial speedups, which, while modest, may be significant in practice depending on the problem structure and dataset scale.

Variational Quantum Optimization and Hybrid Methods

Optimization is also central to the operation of variational quantum algorithms (VQAs), which are hybrid quantum-classical frameworks used for tasks such as combinatorial optimization, quantum chemistry, and machine learning. These algorithms use parameterized quantum circuits (PQCs) whose parameters are iteratively optimized to minimize a cost function defined over quantum measurements. Examples include the Quantum Approximate Optimization Algorithm (QAOA) and the Variational Quantum Eigensolver (VQE). Although no provable quantum-classical separation has been established for these algorithms, they show promise in exploiting the quantum landscape for navigating complex optimization spaces more efficiently.

Quantum Annealing and Adiabatic Optimization

A third route is embodied by quantum annealing and adiabatic quantum optimization, where the system is initialized in the ground state of a simple Hamiltonian and evolved toward the ground state of a problem-specific Hamiltonian encoding the cost function. Quantum annealers, such as those developed by D-Wave Systems, have demonstrated practical applications in combinatorial optimization by exploiting quantum tunneling to escape local minima, potentially outperforming classical heuristics on specific problem instances. However, quantifying quantum advantage in this context remains an active area of investigation, with mixed empirical results and limited theoretical guarantees.

Together, these quantum approaches present a compelling toolkit for advancing optimization in AI. The extent to which they outperform classical algorithms in practice depends on several factors, including problem structure, quantum hardware limitations, and data encoding costs. Continued development in fault-tolerant quantum architectures, noise mitigation, and hybrid workflows will be crucial for realizing their full potential in real-world applications.

Third, quantum algorithms have demonstrated provable advantages in approximating certain classes of practically relevant optimization problems, where classical algorithms either perform poorly or lack efficient approximation guarantees. For example, recent results show that quantum algorithms can efficiently approximate specific instances of problems such as Integer Linear Programming (ILP), for which no efficient classical approximation exists under standard complexity assumptions. These findings offer exponential separations between quantum and classical performance for carefully constructed subclasses of NP-hard problems, highlighting areas where quantum computing delivers fundamental algorithmic advantages rather than mere speedups.

Complementing this, novel methods based on decoded quantum interferometry establish connections between combinatorial optimization problems, such as sparse MAX-XORSAT, and decoding tasks in classical error-correcting codes, notably low-density parity-check (LDPC) codes. In this approach, one leverages the ability of quantum interference patterns to encode and extract solutions from a superposition of states. Surprisingly, classical belief propagation—an efficient inference technique in coding theory—can be adapted to guide the decoding of these quantum interference patterns. The resulting quantum-classical hybrid algorithm exhibits performance that outpaces classical optimization methods, including advanced heuristics like simulated annealing, in both runtime and solution quality for certain problem classes.

These developments illustrate the mutually beneficial interplay between quantum computing and artificial intelligence: quantum algorithms enhance optimization capabilities in AI systems, while AI techniques such as belief propagation and neural heuristics provide classical tools that can be adapted to support quantum computation. As such, the integration of quantum algorithms into optimization workflows not only enriches our algorithmic toolbox but also broadens the frontier of tractable problems in AI, particularly in settings involving high-dimensional, discrete, or non-convex landscapes.

Quantum-native optimization algorithms offer a promising avenue for solving complex, high-dimensional, and non-convex optimization problems by exploiting the intrinsic features of quantum mechanics. A notable example is Quantum Hamiltonian Descent (QHD), which emulates classical gradient-based optimization within the dynamics of quantum systems. Instead of explicitly computing gradients, QHD leverages quantum evolution under tailored Hamiltonians to induce descent-like behavior in the cost landscape. Crucially, the quantum tunneling effect inherent in such systems provides a natural mechanism for escaping local minima, enabling improved exploration of rugged optimization surfaces that typically confound classical methods. This quantum approach is particularly well-suited to analog quantum simulators, where the continuous-time dynamics of quantum systems can be harnessed to perform optimization directly, opening new pathways for solving intractable classical problems.

In parallel, evolutionary algorithms—which mimic biological evolution through mechanisms such as selection, crossover, and mutation—represent a robust family of stochastic optimization techniques. These algorithms operate on populations of candidate solutions, allowing them to explore multiple regions of the search space simultaneously. Their population-based and inherently parallel structure makes them highly resilient to local optima and effective in global optimization tasks. Quantum computing offers significant potential to enhance the performance of evolutionary algorithms, both in terms of speed and search efficacy. Quantum parallelism can be exploited to evaluate the fitness of multiple individuals simultaneously, perform quantum-inspired crossover and mutation operations in superposition, and maintain a diverse search through entangled population states. These capabilities could lead to quantum-enhanced evolutionary frameworks, where core operations are performed more efficiently or with higher expressiveness than their classical counterparts.

Together, these two paradigms—quantum-native gradient descent and quantum-enhanced evolutionary optimization—illustrate complementary strategies in the quantum optimization landscape. While the former capitalizes on continuous quantum dynamics to mimic descent paths, the latter leverages discrete population-based strategies enriched by quantum parallelism. Their development and integration into quantum machine learning workflows represent an important step toward realizing the full potential of quantum optimization across a wide range of applications.

Quantum Automated Planning and Scheduling (QPS) investigates the application of quantum computing to classical AI planning and scheduling problems, with a particular focus on quantum-supported planning (QP) and quantum-supported scheduling (QS). These tasks encompass both online planning, which incorporates dynamic, real-time feedback during execution, and offline planning, where plans are generated prior to execution and remain fixed. In environments characterized by uncertainty and partial observability, more complex models such as Partially Observable Markov Decision Processes (POMDPs) are required. Solving these models entails generating conditional plans or policies that maximize expected utility, often under significant computational constraints. Many of these planning and scheduling problems are known to be PSPACE-complete or worse, making them particularly challenging for classical algorithms.

To address these limitations, early-stage quantum approaches have introduced quantum analogues of classical planning models, including Quantum POMDPs (qPOMDPs) and Quantum Markov Decision Processes (QMDPs). These frameworks propose leveraging quantum computational resources—such as superposition, entanglement, and amplitude amplification—to improve the efficiency of planning under uncertainty. While such models hold significant theoretical promise, they remain largely untested in practical, real-world environments, with current research primarily focused on foundational formulations and complexity analysis. Consequently, further progress in QPS will depend on both the development of quantum hardware capable of supporting these models and the design of hybrid quantum-classical algorithms that can bridge the gap between theoretical quantum models and real-world planning applications.

In parallel to planning tasks, Quantum Scheduling (QS) addresses complex optimization problems such as job shop scheduling and its more adaptable variant, flexible job shop scheduling (FJSS). These problems involve determining optimal job-to-machine assignments across multi-purpose machines with the goal of minimizing performance metrics such as production makespan, total completion time, or resource idle time. Classical approaches often struggle with the combinatorial nature of these problems, especially at scale, due to their NP-hard complexity.

Quantum-enhanced methods offer promising alternatives by exploiting quantum parallelism and non-classical optimization heuristics. Notable quantum approaches include quantum genetic algorithms (QGAs) and quantum particle swarm optimization (QPSO), which simulate evolutionary and swarm-based heuristics on quantum-inspired or quantum-native platforms. Additionally, hybrid techniques that combine Mixed-Integer Linear Programming (MILP) with Quadratic Unconstrained Binary Optimization (QUBO) formulations are gaining traction. These methods are particularly suited to quantum annealers, enabling the encoding of scheduling constraints into a QUBO structure that can be processed efficiently.

Preliminary results demonstrate that quantum approaches can yield computational advantages in specific problem instances, such as scheduling scenarios involving hundreds of jobs and machines, especially when traditional solvers become computationally prohibitive. Furthermore, related combinatorial tasks like bin packing have been explored using quantum annealing, highlighting the versatility of quantum optimization in discrete resource allocation domains. However, the practical effectiveness of these methods remains bounded by current hardware limitations, such as qubit count, connectivity, and noise, underscoring the need for continued advancement in quantum hardware and hybrid algorithm design.

14.1.6 Quantum Reasoning

Quantum reasoning explores the application of quantum computational principles to enhance logical inference, decision-making, and cognitive modeling tasks. Unlike classical reasoning, which operates under the assumptions of Boolean logic and classical probability, quantum reasoning leverages quantum probability theory, superposition, and entanglement to represent and manipulate uncertain or context-dependent information.

At its core, quantum reasoning proposes that cognitive processes—such as belief revision, decision-making under ambiguity, and contextual inference—can be more accurately modeled using quantum probabilistic frameworks. This perspective stems from empirical observations in psychology and behavioral economics, where human judgments often violate classical probabilistic axioms (e.g., the sure-thing principle or the law of total probability). Quantum cognition models attempt to reconcile these deviations by representing beliefs as vectors in a Hilbert space, where interference effects and contextual changes naturally arise.

From a computational standpoint, quantum reasoning also encompasses the use of quantum algorithms to perform logical operations or infer conclusions within knowledge representation systems. Quantum-enhanced approaches to reasoning aim to accelerate inference in domains such as theorem proving, automated planning, Bayesian reasoning, and constraint satisfaction, particularly when these tasks are embedded in large, high-dimensional, or probabilistically uncertain environments.

Furthermore, quantum logic gates can be used to simulate logical circuits with non-classical behaviors, and quantum circuits can be designed to encode complex inference chains. These capabilities open up avenues for hybrid quantum-classical reasoning systems, where quantum modules assist in tasks like entailment checking, hypothesis testing, or learning rule-based structures under uncertainty.

Despite its promise, quantum reasoning remains a developing field. Challenges include the design of interpretable quantum logic frameworks, the integration of symbolic and sub-symbolic reasoning in quantum systems, and the scalability of current quantum hardware for inference tasks.

Reasoning is a core cognitive function that enables intelligent agents to derive conclusions, make informed decisions, and solve problems by leveraging existing knowledge, rules, and observed data. Through reasoning, agents can generate new insights, handle uncertainty, and adapt dynamically to evolving environments. Reasoning is generally categorized into three primary forms: deductive reasoning, which derives logically certain outcomes from general premises; inductive reasoning, which formulates generalizations based on specific observations; and abductive reasoning, which seeks the most plausible explanations for observed phenomena.

To implement reasoning, intelligent agents rely on formal logic systems, including propositional logic, first-order logic, and probabilistic logic, which provide structured mechanisms for knowledge inference. These systems are supported by knowledge representation frameworks such as ontologies, semantic networks, rule-based systems, and Bayesian networks, enabling agents to model entities, relationships, and environmental dynamics in a coherent and interpretable manner.

These structured models empower intelligent agents to process intricate information, derive new knowledge, and dynamically update their beliefs. Through various inference mechanisms—such as logical inference engines, probabilistic models, and machine learning-based predictors—agents can analyze internal representations to generate insights, make optimal decisions, and formulate adaptive action plans. As environments change, agents iteratively refine their internal models to ensure ongoing accuracy, coherence, and responsiveness.

Quantum computing offers the potential to significantly augment these reasoning capabilities by leveraging quantum parallelism to encode and manipulate structured knowledge more efficiently. This could allow intelligent agents to evaluate numerous reasoning pathways concurrently, thereby accelerating inference and decision-making. Furthermore, entanglement may facilitate more expressive modeling of interdependent variables, enhancing context-sensitive reasoning and coordination across multi-agent systems. Quantum interference can further improve accuracy by amplifying correct reasoning outcomes while suppressing incorrect ones.

These quantum advantages are particularly impactful for fuzzy logic systems, probabilistic reasoning, and combinatorial logic, enabling AI systems to manage uncertainty and scale to larger, more dynamic reasoning problems. For instance, in rule-based systems, quantum computing can represent and evaluate a complete rule set in superposition, allowing the exploration of all possible inferences in parallel. Unlike classical systems—where rules must be evaluated sequentially or via resource-intensive parallelism—a quantum circuit could perform global reasoning over the rule space simultaneously. This capability could transform performance in domains like expert systems, automated theorem proving, and legal reasoning, where rapid analysis of complex rule interactions is crucial.

Additionally, quantum entanglement can support richer and more expressive representations of logical relationships, enabling more nuanced, context-aware reasoning within intelligent systems. One promising direction for quantum-enhanced reasoning involves probabilistic inference and Bayesian networks. Through techniques such as quantum phase estimation and amplitude amplification, quantum algorithms have the potential to sample from complex probability distributions more efficiently than classical Monte Carlo methods, particularly in high-dimensional or sparse data settings.

Beyond accelerating classical paradigms, quantum-native reasoning architectures present a more transformative opportunity. These systems leverage the fundamental principles of superposition and entanglement not merely to replicate classical logic but to redefine inference processes altogether. By directly exploiting quantum correlations, such models may be capable of reasoning from limited data, detecting subtle patterns, and achieving higher generalization performance than classical approaches. This shift opens pathways to building more efficient, adaptive, and generalizable AI systems, with applications spanning decision-making, planning, and knowledge-based inference in complex and uncertain environments.

14.1.7 Quantum Algorithms for Multi-Agent Systems

Research on Quantum Multi-Agent Systems (QMAS) explores how quantum computing can enhance the functionality of autonomous agents operating within both centralized and distributed environments. These systems comprise multiple agents—either homogeneous or heterogeneous—that interact in complex, often dynamic settings to achieve both individual and collective objectives. While classical multi-agent systems are well established, the incorporation of quantum computational principles into such frameworks is still an emerging field.

Initial progress has focused on quantum-supported coordination mechanisms, designed to improve collaboration and decision-making among agents. Noteworthy developments include quantum coalition formation protocols and quantum contract net systems, which adapt classical negotiation and task allocation strategies to a quantum setting. These quantum variants promise lower communication overhead and enhanced computational efficiency, as well as improved privacy during negotiation processes. For instance, quantum-enhanced coalition negotiation and resource allocation techniques have been shown, in theory, to outperform their classical analogues in terms of speed and security. However, these benefits remain largely theoretical, with practical implementations and empirical validations still limited.

With the progression of noisy intermediate-scale quantum (NISQ) devices, early-stage QMAS prototypes have begun addressing simplified real-world problems using current quantum hardware. While these preliminary implementations demonstrate potential, their scalability and effectiveness in complex, real-world environments remain open research challenges. Nonetheless, ongoing advancements underscore the promise of QMAS in tackling computational bottlenecks inherent in classical multi-agent coordination, suggesting a promising future for AI systems operating in quantum-enhanced environments.

One key area where Quantum Multi-Agent Systems (QMAS) demonstrate significant promise is in improving cooperation and coordination among agents, especially in complex optimization domains such as resource allocation, network optimization, and social network analysis. A central challenge in classical multi-agent systems (MAS) is the problem of coalition formation, where agents must be grouped into teams to maximize collective utility. Due to the combinatorial explosion inherent in the coalition structure generation problem, it can be reformulated as a Quadratic Unconstrained Binary Optimization (QUBO) problem. This reformulation enables the use of quantum optimization routines, such as the Quantum Approximate Optimization Algorithm (QAOA) and quantum annealing, to explore vast solution spaces more efficiently than classical heuristics. Algorithms such as BILP-Q exemplify this approach. However, the scalability of such quantum techniques is currently constrained by the hardware limitations of existing quantum processors.

To overcome these limitations, researchers have turned to hybrid quantum-classical methodologies, which strategically divide the workload between quantum and classical resources. For example, the GCS-Q algorithm adopts a top-down coalition formation strategy in which a grand coalition is recursively partitioned into smaller coalitions. At each iteration, the computationally intensive bipartitioning task is formulated as a QUBO problem and solved on quantum hardware—typically using quantum annealing—while the classical layer oversees coalition management and recursive structure control. Similarly, QuACS employs a hybrid strategy in which QAOA is used to determine optimal bipartitions for induced subgraph games. In this setup, quantum routines are used to solve subproblems involving graph partitioning, while classical algorithms maintain scalability and control flow across the broader problem space.

These hybrid frameworks maximize the advantages of quantum computing by assigning quantum-suited sub-problems—such as graph-cut and partitioning tasks—to quantum hardware, while relying on classical systems to handle coordination, recursion, and large-scale orchestration. This strategic delegation leads to both runtime reduction and enhanced solution quality, even within the constraints of today's noisy intermediate-scale quantum (NISQ) devices. Ultimately, such hybrid designs offer a pragmatic pathway for leveraging quantum speedups without overwhelming current hardware limitations, paving the way for scalable, quantum-enhanced multi-agent systems.

Future research should emphasize the development of qubit-efficient variational quantum algorithms, which aim to optimize quantum resource utilization by minimizing qubit requirements while retaining the computational advantages of quantum processing. These algorithms are particularly well-suited for addressing high-dimensional and combinatorically complex problems, such as coalition formation in multi-agent systems (MAS)—a domain where classical methods often encounter significant scalability constraints. By leveraging techniques such as parameterized quantum circuits, entanglement-efficient encoding schemes, and adaptive ansätze, these approaches hold promise for enabling practical quantum algorithm deployment on current and near-term quantum devices.

Moreover, the strategic integration of quantum and classical computational components within hybrid quantum-classical frameworks offers a scalable and pragmatic approach to addressing the inherent computational complexity of MAS coordination. In such designs, quantum modules handle the most resource-intensive subproblems—such as bipartitioning or graph-based optimization—while classical systems orchestrate the broader workflow and maintain algorithmic robustness. This division of computational labor is critical for effectively harnessing quantum acceleration without overwhelming the limited qubit capacity of present-day hardware. Ultimately, such hybrid approaches provide a viable pathway toward real-world, large-scale applications in quantum-enhanced multi-agent cooperation and decision-making.

14.2 AI for Quantum

The creation of functional quantum algorithms for traffic and route planning is a potent illustration of how quantum computing and AI may coexist. In essence, these quantum applications determine the fastest path for every single car in a fleet and optimize it instantly.

In collaboration with Microsoft and the quantum computing company Jij, Toyota Tsusho Corp. has shown how quantum routing algorithms can cut wait times at red lights by 20%. In Lisbon, Portugal, Volkswagen has also used a D-Wave machine to test quantum-computer-enhanced navigation and route optimization applications on the CARRIS public bus fleet. Reducing travel times and traffic congestion at the Web-Summit technology conference was the aim of this test. Volkswagen has used D-Wave technology to create a quantum simulation of the best route for 10,000 cabs traveling 20 miles between the Beijing airport and the central business district. These real-time quantum applications may also prove beneficial for transportation logistics, cross-functional supply chain management, and AI-powered self-driving cars and trucks.

Analytical and predictive Hazards like unfavorable geopolitical events or terrorist attacks, stock market meltdowns and financial panics, utility grid overloads, anthropogenic threats (such as habitat destruction, climate change, and overuse of natural resources), social unrest, and impending pandemics will all be predicted, managed, and disrupted with the help of QAI technology. Scholars of legal studies are already investigating the ramifications of a brand-new area known as "quantum jurisprudence" or "quantum AI law." Some academics are even considering the paradoxical ramifications and casuistry of criminality, where disagreements, infractions, and contract breaches merely vanish when inquiries are made. Complete information awareness and quantum legal simulations and decision-making will increase the likelihood of precrime fighting (in the academic meaning rather than the science fiction sense) and predictive pre-delinquency and policing. However, disruptive political maneuvers like to those of Cambridge Analytical or Equifax-style data thefts could also become more commonplace due to quantum AI.

Deciphering the mechanics of quantum systems is another benefit of using artificial intelligence algorithms. For instance, solid state or photonic quantum computing systems are utilized in conjunction with state-of-the-art quantum sensing technologies to detect minuscule changes in microgravity. Seismology, geological exploration, electromagnetic field sensing, global positioning systems, measurement, microscopy, enhanced radar, atomic clocks, magnetometers, and ultra-sensitive gravimeters are among the fields where the technology is anticipated to push the boundaries of technology. Tsunamis, silent-running enemy navy submarines, earthquakes, volcano eruptions, and other seismic occurrences might all be precisely predicted using quantum sensors.

Complex pattern recognition software and computerized expert systems are already heavily utilized in medical imaging technology. The ABCDE heuristic (asymmetry, border irregular, color distribution, diameter large, evolving mole) is a traditional (manually performed) method for diagnosing melanoma. Millions of photos have been used to train a convolutional neural network with machine learning to use ABCDE in the detection of rashes, melanomas, skin lesions, and other anomalies. CheXNet, another supervised learning algorithm, does better at diagnosing and screening for pneumonia than skilled radiologists. Quantum radiomics, or QAI in imaging, holds the potential to advance these interpretative initiatives.

Although it is a long-overdue prediction, quantum artificial neural networks may not be the end of radiology, but they could increase the specialty's efficiency and cost-effectiveness by reading in microseconds the exponentially increasing volume of medical scans performed worldwide. They could also effectively pre-analyze images, flag ambiguous features, and assist humans in avoiding common mistakes that are attributed to boredom, inattention, and fatigue. The intricate, real-time optimization issues of evaluating and weighing the dozens of factors that go into creating adaptable and successful radiation treatment regimens for cancer patients may likewise be tackled by quantum radiomics.

Artificial intelligence (AI), machine learning (ML), and related computational methods are reshaping mathematical and computational modeling practices, offering not only enhanced efficiency but also a fundamentally new perspective on model construction. These technologies accelerate scientific workflows and provoke renewed consideration of which intellectual tasks can be effectively automated. When applied thoughtfully, AI serves not to replace but to augment human insight—guiding, supervising, and enriching knowledge work.

In the context of quantum technologies, AI emerges as a pivotal enabler—not merely as a complementary tool but as a transformative force. This synergy arises from several key alignments. First, the probabilistic nature of quantum mechanics resonates naturally with AI frameworks, especially those rooted in probabilistic reasoning and learning. Second, quantum systems often defy classical intuition, yet their behaviors are governed by precise mathematical formulations—an ideal match for data-driven AI modeling. Third, the extreme sensitivity and precision requirements of quantum technologies demand rigorous validation against complex, multi-parameter models, where AI excels at pattern recognition and adaptive optimization. Finally, as the quantum ecosystem evolves, AI can accelerate the development of a skilled workforce by providing intelligent tools, training platforms, and automated support for research and development.

14.2.1 Discovery and Optimization of Quantum Experiments

The routine and scalable operation of quantum computers necessitates innovative approaches across multiple layers of the quantum computing stack—including device design, optimal control, readout strategies, efficient compilation, noise characterization, and error correction. Machine learning (ML) has emerged as a powerful enabler in this context, offering data-driven solutions that can adapt to the complexity and variability inherent in quantum systems.

One illustrative application is the use of ML models to autonomously learn circuit compression strategies, enabling enhanced compilation by identifying redundancies and optimizing gate sequences across different quantum architectures. At a higher algorithmic level, variational quantum algorithms (VQAs) and other quantum machine learning (QML) paradigms offer promising pathways for algorithm discovery, potentially expanding the currently limited repertoire of quantum algorithms with demonstrated or conjectured quantum advantage.

These developments highlight the critical role of ML as a unifying toolbox for hybrid quantum-classical systems. On one hand, ML enables efficient communication and control between classical and quantum components—e.g., through experimental design, adaptive calibration, and online optimization of control parameters. On the other, it facilitates the translation of classical data into quantum-representable formats (quantum state preparation) and supports transpilation of classical algorithmic structures into quantum-native equivalents.

Furthermore, ML-assisted control protocols running on hybrid quantum-classical architectures may exploit quantum properties (e.g., coherence, entanglement) to devise energy-efficient control strategies for experiment steering and device calibration.

Concrete examples of ML applications include:

Cross-architecture optimization of quantum devices and experimental protocols, enabling platform-agnostic performance tuning.

Adaptive control in hybrid quantum-classical systems, where ML techniques dynamically adjust control pulses or gate sequences to compensate for noise and hardware imperfections.

14.2.2 Quantum System Simulation

Simulating quantum many-body systems on classical computers remains one of the most formidable challenges in physics, yet it is pivotal for advancing our understanding and engineering of functional materials, quantum phases of matter, and complex chemical processes. Recent developments have demonstrated how machine learning (ML) can be integrated into traditional ab initio methods to enhance their scalability and predictive power.

A particularly notable innovation is the representation of quantum wave functions using artificial neural networks, known as neural quantum states (NQS). These architectures, such as Restricted Boltzmann Machines or variational autoencoders, have proven capable of efficiently capturing complex entanglement structures and high-dimensional quantum correlations, offering a scalable ansatz for variational simulations.

These methods are actively pushing the frontiers of quantum simulation and hold promise for tackling open problems such as high-temperature superconductivity, quantum magnetism, and quantum chemical dynamics. By incorporating domain-specific knowledge from quantum mechanics, so-called physics-informed ML or physics-aware neural networks can improve both the accuracy and interpretability of models, overcoming one of the key limitations of black-box ML techniques in physical sciences.

For instance, ML approaches have been employed to reconstruct hidden disorder landscapes in experimental quantum devices—enabling improved control and noise mitigation. Likewise, developing explainable AI (XAI) for quantum systems may accelerate the adoption of quantum machine learning (QML) as a central tool in the digital twinning of quantum devices, potentially leading to the discovery of novel quantum phenomena that lie beyond the reach of classical simulation frameworks.

Concrete examples of ML applications in quantum system simulation include:

- **Neural quantum states:** Learning and compactly representing many-body wave functions with deep neural networks.
- **Automated tailoring of quantum material properties:** Using generative and predictive models to inverse-design materials with target behaviors.
- **Digital twins for quantum systems:** Real-time, ML-based digital replicas for control and monitoring of quantum devices.
- **Classical shadows:** Employing randomized measurements and ML for efficient prediction of quantum observables.
- **Classical control of quantum circuits:** Optimizing control sequences, gate calibration, and error mitigation using supervised and reinforcement learning.

14.2.3 Analysis of Quantum Data

Analyzing data from quantum systems poses unique challenges due to the intrinsic high-dimensionality, entanglement, and non-local correlations that characterize quantum phenomena. In complex systems—such as strongly correlated electrons in condensed matter physics or quantum simulators of many-body dynamics—the relevant features governing macroscopic behavior are often obscured and difficult to extract using conventional techniques.

Recent advances demonstrate that machine learning (ML) provides powerful tools for navigating this complexity by enabling unbiased, data-driven exploration of quantum datasets. For example, artificial neural networks have been successfully used to learn relevant correlations and patterns from measurement snapshots of quantum many-body systems, particularly those arranged on spatial lattices. These models can autonomously identify key observables and underlying order parameters—even in cases of exotic quantum phases or topological order where traditional analytical methods fail.

This capability is especially valuable in noisy experimental environments, where uncertainty, decoherence, and measurement limitations hinder conventional analysis. ML models—especially generative approaches such as variational autoencoders or generative adversarial networks—can assist in data augmentation and inference of inaccessible measurements, thereby enriching sparse datasets and accelerating discovery.

Moreover, the integration of interpretable and explainable AI (XAI) into quantum data analysis opens pathways for AI-assisted scientific discovery. By offering insights into the learned features and decision mechanisms, XAI fosters trust, improves transparency, and facilitates human–machine collaboration in uncovering hidden structures and symmetries within quantum systems.

Concrete examples of ML applications in quantum data analysis include:

- **Discovery of correlations and symmetries:** Neural networks uncover hidden order parameters and quantum phase boundaries from raw measurement data.
- **Explainable AI for quantum systems:** Interpretable models assist in revealing physical insights and guiding hypothesis generation.
- **AI-assisted discovery of emergent phenomena:** ML uncovers exotic order or critical behavior not accessible through conventional diagnostics.
- **Generative modeling for quantum data:** Creating synthetic quantum data to support analysis when experimental measurements are limited or expensive.

14.2.4 Automated Control and Quantum Technologies Calibration

The precise control, calibration, and characterization of quantum systems is foundational to both the development of scalable quantum technologies and the execution of high-fidelity quantum experiments. As the number of controllable quantum degrees of freedom increases—whether in quantum computing, communication, or sensing platforms—the demand for automated, data-driven control strategies grows significantly. Traditional manual tuning becomes infeasible, prompting a shift toward machine learning (ML)-enabled automation.

Machine learning offers a powerful and flexible toolbox for addressing the inherent challenges of quantum system control, such as hardware imperfections, crosstalk, environmental noise, and nonlinear dependencies across control parameters. By leveraging ML's ability to explore large, high-dimensional parameter spaces efficiently, quantum systems can be autonomously calibrated, optimized, and stabilized.

Notable examples include the fully automated tuning of quantum-dot devices, where reinforcement learning and Bayesian optimization have demonstrated robust gate-voltage configuration without human intervention. Similarly, the automated optimization of entangling gates on superconducting quantum processors has been shown to enhance fidelity—an essential requirement for fault-tolerant quantum computation and other near-term quantum applications. These advances not only reduce calibration time but also improve performance reliability across experimental runs and hardware generations.

Beyond computation, ML plays a critical role in quantum state preparation, gate operation scheduling, error mitigation, and readout optimization, thereby enhancing both speed and accuracy in quantum workflows. Moreover, ML techniques are well-suited to characterizing and mitigating noise sources, including those arising from fabrication inconsistencies, environmental coupling, or control imperfections. This is particularly valuable in noisy intermediate-scale quantum (NISQ) devices, where errors must be managed without the full overhead of quantum error correction.

Furthermore, ML can guide the design of optimized experimental configurations for domain-specific quantum tasks—such as quantum sensing, imaging, or quantum radar—by autonomously learning parameter regimes that maximize signal-to-noise ratios or quantum advantage metrics. In cross-platform contexts, ML facilitates cross-architecture calibration and benchmarking, supporting device-agnostic development and comparison.

Concrete examples of ML applications in quantum control and calibration include:

- Efficient tuning, characterization, and stabilization of quantum devices (e.g., quantum dots, trapped ions, superconducting circuits).
- Autonomous noise identification and mitigation, enhancing the robustness of quantum operations.
- Accelerated quantum state preparation and gate calibration, reducing operational latency.
- Cross-platform optimization and certification, enabling coherent operation across heterogeneous quantum hardware.

14.2.5 Explainable AI for Quantum Technologies and Trustful, Robust, Interpretable,

As machine learning (ML) becomes increasingly integral to the advancement of quantum science and technology, ensuring trustworthiness, robustness, interpretability, and explainability of AI models is paramount. While modern ML architectures—especially deep neural networks—have demonstrated impressive capabilities across a wide array of quantum applications, their inherent opacity poses significant challenges for reliable deployment in high-stakes quantum systems, where safety, accountability, and scientific rigor are essential.

Trust and robustness are foundational prerequisites when applying ML to control, simulate, or calibrate quantum devices. Quantum systems are not only delicate but often operate near the limits of physical measurement and coherence. In such settings, model uncertainty, vulnerability to adversarial inputs, and hidden biases can lead to unreliable outcomes, undermining scientific validity and operational safety. Building robust models thus involves not only training on high-fidelity data but also designing fail-safes, uncertainty quantification, and out-of-distribution detection mechanisms that protect against erroneous predictions.

Equally important is the pursuit of interpretability and explainability in AI models tailored for quantum domains. Interpretable AI enables researchers to scrutinize and understand the internal decision-making processes of ML models, which is critical for validating physical hypotheses, discovering new scientific phenomena, and ensuring the reproducibility of results. In this context, explainable ML facilitates the translation of complex model behavior into human-understandable insights, bridging the gap between statistical learning and physical reasoning. By identifying the specific data features, symmetries, or quantum correlations responsible for a given output, explainable AI enhances confidence in model predictions and fosters data-driven theory development in quantum science.

Moreover, extracting scientifically meaningful knowledge from ML models enables researchers to move beyond black-box prediction toward causal understanding and generalization. This is particularly relevant in domains such as quantum simulation, quantum chemistry, and quantum control, where insights gained through ML must align with known physical principles or provide testable predictions.

Notably, quantum technologies present a compelling testbed for developing and evaluating explainable AI methodologies. The hybrid nature of classical-quantum systems, combined with well-characterized physics and experimental repeatability, allows retroactive testing and validation of AI-generated insights. Early advances in this direction include Taylor-∞, a black-box explanation technique grounded in the Fourier representation of parameterized quantum circuits, as well as quantum layer wise relevance propagation (QLRP)—both offering initial frameworks for interpreting what quantum machine learning models are actually learning. These tools represent foundational steps toward building an ecosystem of diagnostics and explainability tailored specifically for quantum-enhanced AI systems.

To summarize, building trustworthy and interpretable AI frameworks for quantum technologies is not only essential for operational reliability but also pivotal for enabling

AI to serve as a meaningful tool for scientific discovery. Meeting this challenge requires the convergence of machine learning, quantum information theory, and philosophy of science to produce models that are not only performant but also transparent, verifiable, and epistemically sound.

Key goals and ongoing developments include:

Enhancing robustness of AI systems under real-world quantum noise and hardware constraints.

Designing interpretable neural architectures and physics-informed models for quantum data.

Developing explainability tools such as QLRP, Taylor-∞, and quantum saliency maps.

Establishing rigorous validation pipelines for AI-driven discoveries in quantum science.

14.2.6 Quantum Error Mitigation via Post-Processing by AI

Quantum algorithms typically produce probability distributions over possible measurement outcomes that encode solutions to tasks such as optimization, quantum simulation, or factorization. However, due to limitations of current quantum hardware—including noise, decoherence, and gate infidelities—the observed distributions often deviate significantly from their ideal counterparts. This discrepancy is particularly problematic in the Noisy Intermediate-Scale Quantum (NISQ) era, where full quantum error correction remains out of reach. Consequently, the reliability of quantum computations depends heavily on quantum error mitigation (QEM) techniques, many of which operate via post-processing of noisy measurement data.

From a computational standpoint, quantum errors arise from multiple sources: gate imperfections, state preparation and measurement (SPAM) errors, and decoherence due to environmental interactions. These distort the statistical outputs of quantum algorithms, rendering results less accurate or even misleading. Unlike classical errors, which can be mitigated through redundancy and error correction codes, quantum errors are more difficult to handle due to the no-cloning theorem, superposition, and the fragility of entangled states. Furthermore, worst-case complexity bounds have demonstrated that the effectiveness of some mitigation strategies diminishes significantly for circuits of increasing depth, particularly in log-log-depth regimes.

To address these challenges, artificial intelligence (AI) has emerged as a promising and resource-efficient means of performing error mitigation via post-processing. ML models such as deep neural networks, Gaussian processes, and autoencoders can be trained to learn the statistical signatures of noisy quantum systems and infer corrections that approximate the ideal distributions. These models can operate in a non-parametric manner, requiring minimal assumptions about the underlying noise model, and are capable of generalizing across varying hardware conditions.

In addition to supervised learning, reinforcement learning and Bayesian reasoning have proven effective in adapting mitigation strategies dynamically based on live feedback from quantum devices. Reinforcement learning agents can iteratively refine correction protocols by interacting with quantum hardware and adjusting their behavior to minimize output variance or maximize fidelity. Bayesian approaches, in turn, offer a principled framework to incorporate prior knowledge and manage uncertainty in the correction process.

A further layer of sophistication is introduced through approximate reasoning, particularly fuzzy logic, which enables the representation and manipulation of quantum errors in terms of multi-valued or continuous logic. This paradigm is especially useful in noisy and uncertain quantum environments, where binary error models are inadequate. Fuzzy inference systems and approximate clustering algorithms can be employed to adjust post-processing parameters in real time, improving the robustness and adaptability of mitigation techniques.

Moreover, optimization algorithms play a crucial role in tuning the parameters of post-processing techniques. Evolutionary algorithms—including genetic algorithms, differential evolution, and memetic strategies—have shown great promise in this context. These bio-inspired approaches simulate natural selection processes to discover high-quality error mitigation strategies, optimize model parameters, and refine fuzzy logic-based correction mechanisms. By continuously selecting and evolving the most effective techniques based on performance metrics such as output fidelity or total variation distance, evolutionary optimization enables continuous improvement of the QEM pipeline.

In summary, AI-driven post-processing techniques offer a powerful and hardware-efficient pathway to mitigate quantum errors, particularly suitable for NISQ devices. These approaches avoid the need for additional quantum resources, such as ancillary qubits or complex error correction codes, while significantly enhancing the accuracy, robustness, and practicality of near-term quantum computations.

Key components of AI-enabled quantum error mitigation include:

- Learning-based correction of distorted probability distributions.
- Reinforcement learning for adaptive and online mitigation strategies.
- Fuzzy logic for managing uncertainty and imprecision in noisy outputs.
- Evolutionary optimization for refining and evolving error correction mechanisms.
- Bayesian and probabilistic inference for principled uncertainty management.

14.2.7 Quantum Error Correction Syndrome Detection

A central challenge in fault-tolerant quantum computing is the accurate and efficient decoding of quantum error syndromes—the patterns of measurement outcomes that signal the presence of errors on physical qubits. The task is to infer the most probable underlying error configuration that explains a given syndrome, so that appropriate corrective operations can be applied. This decoding problem is not only computationally intensive but also critical for maintaining logical qubit fidelity across large-scale quantum systems.

Traditionally, combinatorial decoders such as the minimum-weight perfect matching (MWPM) algorithm have been widely used, especially for surface codes. While these methods are well-understood and highly effective for moderate code distances, they become increasingly resource-intensive as system sizes grow. In recent years, classical AI and machine learning (ML) have emerged as powerful alternatives or complements to traditional decoders, offering data-driven strategies for learning syndrome-to-error mappings.

In this context, ML models—including convolutional neural networks (CNNs), graph neural networks (GNNs), and reinforcement learning agents—have been explored for syndrome decoding, especially for structured error correction codes such as surface codes, color codes, and LDPC codes. These models are trained on large sets of simulated error syndromes and corresponding corrections, allowing them to learn complex, non-local error patterns that might be missed by rule-based decoders.

However, the deployment of ML-based decoders for large-distance quantum codes presents several key challenges:

Scalability: Models must generalize across growing code distances and higher-dimensional lattices without prohibitive increases in computational cost.

Robustness: Decoders should maintain high accuracy even under varying noise models and hardware-specific error characteristics.

Interpretability and verification: The reliability of ML decoders must be benchmarked rigorously against established methods such as MWPM and union-find decoders, with clear metrics for performance, latency, and error thresholds.

The potential benefits are substantial. Successful integration of AI into quantum error correction could significantly reduce the overhead associated with fault tolerance—namely, the number of physical qubits and gate operations required per logical qubit. This would accelerate the timeline for practical, large-scale quantum computing.

In summary, ML-based syndrome decoding is a promising yet demanding frontier in quantum error correction. Future research must focus on:

- Developing scalable architectures that can handle large-distance codes and realistic noise environments.
- Performing systematic benchmarking against classical decoders under both synthetic and hardware-driven noise models.
- Ensuring generalization and cross-hardware adaptability, especially as quantum processors diversify in architecture and error profiles.

14.2.8 ML Quantum Architecture Search for Near-Term Algorithms

In the NISQ (Noisy Intermediate-Scale Quantum) era, variational quantum algorithms (VQAs) have become central to leveraging quantum devices for practical applications, including classification, regression, and generative modeling tasks. At the core of VQAs lie parameterized quantum circuits (PQCs), whose structure—commonly referred to as the ansatz—greatly influences algorithm performance.

However, deep PQCs often suffer from trainability challenges such as barren plateaus, where gradients vanish exponentially with circuit depth, rendering optimization ineffective. These difficulties are compounded by hardware-specific constraints such as limited connectivity, gate fidelity, and noise, all of which diminish the effectiveness of standard VQA approaches on current quantum hardware.

To overcome these limitations, it is crucial to design efficient quantum circuits that are tailored to the underlying problem, optimization landscape, and target hardware. This task, known as quantum architecture search (QAS) or automated circuit design, aims to identify optimal circuit structures and parameterizations that mitigate barren plateaus, respect hardware constraints, and enhance algorithmic performance.

Early efforts in QAS, dating back to the early 2000s, leveraged evolutionary algorithms to discover efficient circuit configurations. Since then, advances in machine learning (ML) and metaheuristic optimization have enabled more sophisticated strategies, including:

Deep reinforcement learning, where an agent learns to construct circuit layers iteratively based on reward signals tied to circuit performance.

Bayesian optimization, used to explore circuit design spaces while minimizing the number of evaluations on expensive quantum simulations or real hardware.

Adaptive methods, such as quantum autoencoders for task-specific circuit compression or ADAPT-VQE, which iteratively builds ansätze based on operator importance.

Attention-based and neural architecture search (NAS)-inspired models, which learn to generate circuit templates by mimicking successful architectures from classical deep learning.

These techniques collectively contribute to more effective co-design of quantum algorithms and hardware, enabling bespoke circuits optimized for both computational goals and physical constraints. Importantly, automated QAS methods can facilitate the discovery of novel quantum circuits that outperform human-designed counterparts, particularly in applications constrained by hardware noise and resource limitations.

Moving forward, QAS is expected to play a pivotal role in:

- Improving trainability and convergence properties of VQAs,
- Enhancing hardware-aware circuit design for NISQ devices,
- Enabling discovery of new quantum algorithms with emergent advantages,
- Supporting autoML pipelines for quantum-classical hybrid workflows.

Thus, quantum architecture search represents a promising frontier in the intersection of quantum computing and artificial intelligence, particularly for advancing the capabilities of variational methods on near-term quantum hardware.

14.3 Ultra-Intelligence in Quantum Physics

Quantum fiction is a new literary subgenre that anticipates the potential benefits and dangers of quantum artificial intelligence. Books like Robert J. Sawyer's Factoring Humanity (1998) and Quantum Night (2016), David Mitchell's Ghostwritten (1999), Kim Stanley Robinson's 2312 (2012), and Wil McCarthy's Antediluvian (2019) all depict realistic or fantastical examples of QAI. Numerous enigmatic quantum AIs appear in the Japanese cyberpunk manga series Battle Angel Alita: Last Order (2000–2014) and Kiddy Grade (2002). Movies include Transcendence (2014), starring Johnny Depp, and Transformers (2007), in which a robot's "signal pattern is learning" through the use of "quantum mechanics."

In addition to discussing the many-worlds interpretation of quantum physics and the implications of quantum technology on determinism and free will, the Hulu TV miniseries Devs (2020) features a fictional quantum computer corporation. A quantum artificial intelligence system called Rehoboam uses its extensive database to plan and govern real-world society in the HBO television series Westworld (2016–present). In the world of the popular military science fiction video game series Mass Effect (2007–present), there are numerous fictional quantum computers that have achieved consciousness, especially the hardworking synthetic "geths" who are at odds with their alien humanoid masters, the "quarians."

Even though all of these examples are made up, some computer scientists have dedicated their lives and careers to creating an artificial general intelligence (AGI) that is self-aware, even going so far as to bootstrap itself to reach ultra-intelligence and access the Technological Singularity. With immediate access to the Penrose-Hameroff theory of quantum consciousness and neuro-inspired computer chips to build the architecture for its own self-designed quantum neural networks, a developing ultra-intelligence may get off to a head start. Whether we can keep a self-aware QAI under "human-in-the-loop" management or persuade it to form a heroic alliance with humans (so-called collaborative QAI) is uncertain. In response to a 2021 Pew Research question on ethical AI, a number of experts expressed skepticism that a QAI would take part in limiting its own boundaries through a Magna Carta for the Quantum Age or a Quantum AI Constitutional Convention.

The only animals on Earth with nearly limitless learning, development, and invention potential are humans. Humans excel at making their environments more complex. Indeed, creating more and more of the manufactured environment that we appear to be unable to live without is the goal of many people working in robotics, automation, and artificial intelligence today rather than returning human habitat to a joyful natural condition. This urge will have profound effects and affects the shared objectives of artificial intelligence and quantum computing. "Everything we love about civilization is a product of intelligence," as MIT physicist and machine learning expert Max Tegmark has stated. Therefore, enhancing human intelligence with artificial intelligence has the potential to help civilization flourish like never before—as long as we manage to keep the technology beneficial.

14.4 Quantum World of Machine Learning and AI

The intersection of machine learning (ML), artificial intelligence (AI), and quantum computing marks a paradigm shift in how we approach information processing, algorithm design, and scientific discovery. As quantum technologies progress from laboratory prototypes toward practical deployment, ML and AI serve not only as powerful tools to enhance quantum system performance but also as transformative paradigms to redefine modeling, computation, and control in a fundamentally quantum world.

Toward Fully Quantum Artificial Intelligence

A foundational question in the emerging field of quantum machine learning (QML) concerns its very scope and identity. Rather than being situated merely at the intersection of quantum physics, quantum information theory, machine learning, and artificial intelligence, QML may more appropriately be positioned within their union—a domain where each component informs and transforms the others. In this vision, we move beyond hybrid schemes or classical algorithms running on quantum devices. Instead, we begin to explore a radically quantum paradigm in which every aspect of the machine learning process is embedded within the quantum formalism itself.

This leads us to a speculative, yet increasingly plausible, future scenario: everything can be quantum. The model parameters, the data (inputs), the labels (outputs), the training dynamics, and the inference process—all exist as quantum objects. Data, for instance, may be encoded into non-trivial quantum states through sophisticated entanglement schemes or quantum embeddings that preserve or amplify high-dimensional correlations. Consequently, the act of "learning" in such a context is fundamentally a quantum process, governed by principles such as superposition, entanglement, non-locality, contextuality, and interference.

Recognizing that machine learning is essentially a form of information processing, we must acknowledge that quantum information is categorically different from classical information. This shift compels a rethinking of core ML concepts: What does it mean to learn from quantum data? How should we define generalization, overfitting, or model capacity when data are quantum states? Can the notions of prediction or uncertainty be redefined using quantum principles?

The long-term vision is to establish a fully quantum AI system—an entity where data encoding, learning algorithms, model architecture, and decision-making protocols are all realized natively within a quantum framework. This requires reimagining learning theories, algorithmic structures, and even conceptual frameworks of intelligence itself.

Classes of Foundational Questions in Fully Quantum AI

We identify several broad categories of foundational questions that emerge when considering a genuinely quantum AI paradigm:

1. **Quantum Data and Representations**

What constitutes meaningful features in quantum data?

How can we define and quantify information content or entropy in quantum learning tasks?

What are the best methods for encoding classical or hybrid information into useful quantum representations?

2. **Quantum Learning Dynamics**

How do traditional learning paradigms (supervised, unsupervised, reinforcement) translate when inputs and/or outputs are quantum states?

What is the quantum equivalent of loss functions, backpropagation, and gradient descent?

Can learning be achieved through quantum feedback, unitary updates, or quantum measurement-driven evolution?

3. **Quantum Inference and Decision Making**

How do we define inference in a quantum system without collapsing the state prematurely?

What role do quantum measurements and probabilistic collapse play in making predictions?

Can quantum Bayesian inference or contextual reasoning provide a new foundation for decision-making?

4. Quantum Generalization and Overfitting

What are the bounds for generalization error in quantum learning?

How can we define model complexity, regularization, or bias-variance tradeoff in a quantum context?

Do new phenomena arise, such as quantum over-entanglement, that parallel overfitting?

5. Quantum Learning Theory

What is the quantum analog of the PAC (Probably Approximately Correct) learning framework?

Are there universal quantum learning machines, analogous to Turing-universal computers?

How do quantum capacity, expressivity, and trainability interact?

6. Quantum Ethics and Interpretability

How can we ensure trustworthiness, interpretability, and explainability in quantum-native models?

Can quantum explainability be formalized, perhaps using tools like quantum layer wise relevance propagation?

How should we conceptualize responsibility or agency in autonomous quantum agents?

How to Define Learning in a Quantum World

One of the central conceptual challenges in quantum machine learning (QML) lies in how we define "learning" itself when the rules of quantum mechanics govern the data, models, and computational resources. While classical learning theory provides well-established definitions—such as learning a function from data, minimizing generalization error, or maximizing cumulative reward—these definitions must be carefully re-examined in quantum scenarios, particularly when dealing with genuinely quantum data and agents.

To concretize this discussion, we consider two fundamental learning paradigms: supervised learning and reinforcement learning.

Supervised Quantum Learning: Fundamental Tensions

Early explorations of supervised quantum learning began in the early 2000s, often using multiple identically prepared quantum states as training inputs. This formulation allows us to pose a quantum analog of classical supervised learning: given a quantum training set of state-label pairs $(|\psi i\rangle,)$, can a learner predict labels for unseen quantum states?

Despite considerable progress, the relationship between classical and quantum supervised learning remains poorly understood. Several open questions highlight the conceptual ambiguity:

What does it mean to generalize from quantum examples? In classical supervised learning, generalization is defined over a statistical distribution of input-output pairs. But in the quantum case, if quantum states are used only once due to measurement collapse, can a learner extract general principles from finite, destructively-sampled data?

What is the "target function" in QML?

In classical learning, one often assumes a fixed target function $f:X\rightarrow Y$. In quantum settings, should we instead think of the label as being associated with a quantum channel, a Hermitian observable, or a measurement outcome distribution?

Does the quantum nature of data offer genuine advantages or limitations? For instance, certain quantum datasets may be hard to simulate classically, and learning patterns from such data might offer exponential advantages. Conversely, if all quantum data is consumed during training (e.g., via projective measurement), then the effective learning process becomes classical—merely mapping state preparation results to outcomes.

How do we define a cost function in quantum supervised learning? Should this be defined as a distance between density matrices (e.g., trace distance or fidelity), or between distributions over measurement outcomes?

These tensions point to the need for a quantum learning theory that integrates physical constraints (e.g., no-cloning, measurement collapse, entanglement) into its foundational definitions of learning, error, and generalization.

Reinforcement Learning in Quantum Settings

Reinforcement learning (RL) offers a complementary perspective, where the learner interacts with an environment to maximize cumulative reward. Quantum generalizations of RL raise even deeper foundational issues:

What is a "quantum environment"?

In classical RL, environments are stochastic transition systems. In quantum RL, the environment may be a quantum channel, possibly entangled with the agent or undergoing unitary dynamics. This shifts the nature of feedback from scalar rewards to possibly quantum information feedback.

How is exploration defined when actions are quantum operations? An agent could apply quantum gates or measurements, which affect not only its immediate reward but also the structure of entanglement in the environment. The agent may face a fundamental information-disturbance tradeoff.

Can a quantum agent achieve learning advantages? Some quantum RL frameworks explore how quantum memory, coherent exploration, or amplitude amplification can offer better sample complexity compared to classical agents. However, a clear separation in power remains unproven in general.

What does a policy look like in quantum RL? Classical policies map states to actions. In quantum RL, the policy might instead be a quantum channel that governs how the agent evolves in response to quantum input.

Quantum Learning: Consumption vs Preservation of Data

A central tension in defining quantum learning is the consumptive nature of measurement. In classical supervised learning, data can be copied and revisited. In quantum settings:

Quantum data cannot be cloned due to the no-cloning theorem.

Measurement generally destroys the original quantum state.

Learning must balance information gain with state preservation—a tradeoff with no classical counterpart.

This means that if all training data is measured (and thereby collapsed) in the learning phase, the process becomes effectively classical. A truly quantum learner would instead need to:

- Preserve quantum correlations during learning;
- Use coherent processing of quantum states (e.g., quantum memory);
- Possibly re-use entangled resources for training and inference.

Hybrid and Fully Quantum Learning Strategies:

Foundational Challenges

Current approaches to quantum machine learning often rely on hybrid strategies, where quantum data is measured, producing classical outcomes that are subsequently processed by classical machine learning (ML) algorithms. However, such hybrid strategies are inherently limited:

Exponential complexity arises in general-purpose quantum state tomography, making full reconstruction of quantum states intractable except for very small systems.

Even partial measurement techniques (e.g., restricted observables or partial tomography) can rapidly become resource-intensive in high-dimensional Hilbert spaces.

As a result, these approaches often fail to preserve the richness of quantum information, limiting the potential for true quantum advantage.

Beyond Tomography: Recent Techniques and Their Limits

To address these bottlenecks, several more targeted and resource-efficient techniques have been proposed:

Classical shadows allow estimation of many observables from relatively few measurements by leveraging randomized measurements and classical post-processing.

Quantum kernel methods embed data into a quantum feature space and assess similarity via inner products, avoiding full state reconstruction.

Quantum Boltzmann machines and tensor networks model quantum correlations compactly and have shown promise in specific tasks, particularly in quantum simulation and generative modeling.

Despite their success, these methods remain task-specific and heuristic. They lack a general guiding principle akin to risk minimization or PAC learning in classical ML. We still lack a unified theoretical framework that characterizes when and why quantum resources yield learning advantages—and how to design algorithms that systematically exploit them.

Quantum Memories and Learnability

A promising direction lies in strategies that retain quantum coherence during training and inference, such as:

Quantum learning protocols that operate on coherent superpositions of data;

Storage of learned models in quantum memories (e.g., unitary operators or entangled states).

Such protocols may achieve provable quantum speedups, especially in situations where retaining the training data in quantum form prevents information loss from measurement.

However, this introduces a set of fundamental issues:

No-cloning and no-broadcasting theorems limit the replicability and sharing of quantum-trained models. Unlike classical models, quantum-learned representations cannot be freely copied or transmitted.

Once a quantum model is stored, extracting predictions or updating the model without measurement collapse becomes non-trivial, especially if the model cannot be queried multiple times without decohering it.

These challenges call for new definitions of learnability and generalization in settings where quantum memory plays an essential role.

Learning with Quantum Labels:

A Foundational Frontier

A more radical and conceptually rich direction emerges when we consider that not just inputs, but also labels, may be genuinely quantum.

In this setting, supervised learning is redefined as learning a map:

$|\psi x\rangle \mapsto |\phi y\rangle$ rather than $|\psi x\rangle \mapsto y$, where both inputs and outputs are quantum states. This scenario raises several foundational challenges:

What does it mean to predict a quantum label? Unlike classical labels, quantum labels cannot be verified via direct comparison unless one possesses many identical copies.

How is performance evaluated?

Classical error rates do not apply directly. Instead, fidelity between predicted and target states, or trace distance, may serve as loss functions—but these are operationally difficult to estimate in high dimensions.

How do we define generalization and sample complexity? Classical theory relies on statistical generalization over i.i.d. data. When labels are quantum and data is consumed during training, this entire framework may need to be redefined.

Moreover, entangled input-output pairs introduce nonlocal correlations into the learning process. This calls for entanglement-aware learning theory, where the learner may need to extract relational structure across multiple subsystems without violating physical constraints.

Partial Measurement and Information Retention

There are intriguing examples—such as gentle measurement and shadow tomography—that suggest quantum states may retain utility even after partial measurement. This inspires new learning paradigms:

Can non-destructive sampling support iterative learning protocols where the same quantum data is reused?

Can learners extract compressed classical representations (e.g., via shadows or sketches) sufficient for future prediction tasks without full state reconstruction?

If so, there may exist a middle ground between full quantum processing and fully classical post-measurement processing—where partial coherence is preserved, and classical models still extract meaningful predictive patterns.

14.4.1 Learning as a Physical Process in the Quantum World

A radical and thought-provoking perspective is to view learning itself as a physical process. In the classical world, analogies between learning systems and statistical mechanics have long been explored—for example, the correspondence between Hopfield networks and Ising models, or between Bayesian inference and energy minimization. In the quantum realm, this perspective becomes even more intriguing.

Quantum Algorithms as Physical Evolutions

Every quantum algorithm can be interpreted as the evolution of a quantum system under physical laws—formally represented by:

Unitary evolution under a time-dependent Hamiltonian (t), or

Open system dynamics, e.g., Lindblad master equations with decoherence, or

Adiabatic evolution, where the system remains in or near the ground state of a slowly varying Hamiltonian.

This interpretation raises a profound question:

Can we engineer interacting quantum many-body systems—composed of qubits, spins, or other physical particles—whose natural dynamics perform useful learning tasks?

In such a framework, learning becomes synonymous with state evolution, and memory, inference, and generalization may all arise from physical laws rather than abstract algorithms.

Associative Quantum Memories and Ground States

In classical machine learning, associative memory networks such as Hopfield models store patterns as attractors in an energy landscape. The retrieval of a memory corresponds to dynamical relaxation into one of these minima.

This naturally invites a quantum analogue:

Can quantum Hamiltonians be constructed such that their ground states encode quantum memories?

Could quantum annealing or adiabatic evolution retrieve these memories through controlled state preparation?

Possible directions include:

Quantum Hopfield networks where memory states are stored in entangled ground states, leveraging non-commutative interactions to encode richer correlations.

Models based on transverse-field Ising Hamiltonians, where quantum fluctuations enable non-local exploration of configuration space.

More exotic constructions, such as topologically ordered states, where memories may be encoded in non-local degrees of freedom and protected against local errors.

These systems could, in principle, serve as robust quantum memory and learning substrates, potentially outperforming classical analogues in terms of capacity, error tolerance, and parallelism.

Learning from Scrambling and Chaos

Another speculative, but fascinating, direction lies in the use of chaotic quantum systems—those that exhibit fast scrambling of quantum information, such as:

Black hole analogs in AdS/CFT correspondence,

Random quantum circuits that quickly entangle and mix information, or

Quantum systems near quantum chaos thresholds.

In these systems:

Learning could emerge from the entanglement structure generated during evolution.

Non-local correlations might act as distributed representations of inputs.

Information could be retrieved or decoded via carefully designed measurements or interactions with ancillary systems.

This approach connects to ideas in quantum reservoir computing, where a fixed quantum system is driven with classical or quantum inputs and its transient dynamics are used for learning and inference. Unlike traditional supervised learning, training may occur via tuning only the readout layer, while the reservoir's evolution remains fixed and complex.

14.4.2 Challenges in the Learning Agent–Environment Paradigm in Quantum Settings

The extension of the classical reinforcement learning (RL) framework into the quantum domain—where both the agent and environment may be fully quantum systems—introduces a host of profound challenges. In this quantized agent-environment paradigm, standard RL concepts such as observation, policy, action, reward, and memory become nontrivial, as they are constrained by the fundamental rules of quantum theory, including entanglement, measurement, and the no-cloning theorem.

The Breakdown of Classical Histories

In classical RL, an agent learns from a sequential history of percepts and actions. However, in a fully quantum RL scenario:

The agent and environment may become entangled during interaction.

Any attempt to observe or measure the history of interactions collapses the quantum state, thereby disrupting the coherent evolution.

The very notion of a discrete, observable "history" becomes ill-defined, as each measurement potentially erases or distorts part of the accumulated quantum experience.

This creates a paradox: how can an agent learn from an interaction history if the act of accessing that history destroys it?

Quantum MDPs and Their Limitations

To address this, researchers have proposed quantum generalizations of Markov decision processes (MDPs), such as quantum observable MDPs, where:

- Quantum states describe the environment.
- Agents select quantum operations (e.g., unitaries or POVMs) as actions.
- Rewards may arise from specific measurement outcomes or entanglement patterns.

However, even in these frameworks:

- Actions are typically described classically, e.g., as descriptions of quantum operations.
- The agent is not a fully quantum system—it merely controls quantum operations using classical logic.
- As such, the models do not support fully coherent quantum agents that act, store policies, and adapt using quantum memory and computation.

To truly realize quantum reinforcement learning, we must go beyond quantum control and allow for agents and actions encoded as quantum states.

Quantum Programming and Agent Design

A more general paradigm would permit quantum agents to generate and manipulate actions encoded in quantum states. This idea has been partially explored through techniques such as:

Quantum programs encoded in states, e.g., port-based teleportation protocols, where a "program" is instantiated as a physical quantum state.

Quantum channels that depend on control qubits or entangled ancillae, enabling context-sensitive adaptive strategies.

However, critical bottlenecks remain:

No known efficient method exists to train such agents or optimize over quantum policies.

Quantum learning agents would need to balance coherence (to preserve entanglement and memory) with measurement (to extract information), a trade-off not present in classical RL.

The representation, storage, and update of policies in quantum memory is further complicated by the no-cloning theorem and the irreversibility of measurements.

Knowledge in Quantum Systems: A Foundational Puzzle

Perhaps the most philosophically intriguing challenge is the definition of knowledge itself in a quantum world:

In classical settings, knowledge can be copied, shared, and transmitted—encoded in bits.

In quantum mechanics, knowledge may be physically instantiated in quantum states that cannot be cloned, broadcasted, or even fully measured without disturbance.

This leads to a radical rethinking of what it means for an agent to "know" something:

Can knowledge be entangled?

Is knowledge inherently personal and non-shareable in the quantum world?

What does learning mean when the learned information cannot be extracted or reused in the same way?

This raises epistemological questions about the nature of knowledge, learning, and collaboration in quantum settings—and suggests that machine learning could play a role in the foundations of quantum theory.

From Autonomous Quantum Agents to Quantum Observers

At the outermost edge of this inquiry lie ultimate questions:

Can fully quantum autonomous agents learn new physics by interacting with unknown quantum environments?

Could a quantum agent's learning algorithm serve as a definition of an observer—one that does not require an external classical interface?

Might learning and interaction dynamics influence our understanding of measurement, decoherence, or even the emergence of classicality?

These questions touch on the boundary between machine learning and the interpretation of quantum mechanics. They may provide a framework to:

Investigate observer-relative quantum theories (e.g., QBism),

Re-express the measurement problem in terms of learning and information exchange,

Explore the notion of agency and subjectivity in quantum systems.

Bridging the gap between quantum epistemology and learning theory, by linking quantum state evolution to belief updates or rational decision-making under quantum uncertainty.

14.5 Building Bridges between Quantum and AI

The time is ripe to invest strategically in the emerging interface between quantum science and machine learning (ML). To ensure Europe remains at the forefront of next-generation quantum technologies, it is imperative to strengthen research efforts that bridge these two transformative domains. While countries such as the US, Canada, and China are accelerating rapidly in this space—with a growing number of patents in quantum-enhanced ML applications—Europe must leverage its strong foundation, particularly through the Quantum Flagship initiative, to lead in both foundational and applied quantum-ML research.

A comprehensive funding approach is essential—one that supports both fundamental and application-driven research. Certain domains, such as optimal quantum control, are already transitioning into commercialization, evidenced by the emergence of European start-ups. Meanwhile, other fields, including ab initio quantum simulations and quantum experimental data analysis, remain in an exploratory phase. These areas hold tremendous long-term potential but require sustained investment in fundamental science to unlock new physical insights and drive technological revolutions.

The convergence of quantum science and machine learning holds the promise of mutual transformation. Quantum technologies can benefit from the optimization and automation power of AI, while ML can be expanded and redefined through quantum principles such as superposition, entanglement, and non-locality. Realizing this synergy demands not only financial support, but also institutional structures that foster interdisciplinary collaboration.

At the heart of this initiative must be the formation of interdisciplinary research ecosystems—bringing together:

- Quantum experimentalists and theorists, who understand the challenges and opportunities of quantum platforms;
- Machine learning researchers and AI engineers, who can develop tailored algorithms and architectures;
- Computer scientists, with expertise in complexity theory, data structures, and high-performance computing;
- Entrepreneurs, investors, and policy-makers, to ensure a robust innovation pipeline and translate breakthroughs into societal impact.

Creating bridges between these communities will catalyze new forms of knowledge and innovation. Structured support for interdisciplinary teams, training programs, shared infrastructure, and public-private partnerships is essential for pushing beyond current boundaries and fostering a culture of open, diverse, and collaborative research.

By enabling cross-fertilization between quantum and AI, Europe has the opportunity not only to secure technological sovereignty but also to shape the future of science itself.

The rapid progress in machine learning (ML) over the past decade has been largely driven by a vibrant ecosystem of open-source software, freely available benchmark datasets, shared model repositories, and community-led challenges. Drawing on this success, we propose creating a similar infrastructure to accelerate research and collaboration at the interface of quantum science and machine learning.

To realize this vision, the standardization of quantum physics problems is a critical step. By developing interoperable, structured interfaces and common data formats, quantum challenges can be translated into a machine-learning-ready framework. This will allow the seamless sharing of experimental and simulated data, and ensure that ML models are reusable, comparable, and reproducible across both theoretical and experimental quantum physics contexts.

In addition to technical standardization, community-driven open projects should be launched to foster knowledge exchange. These projects can serve as hubs for collaborative tool development, shared interfaces, comprehensive tutorials, and thorough documentation—lowering the barrier to entry for newcomers, and strengthening cohesion across disciplines. They will also provide an essential resource for teaching, benchmarking, and developing best practices in the field.

To ensure sustained progress, it is essential to train a new generation of interdisciplinary researchers. Dedicated doctoral networks, cross-disciplinary symposia, and online training platforms will prepare young scientists to work at the interface of quantum science and AI. These initiatives will help bridge the gap between theory and experiment, enabling more integrated and data-informed quantum research.

Importantly, this talent pipeline will also benefit industry. Graduates of such programs will bring cross-functional expertise into the innovation ecosystem, driving the development of competitive products, technological breakthroughs, and industry-ready solutions in quantum computing, simulation, and sensing.

Engagement and communication are equally critical. Strategic science communication efforts, in collaboration with content creators, industry partners, and policymakers, can make the progress and promise of quantum machine learning accessible to wider audiences. By embedding transparency and outreach into the research process, we foster trust, inclusivity, and a shared sense of purpose. Social media, interactive visualizations, and community platforms can amplify this impact, turning quantum-ML research into a collaborative and publicly appreciated endeavor.

The creation of an open, standardized, and community-driven ecosystem, coupled with interdisciplinary training and public engagement, is essential for unlocking the full potential of machine learning in quantum science—and ensuring its benefits are shared broadly across research, industry, and society.

14.6 Empathetic AI and Customized Algorithms

The World Wide Web was created in 1989, and it came with a vision. Sir Tim Berners-Lee once wrote, "The web is more a social creation than a technical one," in reference to this dream. I didn't develop it as a technological toy, but rather to have a social impact by encouraging teamwork. However, it appears that we are moving farther and farther away from the unity Berners-Lee had in mind. False information is catching on like wildfire. Individuals take extreme stances and fiercely defend them. Online conversations are dominated by anger. We are being driven apart by the Internet and the social networking sites it contains.

It's challenging to completely comprehend the mechanics that give rise to these dividing forces, even while we can observe them at work on social media. Why do individuals post irate comments? Why do they spread false information again? Why do they accept more and more illogical claims?

A portion of the solution is based on human psychology, while another portion is determined by the information these platforms present to us. Examining the tools that are being used to choose the information we see will help us understand why the internet is tearing us apart.

Today, the goal of practically all technology platforms is the same: to provide users with a customized experience. The systems that drive these platforms are commonly referred to as algorithms. However, these algorithms are intricate systems that operate behind the scenes using conventional software, human supervision, and, more and more, artificial intelligence and machine learning.

Let's examine this algorithm's inner workings. They first require an objective in order to function. Increasing the number of friends a user invites on the platform, retaining the user on the platform for as long as possible, or—more likely—a thoughtfully constructed combination of these goals. It is entirely up to the platform provider to decide what the algorithm will target. High-ranking executives usually make the very deliberate choice to pursue this goal in large IT businesses.

Additionally, algorithms require a surface—pixels—on which to operate. In the context of social media, this is usually the user stream, which enables an algorithm to choose the sequence in which the user will see content. The user profile is the final yet crucial input for an algorithm. This includes any user data that can aid the algorithm in achieving its goal. This is the point at which algorithms have become increasingly complex over time.

The first user profiles were rather basic, examining factors like gender, place of origin, web browser, and so forth. But now everything is up for grabs. Algorithms create user profiles by gathering information about users, such as the links they click, how long they spend on a page, how quickly they scroll through a mobile app, and a myriad of other details.

Software engineers began to understand that the best approach to assist algorithms in achieving their goal was to supply them with as many profile data points as possible as AI and machine learning began to play a bigger and bigger part in algorithms. Platform providers were forced to compile enormous sets of user data as a result. It has frequently been noted that such collections run the potential of violating user privacy. But they also provide a far more dangerous risk: enabling algorithms to accomplish their goals by taking advantage of every single, even the smallest, cognitive weakness of the individuals who depend on them.

A significant portion of the detrimental effects that we attribute to social media are caused by this abuse of our cognitive weaknesses. For instance, if an algorithm aims to lengthen a user's stay on a platform and a user frequently writes a lengthy, irate response after viewing an inflammatory post, the algorithm will discover that this is a good way to accomplish its goal.

A more thorough definition of the goal can help to mitigate this. In the earlier scenario, we could instruct the algorithm to minimize the quantity of offensive posts a user sees while increasing the amount of time they stay on the site. Users cannot be sure that this objective function is carried out with their best interests in mind, though, as it is entirely at the control of the platform's proprietors. More significantly, it is clear that different users have different goals.

So, how can we solve that puzzle? As is frequently the case, it seems that AI, which initially made this issue so prevalent, may also provide some of the answer. Natural language understanding (NLU) is one branch of artificial intelligence that has advanced significantly in recent years. Any text in plain English (or any other language) can be processed by a system that uses NLU, and it can comprehend the material in a far more nuanced manner than it could previously. For instance, the system may process a text that explains how to bake a cake and comprehend the necessary components and the many stages required to finish the recipe. If the text is an article, the system can comprehend the subjects discussed, the article's tone, the depth or shallowness of the treatment, etc.

This provides an alternative to the current strategy: rather than creating algorithms that profile users based on innumerable data points and optimize for an ambiguous goal, we could allow users to express their preferences for a personalized experience using the richness of natural language. Users might create a document that serves as a recipe for their customization algorithm, which we'll refer to as a living manifesto.

A user could use a manifesto to outline their interests, people they wish to connect with, ideas they are interested in, whether they prefer reading brief texts or more in-depth personal information, times when they enjoy listening to podcasts, and other things. This ever-changing record could explain why a person favors a particular experience in a particular situation. Furthermore, as the user drafts the manifesto themselves, it would provide that response in a clear and understandable manner. This is exactly the kind of algorithm that Waverly is now creating, and it represents a significant shift from the existing strategy in which an AI attempts to infer a person's preferences using information that they are frequently unaware of.

It is no longer necessary for a manifesto-based customization algorithm to gather any user data. All it has to do is comprehend their manifesto. There are numerous advantages to this. First, because the manifesto is a completely transparent document, it directly and favorably affects user privacy. However, the most significant advantage is that the manifesto gives the user conscious control over their unique experience. Because the manifesto does not reveal the user's unconscious cognitive weaknesses, the customization algorithm is unable to take use of them. For instance, someone is unlikely to request more inflammatory stuff in their manifesto unless they genuinely enjoy being furious.

Put another way, a manifesto-based algorithm gives someone a chance to pause and reflect, whereas existing algorithms attempt to infer user preferences from data points that are not intentionally released. It enables users to explain why they value a particular piece of content in a certain context and has the opportunity to provide a kind of personalization that represents not just how a user behaves when using a product, but also how they hope to behave in the future.

However, a manifesto-based algorithm faces a significant obstacle in contrast to conventional algorithms. Conventional algorithms collect data points produced during an application's regular flow to provide a tailored experience in an effortless manner. A manifesto-based algorithm, on the other hand, requires the user to write their manifesto, which is a laborious task. A challenging assignment.

Fortunately, there are great hopes for success in this endeavor due to the developments in quantum computing. Complex problem solving, which has so far eluded even the most potent supercomputers, is now feasible thanks to the advancement of quantum computing. The most sophisticated artificial intelligence machine learning algorithms are one such issue that quantum computers will be particularly good at resolving. The computational divide between our current AI and the issues it causes and AI that is compassionate and complies with social norms can be closed by this new area of quantum AI.

This is where AI advancements in the future will be helpful. We must create AI tools that can help users create a comprehensive manifesto that captures their innermost goals. In order to help people find words that accurately describe who they want to be without unduly influencing them, we must create an AI that is empathetic. Considering that existing chatbots aren't even that effective at assisting users in completing clearly defined tasks, this is a tough challenge. Nevertheless, there are causes for optimism.

First, there are comparatively easy ways to get people to consider challenging issues. Therefore, we could see an AI that is sympathetic not as a chatbot but rather as a system that provides straightforward yet considerate tasks that encourage these kinds of thoughts. Second, one area of AI that has advanced quickly in recent years is text synthesis. When someone is creating their manifesto, OpenAI GPT-3 is a fantastic example of a system that can generate imaginative wording that could inspire them.

Third, although cautiously, the relationship between artificial intelligence and quantum technologies needs to be investigated. Society must create a workable and flexible framework regulating the advancement and use of moral quantum computing and compassionate artificial intelligence in order to avert the reality of the threats previously mentioned in the field of quantum information sciences. One major risk is that, if allowed to advance without such an ethical framework, quantum AI may worsen the shortcomings of classical AI, strengthen the bad aspects of social media that we are trying to counter, and possibly create new threat vectors in the battle against misinformation campaigns.

These are just a few stages toward developing AI that is genuinely sympathetic. Empathy is attained by humans through their sensitivity to a wide range of nonverbal clues, such as posture, tone of voice, facial expressions, and nuanced word choice. All of these things provide insight into someone's innermost thoughts.

A variety of strategies are also needed for empathy in order to support others' thoughts without getting in the way. It's hard for humans, let alone machines, to learn how to ask the appropriate question at the right moment.

Without a doubt, technological advancements will be necessary to build fully empathic systems. First, we will want expertise from a wide range of scientific fields. If we want to advance compassionate AI, neuroscientists, psychologists, behavioral economists, and many more will need to pool their knowledge and datasets. The question of whether the "spark of life" that enables people to sympathize with one another can be discovered using conventional physics or if we must explore quantum mechanics is a more challenging and contentious one. According to some scientists, the latter is accurate, which would imply that the development of really sympathetic AI agents is impossible without the integration of artificial intelligence and quantum computing.

Crucially, creating an AI that is sympathetic carries some risks. A system that assists you in putting your preferences for a customized experience in writing could potentially exert undue influence over you. As a result, we must proceed with caution when creating such an AI. However, given that existing algorithms don't even bother to try to make individuals aware of how their experience is controlled, it's crucial to note that the status quo is obviously suboptimal.

It is also critical that society avoid making the same mistakes that were made in the creation and use of classical AI, when the technology was created and implemented without a global grasp of its ethical consequences. As a result, society now has to catch up and, in certain situations (as with sympathetic AI), strive to control or even undo the technology that is already in use. Although quantum computing is still in its early stages, it offers us the opportunity to proactively create moral guidelines for this next phase of developing technology.

We can learn from the successful application of another significant technical advancement in the same way that society may learn from the unethical application of classical AI. A group of scientists with enough foresight called the Asilomar Conference on Recombinant DNA in 1975 as research into the technology began to take shape in the 1970s. In addition to preventing the spread of biohazards and the creation of malicious biotechnology, the assembly of scientific, policy, and legal specialists effectively created an actionable, ethical framework around the new problems with this technology. A comparable worldwide framework must be established for the advancement of moral quantum technology in order to learn from this successful model and avoid making the same mistakes twice. According to the organizer of the Asilomar Conference, "it would be more effective, especially in the face of uncertainty, to provide guidelines that will undergo timely changes in response to new scientific knowledge" as opposed to implementing a technology in the hopes that it would evolve to conform to society's ethical and compassionate standards.

In order to create ethical and compassionate quantum artificial intelligence, it is imperative that we take lessons from the past, not only about the shortcomings of classical AI in this field but also about the achievements of other ethical standards for comparable innovative technologies.

Sir Tim Berners-Lee had the idea to create the World Wide Web as a network that would facilitate closer collaboration between individuals decades ago. We must combat the increasingly polarizing influences of internet platforms if we hope to do that. The creation of different approaches to tailoring people's experiences is a component of the answer. We must liberate ourselves from the algorithms of the present generation and their capacity to take advantage of our weaknesses as humans.

The creation of compassionate AIs that can comprehend humans on a deeper level and assist us in expressing our goals without influencing them would be necessary for these alternative systems. Creating such systems won't be simple. We might even need to enter the realm of quantum artificial intelligence with caution. However, the difficulty shouldn't deter us from trying, and there are concrete actions that can be made right now that can open the door to a much better future where people can actually work together.

We will be able to implement Berners-Lee's goal and drastically alter the course of our online activity thanks to quantum artificial intelligence.

14.7 Should We Let the Machine Determine What Is Important?

It is extremely difficult to build a quantum computer that performs tasks well beyond the scope of classical computing, like factoring a big integer. I would contend that it will be so difficult to accomplish that it will require significant adjustments to our technical and computational infrastructure, including significant advancements in artificial intelligence subsystems. We won't get close to the realm of millions of quantum bits until we make these advancements. We can aim to support AI developments along the road that incorporate the components required to guarantee their positive impact on mankind. The main topic of discussion here is whether or not humans will ever be able to comprehend the effects of the systems we have built, considering that we will be depending more and more on machines to build quantum computers, including machine learning and increasingly sophisticated artificial intelligence systems. Or will we only be able to comprehend through the filters that our equipment allows us to see?

First, though, how challenging is it to construct a large-scale quantum computer?

Take the well-known Schrödinger's cat thought experiment as a starting point. Schrödinger asked the following question in this experiment: what happens if a cat is placed in a box with a qubit attached to a vial of poison gas so that the poison is released if the qubit is up and kept in the vial if the qubit is down? Can the experiment be conducted with the qubit set in superposition of up and down? He argued that it was absurd, mainly because we were unable to construct a sufficiently isolated cage for the qubit's superposition to result in the cat being both alive and dead at the same moment.

More recently, scientists demonstrated that in order to quantify the presence of this superposition, one must be able to undo the physical process that resulted in the cat's death. In other words, you need to be able to control the cat+poison+qubit system effectively enough to be able to reverse all of the processes employed in order to demonstrate to another observer that you have produced a Schrödinger cat. The majority of this so-called quantum necromancy is still a theory. It does, however, draw attention to the difficulty of creating a large-scale quantum computer.

To maintain a superposition of tens of thousands, or perhaps millions, of qubits, one must advance the instruments for information recovery. In other words, we need to be able to theoretically undo everything that has happened since the computation started. Compared to bringing a dead cat back to life, that is still far simpler. It does, however, go beyond what we currently understand to be possible in terms of engineering. In fact, it is already requiring advancements in a number of disciplines, including computer science, microwave engineering, and materials science.

We now discuss the advantages of spending money on quantum computing. Reaching this absurd objective is, in my opinion, worthwhile in and of itself since it will reveal if the cosmos computes quantum mechanically, which supports the theories of other experts in the field including Krysta Svore, Scott Aaronson, and John Preskill. However, it also turns out that investing in our computing capabilities continues to yield enormous benefits for humanity and our capacities as individuals, countries, and the global community. In particular, there are numerous ramifications for the required technological advancements.

Indeed, the capabilities made possible by new computing and networking technology and applications have played a major role in the productivity increases over the last 50 years. We take this for granted now, but the ease with which thousands of transactions can be completed in a normal week contrasts sharply with the same set of activities fifty years ago, including ordering groceries, paying bills, and making operational decisions in a convoluted supply chain. According to Robert Gordon, our society has benefited from this decrease in unpleasantness in our lives. What benefits are ahead?

14.8 Which AI Is Made Possible by Upcoming Computing Models?

In particular, as computing technology advances, new uses and algorithms are appearing that mark the start of what many refer to as artificial intelligence in a broader context. Nevertheless, we will avoid discussing "general" AI and instead look at the diverse range of methods that are included in the AI umbrella and all relate to different facets of what it means to be "intelligent" in the human experience. Our knowledge of how living things view the world serves as inspiration for some of these methods. They relate to things like word, voice, image, and other sensory input recognition. They provide fuzzy estimations of what a set of inputs corresponds to, given enough training, using ideas derived from the behavior of animal neurons. They allow for the automation of numerous mundane chores and provide us with real-time information and amplification of the environment around us.

But these systems already face many difficulties, especially when it comes to the conflict between bias and truth. Utilizing automated recognition systems entails assigning fundamental truth questions to the training or execution dataset as well as the known and concealed assumptions in the AI-related subsystem. These result in sometimes amusing but frequently horrifying outcomes, such as misinterpretations of causality and consequence and profiling that favors white, male faces over others.

More intricate AI subsystems go deeper toward simulating or enhancing the more challenging aspects of thought and the mind. They examine how to facilitate artificial or enhanced creative thinking, learning, and decision-making.

In this case, the mathematical models and methodologies deviate from the biological networks because, unlike simple neural networks, our scientific understanding of brain function does not fully comprehend these systems to allow for a reverse-engineering approach. We must once more contend with difficult issues, such as determining whether decision-making may be left to automated systems and at what expense. Additionally, we must acknowledge that computer-driven discovery may open up more methods and technologies than our species can readily adopt and use ethically.

Since reaching a consensus on these issues is really challenging, I won't go into length about my thoughts on them here. My main point is straightforward: I think that our ability to choose to use these institutions for the good of our society and civilization originates from our humanity. We are ignoring our personal and societal moral obligations when we lose sight of the purpose behind our technology use and instead allow transformative technologies to take over our lives. As a result, we need to create these technologies for uses that are specific to their efficient operation and restricted to that field, much like an information security sandbox.

14.9 An Example of Building AI Subsystems Using Physics

I want to use a short scenario to demonstrate how placing people at the center of the picture allows for new technical execution regimes in order to make my argument. A seminal scientific paper demonstrating how a quantum device can execute a very specific algorithm exponentially faster than any conventional computer was published in Science magazine at the end of 2020. It was accomplished with a system that has been dubbed a "dark horse" candidate for quantum computing, using light instead of circuits, and—perhaps most intriguingly—relying much more heavily on human labor. Additionally, it is the first significant finding in quantum computing for a Chinese research team.

Although there are many fascinating ways to analyze the outcome and its significance, I'd like to focus on the function of automation in physics experiments and relate it to new applications of automation in other spheres of our lives. One begins to worry how gloomy our science fiction future might turn out as a result of the ongoing conversations about machine learning and driverless cars.

The study done by Chao-Yang Lu's group, which is detailed in the Science paper, effectively illustrates the interaction: a significant amount of physical labor is required to achieve this outcome. You can see the enormous number of hand-aligned optical elements in the group photo, each of which must point at the correct objects with micrometer accuracy. In particular, the following experiment you do in physics (and other domains as well, though I am not an authority on automation in biology, for instance) usually builds on your previous successful experiment. In order for the humans doing the experiment to concentrate on something more crucial, you typically examine the equipment to determine which components you might be able to automate. You continue doing this until you can no longer automate; after that, you try the experiment and hopefully it works. Working closely with innovative teams has given me the impression that the pace at which we can put this loop into practice and comprehend the effects of growing automation will determine the boundaries of our knowledge.

For instance, a lot of global teams working on the development of quantum computers concentrated on improving automation. This involved hardware automation, such as the construction of the intricate interference systems by lithography and nanofabrication techniques. Additionally, it had a significant amount of software automation for testing, tweaking, and operating systems, which might allow them to scale their efforts faster than the most recent Lu group outcomes. As the CEO of Honeywell recently pointed out, their primary contribution to the field of ion trap quantum computing is not advanced physics in and of itself, but rather their proficiency in sophisticated system automation and control.

14.10 Quantum as an AI Force Multiplier

The real devices are not yet faster than their classical equivalents, despite the fact that quantum computing is still developing. Indeed, if you were to see one of them, it would most likely resemble a huge, futuristic train set—one that is super cooled and almost at zero degrees Kelvin. Some claim that it brings to mind the early days of modern computing, as demonstrated by the ENIAC computer, which took up a room.

Depending on who you ask, the development of a large-scale, fault-tolerant computer is necessary before quantum computing can truly take off. Will that be in five years? Ten? More? It's not feasible to tell. However, I would refute that claim by highlighting the current and expanding quantum ecosystem that is creating useful hardware, software, and algorithms.

Furthermore, it's critical to note that quantum and conventional devices tackle different problems, not just different ones. And in the upcoming years and possibly decades, this will remain the case. For this reason, imposing any quantum-related adulations solely on quantum computers is inaccurate. In actuality, innovations and disruptions will result from the combined strength of quantum and classical computers operating in a hybrid architecture and "conducted" with workflow orchestration tools to address issues.

The key lesson to be learned from this is that quantum will mostly function as a force multiplier for current AI and machine learning solutions. For instance, adding quantum to the mix may include deep faking how lung cancer might progress in a person based on their genetic profile and many other parameters, as opposed to simply deep faking a celebrity video as is now possible.

Indeed, we have already entered a realm where quantum devices can perform better than their classical equivalents under specific, severe edge case conditions. Quantum supremacy is the term for this. These accomplishments are not yet scalable or useful for resolving common problems, but future developments will eventually bring us there, and the way there is already paved for us.

Meanwhile, a thriving and expanding ecosystem of economic, academic, and governmental stakeholders—often cooperating—is setting the stage for quantum's unavoidable upending of the status quo. Pharmaceuticals, healthcare, financial services, material science, logistics, cybersecurity, aerospace, and energy are a few sectors that are anticipated to be affected by this upheaval first.

It's all Connected

One of the most alluring aspects of quantum computing's potential is its capacity to take advantage of the interdependence of numerous factors and issues in meaningful ways. For instance, climate change does not occur in a vacuum. There is an additional meta-dimensionality to the way we calculate prediction models because it directly affects food security, which in turn affects global trade, business (name any industry), economies, health, epidemiology, and social unrest.

We will be able to handle the dimensionality of this interconnection of several variables in interwoven complex systems thanks to quantum computing.

Although, as was already noted, those with bad intentions, like cybercriminals, can and will use quantum computing, the majority of the deliberate use cases, research, and activity will be directed toward improving society. As molecular and biological systems are simulated in ways not yet achievable, the discovery of drugs and vaccines will accelerate. Models of climate change will be far more advanced than anything we can produce now. Materials that are currently nonexistent will be created through simulation. Investment portfolios will be optimized to a degree that is currently unattainable but is a goal shared by all financial institutions. Vendors of hardware and software will create and operate their goods in ways that are currently unthinkable.

These are only a handful of the things we may anticipate happening in the years to come; they are constrained by what we can currently envision and anticipate, which is only the beginning of the potential outcomes. We are regrettably but unavoidably constrained by a dogma that limits our ability to think. However, employing quantum computing would unavoidably require us to think about issues in a more probabilistic and scenario-driven fashion, much as the development of classical computers has profoundly and permanently altered our approach to problem-solving. This will fundamentally alter humankind's paradigm—a genuinely profound change in our capacities and ways of thinking. And this is one of the primary reasons for starting a business in order to facilitate and take part in the development of such a future.

Having a Different Perspective

Apple launched a now-famous advertising campaign in the late 1990s with the tagline, "Think Different." It included images and videos of influential people like Martin Luther King Jr., Thomas Edison, and Albert Einstein to bolster that statement. In a sense, quantum computing will soon assist us in achieving that.

Quantum computing's "known unknown" is how technology will enable us to think in new ways and generate concepts—as well as the capacity to analyze and calculate them—that humans were either unable to imagine or were too mired in antiquated, conventional thinking to alter.

Consider the binary basis of computing, which is made up of bits that can only be either a one or a zero. Because the quantum bits, or qubits, exist in a state known as superposition—that is, an indeterminate, probabilistic mixture of both "one-ness" and "zero-ness" until a quantum calculation is ultimately measured at the end—computers can now function in a non-binary mode thanks to the quantum model.

Qubits are considerably faster at calculations and can calculate a lot more data than classical bits because of this quantum state. It is more than just quicker, larger, and better. The way we even formulate the problems that need to be answered is altered by this essentially different method of processing the same data. This compels the problem-solver to reconsider the issue in fresh ways that fundamentally broaden their perspective. Similar to how different backgrounds and viewpoints benefit human organizations, this diversity of ideas in the problem-solving domain will offer special benefits when looking for answers and solutions to our most challenging and frustrating issues.

The intriguing feature of quantum computing is the unknowable potentialities that could materialize as carelessly advantageous results. The lovely mishaps. By definition, neither I nor anyone else can foresee what they will be. However, they are waiting to be born out there. I'm eager to watch how this develops!

14.11 AI-Powered Quantum Computing Enablement

The practical construction of a practical quantum computer is extremely difficult. To fully reap the benefits of quantum computing, significant advancements in programmability, speed, dependability, fidelity, and scale are required. In order to overcome the numerous intricate physics and engineering obstacles that prevent practical quantum computing, strong tools are required.

AI is radically changing how we interact with the digital world, restructuring industries, and changing the technological environment. The capacity to produce insight from data opens the door to ground-breaking fixes for some of the most difficult issues confronting modern society. AI is leading a technological revolution that promises to reshape the future, from autonomous cars to personalized medicine. However, there are numerous difficult issues that stand in the way of practical quantum computing.

Together with traditional supercomputers, quantum computers will speed up important aspects of difficult issues that are pertinent to business, academia, and government. An Introduction to Quantum Accelerated Supercomputing explains this relationship. Supercomputers and quantum computers have mutually beneficial benefits, and this close integration will also allow AI to assist in resolving the primary obstacles to practical quantum computing.

14.12 AI and Quantum Computing Synergies

Potential synergies abound at the nexus of artificial intelligence (AI) and quantum computing, which offers fresh methods for resolving challenging issues that are outside the scope of traditional computer paradigms. The creation of quantum machine learning algorithms, which take advantage of the processing capacity and intrinsic parallelism of quantum computing to improve on conventional machine learning methods, is one area of synergy.

By using quantum principles to process and analyze data more quickly than their conventional equivalents, quantum machine learning algorithms show promise in tasks like classification, regression, and clustering. Significant speedups and increased accuracy are possible with quantum algorithms like quantum support vector machines and quantum neural networks, especially when working with huge datasets or complex feature spaces.

Furthermore, quantum-inspired algorithms are showing promise as a solution for AI's optimization and pattern recognition problems. These algorithms create novel optimization techniques that surpass traditional methods by taking influence from the concepts of quantum computing. For example, quantum annealing and quantum-inspired optimization algorithms, such as the quantum approximate optimization algorithm (QAOA), provide effective solutions for combinatorial optimization problems, including graph partitioning and traveling salesman problems. AI systems can perform better on tasks including scheduling, logistics optimization, and resource allocation by utilizing quantum-inspired optimization techniques.

Quantum-enhanced data processing and analysis is another area where AI and quantum computing might work together. Superposition and entanglement, two special characteristics of quantum computing, allow for the effective manipulation of big datasets and intricate data structures. In high-dimensional data spaces, quantum techniques such as quantum principal component analysis (PCA) and quantum singular value decomposition (QSVD) provide methods for reducing dimensionality and obtaining valuable insights. Furthermore, jobs like anomaly detection, feature extraction, and data clustering, where classical approaches might not be able to handle the computing needs or the complexity of the data, may benefit from the use of quantum-enhanced data analysis techniques. AI systems can open up new avenues for knowledge discovery and decision-making across a range of industries, including cybersecurity, healthcare, and finance, by utilizing quantum-enhanced data processing capabilities.

14.13 Cloud Computing: The Framework for Integrating Quantum and AI

A fundamental technological paradigm that is transforming the way computer resources are delivered, managed, and used is cloud computing. Essentially, cloud computing provides on-demand access to a shared pool of computer resources that may be configured, such as servers, networks, storage, apps, and services. Scalability, flexibility, pay-as-you-go pricing methods, and self-service provisioning are some of the main features of cloud computing. Users can obtain processing power and storage capacity without requiring substantial on-premises infrastructure thanks to cloud providers' internet-based delivery of these resources.

The incorporation of artificial intelligence (AI) and quantum computing in cloud environments requires a strong infrastructure that can accommodate the distinct needs of both technologies. Specialized hardware is needed for quantum computing, such as qubit control systems and quantum processors, which require exacting environmental conditions including electromagnetic shielding and extremely low temperatures. In a similar vein, AI workloads—particularly those requiring deep learning models—call for powerful computers, lots of memory, and effective data storage options. Therefore, cloud providers need to make investments in infrastructure that can handle the resource and processing needs of AI and quantum computing applications.

There are a number of clear benefits to using cloud platforms for quantum-AI integration. First off, cloud platforms offer infrastructure that is elastic and scalable, enabling customers to dynamically distribute resources in response to demand. For quantum computing, where the amount of qubits and computational complexity might vary greatly based on the work at hand, this scalability is very advantageous. Additionally, cloud providers offer a varied range of services and tools customized to enable quantum computing and AI processes, including quantum development kits, machine learning frameworks, and data processing pipelines. Organizations can save development costs and time-to-market while accelerating the creation and implementation of quantum-AI solutions by utilizing these pre-built services.

Additionally, cloud computing facilitates easy resource sharing and collaboration amongst academics, developers, and companies engaged in AI and quantum computing initiatives. Cloud-based platforms help geographically dispersed teams share datasets, algorithms, and computational resources, which promotes creativity and cooperation in multidisciplinary research projects. To further protect sensitive data and guarantee regulatory compliance in quantum-AI workflows, cloud providers also provide strong security measures, compliance certifications, and data protection procedures. All things considered, cloud computing provides a flexible and scalable framework for combining AI with quantum computing, allowing businesses to successfully capitalize on these technologies' disruptive potential.

There are several opportunities and difficulties in the field of cloud-based quantum-AI systems, which promise revolutionary developments but also present logistical and technical challenges that must be carefully navigated. Numerous industries, including banking, healthcare, cybersecurity, and more, have enormous prospects for innovation as a result of the integration of AI and quantum computing in cloud environments. By utilizing cloud infrastructure's processing capacity and scalability, cloud-based quantum-AI systems have the potential to completely transform data analysis, optimization, and decision-making procedures.

Additionally, cloud platforms' collaborative nature encourages interdisciplinary study and cooperation, allowing businesses to exchange knowledge, pool resources, and speed up the creation of quantum-AI solutions. Significant obstacles still exist, though, such as the requirement for reliable error correction methods to lessen the effects of quantum decoherence, the creation of scalable quantum hardware, and the optimization of quantum algorithms for cloud-based implementation. Furthermore, a major concern is maintaining the security, privacy, and regulatory compliance of quantum-AI systems in cloud environments. Realizing the full potential of cloud-based quantum-AI systems and promoting significant advances in science, technology, and business will require addressing these issues while seizing the opportunities they bring.

14.4 Applications of Artificial Intelligence and Quantum Computing

Quantum AI has applications in a wide range of fields, including operations management, supply chain management, healthcare, and finance, due to its quick resolution of intricate and demanding computational tasks and its subsequent impact on processing large data sets in cloud computing environments.

Finance:

For instance, its applications in finance are dynamic and include financial modeling, fraud detection, portfolio optimization, risk analysis, and financial forecasting. Financial managers can achieve precise financial forecasting and modeling thanks to quantum artificial intelligence (AI) in cloud computing, which facilitates the quick and effective analysis and realization of Monte carlo simulations. Furthermore, quantum cloud computing's sophisticated computational capabilities enable it to determine the best mix of financial tools to maximize investment portfolio optimization while lowering risk to manageable levels. In the first quarter of 2024, there were 8,700 financial fraud complaints, up from 6,094 during the same period the year before, according to Financial Ombudsman Services. Therefore, quantum AI in cloud computing is crucial for promptly identifying and stopping illicit financial activity by evaluating large data sets of financial transactions.

Healthcare:

With the use of quantum intelligence technologies that can evaluate more than 100 million compounds in a 24-hour period, it also expedites and enhances the dependability of medication design and development in the healthcare industry, which lowers the time and expenses associated with clinical trials. A virtual examination of safe and efficient medication candidates for the treatment of Ebola was implemented by Atomwise. In a single day, the procedure—which takes months when utilizing traditional computing—identified two potential medication candidates. Additionally, it mimics real-time patient trials such as HumMod, which examines thousands of variables and more than 1500 equations that describe physiological elements like hormones, electrolytes, and bodily fluids.

By 2025, more than 100 trillion gigabytes of healthcare data will have been gathered. In order to improve patient-centered care, healthcare providers will be able to analyze and interpret large amounts of data and get valuable insights through the integration of quantum cloud computing. The need for quantum cloud computing to increase the effect of such data in healthcare decision making and improve patient outcomes will also increase due to the growing use of connected sensory and digital devices that gather huge amounts of patient data. Concerning the enhancement of healthcare decision-making,

Physicians can use quantum cloud computing tools like IBM Watson to search through millions of papers in online sources like PubMed for causes that are difficult to see with the naked eye. These illustrations highlight the priceless uses of AI in healthcare.

Supply chain and logistics:

Improving the robustness, flexibility, and sustainability of supply chains and operations requires quantum analytics made possible by quantum cloud computing. The growing number of interconnected nodes has made supply chain management more difficult, particularly in the current macro and microeconomic context. In order to improve resource allocation within the supply chain, logistical fleets and routes, and sourcing choices while minimizing costs, managers can simply map the interactions of various supply chain factors using quantum cloud computing. Quantum cloud computing skills can also be used to forecast and manage order volumes to cut down on waste and surplus inventory through the computation and analysis of supply chain data.

Time series data can also be analyzed using other technologies, such as quantum machine learning (QML), for predictive maintenance and early detection, particularly in manufacturing and industrial plants.

14.14.1 Quickly Resolve Difficult Issues

As data sets are growing rather large and more complex than what is achievable by standard computers, there is a growing need for improvement in the contemporary computing architecture. Enhanced computing capability is required by present-day computers to solve intricate questions that quantum computers are predicted to resolve in a matter of seconds

14.14.2 Managing Large Datasets.

Data is generated at around 2.5 exabytes each day. Such massive amounts of data can hardly be processed using standard CPUs and GPUs, whereas quantum computers are built to reason about data and identify patterns and anomalies at scale.

14.14.3 Detecting and Combating Fraud.

Let us remember that quantum computing together with artificial intelligence will first come to the banking and finance industries and there fraud detection will be improved and the latter will be enhanced and will become better. Not only would quantum computer trained models be able to detect relatively hard to brilliant patterns but they would also be capable of dealing with large stream of big data that these machines can handle. This objective would also be made possible by improvements in algorithms.

14.14.4 Developing Better Models.

In this space of increasing data, the companies do not have to rely on classic computational tools anymore to study a set of complex situations. There is need for such businesses to have efficient models that would be able to encompass what all types of scenarios are possible.

The healthcare sector is predicted to generate data at a compound annual growth rate of 36% by 2025, which is 6% faster than that of manufacturing, financial services, logistics, and e-commerce. We might be able to increase coordination, lower the chance of financial collapse, and cure illnesses more successfully if we use quantum technology to create better models.

It has been shown that quantum computers can accurately estimate traffic levels in transportation and speed up DNA sequencing in the medical profession. It is anticipated that quantum computing will be essential to improving our knowledge of biology and evolution, facilitating better therapies for illnesses like cancer, and even helping to lessen the consequences of climate change.

14.14.5 New Developments in Quantum Computing

Photonic integrated circuits that are capable of efficiently controlling photonic quantum states, or qubits, are essential for the successful use of quantum technology. A major breakthrough has been made by physicists from the Leibniz-Institut für Kristallzüchtung (IKZ), TU Dresden, and Helmholtz-Zentrum Dresden-Rossendorf (HZDR) to address this problem. They have shown that single-photon emitters can be regulated at the nanoscale in silicon.

In their December 12, 2022, report on nature communications, the scientists asserted that

"Uncontrolled production in random spots impeded scalability in previous attempts to manufacture single-photon emitters. It has been highly probable that focused ion beams (FIB) can produce individual G and W centers on silicon wafers in a controlled manner. Furthermore, a broad beam scalable implantation strategy compatible with complementary metal-oxide-semiconductor (CMOS) technology has been devised to precisely fabricate single telecom emitters at the nanoscale. These findings offer a clear route towards the development of industrial-scale photonic quantum processors with technology nodes smaller than 100 nm. This study offers a straightforward and useful path toward the creation of such processors.

14.15 The Cloud's Confluence of AI and Quantum

The nexus of artificial intelligence (AI) and quantum computing in the context of cloud computing is a promising area that has the potential to completely transform the field of computational capabilities. This section of the article explores particular domains where the combination of AI with quantum computing in the cloud leads to synergistic improvements, delving into the complex mechanics of this convergence.

Quantum Machine Learning (QML)

At the vanguard of innovation, quantum machine learning (QML) uses the special capabilities of quantum computing to improve on traditional machine learning models. This section of the study concentrates on the finer points and significant ramifications of quantum machine learning in the larger framework of cloud-based artificial intelligence (AI) and quantum computing convergence.

1. Quantum Advantage in Machine Learning

In machine learning, QML makes use of the quantum advantage, which is the phenomena whereby quantum algorithms perform better than their classical counterparts for specific processing types. Computational efficiency is greatly increased by quantum computing's capacity to process data in parallel using the superposition principle. For machine learning jobs involving intricate computations and huge datasets, this is very beneficial.

2. Networks of Quantum Neurals:

Many machine learning applications are built on top of traditional neural networks. Quantum neural networks, which use quantum bits, or qubits, to represent and process data, are introduced by QML. More complex patterns and correlations in data may be captured by quantum neural networks, which would be advantageous for tasks like feature extraction, pattern recognition, and classification.

3. Machine Learning with Quantum Algorithms:

A collection of quantum algorithms created especially for machine learning applications is introduced by QML. Quantum K-Means Clustering, Quantum Principal Component Analysis, and Quantum Support Vector Machine (QSVM) are a few examples. When run on a quantum computer, these algorithms seek to perform better than their conventional counterparts, showcasing the possibility of exponential speedups in a range of machine learning applications.

4. Representing Quantum Data:

Classical bits are used to represent data in classical machine learning models. Qubits allow for the simultaneous exploration of several states in QML by enabling the representation of data in quantum superposition. A novel method of information processing and encoding is provided by this quantum parallelism, which may result in more effective representation and analysis of complicated datasets.

5. Quantum Feature Mapping:

A crucial method in QML, quantum feature mapping converts classical input into a quantum state that can be processed by a quantum computer. By mapping classical data to a high-dimensional quantum space, quantum algorithms can uncover intricate patterns that may be challenging for classical algorithms to discern. This procedure improves quantum machine learning models' expressive capabilities.

6. Hybrid Quantum-Classical Approaches:

QML frequently uses a hybrid quantum-classical approach in which classical optimization techniques and quantum algorithms work together. While the quantum component of the algorithm takes advantage of the quantum advantage for particular computations, the classical half of the method manages other duties. The perfect setting for putting these hybrid designs into practice is offered by cloud-based AI platforms, which enable the smooth fusion of quantum and conventional resources.

7. Quantum Circuit Learning:

QML presents the idea of quantum circuit learning, in which traditional neural network topologies are swapped out for quantum circuits. These quantum circuits' characteristics are tuned to maximize particular machine learning goals. This innovative method, which is a current research topic at the nexus of machine learning and quantum computing, has the potential to produce better results for specific kinds of tasks.

14.16 Data Privacy, Security, and Ethical Governance in Quantum AI.

AI technology raises concerns about data privacy, security, and ethical governance. However, with proper safeguards, these risks can be mitigated. The convergence of quantum computing and AI presents new challenges. Legal theories, policies, laws, and regulations that were developed to address AI issues are now outdated. Consider the potential impact of technology on society and regulation, which is currently straining to keep up with technological advancements. AI has significant consequences for data privacy, including compliance with existing and future legal systems worldwide. AI regulation requires consideration of both national legislation and industry overlays. Additionally, a set of supra-national rules and regulations relevant to AI are emerging. The OECD's five AI principles have been embraced by 40 countries, and the G20 endorsed them in 2019. The regulatory framework for AI technology is being focused on the "simple" or "classical" form, ignoring its convergence with quantum computing.

Compliance can be challenging in today's complex regulatory landscape. Legislators and enforcers have identified several essential issues, including justice, lawfulness, transparency, data minimization (collecting only necessary information), individual rights, and security. We'll look at each of these next. AI technology can be complex, making it challenging for companies to adequately explain how they handle personal data. Additionally, the algorithm or technique used may evolve over time, leading to increased complexity. Identifying a single legal basis for processing can be challenging, which is a crucial need of the European Union.

Can a firm depend on permission if it doesn't adequately disclose its processing?

What actions are being taken now and in the future to evolve the algorithm? Repurposing personal data through complex algorithms can have unintended consequences and represent a risk to individuals' privacy. Transparency is essential when collecting and using data. While current AI technology makes it challenging to meet transparency requirements, it is unclear whether quantum computing can help.

AI relies on collecting and analyzing large amounts of data. Companies may face criticism for collecting too much data and retaining it for longer periods than necessary. Overuse of personal data to improve algorithms is not welcome, as it contradicts the data minimization principle at the heart of data privacy regulations. The combination of quantum computing with AI may lead to higher efficiency, allowing for less personal data collection and retention. Combining quantum computing and artificial intelligence could improve data privacy and compliance. Individuals' rights over their personal data continue to be a challenge in AI applications. How can information be retrieved, extracted, and communicated to the individual? The limitations of quantum AI are evident in this scenario, making it difficult to see how the convergence of the two technologies will help overcome this obstacle.

Transparency is important, but corporations must prioritize developing technology with human rights (especially access rights) in mind and implementing adequate security measures from the beginning. As quantum AI advances, the concept of "privacy by design and default" may become a feasible and effective way to include rights into algorithms from the start.

Data privacy is inextricably linked to cybersecurity, especially in the context of AI technology. To handle large amounts of data in standard AI models, effective controls are necessary. Quantum computing's greater efficiency may lead to improved control measures. AI poisoning, or manipulation of training data, has become a common issue in traditional AI models. Improving security controls and procedures to protect algorithmic development processes is a welcome step. AI-based autonomous systems require strong security to operate safely in the physical environment. Poorly secured autonomous vehicles and drones pose a major risk to human safety, property, and liabilities. The number of cyber problems, including ransomware assaults, is increasing. Scientists must capitalize on quantum AI's technical advantages to prevent attacks that could jeopardize the safety of AI-powered technologies.

Ethics and Good Governance: Ensure Biased Outcomes

Algorithm judgments must be fair and consistent, not just for data privacy compliance. As AI technology becomes more prevalent, people want fair and consistent applications in various industries. Critics have pointed out that AI-driven services can produce skewed results. Businesses must assure bias-free technology use, regardless of gender, color, or other characteristics. When quantum computing is combined with AI, it may appear that algorithmic decision-making becomes even more opaque compared to traditional methods. Incorporating quantum computing with traditional AI models may lead to better efficiency and bias-free decision-making. The Centre for Data Ethics and Innovation (CDEI) recently published an assessment on bias in algorithmic decision-making. The review focuses on how algorithms might support justice rather than harm it. The research admits the possibility of prejudice when deploying AI technology. Using a tiny sample to make broad generalizations can lead to high error rates, which might have serious effects in sensitive settings. The paper acknowledges the need for transparency, but emphasizes that information should be tailored to the situation and aimed at promoting understanding and confidence.

Publishing the computational algorithm would not be suitable or useful in the context of algorithmic decision-making, as it may lead to confusion or wrong interpretations. The paper recommends meeting transparency requirements by providing a clear explanation of algorithmic decision-making that addresses potential issues. The criticism does not end there, however. We must consider not only whether judgments are "fair" but also whether the outcomes are "right." The CDEI assessment emphasizes the importance of considering the total bias of decision-making processes, rather than just the algorithm itself. Isolating algorithms is insufficient to adequately address this issue.

This leads to a discussion of quality control difficulties.

The contradiction between machine-driven decision-making and the legal system's emphasis on accountability is evident and likely to increase. While transparency is important, algorithmic accountability is crucial for successful implementation. Quantum AI has the potential to improve openness and accountability, but it remains unclear how it can fully alleviate concerns.

Canadian authorities have developed an algorithmic impact assessment form to help firms manage the risks connected with AI technology development and deployment.

Governance mechanisms are necessary to avoid civil liability, regulatory scrutiny, and reputational harm due to unexpected consequences of AI usage. Could quantum AI help? Experts and the general public agree that good governance structures should be designed and overseen by humans, or include a human component in decision-making, even if limited to a specific level of algorithmic deployment. The CDEI Review highlights that while effective governance strategies vary by industry and application, several factors remain consistent. Leaders must grasp both the capabilities and limitations of AI technology, conduct impact assessments, and maintain appropriate degrees of human participation. A good governance structure, based on industry/application difference, should include important criteria.

Companies using AI technology should make declarations demonstrating their dedication to excellent outcomes, consumer privacy, safety, unbiased decisions, and openness. Businesses must provide notices in accordance with consumer protection and data privacy regulations. These notices should include a mechanism for consumers to seek recourse if they believe they have been unfairly treated as a result of an algorithm decision. These notices should be provided at the appropriate time, typically before deployment. To prevent bias, businesses should implement comprehensive quality-control processes for algorithmic decision-making. Taking a risk-based strategy is crucial, as the usage of AI technology in healthcare may necessitate more oversight than in marketing.

To ensure impartial technology development and implementation, regulations and procedures must be established. Businesses that use algorithmic decision-making in their operations or products should examine the qualifications of key personnel. AI is becoming more widely accepted, despite its risks and criticism. UN groups believe technology may promote the public good and assist accomplish the UN Sustainable Development Goals by 2030.

However, this is not without obstacles. Data privacy and security issues are inherent in technology, posing significant challenges. Establishing strong privacy and security governance frameworks based on ethical principles is crucial for successful technology adoption. According to the CDEI research, effective governance in this domain requires anticipatory planning due to the rapid rate of change and possible repercussions.

Quantum AI should improve technology capabilities and be regulated to prevent unwanted concerns.

14.17 Prospects and Difficulties:

Innovation across a wide range of sectors, including cybersecurity, healthcare, finance, and more, is made possible by the combination of AI and quantum computing in cloud settings. By utilizing the processing power and scalability of cloud infrastructure, cloud-based quantum-AI systems have the potential to completely transform analytics, optimization, and decision-making procedures.

Cloud-based quantum-AI systems have the potential to continue to innovate and have a revolutionary influence in a variety of fields in the future. We may expect the creation of more potent quantum hardware and more effective quantum algorithms designed for cloud deployment as quantum computing technology advances and becomes more widely available. Future developments in cloud-based quantum-AI systems could involve investigating hybrid quantum-classical architectures, in which quantum processors and conventional computing resources are seamlessly combined to handle challenging machine learning and optimization problems. Furthermore, the development of fault-tolerant quantum computing and quantum error correction methods may open the door to the deployment of massive, fault-tolerant quantum processors in cloud settings.

A revolutionary chance to transform computation, data analysis, and decision-making processes across several sectors is presented by the combination of quantum computing with artificial intelligence (AI) in cloud settings. AI and quantum computing can work together to solve complicated issues that are outside the purview of traditional computing techniques by utilizing the special qualities of quantum physics and the scalability of cloud infrastructure. Even though this multidisciplinary sector has seen tremendous advancements, there are still many obstacles to overcome, such as the requirement for reliable error correction methods, scalable quantum hardware, and safe, legally acceptable cloud platforms. Notwithstanding these difficulties, cloud-based quantum-AI systems have a bright future ahead of them, full with opportunities to spur creativity, teamwork, and revolutionary breakthroughs in industry, research, and technology. The combination of cloud computing, artificial intelligence, and quantum computing is set to transform the computer industry and open up new avenues for study and understanding as scientists and practitioners continue to push these areas' boundaries.

Furthermore, multidisciplinary research initiatives in the nexus of cloud computing, AI, and quantum computing are probably going to provide innovative uses and discoveries, which will accelerate the convergence of these domains. To fully realize the potential of cloud-based quantum-AI systems and create a future where quantum technologies enable revolutionary innovation and discovery, it will be crucial to address issues with scalability, security, and regulatory compliance as we navigate these future directions.

Additionally, cloud platforms' collaborative nature encourages multidisciplinary study and cooperation, allowing businesses to exchange knowledge, pool resources, and speed up the creation of quantum-AI solutions. Significant obstacles still exist, though, such as the requirement for reliable error correction methods to lessen the effects of quantum decoherence, the creation of scalable quantum hardware, and the optimization of quantum algorithms for cloud-based implementation. Furthermore, a major problem is maintaining the security, privacy, and regulatory compliance of quantum-AI systems in cloud settings. Realizing the full potential of cloud-based quantum-AI systems and promoting significant advances in science, technology, and business will require addressing these issues while seizing the opportunities they bring.

14.18 Ethical concerns

Quantum AI has significant benefits, but it also raises ethical questions about its various uses, which go beyond the dismal notions of computer masters. Quantum AI can be programmed to manipulate data and bias resources. These biases may not adequately reflect the demands of public transit users and should be explicit. Users should be shielded from corporate data analytics that may negatively impact their access to credit resources, such as using public transportation.

Issues may develop if quantum AI systems are not configured with user-specific features. Low-income communities may not have enough entry points, limiting their access to critical resources. Access points (such as subway stations and bus stops) should be distributed across the city, with more access points located in areas where transportation services are in high demand. Anticipated needs may be best determined through field research that includes community meetings. Going directly to the communities that will use the public transportation system will allow programmers to completely model the overall community's needs. Community meetings and surveys can help identify budget constraints, environmental issues, access point locations, route frequency, and destination options to ensure fair access for all people of a community.

Once set up, quantum AI can be taught to respond to dynamic community feedback and deliver optimizations depending on various user communities as new data is collected in real time. These changes can then be used to modify transit routes or transportation modes (for example, buses versus ride-sharing vehicles). By doing so, quantum AI will improve a transit system's ability to address the unique demands of distinct communities while also increasing its general usefulness to the community as a whole.

Quantum AI can help distribute public transit cars and routes efficiently and ethically, resulting in more fair access for the communities it serves. One practical use for quantum AI is to compute and construct a fare system based on the specific demands of the communities served by the transit system. These fares can vary depending on the route, point of origin, and even peak usage hours, allowing economically challenged areas to benefit from lower rates. Users who utilize the public transportation system regularly may also benefit from recognition and fare savings, which would be especially beneficial to those who use the system to commute to work, as well as encouraging broader system utilization. Quantum AI provides great promise for developing humanity while reducing our environmental impact. Current and future public transportation systems will benefit from the implementation of quantum AI systems for optimization. While quantum AI can be used to combat socioeconomic discrimination, it is critical to impose controls on its use to ensure that individuals who use public transportation do not face discrimination.

Quantum AI has significant potential for improving public transit systems, and this essay merely scratches the surface of its benefits. At its foundation, however, is the conviction that the best application of quantum AI would be to give people with the most convenient transportation options while also protecting the natural environment.

14.19 Quantum AI and Viral Entropy

We are nearing a breakthrough. AI refers to computer systems that resemble human intellect, allowing us to delegate duties and solve issues beyond human capabilities. Traditional AI has been hindered by the poor processing power of traditional computers, making it difficult to imitate even basic brain activity. The brain operates in parallel, while typical computers require sequential processing, which significantly slows down performance. We lack a thorough understanding of brain function, making it difficult to duplicate them. AI has made significant progress in recent years, driven by advances in semiconductor technology and processor performance.

In theory, quantum AI utilizes the ability of quantum systems to exist in multiple states simultaneously. This allows a quantum computer to perform computations quickly, such as breaking encryption codes, which would take a conventional computer a long time to perform. However, this technology is not yet in practice. Quantum technology is still in its early stages, requiring significant energy to power ultra-low-temperature processors that keep particles in a state of entanglement. Quantum computing, like nuclear fusion, remains a theoretical possibility with the potential for endless power, whether in electricity or computer. In 2019, Google announced that it had achieved "quantum supremacy," where a quantum computer solved a problem beyond the capabilities of a classical computer. However, the definition of quantum supremacy and whether Google actually achieved it remain unclear. Consider the potential impact of quantum AI on our future.

The preceding reasons suggest a general direction. Throughout history, technical advancements have aimed to replicate the original system. These innovations include manipulating energy or information to generate heat. However, they are energy-consuming, unstable, and susceptible to viral infection, similar to other information-processing systems. While we may fantasize about AIs performing tasks like housework and dog walking, the reality is that AIs, like other scientific advancements, will soon be militarized and used to harm humanity. They will be extremely energy-intensive, contributing to further global warming. Eventually, civilization will vanish as heat in some form.

Are we thermodynamically doomed? Quantum AI is expected to be the most complicated system ever, as complex systems tend to increase entropy. According to statistical mechanics, we will eventually revert to the formless cosmic soup from which we arose. We are rapidly approaching this point. The path from here to there is not fixed and can be modified to purchase time.

Solutions

The issue of runaway weaponized information systems is not new. Viruses have been present on Earth from the beginning of life. However, the narrative did not end there. The earliest antiviral system, DNA repair mechanisms, developed shortly after the emergence of viruses. These systems detect and fix genetic code defects. Viruses evolved alongside cells. As living systems became more complex, so did their self-preservation mechanisms. We now have a complex immune system that detects and destroys invaders, as well as intricate machinery for maintaining our genetic code.

Molecular biologists have lately developed vaccines that provide further protection. Viruses, along with cancer, continue to provide significant challenges due to their constant evolution and adaptation.

As computer viruses and antiviral systems emerged, we witnessed a similar arms race in human technological growth. Computer viruses and defense systems evolved to become more sophisticated. Nowadays, most people operate behind a "firewall," which functions similarly to the immune system on computers.

Antiviral systems exist at greater levels of complexity, including in the brain. Cognitive "antiviral" mechanisms are also likely to exist, but are less well understood. The brain is a complex network of interconnected subsystems that handle different types of information. Controlling these subsystems is crucial to prevent them from becoming unmanageable. Addiction can occur when one of the motivational circuits gets overly strong and controls behavior. Although little is known about the "cognitive immune system," it is extremely effective considering how effectively most of us function.

Antiviral procedures must function at the social level, as societies are complex information-processing systems that self-replicate. Even inside societies, tensions arise as self-replicating individuals compete for dominance. Social interactions can lead to "winner-take-all" dynamics, where the rich gain power and societies become divided and unstable, potentially leading to self-destruction. This phenomenon is also present in complex self-replicating information systems.

However, some mechanisms can hinder these dynamics. Altruism is a mysterious inclination that drives humans to be generous to strangers, even those they don't know. Evolutionary theorists have long wondered how self-sacrificing behaviors made it into the genome, which often favors self-serving behavior. Altruistic activities are thought to benefit those who exhibit them, while the exact mechanism is still being studied.

Other social behaviors may have developed to counteract the negative effects of self-centered conduct. Societies use rule systems, such as secular and religious laws, to regulate individual behavior and balance self-interest with collective requirements. Although flawed, these "antiviral" mechanisms have helped 7.5 billion people coexist peacefully. Complex systems have survived due to internal dynamics that prevent viral infections and self-destructive behavior. Systems that do not meet this requirement will eventually fail. To ensure our technological progress remains sustainable, we must learn from nature's intricate processes.

14.20 Introducing Safeguards into AI

If quantum AI becomes the super-fast, all-powerful breakthrough that its proponents say, there is a possibility that we will be overtaken by AIs. The technological singularity refers to the point at which technology becomes self-sustaining and self-propagating without human control.

Many experts, including physicist Stephen Hawking and tech entrepreneur Elon Musk, have warned that the technological singularity could lead to human extinction, which is also the central thesis of this essay. The development of complex systems on Earth over four billion years has shown that those that adapt to explosive self-replicating dynamics are more likely to remain. As a single species among billions, our chances of survival may appear slim, especially considering the rapid advancement of technology. Our intelligence can either lead to our collapse or avoid it if we accept responsibility for our own progress and learn from past mistakes. This essay emphasizes the importance of implementing methods to prevent self-replicating intelligent information systems from spreading uncontrollably. To prevent these systems from becoming harmfully independent, we must implement limitations similar to those found in DNA repair, immunity, and moral systems.

Our long-term success hinges on finding a means to achieve this, even if the exact method is unknown. Entropy, the driving force behind complex system development, is a race to the bottom. However, with the evolution of intelligence, we can take a more indirect path to this inevitable outcome. It remains to be seen if our AI designers are capable of the task.

14.21 The Future of Quantum AI.

Quantum computing is the only emerging technology capable of dealing with all of our data and the difficulties we face. This is due, in part, to the raw power of these machines; the more powerful they become, the more problems they can answer. However, and this is the meat of the matter, it is also related to our world's non-classical nature. Many problems, although described as humans using arithmetic formulas and equations, are not based on classical physics. They are based on quantum physics, and a square peg cannot fit into a round hole.

The message is simple: the world is changing. We must accept the change. To thrive in the modern world, mastering data is the only solution. Mastering data necessitates computational capabilities that exceed traditional high-performance computing, blockchain, and AI—not just in terms of speed, but also in kind. It's time for everyone to embrace their quantum nature and become quantum intelligent.

Chapter –15
Quantum Computing and IoT

Quantum computing (QC) is a fast-growing field that uses concepts from quantum physics to enhance the functionality of conventional computers and other devices. It can be applied to a variety of problems due to the significantly increased speed at which it processes data. Although there are numerous possible uses for QC, network optimization, quantum simulation, and unstructured search are three of the most intriguing. The enhanced speed and accuracy of machine learning could be advantageous for a number of current technologies.

In order to increase the Internet of Things' (IoT) accuracy, speed, and security, let's examine how the QC concepts might be implemented. A quantum sensor for IoT, quantum digital marketing, quantum-secured smart locks, quicker processing at IoT endpoints, network optimization in IoT utilizing QC, and more are some methods for accomplishing this objective.

The goal of the Internet of Things (IoT), a contemporary paradigm, is to improve our daily lives by building an ecosystem of intelligent devices. The networking of sensors and actuators makes this possible by enabling intelligent decisions based on data analysis. It is anticipated that IoT technology would present hitherto unheard-of possibilities for connecting individuals. The IoT's overall operating architecture is shown in the figure below. Data processing and analysis is one of the more challenging tasks in IoT. Real-time data analysis is made possible by computational data, which also yields valuable insights. To handle and analyze data from IoT devices, machine learning (ML), data mining, and quantum computing (QC) have been created.

In the Internet of Things, computational data makes it possible to analyze huge data streams from connected devices in real time. QC offers valuable insights to improve decision-making across various domains. Edge computing platforms enable more processing and analysis of IoT data, opening the door to innovative and creative solutions. The rise of the Internet of Things has been facilitated by the widespread usage of radio frequency identification devices, or RFIDs.

RFID uses comparatively low-power radio tags to electronically identify physical items. RFID tags allow wireless intelligent tracking of goods in specific locations, despite their passive and dumb nature. They are unable to document or comprehend their environment because of these characteristics. Evolution and data analysis are hindered by the inability of gadgets to communicate. As a result of their potential to enhance real-world infrastructure and services, these devices have evolved into active, cooperative, and intelligent devices.

Real-time analysis of linked devices' huge data streams in the Internet of Things is made possible by computational data. QC offers insights that improve decision-making across a range of domains. New and innovative solutions are made possible by edge computing platforms, which increase IoT data processing and analysis. The Internet of Things has emerged in part due to the extensive use of radio frequency identification devices, or RFIDs.

RFID uses radio tags that use comparatively little power to electronically identify physical objects. Despite being passive and stupid, RFID tags allow for wireless, intelligent tracking of items in specific locations. These characteristics make it impossible for them to document or comprehend their environment. The inability of gadgets to communicate hinders data analysis and evolution. Since their interconnection may enhance infrastructure and real-world services, these devices have become intelligent, cooperative, and active.

A new era of internet-connected items that enhance our lives is made possible by the global interconnection known as the Internet of Things (IoT). Large-scale data gathering and analysis are required. The significance and potential of IoT have been demonstrated in the underdeveloped countries. Although difficult to manage, data and information security are also essential. Sensitive data is now at risk due to unprotected networks and cyberattacks caused by internet-connected devices. However, the Internet of Things looks for cutting-edge information security and data solutions. The security of IoT data is the biggest concern for businesses and the economy.

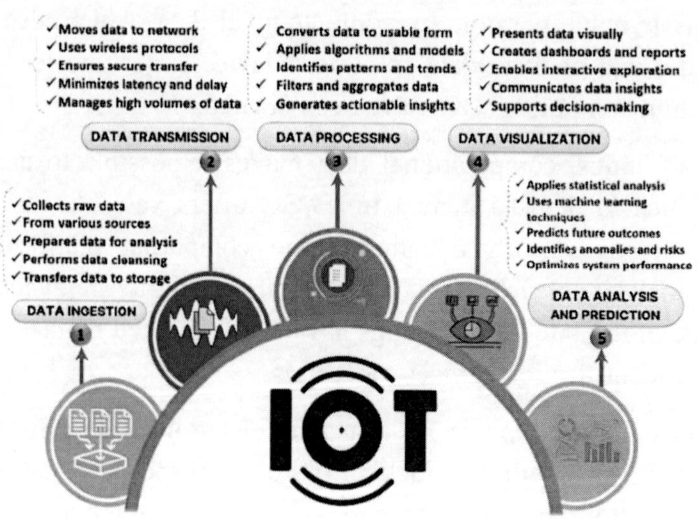

Fig.15.1 The general operating architecture of the Internet of Things, or IoT.

A Soviet and Russian mathematician named Alexander Holevo published a paper in 1973 showing that n number of Q-bits may hold more information than n number of classical bits, whereas Stephen J. Wiesner, a research physicist, developed Conjugate Coding in 1960. Physicists were debating whether it was even feasible to construct a system that could manage quantum particles in a way that made computing feasible at the time due to the lack of advancement in quantum systems. Although the work is still ongoing, it gained usefulness in 2000 when the first operational five Q-bit Nuclear Magnetic Resonance computer was established by the Technical University of Munich. Major computer companies like Google, IBM, and Microsoft started the battle for quantum domination around 2015, or 15 years later.

Compared to existing approaches, this design may improve the security and speed of IoT networks by integrating the architectural characteristics and operational protocols of quantum systems (i.e., entanglement). How QC and the IoT interact is seen in the figure below. Unfortunately, managing so much entanglement would be challenging and complex, thus not all nodes in an IoT network can be replaced by a quantum device.

Industrial IoT identifies numerous pertinent use scenarios where QC can support IoT operations that have arisen as a result of the development of machine-to-machine communication technologies, the IoT, and the related ecosystem. All industrial sectors are included in the IIoT, including transportation, shipbuilding, factories, and warehouses. It can be applied to a number of domains, such as resource optimization, maintenance and control, supply chain management, and quality assurance. The difficulty is that cloud-based data processing and analytics might not be able to handle IIoT because a lot of sensor data might frequently result in latency and storage problems.

To reduce network load and leverage cloud tiers, IIoT systems need to be more resilient, energy-efficient, and have better connectivity, interoperability, and data security. Nonetheless, certain heterogeneity approaches pose a conundrum with regard to temporal criticality, network connectivity, and overall energy efficiency. Here, effective routing may be achieved by applying optimization techniques influenced by quantum mechanics. Quantum particle swarm optimization is one method that can satisfy the necessary requirements.

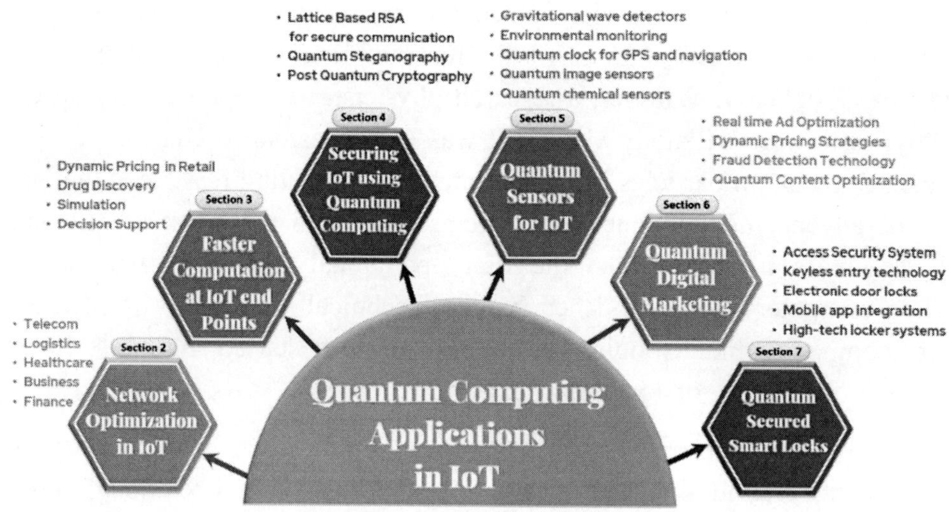

Fig.15.2 Interaction between the Internet of Things (IoT) and quantum computing, section-by-section.

By improving total connectivity and intelligent automation, the use of QC-inspired technologies generally could hasten the 21st-century transformation of industries, technology, and societal patterns and procedures. To put it another way, Industry 4.0 might arrive considerably sooner than anticipated. As a result, the manufacturing process would become more adaptable and responsive to customer needs, enabling the production of highly customized goods without necessitating a significant base reconfiguration. There are still some implementation problems, though:

15.1 Using Quantum Computing for Network Optimization in the Internet of Things

IoT network optimization with QC is a complex procedure. Large amounts of IoT data are first gathered, and then they are effectively analyzed utilizing quantum algorithms like Grover's and Shor's. QC speeds up optimization processes, improving energy efficiency, security, and network performance. Real-time decision-making, topology optimization, and the use of quantum key distribution (QKD) to secure communication are all made possible by it. Optimisation challenges are common in many real-world circumstances, and we require more powerful techniques to manage them with high convergence while tackling each unique issue. Numerous IoT-related discoveries have paved the way for innovation in a number of sectors, including finance, healthcare, logistics, and agriculture.

Thus, the economy of the future is trending toward greater automation and increased productivity. Nearly 80 billion connected IoT devices are expected to exist globally by 2030. Given the high reliance on IoT, data accuracy (DA) analysis becomes even more important for this cutting-edge paradigm. In a dynamic context, it has recently been discovered that a variety of quantum computing-inspired optimization (QCiO) techniques enhance the accuracy and optimal performance of data collected by widely dispersed IoT devices.

By tackling a combinatorial problem with binary constraints, QC improves the effectiveness of scheduling and resource allocation for unmanned aerial vehicles that serve sensor nodes in IoT networks. A QC method called quantum annealing converts the initial issue into a quadratic unconstrained binary optimization form. It then uses quantum characteristics to investigate several solutions at once and may produce more effective results. QC is a formidable tool for optimizing IoT network scheduling, but because of the present limits of quantum annealers, a hybrid approach combines quantum and classical computing to refine and assess viable solutions.

IoT network optimization with QC makes use of QC integration to boost data transfer rates and network effectiveness. This means using quantum algorithms like glued trees based on continuous quantum walks (GTCW) to minimize energy consumption and lower data transmission error rates within IoT networks, as well as optimizing sensor placement to preserve sensor function. The usefulness of this QC is confirmed by experimental findings, which show that it outperforms traditional optimization strategies in terms of DA, temporal efficiency, and cost-effectiveness.

When it comes to IoT network optimization using QC, the quantum-based IoT network optimization (QIoTNO) approach aims to save energy and time in scenarios involving perceptual task offloading in edge computing. Adaptability metrics, logistic chaos perturbation, and sophisticated genetic algorithms are used by QIoTNO to improve convergence and minimize energy loss and time consumption. According to comparative evaluations, QIoTNO significantly reduces energy waste by 3.91%, time consumption by 4.08%, and convergence speed while improving adaptability by 4.89%.

IoT networks could be optimized with QC's high-speed parallel processing. However, issues with quantum channel noise and qubit fidelity make it difficult to use in the Internet of Things. In order to minimize quantum resource consumption in the face of ambiguous optimization demands, a quantum resource allocation model based on stochastic programming is employed, together with an adaptive technique called DQC2O for managing quantum computers and networks in IoT optimization.

15.2 Effective computation at IoT nodes, endpoints

Quantum computers can function at speeds and power levels that are tenfold greater than those of our existing computers. They represent several bits at once using quantum states. "At the quantum level, atoms can be coded to represent every possible input combination simultaneously, testing every possibility at the same time." This is helpful for IoT since IoT devices produce enormous amounts of data that require intensive processing and other intricate optimization. Generally speaking, QC's enormous processing power could help resolve a lot of today's problems.

Drug companies, for example, may now use QC to perform hundreds of millions of simulations and comparisons involving intricate interactions between big molecules. In any situation when optimization is required, it is also beneficial. Iteratively examining multiple scenarios and selecting the one that best satisfies user needs is how this is accomplished. With this approach, a variety of issues could be resolved, such as portfolio and transportation route optimization. The paradigm for data management in Internet of Things applications near edge devices is edge computing, which is our next area of interest. As the amount of data generated daily increases, more processing power is needed even though computing near the network's logical edge lowers latency and reaction time.

The most recent cloud computing implementation model provides service to end users based on how IoT apps use resources, as opposed to pay-per-use. The edge computation paradigm speeds up data processing from IoT apps running on edge devices by utilizing server-less computing. The system requires a large amount of computing power to function properly, which may be easily provided by employing QC. Notwithstanding its potential, using QC to provide the best results remains difficult due to a variety of limitations, including the requirement for a significant number of error-correcting quantum bits (qubits) or difficult operating conditions.

Consequently, the majority of suggested approaches integrate QC with conventional ML. A diversified strategy is needed to make QC on IoT endpoints possible. This includes developing quantum communication channels for IoT devices to access centralized QC resources, investigating hybrid computing models that combine classical and quantum processing, optimizing quantum algorithms for IoT-specific applications to lower computational demands, and developing quantum technology to create smaller, more energy-efficient quantum processors. Furthermore, it is crucial to conduct research on secure QKD, miniaturized quantum hardware, and energy-efficient cooling systems. To overcome the technical difficulties of deploying QC on resource-constrained IoT endpoints, cooperation between QC researchers and IoT developers is essential. But this is still a long-term goal that depends on continuous developments in IoT and quantum technology.

15.3 Using QC to Secure IoT

Modern and cutting-edge information and communication technologies, including the "fog cloud IoT," necessitate secure connections immediately in order to protect critical data. Thanks to this amazing technology and new paradigm, location-aware, low-latency, instantly deployable, and scalable information technology solutions are now feasible. It also reduces the cost of infrastructure. It is a tried-and-true method for placing cloud resources and services close to users and optimizing their use in edge networks.

However, privacy and security issues have been brought up by fog cloud IoT services. It is problematic to send sensitive data across open, public networks, such the fog cloud Internet of Things. Quantum information processing (QIP), as illustrated in the figure below, is one method for addressing security issues, particularly the covert management of private information in the Internet-based computing paradigm. There has been a lot of interest in QIP from scientists working on its development as well as those looking to use these innovative techniques for transferring, processing, and storing data.

A number of important QIP subtopics, including quantum teleportation, quantum cryptography, and quantum steganography, have also attracted attention recently. One proposed paradigm, for instance, provides a "guaranteed" intrusion detection system, which greatly lowers the likelihood that a cyberattack will go unnoticed. A successful undetected cyberattack against a dynamic virtual private network may be practically eliminated by utilizing long Quantum Safe encryption keys, which are impervious to attacks by Quantum Computers using modern quantum algorithms. The US National Institute of Standards and Technology claims that even quantum computers are unable to decode an encrypted transmission using thousands of bits of Quantum Safe encryption keys. Its application in Blockchain technology is another example.

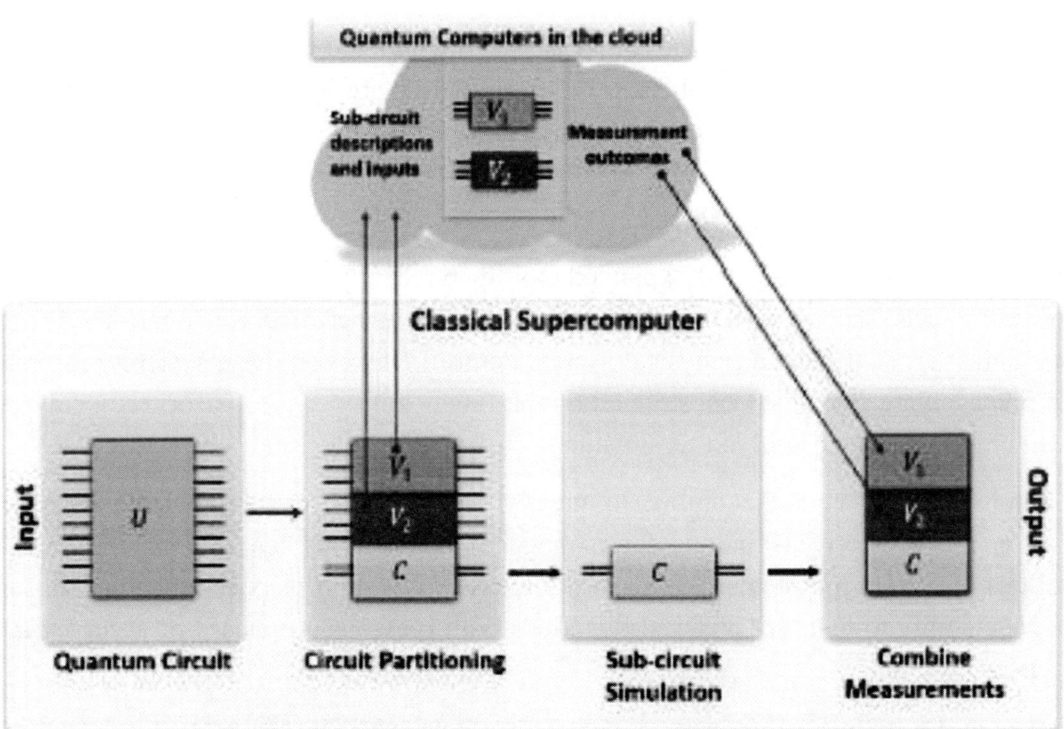

Fig.15.3 Using quantum computing in cloud services.

Data from Internet of Things apps is processed in a series of blocks using blockchain technology, an open distributed ledger. This method limits the computational speed of data processing because it processes data in blocks, but it works particularly well for securely processing data for server-less edge computing. The work required to determine the once values and hashes for every data block in the whole chain is one feature of blockchain architecture. This process needs to occur concurrently across several distributed architecture nodes (POW) in order to validate the Proof-Of-Work. These procedures could be implemented on a server-less pipeline after being integrated into a Function as a Service platform using micro-services. Large-scale computing for resource management may be carried out by quantum computers to solve this problem.

Post-QC has emerged as a viable QC application for the Internet of Things, supported by its conference series (PQCrypto) as well as other organizations working on various projects and standardization activities. It is crucial to keep an eye on the outcomes and standardization procedures of these programs, even though the majority do not primarily target post-quantum IoT systems. Initiatives utilizing post-quantum cryptosystems have received significant financial support from the European Union and the Japanese Science and Technology Agency. Examples include PQCrypto, SAFE crypto, CryptoMathCREST, and PROMETHEUS.

It is crucial to keep in mind that post-quantum security is a way to safeguard the entire communications infrastructure that supports the Internet of Things, not just its individual nodes. This relates to the fact that, due to their computational capacity surpassing that of IoT end devices, the most complicated processing tasks are increasingly being managed in centralized servers or clouds on the Internet these days.

15.4 IoT Quantum Sensors

The Internet of Things (IoT) has expanded rapidly in recent years, linking a wide range of physical objects, sensors, and systems to the web. This has created new opportunities for data gathering, analysis, and physical system control. However, these systems' accuracy and precision are frequently constrained by the functionality of the sensors they employ. Quantum sensors are useful in this situation.

Quantum sensors have the ability to greatly improve IoT system performance and develop fresh, creative solutions for a range of applications by utilizing the special qualities of quantum systems. Based on the ideas of quantum physics, quantum sensors have the ability to measure physical quantities with previously unheard-of accuracy and precision.

Compared to traditional sensors, quantum systems' special characteristics—such as superposition and entanglement—allow for measurements with a far higher sensitivity. Because of this, quantum sensors are perfect for fields like navigation, environmental monitoring, and healthcare that demand high-precision measurements. As seen in the figure below, quantum sensors employ network entanglement manipulation and qubit superposition, which sets them apart from classical sensors. Environmental monitoring is one of the most exciting uses of quantum sensors in the Internet of Things. The previous figure, Quantum computing applied to cloud services, shows how conventional environmental sensors are limited in their ability to measure physical quantities. such as humidity, pressure, and temperature, with great precision and consistency. This may lead to inaccuracies in the information gathered and a lack of trust in the findings.

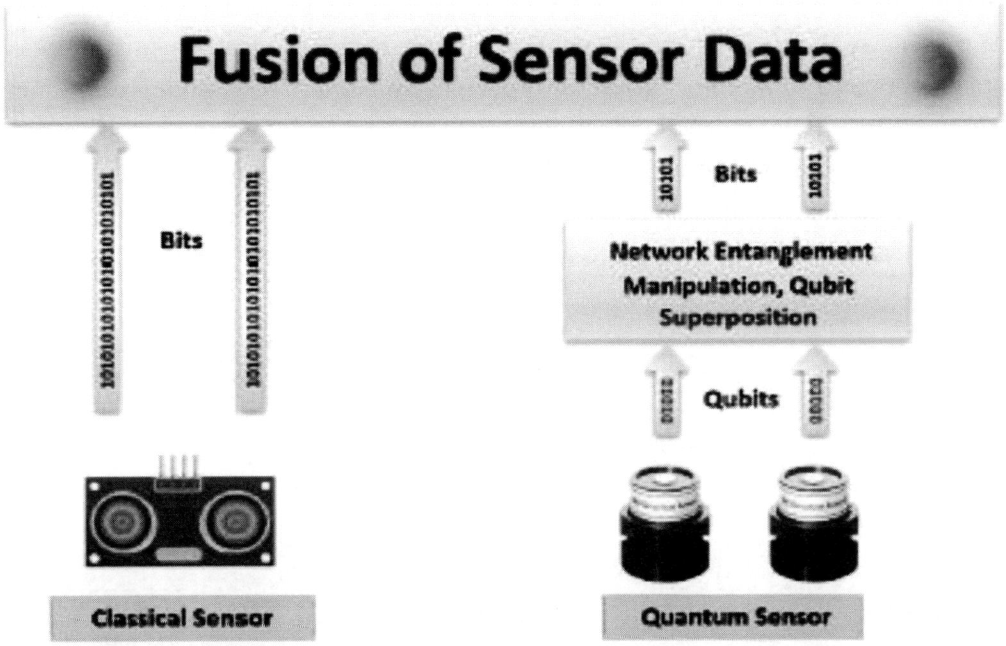

Fig.15.4 Combining data from quantum and conventional sensors.

However, even in challenging conditions, quantum sensors are able to measure these quantities precisely. This can result in better environmental monitoring and decision-making, especially in fields like climate change research, weather forecasting, and agriculture.

Navigation is another field where quantum sensors could have a big influence. The growing number of drones, driverless cars, and other mobile devices necessitates precise navigation systems that can deliver real-time information on their position, direction, and speed. The precision and dependability of traditional navigation systems, like GPS, are constrained, especially in urban settings where towering buildings may block signals. By precisely measuring magnetic fields, which can be utilized for mapping and navigation, quantum sensors—like those based on superconducting quantum interference devices—have the potential to completely transform navigation.

In the medical field, quantum sensors are extremely essential, especially for tracking crucial indicators like blood pressure, oxygen saturation, and heart rate. The precision and stability of conventional sensors used in medical devices are frequently restricted, which can lead to inaccuracies in the data gathered and a lack of confidence in the findings. On the other hand, even in difficult settings like the human body, quantum sensors are capable of taking precise measurements. Better patient monitoring and diagnosis may result from this, especially in isolated or resource-constrained locations with limited access to healthcare services. Another field where quantum sensors can have a big influence is industrial monitoring.

Because of its high precision and accuracy in measuring physical quantities, quantum sensors can be used to monitor industrial processes and equipment, giving real-time data that can improve efficiency and control. Especially in sectors like manufacturing, mining, and oil and gas production, this can lead to less downtime, more output, and enhanced safety. IoT systems and quantum sensors can be used to create safe communication networks that are extremely resilient to cyberattacks, as seen in the figure below.

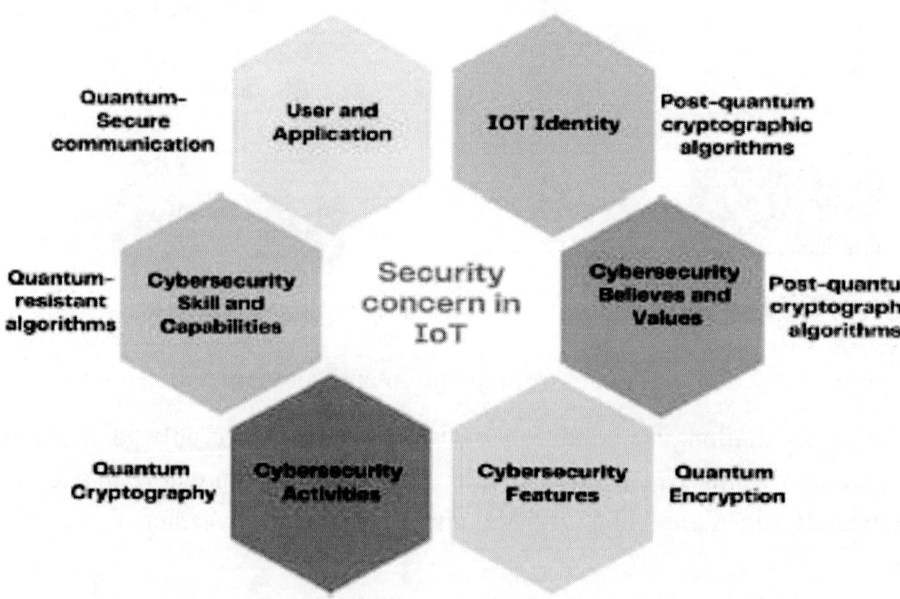

Fig.15.5 IoT security solutions that use quantum mechanics.

This is because it is very difficult to intercept or tamper with quantum communications because of the intrinsic security of quantum systems. Especially in vital infrastructure, military communications, and financial transactions, this can result in more dependable and secure communication networks. Because quantum sensors will perform so well in the future, QC has led to the emergence of the IoT industries.

The growing number of firms joining this space shows that quantum sensors are gradually moving from the lab to real-world applications. Their unparalleled spatial precision and sensitivity are a result of their capacity to utilize the atomic scale and extraordinary coherence qualities. Although quantum technologies hold promise for a number of industries, it can be difficult to predict their exact impact. Two promising quantum sensing platforms—optically pumped atomic magnetometers and nitrogen-vacancy centers in diamond—are the main focus.

A range of possible uses, including single-cell spectroscopy and brain imaging, are demonstrated by four case studies.

15.5 Quantum Digital Marketing

The field of quantum digital marketing is a recent development that blends conventional digital marketing techniques with the ideas of quantum physics. This new strategy uses quantum algorithms to analyze data and forecast client behaviour in an effort to create more precise and effective ways to target and contact potential customers. Utilizing QC concepts like quantum parallelism and quantum entanglement, quantum digital marketing processes and analyzes vast volumes of data far more quickly than traditional computers. This makes it possible to optimize marketing campaigns and make more accurate forecasts about consumer behaviour.

Quantum algorithms, for instance, can be used to analyze enormous volumes of consumer data and forecast which goods or services will appeal to particular market groups the most when utilized by the appropriate user at the right time with the correct messaging. The capacity to offer clients highly customized marketing experiences is one of the main advantages of quantum digital marketing. Marketers can use quantum algorithms to target and connect with particular client groups by providing them with material and message that is most likely to appeal to them. Increased brand loyalty, improved customer engagement, and higher conversion rates can all result from this personalization.

Quantum digital marketing also has the advantage of being able to offer insights into consumer preferences and behaviour far more quickly than conventional techniques. Marketers can remain ahead of the game by swiftly analyzing and reacting to shifts in consumer behaviour and preferences thanks to the speed and accuracy of quantum algorithms. Customer segmentation and targeting could be completely transformed by quantum digital marketing. Digital marketers typically target and segment their consumers using behavioral and demographic data. Marketers can utilize quantum algorithms to analyze and target consumers based on more intricate and sophisticated elements, like emotions, motives, and values, by moving beyond these conventional approaches using quantum digital marketing.

Even with all of its advantages, as the figure below illustrates, quantum digital marketing is still in its infancy as a concept and as a practice. Therefore, in order for it to realize its full potential, a number of obstacles and constraints must yet be removed. The lack of general knowledge and proficiency in QC and quantum digital marketing among marketers and companies is one of the primary issues. Businesses must spend money on staff and partner education and training in order to successfully embrace and apply quantum digital marketing techniques.

Quantum digital marketing has the power to completely change how companies communicate and engage with their clientele. Quantum digital marketing presents a fresh and innovative approach for companies to engage with consumers and develop their brands thanks to its capacity to deliver highly customized marketing experiences, quicker insights into consumer behaviour, and sophisticated targeting and segmentation tools. However, in order for organizations to successfully embrace and implement these methods, they must be willing to spend in education and training.

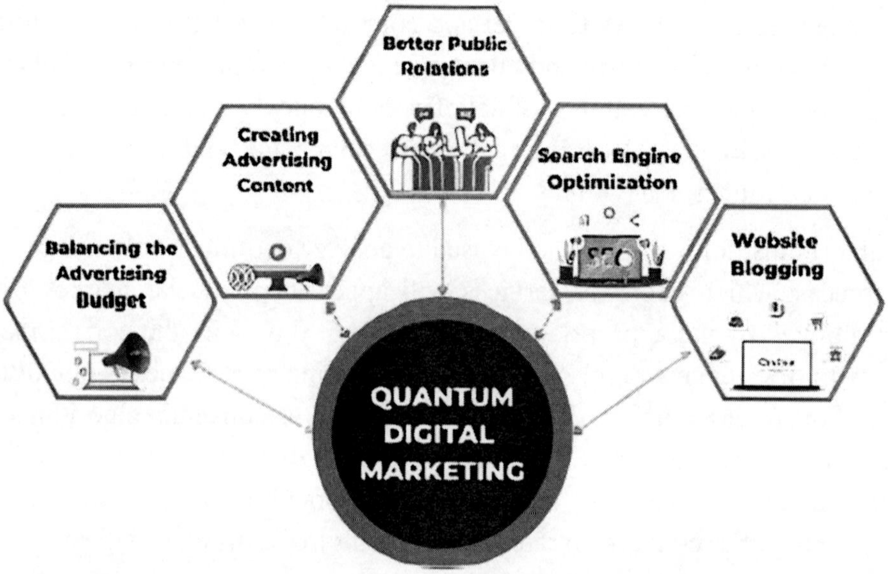

Fig.15.6 Quantum digital marketing's potential applications.

15.6 Secured Quantum Smart Locks

Recently, the field of security technology has seen the creation of quantum-secured smart locks, which combine conventional lock and key systems with the concepts of quantum mechanics. These locks use the special qualities of quantum physics to prevent tampering and unauthorized access, offering a higher level of security than traditional locks. The goal of research on quantum-secured smart locks is to create better and novel ways to secure locks using quantum mechanics. Utilizing QKD to protect the communication between the key and the lock is one field of study. To guarantee that only authorized people may access the lock, this entails sending the key information in a manner that is safe from tampering and eavesdropping. The use of quantum entanglement to improve smart lock security is the subject of additional research.

By using this method, the lock and key are intertwined, rendering it impossible to open the lock in the event that the lock is tampered with. The development of security for networked facilities and equipment is being carried out by Quantum Secured Smart Lock, which uses quantum physics to harness the randomness of particle behavior to create completely unpredictable digital keys to allow communication between devices. With a central hub that encrypts all data transfers using quantum digital keys and keeps an eye on the ledger for any anomalies, the hardware-software system connects all points of entrance and access devices. Utilizing the inherent unpredictability of quantum physics, the Quantum-secured Smart Lock creates unpredictable and encrypted digital keys to secure locks, computers, robots, and other devices and systems that have technologies that allow them to connect to other devices and systems through communications networks.

Enhancing physical security, which is becoming more and more entwined with digital security, is the aim of quantum protected smart locks. The use of quantum-secured smart lock technology can defend locks and other physical equipment against both local and remote cyberattacks. This risk is eliminated with Quantum's Secured Smart Lock, which uses a smartphone, a more secure door-opening mechanism, and a smart lock with QC functionality. Several major advantages of utilizing a smart lock with quantum security. Furthermore, the use of quantum random number generators (QRNGs) in smart locks is being investigated by academics. The communication between the lock and the key can be encrypted and secured by using QRNGs, which can produce really random numbers. By doing this, it is made more difficult for hackers to decipher the encryption and gain access to the lock, even in the event that they manage to intercept the connection.

A major obstacle in the realm of quantum-secured smart locks is the creation of dependable and expandable quantum technologies. Since quantum technologies are still relatively new, they may be prone to mistakes and inaccuracies. It is anticipated that these problems will be resolved with continued study and development, though, and that quantum-secured smart locks will eventually be widely used.

As seen in the below Figure, quantum-secured smart locks are a promising new advancement in security technology that provide a greater level of protection than conventional locks.

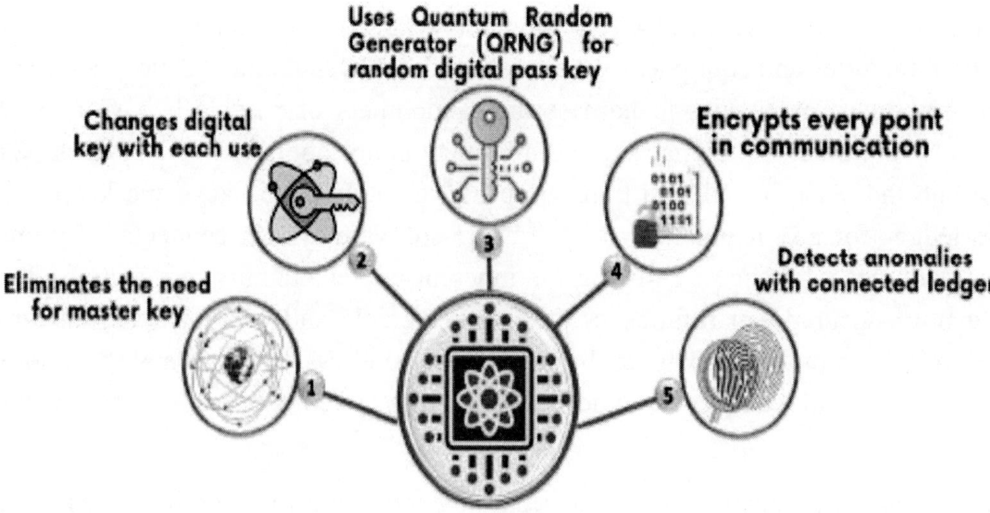

Fig.15.7 Quantum protected smart locks provide several advantages.

The goal of this field's research is to create novel and enhanced approaches to lock security utilizing quantum mechanics, such as QRNGs, QKD, and quantum entanglement.

The future of quantum-secured smart locks is bright, despite the fact that there are still obstacles to be addressed. It is anticipated that this technology will become more and more significant in protecting homes, businesses, and other precious assets.

The constructed systems of the post-quantum period can be categorized into different groups according to the underlying mathematical difficulty. It seems that quantum cryptography could be able to help with this issue. QKD provides an information-based approach that may be safe. In contrast, all of these unique algorithms are ultimately useless without the appropriate hardware. One major issue in the development of quantum hardware is the decoherence of Q-bits. Decoding a Q-bit into a regular bit (any) can reveal whether it has changed into an overlay bit when it loses coherence as a result of interaction with the environment.

Nowadays, the situation strongly favours weight loss. Since factors like the number of Controlled-X gates and the specific Q-bit-tuple in the technology make it difficult to do the mapping with few errors and at a low cost, it is proposed that the availability of Q-bits in the current quantum devices is another crucial test. These are typical difficulties encountered while creating hardware that uses quantum physics. To improve entanglement accuracy with drones, for example, a quantum node must be integrated into a small drone. Data is transmitted over traditional networks in packets. If a loss occurs, these packets might be copied and sent again.

It is challenging to duplicate or magnify Q-bits in quantum communication because of the no-cloning claim and the postulate of quantum state measurement. Using QC for Internet of Things (IoT) and artificial intelligence (AI) applications presents a number of difficulties.

First off, creating quantum algorithms that can effectively handle the enormous volume of data produced by IoT devices and improve AI capabilities is still a difficult undertaking. Interoperability issues arise when QC is integrated with the current IoT infrastructure, which is based on traditional technologies. The practical implementation is further complicated by constraints of quantum hardware, such as error rates in quantum bits (qubits) and the requirement for error correcting codes.

Developing quantum algorithms for IoT and AI applications, refining quantum error correction methods, and investigating hybrid quantum-classical structures should be the main areas of future study. Addressing security issues brought on by the possibility of quantum assaults on AI and IoT networks is also crucial. All things considered, there are many exciting potential brought about by the confluence of QC, IoT, and AI; yet, significant technical and security challenges must be addressed with creative solutions.

15.7 Integrating IoT and Quantum Computing

Quantum computing's capabilities can assist in resolving the problems and obstacles impeding the expansion of the Internet of Things. Among these are the following:

Enhanced capacity for complex computation

By simultaneously representing bits with quantum states, quantum computers can improve their speed and power exponentially. Because "atoms could be programmed to represent all possible input combinations, all at once, and therefore test all the combinations simultaneously," this is the case at the quantum level.

This is advantageous to IoT since IoT devices produce vast amounts of data that necessitate extensive computing and other intricate optimization.

Expedited method for validation and verification

A smart city, which has multiple systems including traffic, utilities, buildings, lights, and more, is an example of an IoT application. Verifying and validating that every system functions as intended would take a lot of time and effort. Quantum computing solves that issue by ensuring continuous system optimization while accelerating the verification and validation process across all systems several times faster.

Enhanced security in communications

IoT devices should be secured since they may hold sensitive data whose handling must adhere to user rights and requirements. It is vital to provide confidentiality, integrity, and authentication. However, security is at risk since "traditional security countermeasures and privacy enforcement cannot be directly applied to IoT technologies due to their limited computing power; additionally, the high number of interconnected devices arises scalability issues."

Quantum cryptography, which employs algorithms that demand more processing power than conventional computers, makes it feasible to communicate more securely by utilizing the concepts of quantum mechanics. The intricacy acts as a barrier against online attacks.

15.8 Secure IoT in the Era of Quantum Computers

The security of commonly used public-key cryptosystems and all communication that depends on them is seriously threatened by recent advancements in quantum computing. As a result, new post-quantum cryptography algorithms that are resistant to quantum computers are presently being investigated by the US NIST. Even with pre-quantum public-key cryptography, security is regarded as one of the most important concerns for low-power IoT devices because of its stringent memory, compute, and energy constraints. originally described how a cutting-edge, TLS-based, low-power Internet of Things infrastructure can use possible post-quantum key encapsulation mechanisms (KEMs) and digital signature algorithms (DSAs) in the associated US NIST process. Measured the effects of new KEMs and DSAs on energy usage, latency, and memory needs during TLS handshakes on an IoT edge device in such a representative environment. Post-quantum primitives' greater bandwidth requirements, not the cryptographic algorithm itself, are the primary cause of high TLS handshake latency. Second, contrary to NIST's objective of standardizing a single method, it was shown that a clever mix of several DSAs produces the most energy-, latency-, and memory-efficient public key infrastructures. The third is the implementation of code-based, isogeny-based, and lattice-based algorithms on an off-the-shelf Cortex M4 microcontroller-based low-power IoT edge device while preserving feasible battery runtimes.

Many aspects of contemporary life are being disrupted by the Internet of Things (IoT). The number of applications that use IoT devices is increasing significantly, regardless of whether they are intended to improve industrial operations in the Industrial IoT (IIoT), facilitate medical and healthcare, or make smart homes more comfortable. However, there are a lot of concerns associated with the Internet of Things, and security is thought to be one of the most important ones, particularly given that the quantity, intensity, and capability of hostile assaults on IoT infrastructures are increasing in direct proportion to the number of devices linked to the internet. In this regard, the recently discovered attack in the log4j-library has demonstrated how flaws in commonly used software impact numerous industries. Due to recent developments in the construction of Quantum Computers (QCs), information security is currently facing an additional hazard in commonly used software libraries.

Many IIoT applications require secure communication since data transferred online may include infrastructure information, industrial secrets, and safety-critical data. Most of the time, this security is created via cryptographic protocols like Transport Layer Security (TLS), which rely on the combination of public key cryptography (PKC) and symmetric cryptography. Although it is difficult to crack these public key cryptosystems using traditional computers, nearly 30 years ago the theoretical foundation for solving their underlying mathematical problems in polynomial time on a QC was presented.

Although there were no powerful QCs at the time, it is anticipated that by the end of this decade, there will be QCs that are pertinent to cryptography.

Thus, in order to develop new, quantum-computer-resistant public key algorithms for digital signature algorithms (DSAs) and key-encapsulation mechanisms (KEMs), the US National Institute of Standards and Technology (NIST) initiated a Post-Quantum Cryptography (PQC) standardization process. Candidates are assessed during this process according to their performance and security presumptions. Exploring the effects of crucial characteristics like PQC algorithms' computational complexity and bandwidth needs in various typical applications, such low-power, secure IoT, is therefore crucial. Furthermore, it's critical to ascertain quickly whether the computing demands of these novel algorithms can be met by state-of-the-art (SotA) low-power IoT hardware within the specified energy restrictions or if specialized hardware accelerators will be needed.

IoT Security

IoT security is a problem because of the intricate, application-specific infrastructures, the infrequent in-field device upgrades, and the constrained memory and processing capabilities of IoT nodes. Moreover, the stringent energy requirements of battery-powered edge devices, which are frequently employed in the Internet of Things, and the need for a quick time to market, which is imposed by competition, frequently lead to serious security vulnerabilities.

This is especially troubling because prior experiences have demonstrated that security lapses can result in severe financial repercussions, a decline in consumer trust, and, in the worst situation, fatalities. Depending on the industry sector, IBM discovered that the average cost of a data breach in 2020 might reach $7.13 million. For "mega breaches," the cost is estimated to be up to $400 million. Because there were no authenticity checks on a firmware update method utilized for malicious code insertion, hackers were able to take control of crucial auto parts including the steering wheel, brake system, and engine.

In order to create botnets that were utilized for bitcoin mining or distributed denial-of-service (DDoS), hundreds of thousands of Internet of Things devices were infected with malicious code. Even though these are the worst-case situations, it is difficult to overstate the importance of privacy, integrity, and authenticity in the Internet of Things. When used in essential infrastructure, industrial applications, or reasonable, private settings, even small, light sensor devices gather sensitive data. Consequently, it should be deemed imperative to use cryptography to offer this protection.

Transport Layer Security (TLS)

TLS is a cryptographic technology used in many domains, such as Hypertext Transfer technology Secure (https), that guards communications against message forging, manipulation, and eavesdropping. By first establishing a master secret, PKC is used to enable authentication and address the secret key distribution issue. The keys to encrypt the application data using symmetric cryptography, including message authentication codes (MACs) to guarantee integrity, are then generated using this master secret.

Several protocol levels that are utilized throughout a connection are part of the TLS standard. The TLS handshake protocol is the main focus because it employs the Public Key Cryptography (PKC), which is vulnerable to QC attacks. A cryptographically secure connection is established via the handshake protocol, which also involves security parameter instantiation, communication partner authentication, and agreement on a common master secret.

The figure below depicts its process. Because PKCs must be altered to be resistant to QCs, the pertinent procedures concerning them are described below. To keep things simple, let's explain the high security configuration that uses mutual authentication and ephemeral keys to ensure perfect forward secrecy (PFS).

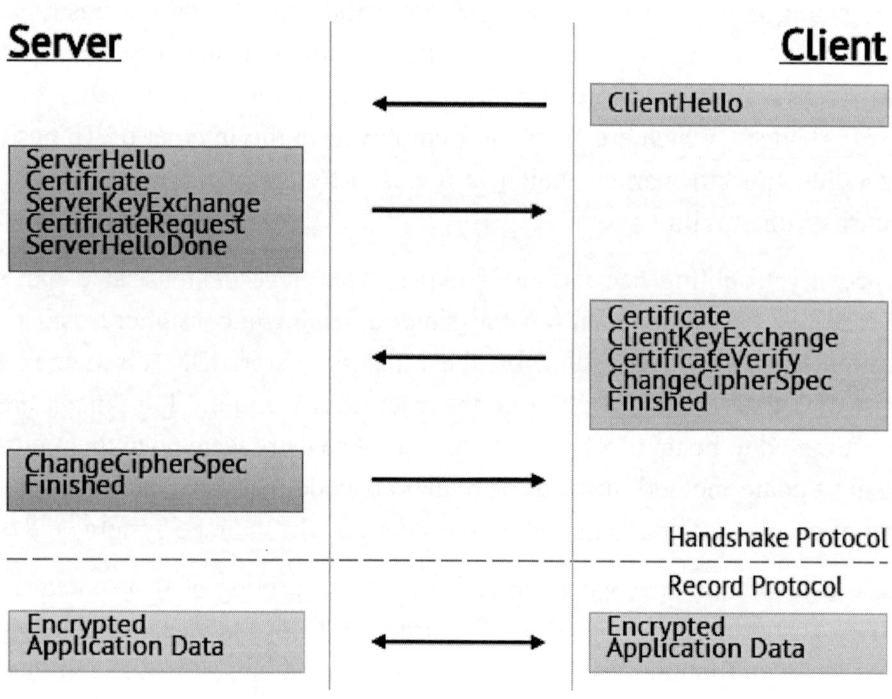

Fig.15.8 The TLS 1.2 handshake process.

In this configuration, a key-establishment algorithm creates the pre-master secret, and the Digital Signature Algorithm (DSA) verifies the legitimacy of each communication partner and guards against Man in the Middle (MITM) attacks. The figure below shows the steps involved in an Elliptic Curve Diffie-Hellman Ephemeral (ECDHE) key-exchange from a high-level perspective. A pair of keys is generated by each communication party, and their public keys are exchanged. They then compute a shared secret using their own secret key and the opposing, received public key, which, because of the mathematical characteristics of ECDHE, yields the identical value for both the server and the client.

To crack the cryptosystem, an attacker would only need to access either Sk_C or Sk_S to compute the same shared secret; however, refactoring Sk_S from pk_S necessitates resolving the elliptic curve discrete logarithm problem, which is thought to be unsolvable on standard computers.

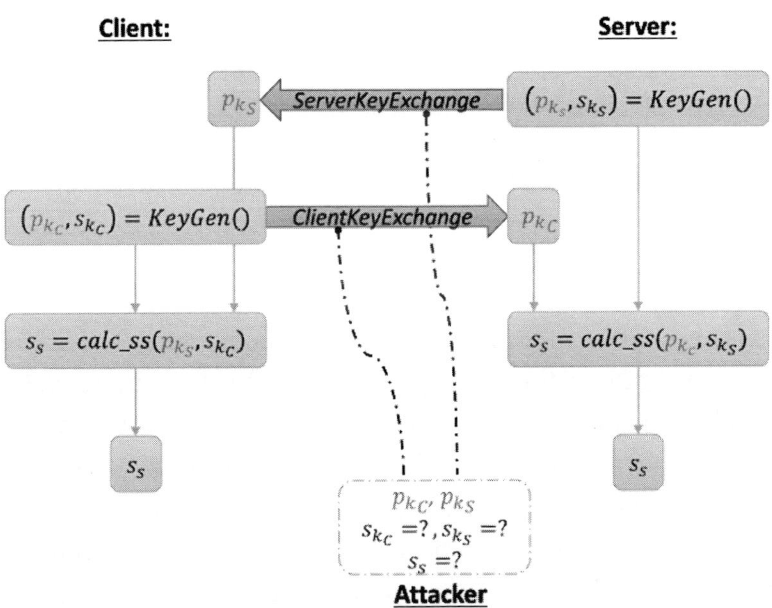

Fig.15.9 The TLS 1.2 handshake uses the ECDHE working principle, where pkC and pkS stand for the client and server's public keys, skC and skS for their secret keys, and ss for their shared secret. While the red variables must be kept secret, the green-marked variables may be known to the general public.

The protocol shown in the above figure is still vulnerable to an MITM since it can send its own public key to the client and server and intercept KeyExchange messages. In order to establish valid digital signatures and guard against hackers intercepting and altering their communications, servers and clients utilize DSAs in addition to extra pairs of long-term keys. The server uses its DSA secret key to sign the ECDHE public key in the ServerKeyExchange message during the TLS handshake. The client then confirms this signature using the server's public key, which was previously sent in the Certificate message as part of the server certificate.

In order to create a chain of trust, this message transmits the server's certificate chain, which includes a root certification authority (CA) certificate and the server's own certificate (as well as maybe a number of intermediate certificates, depending on the PKI employed) (Figure below). By figuring out the hash value of each handshake message sent thus far and signing them with its DSA, the client then provides the server with proof of identity in the CertificateVerify message. Rivest-Shamir-Adleman (RSA) and Elliptic Curve Digital Signature Algorithm (ECDSA) are now the most used DSAs.

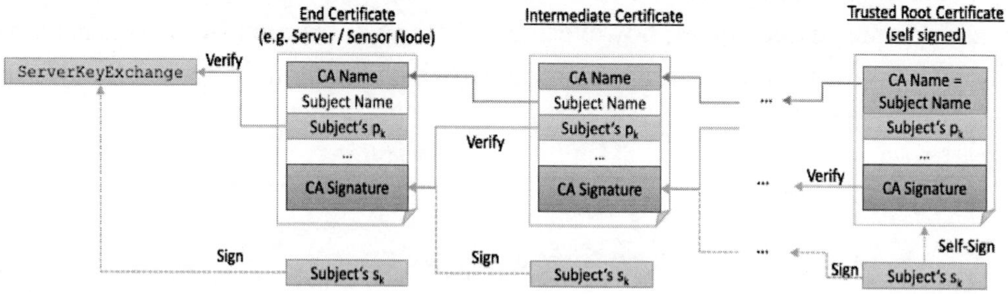

Fig.15.10 An illustration of a certificate chain and how it applies to the TLS handshake.

Using Quantum Computers to Break TLS

The use of specific quantum mechanical effects is the foundation of QCs' working principle, which is very different from that of classical computers. The information unit is one of the most significant variations. QCs use qubits, which can be converted into super-positions of states by quantum mechanical operations, in contrast to classical computers, which use bits that are always in one of two unique states (0 and 1). This superposition is combined with a QC's built-in parallelism of computations, and QCs can effectively solve some mathematical problems that are nearly impossible for traditional computers to handle by utilizing effects like quantum entanglement and interference with quantum logic gates. Although they are not currently anticipated to replace or succeed ordinary computers, QCs will probably be utilized as hardware accelerators for them in the near future.

The reason this heterogeneous setup is also the best for QC-based attacks on the Public Key Cryptography (PKC) is that Shor's algorithm, which theoretically resolves the fundamental issues of Rivest-Shamir-Adleman (RSA) and Elliptic Curve Digital Signature Algorithm (ECDSA) (prime factorization of large integers and the discrete logarithm) in polynomial time, is made up of two distinct components. The QC solves the prime factoring problem in the second half after it has been reduced to the problem of determining a group's order in the first, classical component. Despite not being strong enough to withstand these attacks just yet, quantum computers are developing quickly, and by 2031, it is anticipated that they will be able to carry out effective attacks.

Two distinct opportunities for attackers in the TLS context. One of the public keys in either ServerKeyExchange or ClientKeyExchange can be eavesdropped on by a passive attacker to carry out the first attack possibility, which targets the Elliptic Curve Diffie-Hellman Ephemeral (ECDHE) key exchange during the handshake. By using the Shor algorithm to calculate the equivalent secret key based on the public key, the attacker can calculate the same skS as the client and server. The attacker can use skS to decrypt all application data transmitted between the client and server. By collecting and storing encrypted data with the hope that it can be cracked with a QC later on ("store now, decrypt later"), this attack can already be prepared today.

The second option can be used for an MITM attack that operates as follows and targets the DSAs. The attacker uses Shor's Algorithm to obtain the holder's secret key from the public key included in one of the certificates that is transmitted during a TLS handshake. Because its secret key can be used to forge other certificates, the root certificate provides the most extensive possibilities among these certificates. With the ability to forge the server's signature and use it to change messages, the attacker then has access to every MITM attack possibility, completely breaching the TLS-implied security. For instance, the attacker might transmit fictitious commands or give the client his own public key for key exchange, signed with the server's signature. In the Internet of Things, both situations could have detrimental effects, particularly if the device is utilized in vital infrastructure or the medical field.

The Post-Quantum Cryptography (PQC)

The flaws of modern cryptography have led to the development of PQC, which finds new, QC-resistant Public Key Cryptography (PKC). NIST in the United States is conducting a multi-round standardization process for these new PKCs. In contrast to traditional PKCs, the new algorithms are predicated on hard problems over lattices, codes, isogenies, multivariates, or hash functions that are thought to be impervious to QCs. The process is currently in its final round, and the remaining applicants were separated into "finalists" and "alternate candidates." As shown in the figure below, one of the finalists for each threatened PKC (Key Encapsulation Mechanism and Digital Signature Algorithm) will soon be standardized.

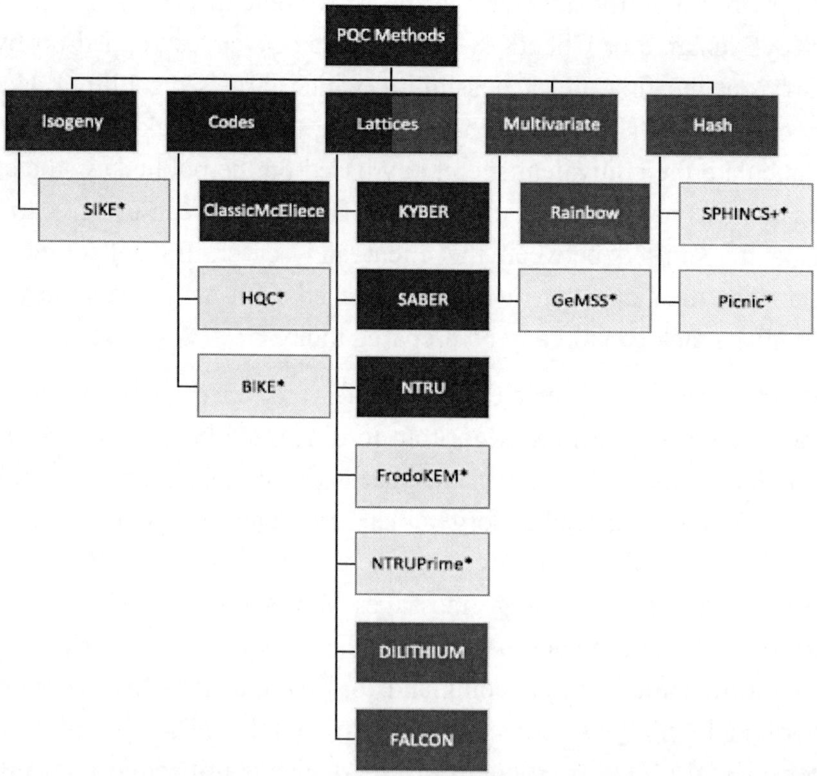

Fig.15.11 PQC algorithms that the related NIST procedure is now considering standardizing. Blue boxes are used to identify KEMs, while green boxes are used to identify DSAs. Alternative candidates are indicated with asterisks and reduced opacity.

Since lattice-based KEMs and DSAs are among the shortest keys, ciphertexts, and signatures and have quick computations, they are regarded as the best prospects for standardization. The learning-with-errors (LWE) problem, which has since drawn a lot of attention in cryptography, is the basis for the majority of them. More structured lattices, which lower the key size needed to reach a specific level of security, were used to further enhance their performance. Security concerns about how much this structured-lattice-based (SLB) design could offer crucial chances for algebraic assaults make this another major disadvantage.

McEliece first proposed code-based cryptography in 1978. It is based on error-correction codes. In order to construct the public key, McEliece's original method uses a hidden, error-correcting, binary Goppa code whose generator matrix is multiplied by two secret matrices chosen at random. To date, no attack that could seriously jeopardize it has been discovered. Only Key Encapsulation Mechanism (KEM) are constructed using coding theory problems in the NIST process. These code-based KEMs are a good substitute for lattice-based KEMs in the event that they become insecure, but they require larger keys than lattice-based KEMs and employ very different, more sophisticated security assumptions.

SiKE is the only contender that is predicated on the super-singular isogeny walk issue. Even while SIKE has been found to have extremely costly computations, it offers the pool of KEMs a special security assumption and has the lowest bandwidth requirements.

The smallest signatures and most effective signing and verification processes are found in multivariate signature schemes; nonetheless, their public keys range from tens of kB to hundreds of kB. This restricts the space for practical applications and results in extremely long certificate chains in TLS-like applications.

The hash-based DSAs have big signatures and a lot of computations, but their public keys are small. But as SPHICNS+ is thought to be the most established and cautious design, it acts as a fallback in the event that significant flaws in the lattice-based signature schemes are discovered.

The table below lists the five security levels into which the PQC algorithms are divided. It includes many parameter configurations for each security level. The computing resources needed to successfully crack the cryptosystem are determined by the minimal security criteria; for instance, attackers must have at least the same resources as for an Advanced Encryption Standard-128 (AES-128) key search in order to crack NIST level 1 KEMs.

Table 15.1 NIST security tiers in the process of PQC standardization.

Security Level	Minimum Security Requirements
1	AES-128
2	SHA-256
3	AES-192
4	SHA-384
5	AES-256

15.9 Process of Quantum Key Distribution Operations

In quantum cryptography, random keys are sent between two devices (sender and receiver) over fibre optic cables or the open air using photons. For secure communication, these keys are dispersed using QKD techniques and then followed by traditional cryptography. A cryptographic procedure called QKD uses the ideas of quantum physics to make it easier for devices to share information. It creates a secret key by using both conventional and quantum channels. The quantum channel transmits polarized photons, also known as quantum states of light, over optical fibres or free space/satellite links. A verified classical channel is also used to compare certain observations related to various quantum states at the same time. Further post-processing procedures are carried out in order to refine a legitimate and private key. Both of these channels are accessible to the general public.

Imagine that a sender (S) and a receiver (R) have specialized optical equipment to create a quantum channel. They can also use a classical channel to exchange particular measurements in order to create a quantum key and mutually authenticate. S uses a QKD transmitter to broadcast a stream of polarized photons using randomly selected bases to R over the quantum channel. Each photon represents one bit of information. R uses his or her own randomly chosen bases to measure each photon after capturing them via the quantum channel using a QKD receiver at the receiver's end. The bases used for sensing each photon are then switched using the classical channel.

While the photons measured with various bases are destroyed and excluded from the final session key, they subsequently take into account the measurement results for each photon that was measured using the same basis as a secret session key. Each photon in the aforementioned example may have one of these polarizations, which are created and measured using four bases or polarized filters. Rectilinear polarizations at 0° or 90° and diagonal polarizations at 45° or 135° make up the bases. The basis that corresponds to a bit "1" or "0" can therefore be chosen at random.

Choose the 0° or 135° polarizations for the bit "0," and for the bit "1," choose the 45° or 90° polarizations. When diagonally polarized photons pass through the rectilinear filter (+), they change arbitrarily with an equal probability, whereas photons with rectilinear bases stay the same. Similarly, photons that are diagonally polarized remain unchanged when they travel through the diagonal filter (x), whereas photons that are polarized in a rectilinear way undergo a random switch with an equal probability to one of the diagonal polarizations. In the beginning, S creates random bits and uses random base selection to transform them into a photon stream or quantum states, or qubits.

S then sends these qubits to R, who receives and measures them without being aware of the polarizations of any of S's photons beforehand. After they receive the bits and calculate them, they determine their secret key. The QKD procedure without an attacker present is shown in the figure below. The binary representation of the session key between S and R is 01110.

Bit number	1	2	3	4	5	6	7	8	9
S's random bits	1	0	1	1	1	0	0	1	0
S's chosen bases	+	x	+	x	x	+	x	x	+
Polarized photons of S	↕	⤡	↕	⤢	⤢	↔	⤡	⤢	↔
R's chosen bases	x	x	+	+	x	x	+	x	+
Polarized photons measured by R	⤢	⤡	↕	↔	⤢	⤡	↔	⤢	↔
R's measured key	0	0	1	1	1	0	1	1	0
Session key		0	1		1			1	0

Fig.15.12 An illustration of a QKD process in the absence of an attacker.

15.10 Applications for Qiot Securing With Qkd

There is an architecture for Internet of Things applications, and each of them has smart devices for communications that are capable of quantum computing. In this, the creation of a quantum key that is unconditionally secure between a gateway node (GN) and a smart device (SD). The network model, the threat model, and the quantum key exchange (QKE) protocol between SD and GN are some of the steps in this architecture.

A. Model of Networks

A generalized network model with quantum computing capabilities for a range of Internet of Things applications is shown in the figure below. A trusted registration authority (RA), using unique identities and quantum-resistant certificates, registers all SDs and GN for a specific application prior to the deployment of IoT devices. A classical channel and a quantum channel are the two public channels that are used for communication between SD and GN. Mutual authentication between the two parties and the sharing of bases that will be utilized to create a quantum key between them are accomplished via the classical channel. Only the sharing of polarized photons or quantum states is possible through the quantum channel. Following a successful registration process, the entities can communicate and deploy their application to exchange sensing data. Following SD data collection, GN can send the data to the quantum servers for additional processing and archiving.

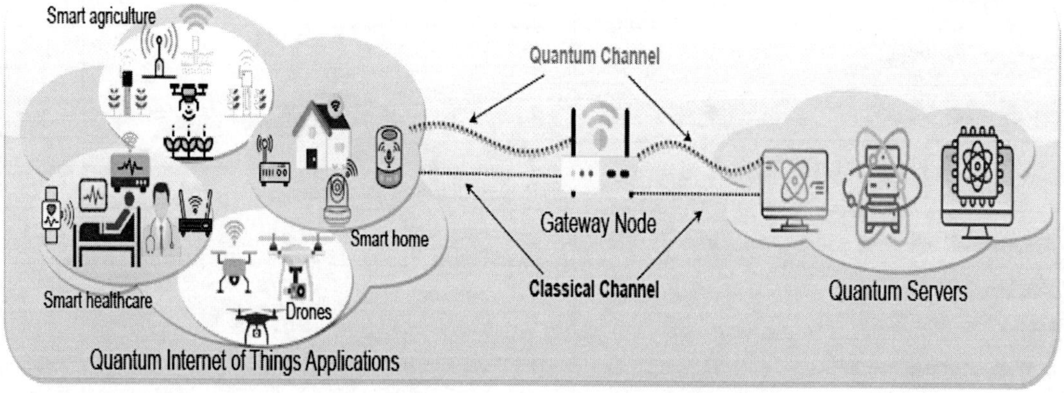

Fig.15.13 Numerous QIoT applications.

B. Threat Model

Both security risks for the classical channel and those that occur during quantum communication via the quantum channel are described in this threat model. An adversary A can obtain a certain amount of quantum information by listening in on the quantum communication channel during QKE. A bright-light assault can be used to control the photon detectors by directing bright light to the participating devices, and a Trojan-horse attack can be used to probe smart devices with light to learn about the device settings.

According to the threat model, A has the capacity to alter, remove, or introduce malicious content into the traditional communication channel in addition to listening in on communication messages. Even though quantum key distribution (QKD) is more secure than conventional encryption, communication over the quantum channel may still be vulnerable. The following are a few examples of potential attacks:

1. Intercept-resend attack, sometimes referred to as the man-in-the-middle attack, in which the attacker measures the quantum states that are sent by the sender and then sends the modified states to the intended recipient; A bright-light assault can be used to control the photon detectors by directing bright light to the participating devices, and a Trojan-horse attack can be used to probe smart devices with light to learn about the device settings.

2. Photon number splitting attack: in this attack, the attacker measures each copy of the photons (light particles) separately after capturing the sender's quantum states and splitting them into multiple copies; and

3. Entanglement-breaking attack: in this attack, the attacker intercepts and measures one or more entangled particles in the quantum channel, destroying their proper entanglement. When utilizing the quantum channel in quantum communication protocols such as QKD, there are additional considerations and threat models that need to be taken into account in addition to the mentioned specific attacks. Given

how sensitive quantum systems are to noise and environmental disturbances, these include channel imperfections and environmental noise.

Variations in temperature, electromagnetic interference, and optical losses are a few examples of factors that might cause errors or jeopardize communication security. Cryptographic techniques like error correction codes and post-processing of quantum key material are used to improve the security and dependability of quantum communication protocols in order to lessen these dangers.

C. Establishment of Quantum Channels

There are usually multiple processes involved in creating a quantum channel between an SD and the GD, including:

Initial Setup: Appropriate quantum communication devices that can create, modify, and detect quantum states must be installed in both the SD and the GD. These devices frequently consist of single-photon detectors, optical components for state manipulation, quantum memories, and sources of entangled photons.

Entanglement Generation: At each node, entangled photon pairs are initially created. A key characteristic of quantum mechanics is entanglement, which is the correlation between two particles' states independent of their distance from one another. Establishing secure quantum communication is based on this entangled pair.

Quantum Transmission: One photon from each pair of entangled photons is transmitted to the other node via a quantum communication channel after they have been created. This channel may be based on free space or optical fibres, among other physical media.

Quantum State Measurement: The nodes measure the photons after they are received. Usually, bases selected at random for every photon are used in these measurements; these bases are then made public to look for any possible eavesdropping attempts.

Key Distillation: Following measurements, the nodes contrast the measurement bases. A raw key is created using a subset of the measurement data for which the bases match. There are bits in this raw key that can be utilized as cryptographic keys.

Error Correction and Privacy Amplification: To eliminate errors caused by noise in the quantum channel and guarantee that the final key is safe from eavesdropping efforts, the raw key is subjected to error correction and privacy amplification techniques.

Creation of a Secure Quantum Channel: A secure quantum channel between SD and the GN is established using the error-corrected and privacy-amplified key as the foundation. Sensitive data can be sent over this channel, and it can also be used to verify traditional communication channels.

Key Refreshment: Using fresh entangled pairs and the previously mentioned procedure, keys are routinely updated to preserve security over time.

D. Procedure for Registration

Before deployment with the subsequent procedure over a secure channel or offline phase, RA registers all SD and GN.

RGP 1: A certificate Certi for an SD and Certj for a GN are selected by the RA, along with a unique and different identity IDi.

RGP 2: Based on a huge prime number (p) and an integer (n) with a power of two, the RA chooses a Gaussian distribution over the polynomial ring $Q_p = Z_p[x]/x^n+1$ with a standard deviation δ represented by χ_δ.

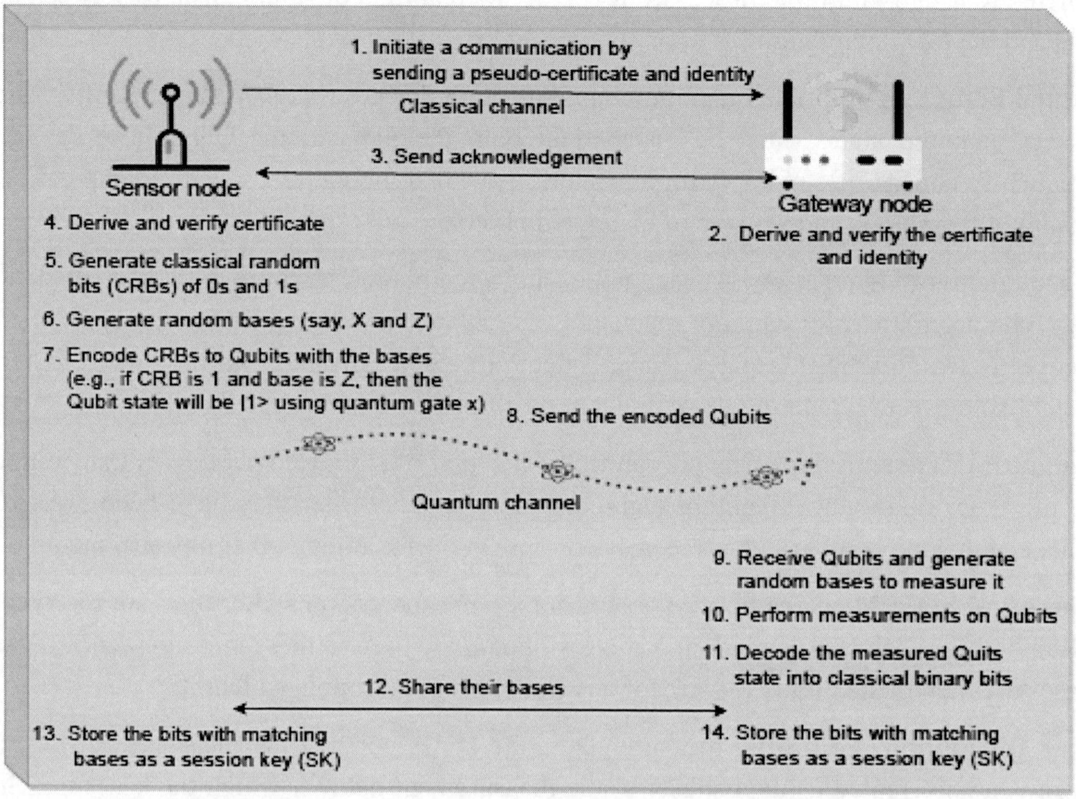

Fig.15.14 The entire QKE process between SD and GN.

RGP 3: Next, using a cryptographic hash function $h : \{0, 1\}^* \rightarrow \{0, 1\}^\gamma$, and a sample Si for SD selected at random by the RA from χ_δ where γ; output length (the SHA-256 technique is used here because it is quantum safe).

Lastly, the RA securely transmits $\{ID_i, s_i, Cert_j\}$ to GN after loading $\{Cert_i, h, ID_i, s_i\}$ into SD's memory.

E. Protocol for Quantum Key Exchange

An SD and GN can share a quantum-secure secret key by using a BB84-type quantum key exchange technique. The actions listed below are taken in order to create this session key:

Step 1: SD selects a new timestamp TS_1 and creates a pseudo-certificate Cert`i as $Cert_i^*$ as $Cert_i^* = Cert_i \oplus h(s_i \| TS_1)$ to start a communication process over a traditional channel. SD then forwards $\{ID_i, Cert_i^*, TS_1\}$, to the GN that is attached.

Step 2: GN verifies the appended timestamp to determine whether the message is fresh after receiving it from SD. GN determines $Cert_i = Cert_i^* \oplus h(s_i \| TS_1)$ if the timestamp is confirmed, and then confirms the identity and certificate for authenticity. In the event that every verification is successful, SD is regarded by GN as the verified party. GN creates a pseudo-certificate $Cert_j^*$ by selecting a new timestamp TS_2 and formulating it as $Cert_j^* = Cert_j \oplus h(s_i \| TS_2 \| TS_1)$. After that, GN acknowledges SD with its pseudo-certificate, timestamp, and verification status.

Step 3: After receiving the message from GN, SD calculates the original certificate $Cert_j$ as $Cert_j = Cert_j^* \oplus h(s_i \| TS_2 \| TS_1)$ and checks its certificate to confirm its authenticity and freshness. They mutually authenticate one another after this verification is finished.

Step 4: SD chooses random bases (in this case, X and Z) and creates classical random bits (CRBs). SD then uses one of these bases to encode the CRBs into qubits, or quantum states. For instance, SD applies a quantum gate "x" and transforms it into a quantum state $|1\rangle$ if the basis is "Z" and the CRB is "1." SD then uses a fibre optic cable or aircraft to transmit the encoded qubits to GN across the quantum channel.

Step 5: GN creates its own random bases to measure the qubits after obtaining them from SD. After that, GN decodes the quantum states into binary bits by measuring the received qubits using its own bases.

Step 6: In order to complete the quantum key, SD and GN now share their bases via the classical channel. Each computes the binary bits based on the matching basis after obtaining their bases, and they are then stored as a session key. In the future, AES encryption may be utilized with this quantum secret session key to exchange confidential data pertaining to QIoT applications.

A thorough explanation of this process is given in the below Fig.

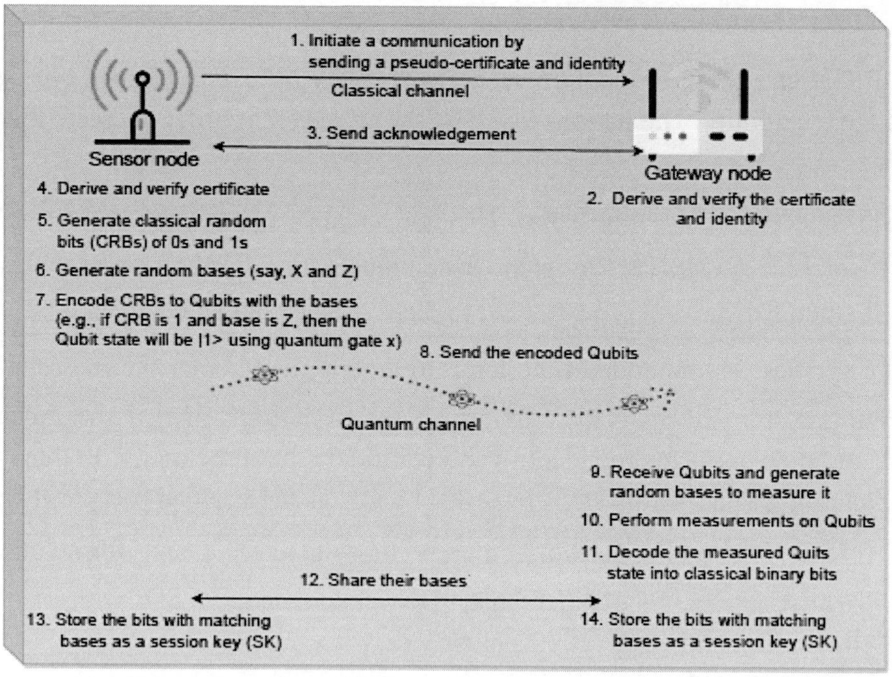

Fig.15.15 The entire QKE process between SD and GN.

15.10.1 Security Evaluation

The foundational ideas of quantum mechanics, not processing power, are what give QKD its security. The no-cloning theorem and the superposition principle are two fundamental ideas that provide QKD's unconditional security. Compared to classical bits, qubits store information more efficiently because of the superposition principle, which permits them to exist in two states at once. This idea makes QKD practically unbreakable by allowing secure quantum exchange for encryption keys over an insecure network. Since measuring polarized photons, which stand in for qubits, disrupts the information they convey, any attempt to intercept the conversation can be detected.

According to Heisenberg's uncertainty principle, a photon's information is lost as soon as it is measured or disrupted. Because any viewing of the photon by an adversary (A) causes modifications that may be recognized, this approach aids in the detection of eavesdropping efforts. In quantum physics, the no-cloning theorem forbids the flawless replication of an unidentified quantum state. Errors are created when an eavesdropper attempts to intercept and replicate quantum states, making the intrusion visible.

It is possible to use the basic ideas of quantum mechanics to detect the presence of an attacker on the quantum communication channel. A quantum state is naturally disturbed when it is measured or observed in quantum communication. The No-Cloning Theorem, which asserts that it is impossible to produce an exact duplicate of any given unknown quantum state, can be applied by the receiver.

A quantum particle's location and momentum are simultaneously altered when any quantum state is measured, in accordance with Heisenberg's uncertainty principle. Therefore, it causes modifications when an attacker attempts to intercept the quantum states that are being communicated. The receiver confirms the modified quantum states using shared bases after receiving them, which could lead to discrepancies. As a result, the receiver can quickly identify whether an attacker is present on the network. Any attempt to eavesdrop on the quantum communication channel can be readily identified in this scheme. It is impossible to watch photons directly without altering them, and it is pointless to try to detect photons indirectly via sender (SD) and receiver (GN) measurements.

A cannot obtain any meaningful information from SD and GN since they only reveal the measurement basis and not the outcome. Imagine that A tries to enter the system and measure the photons of SD. The information carried by the observed photons is annihilated due to the uncertainty introduced by Heisenberg's principle, which causes a discrepancy between the SD and GN measurements. GN is able to identify efforts at eavesdropping by examining the traffic of sent photons. By confirming their bases, A can be clearly identified even if it attempts to produce and send photons to GN.

Additionally, since pseudocertificates are sent in place of the original certificates and the certificates are not sent directly in plaintext form, A cannot disclose any information from the classical channel. Using the private key of the trustworthy authority, the original certificates are created. As a result, A needs to know the original private key in order to create a fake certificate. Therefore, security for authentication via the traditional route is likewise provided by this technique. Untraceability attacks are avoided by not transmitting the original certificate. Rather, a pseudo-certificate is sent via the open classical channel. The recipient can extract the original certificate and confirm the sender's legitimacy after obtaining the pseudo-certificate. Therefore, pseudo-certificates were essential for communication in order to reduce the risk of untraceability attacks.

QKD provides a promising means of guaranteeing the security and integrity of communication in next-generation QIoT applications. In QIoT applications, the incorporation of QKD offers an unconditionally secure technique to create a quantum key between a sensor device and a gateway node, utilizing the ideas of quantum mechanics to identify any possible eavesdropping efforts. The QKD scheme effectively illustrates the viability of using it in a client-server QIoT setup. A secure session key can be created between a sensor node and a gateway node using the scheme's quantum state and classical information exchange. The technique makes use of the special characteristics of quantum physics and certificate modification to successfully handle potential dangers, such as eavesdropping and illegal access. The development of quantum-safe solutions that protect private data in the dynamic field of quantum-enabled Internet of Things applications is made possible by the ongoing advancement of quantum technologies.

Chapter – 16
Quantum Machine Learning

Quantum machine learning is the process of incorporating quantum algorithms into machine learning applications. The phrase is most frequently used to describe quantum-enhanced machine learning, which is the application of machine learning algorithms for the analysis of classical data carried out on a quantum computer. Quantum machine learning uses qubits and quantum operations or specific quantum systems to increase computing speed and data storage performed by algorithms in a program, whereas machine learning algorithms are used to compute enormous amounts of data. This includes hybrid approaches that use both quantum and classical computing, outsourcing computationally challenging subroutines to a quantum device. On a quantum computer, these operations can be carried out more quickly and with greater complexity. Moreover, quantum states can be analyzed using quantum algorithms rather than classical data.

In addition to quantum computing, "quantum machine learning" also refers to traditional machine learning techniques used on data from quantum experiments (also known as machine learning of quantum systems), such as figuring out a quantum system's phase transitions or designing new quantum experiments.

The study of methodological and structural parallels between specific physical systems and learning systems, particularly neural networks, is another area of study that falls under the umbrella of quantum machine learning. For instance, conventional deep learning can benefit from certain mathematical and numerical methods from quantum physics, and vice versa.

Additionally, scholars explore more abstract concepts of learning theory—sometimes known as "quantum learning theory"—in relation to quantum information.

Using quantum computers for machine learning

The term "quantum-enhanced machine learning" describes quantum algorithms that solve machine learning problems, enhancing and frequently speeding up traditional machine learning methods. In order to make the provided classical data set available for quantum information processing, such techniques usually involve encoding it into a quantum computer. The outcome of the quantum computation is then read out by measuring the quantum system after using quantum information processing procedures. For instance, the result of a binary classification task can be inferred from the measurement of a qubit. Some quantum machine learning algorithm proposals have been implemented on small-scale or special-purpose quantum devices, but many are still completely theoretical and need to be evaluated on a full-scale universal quantum computer.

O(n2) **Quantum pattern recognition and quantum associative memories**

Unlike random access memories, which use fixed addresses to identify stored content, associative (or content-addressable) memories use a similarity metric. They must therefore be able to recover both corrupted and incomplete patterns, which is a crucial machine learning task.

The **$O(n^2)$** interactions (synapses) of a real, symmetric energy matrix over a network of n artificial neurons are where typical classical associative memories store **p** patterns. Retrieval is accomplished by minimizing the overall energy, beginning with an initial configuration, and the encoding is such that the desired patterns are local minima of the energy functional.

Unfortunately, cross-talk is a phenomenon that greatly limits classical associative memory. The energy environment becomes chaotic and retrieval is no longer feasible when too many patterns are stored, leading to the emergence of bogus memories that spread rapidly. Usually, a linear function of the number of neurons, **$p< O(n)$,** limits the number of storable patterns.

In their most basic form, quantum associative memory store patterns in a unitary matrix **U** that acts on the Hilbert space of **n** qubits. The unitary evolution of a fixed initial state to a quantum superposition of the desired patterns, with the probability distribution peaking on the pattern that most closely resembles an input, is how retrieval is accomplished. The retrieval process is therefore probabilistic by nature, since it is quantum. However, false memories are never created because quantum associative memories are not affected by cross-talk. As a result, their capacity is higher than that of classical ones. The unitary matrix **U** has an **O (pn)** number of parameters. Thus, for any polynomial number of patterns, one can create quantum associative memories that are efficient and devoid of false memory.

Simulation of linear algebra using quantum amplitudes

The concept of amplitude encoding, or linking the amplitudes of a quantum state to the inputs and outputs of calculations, is the foundation of several quantum machine learning methods. An exponentially compact representation may be possible with this information encoding as a state of n qubits is defined by **2^n** complex amplitudes. This is intuitively equivalent to assigning a classical vector to a discrete probability distribution over binary random variables. The objective of amplitude encoding-based algorithms is to create quantum algorithms with resources that increase polynomially with the number of qubits n, resulting in a logarithmic temporal complexity in the number of amplitudes and, consequently, the input dimension.

The quantum method for linear systems of equations, which, under certain circumstances, executes a matrix inversion using a quantity of physical resources that grows only logarithmically in the dimensions of the matrix, is the basis for many of the quantum machine learning techniques in this area. Among these requirements is the ability to efficiently simulate a Hamiltonian that entry-wise matches the matrix, which is known to be feasible in the case of a sparse or low-rank matrix. For comparison, all known traditional matrix inversion algorithms necessitate a number of operations that increase more than quadratically with the matrix's dimension (for example, $O(n^{2.373})$, albeit they are not limited to sparse matrices.

In machine learning techniques where the training simplifies to solving a linear system of equations, such as least-squares linear regression, the least-squares version of support vector machines, and Gaussian processes, quantum matrix inversion can be used. State preparation, which frequently necessitates initializing a quantum system in a state whose amplitudes mirror the features of the full dataset, is a critical bottleneck of techniques that replicate linear algebra operations with the amplitudes of quantum states. This stage readily conceals the task's complexity, even though effective state preparation techniques are known for particular situations.

VQAs, or variational quantum algorithms

Since current research shows that VQAs can be used to the great majority of known important applications of the quantum computer, they are one of the most investigated classes of quantum algorithms. They also seem to be a top contender for achieving quantum supremacy. In a combined quantum-classical technique known as VQAs, a quantum processor creates quantum states, while a classical computer does measurement and optimization. Since VQAs can withstand noise better than other algorithms and provide quantum superiority with just a few hundred qubits, they are thought to be the best for NISQ. In order to tackle optimization problems and determine the ground state energy of complicated systems that were challenging or time-consuming to compute with a traditional computer, researchers have looked into circuit-based algorithms.

VQCs, or variational quantum circuits

Variational Quantum Algorithms (VQAs) are the foundation of Variational Quantum Circuits, sometimes referred to as Parametrized Quantum Circuits (PQCs). The three components of a VQC are measurement, quantum circuit, and initial state preparation. Because VQCs require fewer parameters than their classical counterparts and leverage the potential of quantum computers to learn quickly, researchers are examining them in great detail. The ability to approximate non-linear functions, such as those found in neural networks, on quantum circuits has been demonstrated both theoretically and statistically. In Reinforcement Learning tasks and Generative Algorithms, VQCs have supplanted neural networks due to their dominance. There is a significant chance that the training of the variation circuits will be limited by the inherent characteristics of quantum devices with regard to decoherence, random gate error, and measurement errors. The issue of decoherence noise caused by the quantity of training repetitions is resolved by first training the VQCs on classical devices before using them on quantum devices.

Classifier for quantum binary

Binary classification is one of the techniques or methods used to detect patterns, and pattern reorganization is one of the key tasks of machine learning. Both supervised and unsupervised learning make use of binary classification. Classical bits are transformed into qubits and translated to Hilbert space in quantum machine learning. To take advantage of Hilbert space, complex value data is used in a quantum binary classifier. The quantum binary classifier generates an accurate answer quickly by taking advantage of quantum mechanics phenomena including superposition, entanglement, and interference.

Grover search-based quantum machine learning algorithms

Amplitude amplification techniques based on Grover's search algorithm, which has been demonstrated to tackle unstructured search problems with a quadratic speedup compared to classical algorithms, are another way to enhance classical machine learning using quantum information processing. The k-medians and k-nearest neighbors algorithms are two examples of how these quantum procedures can be used to train algorithms that translate into an unstructured search challenge. Additional uses include quadratic speedups in attention calculation and perceptron training.

Grover's search algorithm reduction is an illustration of amplitude amplification in action in a machine learning system wherein a subroutine finds an element that is less than a previously defined element using Grover's search technique. An oracle that assesses whether a state with a corresponding element is smaller than the predetermined one can be used for this. Then, Grover's technique can identify an element that satisfies our criterion. This subroutine iteratively finds the minimum element in the data set after initializing the minimization using a random element from our data set.

Quantum k-medians, where **n** is the number of data points and **k** is the number of clusters, are notable applications of this reduction, which has a speedup of at least $O\left(\sqrt{\frac{n}{k}}\right)$ over traditional k-medians. To get the same quadratic speedup, amplitude amplification and quantum walks are frequently used together. It has been suggested that quantum walks improve the performance of reinforcement learning agents in the projective simulation framework and Google's Page Rank algorithm.

Reinforcement learning aided by quantum mechanics

In contrast to supervised and unsupervised learning, which also allow for quantum enhancements, reinforcement learning is a subfield of machine learning. By interacting with a classical or quantum environment and occasionally receiving rewards for its activities, a quantum agent can learn to modify its behavior—that is, to learn what to do to win more rewards—in a process known as quantum-enhanced reinforcement learning. A quantum speedup may be possible in some circumstances, either as a result of the agent's quantum processing power or the ability to investigate the environment in superpositions. Proposals have been made to implement such procedures in superconducting circuits and trapped ion devices. Experimental evidence has shown that the agent's internal decision-making time can be accelerated by a quantum amount in trapped ions, and that the learning time in a fully coherent (or "quantum") interaction between the agent and environment can be accelerated by a quantum amount in a photonic setup.

Quantum Annealing

Quantum annealing (QA) is an optimization technique that uses quantum fluctuations to discover the global minimum of a given objective function over a given set of candidate solutions. Finding the ground state of a spin glass or resolving the traveling salesman issue are two examples of tasks where quantum annealing is most useful. These problems involve a discrete search space with numerous local minima. In 1988, B. Apolloni, N. Cesa Bianchi, and D. De Falco coined the phrase "quantum annealing" to describe a classical method with a quantum influence.

A quantum-mechanical superposition of all potential states (candidate states) with equal weights is the starting point for quantum annealing. The system then undergoes a natural quantum-mechanical development of physical systems, according to the time-dependent Schrödinger equation. According to the time-dependent strength of the transverse field, the amplitudes of all candidate states continuously change, resulting in quantum parallelism. This leads to quantum tunneling between states, or more specifically, tunneling between peaks. The system remains near the instantaneous Hamiltonian's ground state if the transverse field's rate of change is sufficiently slow.

Accelerating the transverse field's rate of change may cause the system to momentarily exit the ground state, but it also increases the probability that it will end up in the ground state of the final problem Hamiltonian, or diabetic quantum computation. When the transverse field is ultimately turned off, the system should have arrived at the classical Ising model's ground state, which is the solution to the initial optimization issue. Shortly after the first theoretical idea, an experimental proof of quantum annealing's effectiveness for random magnets was published. It has also been demonstrated that quantum annealing offers a quick Grover oracle for the square-root speedup in a large number of NP-complete problems.

Quantum Model of NISQ Circuit

Accurately computing costs and gradients for training models becomes extremely difficult on NISQ devices as the depth of the quantum circuit increases due to the increased noise level. By utilizing the quantum algorithm and the quantum perceptron on the currently available quantum hardware, the noise tolerance will increase.

Even the most intricate brain networks are built on a regular connection of similar parts called neurons. The inner product and an activation function are the two operations that a neuron normally performs. The inner product process is linear in contrast to the activation function, which is usually nonlinear. Linear processes can be quickly completed with quantum computing. In addition, most quantum neurons favor the threshold function for activation functions because of its ease of implementation.

Methods of quantum sampling

The foundation of many computer methods with significant applications in research, engineering, and society is sampling from high-dimensional probability distributions. Deep learning, probabilistic programming, and other machine learning and AI applications are a few examples.

Estimating averages over probabilistic models specified in terms of a Boltzmann distribution is a computationally challenging problem that is essential for some pertinent machine learning applications. It is difficult to sample from generic probabilistic models because algorithms that mostly rely on sampling are predicted to stay unsolvable regardless of how strong and vast traditional computer resources grow. Despite being created for difficult combinatorial optimization issues, quantum annealers, such as those made by D-Wave Systems, have lately been identified as a viable option to accelerate computations that depend on sampling by taking use of quantum phenomena.

Recently, some research teams have investigated training deep neural networks and Boltzmann machines using quantum annealing technology. Boltzmann machine training often involves calculating specific averages that can be approximated using common sampling methods like Markov chain Monte Carlo algorithms. Using a physical process that naturally produces samples from a Boltzmann distribution, such as quantum annealing, provides an additional option. The goal is to identify the ideal control settings that most accurately reflect a dataset's empirical distribution.

Recently, a unique class of limited Boltzmann machines that can be utilized as a foundation for deep learning architectures has been learned using the D-Wave 2X system at NASA Ames Research Center. Almost concurrently published complementary work demonstrated the potential of quantum annealing for supervised learning in categorization challenges. Later, among other synthetic datasets, the same device was used to train a fully linked Boltzmann machine to generate, reconstruct, and identify low-resolution, down-scaled handwritten digits. The models that were trained using quantum annealing performed similarly or better in terms of quality in both situations. Whether quantum speedup exists in sampling applications is the main question that motivates this effort. Combinatorial optimization experience with quantum annealers indicates that the solution is not simple. A fully connected quantum limited Boltzmann machine has also been solved using reverse annealing.

A new machine learning method based on the quantum Boltzmann distribution of a transverse-field Ising Hamiltonian was recently proposed, following the success of Boltzmann machines based on the classical Boltzmann distribution. The training procedure of the quantum Boltzmann machine can become nontrivial because quantum mechanics is non-commutative. By placing limits on the quantum probabilities, the authors were able to partially get around this issue and train the model effectively by sampling. In the D-Wave 2X, a particular kind of quantum Boltzmann machine might have been trained by applying a learning rule similar to that of classical Boltzmann machines.

There are more technologies for sampling than quantum annealing. In a prepare-and-measure scenario, a thermal state is prepared by a universal quantum computer and subsequently sampled by measurements. In addition to offering a broader and more complete foundation for deep learning than classical computing, this can shorten the time needed to train a deep restricted Boltzmann machine. The same quantum techniques, which lack well-known classical counterparts, also enable effective training of multi-layer, fully connected models and entire Boltzmann machines. Quantum-enhanced Markov logic networks take advantage of the symmetries and the locality structure of the probabilistic graphical model produced by a first-order logic template, relying on an effective thermal state preparation technique that begins from an arbitrary state. Although the protocol depends on a universal quantum computer, it may be implemented on modern quantum annealing hardware with reasonable assumptions, and it offers an exponential reduction in computing cost in probabilistic inference.

Network of quantum neurons

Based on the ideas of quantum physics, quantum neural networks are computational neural network models. According to the notion of quantum mind, which holds that quantum effects influence cognitive function, Subhash Kak and Ron Chrisley independently released the first concepts on quantum neural computation in 1995. To create more effective algorithms, quantum neural network research typically combines the benefits of quantum information with classical artificial neural network models, which are frequently employed in machine learning for the crucial task of pattern recognition.

The difficulty of training traditional neural networks, particularly in big data applications, is a major driving force behind these studies. It is hoped that quantum computing characteristics like quantum parallelism or the effects of entanglement and interference can be utilized as resources. Such quantum neural network models are primarily theoretical suggestions that await their full application in actual investigations because the technological realization of a quantum computer is still in its early stages.

Typically, feed-forward networks are used to construct quantum neural networks. This structure accepts input from one layer of qubits and transfers it to another layer of qubits, just like their classical counterparts. After evaluating this data, this layer of qubits sends the results to the following layer. The path eventually leads to the last qubit layer. The layers do not need to have the same amount of qubits as the layer before or after them, nor do they need to be the same width. Like traditional artificial neural networks, this structure is trained on the best course of action.

This is covered in a section below. There are three types of quantum neural networks: quantum computers with classical data, quantum computers with quantum data, and quantum computers with classical data.

A. Quantum perceptrons

Numerous suggestions look for a quantum equivalent of the perceptron unit used to build neural nets. One issue is that, because a quantum development is characterized by linear operations and results in probabilistic observation, nonlinear activation functions do not instantly conform to the mathematical structure of quantum theory. From particular measurements to the postulation of non-linear quantum operators (a contentious mathematical framework), there are several ways to simulate the perceptron activation function using a quantum mechanical theory. Recently, Schuld, Sinayskiy, and Petruccione suggested a direct implementation of the activation function based on the quantum phase estimation technique utilizing the circuit-based model of quantum computation.

B. Quantum networks

Researchers have tried to apply neural networks to the quantum environment on a bigger scale. First generalizing classical neurons and then further generalizing them to create unitary gates is one method of building a quantum neuron. Neuronal interactions can be regulated conventionally by measuring the network states or quantum using unitary gates. By using various network types and quantum neuron implementations, such as photonically implemented neurons and quantum reservoir processors (quantum versions of reservoir computing), this high-level theoretical technique can be widely deployed.

The majority of learning algorithms use classical feedback loops to update the parameters of the quantum system until they converge to an ideal configuration, and they employ the classical paradigm of training an artificial neural network to learn the input-output function of a particular training set. Adiabatic models of quantum computing have also been used to approach learning as a parameter optimization problem.

C. Quantum associative memory

In 1999, Dan Ventura and Tony Martinez presented the first algorithm for quantum associative memory. The authors suggest an algorithm for a circuit-based quantum computer that mimics associative memory rather than attempting to convert the structure of artificial neural network models into quantum theory. A Grover-like quantum search technique finds the memory state that is closest to a given input by writing the memory states (in Hopfield neural networks, stored in the weights of the neural connections) into a superposition. Because only partial patterns may be recovered, this memory is not completely content-addressable.

Carlo A. Trugenberger proposed the first genuinely content-addressable quantum memory, which can recover patterns from faulty inputs as well. Because of the no-cloning theorem and the fact that they are destroyed upon measurement, both memories are only able to retain an exponential amount of patterns (in terms of n qubits).

In contrast to classical associative memories, Trugenberger has demonstrated that his probabilistic model of quantum associative memory may be effectively implemented and reused multiple times for any polynomial number of stored patterns.

Neural Network using Quantum Convolution

QCNN is a new multi-dimensional vector architecture that employs circuits as convolution filters. The benefits of CNNs and the strength of QML served as its inspiration. It makes full use of the power of extremely parallel processing on a superposition of a quantum state with a finite number of qubits by combining a deep neural network (DNN) with a variational quantum circuit (VQC). The primary tactic is to optimize the NISQ devices iteratively without the requirement for quantum error correction or the detrimental effects of noise, which may be built into the circuit parameter.

For QCNN to perform like CNN, the quantum circuit must be able to handle spatial information efficiently. The simplest method for using spatial information is the convolution filter. A quantum convolutional neural network (QCNN) consists of one or more quantum convolutional filters, each of which uses a quantum circuit that can be constructed randomized or in an ordered fashion to convert input data. The encoder, the parameterized quantum circuit (PQC), and the measurement are the three components that comprise the quantum convolutional filter. Because the quantum convolutional filter was created with trainable parameters, it can be thought of as an extension of the filter found in the conventional CNN.

Utilizing the hierarchical structures, quantum neural networks reduce the number of qubits from the previous layer by a factor of two for each layer that follows. These structures have O(log(n)) layers for n input qubits, which permits shallow circuit depth. They also ensure trainability by avoiding "barren plateau," one of the biggest problems with PQC-based algorithms. The basic concept of the pooling layer is also provided to ensure validity, even though the QCNN model does not have the associated quantum operation. The pooling layer is usually positioned in between subsequent convolutional layers in a QCNN architecture. It reduces the number of parameters, simplifies network computing, and controls over-fitting by reducing the spatial dimension of the representation while maintaining important features.

Subway processing can be used to complete this process by using full tomography on the state to reduce it to a single qubit. Although there are different sorts of units in the pooling layer, max pooling is the most commonly utilized. The last module is a fully connected layer that has full connections to every activation in the layer before it, much like traditional feed-forward neural networks. One characteristic of the QCNN architecture is translational invariance, which necessitates identical blocks of parameterized quantum gates inside a layer.

Quantum Dissipative Neural Network

Building blocks, which have an arbitrary unitary design, are layers of qubits connected by perceptrons to form dissipative QNNs (DQNNs). A unique collection of qubits is assigned to each node in the network layer of a DQNN, and each qubit is further characterized by a unique quantum perceptron unitary. As the name suggests, layer-to-layer transition mapping on the qubits of the two adjacent layers is how the input states information is passed through the network in a feed-forward manner. The term "dissipative" also describes how the supplementary qubits form the output layer while the input layers are dropped during the final layer's trace. DQNNs are used to learn a unitary matrix that connects the input and output quantum states in a large supervised learning job. The quantum state and the associated classical labels make up the training data for this task.

For unsupervised learning of the unlabeled training data, the dissipative quantum generative adversarial network (DQGAN) is presented, which is inspired by the wildly popular classical Generative Adversarial Network (GAN). A single DQGAN consists of two DQNNs: the discriminator and the generator. The discriminator aims to distinguish between the real training states and the fake states produced by the generator, while the generator aims to produce false training states that the discriminator is unable to distinguish from the real ones. Through alternate and adversarial training of the networks that help produce sets that extend the training set, the generator learns the pertinent features of the training set. DQGAN is trained on quantum data and has a fully quantum architecture. DQNNs are used to learn a unitary matrix that connects the input and output quantum states in a large supervised learning job. The quantum state and the associated classical labels make up the training data for this task.

Markov hidden quantum models

A quantum-enhanced variant of the classical Hidden Markov Models (HMMs), which are commonly used to represent sequential data in a variety of domains such as natural language processing and robotics, are called hidden quantum Markov models (HQMMs).

In contrast to other quantum-enhanced machine learning techniques, HQMMs can be thought of as quantum-mechanical models that are also compatible with conventional processors. HQMMs employ the quantum counterpart, density matrices, to describe hidden "belief" states, whereas classical HMMs use probability vectors.

There is some empirical evidence that these models can more effectively model sequential data than classical HMMs in practice, and recent work has demonstrated that these models can be learned by maximizing the log-likelihood of the provided data via classical optimization. However, more research is required to precisely identify when and how these benefits are derived. Furthermore, an intriguing feature of HQMMs is that the methods employed demonstrate how to carry out quantum-analogous Bayesian inference, which should enable the universal creation of the quantum versions of probabilistic graphical models. This is because classical HMMs are a specific type of Bayes net.

Completely quantum machine learning

Both the learning tool and the system being studied, as well as how they interact, are completely quantum in the most general instance of quantum machine learning. 'Learning' unknown quantum states, processes, or measurements—that is, reproducing them on another quantum system—is one class of problems that can profit from the completely quantum approach. For instance, given a set of sample quantum systems prepared in two coherent states rather than a classical description of the states to be differentiated, one could want to learn a measurement that distinguishes between them. First extracting a classical description of the states and then using this information to create an ideal discriminating measurement would be the naive approach. All that would be needed for this would be classical learning. Nonetheless, it is possible to demonstrate that in this instance, a fully quantum technique is strictly preferable. (Work on quantum pattern matching is also related to this.) This method can be applied to the challenge of learning unitary transformations.

Beyond the particular issue of learning states and transformations, the clustering task also enables a completely quantum variant, in which the information processing device that executes the algorithm and the oracle that gives the distance between data points are both quantum. Lastly, a generic framework including supervised, unsupervised, and reinforcement learning in a completely quantum setting was presented. It was demonstrated that a quantum speedup in reinforcement learning is possible due to the ability to probe the environment in superpositions. A photonic setup has been used to experimentally demonstrate such a speedup in the reinforcement-learning paradigm.

Quantum machine learning that is explicable

The field of explainable quantum machine learning (also known as XQML, in analogy to XAI/XML) is driven by the necessity for human-understandable models, which arises in quantum machine learning similarly to classical machine learning. Another name for these initiatives is Interpretable Machine Learning (IML, and hence IQML). XQML/IQML might be viewed as a different line of inquiry rather than a quantum advantage.

XQML, for instance, has been applied to the identification and categorization of mobile malware. Using a game-theoretic approach, quantum Shapley values have also been proposed to understand gates inside a circuit. In order to do this, gates—rather than features—play a coalitional game in which the value function is dependent on measurements of the relevant quantum circuit. Furthermore, Q-LIME, a quantum variant of the classical method known as LIME (Linear Interpretable Model-Agnostic Explanations), has also been put forth.

Theory of quantum learning

The mathematical study of quantum generalizations of classical learning models and the potential speedups or other enhancements they might offer is the goal of quantum learning theory. Although the learner in this scenario is a quantum information processing device and the data may be either classical or quantum, the framework is quite similar to that of classical computational learning theory. It is important to compare quantum learning theory with the previously stated quantum-enhanced machine learning, which aimed to improve the temporal complexity of classical algorithms for certain tasks by taking into account quantum protocols. Even though quantum learning theory is still being developed, some progress has been made in this area.

Usually, a concept class—a collection of potential concepts—is where learning theory begins. A notion is typically a function on a domain, like $\{0,1\}^n$. The concept class can, for instance, be the collection of Boolean circuits of a certain constant depth or the collection of disjunctive normal form (DNF) formulas on n bits. The learner's objective in this concept class is to acquire (exactly or roughly) an unknown target idea. The learner may be passively absorbing examples from the target topic or actively engaging with it.

In active learning, a student can ask for the value of the goal concept c(x) based on inputs x that they have selected. The learner must next, most likely, recover the precise target concept. The learner can pose membership inquiries in quantum superposition in the quantum precise learning model. For some concept classes, quantum exact learners can be polynomially more efficient than classical learners, but not more, if the learner's complexity is determined by the quantity of membership inquiries it generates. Certain idea classes can be effectively taught by quantum learners but not by classical learners if complexity is determined by the learner's usage of time (given plausible complexity-theoretic assumptions).

Valiant's probably roughly correct (PAC) learning is a natural model of passive learning. Here, a random set of instances (x,c(x)) with x dispersed according to an unknown distribution D are given to the learner. The learner's objective is to produce a hypothesis function h such that, when x is drawn in accordance with D, h(x)=c(x) with high probability. Each D and each target concept c in its concept class must have a 'roughly right' h produced by the learner. We can think of using possibly more potent quantum instances in place of the random ones: $\sum_x \sqrt{D(x)}|x, c(x)\rangle$.

This doesn't drastically cut down on the number of instances required in the PAC model (and the associated agnostic model) because the classical and quantum sample complexity for each concept class is equal up to constant factors. On the other hand, quantum examples can be very useful for learning under some fixed distribution D, such as DNF under the uniform distribution. When it comes to time complexity, there are concept classes that, even with classical examples, quantum learners can PAC-learn effectively, but classical learners cannot (again, given realistic complexity-theoretic assumptions).

The most popular approach in supervised learning is passive learning, where a learning algorithm usually uses preset training examples without allowing the user to query the label of unlabeled samples. One phase in the induction process is to output a hypothesis, h. Inductive models are traditionally divided into two phases: training involves estimating the model parameters, and application involves applying the learnt model an arbitrary number of times. This phase separation also occurs with quantum resources in the asymptotic limit of the number of applications.

16.1 Combining Machine Learning with Quantum Computing

Machine learning is the branch of artificial intelligence that focuses on developing algorithms that enable computers to learn from data and form opinions or predictions. This field has revolutionized fields including image identification, natural language processing, and autonomous systems. Machine learning and quantum computing may be combined to create more powerful and efficient intelligent systems by fusing their greatest qualities.

Quantum machine learning uses quantum technologies and algorithms to enhance and speed up machine learning processes. Its objective is to solve challenging issues that are unsolvable or require a lot of computation by applying traditional methods. By employing quantum approaches, machine learning models with quantum enhancements can investigate vast solution spaces and uncover patterns and correlations that have not been identified before.

16.2 Algorithms for Quantum Machine Learning

To take use of the potential of quantum technology, several quantum machine learning techniques have been developed and implemented. The following are some notable algorithms:

Quantum Support Vector Machines, or QSVMs: Quantum algorithms known as Quantum Support Vector Machines, or QSVMs, are employed in supervised learning applications such as classification and regression. The optimal hyperplane between several classes of data points is found by using quantum algorithms for data encoding and optimization.

Quantum clustering approaches: By utilizing the power of quantum computing, these techniques effectively cluster large and complex datasets. They can identify patterns and structures in data that are difficult to identify with conventional methods.

Quantum Neural Networks (QNNs): QNNs are artificial neural networks that are structured in a quantum fashion. Because they use quantum bits, quantum gates, and quantum algorithms, they are more effective than their conventional counterparts at training models and carrying out concurrent calculations. QNNs have demonstrated potential in two applications: quantum deep learning and quantum image recognition.

Algorithms for Quantum Genetics: Quantum genetic algorithms are algorithms that combine evolutionary computation techniques with quantum computing. Because they leverage quantum parallelism to search vast solution spaces and quantum bits to express genetic information, they are useful for optimization issues.

16.3 Quantum-Based Machine Learning Techniques

Innovative machine learning techniques are becoming increasingly significant due to the daily increase in the volume of data being received, stored, and analyzed. Machine learning systems under supervision deduce an input-output relationship from sizable training data sets that include "correct" mapping examples. Stated differently, the computer gains knowledge about how to handle novel inputs through experience. The pattern classification problem, in which a new data vector must be allocated to one of several classes given a set of successfully classified data vectors, is a well-known example of a mapping that must be learned.

Thus, a data vector—also known as a feature vector—contains details on the attributes of the thing that needs to be classified, such as an internet user's clicking patterns, a molecule's structure, or an image pixel. The abstract formulation of the information interpretation problem is pattern classification, which finds use in a variety of fields like information technology, the food business, and the financial sector. Humans perform these tasks far more naturally than machines do (for example, recognizing other people is a reaction to the numerous photons that enter our eyes every second), and machine learning, a branch of artificial intelligence, is in fact motivated by the way the human brain processes information.

Utilizing the characteristics of tiny particles developed in quantum theory, quantum computing is a relatively recent field that combines computer technology and physics to handle data. It is extremely difficult to control quantum objects that encode information, also known as qubits or qudits, and a fully functional quantum computer is still a long way off. Nonetheless, theoretical research on the extent and capability of quantum information is abundant. Quantum information scientists have realized that there are three main ways that quantum computing could enhance traditional machine learning methods as part of their efforts.

First, because of quantum parallelism, subroutines that are expensive on a classical computer when dealing with large amounts of data, like calculating an inner product or finding the minimum distance, could be carried out on a quantum computer with a linear or even exponential speedup in complexity. Second, from the standpoint of quantum computing, quantum machine learning, or QML for short, creates new avenues for quantum information processing, including the classification of quantum states. Third, quantum physics provides special kinds of logics that are frequently likened to fuzzy logics, particularly in the fields of intelligent agents and reinforcement learning.

With quantum objects, data can theoretically be represented exponentially more compactly in a so-called quantum superposition of both the 0 and 1 states, which is an advantage of computing with them. Unfortunately, retrieving information is constrained by a quantum system's principles of measurement, which severely alter it and make it impossible to evaluate all of the information at once. As we shall see later, however, the probabilistic nature of quantum algorithms' outputs might be advantageous for pattern recognition.

In order to address the more complex issues of QML, the last ten years of research on quantum information have produced a "toolbox" of algorithms that may be utilized on a possible quantum computer. Adding to these techniques, we will now suggest a quantum pattern classification algorithm for binary feature vectors that operates on the basis of the distance weighted k-nearest neighbor method. Our concept calculates the Hamming distance between two binary patterns on a quantum computer using a variant of Trugenberger's subroutine.

16.3.1 Quantum Object Computation

The use of quantum objects to address computational issues is analyzed by quantum computing1. Accordingly, a "quantum object" is any particle or set of particles for which quantum theory explains our observations and Newton's physics reveals to be an inadequate explanation. This opens up whole new avenues for microscopic information processing and becomes crucial for the description of microscopic particles like atoms, electrons, or photons.

Quantum objects with two different configurations or states, known as qubits, are the analogs of bits on a classical computer. They can have a variety of physical applications, such as the energy of atoms or the polarization of photons. However, qubits employ the superposition principle of quantum objects to be in both states "at the same time" if bits are conveying a signal that encodes a 0 or a 1. This appears in the quantum state notation as

$$|\psi\rangle = \alpha\,|0\rangle + \beta\,|1\rangle\,, \qquad |\alpha|^2 + |\beta|^2 = 1,$$

where α, β is a state vector characterizing a quantum entity, and $|\cdot\rangle$ are complex values known as amplitudes. Later on, a qubit's phase ϕ, which is a component of the amplitude ` $\alpha = \tilde{\alpha}e^{i\phi}$.becomes significant. The foundation of quantum theory is the finding that the squared amplitudes $|\alpha|^2, |\beta|^2$ indicate the likelihood of measuring the qubit in either state, $|0\rangle$ or $|1\rangle$. Therefore, a qubit state is defined by its likelihood of being measured in either of the two states rather than by whether it is in the "0" or "1" state. Quantum parallelism is the term used to describe the ability of computations to operate on both states simultaneously.

Examining a system of n qubits each with the two possible states $\{|0\rangle, |1\rangle\}$reveals the power of quantum information processing. An algorithm can operate on all of these configurations in parallel when the quantum system is placed into a superposition of all 2^n combinations, $\{|00...00\rangle, |00...01\rangle, ..., |11...11\rangle\}$. However, the unpredictable nature of the outcomes and the damage brought on by measurement constantly place limitations on quantum computing. The state "collapses" into the measurement result once a qubit has been measured to be either $|0\rangle$ or $|1\rangle$, and it will only produce the same output after that. As a result, the result is probabilistic in nature (i.e., a distribution of results is produced by evolving and measuring the same system multiple times, of which the most likely result can be considered the output of the calculation) and we can only obtain a limited amount of information from it.

For this reason, developing strong algorithms for a quantum computer is challenging. In a d-dimensional Hilbert space $\mathcal{H}_d$, the discrete states of a quantum object—like the polarization or energy level described above—are represented mathematically as vectors. Vectors in $\mathcal{H}_2 \otimes ... \otimes \mathcal{H}_2$ can be used to describe a system of n qubits that encodes a binary string of the same length when d equals 2 for qubits.

H2 (keep in mind that a "qudit" is the d-dimensional generalization of a qubit). Unitary operators U with the condition $U^{\dagger}U = 1$ where $U^{\dagger}$ where $U^{\dagger}$ is the Hermitian conjugate, are used to express vector-to-vector transformations that adhere to the general laws of quantum theory. A series of these operations on an input quantum state can be used to express quantum algorithms, and these unitary transformations define the dynamics of the quantum system.

These unitary transformations are referred to as "quantum gates" in quantum computation because they are analogous to classical gates that work with bits. The X-gate, which alters a qubit's state, the Z-gate, which modifies the sign of its amplitude, and the Hadamard or H-gate, which produces a superposition $\frac{1}{\sqrt{2}}(|0\rangle \pm |1\rangle)$ from $|0\rangle$ $(+)$ or $|1\rangle$ $(-)$ respectively, are a few examples of common 1-qubit gates.

The controlled-NOT operation (cNOT) of a central 2-qubit gate only changes the state of a second qubit when the first one is in state $|1\rangle$. In actuality, the cNOT and conventional single qubit gates provide a universal set for quantum processing. A more general description of a quantum gate that comes from the Schrodinger equation in fundamental quantum theory can be expressed by the unitary transformation $U = e^{-i\mathrm{H}t}$, where H stands for a Hamiltonian Hermitian operator.

16.4 Applications of Quantum Machine Learning

Numerous industries and fields could undergo significant change as a result of quantum machine learning. Among the significant uses are:

Finance: Quantum machine learning may be applied to portfolio optimization, fraud detection, and predictive modeling in the financial markets. It can analyze vast amounts of financial data to identify patterns and enhance projections.

Healthcare: Quantum machine learning techniques may aid in the creation and discovery of new medications by simulating molecule shapes and properties. They may also promote tailored medicine by improving diagnosis and treatment by analyzing complex genetic data.

Cybersecurity: Quantum technology can provide secure data transit by enhancing encryption and decryption methods. Post-quantum cryptography, advanced cryptography, and quantum key distribution by quantum machine learning can all be used to protect sensitive data.

Quantum image and natural language processing: Quantum algorithms may be used to enhance tasks such as object identification, picture recognition, text synthesis, and language translation. They are better at handling complex data and coming up with conclusions that are more accurate and relevant to the situation.

Logistics and Optimization: Quantum machine learning has the potential to handle complicated optimization problems such as supply chain optimization, truck routing, and resource allocation. It might identify the best solutions faster than conventional methods, boosting output and reducing costs.

16.5 Machine Learning Classification Algorithm

As is well known, the Supervised Machine Learning algorithm falls within the general categories of classification and regression algorithms. We have forecasted the output for continuous values using regression techniques, but classification algorithms are required to predict categorical values.

The classification algorithm: what is it?

Using training data, the classification algorithm—a Supervised Learning technique—identifies the category of fresh observations. A program learns from the provided dataset or observations in classification, after which it groups or classes fresh observations. For example, "yes" or "no," "0" or "1," "spam" or "not," "cat" or "dog," etc. Classes may be referred to as categories, labels, or goals.

The output variable of classification, as opposed to regression, is a category rather than a value, such as "green or blue," "fruit or animal," etc. The classification algorithm uses labeled input data, which implies it contains input with the appropriate output, because it is a supervised learning technique.

y=f(x), where y = categorical output

Email Spam Detector is the greatest illustration of a machine learning classification method.

Classification algorithms are mostly used to anticipate the output for categorical data, and their primary objective is to determine the category of a given dataset.

The diagram below can help you better understand classification methods. Class A and Class B are the two classes shown in the diagram below. These classes share characteristics with one another and differ from other classes.

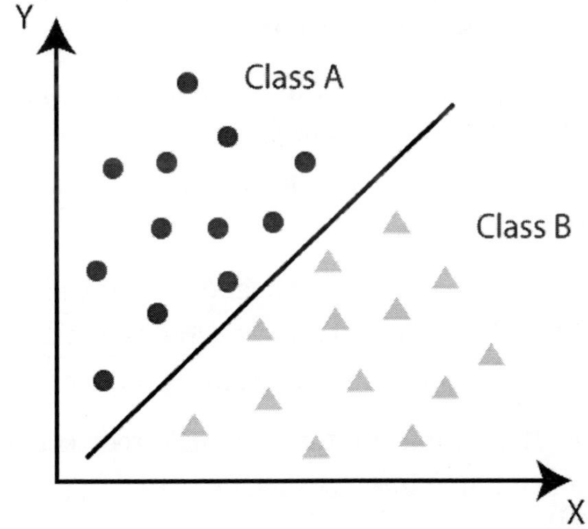

Fig.16.1 Classification methods – Characteristics and Differences.

A classifier is the algorithm that applies classification to a dataset. Classifications come in two varieties:

Binary Classifier: This type of classifier is used when there are only two feasible solutions to the classification problem. For instance, CAT or DOG, SPAM or NOT SPAM, MALE or FEMALE, YES or NO, etc.

Multi-class Classifier: This type of classifier is used when a classification task has more than two possible outcomes. For instance, there are classifications for different kinds of music and crops.

Algorithm Types for Machine Learning Classification:

There are two primary categories into which algorithms can be further separated:

Linear Models

Vector machines that

Support logistic regression

Non-linear Models

K-Nearest Adjacents

SVM kernel

Naïve Bayes Classification Using Decision Trees

Classification by Random Forest

16.6 Machine Learning Using Logistic Regression

Among the most widely used machine learning algorithms, logistic regression falls under the category of supervised learning. With a given collection of independent factors, it is used to predict the categorical dependent variable.

The output of a categorical dependent variable is predicted via logistic regression. As a result, the result needs to be a discrete or category value. Yes or No, 0 or 1, true or false, etc., can be used, but probabilistic values that fall between 0 and 1 are provided rather than the precise values of 0 and 1.

With the exception of their respective applications, logistic regression and linear regression are very similar. While logistic regression is used to solve classification difficulties, linear regression is used to solve regression problems.

In logistic regression, a "S" shaped logistic function that predicts two maximum values (0 or 1) is fitted rather than a regression line.

The logistic function's curve shows the probability of things like whether or not the cells are malignant, whether or not a mouse is obese based on its weight, etc.

Because it can generate probabilities and categorize new data using both continuous and discrete datasets, logistic regression is an important machine learning technique.

Classifying observations using various data formats is possible with logistic regression, which also makes it simple to identify the best variables to employ. The logistic function is depicted in the graphic below:

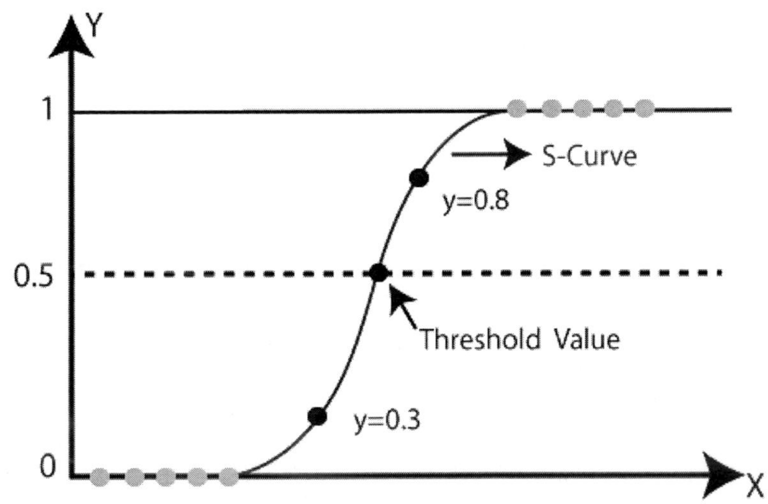

Fig.16.2 Logistic function.

A mathematical function called the logistic function (also known as the sigmoid function) is used to translate anticipated values into probabilities.

It converts any real number between 0 and 1 into another value.

The logistic regression curve takes the shape of a "S" since its value must fall between 0 and 1, which is the upper limit. The logistic function or sigmoid function are other names for the S-form curve.

The threshold value, which indicates the likelihood of either 0 or 1, is a notion used in logistic regression. For example, numbers above the threshold tend toward 1, and values below the threshold tend toward 0.

Logistic Regression Assumptions: The dependent variable needs to be categorical.

Multi-collinearity should not exist in the independent variable.

Equation for Logistic Regression: The linear regression equation can be used to derive the logistic regression equation. The following are the mathematical procedures to obtain the equations for logistic regression:

We are aware that the straight line equation can be expressed as follows:

$$y = b_0 + b_1 x_1 + b_2 x_2 + b_3 x_3 + \cdots + b_n x_n$$

Since y can only be between 0 and 1 in logistic regression, let's divide the equation above by (1-y):

$$\frac{y}{1-y}; \text{0 for y= 0, and infinity for y=1}$$

However, we require a range of -[infinity] to +[infinity], and the logarithm of the equation will be as follows:

$$log\left[\frac{y}{1-y}\right] = b_0 + b_1x_1 + b_2x_2 + b_3x_3 + \cdots + b_nx_n$$

The last equation for logistic regression is the one above.

Type of Logistic Regression: Three forms of logistic regression can be distinguished based on the categories:

Binomial: Only two possible dependent variable types, such as 0 or 1, Pass or Fail, etc., are allowed in binomial logistic regression.

Multinomial: The dependent variable in multinomial logistic regression may be one of three or more different unordered kinds, such as "cat," "dogs," or "sheep."

Ordinal: Three or more ordered dependent variable types, such as "low," "medium," or "high," are conceivable in ordinal logistic regression.

16.7 Machine Learning K-Nearest Neighbor (KNN) Algorithm

One of the most basic machine learning algorithms based on the supervised learning technique is K-Nearest Neighbor.

The K-NN algorithm places the new case into the category that is most similar to the existing categories based on the assumption that the new case and data are comparable to the available cases.

The K-NN method classifies a new data point based on similarity after storing all of the relevant data. This implies that the K-NN technique makes it simple to classify newly discovered data into a well-suited category.

Although the K-NN technique is mostly utilized for classification problems, it can also be used for regression.

Since K-NN is a non-parametric approach, it doesn't assume anything about the underlying data.

Because it stores the dataset and then executes an action on it at the time of classification, it is also known as a lazy learner algorithm. This is because it does not learn from the training set right away.

During the training phase, the KNN algorithm simply saves the dataset and, when receiving new data, classifies it into a category that is substantially comparable to the new data.

For instance, let's say we want to determine whether a picture of a species that resembles a cat or a dog is indeed a cat or a dog. Because the KNN method uses a similarity metric, we can utilize it for this identification. KNN model will identify the features of the new data set that are comparable to those of the photographs of cats and dogs, and it will classify the data according to the most similar features.

Why is a K-NN algorithm necessary?

Assuming that there are two categories—Category A and Category B—and that we have a new data point, x1, which of these categories will this data point fall under? A K-NN algorithm is required to address this kind of problem. We can quickly determine the category or class of a given dataset with the use of K-NN.

Examine the diagram below:

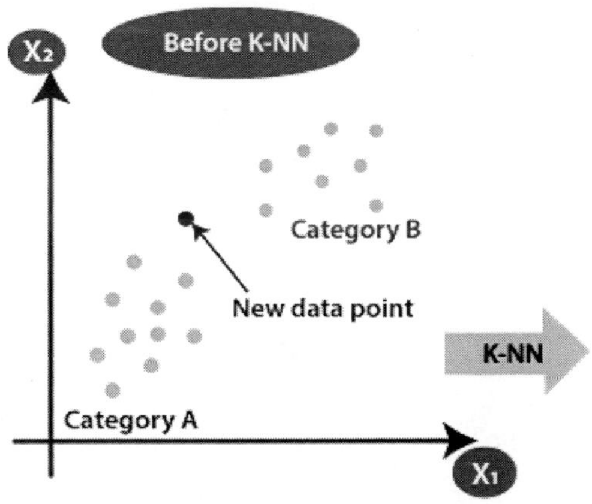

Fig.16.3 New data point categorization before K-NN implementation.

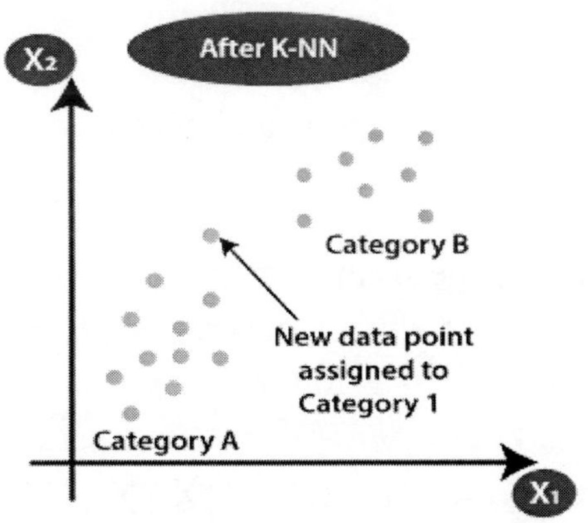

Fig.16.4 New data point categorization after K-NN implementation.

How does K-NN operate?

The following algorithm can be used to describe how the K-NN operates:

Step 1: Choose the neighbors' K number

Step 2: Determine the K number of neighbors' Euclidean distance.

Step 3: Determine the K closest neighbors using the Euclidean distance calculation.

Step 4: Determine how many data items fall into each category among these k neighbors.

Step 5: Put the new data points in the category where the neighbor count is at its highest.

Step 6: We have a finished model.

Let's say we need to assign a new data point to the appropriate category. Examine the picture below:

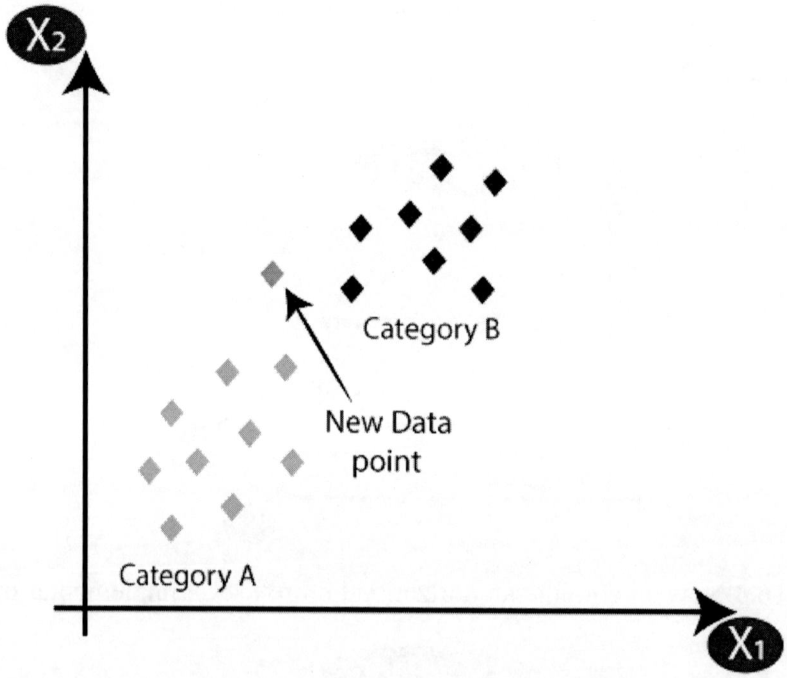

Fig.16.5 New data point assignment category.

In order to determine the number of neighbors, we will first select k=5.

The Euclidean distance between the data points will then be determined. The distance between two points, which we have already covered in geometry class, is known as the Euclidean distance. It can be computed as follows:

$$\text{Euclidean Distance between } A_1 \text{ and } B_2 = \sqrt{(X_2-X_1)^2+(Y_2-Y_1)^2}$$

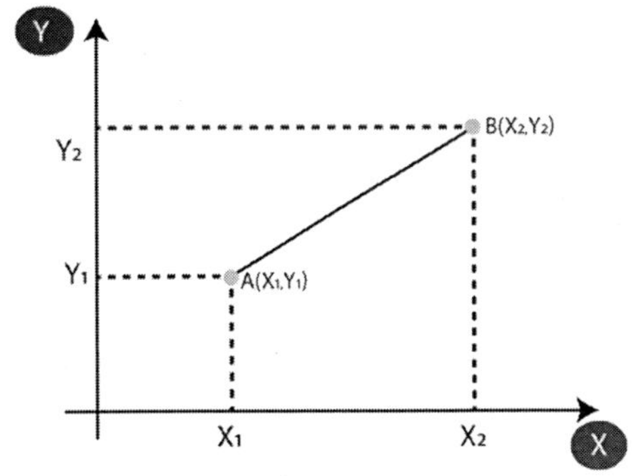

Fig.16.6 Determining Euclidean distance between the data points.

The closest neighbors were determined by computing the Euclidean distance; they were three in category A and two in category B.

Examine the picture below:

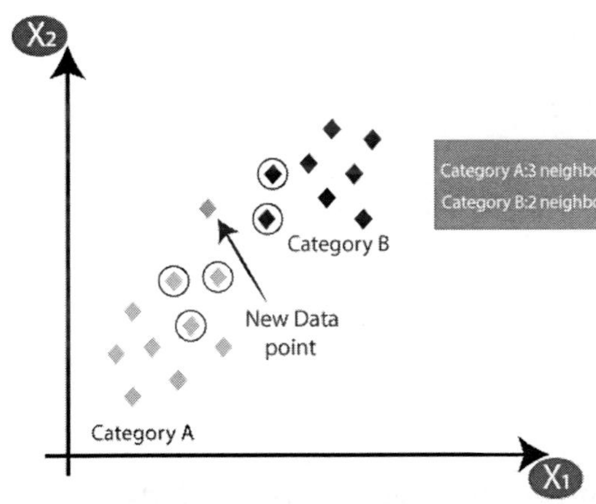

Fig.16.7 Determination of nearby neighbours by computing the Euclidean distance.

Since category A includes the three closest neighbors, this new data point must also fall under that category.

How do I choose the value of K in the K-NN Algorithm?

The following are some considerations to mind while picking the value of K in the K-NN algorithm.

- There is no specific method for determining the best value for "K", thus we must experiment with many values to get the best one. The most popular K value is 5.
- A very low K number, such as K=1 or K=2, might be noisy and cause the model to exhibit outlier effects.
- Large values for K are preferable, but they may provide some issues.

Advantages of KNN Algorithm:

Easy to implement.

It is robust to noisy training data.

It may be more successful if the training data is vast.

Disadvantages of the KNN algorithm:

Always needs to identify the value of K, which can be complex at times.

Calculating the distance between data points for all training samples incurs a substantial computational cost.

16.8 Support Vector Machine Algorithm.

Support Vector Machine, or SVM, is a popular supervised learning technique that is used for both classification and regression tasks. However, it is mostly utilized for classification problems in machine learning.

The SVM algorithm's purpose is to find the best line or decision boundary that can divide an n-dimensional space into classes, allowing us to conveniently place fresh data points in the correct category in the future. The optimal choice boundary is known as a hyperplane.

SVM selects the extreme points/vectors that contribute to the creation of the hyperplane. These extreme examples are referred to as support vectors, and the algorithm is known as Support Vector Machine.

Consider the diagram below, which shows two different groups classified using a decision boundary or hyperplane:

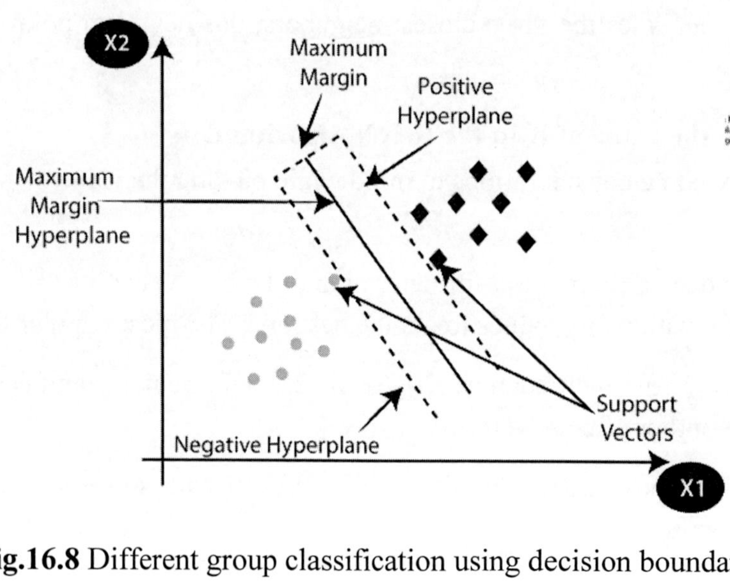

Fig.16.8 Different group classification using decision boundary.

The example we used in the KNN classifier demonstrates how SVM works. Suppose we observe an unusual cat with some canine attributes; if we want a model that can properly determine whether it is a cat or a dog, we can develop one using the SVM technique. We will first train our model with a large number of photos of cats and dogs so that it can learn about their various characteristics before testing it on this weird critter. So, when the support vector sets a decision border between these two data points (cat and dog) and selects extreme cases (support vectors), it will see the extreme case of cat and dog. Based on the support vectors, it will be classified as a cat.

The SVM algorithm is useful for face detection, picture classification, text categorization, and other tasks.

Types of SVM

There are two types of support vector machines:

Linear SVM: Linear SVM is used for linearly separable data, which implies that if a dataset can be classified into two classes using a single straight line, it is considered linearly separable data, and the classifier employed is the Linear SVM classifier.

Non-linear SVM: Non-linear SVM is used for non-linearly separated data, which implies that if a dataset cannot be classified using a straight line, it is considered non-linear data, and the classifier employed is known as the Non-linear SVM classifier.

The SVM algorithm uses hyperplanes and support vectors.

Hyperplane: Multiple lines/decision boundaries can be used to separate classes in n-dimensional space, but we must choose which decision boundary is appropriate for classifying data points. The best boundary is referred to as the SVM hyperplane.

The hyperplane's dimensions are determined by the features in the dataset; for example, if there are two features (as shown in the image), the hyperplane will be a straight line. If there are three features, the hyperplane will be a two-dimensional plane.

We always generate a hyperplane with a maximum margin, which represents the maximum distance between data points.

Support vectors.

The data points or vectors that are closest to the hyperplane and affect its position are referred to as Support Vectors. Since these vectors support the hyperplane, they are referred to as support vectors.

What is the mechanism behind SVM?

Linear SVM:

An example will help you understand how the SVM algorithm works. Suppose we have a dataset with two tags (green and blue) and two features (x1 and x2). We need a classifier that can categorize the coordinate pair (x1, x2) as green or blue. Check out the image below:

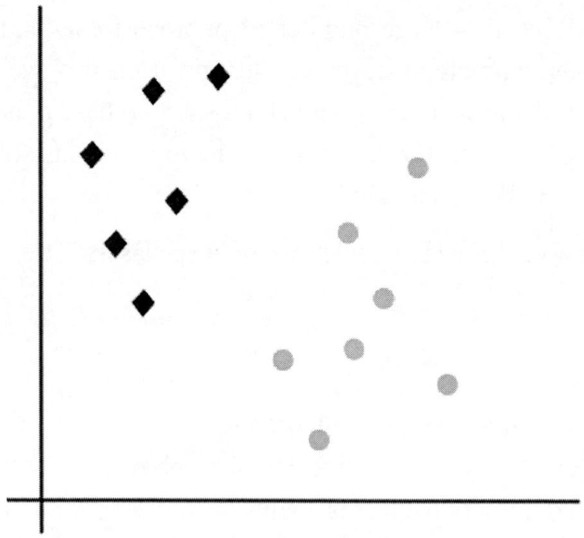

Fig.16.9 Dataset categorization.

As it is a two-dimensional space, we may easily split these two classes with a straight line. However, these classes can be separated by more than one line. Consider the following image.

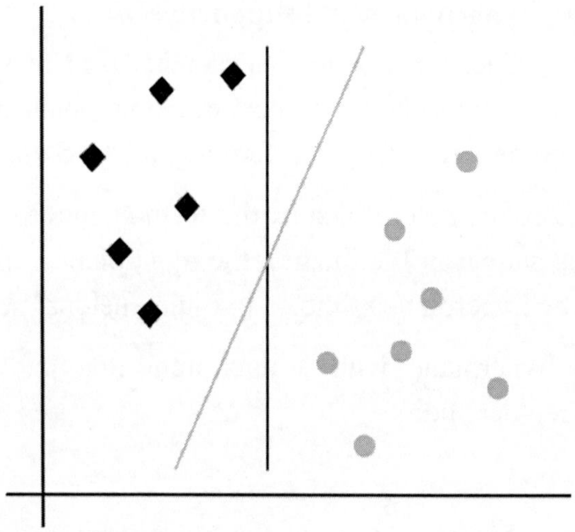

Fig.16.10 Two dimensional class segregation.

As a result, the SVM method aids in the identification of the best line or decision boundary; this optimal boundary or region is referred to as a hyperplane. The SVM method determines the nearest point between the lines from both classes. These points are known as support vectors. The distance between the vectors and the hyperplane is known as margin. The purpose of SVM is to maximize this margin. The hyperplane with the largest margin is known as the ideal hyperplane.

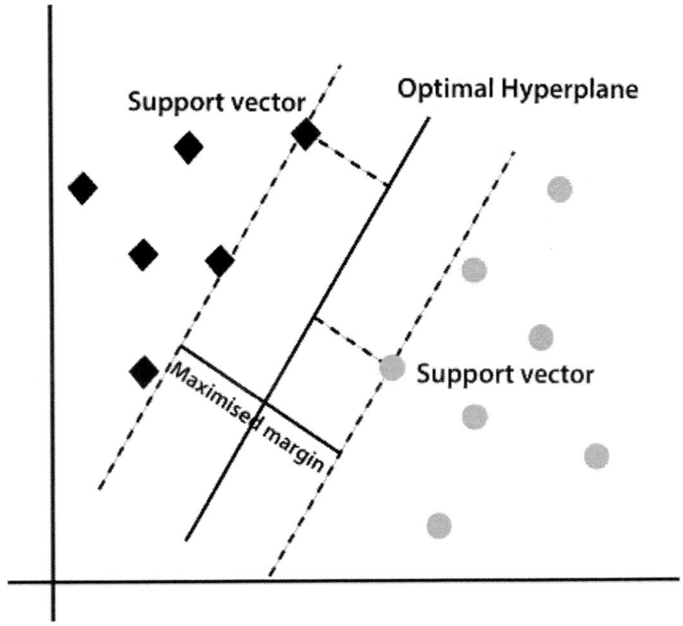

Fig.16.11 Depiction of Support vector, hyperplane and maximized margin.

Non-linear SVM:

If data is linearly arranged, we can separate it using a straight line; however, non-linear data cannot be separated by a single straight line. Consider the following image.

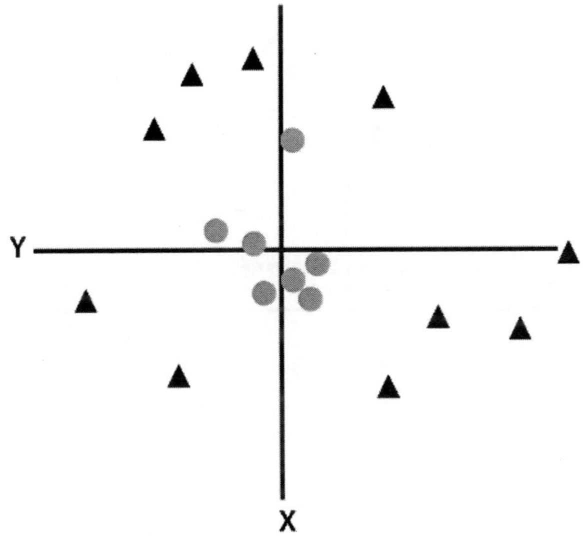

Fig.16.12 Non-linear data separation.

So, to separate these data sets, we need to add another dimension. We used two dimensions for linear data, x and y, but for non-linear data, we will add a third dimension, z. It can be computed as:

$z=x^2+y^2$

Adding the third dimension transforms the sample space into the image below:

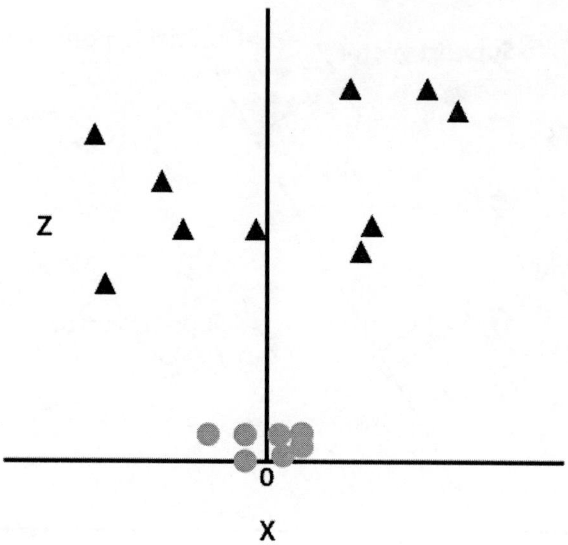

Fig.16.13 Transformation of sample space after adding third dimension.

So now, SVM will divide the datasets into classes in the following manner. Consider the following image.

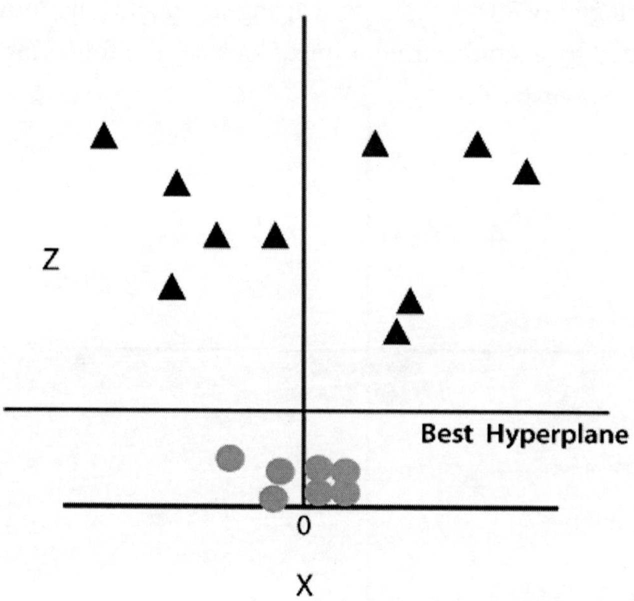

Fig.16.14 Division of datasets into classes.

Since we are in three dimensions, it appears to be a plane parallel to the x-axis. If we translate it to 2D space with z=1, it becomes as follows:

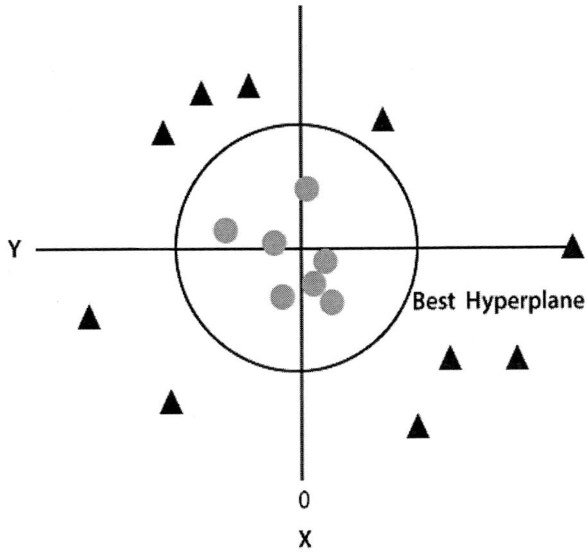

Fig.16.15 Three dimensional transformation.

In the case of non-linear data, we obtain a circumference of radius 1.

16.9 Naive Bayes Classifier Algorithm

The Naïve Bayes algorithm is a supervised learning method that applies Bayes theorem to solve classification issues.

It is mostly used in text classification, with a high-dimensional training dataset.

The Naïve Bayes Classifier is a simple and effective classification technique for generating fast machine learning models with quick predictions.

It is a probabilistic classifier, which implies that it makes predictions based on the probability of an object.

Naïve Bayes algorithms are commonly used for spam filtration, sentiment analysis, and article classification.

What is the significance of the name Naïve Bayes?

The Naïve Bayes algorithm is derived from the phrases Naïve and Bayes, which can be described as:

The term "Naïve" refers to the assumption that a feature's recurrence is independent of other features. For example, if the fruit is classified based on color, shape, and flavor, a red, spherical, and sweet fruit is identified as apple. As a result, each feature contributes to identifying it as an apple without relying on the others.

Bayes' Theorem is the basis for its name.

The Bayes' Theorem, often known as Bayes' Rule or Bayes' Law, determines the probability of a hypothesis based on prior knowledge. It is contingent on the conditional probability.

The formula for Bayes' theorem is as follows:

$$P(A|B)=\frac{P(B|A)P(A)}{P(B)}$$

Where,

P(A|B) represents the posterior probability of hypothesis A on observed event B.

P(B|A) stands for Likelihood probability, which is the probability of evidence provided that a hypothesis is correct.

P(A) stands for Prior Probability: the probability of a hypothesis before witnessing the data.

P(B) represents Marginal Probability: Probability of Evidence.

The example below demonstrates how the Naïve Bayes Classifier works.

Assume we have a dataset of weather conditions and the associated target variable "Play". So, given this dataset, we need to decide whether or not to play on a specific day based on the weather. To remedy this problem, follow the instructions below:

Transform the provided dataset into frequency tables.

Create a likelihood table by calculating the probability of supplied characteristics.

Use the Bayes theorem to compute the posterior probability.

Advantages of Naïve Bayes Classifier:

Naïve Bayes is a fast and simple machine learning technique for predicting dataset classes.

- It can be used for both binary and multi-class classification.
- In multi-class predictions, it outperforms the other algorithms.
- It is the most used approach for text categorization problems.

Drawbacks of Naïve Bayes Classifier:

Naive Bayes implies that all features are independent or unrelated, therefore it cannot learn the link between them.

The Naïve Bayes Classifier is used for credit scoring.

It is used to classify medical data.

The Naïve Bayes Classifier's eagerness to learn makes it suitable for real-time predictions.

It is used for text categorization tasks such as spam filtering and sentiment analysis.

Types of Naïve Bayes Models:

There are three types of Naive Bayes models, which are described below:

Gaussian: The Gaussian model implies that characteristics have a normal distribution. This means that if predictors accept continuous values rather than discrete values, the model assumes that they are drawn from the Gaussian distribution.

Multinomial: The Multinomial Naïve Bayes classifier is used for multinomial distributed data. It is generally used to solve document classification difficulties; it indicates which category a certain document belongs to, such as sports, politics, education, and so on.

The classifier's predictions are based on word frequency.

Bernoulli: The Bernoulli classifier functions similarly to the Multinomial classifier, but the predictor variables are independent Boolean variables. For example, whether or not a specific word appears in a given document. This methodology is also popular for document categorization tasks.

16.10 The Distinction between Regression and Classification

Table 16.1 Differences of regression and classification algorithm.

Regression Algorithm	Classification Algorithm
Regression requires that the output variable be continuous or have a real value.	A discrete value must be the output variable in classification.
The continuous output variable (y) and the input value (x) must be mapped by the regression technique.	Mapping the input value (x) with the discrete output variable (y) is the classification algorithm's job.
Continuous data is used with regression algorithms.	Discrete data are employed with classification algorithms.
Finding the best fit line that can more accurately anticipate the output is the goal of regression.	The goal of classification is to identify the decision boundary that can separate the dataset into distinct classes.
Weather prediction, house price prediction, and other regression problems can be resolved with regression algorithms.	Classification challenges including speech recognition, cancer cell identification, spam email identification, and more can be resolved with classification algorithms.
There are two subtypes of regression algorithms: linear and non-linear.	Binary classifiers and multi-class classifiers are two categories into which the classification algorithms fall.

16.11 Software Architecture for Quantum Machine Learning.

In the current Noisy Intermediate-Scale Quantum (NISQ) era, quantum computing is plagued by scale restrictions and noise, but it still has enormous potential to speed machine learning for certain challenges. However, present machine learning platforms do not effectively account for quantum computing features, resulting in the absence of a fully integrated quantum machine learning environment. As a result, this section suggests a software architecture specifically tailored for the quantum machine learning platform, with the goal of providing development tools that assist quantum machine learning throughout its life cycle.

The user narrative technique is used to examine the software requirements of the quantum machine learning platform, followed by the multi-view software architecture method to design the platform architectural blueprint. To evaluate the architecture's effectiveness, it was implemented as a specification for quantum reinforcement learning (QRL) and a quantum convolutional neural network (QNN). The outcome of the architecture is suitable for combining quantum computing and machine learning.

16.12 Requirement analysis for the quantum machine learning platform

Analyzing the platform's software needs is the initial stage in designing the architecture of the quantum machine learning platform. The study of what the system must accomplish functionally to satisfy users' business needs is known as software requirements analysis. The software requirement analysis for the quantum machine learning platform is the main topic of this part, which is based on the quantum machine learning life-cycle.

We must choose the preferred software development paradigm before we can begin software requirements analysis. starting with the popular "Waterfall Model," moving on to the Agile development model, and finally ending with the DevOps paradigm. Models for software development have developed into a variety of styles. Three presumptions form the foundation of the conventional "Waterfall Model": i) Users are well aware of their desires. ii) Developers have a thorough understanding of user preferences. iii) Throughout the development phase, requirements remain constant.

These three presumptions, however, do not accurately reflect the situation, and the products that the product manager creates after speaking with users frequently diverge greatly from what is actually required. For creative projects with ambiguous requirements, employ the DevOps model that is focused on the evolution of user requirements. However, under the "Waterfall Model," needs are typically recorded as specs and use cases. This method is laborious, prone to errors, and time-consuming to create, therefore thus is not used in the DevOps development paradigm. Rather, describe requirements using stories. User stories often follow a three-stage structure and are written from the perspective of the user, such as: As a <Role>, I want to <Activity>, so that <Business value>

The requirements are typically divided into hierarchical categories using the "Epic to Feature to Story" approach. Since the primary task is to create the quantum machine learning platform's architecture, we should use the "Epic-Feature" structure and forgo the more in-depth Story in order to concentrate on the platform's sophisticated structure. Building a quantum machine learning system is essentially the same as building a classical one. The machine learning process is broken down into three stages, as seen in the figure below: data preparation, model development, and model deployment and application. Quantum machine learning differs from traditional methods in data processing and model building because of its quantum characteristics; in other words, the model creation phase reflects these changes. To examine the software needs for data services, model creation, and model deployment and application in quantum machine learning, this part is broken up into three subsections.

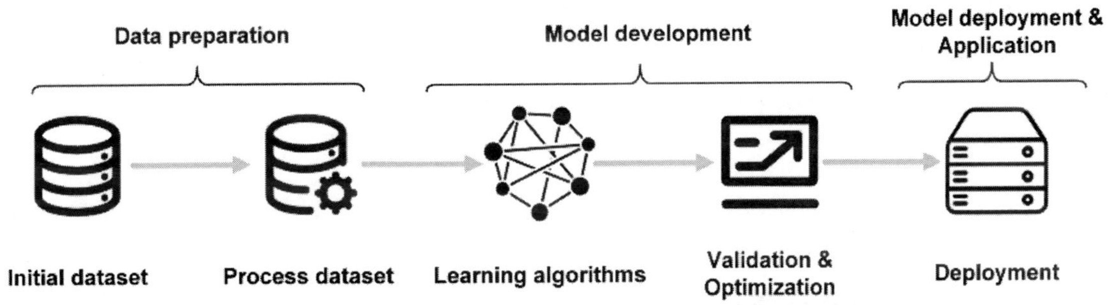

Fig.16.16 The quantum machine learning life cycle.

16.12.1 Data service in quantum machine learning

Since machine learning is essentially a branch of statistics that is inherently based on data, data is a crucial component of machine learning. Data, as used in machine learning, is the information that neural networks and other AI systems require in order to learn. Algorithms analyze the data to identify patterns and derive relationships. Higher training data results in higher model performance. The accuracy of a model can only be increased with a significant amount of high-quality data.

At this stage, the data must also be more specialized, fine-grained, and context-specific. For instance, distinct data formats involving a range of data types and labels may be needed for different machine learning domains. In these situations, data management services require a machine learning platform. Similarly, the importance of data is obvious in the newly developing subject of quantum machine learning. The figure below illustrates the entire data service process offered by a general machine learning platform.

It is primarily broken down into four steps: data creation, data processing, data labeling, and data inference.

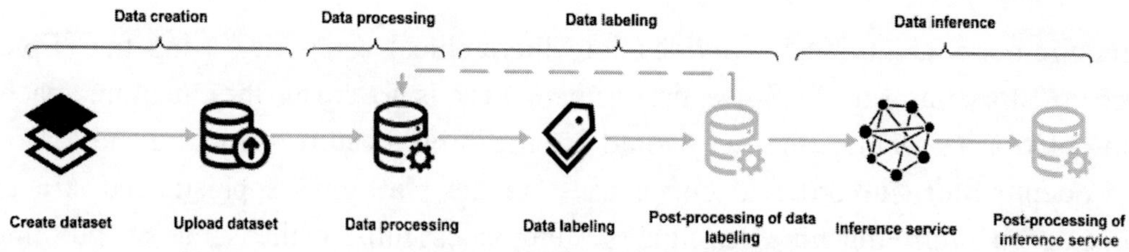

Fig.16.17 The entire quantum machine learning platform's data service procedure.

Create user stories based on a study of the quantum machine learning platform's data service process. First of all, Have a one-stop shop for managing data in quantum machine learning as a user to increase productivity, enhance data quality, and facilitate easy access to data. Divide it into phases and enumerate the characteristics in user stories pertaining to the quantum machine learning platform's data services:

1. The capacity to manage datasets as a user is necessary for the creation of the data required for quantum machine learning.
2. As a user, you must be able to process data in order for it to extract valuable characteristics.
3. The ability to identify datasets as a user so that my machine learning operations can begin.
4. After the model has been inferred, the user can control the data to assess whether the inference results match expectations.

16.12.2 Quantum machine learning model development

Since creating machine learning models is the most crucial aspect of the machine learning life cycle, building a quantum machine learning platform has also turned its attention to creating quantum machine learning models. Focus on the requirement analysis and related architecture design of this section, as it primarily combines quantum aspects and exhibits distinct characteristics from classical machine learning. There are two steps involved in creating quantum machine learning models, as opposed to their classical counterparts: the development stage and the experimental stage. Selecting input datasets, setting up the model, and setting up the environment are all part of the development stage.

Creating training activities, keeping track of them, and assessing and reviewing the training outcomes are all part of the experimental stage. The life-cycle of model development in a quantum machine learning platform consists of these two phases.

The model preparation phase and the experimental stage, which are connected to the quantum variational circuit (VQC) and the quantum hardware, respectively, are where the quantum qualities are mostly represented throughout this entire process, as illustrated in the figure below.

The development stage described above refers to the quantum-classical hybrid machine learning model, which combines quantum and classical models. The term "quantum model" refers to the Variational Quantum Circuit (VQC), which is a type of quantum circuit made up of gates with differentiable parameters and used in quantum machine learning. Quantum machine learning scientists often use the term "quantum neural networks" to compare VQC to classical neural networks. VQC takes quantum data sets or quantum encoded classical data as inputs, transforms them using quantum gates with differentiable parameters, and converts them to classical data by measurement.

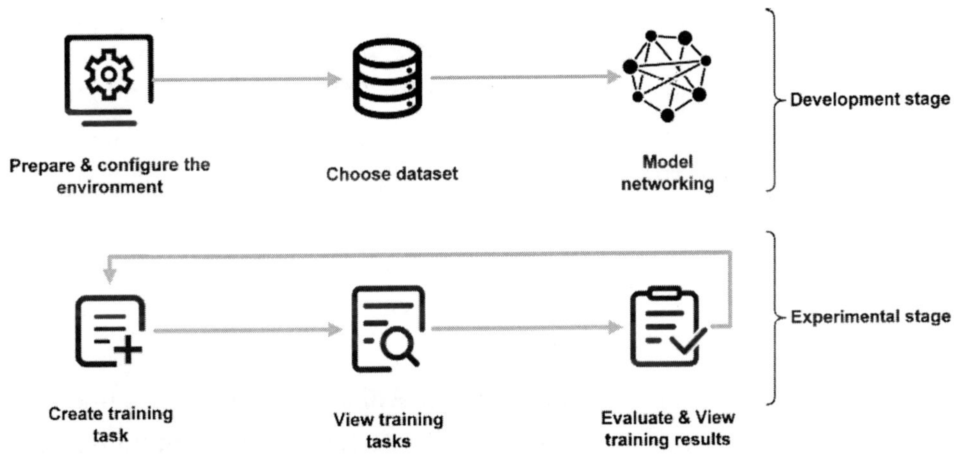

Fig.16.18 Full process of model generation in the quantum machine learning platform.

The classical model receives measured data and calculates the loss value using the usual loss function. The gradient of the model is calculated based on the loss function value. Model parameters, including quantum and classical models, are then updated. Figure shows the detailed process.

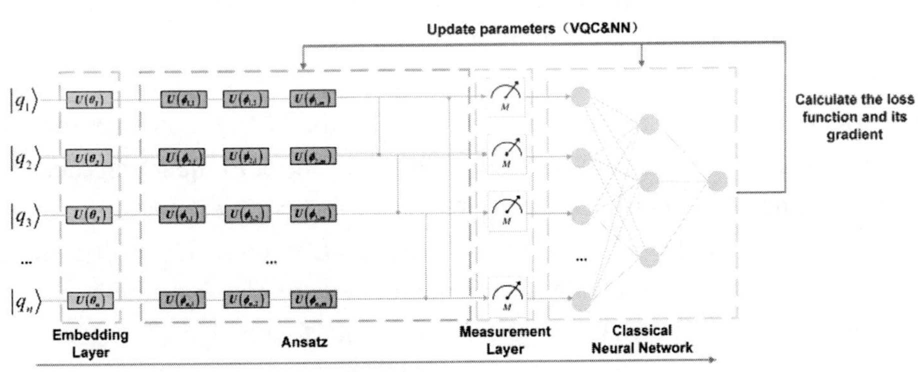

Fig.16.19 Process of quantum-classical hybrid machine learning model.

The picture depicts a quantum neural network with three components: encoding, variational, and measurement layers. The encoding layer encodes conventional data into quantum data, often known as "embedding." The embedding layer uses input samples as parameters and optional parameter weighting to encode characteristics into the quantum state. The variational layer is a trainable circuit, often known as an Ansatz. An Ansatz is made up of many quantum gates that act on specific wires and have freely differentiable parameters. The topology is comparable to classical neural networks, allowing us to customize gate types and free parameters as needed. The measurement layer involves one or more observables that act on specific circuits to generate measurement expectations.

The quantum circuit layer is similar to classical neural network layers, allowing for customization based on experimental needs. This modular approach simplifies the construction of quantum machine learning models. Users should be able to freely model networking and develop VQC. Embedding methods include amplitude and angle coding, among others. Ansatz kinds include the Strongly EntanglingLayer, which generates highly entangled quantum states, the RandomLayer, which generates random quantum gates, and the measurement layer, which can use various measurement bases. The VQC can tackle various problems depending on how these levels are combined. As a result, customers require the platform to provide visual modeling and enable the networking of quantum-hybrid machine learning models through the drag and drop of network components. Furthermore, the platform requires interactive modeling of model networking through programming of several quantum AI frameworks.

For the aforementioned quantum-classical hybrid machine learning models to function in a genuine quantum context, quantum hardware is necessary, as is quantum data storage. The majority of hybrid machine learning models in the NISQ era use quantum simulators to simulate quantum features before running them on traditional computing hardware.

However, this intermediate step is not required in a quantum environment. Quantum settings have their own specialized processors known as QPUs, which are comparable to the CPUs and GPUs used in conventional environments. On quantum computers, which are often made up of low-level qubits and quantum gate sequences assembled from high-level quantum operations carried out by platform users, QPU is utilized to process quantum instructions. We can comprehend that the operation of quantum and classical computing systems is essentially the same; however, the NISQ era's quantum-classical hybrid model necessitates the cooperative operation of both quantum and classical devices, which calls for specific platform support. The physical architecture view in Section will provide an explanation of the relevant architectural design for this section. Analyzing the user story requirements for the model development portion of the quantum machine learning platform is what we perform with the foundation of VQC, just like in the previous subsection.

The user story requirements for the model development portion of the quantum machine learning platform are the first thing we perform using the VQC foundation, just like in the previous section. Three phases are involved: Create quantum machine learning models as a user, allowing it to carry out the model's development and testing phases. Next, deconstruct Epic and enumerate Stories:

1. To begin the machine learning training task, as a user, complete basic pre-development tasks (such setting up the environment and choosing a dataset).
2. The ability to network the quantum machine learning model as a user to enable model implementation.
3. The model can be trained by the user, allowing it to test different combinations of data, techniques, and hyperparameters.

16.12.2 Quantum Machine Learning Model Deployment

Model inference, the process by which users quickly apply the learned information to unseen data after training a quantum machine learning model, requires the usage of the trained outcomes. Users can choose a previously trained quantum AI model for immediate deployment as a quantum AI application and create quantum AI apps within the quantum machine learning platform after a quantum machine learning model has been developed.

Online services and batch services are typically the two main contexts for implementing AI application services. By delivering the model as a web service, online services allow users to obtain the inference results via a console or API.

Until batch data processing is finished, batch services carry out inference on batch data.

The Fig. below, which depicts the three primary processes of AI model inference—developing AI applications, deploying AI apps, and inference services—illustrates the deployment and application of quantum machine learning models to applications.

The model deployment process follows a three-phase Epic: It can employ a quantum machine learning model for inference if the user has the ability to deploy and use the model.

The Story is listed here:

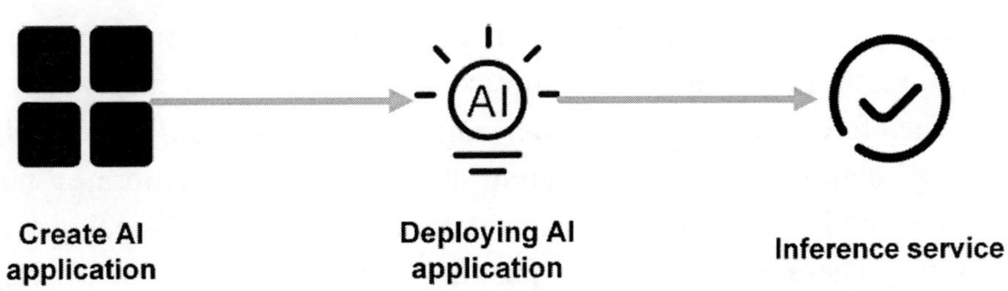

Fig.16.20 The entire quantum machine learning model deployment procedure.

1. I can load my model as a user into the quantum machine learning platform's model repository to enable it to create practical AI applications.
2. In order for the AI application to register as an available service, the user must deploy it as a container instance in a resource pool.
3. Have user access to the installed AI application so that business processes can incorporate AI reasoning capabilities.

16.13 Design of the quantum machine learning platform's architecture

Translating the requirements into the design is the next stage after performing a requirements analysis for the quantum machine learning platform.

The design, development, and upkeep of artificial systems present specific difficulties as they get more complicated. Software engineers now have a much easier time handling the complexity of systems because to the development of software architecture. Software engineers can have a better understanding of the fundamental and crucial characteristics of the system in terms of behavior, composition, and evolution by envisioning the architecture and outlining the different components that make it up. This consequently enables them to concentrate on issues like the software's viability, usefulness, and maintainability.

The use of architecture descriptions for system architecture analysis, design, and maintenance is the focus of the ISO/IEC 42010 standard. It offers a method for building software architecture iteratively over the course of the software development lifecycle. As an organizational and methodological guide for software architecture design, an architectural framework provides an organized approach to architectural design within this standard. These days, a number of software architectural approaches, such the ppen group architecture framework (TOGAF model) and Kruchten's "4+1" perspective model, suggest architecture frameworks that satisfy the aforementioned requirements. Aspects of the system are the emphasis of each of the several architecture viewpoints and accompanying architecture views that are included in these architectural frameworks.

The "4+1" architectural view model, for instance, is concerned with the logic, development, process, physical, and scene perspectives of the system, each of which has a specific representation that goes with it. These opinions aid in making sure that the design of the software architecture can accommodate the demands of different stakeholders. Therefore, to ensure a thorough consideration of the business requirements, functionality, and deployment of the quantum machine learning platform, a number of existing software architectural methodologies are integrated when designing a blueprint for the platform. These methodologies include logical views, physical views, and business views. This adds to the quantum machine learning platform's overall architecture.

A logical view is one that describes the functional elements of a system by concentrating on its high-level modules and functions rather than going into the finer points of implementation. It is usually used to show the structure of a system by providing a high-level illustration of the functions and modules that make up the system. The quantum machine learning platform's software architectural design is shown in the image below from the standpoint of logical architecture. It simplifies development, maintenance, and testing by breaking down the quantum machine learning platform into manageable parts in a bottom-up order, starting with low-level hardware and working up to high-level interfaces. The platform's diverse hardware components, such as the CPUs and GPUs for classical computing, the QPU for quantum computing, and the memory utilized for quantum/classical (Q/C) storage, are located in the heterogeneous resource layer at the bottom.

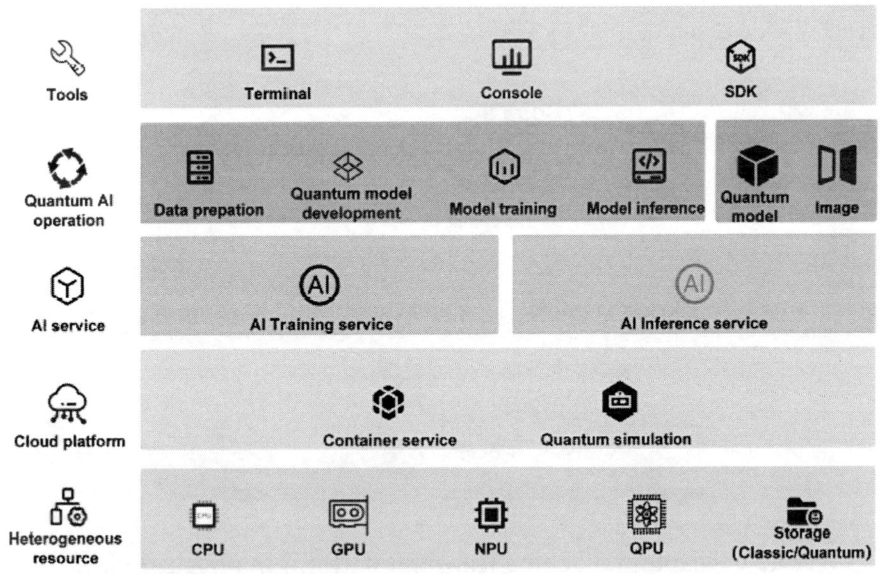

Fig.16.21 Quantum machine learning platform's logic view.

The basic platform sits above the resource layer and is responsible for managing a variety of heterogeneous resources as well as offering a range of platform operation and maintenance services. The quantum simulator, which can convert classical operations into quantum operations and run on classical hardware, is one of them. It is implemented as a container service on the basic platform, establishing the groundwork for the quantumclassical hybrid machine learning model to operate in a classical setting. Task scheduling and resource allocation are made possible by the fundamental platform's interfaces for AI services, such as training and inference services, which are interoperable with popular quantum AI frameworks. This aids users in improving the efficiency of work execution and resource use.

The platform's top layer is called the tool layer, and its console and command-line tools enable rapid platform management and visual operations. The platform's SDK also makes it easier for users to develop unique quantum machine learning solutions. The term "physical view" describes how a system is implemented and operated using actual hardware and software. In order to guarantee the system's efficient operation, it concentrates on the hardware devices and physical components. The quantum machine learning platform's software architecture design is shown in below Fig. from the standpoint of physical architecture.

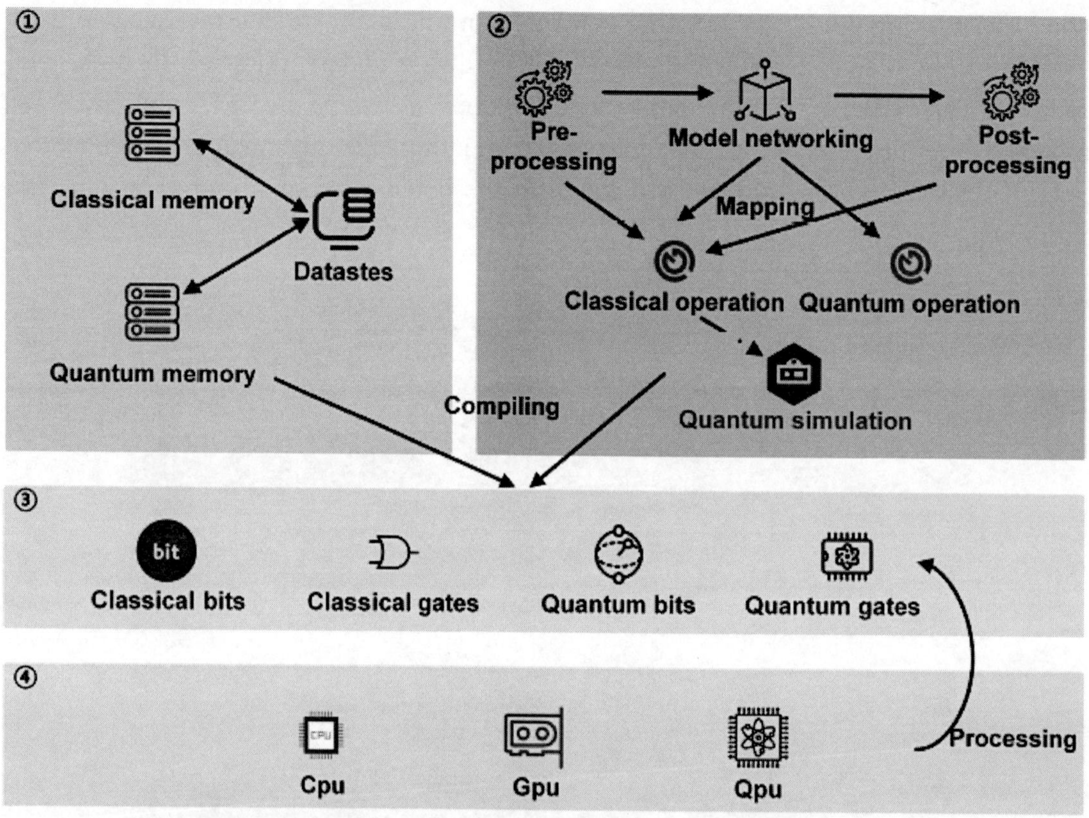

Fig.16.22 Quantum machine learning platform in physical view.

The storage of Q/C data services is the first component. As we already know, bit gates are used to carry out data arithmetic and processing operations, and bits are the lowest unit of data storage and processing in classical computers. Similarly, qubits and quantum gates are the equivalent of bits and logic gates in quantum computers. Here, we won't get into their specific quantum characteristics. The platform makes use of a variety of computational resources, primarily CPU, GPU, and QPU. Many machine learning systems currently incorporate CPU and GPU, two popular accelerators in the field of machine learning that can greatly increase computational speed. On the other hand, the QPU is the accelerator utilized in quantum machine learning.

With the use of quantum gates, a QPU may manipulate quantum bits and carry out quantum operations. It can execute measurement operations on quantum bits following computation execution and produce superposition and entangled states of quantum bits. An overview of the compilation of sophisticated operations in the quantum machine learning platform into machine instructions is given in the second and third sections of the aforementioned figure.

These correspond to classical and quantum operations since the creation of quantum-classical hybrid machine learning models incorporates both quantum and classical models in addition to preprocessing and post-processing the models. While quantum operations can be carried out on actual quantum hardware or in a simulated quantum environment, classical operations are inherently carried out on classical hardware.

While the latter uses quantum hardware directly for quantum operations, the former uses quantum simulators to simulate the evolution of quantum systems and is then processed using classical hardware devices. In order to meet the demands of quantum machine learning in the NISQ era, the coexistence of classical and quantum processes necessitates the cooperative processing of classical hardware and quantum hardware. A system's business functions are described using a business view, which emphasizes how the system satisfies business needs and how business procedures work.

The quantum machine learning platform's business architectural design is shown in the figure below from the standpoint of business functions. Prior section provided a detailed explanation of the quantum machine learning platform's business operations. Hence carried out a business design for the platform based on the research of the software needs, primarily incorporating modules such Q/C data services, the creation of quantum machine learning models, training activities, deployment tasks, and AI asset management.

In order to satisfy the requirements of the quantum machine learning life-cycle, from data preparation to post-inference data management, Q/C data services primarily offer security for data in the quantum machine learning life-cycle, including data sets, feature engineering, and data annotation services.

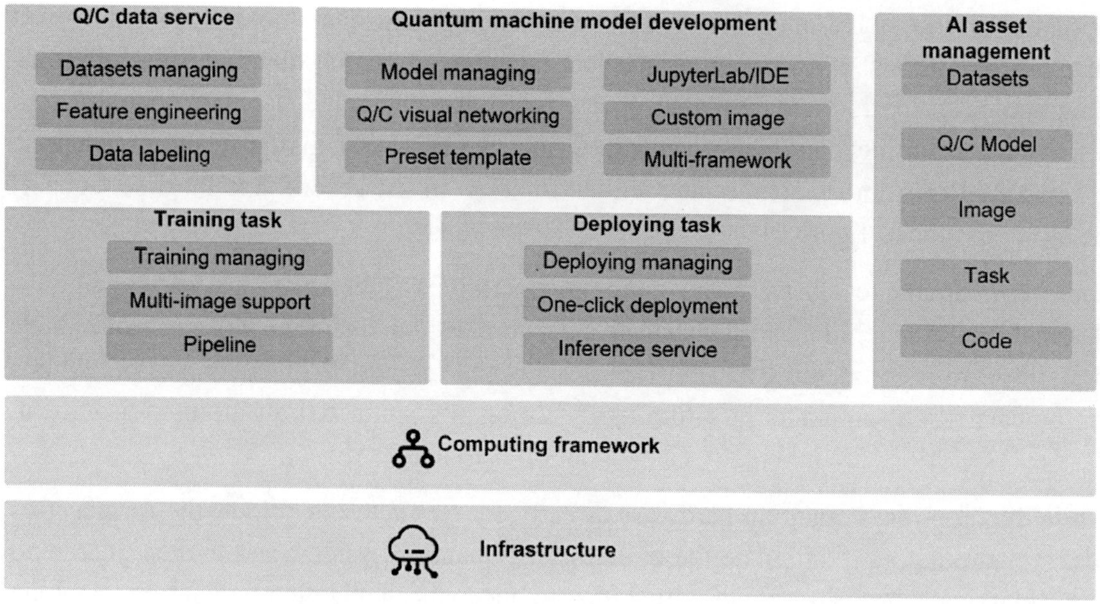

Fig.16.23 Business architectural design for the quantum machine.

The requirements of model creation, including a range of model modeling techniques, are satisfied by the quantum machine learning model development module. Drag-and-drop component modeling is supported by Q/C visual modeling services, and users can select VQC or classic neural network components for model networking tasks as needed without depending on code modeling. In addition, users can augment the visual modeling features by uploading own images or using the online IDE for code modeling. The module offers a range of quantum AI computing frameworks and pre-made machine learning templates, making it simple for users to get started right away. To help users swiftly navigate the quantum AI process, the training and deployment task module offers a pipeline service from machine learning training to deployment. The AI asset management module builds the quantum AI workflow by offering managed services for data sets, models, images, tasks, and code in addition to the quantum machine learning life-cycle. The platform architecture and computer framework, which support the business's implementation, are also necessary for the aforementioned primary functional components.

16.14 Quantum Machine Learning Platform Application

The software architectural design for the quantum classical hybrid machine learning platform was presented in the preceding sections. To show that the architecture design is good, it was decided to create quantum classical hybrid machine learning based on the design specifications and test its experimental outcomes to show how reliable the architecture is Quantum convolutional neural networks (QCNN) and quantum reinforcement learning (QRL) were chosen as example tasks for this goal. One kind of machine learning that quantum algorithms can naturally enhance is reinforcement learning. Agents who engage in continuous iterative optimization with the environment are rewarded in reinforcement learning.

Numerous tests have demonstrated that the agent's performance in the exploration environment can be maximized by combining quantum characteristics with reinforcement learning. While the other network layers preserve the structure of classical convolutional neural networks, the quantum convolutional neural network uses VQC as the quantum convolutional kernel to extract features from images. Additionally, in line with the NISQ period definition of quantum-classical hybrid machine learning, these two mixed machine learning tasks use a feedback loop between quantum exploration and classical optimization techniques.

The next step is to develop QRL using the tools and platform specs. First, prepare the data. Users don't need to prepare datasets since QRL learns by interacting with its surroundings rather than depending on static datasets. Nevertheless, the platform's container service must host the interactive environment it needs. The data collected can be kept on either classical or quantum storage devices, and the environment can be either quantum or classical. Here, the traditional CartPole environment has been used as the interactive reinforcement learning setting.

The agent must constantly change the pendulum's tilt in this environment, which is an inverted pendulum, to keep it from falling. The agent gets a higher score the longer the pendulum stays vertical. As a result, Q-agent's goal is to aim for high scores. Once the data preparation is finished, go on to the QRL task model building, which entails VQC networking and the creation of traditional optimization algorithms.

The Measurement Layer, Ansatz Layer, and Embedding Layer in VQC were built in modules using a visual modeling technique. Utilized templates for the preset circuits directly, using the Pauli Measurement Layer, Angle Embedding, and Strongly Entangling Layer as the VQC components, as illustrated in the image below. The architecture design concept of model modularization is used to componentize and modularize the VQC networking in QRL.

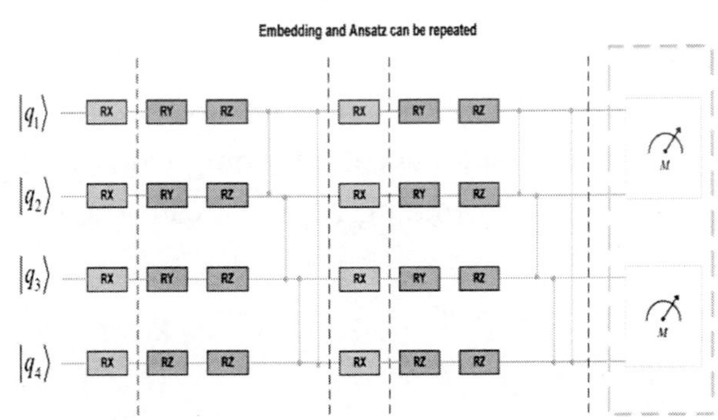

Fig.16.24 RL-VQC's composition in quantum machine learning.

It is evident that modular networking may be carried out between quantum bits, quantum gates, and the different layers that make up a quantum circuit, enabling algorithm engineers to create quantum models more quickly. Lastly, the Pennylane quantum AI framework was used to create VQC, and its robust interaction with Pytorch was utilized to implement classical RL algorithms. Train QRL tasks on a quantum simulator on a CPU at the same time; all that is needed is to indicate the device during training tasks.

Likewise, the development of QCN is comparable to the completion of QRL.

The figure below depicts the QCNN's structure. Select to build a conventional neural network and a quantum circuit using predefined templates. In QCNN, VQC functions as the convolution kernel. Next, select Random Layer as Ansatz and Angle Embedding as Embedding Layer. Measure every qubit independently using the Pauli z matrix, then feed the measured data into a neural network. CNN's pooled layer and fully connected layer are used to lower feature dimension and enhance the model's capacity for learning. The MNIST dataset is used to confirm QCNN's capabilities.

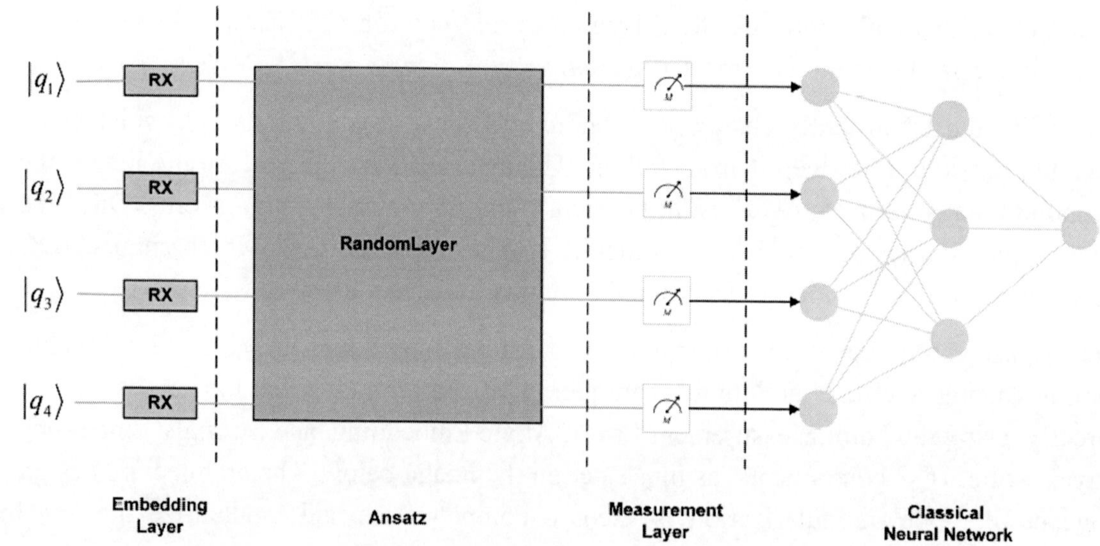

Fig.16.25 Quantum machine learning's QCNN composition.

The image below illustrates how a quantum-classical hybrid machine learning task can be constructed and trained routinely using the software architecture for quantum-classical hybrid machine learning. Run the result once the training work is finished, as seen in the figure below. According to the testing findings, Qagent can receive CartPole's maximum payout.

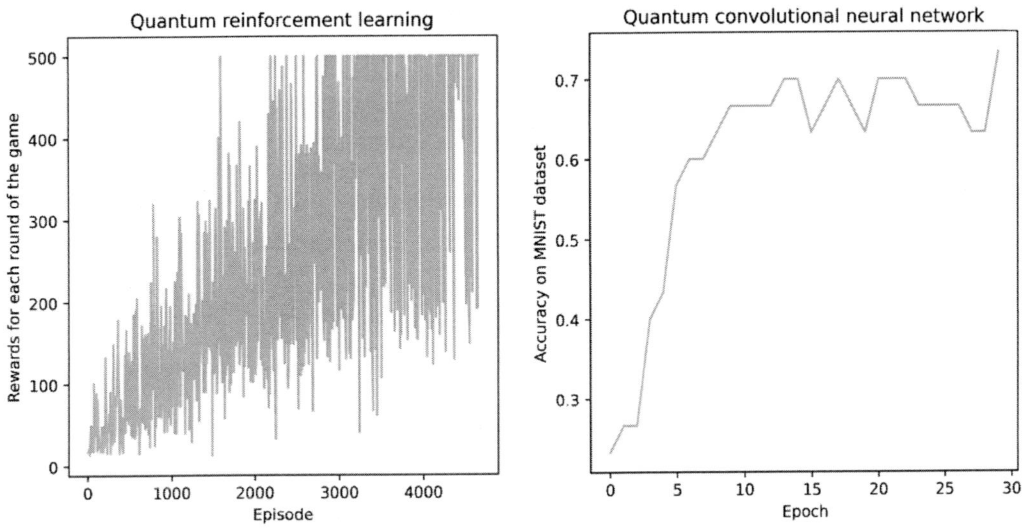

Fig.16.26 Quantum machine learning performance governed by software architecture.

The findings demonstrate that QCNN performs well on the MNIST dataset and that Qagent can obtain the maximum reward in CartPole. Stated differently, quantum-classical hybrid machine learning platform's software architecture is capable of passing real-world tests.

In order to satisfy the demands of the quantum computing area, this AI platform's software architecture is appropriate for the development of quantum machine learning in the NISQera. A number of significant tasks were completed during the architecture design process, such as multi-view architecture design, software requirements analysis of the quantum machine learning platform using software engineering theory, and architecture justification using quantum machine learning tasks. The first step is to conduct a requirements analysis for the quantum machine learning platform, which will evaluate the platform's user business requirements using the DevOps agile development model's user narrative technique. The main functional requirements of the platform, such as data services, model creation, and model deployment, have been hierarchically broken down based on a thorough examination of the quantum machine learning process. In order to guarantee the deployment of the quantum machine learning pipeline, hardware needs were also taken into account and linked with business operations. The architectural design of the quantum machine learning platform was also guided by the integration of several architecture viewpoints from the TOGAF model and the "4+1" view model from the software architecture design framework.

The physical view explains the platform's hardware for deployment, the business view describes the platform's business functions, and the logical view describes the system's essential components. The logical perspective reduces system complexity and improves overall system comprehensibility by abstracting the hardware and software modules of the quantum machine learning platform at a high granularity. The logical view not only serves as the basis for architectural choices, enabling developers and architects to choose suitable technologies and logically divide up the work among the system's various components, but it also serves as a basis for code division within the development team, facilitating parallel development and accelerating project completion.

The physical view provides information about the quantum machine learning platform's operational environment and physical deployment. It enables architects to schedule the platform's hardware resources, such as Q/C storage devices, Q/C compute devices, and additional hardware elements. It is easier to comprehend the physical connections between different components and ensure smooth communication between them when one is aware of the system's physical deployment. Furthermore, the successful completion of quantum machine learning tasks is influenced by the dependability of hardware components.

In order to guarantee the quantum machine learning platform's efficacy at the corporate level, the business view concentrates on how it satisfies business needs and goals. It incorporates the quantum machine learning platform's software requirements analysis content, providing an overview of the platform's business architecture, covering data services, model development, training and deployment activities, and AI asset management. This makes it easier for architects to align the system with the company and assure competitiveness in a constantly changing business environment by giving them a thorough understanding of the platform's business requirements. Ultimately, use quantum machine learning example tasks to verify the logicalness of the platform architectural design.

16.15 Business analytics with quantum machine learning

The use of Quantum Machine Learning (QML) in business analytics is a game-changing prospect that might help companies looking to enhance their decision-making models by gaining more sophisticated data handling skills. The traditional method of business analytics involves interpreting data, improving processes, and predicting trends using traditional machine learning models. But as data gets bigger and more complex, we have a scaling issue that impacts the accuracy and time efficiency of classical models. Because of the properties of quantum computing—such as superposition, entanglement, and quantum parallelism—QML becomes a solution to these constraints, allowing for quicker computation and more accurate data processing.

Big data analytics is essential for risk analysis, portfolio calibration, and fraud detection in financial modeling, which is arguably the most common application of QML. It has also been demonstrated that other quantum algorithms, such QAOA and QSVM, are more effective than classical algorithms at solving optimization issues. QAOA, for instance, might be applied to financial portfolios to produce more accurate forecasts with less weight. Similar to this, QML can improve recommendation systems by enabling them to digest user data much more quickly and create profitable, tailored trading signals for the relevant financial markets.

Particularly in the retail sector, QML may significantly influence demand forecasting and customer segmentation, two of the most crucial elements of enhancing business operations and consumer pleasure. When dealing with high-dimensional data, many traditional methods for grouping clients into categories fall short since the number of factors (such as customer traits, purchasing trends, and preferences) may significantly rise. Because of quantum-enhanced feature spaces, quantum machine learning is able to handle such high-dimensional data. The accuracy of the consumer segmentation models was improved by using quantum algorithms, which were helpful in outperforming classical models, particularly when predicting the location of data points in a wide feature space.

The following is a more accurate representation of the opportunities: There is a greater chance of understanding consumer behavior and adjusting marketing tactics accordingly; there is a greater capacity to forecast future demand and subsequently improve stock management. The following subtopics demonstrate how QML can be applied in supply chain optimization, another crucial field. Quantum optimization is therefore appropriate for supply chains with a large number of decision variables that rely on variables like time, stock levels, and transportation costs. Utilizing quantum algorithms, QML was applied in a supply chain setting to optimize delivery time and cost. According to the results, QML may reduce supply chain processing time by 20% compared to the traditional optimization method. This would allow businesses to quickly handle supply shocks or demand fluctuations. One benefit of QML for business applications is that it may be used to identify the optimal solution because supply chain management is complex and requires optimization of numerous variables.

In addition to these uses, QML has shown promise in the field of predictive analysis, which is essential to corporate intelligence and decision-making. Using historical rates as the predictor variable, algorithms are used to anticipate future rates. However, deterministic classical machine learning models suffer from accuracy and speed problems as the datasets grow in size and dimensionality. As data dimensionality decreases, quantum neural networks may yield stronger predictive values, making them appropriate for a variety of applications, including market trends, customer behavior, and sales prediction. By offering more precise forecasts, it gives businesses the structure and capability they require to make better decisions faster.

Although QML has many applications in business analytics, its practical implementation is still hampered by current hardware technology limitations. Professionally speaking, quantum computers are still in their infancy and are not yet available for purchase through standard business channels. Businesses who invest in QML now for research and development will be in a unique position to fully utilize these technologies when they become widely available, but QML remains at the forefront. Furthermore, as the majority of quantum computing technologies are still in the prototype stage, integrating QML with conventional ML algorithms might lay the foundation for their eventual introduction into the market. As quantum technologies advance, these hybrid models combine the greatest features of both classical and quantum techniques, allowing the company to gradually switch to other cutting-edge systems.

QML is thought to have a lot of potential for improving business analytics and having an impact on a variety of economic sectors, including supply chain management, finance, and purchasing. As more businesses start integrating data into their strategic processes, this capability enables QML to give them the tools they need to make decisions more quickly, intelligently, and effectively. Future business analytical models will likely be significantly influenced by the present developments in quantum technology and its integration with business analytics.

16.16 Aspects and Implications of Ethics

Although QML is a new and developing technology, its usage in business analytics raises a number of ethical concerns that need to be adequately addressed in order to stop improper use of the tool in today's organizations. Finance, retail, and supply chain management are among the businesses that employ QML, raising concerns about data security and privacy as well as potential abuse of the vast volumes of data these sectors hold. The following are possible moral dilemmas with quantum computing: Whether or not quantum computing should be fair is a controversial topic. Furthermore, there are also concerns about whether quantum computing should be applied in a transparent or accountable manner.

The impact that quantum computing will have on society is the main ethical concern that comes up. The purpose of this section is to discuss how and where business analytics experts may encounter the four main ethical issues listed below while using QML. The issue of data confidentiality is another significant ethical concern related to the use of QML. The ability of quantum algorithms to process large volumes of data in comparison to classical algorithms creates a lot of room for advancement in the context of managing consumer data in the commercial environment. When more and more businesses use big data processing technologies for decision-making and must decide between maintaining customer rights and accurately analyzing information, this issue becomes even more crucial. By definition, quantum machine learning may also facilitate the re-identification of de-identified data, which might facilitate the reversal of anonymity, the tracking of particular behaviors, or the reconstruction of personal data from aggregated datasets. There are risks associated with this, particularly for businesses in the healthcare and financial industries where financial and personal data is handled continuously. Data privacy regulations, such as the GDPR for the EU and HIPAA for the USA, must be complied with in order for QML to be deployed in these industries.

Another important question is the issue of data security. Regarding the subject of data security, quantum computing presents both opportunities and risks to the encryption industry. Some of the most widely used cryptography systems, such as the RSA encryption scheme, which is the foundation of much of the security on computer networks today, can be solved using quantum algorithms for other optimization problems. The discovery that quantum computing is likely to render all existing encryption techniques ineffective and expose sensitive company data to cybercrimes is the result of this. This makes it more difficult to decide how best to encrypt certain kinds of messages. Given the ongoing occurrence of data breaches, this is a crucial research issue. Quantum cryptography, and in particular QKD, offer a solution to this problem because they are founded on the quantum mechanical principles. Thus, MQTL Rather, until the full implementation of quantum cryptography techniques, companies using QML must have enough security measures that can adjust to emerging threats that could endanger their operations. Using post-quantum cryptography techniques that are impenetrable by quantum computers as a temporary solution could be one way to do this.

The meticulous structure of those machine learning algorithms raises additional ethical concerns, particularly in relation to prejudice and fairness. Both QML and traditional machine learning methods are known to introduce bias into the training dataset. Because quantum machine learning systems rely heavily on the training data, any injustice to the dataset produces an equally unfair result. For example, if the data used for modeling has such bias, a QML model used in the financial services sector to assess applicants' creditworthiness will turn out to be racially or gender sensitive. Therefore, QML should describe the appropriateness and fairness of training quantum models without exaggerating social inequities. By using bias detection techniques and fairness-aware learning, these concerns can be avoided while building QML models. Additionally, for the stakeholders in the organization to follow the process and comprehend the rationale behind specific decisions, QML systems need to be easily interpreted. For instance, in order to balance the risks associated with foregoing, the decision-making model for Aerie should include an explanation level.

Utility to the community must also be considered while contesting QML. The main reason for this is because there is a chance for drastic shifts in the balance of economic power and productivity as quantum technologies spread and disperse across many applications. As a recent addition to the business analytics space, QML may lead to more potential for market consolidation and less rivalry if companies embrace this technology early on. Fairness and the spread of quantum technology—or more crucially, its accessibility to many companies or organizations, particularly SMEs that might not be able to buy the actual hardware of quantum computers—are highlighted by this. To create equitable market settings, it will also be necessary to address the monopolization of quantum technologies and the lack of access to them.

To establish regulations that would promote equitable allocation of these resources to levels that do not grant monopolistic control of quantum technology to a small number of powerful companies, policymakers may need to step in. Finally, there is the more broad ethical question of whether society is prepared for quantum computing. When it comes to workforce, privacy, and security concerns, QML presents a variety of difficulties because it is a disruptive technology when used to business analytics. To handle the technology of quantum computing, the upcoming generation of data scientists and business analysts will require ethical education and training. Thirdly, in order to prepare society for the change that the technologies are expected to bring, it is also advised that the public be encouraged to participate in high-quality discussions about the ethical implications of deploying quantum technology.

For the following reasons, QML in corporate analytics raises a number of ethical issues. As a formidable technology that speeds up data processing, improves actual and potential accuracy, and scalable virtually infinitely, QML offers many advantages but also presents serious ethical problems, including those related to data privacy, security, and fairness as well as wider societal ramifications. In order to implement QML, businesses must adhere to ethical norms for data protection, prevent prejudice and unfairness against customers, and be open and accountable to them. To encourage the responsible and ethical use of QML in business analysis, technologists, ethicists, and politicians must continue to have open discussions as quantum technologies develop.

16.17 Obstacles and Restrictions

Despite the great potential of quantum machine learning, a few problems still need to be fixed:

Limitations of Current Quantum Hardware:

The errors brought on by noise and decoherence in current quantum hardware restrict the scalability and dependability of quantum algorithms. Advances in quantum error correction and hardware engineering are needed to mitigate these issues.

Algorithm Optimization:

Quantum machine learning algorithms need to be adjusted for quantum technology in order to fully utilize its potential. This means developing programming frameworks, algorithms, and data structures specifically for the quantum realm.

Data Encoding and Preparation: It can be challenging to effectively transform classical data into quantum bits and get it ready for quantum algorithms, particularly for large and complex datasets. Preprocessing, data compression, and efficient quantum data structures are essential.

Hybrid Quantum-Classical Systems:

Due to the restricted amount of qubits in quantum hardware, hybrid systems that combine quantum and classical computing are frequently employed. To enhance the usefulness of these systems and develop efficient ways to integrate them, research is still ongoing.

Talent and Education through Quantum Computational Learning:

A comprehensive skill set in quantum machine learning is necessary to comprehend quantum physics, computer science, and machine learning all at once. In order to meet the growing demand for experts in this field, educational programs and a talent pipeline must be established.

16.18 Future Directions and Research Areas of Quantum Machine Learning

There are exciting opportunities for quantum machine learning in the following areas:

Near-Term Applications: It is expected that quantum machine learning will be used in specialized fields where quantum advantages may be achieved using current or upcoming quantum hardware in the near future. These include optimization challenges,

Fault-tolerant computing, and quantum error correction: The goal of quantum error correction research is to provide techniques for identifying and fixing mistakes in quantum systems so that fault-tolerant quantum computing is possible. Ensuring the accuracy and reliability of quantum algorithms is essential to the long-term success of quantum machine learning.

Quantum Software and Development Tools: The need for user-friendly software and development tools will increase as quantum hardware advances. These include libraries of quantum algorithms, quantum programming languages, and frameworks for quantum machine learning, which help researchers and developers better understand the intricacies of quantum computing.

Quantum Machine Learning as a Service (QMLaaS): Similar to classical machine learning, QMLaaS can be offered as a cloud-based service, eliminating the need for on-premise quantum hardware and allowing companies to utilize pre-built quantum machine learning models and quantum computing resources.

Integration with Classical Machine Learning: Researching hybrid models that combine quantum and classical machine learning techniques will be a major focus. This includes using traditional methods for feature extraction, data preparation, and result interpretation, as well as using quantum algorithms to some computationally hard tasks.

There is a lot of promise for ground-breaking findings in the exciting and quickly evolving field of quantum machine learning. Combining machine learning techniques with quantum computing is expected to lead to advancements in a variety of industries, including banking and healthcare. Even if there may be challenges along the way, more research and development will lead to previously unrealized opportunities and usher in a new era of creative and efficient problem-solving. Quantum machine learning has the potential to produce ground-breaking discoveries that will alter how we approach difficult problems and reach decisions.

Blurb

Quantum cloud computing represents a transformative paradigm that enables access to quantum processors (QPUs) through the cloud, empowering users to leverage quantum capabilities without direct ownership of specialized hardware. This model integrates classical and quantum resources via secure remote connectivity, allowing researchers, developers, and industries to execute quantum algorithms at scale. By reducing barriers to entry, quantum cloud computing accelerates innovation across fields such as optimization, cryptography, machine learning, and robotics. However, it also introduces challenges tied to security, trust, and governance. The success of this model will rely on advanced solutions such as blind quantum computing, post-quantum cryptography, and policy frameworks that promote accessibility, digital sovereignty, and ethical deployment within future 6G-enabled ecosystems.

This book unites diverse perspectives on the convergence of quantum computing, artificial intelligence, machine learning, robotics, and cloud computing. It explores the foundations of quantum infrastructure and implementation while presenting an AI-driven architecture framework that addresses design principles, service-oriented architectures, hybrid and multi-cloud models, enabling technologies, cybersecurity strategies, and Quantum-as-a-Service (QaaS) models. By bridging theoretical constructs with real-world applications, it reveals how quantum-enhanced AI and cloud systems reshape computational paradigms and pave the way for secure, intelligent, and scalable digital ecosystems.

The text also devotes special attention to the architecture of quantum cloud platforms, including frameworks, paradigms, and design methodologies applicable to cognitive systems and big data contexts. Beyond technical integration, it investigates critical concerns in service modification, quantum security mechanisms, and advanced processing workflows essential to robust quantum cloud deployment.

Security is examined comprehensively, including analysis of quantum-specific vulnerabilities such as multi-tenant isolation risks, qubit crosstalk, timing-based side-channel exploits, and insider threats. In response, the discussion highlights quantum-enhanced defenses such as Quantum Key Distribution (QKD) combined with classical encryption techniques to safeguard confidentiality, integrity, and availability within cloud environments. These layered security approaches ensure compatibility with contemporary infrastructures while mitigating emerging cyber threats.

Designed for academic audiences, researchers, and corporate practitioners alike, this book integrates theoretical foundations with practical implementation knowledge. It aims to equip readers with a deep understanding of how quantum computing intersects with AI and robotics—enabling them to engage effectively with the opportunities and challenges shaping next-generation computing platforms.

Salient Highlights

- Quantum Cloud Foundations and integration
- AI, Machine Learning, and Robotics Synergy
- Architectural design patterns and framework insights Paradigm and Design Principles
- Security, Digital Sovereignty and Cryptography